THE AMERICAN POLITICAL SYSTEM
Second Core Edition

THE AMERICAN POLITICAL SYSTEM

Second Core Edition, 2014 Election Update

Ken Kollman
University of Michigan

W. W. Norton & Company
New York ■ London

W. W. Norton & Company has been independent since its founding in 1923, when William Warder Norton and Mary D. Herter Norton first published lectures delivered at the People's Institute, the adult education division of New York City's Cooper Union. The firm soon expanded its program beyond the Institute, publishing books by celebrated academics from America and abroad. By mid-century, the two major pillars of Norton's publishing program—trade books and college texts—were firmly established. In the 1950s, the Norton family transferred control of the company to its employees, and today—with a staff of four hundred and a comparable number of trade, college, and professional titles published each year—W. W. Norton & Company stands as the largest and oldest publishing house owned wholly by its employees.

Editors: Jake Schindel and Peter Lesser
Copyeditor: Jennifer Harris
Project editor: Sujin Hong
Marketing managers: Sasha Levitt and Erin Brown
Assistant editor: Sarah Wolf
Managing editor, College: Marian Johnson
Production manager: Vanessa Nuttry
Book designer: Lissi Sigillo
Photo editor: Stephanie Romeo
Media editor: Toni Magyar
Composition: Jouve North America
Manufacturing: Quad Graphics
Cover design and art by Jennifer Hever

Library of Congress has cataloged the full edition as follows:
Kollman, Ken, 1966–
The American political system / Ken Kollman, University of Michigan. — Second edition.
    pages cm
  Includes bibliographical references and index.
  ISBN 978-0-393-92329-2 (pbk. : alk. paper)   1. United States—Politics and government—Textbooks.   I. Title.
  JK276.K66 2014
  320.473—dc23

                                                                          2013041077

This edition: **ISBN 978-0-393-26421-0**

W. W. Norton & Company, Inc., 500 Fifth Avenue, New York, NY 10110
www.wwnorton.com

W. W. Norton & Company Ltd., Castle House, 75/76 Wells Street, London W1T 3QT

1 2 3 4 5 6 7 8 9 0

This book is dedicated to

Anne M. and Anne C.
Paul V., Jr. and Paul E.

CONTENTS

CHAPTER 3 Federalism **67**

Given the states' interest in protecting their own sovereignty and the American people's
traditional fears of excessive centralized power, why have the states and the American
people allowed the federal government to become more powerful in the past century?

CHAPTER 4 Civil Rights and Liberties 101

At times, protecting the rights and liberties of some people seems to infringe on those of others or to hinder another governmental goal. How have the courts and other branches of government resolved controversies over the extent of Americans' rights and liberties?

CHAPTER 5 Congress 137

Members of Congress constantly think about the interests of their district and their own prospects for re-election. At the same time, Congress is expected to pass laws that benefit the country as a whole. How do legislators rise above self-interest and the narrow interests of their districts to pass important legislation?

CHAPTER 6 The Presidency 185

Today, the American presidency is a far more powerful office than the Founders ever envisioned. How have presidents increased their power at the expense of the legislative and judicial branches of government? And why have Congress and the American people allowed this shift in power?

CHAPTER 7 The Bureaucracy 225

The agencies of the federal bureaucracy are responsible for carrying out the policies passed by Congress and the president. However, bureaucrats are not elected and it is not always clear to whom they answer. Who ultimately are their bosses and how can they avoid defying them?

CHAPTER 8 The Judiciary 263

The courts—especially the Supreme Court—are sometimes seen as being "above" politics, yet court decisions have enormous political consequences, and courts are often subject to strong political pressures. How has the Supreme Court maintained its place as the respected independent arbiter of the Constitution despite these political pressures?

CHAPTER 9 Public Opinion 299

Democratic government emphasizes "the will of the people," and at times politicians
seem very concerned with following public opinion. Yet at other times, the government
goes against what a majority of people want. What is the link between public opinion and
politicians' behavior and expressed views?

CHAPTER 12 Political Parties **409**

Why are political parties and partisanship so widely criticized—but also so indispensable in a democratic system?

CHAPTER 13 Elections and Campaigns **445**

Research shows that most voters have made up their minds how to vote in national elections well before Election Day and are unlikely to be swayed by campaign messages. Do campaigns matter in national elections, and if so, how?

CHAPTER 14 Mass Media and the Press 483

Mass media and the press play an important role in providing the information people need to make political decisions. However, news outlets don't passively report objective facts. Is media bias a problem in American politics?

PREFACE

A common impression is that students entering colleges and universities today do not care about politics or are uninformed, when in fact, many students, even before they arrive at college, are awash in details about politics, public opinion, and international events. They regularly encounter information or opinions about the political world, whether online; through traditional media, personal conversations, and public speeches; or within their clubs and other associations.

Consider the conflicting—and often negative and misleading—messages about the American political system that are broadcast widely and likely to reach the typical student in the United States. Even brief attention to the news or other political programming might lead one to believe some subset of the following: Politicians are venal and corrupt. Lobbyists are venal and corrupt. Congress cannot get anything done. The government meddles too much in the economy and/or in people's lives. The federal government cannot close a military base, reform a bureaucracy, or coordinate relief efforts effectively. The government does not promote jobs effectively enough. No politician wanting to keep his or her job would ever want to raise taxes. Americans' taxes are outrageously high. The Social Security program is going broke. The government spends too much beyond its budget. Political parties get in the way of effective compromise. The Supreme Court is out of touch with public opinion. Interest groups essentially bribe politicians.

Students may try to make sense of the American political system, but understanding can be elusive. The challenge of getting an accurate, coherent picture of American politics is exacerbated by the enormity of the American political system. The bombardment of information about a broad range of topics across different institutions and levels of government may give the impression of incoherence or disorder. The political system can look chaotic, random, and complex, making useful understanding nearly impossible.

What students entering introductory courses often lack is a coherent intellectual framework and set of logical concepts with which they can make sense of political information. I wrote this book to provide such a framework, and this second edition sharpens the original framework even more. My goal is to give a clear introduction to the core facts about American government and an intellectual toolkit to navigate the extraordinarily complex political system in the United States. I want my students to be able to take that toolkit with them after the course, and I hope readers of this book will too. The tools in this book can help students understand the political issues and information that they encounter throughout their lives—in the news, as well as in their own experiences.

Analytical Tools for Understanding American Politics

This textbook conveys the core theoretical insights and analytical tools from modern political science and applies them to the American political system. Political science is a diverse discipline, so this textbook focuses on three core insights:

1. People face recurrent collective dilemmas and principal–agent problems.
2. Political institutions, including those in the United States, are intended to solve collective dilemmas and principal–agent problems.
3. The specific details of those institutions affect how costs and benefits are allocated in society. In other words, institutional details matter for who gets what in society.

After learning about this core and studying various kinds of collective dilemmas and principal–agent problems, students can make better sense of the major topics in American politics. For example, as they learn about Congress in Chapter 5, they can consider the institutional features of congressional elections—including the use of primary elections and legislative action such as agenda-control by the Rules Committee in the House—with a keen eye on how those features are intended to (but do not always) successfully solve social dilemmas. Students learn the consequences of having specific institutions in place in Congress, such as which states will benefit when the filibuster is used on spending bills. They can make sense of why members of Congress are typically re-elected even when a large majority of Americans are unhappy with Congress as a whole. Or how internal congressional politics affects bargaining between the two chambers and between Congress and the president. In every chapter, the analytical tools from Chapter 1 are used to provide insights into the topic at hand.

A Problem-Oriented Approach

Each chapter starts with a puzzle, illustrated through a story about American politics, then uses the concepts and information in the chapter to help "solve" it. Chapter 1, for example, uses the story of the ongoing budget battles between Democratic and Republican party leaders, and asks how the two parties can consistently fail to solve long-term problems. A majority of Americans complain simultaneously about high deficits, their tax burdens, and not enough government spending on programs like education and infrastructure. At first, the situation does not appear to make sense. If deficits are caused by the government spending more than it collects in taxes, increased spending and lower taxes will increase the deficit. So it seems illogical that majorities support both maintaining current levels of spending and retaining existing tax rates, instead of raising more revenue from taxes. Only by further exploring the issue using concepts such as free riding, public goods, and collective dilemmas does the budget conflict (and the public's reaction) begin to make sense.

These types of puzzles motivate not only what follows in the chapters but also the priorities of political science researchers. The book reflects some of the best contemporary scholarship with rich citations, reference lists, and carefully annotated sources for the charts and tables. Students will find the information accessible, accurate, and clearly specified.

Insights through Comparison

To gain insights into how specific institutional details matter, each chapter includes an "In Comparison" section that describes features of the American system as they compare to those in other countries. Students will read about research findings on the consequences of having different institutions and social circumstances in other countries. For example, a section in Chapter 4 explores how France and the United States differ over the interpretation of the separation of church and state. A section in Chapter 13 looks at the differences between simple plurality and proportional electoral systems, and the research connecting those institutional details to certain political and policy outcomes. Sections in other chapters provide data and analysis comparing the United States to other countries on political participation, party systems, public opinion, and constitutional design. While instructors often do not have time to cover comparative material, the comparisons made in this textbook will help students understand the American system better by highlighting the impact of certain kinds of institutions.

Pedagogical Features

This textbook uses innovative pedagogy to help students grasp important concepts and master basic factual material. In each chapter, the following features reinforce the information in the chapter text.

Interests, Institutions, and Outcomes features in every chapter provide students with real-world examples of how institutions work on collective dilemmas to foster specific outcomes. These can serve as models for students' own analysis or as prompts for classroom discussion. Examples include:

- How state and federal policy around marijuana use may differ (Chapter 3: Federalism)
- How the Democrats used budget reconciliation to pass the Affordable Care Act (Chapter 5: Congress)
- The effect of *Citizens United* on campaigns (Chapter 13: Elections and Campaigns)

Know the Facts boxes give the nuts and bolts of American government without cluttering the text with excessive details on features that are relatively straightforward. Using clear tables and outlines, these boxes cover basic factual information that every student taking an American government course should know.

Historical Path boxes highlight important events in history that students should be familiar with, helping them to put these events in historical context and see the long-term trends.

A rich art program includes tables and figures that are an integral part of each chapter, carefully chosen photos that illustrate key points, and marginal definitions of key terms.

New in the Second Edition

In preparing this second edition, I was attentive to the feedback I received from professors who have used the textbook in their courses and from students in my own course. As discussed above, the new Interests, Institutions, and Outcomes feature offers additional material with which students can apply the core concepts from the book, while new opening stories and contemporary examples keep the text fresh and compelling. As an example, Chapter 3 (Federalism) opens with a story about states' attempts (as in Arizona) to adopt immigration laws that may be at odds with federal policy. It poses the puzzle of why, in general, centralization has prevailed in conflicts between the national government and the states.

All chapters have new citations with contemporary scholarship, refreshed "Further Reading" lists, and updated data for charts and tables wherever possible. Finally, professors and students asked for more examples of contemporary real-world events that illustrate the concepts in the book. The Interests, Institutions, and Outcomes feature and the puzzle examples based on real-world events provide both students and professors with plenty of material for lectures, discussions, test questions, and paper topics.

Support Materials for Students and Instructors

This textbook is accompanied by an extensive set of resources developed specifically for instructors and students to use with *The American Political System*.

Coursepacks Available at no cost to professors or students, Norton coursepacks for online or hybrid courses are available in a variety of formats, including all versions of Blackboard and WebCT. Content includes review material, chapter quizzes, and video exercises.

Instructor's Resource Disc

- *PowerPoints:* Written by Sarah Treul (University of North Carolina—Chapel Hill), these PowerPoint slides feature concise text slides, helpful notes and suggestions for instructors, all the figures and photos from the text, and researcher videos.

- *Researcher Videos:* Prominent political scientists talk about the chapter-opening puzzles in the text.

- *Art Files:* All figures, tables, and photos are available in JPEG and PowerPoint formats.

Instructor's Manual Written by Brian Fife (Indiana University–Purdue University, Fort Wayne), the Instructor's Manual includes chapter outlines, lecture ideas, teaching suggestions, in-class activities based on the researcher videos and suggested web activities, supplementary readings, and in-class and homework assignments.

Test Bank Written by John Lovett, Chelsea Phillips, Tamar Malloy, and Nicholas Howard (University of North Carolina–Chapel Hill), the Test Bank includes multiple-choice, true/false, and essay questions for every chapter, all labeled for question type, difficulty, and concept. Available in the following formats: print, CD-ROM, PDF, RTF, Blackboard, WebCT, ANGEL, Desire2Learn, Moodle, and ExamView Assessment Suite.

Ebook An affordable and convenient alternative, Norton ebooks retain the content and design of the print book and allow students to highlight and take notes with ease, print chapters as needed, and search the text for references. Norton ebooks are available online and as downloadable PDFs.

Acknowledgements

I am grateful for the comments, suggestions, and constructive criticisms that the following reviewers provided at various stages of this book's development:

Scott Adler, *University of Colorado Boulder*

Scott Ainsworth, *University of Georgia*

John Anderson, *University of Nebraska, Kearney*

Tama Andrews, *University of New Hampshire*

John Aughenbaugh, *Virginia Commonwealth University*

Julia Azari, *Marquette University*

Paul Bellinger, *Stephen F. Austin State University*

Michael Berkman, *Pennsylvania State University*

Robert Boatright, *Clark University*

Frederick Boehmke, *University of Iowa*

Michael Brown, *Emerson College*

Brian Brox, *Tulane University*

Justin Buchler, *Case Western Reserve University*

Peter Burns, *Loyola University New Orleans*

Michael Burton, *Ohio University*

Jamie Carson, *University of Georgia*

Dan Cassino, *Fairleigh Dickinson University*

Suzanne Chod, *North Central College*

Jeffrey Christiansen, *Seminole State College*

Ann Cohen, *CUNY Hunter College*

Martin Cohen, *James Madison University*

Paul Collins, *University of North Texas*

Michael Crespin, *University of Texas at Dallas*

Sharon Deubreau, *Rhodes State College*

Casey Dominguez, *University of San Diego*

Jamie Druckman, *Northwestern University*

David Dulio, *Oakland University*

Justin Dyer, *University of Missouri*

Chris Ellis, *Bucknell University*

Matthew Eshbaugh-Soha, *University of North Texas*

William Ewell, *Stonehill College*

Kathleen Ferraiolo, *James Madison University*

Femi Ferreira, *Hutchinson Community College*

John Franklin, *Graceland University*

Rodd Freitag, *University of Wisconsin–Eau Claire*

Brad Gomez, *Florida State University*

Craig Goodman, *Texas Tech University*

Andrew Green, *Central College*

Thad Hall, *University of Utah*

Edward Hasecke, *Wittenberg University*

Danny Hayes, *George Washington University*

Diane Heith, *St. John's University*

Roberta Herzberg, *Utah State University*

James Hurtgen, *SUNY Fredonia*

Jessica Ice, *West Virginia University*

Dorothy James, *Connecticut College*

Marc James, *Brock University*

Richard Jankowski, *SUNY Fredonia*

Timothy Johnson, *University of Minnesota*

David Jones, *James Madison University*

Josh Kaplan, *University of Notre Dame*

David Konisky, *Georgetown University*

Chris Koski, *Reed College*

Chris Kypriotis, *Ohio State University*

Christopher Lawrence, *Texas A&M International University*

Beth Leech, *Rutgers University*

Jan Leighley, *University of Arizona*

Christine Lipsmeyer, *Texas A&M University*

Daniel Lipson, *SUNY New Paltz*

James Lutz, *Indiana University–Purdue University Fort Wayne*

Jason MacDonald, *West Virginia University*

Ellie Malone, *United States Naval Academy*

Tom Martin, *Eastern Kentucky University*

Corrine McConnaughy, *The Ohio State University*

Ian McDonald, *Duke University*

Amy McKay, *Georgia State University*

Will Miller, *Southeast Missouri State University*

William Mishler, *University of Arizona*

Jamie Monogan, *University of Georgia*

Joanna Mosser, *Drake University*

Ken Mulligan, *Southern Illinois University*

Michael Nelson, *Rhodes College*

James Newman, *Idaho State University*

Hans Noel, *Georgetown University*

Timothy Nokken, *Texas Tech University*

Paul Nolette, *Marquette University*

Catherine Paden, *Simmons College*

Evan Parker-Stephen, *Texas A&M University*

Michael Reinhard, *Millsaps College*

Kimberly Rice, *Western Illinois University*

Travis Ridout, *Washington State University*

Jason Roberts, *The University of North Carolina at Chapel Hill*

Robert Robinson, *The University of Alabama at Birmingham*

Mark Rom, *Georgetown University*

Beth Rosenson, *University of Florida*

Robert Sahr, *Oregon State University*

Debra Salazar, *Western Washington University*

Pamela Schaal, *Ball State University*

Scot Schraufnagel, *Northern Illinois University*

Jungkun Seo, *University of North Carolina Wilmington*

Emily Shaw, *Thomas College*

James Sheffield, *The University of Oklahoma*

Fred Slocum, *Minnesota State University*

Keith Smith, *University of the Pacific*

Stephen Swindle, *Lee University*

Barry Tadlock, *Ohio University*

Terri Towner, *Oakland University*

Sarah Treul, *University of North Carolina at Chapel Hill*

Jessica Trounstine, *University of California, Merced*

Joseph Ura, *Texas A&M University*

Abby Van Horn, *North Central College*

Renee Van Vechten, *University of Redlands*

Justin Vaughn, *Boise State University*

Greg Vonnahme, *University of Missouri–Kansas City*

Charles Walcott, *Virginia Tech*

Timothy Werner, *University of Texas at Austin*

Stephen Wirls, *Rhodes College*

Frederick Wood, *Coastal Carolina University*

Gina Woodall, *Arizona State University*

Thanks are also due to the following people for helping put this book together: Daniel Magleby, Sang-Jung Han, David Cottrell, Molly Reynolds, Semra Koknar, Sarah Neuman, Michael Robbins, Phil Clark, Nick Marcus, Hannah Bozian, Sarah Danserau, Josh Deyoung, Emma Rew, Peter Gutsche, Zachary Goldsmith, Charles Doriean, Jennifer Miller-Gonzales, Paul Poast, and Tim Ryan. Paul Gargaro was especially helpful in the initial drafting of chapters. The second edition was put together with the help of David Cottrell, Phil Schermer, Richard Anderson, and Erica Mirabitur. The team at Norton—including senior project editor Sujin Hong and production manager Vanessa Nuttry—did a superb job keeping track of the myriad details throughout the development and production process and ensuring the high quality of the printed book. Thanks to Steve Dunn for supporting the original idea, Roby Harrington for key moments of inspiration during lively conversations, and especially Ann Shin, a talented, demanding editor who confidently guided me to the end of a long process for the first edition. With this second edition, Ann began the process as editor, and then handed things over to Pete Lesser, who has been a terrific, creative partner. He was aided by Jake Schindel and Sarah Wolf, who both deserve my gratitude for having the right mix of persistence and patience.

Ken Kollman

THE AMERICAN POLITICAL SYSTEM
Second Core Edition

Conflicts over the nation's debt limit, taxes, and spending priorities seem to exemplify chaos and contradictions in American politics. When we look deeper, however, we begin to see the often predictable ways that American political institutions shape debates about current events and the policy outcomes that ensue.

1

INTRODUCTION

The workings of American government and politics often seem puzzling. How can basic concepts in political science help us to understand the complexities and apparent contradictions of the American political system?

In recent years, the United States national government experienced one budgetary crisis after another. Every time a major decision loomed between 2011 and 2014 over the government's budget and borrowing capacity (its "debt ceiling," as it is known), there was a deadline that provoked grandstanding among political adversaries, threats of economic doom, and intense negotiations among politicians going long into the morning hours. Government officials and commentators used stark words and phrases to describe the consequences of the government's actions, or inactions, in dealing with the basic disagreement between the two major political parties over the budget. If leaders of the two political parties did not come to an agreement over taxes and spending, the government might fall off a "fiscal cliff," funding for many government programs would be subject to "sequestration" (i.e., mandatory budget cuts), or the government might default on its debt obligations.

The disagreements between the parties were not petty or trivial, but instead reflected fundamental differences over policy goals and society outcomes. Leaders of both parties recognized that large, increasing deficit spending could not continue indefinitely. In general, Democrats, led by President Obama and majority leaders in the Senate (until 2015), sought mild cuts to government spending and increased taxes on the wealthy. Republicans, led by majority leaders in the House of Representatives, sought deep cuts to government spending and no tax increases on anyone. Compromises were hard fought, and when they came they followed bitter negotiations, blame in both directions, and a general feeling that nobody won. Many problems were put off until later, and the essential decisions over how to ensure sustainable government budgets were postponed.

In general, Americans do not like to pay taxes. It has never been popular for politicians of either major party to call for an increase in taxes. Aversion to taxes has deep historical antecedents and is ingrained in the American political culture. The War of Independence was sparked by rebellions against British taxation. Periodic tax revolts by citizens groups, especially in states like California in the late twentieth century, have made American politicians wary of raising taxes, even when more tax revenues are needed to pay for popular programs and balance government budgets. This is in spite of the fact that the United States ranks near the bottom among industrialized democracies in the tax burden imposed on citizens and corporations.

At the same time, however, Americans ask a lot of their government. Not only do they want it to educate children, preserve public order, provide health care for the elderly and poor, regulate products and services, build roads and bridges, and provide student loans for college, they also want the government to protect the United States and its interests abroad. Moreover, most Americans prefer government to operate on a balanced budget, spending no more than it collects in taxes and other revenue.

The expectations Americans have for their government often seem incompatible with their dislike of taxes. Politicians commonly complain that the American people want the government to do more than what they are willing to pay. During the crises between 2011 and 2014, many Republicans and some Democrats in Congress expressed misgivings that failure to agree on permanent solutions would increase the budget deficit so much that it would harm the economic future for the next few generations. The deficit was high because of years of low tax revenues from slow growth following the 2009 recession and the huge government spending to stimulate the economy. Meanwhile, the United States was still paying off the costs of expensive wars in Afghanistan and Iraq from the previous decade. Then, in fall 2013, in hopes of delaying or eliminating President Obama's signature health care reform policies, the House of Representatives refused to pass legislation funding the government. This led to a lengthy government shutdown with federal offices closed and employees furloughed. The Republican leaders in the House had drawn the line and were willing to risk the ire of many Americans to get their way on the budget.

Nearly every national leader of both parties agreed that coming to settlement on the budget was necessary, but had different opinions about what that settlement should look like. Most Americans say in surveys that they are in favor of lower taxes in general, higher taxes on the wealthy, and a balanced budget. At the same time, they do not favor cutting certain popular, yet enormously expensive, government programs such as Social Security and Medicare.

The conflicts over the budget seem puzzling and even frustrating when described this way: Why can't they just come to an agreement on a long-term solution? But it is not unexpected or mysterious, given how social scientists think about political systems and institutions. In this chapter, and throughout this book, we will ask—and answer—the question: How can basic concepts in political science help us to understand the complexities and apparent contradictions of the American political system?

Understanding American Politics

This book will deepen your understanding of the elements and operation of the American political system. **Politics** refers to the process of making collective decisions, usually by governments, to allocate public resources and to create and enforce rules for the operation of society. A **political system** is the way a society organizes and manages its politics across various levels of public authority.

The political scientist Harold Lasswell once offered an alternative definition of politics as the struggle over "who gets what, when, [and] how."[1] This definition is too broad for our purposes because it encompasses virtually any social activity involving the allocation of resources, including activities studied in such fields as economics, sociology, psychology, and anthropology.

Lasswell's curt definition is, however, valuable in highlighting the fact that politics fundamentally revolves around satisfying people's needs or wants. These needs or wants can be summarized by saying that people have **preferences** over things that government can potentially provide and they take actions to satisfy those preferences. Generally speaking, people prefer to maximize benefits and minimize costs. Given those preferences, people have ideas about how

politics The process of making collective decisions, usually by governments, to allocate public resources and to create and enforce rules for the operation of society.

political system The way a society organizes and manages its politics across various levels of public authority.

preferences The outcomes or experiences people want or believe they need.

Politics involves the distribution (or redistribution) of goods to satisfy interests. In late 2012, as the "fiscal cliff" political crisis loomed, which entailed heavy spending cuts in many areas, many citizens protested having goods and services that were important to them slashed, including jobs and Medicare benefits.

[1] Harold D. Lasswell, *Politics: Who Gets What, When, How* (New York: Whittlesey House/McGraw-Hill, 1936).

society should be run and expectations about how their own experiences with government actions determine the satisfaction of their preferences. Politics determines the distribution or redistribution of benefits and costs to satisfy those preferences.

It goes without saying that people often do not share the same preferences. One person's costs could be another person's benefits. They can have different interpretations of what is beneficial and what is costly. Nor do people share the same ideas about how society should be run. Politics often involves considerable conflict. It is rare to observe a governmental decision where everyone believes that the government has taken the correct action to satisfy his or her preferences. Much of the time in politics, some people win more benefits and some people pay more costs, and even if everyone wins some benefits, certain people win more than others.

Institutions

In light of people's conflicting preferences and disagreements, there must be means of making collective decisions, of settling on common action. Those decisions happen because of the workings of institutions. Institutions can be broadly defined as constraints on behavior that are usually codified but can also be informally understood by people. In politics, **institutions** are the rules or sets of rules or practices that determine how people make collective decisions. Institutions include the rules and procedures for passing laws, interpreting laws,

institutions Rules or sets of rules or practices that determine how people make collective decisions.

Know the FACTS | Political Institutions

Political institutions include:

- **Branches of government**
  Examples: Congress
  The president
  The federal courts

- **Organizations**
  Examples: The Internal Revenue Service
  The Rules Committee in the House of Representatives
  The electoral college
  Political parties
  Interest groups

- **Rules and procedures**
  Examples: Simple plurality election rules
  Separation of powers
  Judicial review
  Campaign finance laws

enforcing laws, counting votes and electing governments, and appointing government employees, among many other functions. The institutions of government vary across countries, states, and parts of the world, and they can change over time, with important implications for societies. They determine who can legally do what, when, and how, and they affect how the political system distributes benefits and costs among people in society.[2]

The term *institution* may be confusing because it is abstract and can be used in multiple ways. It can refer to large parts of the government or to specific procedures or organizations. It is sometimes used, for instance, to describe an entire branch of the government, as in referring to the presidency as an institution. Indeed, the three major branches of the U.S. government—the executive (the White House and the presidency), the legislative (Congress), and the judicial (the Supreme Court)—are each important institutions in American politics.

The term *institution*, however, is not always used to refer to a branch of government or a particular level of government. It is also used to refer to procedures for decision making or to organizations that make democracy work. The methods by which people are elected to office, for example—the voting rules, including the electoral college—and the procedures adopted for bargaining between the branches of government are also key institutions of government. The major political parties are considered crucial to the functioning of Congress and of elections, and interest groups play a vital role in determining which policies get chosen. These political organizations are key institutional features of the American political system.

One way to think of a political system is that it comprises a bundle of institutions within which many diverse people pursue the satisfaction of their preferences. The national government in the United States sits atop the American political system, but there is much more to a **federal system** like that of the United States. In federal systems, there are multiple levels of government with independent authority over important areas of policy. Each resident of the country is also affected by the policies of the nearly 90,000 state and local governments. People's lives are changed daily by the regulations and budgets decided upon by city, county, state, and regional governments, and by the day-to-day decisions of governors, mayors, council members, attorneys general, prosecutors, assessors, and comptrollers at lower levels of government.

federal system A political system with multiple levels of government, in which each level has independent authority over some important policy areas.

The complicated mixture of multilayered governments and public institutions in the United States, and the various political organizations, businesses, and social movements that influence those governments and other institutions, form an overwhelmingly complex political system.

We will see in this book that the specific nature of these political institutions matters. It is not enough to explain a political outcome by saying that it occurred because "people wanted it that way." *How* they make their collective

[2] Kenneth A. Shepsle, *Analyzing Politics: Rationality, Behavior, and Institutions*, 2nd ed. (New York: Norton, 2010).

An institution can be as big as an entire branch of government, such as Congress, or it can be as specific as a rule for making a particular decision, such as how the Speaker of the House of Representatives is chosen. In 2010, John Boehner was chosen as Speaker through codified rules for electing party leaders.

decisions has consequences. Political outcomes are profoundly shaped by the institutions of government.

Consider the example of the electoral college, an institution that determines which person wins the presidency of the United States. Had the institution for choosing the president been different—in particular, if the presidency were decided purely by which candidate received the most votes—the election of 2000 would have put Al Gore in the White House. Gore won more popular votes than George W. Bush in 2000, but lost the presidency because Bush received more votes in the electoral college. (We will discuss the electoral college in more detail in later chapters.)

In fact, the collection of procedures used to select the president of the United States—the voting rules used by the states, the rules governing the electoral college, the rules the two major parties use to choose their candidates, the tie-breaking rules, and the methods for settling the outcome when it is not determined simply (as in 2000)—constitutes a bundle of institutions with major consequences for determining the winner of the ultimate prize in American politics.

As another example, the institutions described by the U.S. Constitution specify that two senators are to be elected from each state, regardless of population size. Thus, the politics of the Senate are constrained by institutional rules that have had the important effect of giving more representation to people from smaller, more rural states than to those from larger, more urban states. Wyoming, with approximately 570,000 residents, has the same number of senators representing its citizens as California, with approximately 38 million residents. Consequently, the Senate has traditionally been the unit of the U.S. government that is most prone to ensuring generous benefits for farmers. A central question that this book will help answer is how the institutions of the American political system lead to disparities in the apportionment of benefits and costs among people. These benefits and costs are not equitably distributed throughout the United States, and most scholars point to persistent biases in the system as the source of such disparities.

To begin to make sense of the American political system, let us build from individual behavior to institutional design and collective choices. We start by focusing on the "micro" level of politics—the social dilemmas arising among individuals and organizations that require some level of authority to solve.

Collective Dilemmas and the Need for Government

Suppose you live in a house with several other students and share a kitchen. The kitchen is always a mess, with dirty dishes in the sink, food on the counters and floor, and garbage spilling out of the wastebasket. Moreover, the kitchen needs new equipment, particularly a new refrigerator that the landlord refuses to buy. You and your housemates all agree that you want a clean kitchen and a new refrigerator. Yet despite this understanding, the kitchen remains dirty and no one bothers to buy the refrigerator. Why won't anyone take care of these problems?

Imagine that you get mad enough to do something about the situation. You wake up one morning, clean the kitchen, and buy the refrigerator on your credit card. You ask your housemates to help pay for the refrigerator, but only some pay their share. You wish there were a way to enforce a rule that only those who paid for the refrigerator can use it. Furthermore, you wish there were a rule restricting kitchen use to those who clean it. You cannot, however, enforce these rules, so all of your housemates enjoy the newly cleaned kitchen and the new refrigerator, regardless of their contributions.

Your frustration ultimately leads you to propose rules that determine who has to clean the kitchen and when, and who has to pay for the new equipment. Some housemates object, claiming that they don't mind a dirty kitchen and don't use the refrigerator very often. They propose to leave things as they are. Soon after, the kitchen becomes dirty, and when the need arises to replace a broken microwave oven, no one bothers to buy it. The problems begin to mount once again.[3]

Even if you haven't faced this precise situation, you have likely encountered similar collective dilemmas with groups of people. A group is challenged by a

---

[3] For a general statement of one version of this problem, see Garrett Hardin, "The Tragedy of the Commons," *Science* 162 (December 1968): 1243–48.

collective dilemma A situation in which there is conflict between group goals and individual goals or self-interest.

collective dilemma when there is a conflict between group goals and individual goals or self-interest. Such dilemmas can be found everywhere.[4] Take, for example, the economist Thomas Schelling's story of the mattress in the middle of the road.[5] A traffic jam arises as cars slow to a crawl to bypass the mattress. One after another, each driver makes the decision to drive around the mattress and continue on his or her way, and the traffic jam persists. Had one driver taken the time to stop and move the mattress off the road, the traffic snarl would have been eliminated. But for each driver individually, it is easier and faster to simply drive around the mattress.

Maybe you know of a park with trash on the ground that no one will pick up. Or you may belong to an organization that has difficulty recruiting volunteers to work at events or to help pay for food or equipment. These are all situations in which a group of individuals would be better off if some action were taken to resolve the collective dilemma—clean the kitchen, buy the refrigerator, move the mattress, clean the park—yet group goals are often thwarted by individual self-interest. People may be incapable of solving their collective dilemmas without the presence of some authority, or they may lack a personal incentive to resolve the issue for the betterment of the group.

These stories help illustrate the need for government. Some people argue that government is unnecessary because members of society can self-govern by organizing activities that contribute to the common good. Most philosophers and political theorists, however, disagree. In the absence of government, they argue, chaos reigns. Many would concur with Thomas Hobbes, the seventeenth-century English philosopher, who claimed that without a sovereign, society would become a "war of all against all."[6] By sovereign, Hobbes meant a person, group, or government with a monopoly control of force over a well-defined territory. In other words, a sovereign is the final authority—the decision maker of last resort—that can enforce its decisions over others. Imagine a society lacking such authority. There would be no courts or governments to enforce contracts; theft would be rampant, with no threat of prosecution; victims would pursue their own justice, sinking society into a swirl of destruction and unhappiness. A sovereign, therefore, is necessary for an ordered, stable society.

The Hobbesian "war" is a collective dilemma writ large. In the worst-case scenario, society's members have no sovereign to enforce rules and chaos reigns, despite their desire for order and stability. In the much better situation, a sovereign government provides order and other common goods that allow members of society to lead productive, satisfying lives.[7] Sovereign governments are necessary because of underlying collective dilemmas that threaten all societies.

---

[4] Russell Hardin, *Collective Action* (Baltimore: Johns Hopkins University Press, 1982).

[5] Thomas Schelling, *Micromotives and Macrobehavior* (New York: Norton, 2006).

[6] Thomas Hobbes, *Leviathan* (1651; repr., New York: Oxford University Press, 2009).

[7] For the intellectual foundations of American government, especially the foundations that influenced the framers of the U.S. Constitution (discussed in Chapter 2), see John Locke, *The Second Treatise of Government* (1690), and Jean-Jacques Rousseau, *Social Contract* (1762).

Government is not only necessary to solve the fundamental problem that Hobbes identified, it is also essential for solving many of the collective dilemmas that arise in everyday life, such as funding for park maintenance, police protection, education, national defense, and care for the poor. Without the coercive power of government, few services of collective benefit would be provided.

Today, most of us take the need for government for granted. It is true that many governments throughout history have been oppressive and have mistreated their people. All too many have started wars with other countries without justification. The *absence* of government, however, can be at least as bad, if not worse. This is not merely the fanciful imagination of philosophers. In recent decades, some societies have exemplified Hobbes's war. In Somalia in the 1990s, parts of the Congo in the 2000s, and recently in some parts of Afghanistan, Mali, and Yemen, the lack of sovereign governments led to long periods of competition among unchecked militias or roving bands of thugs led by warlords that terrorized people and destroyed cities and towns without regard for loss of life.

Contemporary debates over the appropriate size of government tend not to be about whether we need government at all, but rather about what part the government should play in people's economic, social, and personal lives. Such debates hinge on concerns about the amount of government involvement in resolving collective dilemmas, and whether people should be left alone to solve those dilemmas themselves. Toward one end of the spectrum, libertarians believe that governments should do only the bare minimum to address collective social concerns, such as building roads and bridges and maintaining a small standing army to defend the country. Toward the other end of the spectrum, socialists believe government should provide an extensive social safety net, including generous unemployment benefits; free health coverage, education, and child care; and heavily subsidized utilities, housing, and transportation.[8] Most of the debate within the United States occurs between these two ends of the spectrum; disagreements are matters of degree.

Types of Collective Dilemmas

As we study the American government and political system, it will be useful to consider four types of collective dilemmas common in politics.

Collective-Action Problems

In the housemates example, a clean kitchen is a collective good, or what economists call a public good. A **public good** refers to a benefit provided to a group of people that each member can enjoy without necessarily having to pay costs

public good A benefit provided to a group of people such that each member can enjoy it without necessarily having to pay for it, and one person's enjoyment of it does not inhibit the enjoyment of it by others.

[8] We will discuss these and other political philosophies in later chapters, especially Chapters 9 and 16.

private good A product or benefit provided such that its enjoyment can be limited to specific people, and one individual's consumption of it precludes others from consuming it.

free riding Benefiting from a public good while avoiding the costs of contributing to it.

collective-action problem A situation in which people would be better off if they all cooperated; however, any individual has an incentive not to cooperate as long as others are cooperating.

for it, and for which one person's enjoyment of it does not inhibit the enjoyment of it by others.[9] A classic example of a public good is clean air to breathe. Something like the bite of a hamburger or a sip of a soft drink is a **private good**, which refers to a product or benefit provided to you such that your consumption of it precludes others from consuming it.

The problem is that public goods can be hard to produce without some external enforcer (for example, government) requiring that people pay for them. People will be tempted to **free ride**, which means they will benefit from the public good while avoiding the costs of contributing to it. As with producing the clean kitchen that you and your housemates desire, the public good clashes with individual incentives.[10] A **collective-action problem** is any situation in which people are individually better off free riding and enjoying the public good that others produce without contributing toward the production of that public good.

Your free-riding housemates enjoyed the clean kitchen, and that made you angry because you paid the price and they didn't. Likewise, there are public goods produced by governments—such as parks, national defense, clean air and water, public beaches, traffic lights, and streetlights—that benefit anyone in the vicinity, even if he or she did not pay the taxes to produce those goods.

If there is effective enforcement, however, public goods can be produced with fair systems of payment or contribution by all those who enjoy them. Some kind of authority can be necessary even at the most basic level. Without some form of governance applied to you and your housemates, the kitchen will probably remain dirty. Without some kind of enforcement by the Internal Revenue Service, people would not pay enough taxes to support basic government services.

In later chapters, we will explore a variety of collective-action problems that occur in all modern political systems, including the American system. You will discover that collective-action problems are endemic in politics. For example, the Occupy Wall Street movement in 2011 and 2012 required active participants who were willing to occupy parks and other public areas for days on end as a display of protest. It required participants to volunteer their valuable time and effort in support of the cause. Since the movement was intended to represent and benefit a broad swath of the U.S. population—an intent reflected in the slogan "We are the 99%"—the protesters were paying the costs of participating while having to share the benefits, increased government attention to the plight of 99 percent, with those who chose not to participate. And as the number of days spent in protest increased, the winter temperatures began

[9] Mancur Olson, *The Logic of Collective Action: Public Goods and the Theory of Groups* (Cambridge, MA: Harvard University Press, 1971).

[10] Many goods considered public are not pure in the sense that they contain elements of a private good. For example, the new refrigerator can be subject to crowding: the availability of the refrigerator is a public good to you and your housemates, but each space on a shelf is more of a private good during the period you use it. Public parks are considered public goods, but at some point one person's enjoyment may impinge on another's enjoyment.

to plummet, and run-ins with police became ever more likely, participants had to pay even greater costs, and many of the protesters decided they preferred the alternative course of action—returning to their everyday lives while those who stayed continued to protest on their behalf. Sure enough, eventually the number of protesters dwindled to insignificance.

All voluntary organizations, including movements like Occupy Wall Street, face collective-action problems daily as they seek contributors to their cause. If a voluntary organization cannot solve such problems, it will cease to exist. This is just one example of how collective-action problems occur in politics; they also present challenges in other types of groups and other situations.

Prisoner's Dilemma Situations

A famous parable in modern social science tells the story of two criminal suspects caught after a burglary. The police separate the suspects (we'll call them John and Frank) so that they cannot communicate with each other, and interrogate them individually to try to induce confessions. The police have enough evidence on each man that even if no confessions are forthcoming, they can get them sentenced to a year in prison. However, if either John or Frank provides more evidence against the other man, the police can get a harsher sentence for the one implicated (and get closer to solving the crime). In this context, each man is offered a stark choice: implicate your partner or stay silent. If John implicates Frank and Frank stays silent, John goes free and Frank gets six years

The Occupy Wall Street movement represented a collective-action problem as those who demonstrated absorbed the costs of doing so, including confrontations with police, while many others who did not participate nonetheless benefited from the attention the movement raised. This dilemma contributed to the movement petering out in 2012.

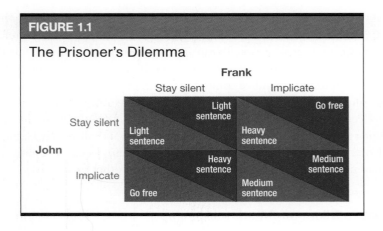

FIGURE 1.1

The Prisoner's Dilemma

		Frank	
		Stay silent	Implicate
John	Stay silent	Light sentence / Light sentence	Go free / Heavy sentence
	Implicate	Heavy sentence / Go free	Medium sentence / Medium sentence

in prison. Likewise, if Frank implicates John and John stays silent, Frank goes free and John gets six years. If they both implicate each other, then they each get three years in prison (less than the six-year sentence, to reward their individual cooperation with the police). If both stay silent, they each get one year. Figure 1.1 shows the four possible outcomes.

The situation is troubling for the prisoners. No matter what Frank does, John receives a lighter sentence—potentially no prison time at all—by implicating Frank. The same goes for Frank. Therefore, both prisoners, if they decide to serve their individual interests, implicate their partner. The expected outcome of this situation is the convergence of the two selfish strategies: each prisoner will implicate the other, and both will receive three years in prison. The **prisoner's dilemma** is that each would be better off if they cooperated and remained silent, but they cannot achieve the better collective outcome unless there is a way to enforce their cooperation.[11]

Note the similarity between the prisoner's dilemma and the collective-action problem. In both situations, what is good for the group of two is difficult to achieve because of individual temptations. In the prisoner's dilemma, the overriding individual temptation is to implicate your partner (to "defect"), while in the collective-action problem the temptation is to free ride off the members of your group who are contributing. Collective-action problems, therefore, are multi-person versions of prisoners dilemmas.

The prisoner's dilemma is also a generic version of situations that regularly occur in American politics. Two candidates campaigning for election to the same office, for example, would both benefit if neither spent much money on television advertising. It's quite possible that the election outcome would be the same if neither one advertised or if both advertised. Yet if one candidate advertises and the other does not, then the former is likely to win. Neither can-

prisoner's dilemma An interaction between two strategic actors in which neither actor has an incentive to cooperate even though both would be better off if they both cooperated.

[11] Robert Axelrod, *The Evolution of Cooperation* (New York: Basic Books, 1984).

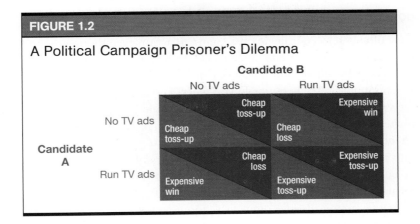

FIGURE 1.2

A Political Campaign Prisoner's Dilemma

Candidate B

		No TV ads	Run TV ads
Candidate A	No TV ads	Cheap toss-up / Cheap toss-up	Expensive win / Cheap loss
	Run TV ads	Cheap loss / Expensive win	Expensive toss-up / Expensive toss-up

didate can escape the trap of spending large amounts on television advertising. The result is expensive advertising by both sides, often with little effect on the election outcome (Figure 1.2).

An external authority or a neutral party, however, can enforce cooperation among people to overcome collective-action obstacles. The political scientist Dennis Chong offers as an example the prisoner's dilemma that arose during the 1960 presidential campaign, when candidate John F. Kennedy sought the endorsement of Adam Clayton Powell, an influential New York politician.

Powell made it known that his endorsement was available only for cash— settling for fifty thousand dollars in return for 10 endorsement speeches. There was a small problem, however: Powell did not trust the Kennedy camp to pay if the speeches were delivered first, and the Kennedy camp did not trust Powell to deliver the speeches if he were paid in advance. The solution? Kennedy turned the money over to an intermediary, who would pay it out in five-thousand-dollar installments following each endorsement speech.[12]

In this case, the intermediary enabled the two men to overcome a collective dilemma, which could be categorized as a repeated prisoner's dilemma, where each faced an individual temptation to "defect" from the agreement to cooperate. Yet even the intermediary could not ensure resolution of the problem's final stage. As Chong adds in an intriguing postscript, "What incentive did Kennedy have to make the final payment?"[13]

Governments play the role of external authorities in many related situations, including the enforcement of contracts among people or organizations. For example, the government helps labor unions and corporations in their negotiations over wages and working conditions by making sure that each side lives up to the agreements reached during labor talks.

[12] Dennis Chong, *Collective Action and the Civil Rights Movement* (Chicago: University of Chicago Press, 1991), p. 38.

[13] Chong, *Collective Action and the Civil Rights Movement*, p. 38.

Coordination Problems

People often fail to coordinate on a course of action even though they all wish they had. If you and a friend agree to meet downtown for lunch at noon but forget to specify where (and at least one of you doesn't have a cell phone, so you can't communicate), where would you meet? Perhaps you would go to the last place you had lunch together. Or maybe you would look for your friend at her favorite place. You may find each other, but it is likely that you won't.

coordination problem A situation in which two or more people are all better off if they coordinate on a common course of action, but there is more than one possible course of action to take.

A **coordination problem** is any situation in which each individual in a group prefers to act in common with the others but there are multiple possible common actions to take, and for a variety of reasons (usually incomplete information), the individuals might have difficulty coordinating on a single, cooperative action. People often face coordination problems either because they can't communicate or because there is a fundamental disagreement over the best action to take. Such situations differ from prisoner's dilemmas, where the expected outcome is that both prisoners implicate the other. With the prisoner's dilemma, there is one expected outcome: that the pair does not cooperate with each other. In coordination problems, each member of the group wants to coordinate on a single outcome with the others, even though more than one outcome is possible.

As mentioned, people are frequently conflicted about the desirability of a given behavior, making it hard to coordinate. For example, let's say your friend would prefer to eat Chinese food and you would prefer pizza. The key, however, is that it is most important to each of you that you eat together rather than eat alone, even at your preferred restaurant. This reflects an important type of coordination problem in which there is a strong desire to coordinate among members of a group, but disagreement over the precise behavior on which to coordinate (Figure 1.3).

A classic example from politics is when members of a political party want to coordinate their support and get behind one candidate in order to defeat their

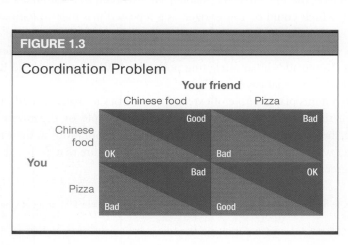

FIGURE 1.3

Coordination Problem

rival party. However, party members may disagree over which candidate to support. The negative scenario for the party is a failure to coordinate, meaning they split their votes among party candidates, enabling the rival candidate from the more united party to win the election. In the positive scenario, party members effectively unite behind a single candidate and defeat the rival contestant.

Because people are sometimes indifferent as to how best to coordinate, many coordination hurdles are easily overcome. Most people simply want a decision to be made so that they can accurately anticipate how others will behave. In the early twentieth century, countries had to choose the side of the road on which cars would drive. Some countries, especially the former British colonies, chose the left side. This is a simple example of government establishing a rule to coordinate people's behavior for everyone's benefit. In terms of safety, it does not matter much which side people drive on as long as there is a consistent rule that everyone follows. A more widespread example of coordination is the worldwide adoption of traffic signals, where red lights mean stop and green lights mean go. If governments didn't make and enforce consistent rules to coordinate such behavior, the world's roadways would be far more dangerous places.

Unstable Coalitions

Politics is about dividing and uniting people. Different interests divide members of society or groups within that society, resulting in disagreements over the best courses for implementing collective action. The ability to accomplish anything in politics, however, demands that people unite into effective coalitions. Unless you are an all-powerful dictator who can force people to bend to your will, a collective effort typically is required to take action for a common cause. The process of forming coalitions, therefore, is a fundamental feature of all politics.

Understanding how coalitions form is not as straightforward as it may sound, however, and collective dilemmas are prevalent. We have already learned about the need to overcome collective-action problems by motivating people to contribute to a public good. Forming a coalition of any kind to create a public good requires solving the basic collective-action problem. We also know that coordinating on a common strategy can be difficult.

Maintaining your coalition in the face of competition presents an additional dilemma, particularly when other coalition leaders make better offers to your coalition partners. To illustrate such instability in coalitions, we can embellish the housemates story. Suppose that there are nine of you in the house but only five parking spaces available, for which you must pay the landlord a flat fee. It's clear to you all that unless you contribute financially to renting the parking spaces, no one can use them. Let's further suppose that the parking spaces altogether cost $500 to rent for a year. You and four others have formed a coalition, and each member of your group promises to contribute $100 toward the parking spaces. Note that you have formed a **minimum winning coalition**, or the smallest-size coalition necessary to achieve your goal. In many situations,

minimum winning coalition
The smallest-size coalition necessary to achieve a goal.

minimum winning coalitions are the most desirable, because larger membership tends to dilute the overall benefits of winning. In this case, for five people and five parking spaces, if you are in the winning coalition, you will always have a place to park your car. If there are any more people in the coalition, you may not have a space when you need it, because there will be more people than spaces.

Problems for your coalition quickly emerge. Just prior to making your rent payment for the parking spaces, two of the excluded housemates, who want to park their cars, make the following offer to three members of your coalition: "If three of you pay only $90, we will pay $115 each." In effect, they have formed a second coalition by "raiding" your coalition. Soon after, two more housemates raid this second coalition by each offering to pay $130, with the remaining three members paying $80 apiece. This third coalition, however, is quickly destabilized when a couple of additional housemates make a better offer to some of its members.

The coalition raiding can continue indefinitely, and in fact, any coalition of five is susceptible to raiders with a better offer. As a result, no coalition will remain in place long enough to accomplish its goal. This collective dilemma is referred to as a problem of **unstable coalitions**.

As with other kinds of collective dilemmas, unstable coalitions are endemic in politics, yet they can be stabilized by external enforcers and by effective institutions. For example, an outside authority (perhaps the landlord) can set up an effective voting system (that is, an institutional solution) and grant one of you

unstable coalition An instance in which three or more people must make a collective choice from a set of alternatives, but any voting coalition in favor of an alternative can be divided by consideration of another alternative.

Know the FACTS — Collective Dilemmas

Any group of people faces **collective dilemmas**, which are situations of conflict between group goals and individual goals or self-interest. We can identify different types of collective dilemmas, including the following:

- **Collective-action problem:** a situation in which many people would be better off if they all cooperated; however, any individual has an incentive not to cooperate as long as the others are cooperating.

- **Prisoner's dilemma situation:** an interaction between two strategic actors in which neither actor has an incentive to cooperate even though both would be better off if they both cooperated.

- **Coordination problem:** a situation in which a group of people want to coordinate, but there are many possible ways to coordinate and people disagree over which way is best.

- **Unstable coalition:** an instance in which any voting coalition in favor of an alternative can be divided by consideration of another alternative.

status as an **agenda setter** to control what options are voted on by your group. Say, for example, that there will be a single, binding vote, with a majority deciding the outcome. The agenda setter then uses his or her power to restrict to two the available options of paying for the parking spaces. Under this arrangement, a decision can be made over payments, and the parking spaces can be allocated.

agenda setter An authority that controls what options are decided on by a group.

Agenda-setting power is essential to avoid coalition raiding, yet those who possess it can use it in a variety of ways. A manipulative agenda setter may rig the results so that he or she pays less for the parking spaces than everyone else while gaining equal access to them. A more beneficent agenda setter with enforcement powers will ensure that a fair scheme emerges, including one option where each of the nine housemates pays just $55.56 for the parking spaces and enjoys access to their use. This type of agenda-setting approach rejects the minimum winning coalition strategy, opting instead to create a consensus among all to enact a program with a unanimous coalition.

In politics, unstable coalitions potentially can occur in legislatures, agency boards, and elections; among groups of judges on the Supreme Court; and within political parties. In the U.S. Senate, for example, it is not uncommon for senators who want to defeat a bill to introduce a "killer" amendment, which reduces support for the bill enough to defeat it. The original coalition of senators in favor of the bill is split apart by the amendment, with some now wanting to vote against the bill. Introducing killer amendments is a form of coalition raiding by opponents. We usually do not witness coalitions being raided and constantly falling apart, however. This is largely because members of vulnerable coalitions anticipate the potential problems and minimize their occurrence by adopting voting rules and granting agenda-setting powers to make raiding difficult. The granting of agenda-setting powers and the establishment of effective voting rules are examples of institutional features to resolve collective dilemmas—in this case, the problem of unstable coalitions.

Principal–Agent Problems

Another kind of situation that commonly arises in politics is called the **principal-agent problem**. It is sometimes referred to as a delegation problem. It is not technically a collective dilemma because it does not at its core involve a conflict between collective goals and individual incentives. Rather, it is a dilemma arising from a direct conflict between at least two individuals. Like the collective dilemmas discussed earlier, the principal-agent problem is found in various guises in politics and can require careful institutional design to solve.[14]

principal–agent problem (delegation problem) An instance in which one actor, a principal, contracts another actor, an agent, to act on the principal's behalf, but the actors may not share the same preferences, and the principal lacks the means to observe all of the agent's behavior.

Principals are those who hire others (agents) to work for them. A classic principal-agent dilemma goes something like this: Suppose your car has

---

[14] D. Roderick Kiewiet and Matthew McCubbins, *The Logic of Delegation: Congressional Parties and the Appropriations Process* (Chicago: University of Chicago Press, 1991).

a knocking sound that worries you. You hire a mechanic to fix whatever is causing the knocking. In this simple example, you are the principal and the mechanic is the agent. You have delegated the task of fixing your car to him. The mechanic tells you that he has found the source of the sound and needs to replace several parts. He promises to order new, high-quality parts from the car's manufacturer. He goes ahead with the work. You get your car back and pay him for his services and for the parts. A happy ending would be that the knocking has gone away and your car is in fine shape.

However, you remain concerned, because you do not know anything about car engines. More troubling, perhaps, is that you did not watch everything the mechanic did to your car. For all you know, he tightened a few screws and did not put in any new parts (but charged you for some), or he put in used parts, or did a sloppy job. Perhaps the car will be back in the repair shop within weeks.

This "problem" or "dilemma," as economists like to point out, is inherent in any relationship between a principal and an agent who does not have exactly the same interests as the principal. You as the principal have limited information about what the agent does in your interests. Without laws to protect you, you are at risk of being taken advantage of by an unscrupulous agent. For a variety of possible reasons, a principal in a contractual relationship may not be able to observe all of an agent's actions. This gives the agent some leeway. He or she could act in a manner that the principal would not want: the agent could shirk his or her responsibilities to the principal, or even steal from the principal. One solution would be to give the principal more information about the agent's actions, but this may be difficult to do. After all, you would need to learn a lot about auto repair to be able to determine what the mechanic was doing, even if you could watch him.

What does the principal-agent problem have to do with politics and government? Much of government involves the delegation of responsibility by principals to agents. A prominent example of a principal-agent problem in politics is the relationship between a bureaucratic agency and elected members of the government. Anyone working for the government who is not part of the ruling powers is called a **bureaucrat**. A **bureaucracy** is an agency or office devoted to carrying out tasks for the government in a manner consistent with the law. In any political system, even nondemocratic ones, bureaucracies can be considered the agents of the sovereign government, as when a king hires an army to fight his wars. In democracies, however, bureaucracies are supposed to carry out the work that elected representatives—the ones who make the rules—want them to do.

In the United States, Congress and the president together pass legislation, and the jobs of the executive-branch bureaucracies are to execute, administer, and enforce the laws. The principal-agent problem looms, however. Executive-branch bureaucracies (the agents) may not always execute the laws in a manner that Congress or the president (the principals) wants. Leaders in government cannot observe all that the millions of employees of the executive-branch

bureaucrat Any government employee who is not part of the ruling powers.

bureaucracy An agency or office devoted to carrying out tasks for the government in a manner consistent with the law.

bureaucracies do. Like the auto mechanic in the preceding example, bureaucrats can shirk their duties, misrepresent their effort, and steal from taxpayers. (We will study these situations in Chapter 7.)

Economists, political scientists, and other social scientists consider ways of setting up institutions so that agents have incentives to do what principals want them to do. The principal-agent problems inherent in any political system require institutional solutions. So Congress requires bureaucratic agencies to adhere to strict rules for documenting administrative decisions. In the auto-mechanic world, many states have laws requiring warrantees on repair work. Warrantees improve the situation because mechanics have an incentive to get the repair right the first time and avoid returns. Some states require that mechanics show the customer the parts being replaced. Of course, one way to hold an agent accountable is to pass along information about the agent to other potential principals. Agents' reputations depend on satisfied principals (or customers, in the case of the mechanic). Honest mechanics hope to get more business over time, because people talk among themselves or can blog about who does good work.

Designing Institutions

We have noted that governments are necessary to solve the most fundamental of all collective dilemmas—namely, the dangerous breakdown in social order. But governments are also necessary to solve many everyday dilemmas, including challenges that arise from prisoner's dilemmas, coordination and coalition problems, and principal-agent problems. Governments accomplish this by establishing rules for decision making or by creating institutions. In the abstract, institutions can be thought of as long-term solutions to the Hobbesian dilemma, as well as to more day-to-day dilemmas.

The institutional details of government are the means by which governments mitigate and control collective dilemmas and principal-agent problems that can bedevil societies. Without effective institutions that survive over the long term, societies can become unstable and fall apart due to people's inabilities to self-organize on a daily basis. The dilemmas described earlier, if unsolved, can destroy a society.

It is not enough to know that institutions solve collective dilemmas and principal-agent problems, however. They *way* they solve these dilemmas matters in determining whose interests are served. In other words, different kinds of institutions will lead to different kinds of outcomes over the long run. Specific institutional designs affect the distribution of power, wealth, status, and other things people prefer and care about in politics.

Everyday **public policies** can distribute benefits and costs to people. Policies are rules for day-to-day life, such as those that establish whether we can turn right on a red light when we are driving, how much we pay in sales tax

public policies Programs and decisions by the government that are enforced by the rule of law.

for a new pair of shoes, or how much the government pays retirees in Social Security benefits. These are policies (which usually take the form of laws) that determine specific conduct in one part of our lives.

Institutions are broader, more stable rules that determine how policies or laws are made and enforced. They are the relatively fixed "rules of the game"—the fundamental rules that dictate how we govern and make future rules or decisions. The Constitution, for example, describes in detail the basic institutions of American government, such as the methods for passing laws and electing representatives and presidents, the authority of the states vis-à-vis the national government, and the fundamental rights of citizens in relation to their government. In short, the Constitution lays out the long-term set of rules (institutions) for making the everyday rules (policies).

Institutions of government are designed purposefully by people who believe such institutions will help them achieve their policy goals.[15] When the leaders of small states argued in the Constitutional Convention of 1787 over the need for a Senate with two senators from each state, they understood that this institutional design would help protect them against policies and laws that would benefit the large states at the expense of the small states. The leaders of the large states understood this, too, and insisted on an institutional design for the House of Representatives that offered them an advantage: representation by the states based on population. The resulting compromise—two legislative houses that are both necessary to approve legislation—was a deliberate attempt to create institutions of government that would allow small and big states to benefit from the union and would encourage all the states to approve the new Constitution.

Now consider two of the Supreme Court's most monumental decisions, *Baker v. Carr* (1962) and *Wesberry v. Sanders* (1964). Together, these decisions effectively mandated that all districts within a state for the U.S. House of Representatives and the state-level house and senate had to be roughly equal in population size. Prior to these rulings, some congressional or state-level districts—mostly in cities—had very large populations, while others—mostly in rural areas—were very small in population. Rural residents had much more representation per person than urban residents in some states. The Court rulings resulted in many more urban districts and increased urban representation in state legislatures and the House of Representatives. The Court claimed that mandating equal-sized districts was consistent with the idea of one person/one vote, an idea it claimed was implied in the Constitution.[16]

These two Supreme Court decisions subsequently changed the nature of politics in some states. Both the people who brought the lawsuits and the

[15] Daniel Diermeier and Keith Krehbiel, "Institutionalism as a Methodology," *Journal of Theoretical Politics* 15 (2003): 123–44.

[16] Note that the Court allowed the Senate to preserve its highly unequal system of representation by population. This was due to the fact that the nature of representation in the Senate was clearly specified in the Constitution.

defendants in the cases were well aware of the consequences, as were the justices of the Supreme Court. The institutional change ordered by the Court fundamentally altered the nature of representation in American legislatures, bringing into the system more representatives from urban populations, including racial minorities, members of new immigrant communities, and those who wanted more federal help for cities. It is no accident that governments at the state and federal level in the U.S. adopted policies friendlier to large cities in the decades following the institutional changes in representation, which meant that people in large cities benefited in concrete ways from new transportation systems, more health clinics, and job training programs paid for by governments. Thus, a change in institutional design produced a different solution or outcome than the previous institution had, or than a different institutional change would have had.

Institutions can be designed or can evolve over time. They continue to shape outcomes long after those who originally designed the institutions have departed the scene. Institutions have lasting effects on societies because they channel political, economic, and social behavior into patterns that can be enduring. As an example, after the national government began to spend a lot of money on space research in the 1950s, a set of interest groups, such as those representing scientists, universities, and research companies, formed to pressure the government to continue these spending policies. In this way, the institutions created to promote space research—new agencies like NASA—became self-reinforcing in that they spawned groups in society applying public pressure for robust budgets for more space research. More generally, the policies chosen as a result of an institutional design create interest groups that resist any institutional changes that would threaten the policies that benefit them. Social scientists often refer to this idea as **path dependence**. Path dependence in this context means that institutional decisions made early on deeply affect current and future policy decisions. The system begins down a "path." Past decisions about institutions leave legacies for the present that make it difficult to change direction, even if that change seems desirable in the present.

Consider our discussion of how representation in the Senate was designed and the consequences of this design: the decision in 1789 to grant each state in the new United States equal representation in the Senate has profoundly shaped the policies of the national government. Because sparsely populated farm states have as many senators as highly populated urban states, the Senate historically has been more sensitive to the plight of farmers than have other parts of the national government, and has tended to thwart changes in policy that threaten farmers' incomes, even when a majority of the population favored such changes. Moreover, as we will see in Chapter 5, the Senate provides opportunities, under its institutional rules, for a small minority of senators to halt legislation they do not like. So once policies are set that happen to favor rural areas, perhaps helped along because of the over-representation of smaller states,

path dependence The notion that earlier events or decisions deeply affect current and future policy decisions or outcomes.

a few senators from those states can block later attempts to undo the policies. In this way, certain institutional design features—such as equal representation by state in the Senate and strong rights of a minority of senators to stop legislation action—not only can cause certain policies to occur but also can freeze those policies in place once they do occur.

Types of Government Institutions

Comparing the American political system with other political systems can help us to understand and evaluate it. We can learn about the consequences of having different institutional forms by examining what happens in other countries. We will compare the United States to other countries throughout this book.

The institutions of government shape the operation of the overall political system, and they differ across countries.[17] All governments, even nondemocratic ones, have some kind of basic institutional structure. A common feature of the various types of **authoritarianism** is the absence of any expectation that the government represents the people. Furthermore, the institutions of government do not give the people a direct voice in choosing their leaders. The institutions within these countries, however, can be different.

Some authoritarian countries are **dictatorships**, vesting sovereign power in one individual. For many decades until his death in 2011, Mu'ammar Qaddafi ruled Libya uncontested as a dictator. He maintained final authority over the government and dealt harshly with his political opponents. In **monarchies**, such as in Saudi Arabia and Jordan, the king (or queen in some instances) rules on the most critical matters, and there is no competition for his (or her) position. Most authoritarian countries are **oligarchies**, meaning that the political power resides in a small segment of society. In the major Middle Eastern monarchies, a parliament that is partially elected and partially appointed shares power with the monarch, and the parliament makes many of the day-to-day policy decisions. Other nations are **one-party states**, another form of oligarchy. In China, for example, the Communist Party runs the government and represses any opposition. It is not subject to real competition in elections. The leader of the Chinese Communist Party conducts foreign policy, but shares with various party committees the responsibility for day-to-day governing.

In the parts of the world accustomed to democratic government, not only do people want governmental institutions to solve collective dilemmas—even the most totalitarian governments can do that—they also demand specific institutions based on democratic principles that will improve the welfare of everyone in society.

Democracy means rule by the people. Although there is disagreement over exactly what democracy means in practice, some consider it an ideal situation

authoritarianism A political system in which there is no expectation that the government represents the people, and the institutions of government do not give the people a direct voice in who will lead.

dictatorship An authoritarian political system in which sovereign power is vested in one individual.

monarchy A political system in which a ruler (usually a king or queen) is chosen by virtue of being the heir of the previous ruler.

oligarchy A political system in which power resides in a small segment of society.

one-party state A political system in which one party controls the government and actively seeks to prevent other parties from contesting for power.

democracy Rule by the people; in practice today this means popular election of the government and basic protections of civil rights and liberties.

[17] Plato's *Republic* is an excellent place to begin a discussion of the various kinds of political systems.

where everyone has an equal voice in all public decisions, a goal that has never been attained and perhaps never will be. There is widespread consensus that, at a minimum, democracy means that the people leading the government are chosen by popular election to rule for a specific period.

Nearly all governments in the world's democracies are also **republics**, meaning that public officials are chosen to represent the people in an assembly, which makes important policy decisions.[18] This is in contrast to direct democracies, in which citizens can vote directly on policy matters. No country operates purely by direct democracy, though some countries, such as Switzerland, and even many of the states in the United States, such as California and Oregon, rely extensively on referendums or initiatives to decide major policy issues.[19]

Today, most people—even those living under authoritarian rule—believe that democracy is a desirable form of government, based on the simple notion that democratic government tends to produce better standards of living and people with their preferences more greatly satisfied compared with those in other systems of government.[20]

In democratic systems, large-scale conflicts among groups of people typically are settled peacefully through legislatures, courts, elections, and administrative agencies. Although peaceful conflict settlement can be reached even in the most authoritarian or dictatorial regimes, democratic regimes offer a better track record of preventing wars, horrible human rights abuses, and oppression. They also tend to be less corrupt than authoritarian regimes.

What makes a country more or less democratic? In classifying political systems, international organizations use specific criteria. For example, Freedom House, a nonprofit organization that monitors the democratization of countries, relies on two general criteria:

- *Political rights*: the degree to which a country's political process allows for open and extensive participation of citizens, with free and fair elections.

- *Civil liberties*: the degree to which a country's people are free to express their views and organize into political parties and other groups, to run for office, to pressure the government, and to insist on the independence of the judiciary.

There is disagreement over how democratic the United States has been in the past, and even how democratic it is today. Some critics argue that the

republic A political system in which public officials are chosen to represent the people in an assembly that makes important policy decisions.

---

[18] This use of the word *republic* should not be confused with the distinction made between a republic and a constitutional monarchy. A republic, of which the United States, Germany, and France are examples, has no monarch, and the head of state is chosen by the people or by representatives of the people. A constitutional monarchy, such as in the United Kingdom or Belgium, formally has a king or queen as its head of state. In practice, there is little difference between these two forms of democratic governance, because monarchs have long since become figureheads and do not retain governing power.

[19] Referendums are direct elections in which voters choose whether to support a law passed by a parliament or legislature. Initiatives are direct elections in which voters choose whether to support a law proposed by a group of fellow citizens.

[20] For evidence on the links between democracy and quality of life, go to www.freedomhouse.org.

FIGURE 1.4

Institutional Features of Select Democracies

	Executive				Legislature		Party System		Legal System		
	Federalism	Parliamentary	Premier-presidential	Presidential	Bicameral	Unicameral	Two-party	Multiparty	Civil Law	Hybrid	Common Law
Australia	X	X			X			X			X
Brazil	X			X	X			X	X		
Canada	X	X			X			X			X
France			X		X			X	X		
Germany	X	X			X			X	X		
India	X	X			X			X			X
Ireland			X		X			X			X
Italy		X			X			X	X		
Japan		X			X			X		X	
Mexico	X			X	X			X		X	
Poland			X		X			X	X		
South Korea						X		X		X	
Spain		X			X			X	X		
Sweden		X				X		X	X		
Turkey		X				X		X	X		
United Kingdom		X			X			X			X
United States	X			X	X		X				X

United States is less than a full democracy because, for example, it has mistreated, and continues to mistreat, specific groups of minorities, or because wealthy people have advantages in influencing electoral politics. We will discuss the first point in Chapter 4 and the second in Chapters 5, 11, and 16.

There is great variety in democratic institutions around the world. In fact, the institutional features of American government are quite rare. Figure 1.4 lists some basic elements of the American political system and shows that most other countries have different institutions. In later chapters, we will study and compare these institutions in more detail.

Although many other countries share one or several institutional features with the United States, none has the identical institutional structure. For example, the Canadian system is also federal and republican, but it is not presidential, nor does it have separation of powers. The American system is particularly unusual because of its combination of federal and presidential structures, as well as the fact that it has only two major political parties.

Political scientists have demonstrated that institutional differences shape not only the nature of politics but also the kinds of policies adopted and the impact of those policies on people's lives. For example, analysts have found differences between countries that are federations and countries with unitary governments (strong central governments with no subnational governments having independent authority) in their approaches to economic policy. They conclude that federal countries do not change their economic policies as abruptly as unitary countries. Political scientists also draw on comparative data to argue that if the United States were to change its method of electing presidents and members of Congress to be more like the methods used in European countries, the country would have more than two major political parties. And systems with more than two major political parties tend to be characterized by more generous government spending on social programs.

Analyzing Politics and Government

The concepts that we have covered in this chapter are those that political scientists use to analyze and understand politics and government. Let us now return to the opening story of the budget crises during President Obama's terms in office to see how these concepts help us make sense of the apparent puzzle in the story.

Two collective-action problems lie at the heart of the story. The first is among the public, who in general do not like to pay taxes despite wanting the government to maintain programs and services at a high level. Each individual would prefer that others pay for the government's programs, as long as the benefits of those programs and a stable economy are available to everyone. In fact, the national government often borrows money rather than raise taxes to pay for its new programs, thus leading to the large deficit. When the government borrows money to pay for services instead of taxing citizens, it is in effect asking future generations (who will have to pay back the loans) to bear the cost of current government programs. Thus, contemporary beneficiaries of the stimulus plan are free riding off their children! The more general point is that it is always tempting for taxpayers to support tax cuts *and* generous government programs on the assumption that citizens other than themselves will pay the bill.

The second collective-action problem occurs among politicians. Suppose a politician prefers to balance the budget by cutting back a popular and expensive program like Medicare, as opposed to raising taxes or cutting other programs. Any politician who takes this stand and declares his or her support for a reduction of government services runs the risk of losing the next election. If a large group of politicians joined together to advocate for reductions in Medicare, then each politician in that group would be somewhat protected. But it is hard for any individual politician to overcome the temptation to go along with the crowd, because that is the easier course of action. From the perspective of those who do not favor continued funding at current levels, fear of the wrath of voters prevents them from publicly supporting deficit-reducing policies like cutting programs or raising taxes. We learned earlier that public goods are hard to produce because of collective-action problems. In this case, the public good such as a balanced budget does not happen because the individual costs of participating in the collective action are high enough that the joint effort to stop the growth of expensive government programs and services never gets off the ground.

We also know that institutions are designed or evolve in response to collective dilemmas and principal-agent problems. The main theme of this book is that the specific political institutions chosen to solve collective dilemmas and principal-agent problems have important consequences for society. Generally, the crises over the budgets indicate that political institutions designed to solve *some* problems cannot solve *all* problems, and so other collective dilemmas will arise. The budget deficit continues to be very large, and politicians continue to battle over which policies are necessary to balance the budget, such as cutting services and programs or raising taxes.

Many details about the institutions in the American political system help to explain the continued recurrence of budgetary crises, but we would be getting ahead of our story to try to incorporate them all here. We will study these institutions in later chapters, but first, we take a closer look at the challenges the Founders faced in designing the basic institutions of American government.

FURTHER READING

★ = Included in *Readings in American Politics*, 3e

Acemoglu, Darren, and James Robinson, *Why Nations Fail: Origins of Power, Poverty and Prosperity* (New York: Crown Publishers, 2012). Nations will fail unless their political and economic institutions encourage the government to serve the needs of most people, as opposed to catering to a small number of elites.

Axelrod, Robert, *The Evolution of Cooperation* (New York: Basic Books, 1984). A close analysis of the prisoner's dilemma, especially situations where people have repeated interactions with one another; tit-for-tat strategies arise over time when people face each other repeatedly in prisoner's dilemma situations.

★ Hardin, Garrett, "The Tragedy of the Commons," *Science* 162 (December 1968): 1243–48. Applies the collective action problem to the study of common pool situations.

Hirschman, Albert, *The Passions and the Interests: Political Arguments for Capitalism before Its Triumph* (Princeton, NJ: Princeton University Press, 1977). An intellectual history showing the relatively recent acceptance of the legitimacy of publicly striving to protect one's material interests.

★ Olson, Mancur, *The Logic of Collective Action: Public Goods and the Theory of Groups* (Cambridge, MA: Harvard University Press, 1971). A classic account defining the collective-action problem and applying it to the study of political organizations.

Ostrom, Elinor, *Governing the Commons: The Evolution of Institutions for Collective Action* (New York: Cambridge University Press, 1990). Under certain conditions, communities are capable of self-regulation, allowing them to sustain long-term yields of a common resource and effectively overcoming the tragedy of the commons.

Shepsle, Kenneth A., and Mark S. Bonchek, *Analyzing Politics: Rationality, Behavior, and Institutions*, 2nd ed. (New York: Norton, 2010). A comprehensive treatment of models of politics using rational choice assumptions, written at a level appropriate for undergraduate students.

KEY TERMS

agenda setter (p. 19)

authoritarianism (p. 24)

bureaucracy (p. 20)

bureaucrat (p. 20)

collective-action problem (p. 12)

collective dilemma (p. 10)

coordination problem (p. 16)

democracy (p. 24)

dictatorship (p. 24)

federal system (p. 7)

free riding (p. 12)

institutions (p. 6)

minimum winning coalition (p. 17)

monarchy (p. 24)

oligarchy (p. 24)

one-party state (p. 24)

path dependence (p. 23)

political system (p. 5)

politics (p. 5)

preferences (p. 5)

principal-agent problem (delegation problem) (p. 19)

prisoner's dilemma (p. 14)

private good (p. 12)

public good (p. 11)

public policies (p. 21)

republic (p. 25)

unstable coalition (p. 18)

Events like Shays's Rebellion, in which poor farmers took up arms against the government in 1786–87, pointed to the need for a strong national government. However, at the time of the Founding, many people were afraid of putting excessive power in the hands of the national government, and this debate over governmental power shaped the Constitution.

2

THE CONSTITUTION

The Founders wanted to establish a set of governmental institutions that were powerful enough to be effective, but not so powerful as to become dangerous to liberty. Why did the Founders who favored a stronger national government prevail over those who preferred a weaker one? Did the Constitution succeed in striking an effective balance, preserving order and liberty?

In 1786, not long after the United States won independence from Britain, a group of several hundred debt-laden, cash-poor farmers in Massachusetts took up arms against their new government. They were led by Daniel Shays, a veteran of the Revolution, who faced the threat of debtor's prison when he returned home from the war. Shays's Rebellion pitted poor farmers like Shays—who had been hurt financially by an economic downturn after the war—against the Massachusetts state militia. The farmers resented the state government's enforcement of foreclosure rules and its alignment with Boston-area merchants. The rebels closed down courts across Massachusetts in an attempt to prevent debt collection. In 1787, Shays led a march to Springfield, Massachusetts, with the intention of seizing the federal arsenal there. Along the way, more farmers, including many war veterans and even some state militia members, joined the rebels, bringing their numbers to around 1,400. The rebellion was eventually crushed in Springfield by a privately funded government militia, but the armed resistance by civilians against state troops alarmed political leaders throughout the young country.

Shays's Rebellion severely tested the governmental institutions in place at the time, which had been established by the Articles of Confederation (ratified in 1781). As Shays's Rebellion and other events following independence showed, the Articles did not provide for effective security in the new country. The rebellion was emblematic of the many collective dilemmas facing the new country. Under the Articles, there was a *unicameral* (one-house) Congress with two to seven delegates from each state. But there was no executive branch to enforce the laws passed by Congress, to protect the states from internal or external threats, or to represent the country in foreign relations.

And Congress could not raise revenue by passing direct taxes, customs, duties, or levies. Instead, it had to "requisition" the states for money, and then wait for them to raise funds and forward those to the national government. Finally, the procedure for amending the Articles was too onerous, making it nearly impossible to address these shortcomings under the Articles.

When delegates from the various states gathered at the Constitutional Convention in Philadelphia in 1787 to improve the institutions of government, they quickly decided to write a new constitution. In summarizing the defects of the Articles, they had events like Shays's Rebellion in mind. They understood that they needed to strengthen the national government so that it could respond to crises like these, and to other collective dilemmas such as the state-by-state economic policies that, by operating distinct from and sometimes at odds with other states, were harming the country as a whole.

A major concern, resulting from the national government's lack of enforcement and direct taxing powers, was that financial free riding among the states was common. Here we see a clear example of a collective-action problem as described in Chapter 1. All of the states would benefit from a stronger national government able to enforce order, but it was in each state's interest to let the other states pay for the military power necessary to keep order. As a result of the incentives to free ride, the national government failed to raise more than 20 percent of the funds owed to it by the states, with some states paying none of what they owed. Moreover, a series of ominous events, including Shays's Rebellion, quickly revealed the problems inherent in having a national government without an executive wielding military powers.

At the same time, the Founders were acutely aware of Americans' fear of excessive governmental power. The Revolution that secured independence from Britain was justified as a fight against tyrannical power, and state leaders had agreed to the Articles of Confederation because they wanted a weak national government that would not interfere too much with the states or individual freedoms. Most citizens believed that the Revolution would lead to less intrusive government and thus to more liberty than they experienced under British colonial rule.

The task for the Founders at the Constitutional Convention was to agree on a set of governmental institutions that were powerful enough to resolve collective dilemmas among the states in times of crisis, but not so powerful as to become dictatorial or dangerous to liberty. As we will learn in this chapter, the Founders held different views as to how this balance should be struck. Some wanted much stronger national powers than were allowed under the Articles, while others preferred to keep national powers weak while perhaps strengthening the state governments. In the end, the former group (called Federalists) won out. Why did the Federalists triumph when there was so much distrust of government among the people? Did the Constitution, which created a set of relatively strong national institutions, strike an effective balance among the competing views of appropriate governmental authority?

What Do Constitutions Accomplish?

In societies governed by the **rule of law**, legal codes are intended to be applied to everyone in an unbiased manner. This implies not only that legal principles guide the behavior of citizens but also that the government, and the officials in that government, are subject to the law and cannot make arbitrary decisions contrary to the law in their capacity as public authorities.

In authoritarian regimes or dictatorships, leaders are often not subject to the same rules that apply to all other citizens. The law in such systems can be what the leaders say it is at any point in time. One of the distinctive features of democratic systems, by contrast, is governance by a body of laws that has been established by the people or their representatives.

Written constitutions form the basis of most societies governed by the rule of law. They establish the basic institutions of government and represent the country's legal core. Legal scholars worldwide share an understanding of a hierarchy of law, which sets constitutional law above statutory law. Statutory laws are those passed by legislatures or by administrative agencies empowered by legislatures. Constitutional law is seen as the collection of fundamental rules for making statutory laws and regulations.

In essence, constitutions specify the most basic institutional rules for making policies. For example, legislatures make statutory law, but constitutions determine who is eligible to be in the legislature, what authority the legislature has, and in many cases, what rules legislators must follow to make decisions. Although the officials elected to legislatures may disagree about what public policy should be, they should not routinely disagree about *who* can make the decisions and *how* those policy decisions should be made. Put more abstractly, a legitimate constitution reflects a shared understanding of who can wield public authority and what kinds of authority public officials should have.

A constitution is therefore a prerequisite for a society based on the rule of law. To use an analogy from biology, the U.S. Constitution is like a skeleton; it provides the fundamental shape and structure of the whole political system. Upon that skeleton hangs the flesh of American politics, which features competition between groups and individuals for resources, influence, and public office. Some parts of the skeleton support muscular institutions such as the American presidency, which has become stronger over time and is today far more powerful than specified in the Constitution. Other parts of the skeleton are more fragile, such as the relationships between the national government and the states. These "bones" were broken during the Civil War in the mid-nineteenth century and rebuilt afterward with new material, including constitutional amendments and court decisions.

The skeleton analogy, however, goes only so far. Although human skeletons age and weaken over time, the Constitution lives on, providing structure to the political system for centuries. And unlike the typical human skeleton, the structure of the Constitution has continued to evolve during the nation's life. A human skeleton can be healed and only slightly amended if defective. The

rule of law A system in which all people in a society, including governing officials, are subject to legal codes that are applied without bias by independent courts.

Constitution, however, has proven remarkably adaptable in the face of national challenges, sprouting new limbs and bones to strengthen its overall structure.

If a constitution is a skeleton that provides structure to the political system, the backbone of that skeleton is the set of institutions of government specifying who has ultimate legislative, executive, and judicial authority, and how those in authority are subject to the laws.

Recall from the last chapter that governments exist to solve the basic problem identified by Thomas Hobbes: without government, society would descend into chaos and few or no public goods would be provided. Sovereign authorities are required to solve societies' fundamental collective dilemmas. In establishing the basic form of government, a constitution provides the plan for solving troublesome collective dilemmas. Indeed, one could regard a constitution as a series of prescriptions for such problems.

Origins of the American Political System

Among the types of collective dilemmas we discussed in Chapter 1 were collective-action problems and coordination problems. Let us now examine these dilemmas in the context of the 13 new states organized under the Articles of Confederation prior to the writing and ratification of the Constitution. When these states faced a collective-action problem, each had a strong incentive to free ride off the efforts of others. Under the Articles of Confederation, the national government could not compel the states to do much of anything. As a result, many states failed to pay their share of the debt incurred during the Revolutionary War, even though all the states enjoyed the benefits of independence from Britain. Likewise, some states refused to participate in cooperative efforts intended to boost the national economy. When several New England states agreed to close their ports to British goods in order to protect their own industries, Connecticut took advantage of the situation by welcoming British goods and securing more favorable terms of trade from England than those extended to other states. Connecticut even imposed a tax on goods from Massachusetts after leaders from that state complained. Such collective-action problems often descended into rounds of punishment, recrimination, and mistrust.

In the case of coordination problems, all states are worse off if the group fails to act in unison. The states may disagree on how precisely to coordinate, but they all have an incentive to pursue a common course of action. For example, under the Articles of Confederation, states printed their own currency. This not only made it difficult for people from foreign countries to trade with or conduct business in the United States, it also led to rampant inflation because states had incentives to print their own money to pay off debts. Most leaders recognized that if the colonies could agree to use one national currency, it would make trading and business investment more attractive to foreigners and also lead to unified policies on inflation.

The Constitutional Convention was called in 1787 largely because leaders in the Continental Congress and in the states acknowledged that the weakness of the national government under the Articles made it impossible to solve these types of collective dilemmas. Most believed that a stronger national government was necessary. Three of the ultimate features of the Constitution—the presidency, the specified national government powers, and an independent judiciary—were specifically designed in response to previous failures to solve free riding and coordination problems. We will start our analysis earlier in history, however, with legacies from the pre-Revolutionary era.

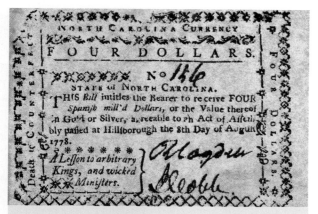

Under the Articles of Confederation, states printed their own currency, such as North Carolina's four-dollar bill pictured above. This system led to a coordination problem that hindered foreign trade with the United States and caused massive inflation, a problem that leaders under the Articles of Confederation were unable to rectify.

Colonial Charters

In the mid-eighteenth century, the American colonies were part of the British Empire. Having defeated the French in the French and Indian War of 1754–63, the British had established political control over most of the Atlantic seaboard, from what is now Virginia to Maine. The colonies provided raw materials for British industry, money for the Crown through taxation of colonial subjects, and space for émigrés from Britain to settle in the New World.

Each colony had a charter describing the powers and responsibilities of the different branches of government. Colonial governments typically consisted of a lower chamber (the assembly), whose members were elected by propertied white males in the colonies; an upper chamber (the council); and a governor. The members of the councils were appointed by British government officials, and the governor was appointed by the governing English noble or company that ran the proprietary colony, or in the case of a royal colony, by the British government.

These charters, and the institutional design they described, presaged later state constitutions and the U.S. Constitution. The North American origins of separation of powers, a single executive, and a two-chambered legislative branch lie in these colonial governments and charters.

The Revolution

Tensions between the British government and the colonies escalated in the 1760s as the colonists grew increasingly weary of being exploited for the economic benefit of England. Many of them especially resented the repressive taxes and unfair trade rules imposed by London. They rebelled against the Crown by various means, including boycotts, riots, attacks on British troops, and formal declarations that the colonies had sole authority to tax themselves ("No taxation

By the 1760s, American colonists were increasingly resistant to the taxes and other rules imposed by the British government. Here, British troops arrive in Boston to enforce compliance in the colonies. Depite the resentment toward British rule, some of the institutions of colonial government were later adopted by the states in the U.S. Constitution.

without representation"). The colonies ignored or flouted a series of measures by which the Crown demonstrated its authority. Radical groups of colonists, such as the Sons of Liberty in Boston, planned public events to highlight the abusive actions of the British government. In one such event, known as the Boston Tea Party, rebels raided British ships in Boston Harbor and dumped hundreds of chests of tea into the harbor to protest increasingly onerous taxes on tea from the East Indies.

In 1774, the Continental Congress, which represented the colonies in communications with the British government, repeatedly passed resolutions deploring the actions of the Crown, asking for relief, and expressing continued loyalty. At the same time, it approved broad boycotts of British goods and indicated that the colonies were willing to risk war with Britain to be free of its tyrannical control. The British government responded to these provocations not through dialogue or by seeking compromises, but by sending troops to America and threatening to arrest the leaders of the rebellious colonies.

In the spring of 1775, under orders to arrest John Hancock and Samuel Adams, two Massachusetts leaders who had been urging the colonies to declare independence, 700 British troops confronted 70 Massachusetts militiamen in Lexington, outside Boston. When the militia refused to disperse, the British redcoats fired, killing eight Americans. The British troops then advanced on nearby Concord and exchanged gunfire with another group of militiamen on a bridge over the Concord River. The British subsequently retreated, only to be attacked by more than 1,000 Americans. By the end of the battle, 73 British troops had been killed and 200 wounded. These opening battles of the war for American independence were humiliating setbacks for the British.

News of the battles spread rapidly on both sides of the Atlantic. The British and the Americans mobilized additional troops, and over the next year they fought to capture key cities and forts from each other. Neither army gained the upper hand, but the escalating war inflamed passions on both sides. Violence by the two armies became more wanton and brutal. In the spring of 1776, realizing that it had a real fight on its hands, the Crown sent tens of thousands of additional troops to put down the troublesome colonists. Throughout the year, thousands of British-paid Hessian mercenaries were dispatched to invade and occupy New York City. It was widely assumed that they would then proceed to conquer the capital city of Philadelphia.

As the colonies prepared for a new British onslaught, they formally announced their separation from Britain in July 1776. Implicitly, the Declaration of Independence was also a declaration of full-scale war against Britain. Discussion within the Continental Congress prior to the signing of the Declaration revealed a bitterly divided group of colonial leaders. There were moments when men charged others with treason and stormed out of the chamber. Those who remained and signed the document did so with considerable trepidation. Had the Revolution failed and the men been captured by the British, they would surely have been shot or hanged as traitors to the Crown. In fact, they wrote a secret agreement into the records of Congress: "To prevent traitors and spies from worming themselves amongst us, no person shall have a seat in Congress until he should have signed the Declaration."[1]

After the Declaration, the war raged for five more years along the Atlantic seaboard, at various locations in the interior of the continent, in the West Indies, and in what is now Canada. With considerable help from the French, who provided badly needed naval power, the Americans eventually were able to isolate British forces and destroy them or induce their surrender.

The Declaration of Independence

The Declaration of Independence and the U.S. Constitution are famous all over the world, not only for being the founding documents of the United States, but also for their influence in promoting specific philosophies of government. Both have been widely imitated or referred to in other countries' founding documents. Because it determined the institutions of American government, the Constitution plays by far the more important role in our daily lives. However, the Declaration of Independence, written by Thomas Jefferson in bold, memorable prose, has long been widely quoted in defense

[1] Cornel A. Lengyel, *Four Days in July: The Story behind the Declaration of Independence* (Garden City, NY: Doubleday, 1958), p. 250.

of revolution and in defiance of abusive authority. It was and continues to be enormously influential in proposing that by virtue of their natural rights, people ought to be self-governing and free from subjugation by foreign powers or tyrannical leaders.

The Declaration comprises three parts. The first offers an argument for rebellion. The more learned members of the Founding generation, including Jefferson, were influenced by the English philosopher John Locke (1632–1704), who was well known for declaring that government was legitimate only if it was based on the consent of the governed. Locke wrote that government exists to protect people's natural rights, which include the right to life and the enjoyment of their property. He also was a proponent of "social contract theory," or the idea that by entering into a society ruled by a popularly elected government, people were obliged to obey the rules determined by the majority. For Locke, decision making by majority rule logically followed from the idea that all humans ought to be treated equally. A government formed by people consenting to being constrained could, in Locke's words, lead to "peace, safety, and public good." These ideas by Locke influenced Jefferson when he wrote the Declaration's famous opening paragraphs asserting that "all men are created equal," that people have the right to "Life, Liberty and the pursuit of Happiness," and that governments derive their "just powers from the consent of the governed."

The Declaration's second and lengthiest section provides political justification for rebellion. It calls King George III a tyrant and cites a litany of grievances against him. In the document's third part, the former colonies took the fateful step: "We, Therefore, the Representatives of the United States of America . . . solemnly publish and declare, That these United Colonies are, and of Right ought to be Free and Independent States; that they are Absolved from all Allegiance to the British Crown."

After considerable debate, the Continental Congress approved the Declaration by an affirmative vote by representatives from 12 of the 13 colonies on July 4, 1776. The New York delegation approved the document two weeks later, after receiving approval to do so from their state convention (as their legislature was called at the time).

The Colonial and State Constitutions of the 1780s

The writers of the U.S. Constitution drew much of their inspiration for institutional design from the state constitutions drafted following independence. In fact, many delegates to the Constitutional Convention had written their own state constitutions.

Between 1776 and 1784, most of the states ratified constitutions establishing forms of government that looked partly, if not entirely, like today's national government. The states typically had separation of powers between a single executive and a legislative assembly, with an independent judiciary. These similarities reflected a widespread appreciation for the ideas of the French philosopher Montesquieu (1689–1755) and of Locke, who believed that power should be fragmented and that to lodge power in one branch of government was to invite abuse of authority and even tyranny.

The powers delegated to the branches of government varied from state to state. Nearly all the powers mentioned in the U.S. Constitution for the various branches could be found in several of the state constitutions. For instance, Georgia, Delaware, Massachusetts, New Hampshire, New York, and South Carolina all declared that their governors or presidents were commanders in chief of state militias. The assemblies, however, had the powers of the purse and sole authority to pass legislation for the common good. Most states also had the equivalent of a bill of rights designed to protect freedom of speech, press, and religion, and to guarantee rights for criminal defendants. The description of basic rights and liberties protected under law given in the Virginia Declaration of Rights (1776), which was attached to the Virginia constitution, formed the basis for the first 10 amendments to the U.S. Constitution, known as the Bill of Rights. It is worth noting, however, that the application of these bills of rights was uneven. Several states in the 1770s and 1780s had established official religions and passed onerous laws restricting free speech. In Connecticut, for example, the Congregationalist Church remained its established church until the 1810s. The states generally forbade speech expressing loyalty to the British Crown, a stand that is unsurprising following the Revolution, but was nevertheless restrictive and at odds with the ideas expressed in their bills of rights.

The Articles of Confederation

As we saw at the start of this chapter, in their first attempt to create a national constitutional system the representatives from the states agreed on a set of institutions that largely failed to address their underlying collective dilemmas. The **Articles of Confederation**, ratified in 1781, created more of a cooperative framework among sovereign states than a sovereign national government with power to govern effectively.

In principle, the Congress established by the Articles had meaningful powers, but in fact it had little means to enforce its laws. Under the Articles, the states agreed on actions that they should not take independently, such as conducting foreign policy or undertaking military operations. They also agreed on how states would respect one another's prerogatives, such as by returning fugitives or honoring each other's contracts. Each state had two to seven delegates but only one vote in the Congress under the Articles, and the voting rules were such that 9 of 13 state delegations were required to approve legislation.

As noted in the opening story of this chapter, in the absence of an executive with powers to enforce the rule of law, and without the power to raise revenue

Articles of Confederation
The constitution drafted by the Second Continental Congress in 1777 and ratified by the states in 1781. It set up a weak central government consisting of a congress with limited legislative power and virtually no authority over the execution of its laws.

for common action, the Confederation under the Articles proved ineffective. Moreover, it lacked the means to correct its shortcomings. The requirement of unanimous consent for any amendments to the Articles meant that any single state could block institutional change. For example, 12 of the 13 states approved an amendment allowing for a levy on imported goods to raise funds for the common defense. Yet when Rhode Island failed to approve the measure, the Confederation was forced to continue to rely on the goodwill of the states to pay what they owed. Inevitably, states were free riders and collective-action problems persisted.

Leaders in several states called for a convention to discuss problems among the states related to trade and finances. A first attempt to hold a convention in Annapolis in 1786 failed when only five state delegations showed up. That meeting, however, resulted in a statement calling for a true national convention. The Continental Congress approved the idea, and the meeting was set for May 1787. Eventually, 55 delegates from all the states except Rhode Island convened in Philadelphia, ostensibly to amend the Articles.

The Constitutional Debates

It quickly became clear at the 1787 Constitutional Convention that amending the Articles would not be sufficient to address the collective dilemmas that the states faced. A new constitution was in order. The document ultimately drafted in Philadelphia that summer was the product of intense negotiations among competing interests represented by the men who wrote and ratified it.

Despite the Constitutional Convention's secretive deliberations, we know a lot about what occurred there thanks to James Madison's detailed journal. His notes reveal major cleavages among both the states and their political leaders. These divisions related to three major issues: liberty versus strong government, large states versus small states, and slavery.

Liberty versus Strong National Government One cleavage existed between those who wanted to preserve the philosophy of individual liberty that animated the Revolution and those who believed that a more vigorous national government was necessary. Individual liberty tended to mean weak government, primarily at the national level but also at the state levels. Several prominent men of the revolutionary generation, including John Hancock, the first signer of the Declaration, and Patrick Henry, a prominent Virginian who had led the fight against the Stamp Act in 1765, declined to attend the convention. They wished to preserve the "spirit of 1776," which reflected a government philosophy more consistent with the Articles—namely, that free and independent states should retain full sovereignty with no external constraints. To Henry and others like him, freedom from the dictates of an American national government was as important as freedom from British tyranny.

In contrast, a majority of Henry's fellow Virginians who attended the Philadelphia gathering proposed a plan for a set of institutions that would replace

FIGURE 2.1

The Virginia and New Jersey Plans and the Connecticut Compromise

Virginia Plan

Upper house

- Members nominated by the state legislatures and elected by the lower house
- Number of representatives determined by state population (or quotas of contribution)

Lower house

- Members elected by the people
- Number of representatives determined by state population (or quotas of contribution)

Executive

- Single, independent executive
- Appointed by the legislature

New Jersey Plan

Unicameral legislature

- Members appointed by the states
- One representative from each state

Executive

- Multi-person, independent executive
- Appointed by the legislature

Connecticut Compromise

Senate

- Members appointed by state legislatures
- Equal number of senators (two representing each state)

House of Representatives

- Members elected by the people
- Number of representatives determined by state population; slaves are counted as three-fifths of a person

Executive

- Single, independent executive
- Elected by the state legislatures through the electoral college

the Articles and create a strong national government. The basic framework of the so-called **Virginia Plan** was eventually incorporated in the Constitution, although important and consequential changes were made to the plan throughout the convention. The plan called for legislative supremacy and an independent executive. The legislature would have two houses, with representation accorded to the states in proportion either to their population or to their contributions to the national treasury. A lower house would be elected by the people, and an upper house would be nominated by the states and elected by the lower house. Finally, the original plan contained the provision that the national legislature could nullify state laws that contradicted the Constitution (Figure 2.1).

Virginia Plan A plan proposed at the Constitutional Convention by Edmund Randolph of Virginia, which outlined a stronger national government, with an independent executive and a bicameral legislature whose membership in both houses would be apportioned according to state population.

Large States versus Small States The debate over the Virginia Plan exposed another cleavage, this time between large and small states. The plan did not sit well with those from smaller states who worried about a legislature in which seats were apportioned by population size. The New Jersey delegation proposed its own plan, which was essentially a series of amendments to the Articles that provided for a single legislative house with equal representation among the states. Under the **New Jersey Plan**, there would be no separation of powers between the executive and the legislature in the sense that the legislature would appoint a plural (multiperson) executive. The legislature would, however, have strong powers to regulate commerce and would retain supreme authority over the states on certain matters. This plan, except for a few aspects, was eventually rejected in favor of a new constitution based on the Virginia Plan. The larger and medium-sized states did not approve of equal representation as proposed under the New Jersey plan.

Slavery A third cleavage divided northern and southern states over slavery. On this issue, which was intertwined with the question of representation, neither the Virginia Plan nor the New Jersey Plan was satisfactory to all the states. If representation in the legislature was to be based on population, as proposed by the Virginians, how were slaves to be counted? Naturally, the southern states, with large slave populations, wished for the slaves to be counted fully for purposes of representation. However, as their northern colleagues pointed out, the same southern states wanted slaves to count for considerably less than full persons in determining the apportionment of taxes and duties owed by the states to the national government. This contradiction between the southern states' position on legislative representation and financial matters bedeviled the negotiations for some time, and it was exacerbated by the discomfort many representatives (mostly from the North) felt toward slavery, and especially toward the continuing slave trade.

Difficult Compromises

Although these three cleavages—over the nature of federation, the representation of big and small states, and slavery—overlapped, the opposing groups were not always the same across all three issues. For instance, some delegates found themselves opposing their colleagues on the question of representation, while agreeing with them on the question of slavery.

The nationalists—later known as Federalists for their support of a strong federal (national) government—largely triumphed at the convention, though only after the idea that the national government could nullify state laws was dropped. As we saw earlier in this chapter, a series of events, including Shays's Rebellion and the states' failure to cooperate on important matters such as international trade, gave increasing momentum to the belief that a strong national government could solve collective dilemmas. Nonetheless, the question of the national government's power would continue to be debated, as we will see later in this chapter.

The other two cleavages resulted in painful compromises. The Constitution would not have been approved by the convention or ratified by the states had the delegates stuck firmly to their positions on the issues of representation and slavery.

The Connecticut Compromise The issue of representation was the most difficult to resolve. Delegates remained deadlocked over it for several weeks. Finally, a committee composed of one delegate from each of the participating states hammered out the **Connecticut Compromise**. It was a compromise between the essential elements of the Virginia and New Jersey plans. The compromise determined that Congress would be composed of two houses, with representation in the lower house apportioned by population and the upper house having equal representation across the states. The nationalists insisted that the lower house, elected by the people, would initiate all spending bills. The southern states insisted, for the purposes of representation in the lower house, that slaves would have to be counted in some fashion acceptable to them. Ultimately, on the question of slave representation, northern and southern delegates compromised on a formula such that five slaves were to be counted for representational purposes as three people. Only after the southern states accepted a northern counterproposal did they come to agreement. Northern delegates insisted that for them to go along with the so-called three-fifths compromise on lower house representation, in a similar way five slaves would count as three persons for the purposes of apportioning financial levies on the states. With all finally agreed on the compromises on these representational issues, which were of immense importance to the design of the new government, the convention could move forward on other issues.

Connecticut Compromise
An agreement reached at the Constitutional Convention that there would be a bicameral legislature, with an upper house (the Senate) composed of equal representation from each state and a lower house (the House of Representatives) composed of representation from each state in proportion to its population.

Know the FACTS	Three Cleavages at the Constitutional Convention

Cleavage 1: Strength of National Government
- Some delegates favored a weak national government.
- Some delegates favored a strong national government.

Cleavage 2: Representation in the Legislature
- States with a large population wanted a system based on state population.
- States with a small population wanted equal representation for all states.

Cleavage 3: Slavery
- Slave states wanted slaves counted fully when apportioning seats in the legislature.
- Nonslave states insisted that slaves also be counted fully in apportioning costs associated with national government.

Compromising on Slavery The issue of slavery came up several more times in the convention, and each time delegates recognized that the fate of the Constitution depended on compromise. Even delegates from the North, who generally favored abolishing the slave trade (or banning slavery altogether), understood that any move to change the status quo in the South would doom the entire constitutional enterprise. Neither delegates from the major slaveholding states nor southern state legislatures would have approved the Constitution without the inclusion of protections of the institution of slavery. Some of the northern delegates deeply regretted having to compromise on this particular issue, but expected that the issue would eventually go away, either because slavery would become economically less feasible or because future generations would settle this delicate matter.

As a result of the southerners' intransigence, four articles in the Constitution were included that implicitly sanctioned slavery (although the word *slavery* does not appear in the document). The first was Article I, Section 2, which, as mentioned earlier, declared that for purposes of representation in the House and the electoral college, and for apportionment of direct taxes owed by the states, every five slaves were to be counted as three persons. (This was superseded by the Thirteenth and Fourteenth Amendments after the Civil War.) The second was Article I, Section 9, which stated that the importation of slaves could not be prohibited by Congress until after 1807, although Congress could approve a limited tax on the importation of slaves. (Congress did in fact ban the importation of slaves in 1808.) Third, Article V said that no constitutional amendment was allowed that would change Article I, Section 9, until after 1807. Finally, Article IV, Section 3, stated that fugitive slaves fleeing to another state were to be returned to their owners (superseded by the Thirteenth Amendment). These passages would later be rendered obsolete by congressional action in the early nineteenth century and by constitutional amendments after the Civil War.

The Constitution was finally agreed to and signed by all but three of the delegates present in Philadelphia. Many gave speeches indicating that they were unhappy with specific aspects of the Constitution but felt it was important to approve the document as it stood. The last signer was Benjamin Franklin, old and frail, but still eloquent. He said to those present that, throughout the convention and its debates, he had been concerned that the divisions in the young country might doom it to failure. Now, he said, comparing the young country to the sun pouring into the chamber, he had "the happiness to know that it is a rising, and not a setting sun."

Institutional Features of the Constitution

The U.S. Constitution is the oldest written constitution among those in use by nation-states around the world. Although it has served as a model for many other constitutions, the form of government it established remains, on the whole, distinctively American. Upon its ratification in 1788, the Constitution provided the new country with the critical governance features it had lacked under the Articles of Confederation. These features helped to strengthen the national government by enabling it to overcome collective dilemmas among the states and the people. The Founders, however, deliberately designed a constitutional system with limited popular control because they feared that too much democracy would lead to poor government and mob rule. Only one unit of government, the House of Representatives, was directly elected; the Senate, the president, and federal court judges were appointed by officials chosen in some way by the people—the Senate by state governments, the president by the electoral college, and federal court judges by the president and the Senate.

The complete text of the Constitution is included in the Appendix. Here we consider its main institutional features.

A President as Executive

Various ideas were proposed at the Constitutional Convention regarding the executive branch. They ranged from a plural executive, consisting of three or more people, to a president who served for life. The delegates eventually settled on the idea of one person serving as president for a four-year term. Unlike the Articles, which made it difficult for the states to join together to quell rebellions and negotiate with foreign powers, the individually held executive powers outlined in the Constitution were intended to bring decisiveness to the national government in the face of collective dilemmas. Under the Constitution, the president has relatively broad powers to execute laws, protect the country against internal and external military threats, negotiate with foreign countries, and appoint officials to the executive branch. The president is indirectly elected by state-level groups of electors, which together make up the **electoral college.** This method of presidential selection reflected a compromise between those who wished for an executive elected by Congress and those who wished for an executive elected directly by the people in a popular election.

electoral college The electors appointed by each state to vote for the president.

A Bicameral Legislature

The delegates agreed on a Congress with two chambers or houses (we call this a **bicameral legislature**), both of which must approve legislation before it can become law. Because the House of Representatives is intended to represent the people, its members are directly elected by the voters. Representation in the House is in proportion to state population, and each representative serves a two-year term. The Senate is intended to represent the states. Each state has two senators, who originally were appointed by the state governments for six-year terms. Since 1913, after ratification of the Seventeenth Amendment to the Constitution, senators have been directly elected by the people in their respective states.

bicameral legislature A legislature consisting of two chambers or houses.

The constitution that was signed in Philadelphia in 1787 was the product of bargaining and compromise. Although the delegates to the convention did not agree on all the institutional features of the new government, in the end, most felt that it was important to establish a more effective government than the one under the Articles of Confederation.

expressed powers (enumerated powers) Those powers specifically described in the Constitution.

elastic clause (necessary and proper clause) The provision in Article I, Section 8, of the Constitution that states that Congress can make whatever laws are "necessary and proper" in order to provide the means to carry out its enumerated powers.

The Founders intended Congress to be the center of the national government, and endowed it with the greatest number of **expressed powers** in the Constitution, more than those given to the executive or judicial branch. The general language of the so-called **elastic clause**, referring to the power to make "all laws necessary and proper," grants Congress wide authority to legislate to provide the means to carry out its enumerated powers.

An Independent Judiciary

Judicial power for the entire country rests with the federal courts, headed by the Supreme Court, which has very broad jurisdiction, including all cases "arising under this Constitution." Congress, charged by the Founders to decide whether to establish "inferior" federal courts, early on set up a system of federal district and appeals courts. Courts that are independent of other branches of government and of the interests of their particular states or localities play an extremely important role in maintaining social order and promoting the common good in modern societies. The courts settle disputes over the meaning and applicability of laws and contracts. Without neutral, unbiased courts, people, states, or organizations would regularly settle their conflicts by other means, including violence or intimidation.

Furthermore, a federal court can resolve disputes among states or among sub-units of the national government. A strong Supreme Court was seen as necessary to settle conflicts among the states, as much as to resolve cases involving more general legal or constitutional issues. The states have maintained their own court systems to manage state-level matters, but cases involving conflicts among states, between citizens residing in different states, and between representatives of foreign countries and the United States are all the prerogative of the federal courts.

Soon after the Founding, the Supreme Court took the further step of declaring that it had the authority to determine the constitutionality of actions by any government within the United States. Although the Court's power to review the constitutionality of laws or acts of government was not mentioned in the Constitution, it was asserted by the Federalists and applied by the Supreme Court in the *Marbury v. Madison* decision of 1803, as we will see in Chapter 8.

Separation of Powers

The executive, legislative, and judicial functions are separated into three distinct branches of government in the United States. This is known as **separation of powers**. One way to think of separation of powers is to consider what it is not. Separation of powers does not have the various branches as part of a hierarchy with one branch above the others. No single branch can determine the people leading any other branch. Rather, the branches are coequal and have different functions to perform. Separation of powers contrasts with a parliamentary system (as in the UK), where the executive (typically the prime minister, as he or she is known) is chosen by the parliament and remains in power at the parliament's discretion. In other words, in parliamentary systems, the parliament sits atop a hierarchy and can hire and fire the executive. Thus, in practice, having a president elected independently of the legislature is the distinctive feature of a separation-of-powers system. The American-style separation-of-powers system, whereby the legislature does not choose the executive but rather determines the laws that the executive must carry out, is increasingly common among new democracies around the world. In Latin America, Africa, and Asia, many countries have systems with elected presidents who hold considerable powers. Among older democracies, especially in Europe, parliamentary systems—in which the legislative and executive functions are fused together by virtue of the parliament choosing the executive—are more common. When the Founders chose to devise a separation-of-powers system, they were deliberately avoiding a model of government with a single sovereign, based on their experiences with the British government. For the Founders, dividing governmental authority was a bulwark against oppression.

separation of powers An arrangement in which specific governmental powers are divided among distinct branches of government; typically, this means having an executive who is chosen independently of the legislature, and thus executive power and legislative power are separated.

Checks and Balances

checks and balances An arrangement in which no one branch of government can conduct its core business without the approval, tacit or expressed, of the other branches.

The concept of **checks and balances** (as distinct from the notion of separation of powers) refers to the ways in which the three branches of government share power (Figure 2.2). The Founders built various "checks" into the political system to help ensure that power would not be concentrated anywhere within the three branches. No one branch can conduct its core business without the approval or acquiescence of the others. While separation of powers divides the primary functions among multiple branches, checks and balances ensures that no one branch has total control over any function. For example, Congress primarily legislates, but the president (or the executive branch) has some legislative powers, including the power to veto legislation and to call Congress into special session in emergencies. The judicial branch runs the courts and interprets the law, but the president appoints judges to federal courts with Senate approval. Congress (or the legislative branch) can override the president's veto, impeach the president and federal judges, and set up new federal courts. It must also pass laws to raise funds for anything the other branches wish to do. The Senate must approve many executive-branch appointments, including federal judges, as well as all treaties. The Supreme Court, under the doctrine of judicial review, can declare acts of Congress or the president unconstitutional. The chief justice on the Supreme Court presides over impeachment trials in Congress.

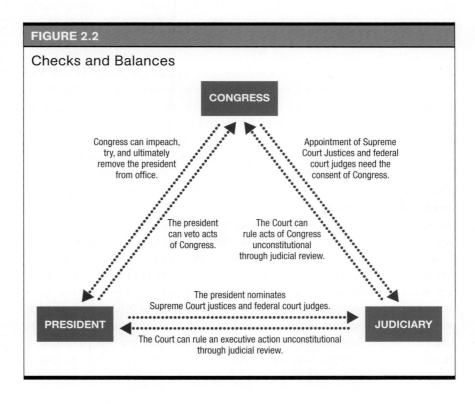

FIGURE 2.2

Checks and Balances

CONGRESS

Congress can impeach, try, and ultimately remove the president from office.

Appointment of Supreme Court Justices and federal court judges need the consent of Congress.

The president can veto acts of Congress.

The Court can rule acts of Congress unconstitutional through judicial review.

The president nominates Supreme Court justices and federal court judges.

PRESIDENT

The Court can rule an executive action unconstitutional through judicial review.

JUDICIARY

Federalism with National Authority over the States

There was never any doubt among the delegates to the Constitutional Convention that the states would retain considerable authority over their own affairs. The issue of the national government's authority, however, was highly controversial. Proponents of a strong national government eventually held sway because they were able to convince enough leaders that a weak national government, such as existed under the Articles of Confederation, would lead to continued squabbling among the states, ineffective response to threats, and lack of coordination on appropriate policies. (These same arguments were used to support the creation of a single executive.) By acknowledging the need for a central government to solve the collective-action problem inherent in getting states to contribute to national defense, the delegates included in Article IV, Section 4, of the Constitution the declaration that the national government (rather than individual states through state militias) is responsible for protecting the states against invasion. Under Sections 2 and 3 of the same article, the national government has the power to approve the boundaries of new states coming into the union and to enforce the rule that states return fugitives to the state from which they fled. These important coordination and enforcement functions were designed to avoid disputes between the states and/or new territories that might lead to war. Article VI of the Constitution contains the most important such language, the **supremacy clause**, which states that the laws and treaties of the United States are supreme throughout the land, including superseding rulings by state courts. Moreover, all government officials in the states must swear allegiance to the Constitution. Finally, Article I, Section 10, lists a series of actions that states cannot take, such as making treaties with foreign nations, placing tariffs on foreign goods, and coining their own money. If taken by the states individually, such actions would harm the collective good of the entire group of states.

supremacy clause The section of Article VI of the Constitution that states that the Constitution and the subsequent laws of the United States are to be the "supreme law of the land," meaning that they supersede any state and local laws.

Reserved Powers for the States

Although the Constitution lists many things that the states cannot do, it also protects them in critical ways from intrusion by the national government or by other states. States cannot be subdivided into other states. One state cannot have fewer senators than any other state unless that state approves. That is, according to Article V, the Constitution cannot be amended to allow for unequal representation in the Senate unless states receiving less representation approve. The states are guaranteed protection as republican forms of government. Most directly, as part of the Bill of Rights, the Tenth Amendment decrees that all powers not granted to the national government in the Constitution are reserved to the states (and therefore known as **reserved powers**). For a long time, this amendment was seen as having little meaning, especially in light of the previously mentioned elastic clause. In recent years, however, the Supreme

reserved powers Those powers not granted to the national government by the Constitution, and therefore reserved to the states.

Court has used the amendment to limit the power of the national government relative to the states on certain matters.

Amending the Constitution

The delegates to the Constitutional Convention agreed on the need for a process to amend the Constitution, and unlike the Articles of Confederation, amendments did not need unanimous approval of the states. They designed two methods for amendment. Under the first method, an amendment becomes law when two-thirds of both houses of Congress and three-quarters of the state legislatures approve it. Under the second method, two-thirds of the state legislatures can together call for a national convention to propose an amendment or a set of amendments, any of which must be approved by three-quarters of the state legislatures. Only the first method has been used in a successful amendment. The very fabric of the country has been changed by constitutional amendment, including the Thirteenth, banning slavery (1865), the Fourteenth, which laid the basis for anti-discrimination laws (1868), and the Sixteenth, permitting a national income tax (1913). Amendments have greatly expanded the right to vote, declaring that racial minorities (1870), women (1920), people of Washington, D.C. (1961), and 18- to 20-year-olds (1971) can vote in all elections. In recent years, Congress has debated amendments banning the burning of the American flag, another one banning abortion, and yet another banning same-sex marriage. In 2011, a senator proposed an amendment mandating term limits for members of Congress—three terms maximum for representatives in the House and two terms maximum for senators. (It did not get very far in Congress.) Only 27 amendments, out of the thousands that have been proposed, have made it through the process. The first 10 (the Bill of Rights) were approved together in one process soon after the ratification of the Constitution, as we will see later in this chapter.

The Ratification Debate

Federalists Those who favored adopting the Constitution as written because they believed that a strong national government was needed to solve the collective dilemmas facing the states.

Antifederalists Those who opposed adopting the Constitution as written because they feared that it created an overly strong national government.

According to Article VII, the Constitution required the approval of conventions in nine states for it to take effect. By implication, any state that withheld its approval would be excluded from the federation. Those who favored adopting the Constitution as written, with its strong national institutions, became known as the **Federalists**, while those opposed were called **Antifederalists**. In the seven states dominated by Federalists, the Constitution was ratified by the spring of 1788 with comfortable majorities, but there was serious opposition in all the other states. Three—Virginia, Massachusetts, and New York—had strong Antifederalists among their leadership, while Rhode Island didn't even send delegates to the convention and remained opposed to the Constitution for several more years.

Federalists versus Antifederalists

The Antifederalist positions were published as letters in various periodicals and summarized in a pamphlet titled "Letters from the Federal Farmer to the Republican," written anonymously.[2] These letters complained that the new constitution trampled on the sovereignty of the states, that the Constitutional Convention had gone far beyond its mandate to amend the Articles of Confederation, and that the people of the states could potentially be tyrannized by a new national government. The Antifederalists adamantly opposed ratifying the new constitution because they felt it betrayed the principle of the Revolution—namely, that men should live in freedom apart from strong, vigorous government, such as the one they believed would be established by the Constitution. They were particularly opposed to the elastic clause and the supremacy clause (see the preceding text), which in their view together gave the national government such power that "there is no need of any intervention of the state governments . . . with this constitution . . . the government then, so far as extends, is a complete one, and not a confederation."[3] To the Antifederalists, federalism as described in the Constitution meant a return to what they despised about the British: remote government with overriding authority to tax without the approval of popularly elected local or state governments, a standing army ready to oppress the people, and one-size-fits-all policies that did not recognize the diversity of the various states spread across a huge land area.

In response, three proponents of the Constitution—James Madison, Alexander Hamilton, and John Jay—published (under a pseudonym) a series of articles in New York newspapers extolling the virtues of the proposed constitution. These articles, which eventually became known as the *Federalist Papers*, not only urged approval of the Constitution, but also advanced a political philosophy that provided much of the intellectual basis for the American form of government. Among other themes raised in the *Federalist Papers*, a strong national government was considered crucial to solving collective dilemmas facing the states and the people.

Several of the *Federalist Papers* have become classics in political theory across the world. The institutions of government, the Federalists argued, are designed to constrain the behavior of ambitious people and lead to better collective outcomes. A strong national government was essential to protect states from threatening foreign powers, to prevent war between the states, and to forestall damaging internal competition among the states for trade and commerce with other countries. Furthermore, a combination of federalism with separation of powers was desirable to ensure that power did not become lodged in

[2] Its full title was "Observations Leading to a Fair Examination of the System of Government Proposed by the Late Convention; and to Several Essential and Necessary Alterations in It. In a Number of Letters from the Federal Farmer to the Republican." Historians now know that the letters were written by Richard Henry Lee of Virginia.

[3] Brutus, "Antifederalist No. 1," in *The Complete Anti-Federalist*, vol. II, ed. Herbert J. Storing (Chicago: University of Chicago Press, 1981), p. 365.

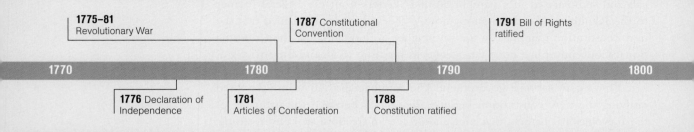

one branch of the government, where it could be controlled by one faction of the society. Finally, the Federalists sought to dispel the fears of those opposed to a stronger national government, arguing that the Constitution reserved important powers for the states, and that citizens would retain their loyalties to the states and not transfer that loyalty to the national government.

Massachusetts and New Hampshire approved the Constitution in early summer, providing the two additional approvals required for ratification. June 21, 1788, the date of New Hampshire's ratification, marks the formal beginning of the new constitutional era. However, it was not until Virginia and New York, the two largest and most important states, ratified the Constitution later that summer that the Federalists knew they had won their struggle. A new Congress and the new president, George Washington, took office on April 30, 1789. Eventually, North Carolina (in November) and Rhode Island (in 1790) approved the Constitution and joined the rest of the states within the new system. The Historical Path box above shows the timeline of major developments in the Founding era.

The Bill of Rights

In the debates over ratification, the Antifederalists complained that the Constitution did not contain a list of individual rights to be protected against government intrusion. Many of the state constitutions contained such lists, particularly Virginia's. To address these concerns, supporters of the Constitution promised that a list of rights would be added as amendments soon after ratification. Consequently, the first 10 amendments were approved by Congress in September 1789 and ratified by three-quarters of the states in December 1791.[4]

Bill of Rights The first 10 amendments to the Constitution, which enumerate a set of liberties not to be violated by the government and a set of rights to be protected by the government.

These 10 amendments, known as the **Bill of Rights**, specify the limits of government action. Among the rights listed are freedom of speech, assembly,

[4] In fact, Congress approved 12 amendments in 1789, but only 10 were ratified by the states. One of the two remaining amendments, concerning congressional salaries, was finally ratified by the states in 1992 as the Twenty-seventh Amendment.

and religious practice; a criminal defendant's right to counsel; the right to bear arms; and the right to security against government intrusion on private property unless a warrant is granted by a court of law. The Bill of Rights is as fundamental to the American political system as the governmental institutions established by the original Constitution. Its protections have been central in determining how individuals and government relate to each other in American society, operating as a kind of buffer against government intrusion on individual liberty. Figure 2.3 shows how the Constitution created a national government that was stronger than under the Articles of Confederation, but the Bill of Rights put limits on government power. As we will discuss in more detail in Chapter 4, controversies over whether the Bill of Rights applies to state as well as to national laws, and over the meaning of the particular rights listed, have

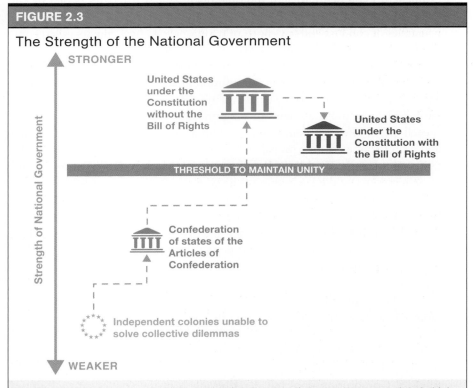

FIGURE 2.3

The Strength of the National Government

STRONGER

Strength of National Government

United States under the Constitution without the Bill of Rights

United States under the Constitution with the Bill of Rights

THRESHOLD TO MAINTAIN UNITY

Confederation of states of the Articles of Confederation

Independent colonies unable to solve collective dilemmas

WEAKER

The Founders attempted to establish a national government that was strong enough to hold the Union together, but not so strong as to infringe on state prerogatives and individual freedoms. The Articles of Confederation represented a step toward unity, but its provisions were not strong enough to solve the states' collective dilemmas. The Constitution created a stronger national government that could effectively hold the states together. The Bill of Rights then placed limits on the national government, reducing its powers toward the minimum strength needed to maintain unity.

occurred throughout American history. These controversies underlie many of the most important political struggles past and present over federalism, slavery, voting rights, taxation, discrimination, and abortion.

In Comparison: National Constitutions

Although our main focus is on the U.S. Constitution, it is useful to consider how it differs in structure and purpose from the constitutions of other countries. There is great diversity among the world's constitutions, mirroring the differences in the institutional structures of the countries discussed in Chapter 1. A few countries, such as the United Kingdom, Israel, and New Zealand, do not have written constitutions. Instead, the "constitutional structure" of government is expressed either in multiple documents or by laws passed by the legislature that are given constitutional stature. In the United Kingdom, basic principles of conduct and laws born of traditional practices (the so-called common law) constitute the foundational legal structure.

Some countries have written constitutions that are essentially meaningless. For example, the North Korean constitution guarantees equal rights "irrespective of sex, race, occupation, length of residence, property status, education, party affiliation, political views or religion" and claims to protect freedom of speech, press, assembly demonstration, and association. However, these rights and protections exist only on paper. North Korea established a communist dictatorship following World War II and mandated that the country "shall conduct all activities under the leadership of the Workers' Party of Korea." The country has one of the most repressive governments in the world, which regularly jails or executes dissidents and critics of the ruling regime. Iran's constitution guarantees equal rights for men and women and divides power equally among three branches of government. In fact, all power in Iran resides with the religious hierarchy, and men and women are treated very differently, both legally and in the broader society.

The U.S. Constitution, at approximately 4,600 words in its original form (approximately 8,000 words including the amendments), is reported to be the shortest among any of the world's nation-states. Unlike some constitutions, such as those of Brazil and Portugal, the U.S. document does not delve into detailed social and political goals. And unlike those of many other countries, the U.S. Constitution does not describe much in the way of citizens' duties. Rather, it focuses on the powers of government and the rights of individuals that are to be protected by the government and from the government. The U.S. Constitution is less specific about several important matters than those of other countries. For instance, it is vague on the powers of the Supreme Court relative to the other branches of government; as we have seen, it was only through later court decisions that the principle of judicial review—the power of the Supreme

Court to declare acts of government at any level unconstitutional—was established. The U.S. Constitution is also relatively vague on the exact powers of the president to wage war. Although the document appears highly specific about Congress's powers, in practice the president's war powers relative to those of Congress go far beyond what the Constitution states.

Nevertheless, the basic elements of the U.S. Constitution have been adopted by many other countries. Following the American model, nearly all constitutions contain a preamble that sets forth guiding principles, a section that describes the institutions of government and how they are to function, and guidelines for amending the constitution.

The "Living Constitution"

The text of the Constitution should be understood as a starting point and not the entire story of constitutional government in the United States. Amendments, court decisions, and the practices of politicians have significantly shaped the constitutional structure of government as it applies to the political system today. The Constitution is a "living document" because its meaning evolves over time in response to changing circumstances and through changes to the text itself. Let's consider some of the major areas in which the original provisions in the Constitution have evolved.

Relative Powers of the Branches of Government

Take, for instance, the military powers of the president, which have changed significantly from what the Founders delineated in the Constitution, mostly through the actions of presidents and decisions of Congress and the federal courts. After much debate, the Founders decided to divide responsibilities on matters of war, foreign policy, and domestic peace between Congress and the president.

The Constitution states in Article I, Section 8, that Congress has the power to:

- declare war;
- make rules concerning captures on land and water;
- call forth the militia to execute the laws of the union, suppress insurrections, and repel invasions;
- raise and support armies;
- provide and maintain a navy.

The president's powers, in contrast, are tersely summarized in the first clause of Article II, Section 2: "The President shall be Commander in Chief of the Army and Navy of the United States, and of the Militia of the several States, when called into the actual Service of the United States."

The Constitution and Religion in Politics

The U.S. Constitution is often said to have created a political system with separation of church and state. Yet public religious expression is common and religious symbolism pervades some government buildings and schools throughout the country. What leads to religious expression being tolerated and even promoted in American politics?

Interests

Compared to populations in most other industrialized countries, Americans are notably religious. According to national surveys, 80–90 percent of Americans say they believe in God. Many Americans who are religious support candidates with similar views and invocations of God and religious beliefs in public life. A majority of Americans expect that viable presidential candidates be Christians who practice their faith. Alternatively, there are other Americans (even many who are religious) who oppose the promotion of religion in public life. They advocate a strict separation of church and state and want religion to be a private matter, and not promoted in any way by government.

Institutions

The words of the Constitution matter greatly, and this can be seen when we contrast the United States with France on religious liberties. In France, the words in the *Declaration of the Rights of Man and of the Citizen* guide French constitutional law: "No one shall be disquieted on account of his opinions, including his religious views, provided their manifestation does not disturb the public order established by law." By comparison, the relevant language of the First Amendment in the U.S. Constitution reads: "Congress shall make no law respecting an establishment of religion, or prohibiting the free exercise thereof." Unlike the French declaration, this American clause makes no mention of public order.

Outcomes

While the U.S. federal courts have required that the American governments not favor one religion over another, constitutional interpretation does not aim to purge all religious expression from the public sphere. Open religious expression, even by politicians, is tolerated and widespread. Prayers are said regularly in legislative sessions in Congress, and "In God We Trust" is engraved and printed on U.S. currency. It is common for political

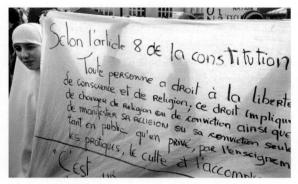

A demonstrator in France protesting a ban on overt displays of religion in schools.

candidates for federal and state offices to discuss their religious views openly, and all serious presidential candidates feel the need to express and show their belief in God. The federal courts have permitted religious expression, even on public property, as long as the government is not promoting one sect or point of view.

The French government, in contrast, grants more legal weight to the secularity of the public space than it does to the individual's freedom of expression. For over 10 years, the French government has prohibited students in public schools from wearing conspicuous religious items such as Muslim head scarves or large crosses around their necks.

Ultimately, the United States and France have responded differently to the challenge of the separation of church and state; the former has favored the coexistence of varied religious expression in the public sphere, while the latter has favored the removal of all religious expression. Due to differences in the language enshrined in their constitutional law, a public-school student of the Islamic faith in the United States enjoys the constitutional guarantee to wear a religious head scarf to express her religious belief, whereas a similar student in France does not.

Think About It

Is American implementation of the separation of church and state appropriate, given the language of the First Amendment? Or is the French model better by keeping religious expression out of the public sphere?

One might assume that the last phrase, "when called into the actual Service," in combination with the powers granted to the Congress, implies that, under the Constitution, Congress alone is empowered to call the military into service, while the president's duty is to determine *how* the military will carry out its task. The Constitution clearly states that Congress shall play the preeminent role in military decision making, while the president is in charge of implementing congressional decisions.

The Constitution's words, however, do not match up against the events that have taken place since its ratification. As a result of important court rulings and acts of Congress dating back to the 1790s, the president has had predominant authority and wide discretion over executing the law, and over foreign policy and defense matters. George Washington set the tone in 1794 by vigorously suppressing a rebellion against a tax on whiskey in rural Pennsylvania. Indeed, Washington deliberately set out to demonstrate that the national government, which had been exposed as weak at the time of Shays's Rebellion seven years earlier under the Articles of Confederation, had gained considerable strength under the new Constitution.

Recent presidents have exercised broad war powers. President Ronald Reagan sent troops to Lebanon in 1982 and invaded and occupied Grenada in 1983 without congressional authorization. President Bill Clinton sent a military force to Haiti in 1994 after stating that he was not constitutionally mandated to seek prior congressional approval for the action. President George W. Bush invaded Iraq and toppled Saddam Hussein's government in 2003 after receiving a vaguely worded congressional authorization to use force under certain conditions. President Barack Obama bombed Libyan armed forces in 2011 in order to oust dictator Mu'ammar Qaddafi and claimed that he did not need congressional approval to do so. Congress sometimes passes resolutions giving presidents wide latitude as international crises unfold; when that happens, these decisions are the presidents' to make without any legal controversy. While the decisions to use military force can be controversial, and opponents complain because they believe either the decision was wrong or presidential authority was overstepped, recent presidents have ordered troops into battle with little or no legal consequence.

This may all seem strange to those who look to the words of the Constitution for guidance on the conduct of foreign affairs and defense. Why is there such divergence between what the Constitution says and what presidents actually do? In fact, any constitutional text, regardless of what country it covers or when it was written, invariably contains passages that are ambiguous in their application to real situations, or that will become outdated by historical events. Military policy is not the only area where the operation of American political institutions has departed from the original text of the Constitution. In later chapters, we will discuss how historical events have changed the relative authority of different parts of the American political system as set forth in the

Constitution. We must bear in mind, however, that it is not only the meaning of a given constitutional text that is subject to change over time, but the text itself.

National Power versus States' Rights

The Constitution itself contains a number of apparent contradictions. For instance, the elastic clause (Article I, Section 8) states that Congress has the power to make laws to carry out a wide range of powers listed in the Constitution, including those providing for "the common Defence and general Welfare of the United States." This could in principle mean that Congress can pass any law with the common good of the country as its goal, leaving little power to the states. The Tenth Amendment, however, appears to contradict this interpretation. It reserves all residual powers not mentioned in the Constitution to the states or to the people. Without the benefit of judicial interpretation over the years, such contradictions could be problematic in the elastic clause's application for governance. Only in later decisions did the courts rule on the kinds of national laws that are allowable under the standard of providing for the "general Welfare."

commerce clause An enumerated power listed in Article I, Section 8, of the Constitution that grants Congress the power to "regulate Commerce with foreign Nations, and among the several States, and with the Indian Tribes."

The courts have mainly focused on the **commerce clause** (Article I, Section 8) as a guide to what policy areas Congress is allowed to act on. Under this clause, the Constitution grants Congress the power to regulate commerce when it is conducted with foreign nations and when it involves more than one state. Court decisions in the twentieth century made it clear, however, that just about any commercial activity occurring in the United States constitutes interstate commerce and thus is fair game for regulation by the national government. Beginning in the 1930s, the courts gave all but complete discretion to the national government to regulate business and commercial activity, stretching congressional authority far beyond what the original text of the commerce clause implies. Recent Supreme Court decisions (on health care, for example), however, have indicated that the legal pendulum may be swinging in the other direction. The Roberts Supreme Court has backed away from this expansive interpretation and limited congressional action based on a stricter reading of the commerce clause, a subject we return to in later chapters.

Direct Election of the President and Senators

The institutions described by the first version of the Constitution were designed to limit popular participation and shield policy makers from public pressure. Among the major branches of the national government, only the House of Representatives was directly elected. The president and senators were not elected directly by the people, but were appointed by the states through a group of electors or legislators. The president and senators were given longer terms in office to protect them from short-term changes in the popular will. Furthermore, the right to vote, known as suffrage, was controlled by the state governments that mostly restricted voting to property-owning white males. Overall, the original Constitution did not specify or encourage a highly democratic political system sensitive to public opinion.

Over the course of American history, however, constitutional amendments and court decisions provided for—and even encouraged—popular participation in government. This evolution not only enabled new groups in society to vote, such as former slaves, women, and 18- to 20-year-olds, it also empowered the national government to enforce this right. Since the early twentieth century, the Constitution also has been applied by the courts to protect vigorously the rights of people to organize, speak out, and protest against the government.

Under the original Constitution, senators were appointed by state legislatures. Since the passage of the Seventeenth Amendment in 1913, senators are elected directly by the people. Here, Joni Ernst (R–IA) celebrates her 2014 election victory.

Rights and Liberties

Many of the rights established by the Bill of Rights are clearly stated, such as the rights of free speech, assembly, and the press. The application of those rights to specific circumstances, however, is not always so clear. Thus, as one Supreme Court decision states, freedom of speech does not permit someone to yell "Fire!" in a crowded theater. The lines defining what is permissible and what is not continue to be drawn and redrawn by the courts.

Other rights not specified in the text have been discovered in the *penumbras* (implied rights) of the Bill of Rights. For instance, current applications of constitutional law identify a "right to privacy," which has been used to protect people from certain kinds of warrantless searches by police and to strike down laws banning birth control, abortion, homosexual sex, and sodomy. Nowhere is the right to privacy mentioned in the Constitution. But, according to the Supreme Court in *Griswold v. Connecticut* (1965), marital privacy is a fundamental right that exists due to the Ninth Amendment ("certain rights shall not be construed to deny or disparage others retained by the people") and also "within the penumbra of the specific guarantees of the Bill of Rights."[5] In the *Griswold* case, the Court discovered meanings in the text to establish that the right to privacy exists, and then used the concept to strike down state laws banning contraception that had been in place for decades.

Despite the evolution of the meaning of the Constitution, the original document and the constitutional framework it established in 1789 remain

[5] From Justice Arthur Goldberg's concurring opinion in *Griswold v. Connecticut*, 381 U.S. 479 (1965).

important today. The institutions set forth in the original Constitution remain the most critical factors in shaping the nature of conflict and cooperation within the American political system. The document was written by people who disagreed bitterly over the fundamental structure of government because they knew that structure would help determine who wins and who loses in American society as a result of government decisions. In short, the Founders understood the importance of institutional design for shaping the country's future.

Consequences of the Constitution

We began this chapter by puzzling over why the Federalists ended up winning most of the conflicts surrounding constitutional design at the Founding. After all, Americans at the time were, and to some extent still are, distrustful of strong government. Yet the Federalists wanted a stronger national government than the one that existed under the Articles of Confederation. In light of what we have learned in this chapter, the answer to our puzzle comes down to this: the Federalists provided convincing arguments to enough groups in society that a government that was too weak would not work to solve collective dilemmas. Unsolved collective dilemmas, leading to events like Shays's Rebellion and to possible threats from foreign powers such as France and Britain, were considered worse than the potential threats from the stronger government put in place by the new Constitution.

Were the Federalists correct that the new Constitution would improve things dramatically for the new country? Most political scientists believe that governmental institutions, especially those established by constitutions, have real consequences. Certainly, the Founders believed this, as do the people who write or amend constitutions in other countries or in the United States. So what have been the consequences of the governmental institutions that were established by the original U.S. Constitution?

Answering this question is not as straightforward as it seems. First, we cannot simply rerun American history multiple times under different institutional conditions and see how it would play out in each scenario. How would American history have been different if the country had not had a strong president but a weak figurehead appointed to a ceremonial position by Congress? We can never know the answer to such questions with certainty. Second, we cannot know for certain if outcomes were caused by the original aspects of the Constitution, by the Constitution as it was amended later, or by other factors in society. As previously discussed, the structure of the American political system only partly reflects the text of the original Constitution. Later developments, including court cases, constitutional amendments, legislation, and even the Civil War, have reshaped its meaning over time, leading to a constitutional system that is different today than the one the Founders intended.

Despite these obstacles to determining cause and effect, there are two promising approaches to understanding the consequences of governmental institutions. One is to compare what happens in other countries that have different constitutional or institutional frameworks. Another is to compare what happens over time as institutions change.

Extensive research has focused on the consequences of having specific institutional features in place. This research confirms that there is an overall benefit to having a democratic system, or what the Founders called a *republican system* (meaning that representatives of the people govern). Political scientists have learned, for example, that democratic institutions across the world tend to lead to better economic growth, improved health among citizens, a higher level of educational achievement, and lower incidences of infant mortality.[6]

In addition, researchers who have studied emerging democracies have demonstrated that those with presidential systems have different kinds of public policies in comparison with parliamentary democracies. More specifically, presidential systems, relative to parliamentary systems, have more incremental changes in governmental budgets and fall back into authoritarian rule more often.[7] Democracy is significantly less likely to be sustained under a presidential system than a parliamentary system[8] (Figure 2.4).

Finally, there is widespread agreement among scholars that the rule of law, with independent courts and enforcement of individual rights and liberties such as those in the Bill of Rights, leads to better economic growth and to richer associational life in the country.[9] In other words, people living under the rule of law tend to be more active in local and national governance in their societies by belonging to civic organizations and participating in politics, in comparison with those in countries without such constitutional protections and judicial independence.

Taking a more historical approach, it is worth stating the obvious point that the U.S. Constitution's reputation is overwhelmingly positive. By the 1820s, three decades after the Constitution was ratified, the document itself and the men who wrote it took on exalted status in the mythology of the country. By

The Constitution and the Bill of Rights are very clear about some rights and liberties, but somewhat vague about others, leaving the door open to interpretation and debate. Opponents of same-sex marriage have tried to pass a constitutional amendment limiting marriage to one man and one woman in order to clarify the limits of gay rights.

[6] William R. Clark, Matt Golder, and Sona N. Golder, *Principles of Comparative Politics* (Washington, DC: CQ Press, 2009).

[7] George Tsebelis, *Veto Players: How Political Institutions Work* (New York: Russell Sage Foundation, 2002); Matthew S. Shugart and John M. Carey, *Presidents and Assemblies: Constitutional Design and Electoral Dynamics* (Cambridge, UK: Cambridge University Press, 1992); Adam Przeworski, Michael E. Alvarez, José A. Cheibub, and Fernando Limongi, *Democracy and Development: Political Institutions and Well-Being in the World, 1950–1990* (New York: Cambridge University Press, 2000).

[8] Alfred Stepan and Cindy Skach, "Constitutional Frameworks and Democratic Consolidation: Parliamentarianism versus Presidentialism," *World Politics* 46, no. 1 (1993): 1–22.

[9] Douglass C. North, *Institutions, Institutional Change, and Economic Performance* (Cambridge, UK: Cambridge University Press, 1990); Robert D. Putnam, *Making Democracy Work: Civic Traditions in Modern Italy* (Princeton, NJ: Princeton University Press, 1993).

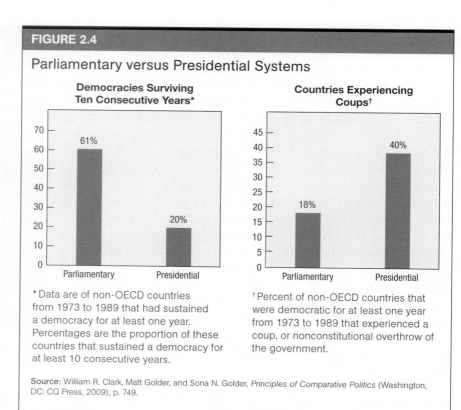

FIGURE 2.4

Parliamentary versus Presidential Systems

Democracies Surviving Ten Consecutive Years*

- Parliamentary: 61%
- Presidential: 20%

Countries Experiencing Coups†

- Parliamentary: 18%
- Presidential: 40%

* Data are of non-OECD countries from 1973 to 1989 that had sustained a democracy for at least one year. Percentages are the proportion of these countries that sustained a democracy for at least 10 consecutive years.

† Percent of non-OECD countries that were democratic for at least one year from 1973 to 1989 that experienced a coup, or nonconstitutional overthrow of the government.

Source: William R. Clark, Matt Golder, and Sona N. Golder, *Principles of Comparative Politics* (Washington, DC: CQ Press, 2009), p. 749.

the mid–nineteenth century, in the minds of most Americans, the Constitution was fundamental to the thriving of the country.

Historians and political scientists in our own era credit the Constitution with establishing a stable political system that became more democratic over time, and that has enabled the country to grow in three important ways: geographically, by population, and by wealth. The Founders fully expected westward expansion of the country to take place and included provisions for expanding the size of Congress and the electoral college to keep up with the increasing number of states, making it relatively easy for new states to join the union. The Constitution, especially through the Bill of Rights, also paved the way for the nation to grow as wave after wave of immigrants swelled the population. Finally, there is widespread agreement among economic historians that the constitutional basis for protection of private property, for enforcing contracts and bills of credit, and for ensuring that courts remained independent of political manipulation, was instrumental in the unprecedented economic growth experienced by the United States throughout its history, especially in the nineteenth century.[10]

[10] North, *Institutions, Institutional Change, and Economic Performance.*

The institutions established by the Constitution have survived, even if not working exactly in the way the Founders intended. To answer one of the questions posed at the beginning of this chapter, the Constitution, by its flexibility, seems to have survived by virtue of striking a workable, amendable balance between strong government and liberty. Although it has changed in many ways, the Constitution—if measured objectively by its longevity and its role in fostering a strong, wealthy country—has been a rousing success. And with the notable exceptions of the Civil War and the political system's long tolerance of racial and gender discrimination, the Constitution has been able to solve the most threatening collective dilemmas faced by the states.

Is this conclusion too rosy? The Constitution and the consequences that flow from it have their critics. Among the most notable are those, such as the historian Charles Beard, who believe that the Founders—who were almost entirely wealthy men with large landholdings or considerable capital—deliberately wrote a Constitution to protect the economic interests of people in their own class.[11] Other critics have complained that the American system of government, supported by the legal and political institutions established by the Constitution, has led to extreme inequality and racial subjugation.[12] These criticisms, especially of the Constitution's implicit sanctioning of slavery, undoubtedly have merit. The Constitution generally changes slowly. Even slower has been the appropriate application by courts and legislatures of constitutionally enshrined protections for individual rights and liberties, such as freedom of speech and the right to vote.

Other critics of the American constitutional system suggest that it creates partisan conflict that does not adequately represent public opinion, or that it encourages inefficient government that is better at doling out benefits to special interests than at formulating policies that promote the public good.[13] We will be in a better position to evaluate such criticisms after examining in later chapters the consequences of the specific features of the American political system.

---

[11] Charles A. Beard, *An Economic Interpretation of the Constitution of the United States* (New York: Macmillan, 1913).

[12] Mary F. Berry, "Slavery, the Constitution, and the Founding Fathers: The African American Vision," in *African Americans and the Living Constitution*, ed. J. H. Franklin and G. R. McNeil (Washington, DC: Smithsonian Institution Press, 1995); Howard Zinn, *A People's History of the United States: 1492–Present* (repr., New York: Harper Perennial, 2005).

[13] Theodore J. Lowi, *The End of Liberalism: The Second Republic of the United States* (New York: Norton, 1969); E. E. Schattschneider, *The Semisovereign People: A Realist's View of Democracy in America* (New York: Holt, Rinehart, and Winston, 1960); A. Ranney, *The Doctrine of Responsible Party Government, Its Origin and Present State* (Urbana: University of Illinois Press, 1954); Morris P. Fiorina, *Divided Government* (New York: Macmillan, 1992); Bruce E. Cain, John A. Ferejohn, and Morris P. Fiorina, *The Personal Vote: Constituency Service and Electoral Independence* (Cambridge, MA: Harvard University Press, 1987); Robert A. Dahl, *How Democratic Is the American Constitution?*, 2nd ed. (New Haven, CT: Yale University Press, 2003).

FURTHER READING

★ = Included in *Readings in American Politics*, 3e

Anonymous, *Letters from the Federal Farmer*, No. 2, 1788. Critics of the Constitution (the Antifederalists) wrote under pseudonyms urging state legislatures not to approve the new Constitution.

Beard, Charles, *An Economic Interpretation of the Constitution* (New York: Macmillan, 1913). A classic account arguing that the Founders intentionally created a document that primarily led to preserving their own wealth and position.

★ Dahl, Robert, *How Democratic Is the Constitution?*, 2nd ed. (New Haven, CT: Yale University Press, 2003). A critical look at the Constitution, arguing that the Senate and the judiciary are highly undemocratic features.

★ Hamilton, Alexander, James Madison, and John Jay, *The Federalist Papers*, No. 10 and No. 51, 1788. Letters written by Madison (under a pseudonym) describing the virtues of republican government. Other *Federalist Papers* were written by Alexander Hamilton and John Jay (also under pseudonyms).

North, Douglass, *Institutions, Institutional Change, and Economic Performance* (Cambridge, UK: Cambridge University Press, 1990). A comparative and historical sweep through Europe and the United States showing the intimate relationship between economic growth and the establishment of stable political institutions.

Rakove, Jack, *Original Meanings: Politics and Ideas in the Making of the Constitution* (New York: Alfred Knopf, 1996). A careful, detailed examination of the debates and intentions of the Founders.

Schwarzenbach, Sibyl A., and Patricia Smith, eds., *Women and the U.S. Constitution: History, Interpretation, and Practice* (New York: Columbia University Press, 2004).

KEY TERMS

Antifederalists (p. 50)

Articles of Confederation (p. 39)

bicameral legislature (p. 45)

Bill of Rights (p. 52)

checks and balances (p. 48)

commerce clause (p. 58)

Connecticut Compromise (p. 43)

elastic clause (necessary and proper clause) (p. 46)

electoral college (p. 45)

An Arizona law passed in 2010 gave local law enforcement increased and controversial means to target illegal immigrants. Many observers felt that, in addition to raising civil liberties concerns, the law conflicted with national authority over immigration policy. Others claimed the state was merely enacting a federal law that the national government was failing to enforce. A divided Supreme Court narrowly decided in favor of federal supremacy on immigration policy.

3

FEDERALISM

Given the states' interest in protecting their own sovereignty and the American people's traditional fears of excessive centralized power, why have the states and the American people allowed the federal government to become more powerful in the past century?

I n 2010, Arizona Governor Jan Brewer signed a controversial state law and said at the time, "The bill I'm about to sign into law—Senate Bill 1070—represents another tool for our state to use as we work to solve a crisis we did not create and the federal government has refused to fix."[1] The "crisis" she referred to was that unauthorized immigrants constituted at least 6 percent of Arizona's population; the national average was 3.7 percent.[2] The law she signed was intended to provide Arizona law enforcement better tools to find, report, and remove undocumented immigrants.

The Arizona bill garnered mixed but heated reception. Many saw it as an invitation for law enforcement to employ racial profiling, while others applauded the effort for enforcing federal law where the federal government seemed either unable or unwilling. While the law, and the tools afforded by it, exposed issues of prejudice and civil rights, they also drew attention for what it meant for federalism. The bill seemed to pose a threat to the federal government's supremacy on immigration policy. Despite the controversy, five states—Alabama, Georgia, Indiana, South Carolina, and Utah[3]—followed Arizona's example and passed similar legislation.

Several of the most controversial elements of the law were later struck down by the U.S. Supreme Court in *Arizona v. United States* (2012), for reasons having precisely to do with federalism. The Court declared that parts of the law violated the supremacy

---

[1] Office of the Governor, "Statement by Governor Jan Brewer on Senate Bill 1070," press release, Phoenix, AZ, April 23, 2010.

[2] Pew Research Center, "Unauthorized Immigrant Population: National and State Trends, 2010," February 1, 2011, p. 29, www.pewhispanic.org/files/reports/133.pdf (accessed 4/8/13).

[3] American Civil Liberties Union, "Arizona's SB 1070," www.aclu.org/arizonas-sb-1070 (accessed 4/8/13).

clause of the Constitution because the law intended to grant Arizona officials more authority to arrest and charge suspected undocumented immigrants than the U.S. Congress had granted to federal officials with its own previous legislation. Writing for the majority on the Court, Justice Anthony Kennedy declared that states "may not enter, in any respect, an area the Federal Government has reserved for itself." Since the federal government had, through its lawmaking, established itself as the authority on regulating immigration for the entire United States, Arizona and other states could not preempt or encroach upon that authority, nor hinder its exercise in any way.

The Court's decision was itself controversial, and Governor Brewer and other conservatives in Arizona were critical. They believed that the federal government had not been doing enough to enforce immigration laws along the Mexico–U.S. border. Three justices dissented from the ruling, and writing for the dissent, Justice Antonin Scalia stated, "Arizona has moved to protect its sovereignty—not in contradiction of federal law, but in complete compliance with it. The laws under challenge here do not extend or revise federal immigration restrictions, but merely enforce those restrictions more effectively."[4]

The Arizona legislation and the Court's response highlight the difficult balance between state sovereignty and its relationship to federal supremacy. Here was a direct conflict between what a state government wanted to do and what the national government would allow. The genesis of SB 1070 and the pushback it received from those interpreting national law mark a tension in the federal character of the nation. The boundaries between state and federal authority often remain contested and sometimes unclear.

Those boundaries have been contested throughout American history due, in part, to the Constitution's fundamental ambiguity about the nature of American federalism. Constitutional language about federalism was not straightforward, and political leaders in the years after the Founding left crucial questions about the sovereignty and authority of different levels of government unresolved. Such ambiguity played a major role in the run-up to the Civil War in 1860 (discussed later). Debates over many other aspects of federalism continue to this day.

Throughout the twentieth century, federalism questions were most often decided in favor of greater power for the national government. As a result, the national government has grown in power over time relative to the states. Perhaps surprisingly, this centralization of authority is largely the result of public pressure and even state governments requesting and assenting to increased national power. The state government of Arizona's actions are noteworthy, but the final outcome in favor of national authority has been the general norm. All it would take would be a change in federal law to allow Arizona to have its separate immigration enforcement policies, but laws granting authority back to the states are rare. In general, the representatives of the people in the states (in Congress) consent to national authority and keep it in place. Why? Given the states' interest in protecting their own sovereignty and the American people's traditional fears of excessive centralized power, why have the states and the American people allowed the federal government to become more powerful in the last century?

[4] American Civil Liberties Union, "Arizona's SB 1070."

Federation and Confederation

Federalism can be defined as a political system that includes multiple levels of government where at least one lower level has constitutionally protected status and exercises independent authority over important areas of policy.[5] "Constitutionally protected status" means that subunit governments (such as states or provinces) are woven into the very fabric of the political system; they coexist with the central government according to constitutional tradition and cannot be abolished unilaterally by the central government. In the United States, for example, the states always have been the constituent units of the federation, and Congress is explicitly forbidden under the Constitution from unilaterally changing an existing state's boundaries or altering its government so long as it is of a republican nature. In contrast, U.S. cities and counties do not have the same protected status that states have. They are "creatures" of the states, which means they can be set up, abolished, or amended in form by state law.

Compared with a federation, a **confederation** is a weaker form of union. As commonly used, the term *confederation* implies that the subunit governments retain full sovereignty and that the national government cannot compel them to act. In practice, united action by a confederation requires voluntary compliance. In this situation, as when the American colonies operated under the Articles of Confederation (discussed in Chapter 2), subunit governments typically face serious collective-action problems that inhibit them from achieving the common good. If confederation was as far as the states would allow the country to go down the path of centralization, the states could refuse to pay the costs of union—as many did under the Articles—or even leave the Union, as the 11 Confederate states did in 1860 and 1861.

After the Founding, the Civil War was the most important event in the development of the American political system. The war began after the southern states left and formed a new country called the Confederate States of America. In response, the U.S. government, composed of the remaining states and led by President Abraham Lincoln, mobilized an army and invaded the South to preserve the Union. Approximately 620,000 Americans died in the Civil War; one out of every 10 able-bodied men in the North and one out of 4 in the South

federalism A political system with multiple levels of government, in which each level has independent authority over some important policy areas.

confederation A political system with multiple levels of government, in which lower-level governments retain full sovereignty and cannot be compelled by the national government to act.

In a federal system, the national government has jurisdiction over some policy areas, while states control other areas like public schools and education. In yet other areas, state and national government powers overlap.

---

[5] See William H. Riker, *Federalism: Origin, Operation, Significance* (Boston: Little, Brown, 1964).

were killed or injured. The Union army finally defeated the Confederate army in 1865, ending the war and southern secession.

The Civil War stemmed from a variety of deep splits between the states of the North and the South during the first 80 years of the nation's history, including slavery and economic policies. The two sides also interpreted the Constitution differently when it came to the relationship between the states and the federal government. In deciding to secede, the leaders of the Confederacy relied on a view of American federalism that held that the country was created by agreement among sovereign states. They took the position that the United States are together *voluntarily* under one confederation and, as sovereign states, could leave the Union if they wished.[6] Unless the Constitution expressly forbade states from taking certain actions or adopting certain policies—such as making treaties with foreign countries—the national government, according to the Tenth Amendment, granted them full discretion. In the Confederate view, state sovereignty was the hallmark of the American federal republic.

Reflecting on what we learned in Chapter 2, we can see that this interpretation of the Constitution springs from a view resembling the Antifederalists' philosophy. The Confederation's subsequent defeat at the hands of the Union army could be seen as vindication of the Antifederalists' prediction that the Constitution would lead to the trampling of states' rights. While the Antifederalists after the Founding pushed the Bill of Rights, including the Tenth Amendment designed to protect the states from a vigorous national government, Confederation leaders could only conclude that the Tenth Amendment was not enough.

The Lincoln administration and most northern politicians, particularly members of Lincoln's Republican Party, promoted a different version of federalism and the Constitution. In their view, the Constitution meant the United States is a *sovereign* country, and the preamble declared that "the people" had created an indissoluble union. The national government had authority granted to it by the sovereign people of the United States as a whole. As such, the national government could make decisions and expect compliance even if a united South was opposed to those decisions. More important for Lincoln, secession was not only an illegal act, it also broke the "sacred" bond created at the Founding. Lingering notions from the Antifederalists, in this view, were dangerous precisely because they could lead to disorder, including secession. The Civil War and its aftermath settled the issues of secession and slavery and emphatically shifted the country in a more federal direction.

Figure 3.1 illustrates the continuum in the centralization of political control from a loosely organized confederation to a highly centralized "unitary system" of government.[7] As one moves toward the left in the figure, the central government's power increases relative to that of the subunit governments. During the ratification debates between Federalists and Antifederalists following

---

[6] Geoffrey Ward, with Ken Burns and Ric Burns, *The Civil War: An Illustrated History* (New York: Alfred Knopf, 1996), p. 404.

[7] See Daniel Elazar, *American Federalism: A View from the States* (New York: Crowell & Company, 1966).

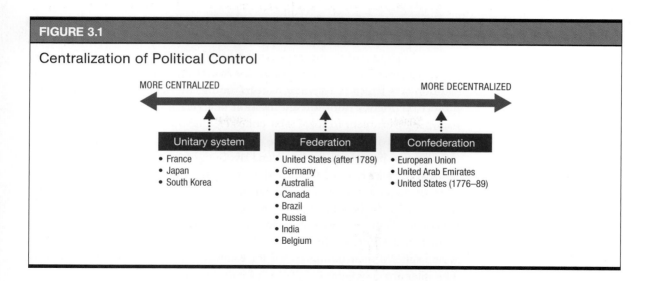

FIGURE 3.1

Centralization of Political Control

MORE CENTRALIZED

MORE DECENTRALIZED

Unitary system	Federation	Confederation
• France • Japan • South Korea	• United States (after 1789) • Germany • Australia • Canada • Brazil • Russia • India • Belgium	• European Union • United Arab Emirates • United States (1776–89)

the Constitutional Convention, much of the discussion centered on where along this continuum the United States should stand. The issue continued to be debated up to and during the Civil War.

An example from another part of the world can help clarify the distinction between federation and confederation. Most scholars consider the European Union to be a confederation. The 28 member countries have agreed to join together to create a single economic market. To that end, they have developed a set of political institutions, such as a European parliament, an executive commission, and a court, to coordinate action and solve their collective dilemmas. The European Union government in Brussels, however, cannot compel the member countries to act in the same way that the national governments of the world's federations can compel states and provinces. Brussels exacts fines from member countries when they do not comply with its decisions, but there is no legal basis for the idea that the Brussels government has sovereignty over the territory of the European Union. If the member countries were to vest sovereign military authority in the Brussels government, then Europe would begin to look more like other federations around the world. Until then, however, compliance is essentially voluntary because punishments for noncompliance are financial (and typically moderate) and do not entail force.

Federalism as a Response to Collective Dilemmas

The United States and the European Union provide stark examples of how centralization evolves when subunit governments cannot solve certain problems on their own. Central governments often gain power and become either confederated or federated when the subunits face collective dilemmas. The European Union originated in the 1950s as a confederation among six countries, largely in response to two devastating world wars resulting from conflict between Germany and France. The idea was that a political confederation, even a weak one, would prevent wars between member countries. Likewise, we saw in Chapter 2 how the creation of the American federation under the Constitution was largely a response to fears among the states that they could not protect themselves from foreign invasion or internal strife without a stronger national government to solve their collective dilemmas.

The following hypothetical situation highlights the advantages of national coordination brought about by federal law. Suppose there were no federal minimum wage and Kentucky adopted a lower minimum wage than other states in order to attract businesses seeking to offer cheaper products to consumers. Kentucky might benefit from the influx of new businesses, as would its business owners and their price-conscious consumers. However, not only would the workers in Kentucky suffer from low wages, but other states and their workers would suffer if their businesses left for Kentucky in search of lower labor costs. This dilemma—sometimes called a "race to the bottom," referring to how competition gives incentives for states to go lower and lower on something of value to their own citizens in order to attract business—might lead to calls for the national government to set a uniform minimum wage for all the states, eliminating the collective-action problem by reducing the temptation to free ride off higher-minimum-wage states. In fact, the United States *does* have a national minimum wage. Congress first established it in 1938 to resolve the collective-action problem among states and city governments. By passing a national law mandating a minimum wage enforceable everywhere, the national government uses its authority over the states to solve a problem that they cannot solve on their own.[8]

Most people would agree that the states often need coordination and enforcement to avoid the problem of free riding, but not always and not on every issue. When and on what issues should the national government make policies that apply to all the states? On what issues should the states be given the discretion to adopt their own policies? Most controversies over federalism stem from differences of opinion about these questions. It is fair to say that, although the balance of power between the states and the national government is constantly in flux, depending on the nature of the times and the issues that confront the nation, the historical trend has been toward greater centralization, shifting more power to the national level.

The Dynamics of American Federalism

dual federalism A political system in which each level of government—national and state—is sovereign in its own sphere of policy authority.

Some scholars have depicted the set of American governmental institutions as a system of **dual federalism**, whereby each level—national and state—is sovereign in its own sphere and operates largely independently of the other.

[8] The federal government's minimum wage is the *minimum* legal wage. However, states and localities can impose a *higher* minimum wage than the national standard.

This kind of federalism is often likened to a layer cake. Critics of this depiction describe the system instead as **cooperative federalism**, whereby both national and state governments are active in nearly all spheres, sharing powers and working together to solve problems. A marble cake is a more apt metaphor for this kind of federalism, because no matter how you slice it, both levels of government are present in every piece.

In fact, the American political system is a mixture of dual and cooperative federalism, although as the national government has grown stronger over time, the more the system has come to resemble a marble cake. As Figure 3.2 shows, some policy areas are almost completely the prerogative of one or the other level of government. In many policy areas, however, the two levels cooperate or share resources. This is sometimes called **intergovernmentalism**. When both the states and the national government are active in a given area, the precise boundaries of their authority can be difficult to define. One example is education policy. Congress has mandated federal standards for states in designing and operating school systems. Schools are run by the states and by local school districts, but the federal government has used strong financial incentives (fines as punishments in some cases and grants as rewards in others) to induce the states to comply with federal standards. Because the education of children has

cooperative federalism A political system in which both levels of government—national and state—are active in nearly all areas of policy and share sovereign authority.

intergovernmentalism A system in which multiple levels of government are active in a given policy area.

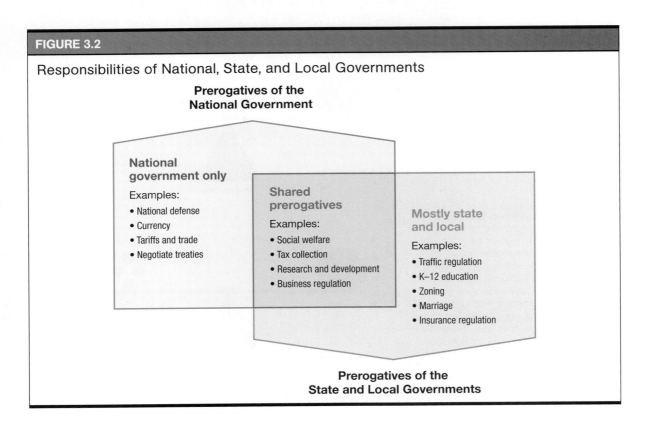

FIGURE 3.2

Responsibilities of National, State, and Local Governments

Prerogatives of the National Government

National government only

Examples:
- National defense
- Currency
- Tariffs and trade
- Negotiate treaties

Shared prerogatives

Examples:
- Social welfare
- Tax collection
- Research and development
- Business regulation

Mostly state and local

Examples:
- Traffic regulation
- K–12 education
- Zoning
- Marriage
- Insurance regulation

Prerogatives of the State and Local Governments

long been the prerogative of the states, the extension of federal power into the domain of education remains controversial.

In many policy domains, the states and the national government have no choice but to work together, but the underlying question remains: How much sovereign authority do states have to do what they want? The need for clarity has repeatedly forced this issue to the forefront throughout American history, and the outcome has generally not been in favor of states' rights. To understand why the national government has so often prevailed in struggles involving **intergovernmental relations**, we need to consider the dynamics of American federalism. Some scholars like to depict federalism as a seesaw, where equal power between the states and the federal government would mean an evenly balanced beam on the fulcrum (see Figure 3.3). In any federation there is constant tussling between the subunit governments and the central government over which side has legitimate authority over select policy areas, and the seesaw can swing accordingly. If we use this metaphor, we can convey the possible extremes in a confederation or federation, and we can also convey the historical pattern in the United States. If one end of the seesaw touches the ground, the federation experiences complete domination by the national government.

intergovernmental relations
The relationship between the different levels of government. For example, it may pertain to the struggle between the national government and the states for authority over a specific policy domain, or it may pertain to the coordination of action between the levels in an effort to achieve common goals.

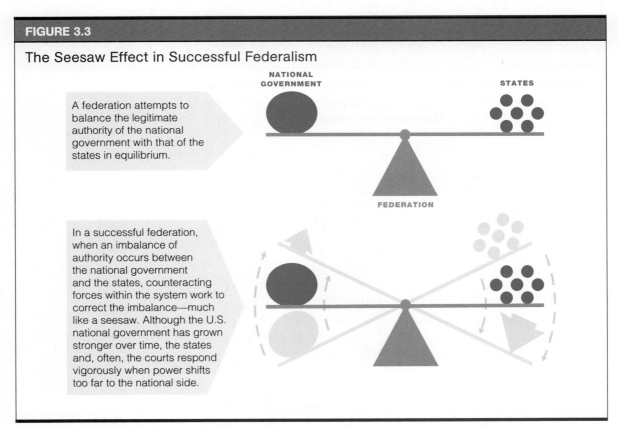

FIGURE 3.3

The Seesaw Effect in Successful Federalism

A federation attempts to balance the legitimate authority of the national government with that of the states in equilibrium.

In a successful federation, when an imbalance of authority occurs between the national government and the states, counteracting forces within the system work to correct the imbalance—much like a seesaw. Although the U.S. national government has grown stronger over time, the states and, often, the courts respond vigorously when power shifts too far to the national side.

NATIONAL GOVERNMENT

STATES

FEDERATION

If it touches down on the other side, the federation is effectively replaced by a confederation in which the states do not need to abide by national government mandates. A working federal system at times self-corrects and never tilts too far one way or the other. As the seesaw begins to dip down on one side, the other side responds vigorously to redress the balance.[9] Nevertheless, the U.S. federal system has tilted over time, and if it has not touched the ground, it has nearly always tilted in the national government's direction. There have been moments when some feared the imbalance was becoming so great that it might indeed touch the ground. Some conservatives believe, for instance, that established legal interpretations of parts of the Constitution (e.g., the commerce clause, as discussed below) have become so favorable to the federal government that states have no authority left to regulate the businesses in their local communities. The federal courts have often played a role in tilting the seesaw in one direction or restoring a semblance of balance.

The Courts and the Constitution

Throughout American history, the federal courts have helped determine the balance between the national government and the states. Decisions by the Supreme Court and other federal courts have played a large role in enabling the national government to increase its authority, while also maintaining state authority over certain policy areas. In other words, the courts have occasionally caused our metaphorical seesaw to tilt, but they have also kept it from hitting the ground.[10]

The courts rely on the language of the Constitution for guidance, but as we have seen, there has always been ambiguity about how that language applies to actual practice. Recall our discussion of national power versus states' rights in Chapter 2. In various places, the Constitution specifically defines the limits of state and federal authority. For example:

- Article I, Section 10, clearly lists the things states cannot do, such as negotiate treaties with foreign countries or coin money.

- Article IV, Sections 2–4, declare that the national government has key responsibilities to protect the states, to approve state boundaries and new states joining the Union, and to enforce laws about fugitives crossing state boundaries.

- Article VI contains the "supremacy clause," which declares national law supreme over the entire nation (that is, if state law conflicts with federal law, federal law overrides it) and mandates that all public officials, including state officials, swear allegiance to the United States.

[9] Jenna Bednar, *The Robust Federation: Principles of Design* (New York: Cambridge University Press, 2007).

[10] William Eskridge and John Ferejohn, "The Elastic Commerce Clause: A Political Theory of American Federalism," *Vanderbilt Law Review* 47 (1994): 1355.

In the main, however, the Founders left it for later generations to decide what the national government and the states can do. For instance, the Constitution gives Congress broad powers to make all laws "necessary and proper for carrying into Execution the foregoing Powers" (Article I, Section 8, Clause 18) and says that Congress has the power to "regulate Commerce ... among the several States" (Article I, Section 8, Clause 3). These are referred to as the **elastic clause** and the **commerce clause**, respectively. People ever since have struggled to define the boundaries of authority prescribed by these words. Furthermore, the Tenth Amendment reserves to the states all powers not specified as the prerogative of the national government. But what powers are *not* the prerogative of the national government? The text of Article I, in and of itself, does not provide a conclusive answer.

elastic clause (necessary and proper clause) The provision in Article I, Section 8, of the Constitution that states that Congress can make whatever laws are "necessary and proper" in order to provide the means to carry out its enumerated powers.

commerce clause An enumerated power listed in Article I, Section 8, of the Constitution that grants Congress the power to "regulate Commerce with foreign Nations, and among the several States, and with the Indian Tribes."

The Antifederalists thought they had the answer, which was that the national government ought to have very limited powers. The Constitution as written, they argued, would lead to national government domination over the states and ultimately make the states powerless. In their writings, they focused on the elastic clause and the commerce clause, and indeed subsequent tensions over federalism have occurred largely because of interpretations of those parts of the Constitution. The elastic clause in particular, they feared, could open the door for the national government to make policies that override state law in virtually any domain. The Antifederalists may have predicted accurately the rising power of the national government as a whole, but they were most worried about Congress. They failed to anticipate the role of the courts in not only fostering national authority, but also at times in maintaining some balance.

When there is disagreement over the limits of American federalism, the courts are often called in to adjudicate between states, or between states and the national government. In fact, legal wrangling over where sovereignty should lie is a constant feature of the American federal system. In perhaps the two most important Supreme Court cases concerning national government authority over the states, the majority opinions in *McCulloch v. Maryland* (1819) and *Gibbons v. Ogden* (1824) declared that the national government had wide latitude to regulate commercial activity, even within the states. In *Gibbons*, for instance, the Court took a particularly expansive view of the commerce clause. It decided that national power over interstate commerce includes commerce that occurs within state boundaries but involves enterprises from other states. In the increasingly nationalized economy of the 1820s, this ruling meant that virtually any commercial activity occurring anywhere in the country was subject to national regulation.

The courts have also helped the states preserve their autonomy in many areas. In the late nineteenth and early twentieth centuries, the Supreme Court limited the scope of national powers to regulate certain forms of commerce. Taking a narrow view of the commerce clause, the Court struck down efforts by the national government to regulate things like working hours and child labor, and to impose a national minimum wage. Only in the 1930s, at the height of the New Deal, did the Court begin to expand its reading of the commerce clause. In particular, new judicial theories led the Court increasingly to view "Commerce . . . among the several States" as incorporating nearly any activity related to commerce, including employment and wages, the purchasing of products, and even racial exclusion. This was the legal opening the Roosevelt administration needed to assert substantial powers to regulate and stabilize the economy within and across the states, with virtually no restrictions imposed by the Tenth Amendment. In recent decades, however, the Supreme Court has

---

Know the FACTS — Sources of National Government Power and State Power

Constitutional Provisions: The Constitution outlines national and state authority, leaving some areas ambiguous.

- Centralization of power

  - *The commerce clause*—Article I, Section 8, enumerates the responsibilities of Congress, giving Congress significant powers over the states.

  - *The elastic (necessary and proper) clause*—This clause, also found in Article I, Section 8, grants Congress the authority to do whatever is "necessary and proper" to execute its powers enumerated within the Constitution.

  - *Article I, Section 10*—This section of the Constitution lists numerous restrictions on the powers of the states.

  - *The supremacy clause*—Through this clause, the Constitution, subsequent federal law, and all U.S. treaties become the "supreme law of the land" to which all states are bound.

- Decentralization of power

  - *Article I, Section 9*—Much like Section 10 for the states, this section lists restrictions placed on federal power.

  - *The Bill of Rights*—The first 10 amendments to the Constitution place further limits on the actions of the federal government. The First Amendment begins with "Congress shall make no law. . ."

  - *The Tenth Amendment*—The Tenth Amendment establishes what are referred to as the reserved powers. It says that "the powers not delegated to the United States by the Constitution, nor prohibited by it to the states, are reserved to the states respectively, or to the people."

Major Supreme Court Decisions: The text of the Constitution is not always clear in its meaning, and disputes over federalism are often settled in court.

- Centralization of power

  - *McCulloch v. Maryland* (1819)—The Court ruled that although not expressed in the Constitution, Congress has the authority to establish a national bank according to the powers implied by the necessary and proper clause, giving the national government wide latitude.

  - *Gibbons v. Ogden* (1824)—The Court affirmed that Congress has the authority to regulate commerce as long as it involves more than one state.

- Decentralization of power

  - *United States v. Lopez* (1995)—The Court ruled that the Gun-Free School Zones Act passed by Congress in 1990 is unconstitutional because regulating firearms in public schools is not regulating interstate commerce. Thus the Court recognizes limitations on national government authority granted by the commerce clause.

While Supreme Court decisions have been very influential in shaping state–national relations, they have often relied on the actions of the other branches of government to achieve their impact. Despite the Court's ruling in *Brown v. Board of Education* that public schools were required to integrate, it took President Eisenhower's sending of federal troops into Little Rock, Arkansas, to ensure state compliance.

begun to return to a narrower interpretation of the commerce clause, a topic we expand upon later.

To be sure, court decisions, and even changes to the Constitution, are often limited in their impact. In part, this is because courts generally lack the means to enforce their rulings and must rely instead on other branches of government. In many instances, the executive and legislative branches are responsible for enforcing court decisions. But which level of executive or legislative authority shoulders this responsibility: the local, state, or federal? Uncertainty and disagreement over such jurisdiction within the federal system can lead to dangerous confrontations. For example, in 1957, a Little Rock, Arkansas, school district failed to comply with federal court rulings mandating racial integration of its schools. The state of Arkansas likewise refused to enforce the federal law. President Dwight D. Eisenhower as a last resort sent federal troops to Little Rock to enforce the court order. The president's decision was controversial not only because it involved the issue of race relations in the South in the 1950s but also because it involved the federal government using force to bring a state into compliance on an issue usually reserved for the states—education. In a different realm of law, beginning in the mid-1960s, federal courts ruled on a number of cases concerning poor conditions in state prisons. To ensure compliance by the states, the courts set up a system whereby state officials who do not comply face arrest on contempt-of-court charges.

Toward a Stronger National Government

Although the courts have at times interpreted the Constitution in favor of national power and at other times in favor of states' rights, the overall trend, in court decisions and in subsequent legislation and executive action, has been toward greater power for the national government. Since the Civil War, broad political movements in three distinct eras have shifted the balance toward the national government. Each of these movements culminated in sweeping legislative changes, and each were the product of public pressure in favor of national government action to solve problems that were seen as beyond the scope of the states either individually or collectively.

Progressive Era, 1896–1913

Around the turn of the twentieth century, the national government began to develop a substantial administrative capacity to regulate the newly industrialized, urbanized economy. Although some Supreme Court cases upheld states' rights, and thus slowed down the efforts of the national government, it became increasingly accepted by both major political parties and the public that the national government had legitimate authority to regulate certain areas of commerce: the safety of food, medicine, clothing, and household fabrics; the control

HISTORICAL PATH A Conceptual Depiction of the Rise of National Government Power since 1861

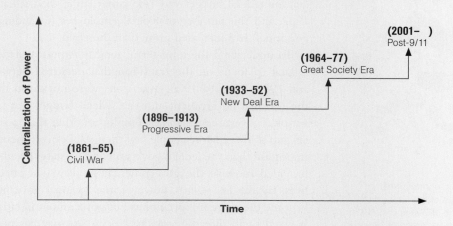

Note: This figure provides a conceptual depiction of the increases in national government power corresponding to important historical eras and is not intended to be a historical timeline.

or break up of monopolies in oil, railroads, and utilities; and the management of mineral and wood extraction from federal lands. Although some national bureaus, such as the Interstate Commerce Commission (1877), were created earlier, it was not until the administration of President Theodore Roosevelt (1900–1908) that these units were given much real authority or substantial personnel to regulate interstate business activity. To cap off the so-called Progressive Era, the national government was granted authority by constitutional amendment to institute an income tax on individuals in 1913. This meant that, for the first time, the national government could tax individuals directly, a power the states had always had.

New Deal Era, 1933–52

The New Deal Era saw the most far-reaching political and economic centralization in American history. Following the election of President Franklin Delano Roosevelt and overwhelming Democratic majorities in Congress in 1932, the national government embarked on a massive effort to bring the country out of the Great Depression and to prevent such shocks to the economic system in the future. It established bureaus to regulate the activities of banks, financial trading companies, public employees, airlines, railroads, unions, and utilities. It set up programs to promote the building of transportation, recreation, and utilities infrastructure nationwide. It also created a social security system that for the first time guaranteed a minimum level of income for retirees and the disabled. The national government grew to unprecedented size with the creation of numerous advisory agencies and oversight boards to help make informed decisions on macroeconomic and fiscal policies. By the end of the era, the federal budget was 14.5 times larger than it had been in 1932, and the number of federal employees (excluding military personnel) had increased more than threefold.

To understand the long-term trend in American federalism, it is vital to focus on the transition that occurred between 1900 and 1950. Prior to 1900, Americans were not taxed directly by the national government and the federal budget was small. The national government had few employees other than postal workers and soldiers. Most people saw their state governments as more important than the federal government. The states taxed them and provided most of the governmental services that affected their lives. By the late 1940s, however, the national government had become the more important level of government in citizens' lives. It taxed them directly, provided Social Security payments, regulated many household products, and was responsible for the overall health of the economy. The changes that took place in the early twentieth century gave the national government preeminent

FDR's New Deal programs greatly expanded the size of the national government in the 1930s and 1940s. In this 1938 cartoon, various new national programs were depicted as young children with the caption, "Ring a round a Roosevelt, pockets full of dough."

authority, not only over the status of the Union itself, which had been settled by the Civil War, but also over the country's entire economic system.

Great Society Era, 1964–77

Continuing the legacy of the New Deal, Presidents John F. Kennedy, Lyndon B. Johnson, and Richard M. Nixon, supported (or sometimes compelled) by Democratic majorities in Congress, sought to use the powers of the national government to correct various social problems such as poverty and inequality across groups in housing, education, and health care. To a greater extent than during the New Deal, the national government of the Great Society Era worked directly with state and local governments to enact new programs. States and cities received large grants and loans from the national government to improve conditions in inner cities, build transportation infrastructure, enforce racial integration, and provide basic health care and education. Moreover, the period was defined by another surge in the creation of federal bureaucracies, this time to enforce regulatory laws relating to the natural environment, worker safety, highway safety, health care, product safety, and access to education and housing.

Recent Trends

Since the 1990s, the development of American federalism has been characterized by two opposing trends. On the one hand, in the federal courts the balance between the national government and the states has tipped back toward the states. Between 1995 and 2012, the Supreme Court handed down decisions favoring state autonomy under federal laws regarding gun control, violence against women, rights of the disabled, medical marijuana, endangered species, and voting rights. In *United States v. Lopez* (1995), for example, the majority asserted states' rights against the national government by striking down a national law banning handguns near schools, deciding that the commerce clause did not justify congressional regulation of this issue area. In *National Federation of Independent Business v. Sebelius* (2012), the majority, while upholding President Obama's signature health care law on other grounds, also declared that the law violated the commerce clause because the Founders "gave the Congress power to *regulate* commerce, not *compel* it." The majority construed the Constitution as protecting individuals and the states from an overly vigorous national government, and a law mandating that someone buy health insurance was beyond what the commerce clause permits Congress to do. Thus, in specific areas, the courts have reserved powers for the states, causing consternation among some national lawmakers who believe that the states cannot do it themselves and that the national government's power is needed to solve specific social and economic problems.

On the other hand, enormous increases in federal spending resulting from the terrorist attacks on September 11, 2001, and the financial crisis in 2008 have made the states increasingly dependent on the national government for funding. Beginning in 2002, a series of homeland security policies by the national government infused state budgets with money for policing, monitoring of potential criminal activity, and disaster-response preparedness. The money came with requirements for cooperation with other states and compliance with federal guidelines. Following the major economic downturn in 2008, the economic stimulus policies of the George W. Bush and Obama administrations again channeled huge amounts of federal money to the states, this time for education, research, small-business development, and incentives to hire new workers both in the private sector and in government. Proponents of these policies argued that both of these situations called for strong responses at the national level, and by and large their arguments won the day. Public pressure to have the national government act came from those convinced that the states themselves would not be able to take strong enough action, because the states either would not be able to unite around coordinated policies or would not have the capacity to deal with problems at such a grand scale. Critics, such as those in the Tea Party movement beginning in 2009 and continuing through the 2012 election, harkened back to the symbols from the Founding and lamented the increasing power of the national government relative to the states. In their interpretation, the national government had far overreached its appropriate authority under the Constitution. Some also claimed that the large-scale national-level solutions were simply too expensive for taxpayers. Let us now examine the role of federal money in more detail.

Federal Financing

grants-in-aid Money that is distributed to lower-level governments with the purpose of funding special projects.

categorical grants Grants that narrowly define how the funds are to be spent. These grants normally come with conditions that need to be satisfied in order for the money to be used.

revenue–sharing A principle whereby the national government and the lower-level governments cooperate in funding a project.

As part of the overall shift toward greater national power, the federal government since the 1950s has provided significant funding to states and cities for such things as highways and roads, education, research and development, environmental cleanup, urban renewal, and mass transportation. **Grants-in-aid** are given to state or local governments to fund special projects, such as school lunch programs or new transportation infrastructure. The national government often awards **categorical grants**, which specify exactly how the money is to be spent and attach many conditions. For example, a state can receive federal grant money for school lunches, but the national government attaches regulations on the kinds of food that must be served, the nutritional value, and the total number of calories per child. These grant programs frequently operate on a **revenue–sharing** principle, which means that the state or local government must partner with the national government to fund a project.

Block grants are given by the national government for more general purposes. With block grants, states or localities have considerable freedom to use the money as they see fit, as long as the purpose is in line with the broad goals set by the national government. Block grants were created in the 1970s in part because of complaints by the states that other kinds of federal grants had too many strings attached and led to excessive meddling by the national government in state affairs. In some circumstances, the national government provides loans to state or local governments on more favorable terms than are available on the private financial market, such as loans to rebuild after natural disasters.

Figure 3.4 shows the proportion of state revenues that came from national government grants (also called *transfers*) in 2012. Such grants represent a double-edged sword for state and local governments. Because the original legislation authorizing much of this funding—especially for block grants—was intended to give states and localities more autonomy relative to the national government, it was supported by state governments. However, the national government can always threaten to deny states money if the states do not comply with national standards. One classic example occurred in 1984–85 when President Ronald Reagan effectively mandated that states not complying with the national drinking-age standard of 21 would not receive federal highway funds. South Dakota resisted and then appealed to the federal courts, claiming that the national government had overreached its powers. The courts sided with Reagan, but the Court recently clarified their position. In the 2012 health care decision mentioned earlier (*Federation of Independent Business v. Sebelius*), the court said that the federal government can use money as a "mild encouragement" to the states but cannot use money as a "gun to the head." By this, the Court meant that financial penalties cannot be so severe that a state failing to comply with a federal requirement would need to eliminate core services due to budget losses.

In spite of the Court's prohibition against onerous financial penalties on the states, the question arises: Are the states so dependent on the federal government in total that they have lost their freedom to act based on their own populations' preferences? Since the early 2000s, federal funding for homeland security and for stimulating the economy has come to make up a large portion of state budgets. The more states and localities come to depend on national grants to conduct their day-to-day operations, the more control the national government has over what the states can and cannot do.

The opposite problem is when the national government *fails* to provide funding but requires states to undertake actions that cost the states money. The states have complained repeatedly about "unfunded mandates" by the national government. One example is the list of requirements for states to comply with the Healthy, Hunger-Free Kids Act (2010). States have had to use their own money to meet federal standards for menu planning and nutrition and to make free water available at meal times for all school children.

block grants Sums of money transferred to lower-level governments such that, as long as the general purpose of the grant is met, the lower-level governments are allowed considerable freedom in deciding how the money is spent.

FIGURE 3.4

Proportion of State Revenues from Intergovernmental Transfers, 2012

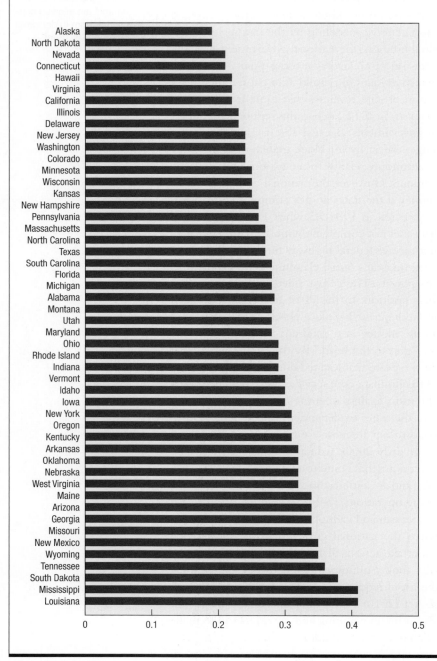

Source: U.S. Census Bureau, "State Government Finances," Summary Table, 2012, www.census.gov/govs/state (accessed 11/6/14).

Federalism and Race

Shifts in the state-federal seesaw have had especially serious consequences for racial politics and for minorities. For example, constitutional amendments passed after the Civil War were intended to change the legal status of African Americans throughout the United States. The Fourteenth Amendment stipulated that all persons, including former slaves, would now count equally for purposes of representation in the House of Representatives and the electoral college. (In other words, the amendment repealed parts of Article I, Section 2, of the original Constitution, which counted every five slaves as three persons.) Moreover, all persons, regardless of color, were to be guaranteed the right to vote under the Fifteenth Amendment.

As we will discuss in Chapter 4, the Fourteenth Amendment was key in extending protections guaranteed at the federal level to lower levels of government. The amendment explicitly declared that not only the national government but also the states must provide for equal protection under the laws and shall not deprive persons of "life, liberty, or property, without due process of law." Unfortunately, many states continued to violate the principles established by the Fourteenth Amendment for many years after its passage. Well into the mid-twentieth century, for example, southern leaders used the doctrine of "states' rights" to justify the oppression and segregation of African Americans. The treatment of former slaves, and of African Americans in general, often included the denial of basic rights (including voting rights), little protection from mob violence, unfair juries in criminal trials, discrimination and separation under Jim Crow laws in the South, and inferior public facilities and infrastructure for black areas. For a hundred years after the Civil War, many white southern leaders continued to assert that the states had the right to regulate relations between races within their territory, an interpretation of the law that the Supreme Court and the national government ultimately rejected in the latter part of the twentieth century because it led to systematic civil rights violations.

Starting in the 1940s, and especially in the 1960s, the national government began to use its power to enforce the ideals stated in the Fourteenth Amendment. Through additional constitutional amendments, enforcement of Supreme Court decisions, and civil rights legislation, the seesaw tilted strongly in the direction of the national government on matters of race, and by the 1970s the national government had become the main protector of racial equality. In the wake of the 1965 Voting Rights Act, for example, the national government used the full power of the Justice Department to oversee elections in the southern states. In some cases, federal workers manned polls and counted ballots in southern counties.

The writers of the *Federalist Papers* argued that federalism had the advantage over other forms of government in that one level of government can check the abuses of another level. In theory, governments at any level can oppress or fail to protect the vulnerable. The national government has in past history been complicit or actively involved in the unjust killing and mistreatment of Native Americans, immigrants, slaves, and enemy combatants. But beginning in the mid-twentieth century, racial oppression and discrimination were undoubtedly lessened because of the active role of the national government in upholding individual rights and liberties that were flouted by the states. This is an area where arguments in favor of states' rights were made to protect those violating basic human rights. We will discuss in greater detail in the next chapter how federalism issues become intertwined with the politics of civil rights and liberties.

State Governments

The growth of the national government's power does not mean that the American states are powerless. As we have seen, the states retain important powers and have control over many aspects of the political system that touch the everyday lives of Americans. State government continues to flourish under American federalism, despite the increasing centralization since the Civil War. In fact, both federal and state governments in general play a larger role in people's lives today than they did in the late nineteenth century. Thus, in our seesaw metaphor, although the balance may have tilted toward the national government over time, both riders on the seesaw (the states and the national government) have grown in size.

The Institutions of State Government

The institutions of state governments are very similar to those of the national government. All state governments have separation of powers, with a directly elected governor as executive, a legislative branch with powers of the purse, and a judicial system headed by a state supreme court. Except for Nebraska, every state has two chambers in the legislature, typically a house and a senate. (Nebraska eliminated its senate in 1937 in a statewide referendum.)

Governors' powers vary from state to state, as do the structures of legislatures. For example, in states such as Texas and New Hampshire, the legislatures meet irregularly and members receive very low pay for what is often their second job. In other states, such as New York, California, Illinois, and Michigan, legislators are well paid, have large staffs, and work full time year-round.

By and large, state-level governance, like national governance, is accomplished by elected representatives in the executive and legislative branches. Unlike the national government, however, several states allow for direct democracy in which citizens vote directly on laws or vote to remove an elected official before completion of his or her term. Such action is often achieved through **ballot initiatives**, **referendums**, or **recall elections**. For instance, in 2014, the people of Oregon and Alaska were asked to vote in ballot initiatives to decide whether marijuana, or cannabis, should be legal for recreational use in those states. In both states, voters approved the initiatives. We will take a closer look at these forms of direct democracy in Chapter 13.

Governors and (in most states) other officers, such as state attorneys general and secretaries of state, are chosen in statewide elections. Representatives and senators are usually selected in a manner similar to U.S. House and Senate elections. For each chamber, the states are divided into electoral districts and one person is elected from each district. As noted in Chapter 1, electoral politics in the states was changed drastically by the U.S. Supreme Court decisions in *Baker v. Carr* (1962) and *Wesberry v. Sanders* (1964). Together, these rulings mandated that all electoral districts of state and national legislatures (with the important exception of the U.S. Senate) must be equal in size by population within each state. When districts for state houses and senates were subsequently redrawn to reflect equality by population, cities immediately had a dramatic increase in representation in state legislatures.

ballot initiative An election in which citizens vote directly on a proposition raised by a group of fellow citizens.

referendum An election in which citizens vote directly on whether to overturn a bill or a constitutional amendment that has been passed by the legislature.

recall election An election during the term of an elected government official in which citizens vote directly on whether to remove the individual from office.

State Power

Over the past three decades, the states have begun to play a somewhat larger role in the American political system. This resurgence in state power stems from several sources. First, the Supreme Court in the 1990s handed down a series of decisions that narrowly interpreted federal powers, thereby granting states more discretion in complying with national law. Second, the national government in the mid-1990s shed some of its responsibility for social welfare programs, giving states considerably more freedom than before to adopt their own welfare standards (see Chapter 16). Third, the national government has become increasingly strained financially as a result of cuts in federal tax rates since the 1980s and international military interventions since the early 2000s. With the exception of the temporary economic-stimulus funding enacted in 2009, Washington has cut back spending in many categories, including scientific and industrial research, roads and highways, job training, loans to students and businesses, and enforcement of antidiscrimination laws. In states where voters tend to favor such programs, the states have had to pick up where the federal government has left off. State budgets have generally grown since the 1980s (Figure 3.5).

FIGURE 3.5

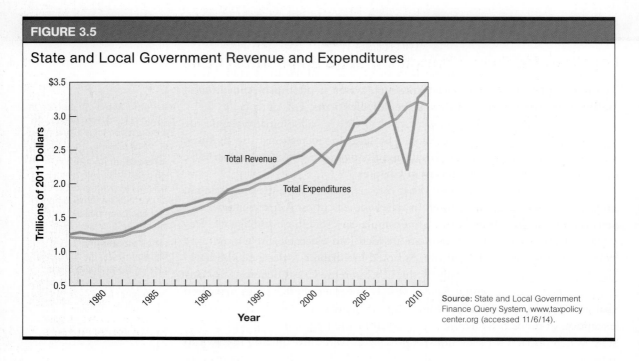

State and Local Government Revenue and Expenditures

Source: State and Local Government Finance Query System, www.taxpolicy center.org (accessed 11/6/14).

Local Governments

There are nearly 90,000 local governments in the United States. They include the most recognizable types: cities, towns, and counties. They also include school districts, regional councils, and special districts that deal with particular issues such as water, zoning and urban planning, transportation, business development, port and lake management, and utilities. The boundaries of special districts typically overlap or cut across multiple cities or counties, and they often are dedicated to coordinating the efforts of several local governments. There are even instances of cross-state regional governments, such as the Port Authority of New York and New Jersey, which operates within both states' territories and is governed by a 12-person board appointed by the governors of each state. In this case, the two states have agreed to grant the Port Authority considerable leeway in regulating transportation, water management, and commercial interactions within their territories, although with oversight by the individual state governments.

Although some leaders, managers, and representatives are appointed, nearly all local governments are led by elected officials. Thus, Americans vote to elect an enormous number of people to run local governments. Sometimes these elections are small in scope and occur throughout the year, with low voter turnout. Yet even when Americans go to the polls in November for the national elections, their ballots are often long because of the large number of local races. They vote not only for mayors, council representatives, and state and county judges but also for coroners, sheriffs, drainage commissioners, zoning board members, and dogcatchers.

Legalized Marijuana: Navigating State and Federal Laws

The U.S. federal law prohibits the cultivation, sale, distribution, or possession of marijuana. Yet nearly half of the states have established policies that legalize medical marijuana. Moreover, between 2012 and 2014, Washington, Colorado, Oregon, and Alaska legalized recreational use of marijuana. How have these states been able to deviate from federal policy?

Interests

Leaders in the federal government have a strong interest in preserving public safety while appearing tough on crime. They also have an interest in preserving national power over the states, as well as retaining favorability with the public. In contrast, the leaders and a majority of people in the states that legalized marijuana believe marijuana is necessary for certain health practices and recreational use is no more harmful than alcohol or tobacco. They claim the issue is one that rightfully belongs under state jurisdiction, not federal.

Institutions

Two key institutional features of American federalism are especially relevant in this issue. First, the supremacy clause of Article VI of the Constitution and subsequent court decisions interpreting its application establish that the federal government's laws have ultimate authority over state laws. This clause gives the national government power to enforce national law prohibiting marijuana, even in states that have legalized it. Second, direct democracy in the states allows citizens to pass laws through an initiative or referendum. In both Colorado and Washington, the legalization of recreational marijuana was decided through voter initiatives. These public-driven efforts cue officials at both the state and federal levels about their constituents' preferences. If federal officials believe the public would react negatively to attempts to assert federal power in this matter, they may decide to leave the states alone to implement their own policies.

Outcomes

The federal government for several years put little effort into combating state laws that conflict with the national criminalization of marijuana. However, that policy has been slowly changing. The Obama administration's published guidelines for federal prosecutors in 2012 indicate that federal law enforcement personnel have discretion: "[I]t is likely not an efficient use of federal resources to

After Washington voters legalized recreational use of marijuana, the Seattle Police Department published guidelines for new enforcement rules.

focus enforcement efforts on individuals with serious illnesses who use marijuana as part of a recommended treatment regimen consistent with applicable state law or their individual noncommercial caregiver. However, persons who are in the business of cultivating, selling, or distributing marijuana, and those who knowingly facilitate such activities, are in violation of Federal law, and are subject to Federal enforcement action, including potential prosecution."[1]

Such an approach may be a way of balancing the federal government's conflicting interests to avoid unpopular law enforcement actions while also being seen as retaining its supremacy over the states and being strong on crime. The current ambiguous situation seems untenable in the long run. People who use marijuana in many states are simultaneously breaking federal law *and* acting consistently with state law. They face risks of prosecution, but do not know what to expect from law enforcement at federal and state levels.

Think About It

How do you think this situation will resolve? Will the national ban on marijuana be preserved and the state laws negated? Or will the states ultimately prevail?

[1] The White House Office of National Drug Control Policy, "Marijuana Resource Center: Federal Laws Pertaining to Marijuana," www.whitehouse .gov/ondcp/federal-laws-pertaining-to-marijuana (accessed 5/10/13).

City governments can take on various forms. Many cities have a *mayoral* form with direct elections for a mayor and a city council; this is essentially a local version of a separation-of-powers system. For instance, the mayor appoints people to head administrative departments, but the council must approve those appointments. This form of city government is common among small cities with fewer than 10,000 people, and in large cities of more than 250,000. The most common form of government for cities, however, is *council-manager*. Under this setup, the city council is directly elected and then appoints a city manager to run the day-to-day operations of the city and to appoint heads of departments.

Scholarship on city politics has demonstrated that the type of governmental institutions in cities affects who is represented in city government, the quality of services delivered to residents, and overall success in attracting investment and jobs. For example, numerous studies have shown how at-large election rules—which require city council members to be elected by the city as a whole, rather than by district—lead to councils with fewer racial minorities and advocates for the poor than those relying on districted elections.[11] Also, different methods of budgeting have led to systematically different distributions of services among rich and poor neighborhoods.[12]

With respect to the powers of local government relative to the states, the prevailing legal theory, known as Dillon's Rule, holds that local governments are the "creatures" of the states, that states have sovereign authority to create, abolish, or amend local governments, and that all local matters must be approved by the states. If interpreted literally, this theory would mean that state governments have to deal constantly with minute decisions for every local government. In practice, what it means is that when there is a dispute over jurisdiction between states and local governments, the courts usually side with the states. When states set up a local government or a special district, for example, they authorize the new government to make decisions in accordance with state law. Nearly all states also have **home rule** as part of their constitutions or laws. Home rule gives a local government wide authority and even forbids states from interfering in local matters. In 37 states, for example, counties have home rule. Most of the nation's largest cities have home rule. States can revoke home rule either by legislation or by constitutional change, depending on the state. Also, states do sometimes infringe on cities' home rule, and courts have allowed that under certain circumstances.

home rule The constitutional or legal authority held by local governments that allows them to govern themselves with little or no interference from the state.

Special Districts

The growth in the number of special districts is one of the most striking recent developments in American local government (Figure 3.6). It signifies a recognition by local politicians and public administrators that many problems—such as

[11] Bernard Grofman, Lisa Handley, and Richard Niemi, *Minority Representation and the Quest for Voting Equality* (New York: Cambridge University Press, 1992).

[12] Paul Peterson, *The Price of Federalism* (Washington, DC: Brookings Institution, 1995).

FIGURE 3.6

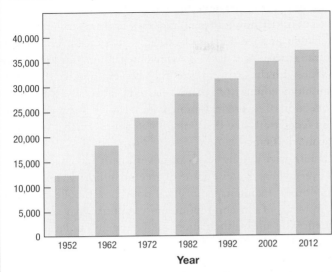

Number of Special Districts, 1952–2012

Sources: U.S. Census Bureau, Local Governments by Type and State: 2012, 2012 Census of Governments, Table 2, and Census of Governments 1952, 1962, 1972, 1982, 1992, 2002, www.census.gov (accessed 11/6/14).

the management of transportation and waterways—call for solutions that cut across the boundaries of cities, towns, and counties. In fact, many of these special districts are created in response to collective dilemmas occurring among local governments. Problems such as polluted waterways or lakes, overcrowded airports, or terrible traffic require multiple governments to coordinate their efforts, or a central enforcer to make sure that local governments pay their fair share for the public good. Special districts can play the role of coordinators or enforcers.

There is also a downside to the creation of special districts. Some research has shown that a large portion of new governments in the United States created between the 1960s and the 1980s—especially school districts and special districts—occurred in response to demands by whites to separate themselves politically from cities with diverse populations that included many blacks and immigrants.[13] On the one hand, we can praise the flexibility of the American federal system in enabling groups of citizens and of local governments to craft new governmental institutions to deal with problems that span multiple jurisdictions. On the other hand, that same flexibility also allows groups that no longer want to be part of jurisdictions struggling to manage problems associated with poverty, immigration, and racial diversity to exit those jurisdictions and create a new space and a new government that faces fewer social problems.

[13] Nancy Burns, *The Formation of American Local Governments: Private Values in Public Institutions* (New York: Oxford University Press, 1994).

In Comparison: American Federalism

Some countries have strong central governments, while others are looser federations with relatively weak national governments. In studying American federalism, it is useful to consider how other political systems are structured, and to consider whether it makes a difference in policy outcomes. Countries or international organizations can be placed somewhere along the continuum illustrated in Figure 3.1, with those toward the right being more like the European Union (which is not a country, or what is referred to formally as a nation-state, but rather a collection of sovereign nation-states). Moving toward the left, countries range from federations like the United States and Canada to unitary countries such as Japan and France.

Countries divide authority among levels of government in different ways. Local governments everywhere exercise some degree of authority and responsibility for such functions as maintenance of local police, trash collection, and street cleaning. But in terms of our continuum, most countries have a **unitary system** of government. This means the national government has legal control over the creation and amendment of lower levels of government, much as U.S. states have control over their cities, counties, and townships. In Japan, for example, the central government is completely predominant over the 47 subunits (called prefectures) and the approximately 3,200 cities, towns, and villages that dot the country. Similarly, French subnational governments are considered to be the administrative arms of the national government, although some discretion has been granted to the 22 French regions in recent years.

Among federations, there is variation in the degree of autonomy granted to subunit governments. Switzerland and Canada are among the world's most decentralized countries, with considerable autonomy granted to cantons and provinces, respectively. In Canada, for example, provinces play the predominant role in the provision of the generous welfare state, including pensions and health care, and in licensing businesses. The cantons and half-cantons in Switzerland are granted wide latitude to implement national laws and to be involved in rules for lawmaking, including direct voting by citizens on laws. Consequently, a small number of cantons can thwart national action. The Swiss refer to their country as a confederation, although by our definition it qualifies as a federation. In contrast, Brazil's 27 state governments are extremely weak in their administrative capacity relative to the national government, although the political clout and electoral independence of Brazilian governors make them heavyweights in Brazilian politics. Most scholars consider the United States somewhere between these two extremes among federations, with both a strong national government and important **reserved powers** for the states, which have substantial administrative capacity.

Why have some countries set up federations instead of establishing a weaker form of union among sovereign states or provinces, as with the European Union? Alternatively, why have they not chosen a unified form of government in which

unitary system A political system in which the national government holds ultimate authority over all areas of policy and over the actions of subunit governments.

reserved powers Those powers not granted to the national government by the Constitution, and therefore reserved to the states.

the national government holds complete sovereign authority, as in Japan? It may seem at times as if the founders of countries had a lot of choice in the matter. But in the United States, for example, there was never any doubt at the Founding that the country would be federal (or, some thought, strongly confederal). The Founders debated how powerful the national government should be relative to the state governments, but they never considered setting up a unitary government.

To understand why one country is federal and another is unitary, it is most useful to consider the conditions at the time of their founding. (Recall our discussion of path dependence in Chapter 1.) For most federal countries, including the United States, their founding involved the uniting of disparate units under one central government for purposes of security or economic prosperity. The Canadian federation, for instance, was formed in 1867 to unite English and French Canada. It was simply assumed that the provinces would have considerable sovereign authority. The same goes for such countries as Belgium, Switzerland, and Germany. Following the breakup of the Soviet Union, the Russian federation was formed among existing subunits that either chose, or were forced, to remain under Moscow's umbrella. Although these subunits have varying levels of autonomy, it has always been assumed that they would be separate parts of the federation, with constitutionally protected status.

It is also worth noting that most of the countries in the world with very large landmasses are federations: India, Canada, the United States, Russia, and Brazil. Before the modern era of jet travel, having populations spread across vast spaces made it difficult for unitary governments to retain complete authority over far-reaching areas. Vesting authority in local subunits was the only practical way to hold a country like Russia or Canada together. Thus, a nation's large geographic size may lead it to adopt federation.

In contrast, countries that are unitary had founding moments when the creation of a unified national language and identity was seen as a more pressing need than permitting diversity among regions. France and Japan, for instance, were each unified under royal families who wanted to crush rival principalities and force them under one imperial domain. The French kings (in the late seventeenth and early eighteenth centuries) and the Japanese emperors (in the nineteenth century) imposed uniformity on all their regions and saw federated forms of governance as a threat to their power. Better, in their view, to have compliant regions under tight central control than to have semiautonomous regions where secessionist or revolutionary sentiment could gain traction. The decisions of these founding rulers shaped the ultimate nature of the modern countries of France and Japan.

Does it make a difference if a country is federal or not? Scholars who have studied this question have generally agreed that federalism matters but they come to mixed conclusions about whether it is good or bad. There is evidence that among low-income countries, federalism leads to more regime stability, including fewer coups and civil wars. But there is also evidence that federal countries have historically had higher rates of corruption and less effective government in producing public goods. While the actual outcomes associated with federalism may have varied historically among many countries, the potential benefits of federalism in the American context are worth exploring further.[14]

Evaluating American Federalism

The American federal system has been influential around the world and often serves as a model when constitutions are designed for new democracies. Scholars have argued that the American system has both advantages and disadvantages.

Avoiding Tyranny

One of the original justifications for the American system given by the writers of the *Federalist Papers* was that, just as with the separation of powers among the three branches of government (executive, legislative, and judicial), federalism fragments power and protects against tyranny. By dividing authority between the states and the national government, constitutional federalism has helped different levels of government check each other's power so that one level cannot dominate. The *Federalist Papers* claim repeatedly, in response to the Antifederalist fears of national government dominance, that the important powers reserved for the states check the power of the national government.

This observation brings us back to the puzzle set forth at the beginning of this chapter: If one advantage of federalism is that each level of government has the ability to check the other, why has the United States centralized authority and granted more power to the national government over time? And has the increase in national power protected citizens from bad government (as someone sympathetic to the Federalists might conclude) or made government worse and even more threatening (as an Antifederalist would have predicted)? As we have seen, the national government has become dominant in response to public pressure amid collective dilemmas among the states. During urgent crises, such as wars, depressions, and labor unrest, the states and the people in the states often come to recognize that collective dilemmas make it difficult to mobilize and coordinate effectively. When voters elect national leaders who propose *national* solutions to problems, they support authorizing the *national* government to lead the country out of trouble. In doing so, the national government amasses resources and capacity to carry out policies to deal with the crisis. And those resources and capacity often stay in place after the crisis passes.

---

[14] For the relationship between regime stability and federalism, see Alicia Adsera and Carlos Boix, "Constitutions and Democratic Breakdowns," in *Controlling Governments*, ed. José M. Maravall and Ignacio S. Cuenca (New York: Cambridge University Press, 2008), pp. 247–301. For a summary of research linking federalism to corruption, see Daniel Treisman, *The Architecture of Government* (New York: Cambridge University Press, 2007), pp. 247–69.

Nevertheless, there have been institutional checks on national government powers. The Supreme Court, for example, has protected the states from national government encroachment on a variety of occasions. More generally, courts have been careful to define areas where, under the Constitution and existing national law, the states retain virtually complete sovereign authority. A federal court system independent of interference from the other branches of the national government is a critical institutional feature that preserves balance in the federal system.

Holding elections at multiple levels of government provides another important institutional check on the national government's power. Political scientists have long argued that federalism opens the door for voters to choose different types of politicians for different levels of government. For instance, a voter may prefer strong law-and-order politicians at the local level (let us say they are Republicans, for the sake of argument), but relatively liberal politicians who might restrict gun sales at the national level (Democrats, in this example). Thus, instead of pursuing one party's dominance at all levels of government, some voters may have different ideological preferences for different levels and can "split" their partisan loyalties accordingly. This idea indicates that federalism allows for a curious kind of partisan competition. Political scientists have found evidence that some voters intentionally split their votes between the parties in state and national elections so that no one party has complete control over all levels of government.[15]

Preserving Diversity

Federalism enables the citizens of a country to have it both ways: it preserves *diversity* across geographic areas while instilling *unity* to fight common enemies and solve collective problems. Providing states with powers preserved by constitutional mandate and court rulings allows people to live under different laws appropriate for their unique circumstances, requirements, or geographic location. For example, residents of Utah may prefer more restrictive laws regarding liquor, pornography, or drug treatment than residents of New York State. California residents may be more willing to pay higher gasoline prices to provide for tighter pollution regulations than Texans, while rules regulating farming may be different in Vermont than in Florida.

Yet this capacity for diverse policies across states or regions can be problematic. Some of these problems can be traced to what economists call *externalities*, which are the costs or benefits experienced by people who are not directly engaged in a specific activity (see Chapter 15).[16] Our earlier example of Kentucky potentially

[15] Morris Fiorina, *Divided Government,* 2nd ed. (New York: Longman, 1995); Alberto Alesina and Howard Rosenthal, *Partisan Politics, Divided Government, and the Economy* (Cambridge, UK: Cambridge University Press, 1995).

[16] Michael Bailey and Mark Carl Rom, "A Wider Race? Interstate Competition across Health and Welfare Programs," *Journal of Politics* 66, no. 2 (2004): 326–47. See also Barry Weingast, "The Economic Role of Political Institutions: Market-Preserving Federalism and Economic Development," *Journal of Law, Economics, and Organization* 11 (1995): 1–31.

having a lower minimum wage than other states is an example of an externality: Kentucky's policies would indirectly affect the actions of businesses in other states. It might lead to a "race to the bottom," as discussed earlier. As another example, if a factory pollutes the water in Pennsylvania and the pollution floats down the Ohio River to parts of Ohio and Kentucky, then people in the latter two states would suffer negative externalities caused by the factories in Pennsylvania. Negative externalities in a federal system arise when states can take actions or conduct business irrespective of the consequences for other states. This is essentially a form of free riding in that all states might generally agree to keep the air and water clean, but one state might avoid paying the costs of regulation because the externalities fall elsewhere. Midwestern states, for example, may oppose onerous pollution-control laws that deter business investment if most of the air pollution—from coal-burning power plants, for example—flows toward states to their east.

Today, disputes over federalism persist in several areas. For example, as of 2015, 23 states and the District of Columbia allow the use and sale of medical marijuana in defiance of federal drug laws, as shown in this Washington state dispensary.

Fostering Competition

Economist Charles Tiebout argued that competition among states or localities for people and business leads to more efficient government and more generous public programs.[17] Because people and businesses can migrate to whatever town, city, or state they choose, those entities compete among each other to find the mixture of taxes and public policies that promotes the greatest efficiency. If taxes are too high relative to what residents receive from the government in services, then another city, town, or state will find a better set of policies to attract those people. In Tiebout's view, competition induces innovation in government and leads to better outcomes.

Some scholars, notably Paul Peterson, argue that competition among states or local areas for business investment creates a countervailing negative effect—namely, harm to the poor.[18] As in our Kentucky example, areas will compete

---

[17] Charles M. Tiebout, "A Pure Theory of Local Expenditures," *Journal of Political Economy* 64, no. 5 (1956): 416–24. See also Craig Volden, "The Politics of Competitive Federalism: A Race to the Bottom in Welfare Benefits?" *American Journal of Political Science* 46, no. 2 (2002): 352–64; and Michael Bailey and Mark Carl Rom, "A Wider Race? Interstate Competition across Health and Welfare Programs," *Journal of Politics* 66, no. 2 (2004): 326.

[18] Peterson, *The Price of Federalism*.

actively with each other for business investment, not only by reducing the burden of regulations but also by lowering taxes on businesses and on wealthy people who run or own those businesses. Lower taxes on businesses and on wealthy people mean fewer funds to pay for social programs for the poor and for public goods, such as schools and parks, that benefit poor people who cannot afford to pay for them privately. In much the same way, migration of people and investment can also harm the poor. Cities or states with generous social programs for the poor (and higher taxes to pay for those programs) will lose wealthier residents and businesses to other cities or states with lower taxes and less generous programs, thus reducing the resources available for the poor in the former locales.

The Tiebout and Peterson theories are difficult to reconcile. Peterson argues that migration from the 1960s through the 1990s has overwhelmingly occurred among wealthier people leaving inner cities to live in suburbs, which have historically offered lower taxes and fewer social services. He notes that large urban areas with many poor residents have struggled to retain business investment as well as their upper-middle-class and wealthy inhabitants. Some economists in the Tiebout tradition argue that such migration is inevitable as people seek out better places to live, and that it forces urban areas to reform their governments. From either perspective, finding the right mixture of taxes and public policies to attract business investment and maintain generous social programs is very difficult for a city or state, and many cities have fared poorly as a result. Cities like Detroit, Gary (Indiana), and Newark (New Jersey) have suffered as people with higher incomes migrated to the suburbs, leaving behind large poor populations that have little means to pay for the services they need.

Promoting Unity and Experimentation

The national government promotes unity and helps to solve collective dilemmas in three ways.[19] First, it sets common national standards to avoid the problem of negative externalities that result from differing state standards. Thus, national pollution standards have become the norm, with states having the freedom to set even stricter standards.

Second, many national agencies cooperate with the states to coordinate activity for better effectiveness. The Department of Homeland Security attempts to coordinate the activities of state and local police forces to establish procedures for preventing and responding to terrorist attacks. Other national agencies that work closely with state agencies to coordinate efforts include the Department of Transportation, the Environmental Protection Agency, and the Department of Agriculture. These national-level agencies often work with parallel state-level agencies to design and implement policies passed by the national government.

[19] For a paper that addresses these issues in depth, see Rui J. De Figueiredo Jr. and Barry R. Weingast, "Self-Enforcing Federalism: Solving the Two Fundamental Dilemmas," *Journal of Law, Organizations, and Economics* 21 (2005): 103–35.

The national government can also encourage states to try out new policies and report on the experiments for the benefit of all the states.[20] Former Supreme Court Justice Louis Brandeis wrote that one justification for maintaining strong states was that they can be "laboratories of democracy." For example, national welfare reform in the 1990s that gave greater authority to the states was modeled on initiatives in Michigan and Wisconsin that were deemed largely successful.[21]

Third, the national government can subsidize state efforts, and does so with regularity and purpose. It can also use that funding to give states incentives to go along with the rest of the country, as the Reagan administration did in establishing a national drinking age and as the Obama administration did with education standards. Although such federal funds have been unreliable in recent years—the huge boost provided by the stimulus package in 2009 soon dropped off—they are substantial even during economic downturns.

Federalism as a Difficult but Important Balance

The federal aspects of the American political system contain tensions in design and implementation. The nation is comprised of states with considerable authority. Yet over time, the national government has grown in authority and power, often eclipsing the role of the states. The system honors diversity across geographic areas, but the states need, and their residents demand, a high degree of uniformity in coordination and enforcement by the national government to solve their collective dilemmas. In reality, the basic requirements and actions of the various states are not all that different. They tend to copy each other and to converge on similar policies.

The United States operates on the principle of two levels of sovereignty—the people of Iowa, for example, are sovereign over the territory of Iowa, and the people of the United States are sovereign over the entire country. Contrary to what the Founders envisioned, however, most Americans are not primarily loyal to their states; they relocate from state to state with regularity and, with few exceptions, patriotism among Americans is reserved more for the nation as a whole than for individual states. Studies show that more people pay attention to national politics than to their own state politics and recognize their national leaders more readily than their state leaders.[22]

All of these characteristics are consistent with the notion that the political system in the United States has tipped strongly in the national government's direction, but it has not tipped so far as to undo the fundamental federal design.

[20] Charles Shipan and Craig Volden, "Bottom-Up Federalism: The Diffusion of Antismoking Policies from U.S. Cities to States," *American Journal of Political Science* 50 (2006): 825–43.

[21] For an interesting and different approach to studying innovation, see Virginia Gray, "Innovation in the States: A Diffusion Study," *American Political Science Review* 67 (1973): 1174–85.

[22] For a paper that addresses some of these issues, see Cindy D. Kam and Robert A. Mikos, "Do Citizens Care about Federalism? An Experimental Test," *Journal of Empirical Legal Studies* 4, no. 3 (2007): 589–624.

FURTHER READING

★ = Included in *Readings in American Politics*, 3e

★ *Arizona v. United States* (2012). A Supreme Court decision that struck down aspects of an Arizona law that empowered local police to enforce immigration regulations, thus siding with national government authority over the states on matters of immigration.

Bednar, Jenna, *The Robust Federation: Principles of Design* (New York: Cambridge University Press, 2009). Details the tensions and dynamics of federalism.

★ Hamilton, Alexander, James Madison, and John Jay, *The Federalist Papers*, No. 39, 1788. Madison's classic account of the differences between American political institutions that reflect the will of the people and political institutions that represent the states.

Ostrom, Vincent, *The Political Theory of a Compound Republic: Designing the American Experiment* (Lincoln: University of Nebraska Press, 1987). A book that places federalism at the very heart of the American political system.

Peterson, Paul, *The Price of Federalism* (Washington, DC: Brookings Institution, 1995). The argument that cities lose their tax-paying residents to suburbs and keep their poorer residents, thus reducing resources at the local level for services that benefit the poor.

★ Riker, William, *Federalism: Origin, Operation, Significance* (Boston: Little, Brown, 1964). A classic account of American federalism in comparative context, with special emphasis on civil rights.

Rodden, Jonathan, *Hamilton's Paradox: The Promise and Peril of Fiscal Federalism* (New York: Cambridge University Press, 2006). Describes the problems that arise when state governments take bad risks, knowing that the national government will bail them out if things go poorly.

KEY TERMS

ballot initiative (p. 87)

block grants (p. 83)

categorical grants (p. 82)

commerce clause (p. 76)

confederation (p. 69)

cooperative federalism (p. 73)

dual federalism (p. 72)

elastic clause (necessary and proper clause) (p. 76)

federalism (p. 69)

grants-in-aid (p. 82)

home rule (p. 90)

intergovernmentalism (p. 73)

intergovernmental relations (p. 74)

recall election (p. 87)

referendum (p. 87)

reserved powers (p. 92)

revenue–sharing (p. 82)

unitary system (p. 92)

Civil liberties, such as the right to bear arms, are protected from improper government interference. However, the meaning and boundary of such rights are often unclear and in dispute. Moreover, when the rights and liberties of one group (for example, gun owners) threaten the rights and liberties of others (potential victims of gun violence), a question arises over what action the government should take.

4

CIVIL RIGHTS AND LIBERTIES

At times, protecting the rights and liberties of some people seems to infringe on those of others or to hinder another governmental goal. How have the courts and other branches of government resolved controversies over the extent of Americans' rights and liberties?

I n 1975, in response to rising rates of crime, the District of Columbia (Washington, D.C.) passed a law that severely limited the freedom of people to buy and own handguns. The stated objective was simple: to reduce the number of guns and thus reduce crimes involving guns.

To some, the new gun restrictions and others like them passed by other cities were justified because a major purpose of government is to protect the safety of its citizens. Citizens have an interest in security and order. But to others, the restrictions violated individual liberty, and some argued that gun restrictions do little to deter crime and may even permit more crime to occur. As a matter of constitutional interpretation, they argued, restricting the possession of handguns is a violation of the fundamental right to own and possess a firearm enshrined in the U.S. Constitution. This is a right they say is protected by the Second Amendment of the Constitution, which says, "A well regulated Militia, being necessary to the security of a free State, the right of the people to keep and bear Arms, shall not be infringed."

The appropriate interpretation of this amendment, especially with regard to how much the government can restrict gun ownership, has been a subject of intense political and legal controversy. Political conflicts over these laws often pit hunters and sporting organizations who oppose gun control against police associations and big-city mayors who favor more restrictions on gun ownership. There is always the question of what kinds of guns fall under the purview of the amendment. After all, it has never been controversial for the government to ban ownership of howitzers or machine guns, weapons that can kill indiscriminately and that require intensive training to use properly. But what about handguns or assault rifles?

The law remained in effect for 33 years until Dick Heller, a Washington, D.C., police officer who was denied a registration for his personal firearm, took his case against the law all the way to the Supreme Court. In 2008, the Court agreed to decide on the case to determine what exactly the Constitution's Second Amendment protects when it comes to the possession of firearms. Does it protect the right of an individual to keep and bear arms, or is it a protection that applied only in the context of those acting in common defense—as in a state militia? If it is an individual's right, does it protect all individuals—including felons and the mentally ill—or can governments limit who is allowed to own guns? Does the protection apply everywhere, such as in a school or in a government building? And what, exactly, constitutes a firearm? If the possession of handguns is protected, what about the possession of assault rifles?

Justice Antonin Scalia wrote the majority opinion and provided the Court's answers to these questions. With the support of four other judges he wrote that the Washington, D.C., law violated the Second Amendment. The amendment guarantees individual rights to possess a firearm, even for purposes unconnected to a militia. However, this right, as is the case with all rights or liberties, has its limits. Although the right does protect the possession of firearms, it does not protect the ability of any-one anywhere to possess any type of firearm for whatever purpose. Rather, the Court determined that the right applies to gun possession only in the context of traditionally lawful purposes, such as self-defense in one's home. It determined that not all weap-ons were covered under the term *firearms*, but rather only those "in common use at the time." This includes handguns, but excludes machine guns. The Court determined that local governments prohibiting felons and the mentally ill from possessing fire-arms is constitutional, as is prohibiting the possession of concealed weapons in sen-sitive locations. In a later case, *McDonald v. Chicago* (2010), the Court held that its legal reasoning in the *Heller* decision applies to any jurisdiction in the United States, not just Washington, D.C., and federal property.

The coexistence of some legal restrictions on gun ownership and the Court's rul-ings limiting government regulation of guns is emblematic of the difficult balancing act that often occurs when rights and liberties conflict. The trade-offs among rights and goals can be stark. We can protect people's rights to own a gun, but a gun can be used to harm others, infringing on their right to security. The government is at once responsible for protecting one's life and property while also respecting one's freedom to be armed. Thus, the principles of liberty and security can be posed as in opposi-tion. The Court was split 5–4 in the *Heller* decision, and the controversy continues in fierce public and legislative debate today. Some want to overturn *Heller* or change laws to work around it. And in spite of and in response to court decisions, powerful interest groups, such as the National Rifle Association (see Chapter 11) and the Brady Campaign to Prevent Gun Violence, put enormous pressure on Congress and state legislatures to influence gun control laws.

Ultimately, for controversies like these, the questions must be asked: Which princi-ple should be upheld? How do we determine the proper balance between opposing rights and liberties? How have the courts and other branches of government resolved these controversies?

Defining Civil Rights and Liberties

To answer our chapter-opening questions, we need to learn how the boundaries on governmental behavior and on individuals' rights and liberties arose and continue to change within the United States. In Chapter 3, we focused on federalism, which has to do with the relationships among the states and between the states and the national government. Now we will build on that discussion to address the relationships between individuals and the government. Civil rights and liberties primarily concern limits on or the responsibilities of government in relation to individuals, yet as we will learn, issues relating to federalism are crucial to understanding the development of civil rights and liberties in the American political system.

Civil rights and **civil liberties** fall into two general categories. First, there are guarantees that individuals can engage in activities central to citizenship or legal immigrant status, such as the right to vote or petition the government, and that individuals are assured due process and equal protection under the law. This category generally refers to protections that the government must actively provide. As an example, when people are charged with a crime, they have rights as criminal defendants to certain protections, like a court-appointed lawyer if necessary, that the government is obligated to make available. Second, rights and liberties entail freedom from undue or unjust interference by government, such as interference with citizens' freedom of speech or freedom of religion. This category refers to protections from government, and thus obligates nonaction by the government.

The terms *rights* and *liberties* often are used interchangeably and were lumped together under the concept of "rights" in the Founding era. (Thus, the Bill of Rights included both categories.) Today, in legal circles, lawyers and judges refer to the first category as rights and the latter category as liberties, but for our purposes we can mostly treat them together.

The laws and constitutional interpretations about rights and liberties in effect oblige the government to take certain actions and to refrain from taking certain other actions. They can change over time due to new legislation or to court decisions reinterpreting specific language in laws or in constitutional passages. These obligations and boundaries on behavior, once set, become vital pieces of the institutional framework in the American political system. As with all political institutions, the obligation and boundaries constrain and coordinate behavior. An example of a particular obligation or boundary is in the *Heller* case, which determined that state and city governments are able to regulate where handguns are allowed to be possessed (for example, not on university campuses) but not to ban all handgun ownership. The Court's decision clarified, in light of the Second Amendment, where the constitutional boundary should exist for states and cities writing laws, and for lower-level courts in future legal cases.

Decisions by courts or other branches establishing these boundaries are often highly controversial and, as we have seen, involve difficult trade-offs. The set of

civil rights Rights that (1) enable individuals to engage in activities central to citizenship or legal immigrant status, such as voting or petitioning the government; (2) ensure all individuals receive due process and equal treatment under the law; or (3) guarantee freedom from discriminatory actions by others that seek to deny an individual's full status as an equal member of society.

civil liberties Freedoms protected from interference by the government, such as freedom of speech and freedom of religion.

civil rights and liberties to be protected is not always obvious. Moreover, the rights and liberties evolve in response to changing social conditions, values, and norms of behavior, as well as occasional emergencies and threats. In the context of voting rights, consider that at one time it was widely accepted that only men should be permitted to vote. In our own time, most people in nearly every country agree that men and women should have an equal right to vote in all public elections. The United States, through the Nineteenth Amendment, mandated in 1920 that women be allowed to vote. In Switzerland, however, women were not guaranteed the right to vote until 1971, and in Lichtenstein not until 1984. Rights and liberties vary across countries and over time, and these variations have consequences for the entire political system and for who can do what in society.

The Origins of Rights and Liberties

The values of equality and human dignity stand at the heart of the intellectual tradition that the Founders relied upon when they debated and ultimately crafted the Declaration of Independence and the Constitution, especially in appending the Bill of Rights at the end of the Constitution. The Founders followed a long line of thinking from specific theologians and philosophers since ancient times who wrote that all humans were born equal. These ideas have theological roots, and most of the Founders would have believed in a God-given "natural law" that exists independent of government. Because God created them thus or because of their inherent value as human beings (or both), all persons ought to be treated equally by governments. Similarly, values associated with the eighteenth-century Age of Enlightenment, and embodied in the principles expressed by the leaders of the American and French Revolutions, placed special emphasis on limiting the powers of government, in particular on protecting unpopular minorities from oppression by majorities or majority-elected governments.[1] Because of inherent human dignity and equality, people deserve protection from oppression. The Declaration of Independence, for example, states that "all men are created equal" and enjoy "certain unalienable rights" that no government should infringe upon. Among these are the rights to "Life, Liberty, and the pursuit of Happiness." Similarly, the French revolutionaries' slogan of "Liberty, Equality, Fraternity" reflected an emphasis on individual rights and shared norms to protect them.[2]

Following the American Revolution, the Commonwealth (State) of Virginia paved an important path when its constitution contained a bill of rights, which is a detailed list of rights and liberties that the state government was obligated to

[1] Many of these principles have their modern origins in the writings of John Locke, the English political philosopher. See John Locke, *Second Treatise on Government* (1690; repr., Indianapolis: Hackett, 1980), and *A Letter Concerning Toleration: Humbly Submitted* (1689; repr., Indianapolis: Hackett, 1983).

[2] Max Ferrand, *The Framing of the Constitution of the United States* (1930; repr., Frederick, MD: Beard Books, 2000).

protect. The Virginia Declaration of Rights in that constitution instantly became the reference for other state constitutions and served as the basis for the U.S. Bill of Rights. As discussed in Chapter 2, the U.S. Bill of Rights was ratified in 1791 as the first 10 amendments to the U.S. Constitution.

The rights and liberties specified in the U.S. **Bill of Rights** fall into several categories:

- Basic individual rights and liberties, such as freedom of religion and the right to bear arms.

- Rights and liberties having to do with the process of republican government, such as freedom of speech, assembly, and the press, and the right to petition the government.

- Rights of criminal defendants, such as the right to a fair trial and to a trial by an impartial jury, and freedom from unreasonable search and seizure.

- Rights protecting citizens against excessive government force—for example, against seizure of property without just compensation, against soldiers occupying private property in times of peace, and against deprivation of "life, liberty, property, or without due process of law."[3]

> **Bill of Rights** The first 10 amendments to the Constitution, which enumerate a set of liberties not to be violated by the government and a set of rights to be protected by the government.

Subsequent constitutional amendments either added to or clarified the rights and liberties enumerated in the Bill of Rights. Amendments ratified in the late nineteenth and twentieth centuries have been particularly important in making the American political system more democratic. Specifically, these amendments have:

- abolished slavery (Thirteenth Amendment).

- expanded the right to vote to new groups (Fifteenth, Nineteenth, Twenty-fourth, and Twenty-sixth Amendments).

- required the states to abide by the U.S. Bill of Rights and granted former slaves full rights of citizenship (Fourteenth Amendment).

In addition to expanding the right to vote and freeing the slaves, these amendments required all governments at any level to enforce the laws that applied to individuals and governments. The Fourteenth Amendment in particular advanced critical issues of federalism that not only gradually enhanced the role and stature of the national government but also resulted in a more humane and morally defensible government.

Beyond those rights and liberties directly mentioned in the Constitution, there are others that are set forth in statutory laws (for instance, laws passed by legislatures or other elected assemblies). Laws concerning civil rights and liberties have been passed by legislatures at the national and state levels, and by city and council governments. These laws can exist, according to the courts, as long as they do not violate the Constitution. For example, numerous laws at all levels of government in the United States ban discrimination in public places

---

[3] The Tenth Amendment mostly concerns federalism, but its application has been important to the development of civil rights and liberties, as discussed later in this chapter.

The Bill of Rights is made up of the first 10 amendments to the Constitution and includes the following protections.

- **First Amendment:** protects the freedoms of religion, speech, press, assembly, and petition.

- **Second Amendment:** guarantees the states the right to establish a militia, and individuals the right to bear arms (own weapons).

- **Third Amendment:** ensures that citizens are not required to quarter troops in their home.

- **Fourth Amendment:** protects individuals from unreasonable search and seizure by government agents.

- **Fifth Amendment:** guarantees that an individual will not stand trial more than once for the same offense or have to testify against him- or herself. Also ensures that no individual is deprived of "life, liberty, or property" without a fair procedure or compensation.

- **Sixth Amendment:** guarantees criminal defendants the right to a speedy and public trial by an impartial jury.

- **Seventh Amendment:** provides the right to a trial by jury in civil cases.

- **Eighth Amendment:** protects the accused from excessive bail and cruel and unusual punishments.

- **Ninth Amendment:** guarantees rights not specifically enumerated in the Constitution or Bill of Rights.

- **Tenth Amendment:** reserves powers not specifically given to the national government for the states and the people.

on the basis of race, ethnicity, religion, place of origin, gender, sexual orientation, political beliefs, or disability.

Other rights and liberties not explicitly mentioned in the Constitution have been "discovered" by courts in vague phrases in the Constitution or established by reference to tradition. For example, the Supreme Court declared in *Griswold v. Connecticut* (1965) that the Constitution implies a right to privacy, making laws banning contraception unconstitutional. Also implied are the right to travel within the United States (if not fleeing justice) and the right to marry someone of the opposite sex as one chooses. The justification for treating these rights as constitutionally protected is a combination of constitutional interpretation, history, and tradition. For example, the courts have inferred that the right to marital privacy exists in the Ninth Amendment clause stating that other rights not mentioned in the Constitution are "retained by the people."

The Special Role of the Courts

The Founders understood well the dangers that a government elected by a majority might pose in oppressing minorities or in permitting mistreatment of minorities in society. Through civil rights and liberties protections, including the Bill of Rights, they attempted to design the American system to protect minorities, even from the government.[4] During debates over ratification of the Constitution, the minorities often mentioned by the Founders as needing protection were property owners whose rights to own and enjoy property were threatened by local and state governments' ability to impose onerous taxes or even redistribute property. Not long after the Founding and the ratification of the Bill of Rights, however, another kind of threat to rights and liberties emerged. The presidential administration of John Adams blatantly violated the First Amendment by passing the Alien and Sedition Acts in 1798. The Acts permitted the harassment and jailing of people critical of the administration and its policies. In the heat of political competition, the Adams administration forbade certain kinds of legitimate political assembly and speech guaranteed by the First Amendment.[5] Critics at the time claimed that the Acts also violated the Tenth Amendment by giving the national government more power than the Constitution allowed. The Acts became an embarrassment to Adams and did not ultimately result in large-scale oppression of dissent. The legislation expired in 1801, when Adams left the presidency.

Legislatures and executives, in trying to be responsive to majorities that elected them, can be tempted to violate basic freedoms of minorities. For that reason, the courts as unelected bodies interpreting the law are often considered the protectors of individuals against the government and against other individuals. Not only do courts act as independent enforcers of behavior by both individuals and governments, they also play the crucial role in defining the obligations and boundaries of behavior.[6] Governments sometimes violate their own rules or try to change them. The courts can overturn rule violations or decide whether a rule change is constitutional. As the final arbiters of what the law means, including the legal protections or rights and liberties enshrined in the Bill of Rights and other parts of the Constitution, the federal courts have often drawn the lines between acceptable and unacceptable laws or government actions.

As an example, the Supreme Court in *United States v. Jones* (2012) ruled that attaching a global positioning system (GPS) device to the car of someone being investigated for crimes (without the person's knowledge) constituted "search" under the Fourth Amendment. That amendment bars search and seizure by the government without probable cause (and usually a warrant). The question for the court was, given new technologies enabling law enforcement to track movements using GPS devices, whether installing these devices was legally

[4] Robert Dahl, *How Democratic Is the American Constitution?* (New Haven, CT: Yale University Press, 2001).

[5] Leonard Levy, *Freedom of Speech and Press in Early American History: Legacy of Suppression* (New York: Harper & Row, 1963).

[6] Howard Gillman and Cornell Clayton, *The Supreme Court in American Politics: New Institutionalist Interpretations* (Lawrence: University Press of Kansas, 1999).

Evolving technology and social norms have required the courts to continually revisit certain civil rights and liberties issues in new contexts. In 2012, the Supreme Court decided that police affixing GPS devices to the cars of unwitting investigation subjects violated the Fourth Amendment.

considered to be searching for evidence and thus subject to the restrictions mandated by the Fourth Amendment. The Court ruled that GPS devices do indeed fall into that category.[7] Through hundreds of such cases, the Supreme Court has played a key role in defining the institutional boundaries on individual and governmental conduct, having to make new rulings in response to changes in technologies and in the nature of people's behavior.

Other examples have come in the area of freedom of speech and freedom of association. As the example of the Alien and Sedition Acts shows, the government can be tempted to suppress the critical speech of an unpopular minority group. Governments especially come under pressure to crack down on dissent in times of crisis such as wars, after terror attacks, or amid fear of sabotage. During the so-called McCarthy era in the late 1940s and early 1950s, numerous members of Congress, led by Senator Joseph McCarthy of Wisconsin, falsely accused hundreds of people in the U.S. State Department and other federal agencies of conspiring against the United States. Many of those accused of belonging to the Communist Party lost their jobs or experienced other forms of harassment. In addition, the government banned more than 30,000 books from library shelves and pressured newspapers and magazines not to publish the writings of accused communists. The government later rescinded all its censorship provisions, and in 1954 the Senate put an end to the "witch hunts" by officially censuring McCarthy.

[7] *United States v. Jones*, 132 S.Ct. 945 (2012).

The McCarthy era treatment of suspected communists is now widely considered to be unjust, but at the time there was widespread fear of communist infiltration of the U.S. government. In some circumstances, it can be difficult to find the right balance between maintaining order and security while preserving rights and liberties, and there can be legitimate disagreements over appropriate government action. Groups can move beyond engaging in legitimate criticism to spreading damaging rumors or, more seriously, advocating violence or other illegitimate means of bringing down the government. Such actions risk provoking the government into cracking down on dissent. In the 1960s, for example, some fringe anti–Vietnam War groups that advocated violence against government institutions elicited fierce reprisals from the police and other government agencies. A few groups actually bombed government offices, and the reaction of some law enforcement agencies was to spy on and infiltrate many groups that were critical of the government's policies, even if most of them did not advocate violence. Elected officials disagreed, and historians still disagree, over whether this was legitimate law enforcement or a violation of civil rights and liberties.

Although popularly elected branches of government can pass laws proposing specific means to restrict actions in order to maintain security or to respond to majority sentiment, it is often left to the courts to decide whether the rules passed by governments are constitutional. In the area of freedom of speech, because of Supreme Court decisions beginning in the early twentieth century, generally people today are free to express their opinions with few legal limitations. Exceptions defined by the courts include pronouncements advocating the overthrow of the government or the killing of people in positions of public authority, or speeches designed to incite immediate violence or panic. For its part, because of court decisions interpreting the Constitution, the government is not allowed to engage in most forms of censorship, even of very unpopular opinions.

The courts can play this role because of the establishment of an independent judiciary, a key institutional hallmark of most modern democracies. (We discuss this in more detail in Chapter 8.) Because courts make decisions but cannot enforce the law themselves, they must rely on the branches of government that control the military and the police—usually the executive branch. So even when the courts rule against the majority-elected government, they still have to count on parts of that government to enforce the decision. Therefore, the courts must have enough legitimacy in society to ensure that their decisions are ultimately enforced by the executive branch or by the states. This legitimacy has long been in place in the United States, where even the most unpopular court decisions eventually have been enforced.

As an example, opinion polls indicate that a clear majority of Americans support allowing religious prayer in public schools and the display of the biblical Ten Commandments on public buildings (see Chapter 9). If it were up to the elected branches of the national government—the Congress and some

The First Amendment protects religious freedom partly by prohibiting the establishment of an official state religion. The courts have interpreted this to mean that religious displays in government offices—such as this monument of the Ten Commandments in an Alabama courthouse—are unconstitutional, even if a majority of people like them.

recent presidents—or to individual school districts, prayer in public schools would most likely be allowed and courts would be free to display the Ten Commandments on their buildings and in their courtrooms. However, following two cases—*Engel v. Vitale* (1962) and *Abington School District v. Schempp* (1963)—the Supreme Court has maintained that school-sponsored prayer violates First Amendment prohibitions against the establishment of an official state religion.[8] In two cases decided in 2005, the Court ruled that unless the display of the Ten Commandments was clearly part of a secular display of lawmaking throughout human history, such displays on publicly funded buildings were unconstitutional.[9] Despite the unpopularity of the Court's rulings, state and local governments have taken down such displays. Likewise, most school districts throughout the country comply with the Court's mandate to keep organized prayer out of public school activities, even though many districts would receive overwhelming public support for allowing prayer in the schools. This compliance is an indication of the courts' legitimacy in the United States.

Civil Rights and Liberties Failures

Courts are not perfect arbiters and can err egregiously in civil rights and liberties cases. In one of the most notorious Supreme Court decisions, the majority opinion in the *Dred Scott* case in 1857, written by Chief Justice Roger Taney, stated that the Founders did not consider African Americans to be part of the "people of the United States." Thus, blacks did not possess the rights and privileges granted to the people under the Constitution. By providing legal justification for the continued oppression of blacks, the Court's decision went against the norms of human rights and liberties that were generally promoted during the Founding era. *Dred Scott* was soon overturned by the Fourteenth Amendment in 1868, but the civil rights of African Americans were not well protected in practice for another 100 years.

Like the courts, American legislatures and executives have also grossly violated the principles enshrined in the Bill of Rights and failed at various times

[8] *Engel v. Vitale*, 370 U.S. 421 (1962); *Abington School District v. Schempp*, 374 U.S. 203 (1963).
[9] *Van Orden v. Perry*, 545 U.S. 677 (2005); *McCreary County v. ACLU of Kentucky*, 545 U.S. 844 (2005).

to protect the basic civil rights and liberties of certain groups in society. We have already considered the Alien and Sedition Acts that Congress passed in 1798 and the actions of the government during the McCarthy era. Even worse have been legally sanctioned systemic patterns of oppression and discrimination based on race, ethnicity, or national origin. With widespread public support among citizens, the U.S. government in the nineteenth century forcibly relocated or killed a substantial portion of the Native American population in order to settle the continent for white Americans. Two other shameful failures have concerned slavery and its aftermath, and the treatment of immigrants.

Slavery and African Americans

The existence of slavery and the continuing discrimination against black people following the Civil War represent terrible breaches of the principles expressed in the Founding documents. In the eyes of many who participated in the debates over the drafting and ratification of the Constitution and the new institutions of American government, slavery, the slave trade, and the mistreatment of former slaves were fundamentally at odds with the ideals of the American Revolution and the new United States.[10] How could the institution of slavery be allowed to exist, they argued, in a land governed by a Constitution that was based on the revolutionary idea that all men are created equal? Proposals were made at the Constitutional Convention to outlaw slavery throughout the country, but in the end the issue was left to the states to resolve, ensuring the continuance of slavery for the next several decades.[11] Although owning or trading slaves was gradually outlawed in the northern states between 1790 and 1804, it remained a basic feature of southern society and the region's economy for another half-century and more.

By the start of the Civil War, slaves accounted for one-third of the total southern population. Among white leaders in the South, there were deep fears of slave uprisings and of the revenge that slaves would exact if they were freed en masse. Even after slavery was formally abolished throughout the United States in 1865, most black Americans were still denied their basic rights in many parts of the country. Segregated into areas with poor infrastructures and inadequate public institutions, blacks were discriminated against in schools, in the workplace, and in hospitals, stores, government offices, restaurants, and courts of law.

It was common for former slaves to continue working as poorly paid servants on farms in the South, often living in hovels and shacks with little access to education and basic services. Many southern states enacted **Jim Crow laws**

Jim Crow laws Laws passed after the Civil War to establish a system of segregation of public facilities and private establishments that made African Americans second-class citizens.

[10] James D. Anderson, "Race-Conscious Educational Policies versus a 'Color-Blind Constitution': A Historical Perspective," *Educational Researcher* 36, no. 5 (2007): 249–57.

[11] David Waldstreicher, *Slavery's Constitution: From Revolution to Ratification* (New York: Hill & Wang, 2009).

that codified the second-class citizenship of blacks. Blacks living in the North and in cities also suffered relative to other racial groups. Ever since the Civil War and the emancipation of the slaves, American blacks have consistently experienced higher levels of unemployment; been poorer, less educated, and more disease-prone; and been subject to greater rates of discrimination in education, housing, and employment than any other major racial group in the United States, particularly whites.

The black-white cleavage in American society remains the nation's most enduring and troublesome divide. Slavery, the discriminatory post–Civil War social and economic system, and long-standing prejudice have scarred the African American population.[12] The legacy of slavery represents a massive systemic failure on the part of the country's political institutions and is the worst stain on its reputation for democratic governance.

The Treatment of Immigrants

The treatment of immigrants, and their experiences of discrimination throughout the nineteenth and early twentieth centuries, similarly defies justification in light of constitutional principles. Since the sixteenth century, the American nation has been built on successive waves of immigration. In terms of the proportion of the population born outside the United States, immigration peaked in the 1840s when 1.7 million newcomers arrived. (In 1850, the nation's total population was just 27 million.) In terms of sheer numbers, the flow peaked between 1900 and 1910 when nearly 9 million immigrants arrived, and again in the decade of the 1990s when it reached a similar number.

Racial, ethnic, or religious discrimination against immigrants was common in each of these eras. Established residents—the majority of whom were of English or Scottish origin—justified their hostility by claiming that the immigrants were of inferior genetic stock with strange religions, languages, accents, and dress. It did not help that most immigrants until the mid-twentieth century arrived poor. Residents resented competing with the new immigrants for jobs.

Irish immigrants endured some of the harshest discrimination. It was common in the 1850s for businesses in Boston and New York to post help-wanted signs that read, "Irish need not apply." The Chinese who came to work on the railroads in the West in the nineteenth century also suffered terrible exploitation, mistreatment, and denial of citizenship for years after their arrival. Italians and Greeks who arrived in the early twentieth century were often denied access to jobs and housing close to that of the better-established ethnic groups. Mexican Americans who arrived in the twentieth century to fill low-wage jobs in the South and Southwest often found living and employment conditions

[12] Michael Klarman, *From Jim Crow to Civil Rights: The Supreme Court and the Struggle for Racial Equality* (New York: Oxford University Press, 2004).

difficult at best. In the wake of the September 11, 2001 terrorist attacks, many Arab immigrants reported intimidation by immigration officials, employers, and law-enforcement agents, and were deported for such minor infractions as making typos on their immigration forms.

In a blatant act of state-sponsored discrimination during World War II, the U.S. government, responding to fears that Japanese Americans would sabotage the American war effort, set up prisonlike internment camps to isolate them from society. Over the course of the war, more than 120,000 Japanese Americans—a large majority of whom were American citizens—were confined to 10 relocation camps in the western United States. In 1944, the Supreme Court upheld the government's internment policy in its controversial decision in *Korematsu v. United States*. The Court majority held that during wartime the needs of national security trumped the individual rights of Japanese Americans and Japanese immigrants.

Hispanics now represent the largest nonwhite demographic group in the United States, comprising approximately 17 percent of the total population. Although the vast majority of Hispanics are in the United States legally, and many are American citizens, the large number of illegal Hispanic immigrants in recent years has sparked a backlash from citizens demanding that the government crack down on illegal immigration.

Historically, most immigrants have not had citizen status when they arrived in the United States and therefore were not entitled to all the civil rights and liberties protections afforded by the American legal system. However, a series of Supreme Court decisions has established that all immigrants are entitled to certain protections, including the right to life, the pursuit of material gain, and a basic education.[13]

Other Failures

There have been other prominent failures to protect rights and liberties in American history besides discrimination based on race or ethnicity. For instance, states and localities have denied voting rights to various other groups. Not only African Americans but also vagrants, Catholics, Mormons, women, Native Americans, paupers, and illiterates were systematically denied the right to vote by some or all states at various stages in the nation's history. These rights were recovered or won through mass political action and sometimes turbulent struggle, as we will see below and in Chapter 10.

There have also been repeated attempts—some successful—by various governments within the United States to harass political opponents or those deemed (but not proven) to be dangerous, to grant police broad powers to investigate legitimate democratic activities, or to suppress freedom of the press.

[13] For example, the Supreme Court's decision in *Plyler v. Doe* (1982) affirmed that the children of illegal immigrants had a constitutional right to primary education.

Activists in the civil rights movement of the 1950s and 1960s, like Martin Luther King, Jr., argued that the national government has an obligation to protect the constitutional rights of all Americans, including African Americans and other minorities.

In the 1970s, for example, the U.S. Justice Department tried unsuccessfully to prevent the *New York Times* and *Washington Post* from publishing the documents known as the *Pentagon Papers*, which cast the government's conduct of the Vietnam War in an unfavorable light. In another example, from the 1950s into the 1970s, the Federal Bureau of Investigation (FBI), led by J. Edgar Hoover, adopted McCarthyesque tactics in investigating and harassing hundreds of people whose activities were deemed to threaten public order, including Martin Luther King, Jr., and Albert Einstein. More recently, Congress responded to heightened fears of terrorism in the post–September 11 era by passing the controversial USA PATRIOT Act, some provisions of which have been ruled unconstitutional by the courts.

Our purpose in highlighting failures of the American political system to protect rights and liberties is to emphasize, first, that democratic government is not a guarantee of protection from unjust government, and second, that the obligations and boundaries placed on individual and government conduct are fluid in nature. These obligations and boundaries have important effects on American politics, but they can and do change over time in response to historical circumstances. In this respect, they resemble other aspects of government that have changed over time, such as federalism (that is, the relationship between the states and the national government).

Egregious violations of the Bill of Rights, such as the Alien and Sedition Acts of 1798 or the internments of Japanese Americans in World War II, seem embarrassing and even absurd today. Such actions highlight the need for perspective and wariness when political leaders consider restrictions of basic rights and liberties, even in the face of such real threats as terrorism. Although few people deny in principle that rights and liberties ought to be protected vigorously, the obligations and boundaries in any era are hotly contested. Often, competing rights have to be traded off against each other. Three areas that continue to be particularly controversial—affirmative action, abortion, and gay rights—will be discussed later in this chapter.

Popular Demands for More Rights

Democratic political systems permit legitimate expressions of dissent, and institutions of government can change to address violations of civil rights and liberties. In other words, the political system can adapt and move the obligations and boundaries when called for. However, expanded rights and better protected liberties have rarely been won by oppressed groups without a long struggle and major political action leading to changes in laws.

The Civil Rights Movement

The **civil rights movement** in the 1950s and 1960s focused on the rights of African Americans, but it also promoted broader goals, such as the principle that all people should be treated as equals under the law; that discrimination based on race, religion, ethnicity, gender, and place of origin should be eliminated; and that more generous programs should be created to help oppressed minorities and the impoverished. The results of the civil rights movement go well beyond the winning of basic civil and political rights for African Americans. The movement continues to serve as a model for efforts to expand access by minority groups to the American and other political systems and the economic rewards these societies offer. Other groups have applied the tactics used by civil rights leaders to force changes in government policy, establish new institutions, and open representational assemblies and voting booths to communities that were formerly disenfranchised.

civil rights movement
A social movement of the 1950s and 1960s focused primarily on the situation of African Americans, but also promoting the goals that all people be treated as equals under the law and that discrimination based on race, religion, ethnicity, gender, and place of origin be eliminated.

The civil rights movement presented the case to the American people and political leaders that the national government had the obligation and the authority to protect the basic civil and political rights of citizens, even overriding state and local laws. Rather than support governmental institutions that perpetuated racial discrimination by deferring to state or local authority, civil rights leaders called for stronger federal institutions that would prevent unequal treatment and living conditions for blacks. Their argument was based on the ideal of equal rights for all.

Southern political leaders in the first half of the twentieth century used the federated nature of the American system of government to perpetuate practices of racial discrimination and oppression that contradicted the basic ideals of the American Revolution and the Constitution. Many leaders justified the government's failure to take action against the mistreatment of African Americans by claiming that the authority to regulate race relations rested with the states. They maintained that the national government had no business stepping in to protect voting rights, the right of children to decent education, and the right to equal treatment before the law.

Opposition to this viewpoint gathered momentum in the 1950s, led by figures such as Martin Luther King, Jr., who advocated nonviolent protest as a means to draw attention to the civil rights cause. Through boycotts, marches, and sit-ins, members of the movement pressured government to change the laws and practices of the United States, especially in the Deep South. They worked to eliminate racial segregation, while protecting the basic civil and political rights of blacks and other minorities and improving their economic condition.[14]

[14] David J. Garrow, *Bearing the Cross: Martin Luther King, Jr., and the Southern Christian Leadership Conference* (New York: William Morrow, 1986).

The movement sparked a violent reaction from white supremacists, states' rights advocates, and others. Medgar Evers, a prominent civil rights leader from Mississippi, was killed in front of his house in 1963. In Birmingham, Alabama, that summer, police were televised beating, kicking, and unleashing attack dogs against peaceful civil rights advocates. Not long after, four young black girls died in the bombing of a Birmingham Baptist church.

Yet despite this brutal opposition, the movement largely achieved its legal goals. It set in motion a series of monumental changes in the American political system, including landmark legislation in civil rights and voting rights that left deep imprints on race relations throughout the United States. As a result of the movement, the U.S. Justice Department played a major role over the next three decades in enforcing voting rights for racial minorities; equal access to housing, education, and public benefits for all; and even affirmative action in university admissions and government contracts. (We will learn more about affirmative action later in this chapter.) By the late 1970s, significant progress had been made in the eradication of discriminatory laws and in the enforcement of regulations banning discrimination in many aspects of political, economic, and social life.

The civil rights movement highlights the importance of popular movements in pressing for political institutions to change and reset the boundaries of government action in support of civil rights. Early institutions of American government, while created out of the principles enshrined in the Constitution, failed to protect certain vulnerable minorities and to promote the common good that can be enjoyed by all persons. In other words, these initial institutions failed to safeguard minorities from the "tyranny of the majority," a mission outlined by the Founders.

Although contemporary civil rights leaders acknowledge the progress that has been made on the legal and regulatory front, many remain disappointed by the limited progress made in advancing racial equality in education and the workplace. Such gaps are still among the most troubling and urgent problems in American society.

Other Movements

As we will see in Chapter 11, along with the civil rights movement there have been other social movements to expand the civil and political rights of groups experiencing discrimination. Prominent examples include the efforts of women and of 18- to 20-year-olds to win the right to vote. Both initiatives culminated in constitutional amendments expanding the franchise. For women, the movement to win voting rights started in the mid-nineteenth century and only came to fruition in 1920. Women's rights activists in the mid-twentieth century sought another constitutional amendment banning all discrimination based on sex. The Equal Rights Amendment was passed by Congress in 1972 and submitted to the states for approval, but it narrowly failed a decade later after falling two states short of the 37 required for ratification.[15]

The national government often needs prodding to improve the lot of minorities who have experienced discrimination. Groups throughout American history, especially since the 1960s, have sought laws to prohibit discrimination, promote respect from the rest of the population, and provide for the concrete, economic rewards that flow from being part of the mainstream of American society. Only after public protests in the 1960s, for instance, did the federal government respond to repeated demands by Native Americans for more rights. In recent years, gays and lesbians have organized to pressure governments within the United States to extend to them basic civil rights protections and privileges, such as the rights to adopt children, marry, and serve as openly gay in the military. Christian conservatives have pressured governments to allow for more freedom of religious expression in public schools, and groups representing the disabled were successful in getting the national government to pass laws requiring easy access to all public buildings.

Women also faced a long struggle to achieve equal rights and liberties in the United States. In the late nineteenth and early twentieth centuries, the movement for women's political rights intensified, resulting in the passage of the Nineteenth Amendment in 1920, which guaranteed women the right to vote.

Equal treatment, however, is in the eye of the beholder, and the line between it and special treatment is fiercely debated. As we will discuss later when we examine the controversies over affirmative action, abortion, and gay rights, the boundaries for how far government can or should go to ensure equal rights end up being settled by political struggles waged in legislatures, elections, and courts.

Incorporating the Bill of Rights into the Fourteenth Amendment

In Chapters 2 and 3, we learned that the Constitution is ambiguous on certain key points and that the American constitutional system continues to evolve. Particular historical circumstances are important in determining how constitutional

[15] Judith Baer and Leslie Goldstein, *The Constitutional and Legal Rights of Women: Cases in Law and Social Change* (Los Angeles: Roxbury, 2006).

institutions or ideals are applied in practice. The gun control issue shows that the Supreme Court must decide among various possible interpretations of the Second Amendment's protection of the right to "keep and bear arms," including the allowable policies of local governments. This is one example of how the Court rules on major issues of federalism as they relate to civil rights and liberties.

Prior to the Civil War, the Bill of Rights applied only to national laws and actions by the national government, not to the actions of state or local governments. The Supreme Court affirmed this view in *Barron v. Baltimore* (1833) when Chief Justice John Marshall, writing for the majority, ruled that a Maryland man would have been entitled to government compensation under the Fifth Amendment if the national government had ruined his property. Instead, because Maryland did not have a similar guarantee in its constitution, and because the harm to his property occurred as a result of actions by the city of Baltimore (a "creature" of the state of Maryland), the man was not legally protected under the Fifth Amendment.

The Fourteenth Amendment, ratified in 1868, began a process that dramatically changed the nature of civil rights and liberties in the United States. The key passage in the amendment declares, "No State shall make or enforce any law which shall abridge the privileges or immunities of citizens of the United States; nor shall any State deprive any person of life, liberty, or property, without **due process** of law; nor deny to any person within its jurisdiction the **equal protection** of the laws."

due process The right to legal protections against arbitrary deprivation of life, liberty, or property.

equal protection The principle that laws passed and enforced by the states must apply fairly to all individuals.

The language would seem to be clear in stating that the Bill of Rights, which summarizes all the "privileges and immunities of citizens," should apply to the states. The Supreme Court, however, was slow to embrace this idea, with unfortunate consequences. In the famous *Slaughter-House Cases* (1873), the Court ruled that the Fourteenth Amendment applied only to discrimination against African Americans, thus severely limiting its reach.[16] Furthermore, the Court decided soon thereafter that the language about equal protection applied only to laws and not to private conduct, even in the case of African Americans. It reasoned in both cases that the authors of the Fourteenth Amendment could not possibly have meant it to apply to the entire Bill of Rights. This legal understanding held sway for more than 60 years and opened the way for states, mostly in the South, to permit blatant discrimination of African Americans under Jim Crow laws. Those laws established a system of segregation of public facilities and private establishments that made African Americans second-class citizens. Other laws and practices in the rest of the country were patently discriminatory toward immigrants and other racial and ethnic minorities. The Supreme Court's initial refusal to apply the Fourteenth Amendment to the states set back progress on civil rights for many decades.

incorporation The process by which rights and liberties established by the Bill of Rights are applied to state and local governments through the Fourteenth Amendment.

Nevertheless, court rulings and congressional legislation in the century following the ratification of the Fourteenth Amendment gradually **incorporated**

[16] *Slaughter-House Cases*, 83 U.S. 36 (1873).

HISTORICAL PATH Incorporation of the Bill of Rights into the Fourteenth Amendment

Freedom/Right	Amendment	Case	Year
Of speech and press	First	Gitlow v. New York	1925
To have attorney in capital cases	Sixth	Powell v. Alabama	1932
To exercise any religion	First	Hamilton v. Regents of the University of California	1934
Of assembly and petition	First	DeJonge v. Oregon	1937
From establishment of religion	First	Everson v. Board of Education	1947
To have a public trial	Sixth	In re Oliver	1948
From unreasonable searches and seizures	Fourth	Mapp v. Ohio	1961
From cruel and unusual punishments	Eighth	Robinson v. California	1962
To have attorney for felony cases	Sixth	Gideon v. Wainwright	1963
From self-incrimination	Fifth	Malloy v. Hogan	1964
To confront witnesses	Sixth	Pointer v. Texas	1965
To have an impartial jury trial	Sixth	Parker v. Gladden	1966
To have a speedy trial	Sixth	Klopfer v. North Carolina	1967
To compel witnesses to testify	Sixth	Washington v. Texas	1967
To trial by jury	Sixth	Duncan v. Louisiana	1968
From double jeopardy	Fifth	Benton v. Maryland	1969
To have attorney for charges that could result in jail time	Sixth	Argersinger v. Hamlin	1972
To bear arms	Second	McDonald v. Chicago	2010

into the amendment many of the protections for rights and liberties established by the Bill of Rights, so that they applied to state and local governments as well as to the national government. By the 1970s, the amendment had incorporated nearly all of the Bill of Rights, including freedom of speech and assembly, and the rights to counsel, privacy, and just compensation for forfeiture of property. It incorporated rights against warrantless searches, double jeopardy (being tried twice for the same offense), self-incrimination, the admission of illegal evidence, and forced confessions in criminal cases. In our own era, the Fourteenth Amendment's due process and equal protection clauses essentially apply to the entire Bill of Rights.[17]

This evolution in legal doctrine not only affected the progress of civil rights and liberties in the United States, it also altered the nature of American federalism. The incorporation of most of the Bill of Rights has been important

[17] Sue Davis and J. W. Peltason, *Corwin and Peltason's Understanding the Constitution* (Belmont, CA: Wadsworth, 2007). There are some exceptions: the Fifth Amendment right to indictment by a grand jury and the Eighth Amendment right against excessive bail have not yet been incorporated.

in tipping the balance of authority in the United States away from the states and toward the national government. The national government not only has the authority through the Court to enforce the Bill of Rights in the states, it also has the obligation to protect civil rights actively through legislation and administrative procedures.

Government Responses to Discrimination

American governmental institutions are both *restrained* from interfering in certain individual activities, such as practicing one's religion or expressing dissent over government policies, and *empowered* or *obligated* to protect individuals when they exercise their rights as citizens or residents of the country. Since the mid-twentieth century, the emphasis has been on the latter role. Governmental institutions have not only stepped in to protect people in certain groups (especially racial, ethnic, or religious minorities; women; and the disabled) from discrimination. In many cases, legislation and court decisions have required some governments in the United States to provide expensive and vital services to criminal defendants, minority school children, illegal immigrants, and prisoners. Indeed, in the area of civil rights, especially in relation to the equal protection and due process clauses of the Fourteenth Amendment, governments in the United States have become notably active in trying to limit discrimination and provide support for vulnerable people.

New laws beginning in the mid-twentieth century were crucial. Of foundational importance was passage of the Civil Rights Act of 1964, a sweeping law that banned most forms of discrimination on the basis of race, color, national origin, or religion, and required the government to be active in guaranteeing equal treatment of people traditionally discriminated against in employment, housing, educational admissions, and public funding. Passing the law took several years and started before President John Kennedy was assassinated in 1963. The law was passed by Congress after Kennedy's assassination, following intense public pressure brought by the civil rights movement and by the culmination of changes in public opinion overall toward tolerance of and sympathy for oppressed minorities. Martin Luther King, Jr., in late 1963 gave his famous "I Have a Dream" speech urging passage. It took sustained effort by proponents of the law in the government, including President Lyndon Johnson, to overcome opposition among southern senators.

The 1964 Act formed the basis upon which many other national and state-level laws have been passed since banning discrimination and requiring government redress of past discrimination. The law in 1964 included some bans on discrimination on the basis of gender, but applied those bans only to public institutions or those supported by public funds or engaging in interstate commerce. Since then, however, many other protections for women and other groups, including the disabled, Native Americans, veterans, and homosexuals, have been included in certain states and localities. Moreover, the government has moved beyond protection to actively promoting minority well-being through affirmative action (discussed later in this chapter).

New laws have reshaped the landscape of civil rights and liberties, and so have court decisions. The Supreme Court, in wrestling with how to interpret the Constitution and the new laws about discrimination, has applied the equal protection and due process clauses of the Fourteenth Amendment by devising a three-tiered classification scheme to evaluate whether a state law or state government action violates someone's constitutional rights. If confronted with a case involving a potential violation of the equal protection clause, all courts in the nation must use this three-tiered scheme as guidance.

To understand the Court's scheme for making decisions, we first need to acknowledge that laws about civil rights do not prohibit *all* discrimination. In fact, there are many laws that allow for, and situations that require, discrimination. Only Native Americans can receive benefits accorded specifically to members of recognized Indian tribes. Insurance companies can discriminate by charging men higher auto insurance rates than women, and hairstylists can legally charge higher rates for women than for men. Movie studios are allowed to search for actors of particular races for parts in movies. Colleges and universities are allowed to employ a form of sex discrimination by admitting an incoming freshman class divided more or less equally between male and female students.

Nevertheless, the Supreme Court has declared that if a state law or state government action allows for discrimination (or results in discrimination) based on what are called "suspect" classifications such as race, ethnicity, religion, creed, or national origin, or involves a fundamental right, it is subject to **strict scrutiny**. If the Court uses this standard, it means that the law is presumed to be unconstitutional unless the government can convince the Court that it advances a "compelling state interest" and that the means used to achieve the state's ends are the least intrusive on the fundamental right. This strict scrutiny standard is the highest of the three tiers, and laws allowing for or resulting in discrimination rarely pass this constitutional standard; in other words, most such laws or government actions are struck down by the Court.

When state laws or government actions discriminate (or result in discrimination) based on what are called "disfavored" criteria—usually economic in nature, such as income levels—then the Court uses the **rational basis test**, which presumes the law is constitutional as long as there is a reasonable link between the means and the goals of the law or action. Most laws or actions pass this hurdle, the lowest of the Court's prescribed tests.

Since the 1970s, the Supreme Court has also used an **intermediate scrutiny** standard in cases of discrimination that are not "suspect" but are nevertheless "disfavored." If a law serves "an important government objective" and

strict scrutiny The highest-level standard used by the Supreme Court to determine whether a law is compatible with the Constitution. A law subject to this standard is considered unconstitutional unless it advances a "compelling state interest" and represents the least intrusive means.

rational basis test The lowest-level standard used by the Supreme Court to determine whether a law is compatible with the Constitution. A law subject to this standard is assumed to be constitutional as long as its goals are clearly linked to its means.

intermediate scrutiny An intermediate standard used by the Supreme Court to determine whether a law is compatible with the Constitution. A law subject to this standard is considered constitutional if it advances "an important government objective" and is "substantially related" to the objective.

"is substantially related to the achievement" of the objective, then the law can stand. Otherwise, it is unconstitutional. Since the 1980s, for example, the Court has tended to use this intermediate standard for laws that allow for (or result in) discrimination based on sex. This means that the Court has yet to make sex difference a "suspect" classification that deserves strict scrutiny, but examines such laws more closely than those involving discrimination based on economic differences, for which it uses the rational basis test.

To summarize, the U.S. legal code has made it virtually impossible for state or local governments to tolerate or promote discrimination based on certain characteristics such as race or religion; the exceptions include certain kinds of affirmative action (discussed in the next section). But interpretations of the legal code have made it easy to discriminate based on economic criteria, and moderately easy to discriminate in categories such as sex. This three-tiered scheme has been criticized for being arbitrary and giving the Court too much leeway in defining which discriminatory categories fit into each tier. Critics, however, often miss the point that the obligations and boundaries drawn in the areas of civil rights and liberties, while meaningful and consequential, are continually being redrawn in response to particular historical circumstances and political trends.

When the Court declares that past discrimination or injustice has harmed a particular group in society, it often mandates that governments either change the laws to make discrimination illegal or provide remedies for that group. For example, when the Supreme Court decided in *Estelle v. Gamble* (1976) that the Eighth Amendment's prohibition against "cruel and unusual punishments" was violated when states packed prisoners into jail cells and denied them adequate food and sanitary conditions,[18] some lower federal courts subsequently forced states to submit plans for improving prison conditions so that the courts could decide whether the plans met constitutional standards. Starting in the 1970s, when local districts were seen to be operating highly segregated schools, contrary to the *Brown v. Board of Education* (1954) decision and subsequent rulings that racial segregation in schools violated the equal protection clause, the federal courts required the districts to bus students to various locations to ensure a more integrated and racially diverse student body among the schools.[19] The controversy over busing was particularly bitter, given that the government's attempts to force school districts to comply with court decisions mandating desegregation meant that children were often sent to schools far outside their neighborhoods and apart from their friends or siblings.

The trade-offs that governments have to make in pursuit of civil rights and liberties make many issues in this area controversial. We will now take a closer look at three issues in which the proper degree of government activism or restraint is often debated.

[18] *Estelle v. Gamble*, 429 U.S. 97 (1976).
[19] *Brown v. Board of Education of Topeka*, 347 U.S. 483 (1954).

Affirmative Action

Among the most controversial issues in the area of civil rights and liberties is **affirmative action**, defined in the American context as the effort to redress previous discrimination against women and minorities through active measures to promote their employment and educational opportunities. Many U.S. colleges and universities, for instance, have programs designed to bolster the admission of students from certain racial or ethnic groups, including African Americans, Latinos, and Native Americans. Departments in certain disciplines, especially in the sciences, actively try to attract women to undergraduate and graduate programs. Government agencies at the federal and state levels typically request bids from companies owned by women or racial minorities and give those bids special consideration when awarding contracts. Fire departments and police forces are required by local and federal laws to take steps to hire women and minorities, and to maintain a certain proportion of such people in their ranks, even when they have to lay off workers.

affirmative action Efforts to redress previous discrimination against women and minorities through active measures to promote their employment and educational opportunities.

The rationale for affirmative action is that certain groups in society, having faced previous discrimination, are disadvantaged in employment and education and need active government intervention to promote equal opportunities. Merely allowing social processes, such as admissions to colleges or the awarding of government contracts, to operate normally perpetuates inequalities and the discrimination that underlies them.[20] Yet affirmative action, it has been argued, creates one form of discrimination in the interest of redressing another. Critics charge that when a college devotes special efforts to recruit African American or Hispanic students, it can have the effect of discriminating against whites because of their race. Much of the criticism of affirmative action comes from people who claim that the government should not be using race, sex, or ethnic heritage to make decisions about access to education, government contracts, or jobs. They argue that even if the goal of equal opportunity is worthwhile, open preference for people based on race, sex, or ethnicity detracts from other goals, such as promotion of a society in which merit is the only criteria for educational or professional success.

Courts and other branches of government at all levels in the American political system have wrestled with the challenges raised by affirmative action. Can organizations set quotas for racial minorities or women? Should affirmative action for a particular group go on indefinitely, or should it end after a set period? These are only two of the many thorny questions that confront lawmakers and judges. The Supreme Court has issued a number of rulings on affirmative action that have attempted to define the boundaries of acceptable promotion of group attainment. In its *Regents of the University of California v. Bakke* decision (1978), the Court permitted affirmative action in university

[20] W. Avon Drake and Robert Holsworth, *Affirmative Action and the Stalled Quest for Black Progress* (Urbana: University of Illinois Press, 1996).

admissions as long as race or sex was only one consideration among others.[21] Quotas, however, were declared unconstitutional. In its several *Bollinger* cases (2003) and the *Fischer* case (2013), the Court drew the line between university admissions policies that gave extra points to people if they were a racial minority (not allowed)[22] and policies that, consistent with *Bakke*, treated race as one of several factors considered in deciding on admission (allowed).[23]

Abortion Rights

The politics surrounding abortion rights have been among the most divisive of all issues in the American political system since the 1970s. At its core, the controversy over abortion entails differing understandings of whose rights and liberties deserve protection from government or by government.

Abortion, or the deliberate termination of a pregnancy, was only in recent history permitted under the law. Some states in the 1960s began allowing abortion. In 1973, with the decision *Roe v. Wade*, the Supreme Court mandated that no governments in the United States could restrict women from having abortions within the first trimester of their pregnancy.[24] This "right to choose" abortion was established as a matter of constitutional law under the interpretation of several amendments implying, in the Court's view, a right to privacy. (This is discussed in Chapter 2.)

For those opposed to abortion rights, attention on women's rights to choose abortion is misplaced, and instead unborn fetuses need protection by government. Many (though certainly not all) opponents are motivated by religious convictions that the life of a person deserving of protection begins at the moment of conception, and that allowing abortion amounts to the killing of a human being. To them, unborn fetuses should be included when the Constitution says governments should protect "life, liberty, and the pursuit of happiness." The Supreme Court in *Roe* rejected the idea that fetuses are included in this constitutional language. Those supporting abortion rights instead focus attention on the rights of women to control their reproduction, and that intrusion into women's freedom to choose abortion amounts to governmental invasion of privacy. For the majority in *Roe*, they mostly justified their decision by saying that women have a right to private decisions over their reproduction in consultation with their physicians.

Political battles over abortion continue. The controversy over abortion has been front and center in presidential politics, in the differences between the two major political parties, and in Supreme Court nominations. In general, Republicans have defined themselves as *pro-life*, meaning that they oppose abortion

[21] *Regents of the University of California v. Bakke*, 438 U.S. 265 (1978).
[22] *Gratz v. Bollinger*, 539 U.S. 244 (2003).
[23] *Grutter v. Bollinger*, 539 U.S. 306 (2003). See also *Fischer v. University of Texas*, 570 U.S. 345 (2013).
[24] *Roe v. Wade*, 410 U.S. 113 (1973).

rights or at least support more restrictions on abortion. Democrats have mostly defined themselves as *pro-choice*, meaning that they support the legal reasoning in *Roe* and work to protect women's reproductive rights as defined by that decision. Supreme Court justices are known to have legal positions either for or against the legal reasoning in *Roe*, and recent Court cases on abortion rights have been very close (typically 5–4 or 6–3). Meanwhile, at the state and local levels policies are passed to restrict access to abortion, and sometimes these policies are struck down by the federal courts and sometimes they are allowed to stand.

Should government protect the right of women to terminate their pregnancies toward the beginning of term? Or should government protect unborn fetuses from being aborted? These are deep questions that divide people passionately. For our purposes we can ask, Why did the Court choose the boundary between the first and second trimester as the point demarcating when governments could and could not regulate abortion access? The majority in the *Roe* decision reasoned that as a pregnancy progresses the state has increasing room to regulate abortion and that the rights of the mother to privacy in determining her reproduction decrease relative to the right of states to protect the life of the fetus. Defining the line as between the first and second trimester was the Court's attempt, in effect, to balance the rights of the woman and the rights of the state to protect the fetus if that is what state governments through their democratic processes decide to do. The line was set to establish a boundary at the moment when a fetus could be, given medical technology available at the time, viable outside of the womb. The author of the *Roe* decision, Justice Harry Blackmun, stated that "the end of the first trimester . . . is arbitrary . . . but perhaps any other selection point . . . is equally arbitrary."[25]

Gay Rights

The treatment of gays and lesbians is an increasingly important area of civil rights. Until a few decades ago homosexuality was a taboo topic, little discussed in public. Very few people were openly gay. People known to be gay often faced discrimination. Violence against gays and lesbians was not only widespread but local governments in some places often looked the other way. Discrimination continues in many situations, but homosexuality is now widely discussed. According to recent studies, millions of Americans acknowledge being gay and have stable homosexual relationships. Compared with past decades, homosexuality in many parts of American society is out in the open and accepted.

Nevertheless, there is still widespread hostility toward homosexuality and homosexuals, especially outside of the largest cities and in more traditional communities. Even the many Americans who claim to be sympathetic to the rights of gays and lesbians to be free of discrimination often feel discomfort

[25] Bob Woodward, "The Abortion Papers," *Washington Post*, January 22, 1989.

arising from religious or traditional beliefs about sexual practices, the importance of the traditional family, and child-rearing.

The gay rights movement (which we will discuss further in Chapter 11) has been pushing for a variety of policy changes. A major effort has been made to add bias against homosexuals to the list of discriminatory practices in housing, school admissions, and employment proscribed by national and state laws. Many cities and some states have outlawed discrimination based on sexual orientation (as well as race, ethnicity, sex, or religious belief), and the gay rights movement seeks to expand the reach of such laws.

Another change sought by the gay rights movement has been particularly controversial: expanding the legal definition of marriage to include homosexual unions (same-sex marriages).[26] Marriage confers on a couple substantial legal and financial benefits, including the right of inheritance and the right to pass on Social Security benefits if one member of the couple dies. As important as the financial stakes for gay rights groups is the basic recognition of equality before the law. The movement for same-sex marriage has so far met with mixed but growing success. The national government passed the Defense of Marriage Act (DOMA) in 1996, which defined marriage as between a man and a woman. The Supreme Court in 2013 struck down the core of DOMA, which denied federal benefits to gay married couples even when legally married in their home states. The Court stated that DOMA violated the liberty protections of the Fifth Amendment. Still, under federal law, no state or locality is required to recognize a same-sex marriage from another state. The legal and political momentum, however, has shifted in favor of gay marriage. As of the end of 2014, about two-thirds of the states allowed gays and lesbians to marry. Election results and opinion surveys indicate that a majority approves of gay marriage, though a large proportion continues to be uncomfortable with the notion. A move that represented a major boost for activists in favor was when President Barack Obama expressed his support for allowing same-sex marriage during the 2012 campaign.

For some people, same-sex marriage presents a difficult trade-off between their freedom to practice their religion and the freedom of homosexuals to enjoy the benefits of marriage. A large proportion of Americans belong to religious faiths that consider homosexual practices to be morally wrong. Both in doctrine and among church leaders, several major religions oppose same-sex marriage. If a religious person agrees with his or her religious authorities on the issue, and same-sex marriage is legal, should that person be required to recognize homosexual couples as legally equivalent to heterosexual couples? Especially for those opposed to same-sex marriage, the gay rights movement may pit religious freedom against equal rights to the benefits of marriage.

The challenge of trading off the rights of different people is apparent in all three of these policy areas. In trying to redress past discrimination, is it acceptable,

[26] Evan Gerstmann, *Same-Sex Marriage and the Constitution* (New York: Cambridge University Press, 2004).

Access to What Others Have: Rights of the Disabled

It would seem unobjectionable to create buildings and provide services that accommodate people with disabilities. If workplaces did not have ramps and elevators to accommodate people with wheelchairs, many disabled people would not be able to work, even if they were qualified. If schools did not provide textbooks in Braille or texts of audio recordings, blind and deaf students would not be able to learn. Yet, as of the late 1980s, there was no recourse for the disabled to sue a person or an institution when faced with blatant discrimination.

As admirable as it is to provide access to people with disabilities, however, offering access to anything for anyone with any disability is, according to some, unreasonably expensive. And making such changes take money away from serving the vast majority of people without disabilities.

President George H. W. Bush signing the Americans with Disabilities Act in 1990.

Interests

People with disabilities want access to what others experience and enjoy. They want to travel, attend baseball games, and enjoy parks, movies, and the latest technology. Interest groups that lobby on behalf of people with disabilities have long pressured the government to have strict laws requiring businesses and all public institutions to change their facilities and programs to allow people with disabilities full access. Meanwhile, people who own businesses and run facilities that admit the public and numerous employees have interest in keeping costs down. They may claim that they can make reasonable accommodations, but cannot afford expensive changes for a few people with disabilities.

Institutions

The Fifth and Fourteenth Amendments to the U.S. Constitution mandate the protection of liberties and equal protection of the laws. These two amendments provide a legal framework from which Congress can act to protect the liberties of people with disabilities. Also, since the 1960s, Congress has tried to "fill in" the details on how government ought to protect liberties and determine equal protection of the laws. Instead of waiting for courts to settle disputes over discrimination, Congress passed legislation that required governments and all public institutions to not only avoid unjust discrimination but also bring about changes leading to equal treatment. Finally, the supremacy clause of the Constitution allowed the federal government to pass laws mandating all jurisdictions in the country be responsible for implementing changes in favor of the rights of the disabled.

Outcomes

Congress passed the Americans with Disabilities Act (ADA) in 1990 and subsequently amended and updated the Act in 2008. This landmark law banned discrimination of people with disabilities in many circumstances, such as employment, schools, and public spaces, and required that most entities in society make reasonable accommodations for people with disabilities. Among the many sections of the law are descriptions of who and what places in society are exempt from the requirements, what aspects of technology have to conform, and what bodily functions count as major life activities that people are entitled to enjoy, even if it is costly on society to ensure that they can. The law has been criticized as burdening businesses and public institutions with enormous costs; nevertheless, the law and the regulations by agencies to implement the law are highly detailed as it tries to strike a balance between the overall costs of complying with the law and ensuring equal access to those with disabilities.

Think About It

How far should society go to accommodate people with disabilities? What requirements should government set for society? Does American society, following passage of the ADA in 1990, strike the right balance?

Gay rights activists argue that discrimination based on sexual orientation should be outlawed by the federal government as a violation of civil rights. They have succeeded in recent years in getting same-sex marriage legalized through voter referendum in certain states, including Maryland in 2012.

given the Fourteenth Amendment, to tilt competition for admission or employment in favor of some groups over other groups? In trying to protect women's reproductive rights, is it acceptable to permit abortion that kills a fetus? In trying to allow for equal access to the benefits of marriage, is it acceptable, given the First Amendment, to force members of religious groups to recognize gay marriage contrary to their doctrines or the advice of their religious authorities?

In Comparison: Rights and Liberties around the World

Other countries face similarly controversial issues, and often the same issues. Comparison helps to put the American experience in context and enables us to consider more systematically the consequences of the specific American interpretations of rights and liberties.

Compared with the rest of the world, people living in the United States today are remarkably free to speak, practice religion, publish, or assemble together. In terms of liberty from government interference, the American political system places fewer restrictions on its citizens than most other democratic countries.

Of course, civil rights and liberties are not absolute, and all countries place boundaries somewhere. Note the line drawn by the Supreme Court on owning guns: handguns are permitted, but governments can restrict ownership of machine guns. Other countries draw slightly different boundaries across a variety of issues that are typically tighter than in the United States.

Germany, France, and Canada, for example, do not allow any speech that incites hatred, especially hatred based on ethnicity or religion. In Germany and France, it is illegal to deny that the Holocaust (the Nazi genocide of Jews in World War II) occurred, and in both countries, items with the Nazi swastika cannot be sold or displayed in public. In 2005, the United Kingdom passed a law banning speech inciting religious hatred in response to bombings in London by Islamic extremists. The United States, on the other hand, permits such expressions in most situations. In the United States, you are permitted to burn crosses (a long-standing practice of racist groups including the Ku Klux Klan) as long as you are not directly intimidating someone but are instead making a political statement.

The United States has relatively tolerant laws regarding assembly and the press, including organizing and publishing by groups that may advocate radical mass action or violence, such as communists, Nazis, and the Ku Klux Klan. More generally, the United States has liberal laws regarding pornography and strictures against "prior restraint" (government prohibition of speech in advance of publication). As for libel, nearly every other country has laws that make it easier than in the United States for people to sue journalists or the press successfully for spreading false information about them. In the United States, the hurdle for winning a libel lawsuit is relatively high; plaintiffs must demonstrate that the defendant not only published false information, but knowingly published it with the intention of harming the plaintiff. This standard is almost never met, and libel lawsuits in the United States rarely succeed. Many other countries require plaintiffs to meet a lower standard in libel suits. For instance, the defendant may have to show that the accusation made in print is true, placing the onus on the journalist or author. Such standards give the U.S. press far more freedom to publish criticism of public figures than in other countries.

The United States is not as distinctively vigorous in the protection of civil rights, although the nation has earned its place as a leader in some respects. Through the early twentieth century, for example, the United States was historically at the forefront on the issue of voting rights. It extended the voting franchise earlier to major groups of people (non-property holders, religious minorities, women) than any other major country except Great Britain. Of course, from the late nineteenth century until well into the 1960s, the United States also allowed states and localities to inhibit voting by many of their citizens, especially African Americans and other racial minorities. The United States also grants criminal defendants more rights than do most other countries.

Many countries, such as Germany, do not have jury trials. In Europe, criminal defendants commonly do not to have the right to refuse self-incrimination, and prosecutors in many countries, unlike their American counterparts, may introduce evidence at trial that has been gathered illegally.

In contrast to legal traditions in such countries as Norway, Denmark, India, Brazil, and Canada, the U.S. courts have specifically declared that so-called social rights—such as the right to shelter, food, education, or health care—are not fundamental and do not have the same status as those rights mentioned in the Bill of Rights or declared in later court decisions. Of course, American governments at any level may legally provide these social benefits, but they are not mandated to do so. In the late twentieth century, however, the Supreme Court placed education in a somewhat intermediate category by implying in several rulings that, under equal protection clauses, the right to a minimal education enabling someone to read and write might approach the status of a fundamental right in the contemporary United States.

Why do such differences exist across countries? Why is the United States comparatively vigorous in protecting liberties and more typical with regard to rights? The latter question is not easy to answer. In such areas as freedom of speech, religion, and the press, the differences among countries may well reflect the fact that the United States is one of the few nations (even among democracies) that does not have a state-sponsored religion or a monarchy. Countries with state-sponsored religions and/or monarchies are more likely than nations that do not have such institutions to place greater restrictions on at least some of these civil liberties. Moreover, countries with constitutions designed after their loss in a war—Germany and Japan, for instance—are likely to place more restrictions on allowable political speech or publications.

France may be the largest nation that closely resembles the United States in both its history and its approach to civil rights and liberties. It has no state religion or monarchy and was founded by a revolution based on Enlightenment principles. France, like the United States, has a relatively liberal record on civil rights and liberties. There is, however, an important distinction between the French and American approaches to religious freedom. In the United States, the government may not support any particular religion, yet it vigorously protects the rights of people to be religious and to express religious points of view. In France, the government also may not support any particular religion and protects the rights of people to be religious. Both societies have a constitutional tradition of "separation of church and state." However, in state-supported public buildings in France, such as schools or courts, people may not express their religious views openly because these places are considered "secular." Thus, bitter controversy has arisen in recent years when France banned Muslim girls from wearing head scarves and Christian students from wearing large crosses in public schools. There are further efforts to ban all Muslim women from wearing certain head coverings in public. According to French law, secular society is to be protected from religious zealotry. Under American law, government can neither promote nor inhibit religion. These are two fundamentally different ways to conceive of and apply meaning to "separation of church and state" and freedom of religion. (See Institutions, Interests, and Outcomes box in Chapter 2.)

Why Protect Rights and Liberties?

Situations constantly arise that pit people's competing civil rights or liberties against each other. It may seem at times as if the Supreme Court splits hairs with its rulings. In the gun control cases discussed at the beginning of this chapter, for example, the Court drew a boundary between governmental laws that violated the Constitution and those that did not. Court decisions on difficult cases often expose trade-offs inherent in a democratic society's values. The Court defined the group needing protection to be gun owners, the people wanting to use firearms to protect themselves, not the people who might be harmed, even inadvertently, by gun violence.

This is the key to answering our questions at the beginning of the chapter: The Court's decision might seem arbitrary, as in the *Roe* decision on abortion, but it was one way to strike a balance between two alternatives. And striking a balance serves an important purpose for the maintenance of a society that is both ordered and protects rights and liberties. We may not think the courts or the government has struck the right balance on a particular issue, but we ought to recognize that for most civil rights and liberties issues it would not be desirable if one group's rights or liberties were taken to the extreme. Certainly people should not be able to own any kind of weapon and carry it anywhere they want. To paraphrase a folksy adage, someone's liberty to swing a fist ends at someone else's nose.

Free speech situations can illustrate the need for balance as reflected in political institutions and legal codes. Consider whether people should be able to call each other names, even racist or offensive names. In principle, people should be free to express their political views, and equally free from threats and harassment. But where should boundaries be drawn between the protection of free speech and the prevention of speech that foments hate or even incites violence? Shouldn't people be free from hate speech? Should people be allowed to publicize and even broadcast racist messages? Should the government restrict speech by groups preaching hate? The federal courts have balanced the competing interests by saying (over many cases) that governments in the United States can restrict speech that is directly intimidating, but in almost all situations they cannot restrict political speech—for example, by candidates during a campaign—even if that speech is offensive. Moreover, constitutional protections of speech depend on whether the target of critical speech is someone well-known to the public, and whether the speech occurs in a situation that could become disorderly or violent. In drawing legal boundaries on behavior and taking contexts into account, courts and governments are institutionalizing expectations among people over what is permitted for the intended purpose of ensuring order and freedom together. Not one without the other, but both.

Consider that we can divide justifications for protecting civil rights and liberties into two categories: those based on moral claims of inherent human dignity, and those based on "utilitarian" claims. Utilitarianism is a general philosophy that promotes social institutions in order to create the most good for the greatest number of people. The Founders were motivated by both justifications; let's discuss them in more detail.

The traditional moral justification for protecting civil rights and liberties as stated in the Declaration of Independence, and in the writings of philosophers such as John Stuart Mill or Isaiah Berlin, is that people possess certain rights simply by virtue of being human. Those rights could come from religious sources (as claimed in the writings of Saint Thomas Aquinas, for instance) or from a sense of shared values or experience as human beings (as claimed in the writings of Isaiah Berlin[27]). Many of us experience a sense of shame or anger at the way groups in American society have been treated in the past. Such responses undoubtedly come from a notion that discrimination, oppression, torture, or unjust bondage are morally wrong. We are offended by stories of slavery, of the Japanese American internments, and of failings by various American governments to protect people's voting rights regardless of their race, ethnicity, sex, or religion. It is hard to explain why we feel offended without some reference to an ethical system that is shared by a vast majority of people, not only in the United States but also around the world. Simply put, most of us believe in the basic morality of a political system where the government is obligated to protect fundamental liberties and equal treatment of persons under the law.

Beyond the general moral claims of basic rights and liberties as fundamental to human dignity, there exist utilitarian justifications for the protection of liberties—specifically for freedom of speech, travel, assembly, and the press. These justifications share the idea that the entire society benefits from allowing many voices to be heard and from giving people the freedom to be creative. To stifle these freedoms is to stifle innovation, creativity, and the ability to learn from others.

On the political and social side, a system of government characterized by vigorous protection of civil rights and, especially, civil liberties fosters discussion, debate, deliberation, and competition among ideas. Thus, closed societies—those with few protections for rights and liberties—tend to stifle innovation, have little creativity and entrepreneurship, and, not incidentally, have low economic growth rates and fewer healthy and wealthy people. On the economic

---

[27] Isaiah Berlin, *Liberty* (New York: Oxford University Press, 2002).

side, the arguments are similar. The freedoms to assemble, speak, and travel are related to the freedom to create new products and make associations with business partners, which spurs economic growth. Such freedoms, especially from government intrusion, regulation, and monopoly on investment, allow for creativity and entrepreneurship.

The utilitarian justification for protecting civil rights and liberties would not only say that the institutional boundaries on individual and governmental behavior that evolved in the United States have been successful in creating a dynamic, wealthy, and free society. It would also say that the boundaries were deliberately designed to achieve these goals. Far from enforcing freedoms to tolerate dissent merely because it is morally the right thing to do, dissent is tolerated because it is the smart thing to do.

It might be said that there is a downside, especially with regard to economic inequalities, to allowing too much freedom. Some might argue that allowing more economic freedom creates inequalities, and allows people with the most resources to have the loudest voices and the most influence in a democracy. Instead of allowing for the orderly operation of a society, extreme versions of freedom of speech can stack the deck against real dissent.

Finally, consider the political interests that pursue changes in civil rights and liberties. Many expansions of civil liberties and rights, especially voting rights, have occurred because of opportunistic behavior by groups of politicians, and specifically by political parties seeking to expand their electoral support. In the early to mid-1800s, for example, both major parties, the Democrats and the Whigs, sought the support of immigrant groups, often by promising or providing them with an expansion of the franchise. Moreover, Democrats reasoned in the 1960s and 1970s that promoting voting rights for African Americans in the South would bring more Democratic voters to the polls in those regions. Undoubtedly, part of President Lyndon Johnson's motivation in seeking to expand the franchise to 18- to 20-year-olds in the late 1960s was to improve Democratic vote totals nationwide.

That rights frequently are expanded as a consequence of politicians seeking to achieve their goals does not necessarily mean that the expansion was wrong or led to bad consequences. This observation helps us to understand that the institutions of government are typically designed intentionally and are not neutral regarding boundaries on individual and government behavior.

To return to our questions from the opening of the chapter, there is no definitive answer to the question of where the lines should be drawn in civil rights and liberties issues. The obligations of and boundaries on governmental behavior shift in response to changing values in society and among governmental leaders. But defining obligations and boundaries is often important, if not critical for society, to maintain a balance among competing rights and liberties. The obligations and boundaries have consequences for how people live day-to-day and make up vital institutional pieces of the American political system.

FURTHER READING

★ = Included in *Readings in American Politics*, 3e

★ *Brown v. Board of Education* (1954). The ruling that nullified the logic of *Plessy v. Ferguson* (1896) and declared "separate but equal" educational institutions for different races unconstitutional.

★ Dawson, Michael, *Not in Our Lifetimes: The Future of Black Politics* (Chicago: University of Chicago Press, 2011). Some believe that the election of President Barack Obama indicates that the United States is now a post-racial society. Dawson argues that events surroundings Obama's election and his time in office strongly indicate otherwise.

Grutter v. Bollinger (2003). The ruling that delineated the constitutionality of college and university affirmative action programs.

Katznelson, Ira, *When Affirmative Action Was White* (New York: Norton, 2005). A revealing examination of how federal social policies from the 1930s to the 1960s discriminated against African Americans.

King, Martin Luther, Jr., "I Have a Dream" Speech on the Mall, Washington, DC, August 28, 1963. King's electrifying speech laying bare the inequalities in American society that were contrary to common sense and common values.

Plessy v. Ferguson (1896). The ruling that declared it constitutional for states to have "separate but equal" facilities for different races; overturned by *Brown v. Board of Education* (1954).

Roe v. Wade (1973). The ruling that established that women have a right to an abortion during the first trimester of their pregnancy.

★ Rosenberg, Gerald, *The Hollow Hope: Can Courts Bring about Social Change?* (Chicago: University of Chicago Press, 1991). A controversial book that questions the view that the federal courts led the way on civil and political rights, instead arguing that the courts lagged behind the elected branches in improving matters for minorities.

KEY TERMS

Controversies around legislation to fund relief efforts after hurricane Sandy epitomize the tensions members of Congress face between promoting national interests and helping their home districts. Here, Representative Peter King (R–NY) expresses his anger that the legislative session ended without Congress passing a relief bill. When the bill finally passed, it included spending provisions that had little to nothing to do with disaster relief, some proposed by fiscal conservatives.

5

CONGRESS

Members of Congress constantly think about the interests of their district and their own prospects for re-election. At the same time, Congress is expected to pass laws that benefit the country as a whole. How do legislators rise above self-interest and the narrow interests of their districts to pass important legislation?

Regardless of their party or ideology, legislators find some bills in Congress tough to vote against. Take, for example, the Disaster Relief Appropriations Act of 2013, H.R. 152. As its name suggests, this $60 billion spending bill sought to alleviate the immediate needs of citizens suffering from massive storms that devastated parts of the East Coast in fall 2012, including Hurricane Sandy. The bill passed both chambers of Congress in January 2013, and President Obama signed the bill into law the following day.

No one doubted that some kind of bill for disaster relief would be enacted. Yet, as is often the case with such legislation, representatives and senators added spending items unrelated to disaster relief. Most tried to insert pork-barrel spending items into the bill, and some succeeded. The term *pork barrel* refers to government spending that benefits a narrow constituency in return for electoral or some other kind of political support.

An early version of the relief bill included $150 million for fisheries in Alaska and Mississippi, and $56 million to the West Coast to clean up residual debris from the 2011 Japan tsunami, though these two parts were eventually removed.[1] The bill that did pass, however, included $2 billion for *nationwide* highway spending and $100 million for Head Start, a federal preschooling initiative for low-income families.[2] Representative Nydia Velázquez, a Democrat from New York, succeeded in including an amendment that allotted an additional $1 billion to the National Cemetery Administration for repairs to veterans' cemeteries.[3]

[1] Raymond Hernandez and Jonathan Weisman, "House to Take Up Storm Relief Bill Amid Battle Over Spending," *New York Times*, January 13, 2013, www.nytimes.com (accessed 5/28/13).
[2] Raymond Hernandez and Jonathan Weisman, "House to Take Up Storm Relief Bill Amid Battle Over Spending."
[3] U.S. House Republican Majority, "H.R. 152 Amendments," *Legislative Digest*, January 15, 2013, www.gop.gov /legdigest (accessed 5/28/13).

Taken individually, each of these special-funding projects may have merit. Funding for any of these critical needs was politically difficult to oppose. Indeed, what member of Congress would want to go on record for voting against support for veterans' cemeteries? When tacked onto the original bill, however, they raised the question of whether the legislation had more to do with other spending such as the pork-barrel projects than with critical disaster relief.

Bills like H.R. 152 may inspire cynicism regarding the motivations and behavior of federal lawmakers. For example, why would Representative Rodney Frelinghuysen, a fiscally conservative Republican from New Jersey, who ostensibly wanted government to cut back on domestic spending, succeed in adding almost $34 billion in spending into the bill?

Opinion polls show that the public has little confidence in the institution of Congress. In fact, Americans' trust in the legislative branch of government has long been declining. More than a century ago, Mark Twain captured the view of many people when he wrote, "It could probably be shown by facts and figures that there is no distinctly American criminal class except Congress." Media coverage of Congress is often critical, and headline-grabbing scandals have beset the institution throughout its history. Leaders of every major political party have been found guilty of well-publicized misdeeds, ranging from influence peddling and bribery to sexual impropriety and extortion.

When political scientists question legislators' commitment to broad national goals, their doubts are not necessarily rooted in a belief that members of Congress are more prone to criminal activity than other professionals. Rather, they believe that congressional lawmakers place the interests of their districts and their own prospects for winning re-election ahead of the welfare of the country as a whole. It is widely assumed that members of Congress expend most of their energy on massive public relations efforts aimed at their constituents, rather than on making laws to benefit the entire nation.[4] If given the choice between delivering targeted benefits to people in their district or working with their colleagues to craft careful, meaningful legislation, members of Congress will choose the former. The political payoffs are simply much higher for helping constituents with specific requests than contributing to broad national policy outcomes. As one representative stated, "Before you save the world, you have to save your seat."[5]

This is one version of what we will describe later as the distributional model of congressional politics, and it has more than a kernel of truth to it. Instead of producing the best, most efficient public goods, members spend time cooperating with each other to produce pork for their districts and ensure re-election.

Yet, if this distributional model is accurate, and members of Congress focus mostly on the needs of their own districts above broader goals, how are they ever able to pass meaningful legislation? How do historic laws get passed, such as the legislation establishing the New Deal, the Civil Rights Act of 1964, the Voting Rights Act of 1965, or the stimulus bill, the health care and financial reforms, and a major farm bill that Congress enacted between 2009 and 2014? What explains the occasions when the members rise above their individual self-interest or the interests of their district and create meaningful, lasting legislative accomplishments?

---

[4] David R. Mayhew, *Congress: The Electoral Connection*, 2nd ed. (New Haven, CT: Yale University Press, 2004).

[5] Representative George Miller, quoted in Leroy N. Rieselbach, *Congressional Politics: The Evolving Legislative System*, 2nd ed. (Boulder, CO: Westview, 1995), p. 39.

Constitutional Prerogatives

The Founders intended Congress to be the most powerful branch of the national government. The Constitution describes dozens of specific congressional responsibilities and powers, and it also gives Congress broad authority as the primary lawmaking body in the national government. Specific congressional powers outlined by the Founders, as listed in Article 1, Section 8, include the authority to tax; borrow and coin money; operate a postal service; promote science and the arts; declare war; raise and support armies and a navy; suppress insurrections; and build a capital city.

Broad responsibility, however, is found in the concluding clause of Article I, Section 8, which states that Congress has the power to "make all Laws which shall be necessary and proper for carrying into Execution the foregoing Powers, and all other Powers vested by this Constitution in the Government of the United States, or in any Department or Officer thereof." This elastic clause (also called the necessary and proper clause) grants Congress virtually blanket authority to make laws in the national interest, as long as those laws do not violate other precepts of the Constitution. No phrase in the Constitution gives any other branch such substantial powers.[6]

From the *Federalist Papers*, we know that leading constitutional advocates James Madison, Alexander Hamilton, and John Jay believed not only that Congress would play a preeminent role in a strong national government but also that a strong legislative branch was essential to the proper functioning of the new government and the protection of the population from injustice. Using the *Federalist Papers* to argue against skeptics who feared that under the new Constitution the presidency would be too powerful, or that the states would lose their identities, Madison, Hamilton, and Jay repeatedly claimed that strong congressional authority was key to a functioning federal republic with a separation-of-powers system that prevented the rise of a tyrannical president.

Bicameralism

The Constitution specifies that Congress will consist of two legislative chambers, the House of Representatives and the Senate. The **bicameral legislature** reflects the dual character of the American republic, blending popular government with federalism.[7] Congress not only makes the laws, it also plays the critical role of representing the people and the states in the national government.

bicameral legislature
A legislature consisting of two chambers or houses.

---

[6] The "Take Care" clause for the president (discussed in Chapter 6) is similarly broad and under a reasonable interpretation gives the president substantial discretionary power. But given that we know the Founders generally preferred Congress to be the primary locus of power in the national government, and given how federal courts have interpreted the Constitution, the elastic clause has had the biggest effect on national power relative to the states and on the relative powers of the branches within the national government.

[7] George Tsebelis and Jeannette Money, *Bicameralism* (New York: Cambridge University Press, 1997).

In *Federalist 39*, for example, Madison compares the House to the Senate. Because the House was intended to represent the people, states are apportioned seats in the House according to the size of their population. Furthermore, members of the House have two-year terms of office, and all members can stand for re-election every two years to ensure that they remain responsive to the people. If their behavior diverges significantly from the wishes of their constituents, voters have frequent opportunities to replace them. For the House, the principals (voters) hold the agents (representatives) on a tight leash.

The Senate, in contrast, was designed to represent the states. Each state has two senators, regardless of size. Senators serve six-year terms and were originally appointed by the state governments. (Senators began to be elected directly by the people in the early twentieth century, as we will see later.) Although each Senate seat is up for renewal after six years, in any given even-numbered year, only one-third of the members' terms expire. Thus, in 2012, 33 senators faced re-election; in 2014, a different set of 34 senators faced re-election; and in 2016, the final set of 33 senators faces re-election. This design—the longer terms in office and the rotation of term-expiration dates—reflects the intention of the Founders that the Senate was to be the more deliberative chamber, acting to maintain continuity in government in the face of popular whims and shifts in public opinion. For the Senate today, the principals (voters) hold the agents (senators) on a looser leash than is the case for the House.

Making Law

Congress, by constitutional mandate, bears ultimate responsibility for lawmaking. Both chambers of Congress must approve a piece of legislation, which must then be signed by the president to become law. Although the methods of approval by a chamber for the initial passage of bills are not specified in the Constitution, tradition and practice dictate that at least a majority in each chamber must be in favor of a bill before it can become law.[8] After approval by both chambers, the president can choose to sign the bill into law or veto it. The Constitution specifies that Congress can "override," or overturn, a presidential veto by a vote of two-thirds of the members in each chamber. (We will look at the lawmaking process more closely later in this chapter.) The Constitution also specifies voting rules for the approval of treaties, which require the votes of two-thirds of the Senate. The House must be the formal originator of all taxing and spending decisions for the American national government.

Constitutional prerogatives aside, in some areas, especially foreign policy and war making, the president's power has eclipsed congressional authority. Over time, the presidency has become the locus for many legislative initiatives,

---

[8] The chambers can impose other rules for debate that make passage of a bill in practice require more than a majority. The Senate's cloture rule, for instance, requires three-fifths of the members' support for a bill to be introduced on the floor for debate. We will discuss this subject later in this chapter.

for federal budget planning, and for foreign policy decision making. Madison, Hamilton, and Jay, therefore, were mistaken about what the relative powers of the Congress and the president would be; in particular, they failed to foresee how those powers would evolve over the course of the twentieth century. We will take a closer look at the expansion of presidential power in Chapter 6.

Congressional responsibilities as outlined in the Constitution and the growing role of the national government (see Chapter 3) mean that much of national politics swirls around Congress. As the formal originator of all taxing and spending decisions for the American national government, and as the locus of debate over business regulation, foreign and domestic aid, public works, approval for executive appointments and treaties, and the general direction of government, Congress is subject to intense media scrutiny. It attracts more lobbyists than any other legislative body in the world. Congress also draws the attention—either ire or appreciation—of the voters who elect its members. We turn now to the choosing of members of Congress.

Congressional Elections

According to the Constitution, the states are responsible for deciding how to choose their congressional representation, provided these methods comply with constitutional tenets, such as the requirement that representatives must be at least 25 years old and senators at least 30.

Distinctive features of congressional elections have emerged over time as a result of laws passed by Congress and of traditions dating back to the eighteenth century. In the following sections, we will see how plurality elections, primaries, and redistricting every 10 years encourages individualism in Congress. Individualism in this context means that members of Congress to a large extent see their own political fortunes as tied primarily to their own behavior and that voters consider their representation in Congress to be tied to individual legislators who represent them, and secondarily to political parties or ideological groupings. Political representation, therefore, occurs more by individual politicians and less by groupings of politicians. We will learn how these institutional features and other historical trends have led to high incumbency re-election rates, but also to increasing minority representation in Congress.

The features of congressional elections have exacerbated the collective dilemmas that members face once they are inside their respective chambers. As we will see, the specific electoral *institutions* encourage candidates and members of Congress seeking re-election to maintain personal reputations among voters. In most other democracies, candidates for national legislatures are more closely linked to the reputations of their political parties. There is more individualism among members of the U.S. Congress than there is among legislators in most other democracies, and this individualism increased during the twentieth century.

Causes of Individualism in Congress

The main causes of individualism in Congress are institutional: the nature of electoral districts is one factor that leads to individualism, and other electoral rules also create incentives for legislators to make strong personal connections to voters in their districts.

Single-Member Districts and Plurality Rule Drawing on the example set by the British House of Commons, nearly all states have elected their representatives for the House and Senate using **single-member districts** and **plurality rule**, sometimes known as "first-past-the-post." In single-member districts, each electoral district or state chooses one representative. The plurality method of voting means that whoever receives the most votes wins. Note that this is distinct from a majority-rule voting method. Under majority rule, if no candidate receives at least 50 percent of the total vote, then there is a runoff between the top two vote-getters. Under plurality rule, there is no need for a runoff election.

Strictly speaking, under the current system, senators are elected in double-member districts (states have two senators), but each senatorial election occurs as a contest for one seat only, based on plurality voting rules. These elections are also first-past-the-post. Until the early twentieth century, senators were not

single-member district An electoral district in which a single person is elected to a given office.

plurality rule A method for determining an election's winner in which the candidate who receives the most votes wins.

Members of Congress need their constituents' support—in the form of votes and campaign donations—to win re-election. This creates a strong incentive to focus on the needs of their districts rather than on the country as a whole. Here, Lloyd Doggett of Texas meets with constituents.

elected by popular vote but were appointed by their state governments. This process was revised in 1913 by the Seventeenth Amendment, which provided for the direct election of senators.

For Americans, the single-member, simple-plurality system is so familiar that it may be surprising to learn that few other countries use it. France, for example, requires that candidates win an outright majority of the votes in a district, which means that runoff elections between the top two vote-getters are often held if neither candidate wins a majority. Many other countries either elect multiple candidates from a district or use a form of **proportional representation**, or both. Under proportional-representation systems, the number of seats a party receives in a district or nationwide is proportional to the votes it receives in the elections. For instance, if a party receives 30 percent of the vote under proportional representation, it can expect to hold about 30 percent of the legislative seats. Under single-member, simple-plurality systems, the winning candidate receives 100 percent representation of that district (its one and only seat) simply by getting more votes than any other candidate.

Historically, there have been a few exceptions whereby states have elected representatives using methods other than plurality rule, and some states have recently switched to a system not unlike the French one, requiring a runoff election if no one wins a majority. Nevertheless, the pervasive use of the plurality rule and single-member districts has had a strong influence on the nature of the U.S. Congress, especially in combination with other features such as primary elections and redistricting.

Primary Elections For both chambers, being chosen to run for Congress once depended on establishing a record of loyalty to state-level political parties. Party leaders in the states controlled which candidates got on the ballot and who was nominated to serve in the Senate. Beginning in the first half of the twentieth century, however, voters began to select which congressional candidates would appear on ballots through the primary election process. Primary elections allow voters to choose who will appear under the party label on general-election ballots. These primary elections are akin to the semifinals of a sports tournament, with competition *within* the parties (like within a sports conference), whereas the finals are the general election *between* the candidates of the parties (like an overall champion). As long as someone can win a primary election, he or she can run for Congress under that party label without having to please the party leadership.

One consequence of single-member, simple-plurality election rules in combination with primary elections is that representatives and senators work extremely hard to cultivate reputations as individualistic politicians who are not completely beholden to their political parties. Candidates for Congress in the United States can focus mostly on satisfying voters in their own constituencies, whereas in most other countries politicians are much more loyal to their parties because they depend on the party leadership for their job security.

proportional representation
A method for allocating seats in a legislature in which the number of seats a party receives in a district or nationwide is proportional to the votes it receives in the elections.

Drawing District Boundaries Congressional district boundaries determine the actual constituencies for representatives to the House. The American states are allocated seats in the House according to population, but no state can have fewer than one representative. Wyoming, for example, with a half-million people, has one representative for the entire state. Six other states also have a single representative in the House—Alaska, Delaware, Montana, North Dakota, South Dakota, and Vermont. Voters in the remaining 43 states are divided into districts.

House districts, according to Article I, Section 2, of the Constitution, cannot have fewer than 30,000 people. This was stipulated at the time to ensure that state governments would not create tiny districts easily controlled by a given political faction or interest groups, something that was a problem in the British system. The British House of Commons for a long time contained representatives from so-called rotten boroughs, which were tiny electoral districts dominated by one person who could bribe the small number of voters to win reelection. The Founders placed the 30,000 person minimum to avoid the American equivalent of rotten boroughs, and also to set the size of the House at a bit more than twice the size of the Senate at the time (64 members in the House, as compared to 26 members in the Senate). As the country grew in population, Congress occasionally increased the size of the House, until it was decided to cap the number permanently. The total number of representatives was set at 435 in 1911; the main argument for fixing the number at what was then the status quo was that a parliament approaching 500 members in size would be unworkable.

The number of representatives allocated to each state and the boundaries of congressional districts are reset after the national census is taken every 10 years. A state can gain or lose seats if its population grows or shrinks relative to other states. If a state gains or loses seats, it must redraw its district boundaries. Because of population shifts within the states, most states redraw their district boundaries every decade regardless of whether they have gained or lost seats.

For much of American history, states could draw their boundaries as they wished. This meant that districts were of varying population size even within states, and that it was possible (and common) for rural districts with few residents to have representation equal to the more populous urban districts. In the 1960s, however, the national government, through legislation (discussed later in this chapter) and through Supreme Court rulings, began to place restrictions on the states. The Court's rulings in *Baker v. Carr* (1962) and *Wesberry v. Sanders* (1964) paved the way for a major change in congressional districts. The Court concluded in those two cases that all House districts and all state house and senate districts in a given state must be of approximately equal population size. The *Baker* and *Wesberry* rulings not only mandated a dramatic change in districts all over the country, they also strengthened congressional representation of heavily populated cities. Following the ruling, large cities were divided into multiple congressional districts, each with one representative in the House.

Partisan Redistricting

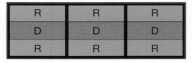

Imagine a rectangular state with nine voters and three House seats. If the district lines are drawn one way, there is a mix of Republicans and Democrats in each district. In this scenario, Republicans have a majority in each district and will likely win all three seats.

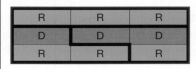

However, district boundaries could also be drawn to give Democrats a majority in at least one district. In this second scenario, Democrats would be expected to win one of the three seats.

Determining congressional district boundaries is fraught with politics because it is possible to draw districts in ways that give one political party or population group more representation or power (Figure 5.1A).[9] For many states, the political party in control of the state government appoints a commission to redraw the boundaries. These commissions tend to draw the boundaries to the advantage of the political party that appointed them. In states with divided government—one party controls the governorship, while another party controls the state legislature—the makeup of the commission typically reflects the proportion of each party's representation in government. Some states try to divorce the process from partisan politics by appointing a bipartisan commission to decide on district boundaries.

To see how politics can easily intrude into the drawing of district boundaries, consider the simplified example shown in Figure 5.1B. In this example,

Racial Gerrymandering

The same approaches have been used to try to manipulate the voting power and representation of minorities. In a hypothetical state with six white voters and three black voters, lines could be drawn such that black voters do not constitute a majority in any district.

Or, boundaries could be drawn to create at least one "minority-majority" district, where members of the minority group constitute a majority of voters. Although this configuration may result in a black candidate being elected from the minority-majority district, some scholars have questioned whether this approach ultimately improves the overall representation of minorities in legislatures.

[9] David Butler and Bruce Cain, *Congressional Redistricting: Comparative and Theoretical Perspectives* (New York: Macmillan, 1992).

drawing boundaries one way results in a situation where African Americans do not have a majority in any district, while drawing boundaries another way ensures that there is a majority of African Americans in one district. Assuming, for the sake of argument, that blacks are more likely than whites to support an African American candidate, then the latter set of boundaries will virtually ensure that at least one African American is elected.

The process of drawing strangely shaped district boundaries in order to gain political advantage is known as **gerrymandering**. The term is derived from a district drawn for the 1812 election in Massachusetts to ensure the election of Governor Elbridge Gerry's allies, known as the Jeffersonians. The district looked like a salamander, or so Gerry's opponents thought. They accused the Jeffersonians of drawing, not a salamander, but a "Gerrymander." One district in Texas in the 1990s was accused of looking like "four spiders having an orgy"[10] (Figure 5.2).

gerrymandering Drawing strangely shaped district boundaries to gain political advantage.

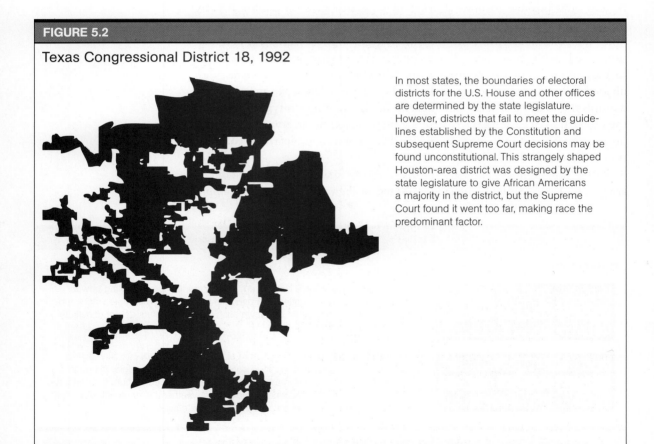

FIGURE 5.2

Texas Congressional District 18, 1992

In most states, the boundaries of electoral districts for the U.S. House and other offices are determined by the state legislature. However, districts that fail to meet the guidelines established by the Constitution and subsequent Supreme Court decisions may be found unconstitutional. This strangely shaped Houston-area district was designed by the state legislature to give African Americans a majority in the district, but the Supreme Court found it went too far, making race the predominant factor.

[10] Sam Roberts, "Will District Mappers Ever Draw the Line?" *New York Times*, March 23, 1992.

The Supreme Court has generally allowed gerrymandering by state governments, but only within limits. Congressional districts must be contiguous, or "all of one piece" geographically. Political parties can draw districts to give them an advantage in elections, but districts cannot be drawn in ways that systematically disadvantage population groups that historically have been discriminated against in elections. The Court, for example, carefully examines districts drawn in southern states because of the region's long history of discrimination against former slaves and their descendants. In fact, the Court has permitted states to draw districts for the express purpose of enhancing minority-group representation. It has struck down redistricting efforts that led to reductions in the number of black representatives and other minority representatives to state legislatures or the U.S. Congress, and it has allowed redistricting that has deliberately led to increases in the number of black or Latino representatives.

As for individualism in Congress, districting for House seats can certainly intensify the need for members of Congress to make personal connections to voters. Redistricting after a census can sometimes make an incumbent safer in his or her seat by drawing the lines so that voters of the other party are now in another district. Conversely, redistricting can make the incumbent's district more competitive and thus hurt re-election efforts. Not surprisingly, the redistricting process is closely watched by members of Congress, who often feel that state-level politics determines their re-election fate. The best way for incumbents to protect themselves against the vagaries of redistricting is to make sure that constituents appreciate the members' work on their behalf regardless of party affiliation.

Other Electoral Factors The individualism of American congressional candidates and members of Congress has increased over time, not only because of institutional changes such as the rise of primary elections for ballot access but also because of methods of campaigning and the kinds of policies the national government adopts. Since the latter half of the twentieth century, candidates have increasingly used television advertising to gain personal name recognition. Television advertising takes a lot of money, and to earn a seat in Congress candidates need to raise money from individual donors, interest groups, corporations, and political party fund-raising organizations so that they can hire a campaign staff and advertise their candidacy. Congressional candidates have to raise their own money for campaigns, and critics of Congress focus on the potential benefits that Congress can bestow on specific industries or companies that donate money to campaigns. Critics argue that members of Congress rely on wealthy donors to win and retain their seats, and therefore the legislation they pass mostly benefits contributors to campaigns. (We will discuss the ideas of these critics in more detail at the end of this chapter.)

The growth of the national government's power has also contributed to making elections more candidate-centered. In the nineteenth century, when the federal government played a smaller role in the economic life of the country than it does now, state-level parties dominated congressional elections. In the early twentieth century, about the same time as the switch toward primary elections, the federal government began to enact legislation affecting the economic well-being of every congressional district in the country. The increase in national government power and wealth relative to the states meant that members of Congress could plausibly take credit as individual politicians for protecting their districts from such potentially harmful legislation as taxes or regulations. They could also claim credit for bringing home as many government benefits as possible, such as research grants or public works projects. Recall our brief discussion of the distributional model of Congress (discussed in more detail later). Those who favor this model find the most convincing evidence to be from the era post-1930s.

The individualism in Congress is real and consequential, and as we will discuss shortly, it makes solving collective dilemmas inside the chambers a daunting task. But this individualism should not be overstated. Members of Congress do cooperate and do feel constrained by collective goals.[11] It is not that political parties are unimportant in congressional elections, or that members have little incentive to follow their party's line or work on its behalf once inside Congress. In fact, legislators work closely with their fellow party members, as we will see later and again in Chapter 12. Nevertheless, Congress needs effective institutions inside its chambers to do anything collectively.

Representing the District or State

Those who sit in Congress win their seats because they are good at determining what their constituents want from government. If they are effective enough as representatives, they will be re-elected as a matter of course. As a rule, conservative representatives come from relatively conservative districts, and liberal representatives from relatively liberal districts. If representatives or senators are consistently out of step with their constituents, they will likely lose their jobs.

As noted earlier, a representative or senator is essentially an agent of the voters (the principals). What kinds of agents should members of Congress be for their principals? The principal-agent problem is a modern conceptualization, but the question of how one should best represent constituents is very old. Edmund Burke, a nineteenth-century British member of Parliament, proposed that representatives of a constituency sometimes act like trustees and at other times like delegates. **Trustees** make decisions within the legislature—voting, crafting bills, adding amendments—using their own judgments about what is best for their constituents. **Delegates** listen carefully to what their constituents want and make decisions based on feedback. We can think of trustees as being agents with more discretion to make their own decisions in comparison to delegates, who need to obey principals closely.

trustees Representatives who make decisions using their own judgments about what is best for their constituents.

delegates Representatives who listen carefully to what their constituents want and make decisions based on feedback from constituents.

[11] Nelson Polsby, *How Congress Evolves* (New York: Oxford University Press, 2004).

When asked in surveys, members of Congress claim that they try to balance these competing visions of representation.[12] The trustee-delegate trade-off is conspicuous when members publicly take policy positions in a manner inconsistent with what a majority of their constituents want. More than a dozen House Republican incumbents lost their seats to Democrats in 2012, and evidence from exit polls indicates that their positions on issues like abortion swung key votes toward the Democratic challengers.

The use of primary elections, however, means that the principals in the local election within a candidate's state or district may not match the principals in the general state or national election. Indeed, primary election voters tend to be more intensely partisan than general election voters, and it can be hazardous for a candidate to vote in a manner inconsistent with what his or her party's primary voters want, even if doing so makes it harder to appeal to the broader electorate for the general election campaign. For example, Senator Richard Lugar (R–IN) voted in favor of President Obama's stimulus policies in 2009 and 2010, publicly announced his support for the practice of earmarking (inserting pork into a bill), and came out in favor of an immigration plan that many in his party felt offered amnesty to illegal immigrants. Lugar was well aware that many people who voted for him, and especially Republican primary voters in his state, would be upset with him, but nonetheless he chose to act as a trustee and use his own judgment about what he thought was best for the country. Indiana has a strongly conservative state-level Republican Party, and in March 2012 Republican voters in Indiana ousted Lugar in the primary election in favor of a more conservative candidate, Richard Mourdock. Mourdock subsequently lost in the general election to the Democratic candidate, Joe Donnelly, in part because of comments Mourdock made about abortion that made him seem too extreme to many voters.

Constituency Service An important part of the job of members of Congress is to help constituents in their interactions with the federal government. As an example, if a business owner believes that his or her company has been treated unfairly by the tax authorities or by another federal agency, it is common for that person to ask the congressional representative or senator to help clear things up, perhaps write a letter to the appropriate people in the agency or make a phone call on behalf of the business owner. Or if someone has been waiting too long to get a passport for foreign travel, a phone call from a senator's office to the Department of State (which issues passports) can speed things along. Complaints from ordinary people about the federal bureaucracy are plentiful, but when a federal agency receives a communication from a member of Congress, especially from a member of Congress on the relevant Congressional committee with jurisdiction over that agency, people in that agency will

---

[12] John Kingdon, *Congressmen's Voting Decisions* (New York: Harper and Row, 1981); Richard Fenno, *Home Style: House Members and Their Districts* (Boston: Little, Brown, 1978).

pay more attention. Members of Congress of course wish to avoid a reputation for being uncaring or unhelpful. Thus they devote staff time to what is called **constituency service**, the direct help of specific constituents with governmental matters.

If done successfully, constituency service can build tremendous goodwill among constituents. Developing a reputation for being a helpful, concerned representative or senator, especially among constituents who might be influential with other constituents (such as business owners or union leaders) or who might provide generous campaign donations, can bolster reelection chances considerably. Along with delivering pork to the local area or state, constituency service forms a basis of the individual reputations of members of Congress. However, if a member's staff devotes many hours to constituency service, and the member likewise devotes time in making phone calls or writing letters to federal agencies, this is less time available to engage in collective activities such as working on legislation with broad benefits for the country or for the home state, or working with partisan allies inside Congress to pull the party together to pass or block legislation. In other words, constituency service provides individual benefits to constituents and to members of Congress, and helps with individual reputations, yet often competes with the pursuit of collective goals. As the role of the federal government in people's lives has grown since the early twentieth century, there have arisen many more opportunities for members to come to the rescue of constituents vis-à-vis that federal government. This is among the reasons why incumbent members of Congress have advantages over their challengers at election time.

The Incumbency Advantage Members of Congress, especially in the House, are re-elected in very high numbers. This **incumbency advantage** is indicated by Figure 5.3, which shows the proportion of incumbent House and Senate candidates that wins re-election. In a typical election, it is extremely rare to defeat a sitting House member, and it is only somewhat more common to unseat a senator. The elections immediately following a census reapportionment, such as in 2012, produce more incumbent losses simply because redistricting often leads to situations where incumbents are running against incumbents, either in the primary or general election. Thus, because Ohio lost two House seats after the 2010 census, Democrats Dennis Kucinich and Marcy Kaptur were forced to run against each other in the 2012 Democratic primary. Kaptur won the primary and then went on to win the general election. Kucinich, after the redrawing of his Cleveland-area district led to his defeat, said that he briefly considered moving to Washington state and running in the district that Washington gained through reapportionment.

This measure of the incumbency advantage shown in Figure 5.3 probably overstates, though, the extent to which incumbent legislators are protected from electoral pressures. When considering whether or not to run for re-election, members consider their probability of winning. A political

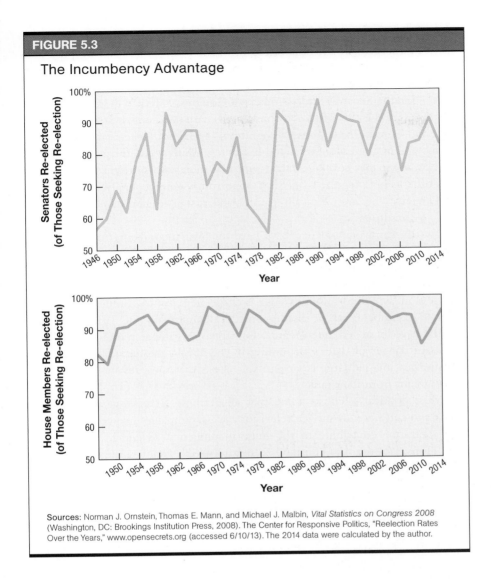

FIGURE 5.3

The Incumbency Advantage

Sources: Norman J. Ornstein, Thomas E. Mann, and Michael J. Malbin, *Vital Statistics on Congress 2008* (Washington, DC: Brookings Institution Press, 2008). The Center for Responsive Politics, "Reelection Rates Over the Years," www.opensecrets.org (accessed 6/10/13). The 2014 data were calculated by the author.

campaign is a grueling process, and few would willingly subject themselves to a campaign if they were certain that they would ultimately lose. Therefore, counting only incumbents who decide to run removes from the sample several members who likely would have lost had they decided to run. Despite this, the overall levels of incumbent re-election are remarkably high and have been trending upward.

Political scientists have proposed various theories to account for this upward trend. First, state parties have had growing success, through enhanced computing technology, in gerrymandering districts to ensure their incumbents' re-election. Second, congressional members have demonstrated increasing skill, aided by the growth and sophistication of their staffs, in delivering pork and constituency service. This has been especially true in the decades since the 1960s, when the size of congressional staff doubled in the House and increased fourfold in the Senate. Third, members of Congress have had increasing opportunities since the 1950s to flood constituents with inexpensive or free television appearances to enhance name recognition. Throughout a session of Congress, members can grant interviews and hold press conferences to earn local television or newspaper coverage and ensure that their names are heard or read by constituents on a regular basis. Such opportunities are generally unavailable to challengers, who must typically pay for advertising to gain name recognition among constituents.

Fourth, campaign finance laws have enabled incumbents to amass huge amounts of money ("war chests") and ward off potential challengers. The laws permit candidates to roll over money not spent in one election for use in the next election, and also to raise money continuously during the congressional session. The fund-raising needs for challengers just to compete with well-funded incumbents can be discouraging. Fifth and finally, the national political parties have improved their organizations to target campaign money to incumbents in danger of defeat. Beginning in the 1980s, the national parties have themselves amassed large campaign war chests that they devote to protecting incumbents from their ranks.

Most political scientists argue that all of these factors—gerrymandering, pork and constituency service, television access, campaign finance, and national party efforts—contribute to the huge incumbency advantage, especially in the House. Yet scholars continue to debate which factor is the most important. Many critics of Congress see the incumbency advantage—especially as it is fueled by readily available campaign funding from wealthy segments of society—as evidence of a bias in American government toward entrenched, moneyed interests (an idea discussed again at the end of the chapter). Members of Congress and other defenders of the institution argue that the incumbency advantage is so strong because members are good at discerning and acting on constituents' preferences. Besides, the counterargument goes, the money members of Congress receive for re-election comes from people and organizations on all sides of controversial policy issues (discussed again in Chapter 13).

Minority Representation Although incumbents win at high rates, changes since the mid-twentieth century have also increased the rates of election of minorities and women. An increase in minority voting followed the Voting Rights Act of 1965 and the heightened federal court scrutiny of congressional redistricting. Some scholars have speculated that the increased representation of minorities stems from efforts by state Republican parties to concentrate minority voters (who tend to vote Democratic) into a few predominantly urban districts. This strategy allegedly grants voters in those districts the minority representatives that they seek, while enabling the Republicans to remain dominant in the state's other districts. This claim, however, remains controversial.[13]

What is not disputed by scholars is that the increase in minority representation has had notable consequences both for Congress and for American politics in general. The Congressional Black Caucus (discussed later in this chapter) has become an important organization on Capitol Hill, especially within the Democratic Party. The voting behavior of minority and women members of Congress has differed on a range of policy issues from that of their white male counterparts.[14] And the first female Speaker of the House, Nancy Pelosi, rose to that position in 2007 after the Democrats gained majority status in the 2006 election.

Understanding Congressional Politics

Congress is not only the center of lawmaking activity in the American political system, it has also evolved into a highly complex political system in its own right, with its own institutions, norms of behavior, and cultural practices. It is worth studying as a microcosm of the entire American political system and, indeed, of any political system based on democratic principles.

The collective dilemmas outlined in Chapter 1 are prevalent in Congress. Members of Congress face recurring collective-action problems. They have incentives to free ride off the efforts of their colleagues—for example, by taking credit for producing public goods while spending most of their time working on bills that benefit their district, even though these bills may not be good for their party or for the country as a whole. Members of Congress also face coordination problems. They must find ways to coordinate their behavior in order to accomplish anything. Coordination can include voting for one another's **pork-barrel** bills, but it can also include coordinating efforts on a compromise bill that no one is perfectly happy with. Moreover, members face the possibility of coalition raiding. If there were no one to control the agenda and prevent repeated introductions of competing bills, then coalition raiding could continue indefinitely as members presented alternative versions of bills in an effort to attract support for their favored version.

Consider the collective-action problem highlighted in our opening story: how to get members of Congress to work for the common good of the country

pork barrel Government spending that benefits a narrow constituency in return for electoral support or some other kind of political support, including campaign donations.

[13] Carol Swain, *Black Faces, Black Interests* (Cambridge, MA: Harvard University Press, 1993); David Lublin, *The Paradox of Representation: Racial Gerrymandering and Minority Interests in Congress* (Princeton, NJ: Princeton University Press, 1997); David Epstein and Sharyn O'Halloran, "Measuring the Electoral and Policy Impact of Majority-Minority Voting Districts," *American Journal of Political Science* 42 (1999): 367–95.

[14] Katrina L. Gamble, "Black Political Representation," *Legislative Studies Quarterly* 32, no. 3 (2007): 421–47; Michele L. Swers, "Are Women More Likely to Vote for Women's Issue Bills than Their Male Colleagues?" *Legislative Studies Quarterly* 23, no. 3 (1998): 435–48.

as opposed to that of their own district or state. As a group, members want to pass broad legislation and earn a collective reputation as an efficient body. As members of a political party, they want that party to have a good reputation among voters. As individual representatives, however, they engage in activities to sustain their political popularity by delivering pork to their constituents and supporters.[15] Pork-barrel projects and constituency service can undercut their collective goals. The collective-action problems spring from this disconnect between individual and group interests: each individual legislator would prefer that his or her colleagues do the hard and sometimes unpopular work of crafting legislation for the good of the entire country. At the same time, each is tempted to free ride off the efforts of the group and bring home as much pork as possible for his or her own district. If every member of Congress spent all of his or her time getting pork and doing constituency service, then nothing that benefits the entire country would be accomplished.

Our legislative system also presents a principal-agent problem. The voters are the principals who elect members of Congress to be their agents and work on behalf of the people in the district. As we saw in Chapter 1, a principal-agent problem exists when principals cannot adequately observe the actions of agents. Voters evaluate members of Congress at election time and decide whether to keep them in office, yet voters may not have enough information to make intelligent voting decisions. And because voters cannot observe all that goes on in Congress, representatives may at times have incentives to act contrary to the interests of their districts—to vote against the wishes of a majority of their constituents, for instance. The principal-agent problem between voters and congressional representatives hinges on the degree to which voters can monitor effectively what happens in Congress.[16]

In Chapter 1, we discussed how various political institutions solve collective dilemmas. The way these institutions operate also has consequences. The details of the institutions determine who gets what in society and the quality of government policies. When Congress, for example, makes rules about who can propose amendments to legislation and when they can propose them, those rules have implications for what legislation gets passed.

Three Models for Analyzing Congress

Although scholars generally agree that Congress faces collective dilemmas, that principal-agent problems exist in legislative politics, and that the internal institutional features of Congress help overcome these dilemmas, they come to different conclusions about which specific institutions are most important in

---

[15] Morris Fiorina, *Congress: Keystone of the Washington Establishment*, 2nd ed. (New Haven, CT: Yale University Press, 1989).

[16] The principal-agent problem is also present in the relationship between congressional committees and other actors in the chambers. We will discuss these relationships later in the chapter.

Congress. They also disagree about the consequences of the institutions that make Congress operate. Various models of how congressional institutions work have been proposed. Here we will use three prominent models to help us gain a deeper understanding of the internal workings of Congress—namely, the distributional, informational, and partisan models. All three models have as an underlying assumption that members of Congress want to be reelected, and for that reason want to be considered good representatives. The differences between the models have to do with how members go about this.

The Distributional Model The **distributional model** of Congress focuses on the ways members of Congress help each other deliver specific benefits to specific groups of people.[17] Although valuable legislation that supports the general public is occasionally passed, congressional lawmakers devote much of their energy to securing programs that benefit their narrow constituencies and make sure that their own constituents do not face undue burdens in paying for government. Bills of broad national interest are frequently loaded with pork or with special provisions for relatively small groups of constituents, and members of Congress devote their time and their staffs' time to constituency service. This, according to the model, is key to understanding the workings of Congress.

> **distributional model** The view that the internal institutions of the congressional chambers are designed primarily to help members of Congress secure economic benefits for only their constituents, not the general public.

Why do members agree to each other's pork projects? The mechanism used to pass pork-barrel legislation is called **logrolling**. The name comes from an era of timber cutting when men stood on logs floating in a river and helped each other roll their logs along the river toward the mill. It is an apt analogy for legislative voting behavior. When Nydia Velázquez (discussed earlier) proposed to include $1 billion to fund veterans' cemeteries that concerned many in her district, she was asking her fellow representatives to vote in favor of it even though they have little interest in this particular allocation. Velázquez's request was made with the understanding that when a colleague's pet project is proposed, she will vote in its favor. It is a classic *quid pro quo*.

> **logrolling** An instance of two or more legislators agreeing to vote in favor of one another's proposed bills or amendments.

The Informational Model The **informational model** of Congress proposes that members of Congress are mostly interested in gathering the best information possible to help them choose effective public policies that make voters happy and help incumbents win re-election.[18] According to this view, the institutions are designed to help Congress make more informed decisions. Given that it would be impossible for every member to become an expert on every issue, the only way Congress as a whole can make good public policy is to divide the tasks of determining which policies will work given the goals of the majority in Congress. Thus, when Congress is considering a bill to fund the Department of Defense, it must rely on members with some expertise in international aid and foreign affairs to play a large role in drafting the bill.

> **informational model** The view that the internal institutions of the congressional chambers are designed to help Congress make more informed decisions.

[17] Kenneth Shepsle and Barry Weingast, "The Institutional Foundations of Committee Power," *The American Political Science Review* 81, no. 1 (1987): 85–104.

[18] Keith Krehbiel, *Information and Legislative Organization* (Ann Arbor, MI: University of Michigan Press, 1992).

Congressional leaders then can ensure that knowledgeable members on the appropriate committees review the bill.

partisan model The view that majority-party leaders dominate the workings of Congress and ensure that most legislative benefits come to majority-party members.

The Partisan Model The **partisan model** of Congress revolves around the significant role that political parties play in the organization and work of the chambers. Party leaders in particular play a crucial role. This model devotes attention to the intensity with which party leaders, especially in the House, try to control the agenda and enforce party discipline on key votes in Congress.[19] As we will discuss later, the powerful Rules Committee is a strong tool that party leaders use in running the House.

We will highlight these three models at various points in the remainder of this chapter. The purpose of describing and comparing them is to provide you with some tools to evaluate Congress. None of the models is perfectly true, but perhaps one or more of them captures the essence of how Congress works. These models are analytical tools that you can use to categorize information about Congress and try to fit that information into a coherent overall picture of the chambers. For our purposes, the models help you to understand the various moving parts of Congress in relation to each other—committees, party leaders, congressional elections, and voting on the floor of the chambers. Each model emphasizes different connections among these parts of Congress and ascribes different importance to each of them. The models lead to different conclusions about consequences for society at large, in terms of how costs and benefits are distributed. We will consider these possible consequences more fully at the end of the chapter.

While reading the remainder of this chapter, you will want to remind yourself of the links between the models and the aspects of Congress they emphasize. These three models are not entirely at odds with one another. They all make the case for the importance of congressional institutions in helping members to solve their collective dilemmas and accomplish their goals. Even the distributional model suggests that although members occasionally free ride off their colleagues, they also cooperate with each other in order to divide up the government largesse for their home constituents. Furthermore, your own analysis of Congress may combine aspects of more than one model. As an example, one could propose a distributional-partisan model that emphasizes how members of the majority party secure pork for their own constituencies at the expense of the constituencies of members from the minority party.

Internal Institutions of Congress

As we have seen, several features of congressional elections have tended to promote highly individualistic behavior by members, at least in comparison to legislative behavior in most other democracies. The free-riding problem among

[19] Gary Cox and Mathew McCubbins, *Setting the Agenda: Responsible Party Government in the U.S. House of Representatives* (New York: Cambridge University Press, 2005).

members, for example, presents one kind of collective dilemma made more salient by increasing individualism. When a party's leaders and most of its members in Congress agree on the need to raise taxes, to raise the pay of federal employees, or to cut spending on popular programs, it is tempting for individual members to let others in their party pay the political costs of casting the difficult votes. In other words, there is a strong incentive for members to do the most popular thing in the eyes of their constituents, rather than to support legislation that is seen within the party as best for the country as a whole.

The problem of unstable coalitions represents another kind of collective dilemma. Recall from Chapter 1 the problem in voting situations where any coalition can be "raided" by an alternative proposal. This endemic problem always lurks in legislative bodies. Even if a given coalition of people agrees to vote in favor of a bill, if opponents are able to propose any alternative bill they wish, it is possible that some supporters of the original bill will vote for the alternative and thus defect from their previous agreement. (Figure 5.4 goes through hypothetical examples.)

The possibility of unstable coalitions highlights the importance of agenda control: who controls the agenda often determines which group wins its favored policies. If a group controls the agenda and wants the status quo to prevail, that group can prevent any vote on alternative policies. Or, as Figure 5.4 shows, if a group wants a specific change to the status quo, it can control the alternatives being voted upon to get its preferred policy outcome. A group needs to control not only what alternatives are proposed but also the order of the votes. The key insight is in the importance of maintaining agenda control and not giving it up. In fact, Figure 5.4 shows how three different agenda setters would result in three different policy outcomes. If the floor is open for anyone to propose any alternative and no one controls the agenda, cycling between different alternatives can continue indefinitely.[20]

The institutions and procedures of Congress are designed to grant agenda control to a small subset of people who carefully manage the flow of legislation.

FIGURE 5.4

Agenda Control and Coalition Raiding

Assume legislators belong to groups that receive either high, medium, or low benefits from a particular alternative.

		Alternative		
	Size	SQ	A	B
X	25	High	Medium	Low
Y	35	Medium	Low	High
Z	40	Low	High	Medium

(rows labeled under "Group")

If group X controls the agenda and wants the status quo to prevail, it could simply not allow a vote against either alternative, and get its preferred outcome (the status quo). If group Z controls the agenda and wants policy A, then it would first allow B to be voted on against the status quo. B would win. Then group Z would allow A to be voted on against the new status quo (alternative B), and A would win. Thus group Z would get its preferred outcome, A. Finally, if group Y controls the agenda, it would permit only one vote, B against the status quo. B would win against the status quo, and thus the group Y would get its preferred outcome. Three different agenda setters would result in three different policy outcomes.

Pairing	Outcome	Winning Coalition
SQ beats A	60 to 40	XY
A beats B	65 to 35	XZ
B beats SQ	75 to 25	YZ

[20] There are real examples of cycles occurring in Congress. See William Riker, "The Paradox of Voting and Congressional Rules for Voting on Amendments," *American Political Science Review* 52 (1958): 349–66; or John Blydenburgh, "The Closed Rule and the Paradox of Voting," *Journal of Politics* 33 (1971): 57–71.

Not only do these institutions help overcome free-riding problems, but they also help prevent potential coalition raiding in legislation. As we will see, the institutions inside Congress solve many kinds of collective dilemmas and principal-agent problems. Before describing these institutions in detail, let us gain some historical perspective.

An Increasingly Institutionalized Congress

The Constitution says virtually nothing about how Congress should conduct its internal business apart from specifying a few voting rules, such as the two-thirds requirement to overcome vetoes or pass treaties. The first meeting of Congress in 1789 in New York City included 65 members in the House and 26 members in the Senate. It was composed of the leading politicians of the day, including many of the Founders. Members initially met as a full body to conduct business, rather than breaking into smaller committees. The House, however, quickly established its first committee, Ways and Means, and went on to develop several others. Only 144 bills were proposed in the first Congress (as compared with thousands today), though they involved such weighty matters as the future location of the nation's capital, Revolutionary War debt, foreign relations, domestic relations with Native Americans, national expansion, and postal services.

Congress changed over time in ways that mirrored the nation's development. Congress grew in size as new states were added. As discussed, House membership reached its peak and was capped in 1911 at 435 voting members. There are now 100 Senators, two from each of the 50 states. As the national government's responsibilities expanded in relation to those of the states, so too did the prestige of congressional membership versus membership in state legislatures. It was common in the early nineteenth century for state-level politicians to spend short spells in Congress and then return to the state level where they could exert real influence. Between the mid-nineteenth century and the 1960s, however, the average tenure for a member of the House increased from two to five terms.

Furthermore, as the country became an industrial and military power, and as the national government took on greater responsibilities, Congress developed an increasingly elaborate committee system to deal with the volume and complexity of legislation. Its operations became more organized and rule-based. Political scientists have summarized this process by saying that Congress became increasingly *institutionalized* over time.[21] The Congress we know today would not be recognizable to the Founders. Although the atmosphere on the floor of the House and Senate might seem to be on the whole dignified and relatively quiet, behind the scenes Congress is a very busy place. Hallways, members'

[21] Nelson W. Polsby, "The Institutionalization of the U.S. House of Representatives," *American Political Science Review* 62, no. 1 (1968): 144–68.

offices, and committee meetings swarm with politicians, lobbyists, reporters, foreign dignitaries, experts, and citizens. Yet through remarkably efficient organization, Congress manages, in an average year, to deal with approximately 9,000 proposed bills and pass 400 to 500 into law. Its professional, well-paid legislators are assisted by some 11,000 staff members and a large number of congressional bureaus that conduct research and provide other services. Roughly 250 committees and subcommittees work in both chambers. More than 10,000 officially registered lobbyists try to influence congressional policy making.[22]

The internal operations of Congress are highly bureaucratic and follow codified rules. Recall our definition of a political institution from Chapter 1: a rule or set of rules or practices that determines how people make collective decisions. Congress, especially the House, is considered to be highly institutionalized today because it has elaborate, codified rules of conduct.

These codes for behavior are expressed both in the internal rules of the two chambers, which are voted on by all the members, and in rules established by the political parties. Two institutional aspects of internal congressional politics are paramount: party leadership and committees. Party leaders, especially those from the majority, are like orchestra conductors: they make sure that things run smoothly and allocate resources and time to different members of the legislature. The committees function more like specific sections of the orchestra by doing their part to contribute to the body's overall performance. The party leaders orchestrate, while the committees specialize. Their combination provides the final product.

Party Leaders

The majority and the minority parties in Congress each elect their leaders within the House and Senate. Leaders are elected in their party's caucus, which typically occurs at the beginning of each two-year congressional session. By orchestrating the conduct of members, party leaders can be seen as repeatedly solving coordination problems. They do this partly by trying to enforce **party discipline**—pressure on party members to vote on bills that have the support of the party leadership—on important votes, but they also help organize congressional business in other ways. If different committees or factions in Congress fail to coordinate, then nothing can get done and all members of the parties will be worse off. The party leaders make their members better off by getting them to coordinate on common action.[23]

The House members vote to choose the **Speaker of the House**, the most important legislator in that chamber and in the country. The Speaker's position is

party discipline Pressure on party members to vote on bills that have the support of the party leadership.

Speaker of the House The constitutionally designated leader of the House of Representatives. In the modern House, he or she is always the leader of the majority party.

---

[22] Those who support the expertise model of Congress note how a good deal of the machinery of Congress is devoted to providing specialized expertise to members. We will return to this idea later.

[23] Gary Cox and Mathew McCubbins, *Legislative Leviathan*, 2nd ed. (New York: Cambridge University Press, 2007).

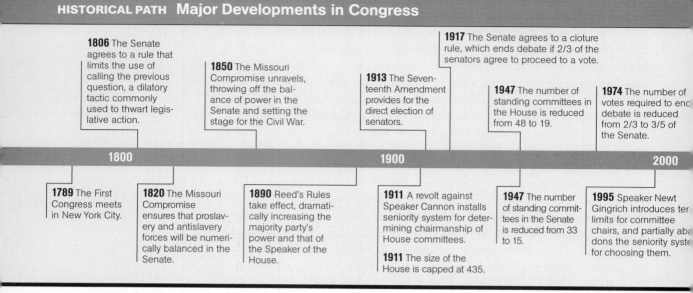

1806 The Senate agrees to a rule that limits the use of calling the previous question, a dilatory tactic commonly used to thwart legislative action.

1850 The Missouri Compromise unravels, throwing off the balance of power in the Senate and setting the stage for the Civil War.

1913 The Seventeenth Amendment provides for the direct election of senators.

1917 The Senate agrees to a cloture rule, which ends debate if 2/3 of the senators agree to proceed to a vote.

1947 The number of standing committees in the House is reduced from 48 to 19.

1974 The number of votes required to end debate is reduced from 2/3 to 3/5 of the Senate.

1800

1900

2000

1789 The First Congress meets in New York City.

1820 The Missouri Compromise ensures that proslavery and antislavery forces will be numerically balanced in the Senate.

1890 Reed's Rules take effect, dramatically increasing the majority party's power and that of the Speaker of the House.

1911 A revolt against Speaker Cannon installs seniority system for determining chairmanship of House committees.

1911 The size of the House is capped at 435.

1947 The number of standing committees in the Senate is reduced from 33 to 15.

1995 Speaker Newt Gingrich introduces term limits for committee chairs, and partially abandons the seniority system for choosing them.

considered so central to American politics that, by law, he or she is second in line behind the vice president in the presidential succession. Should the president and vice president both die or otherwise become unable to serve out the term, the Speaker automatically becomes president. In fact, the Speaker of the House and his or her counterpart in the Senate, the Senate majority leader, often meet together and with the president on weighty matters of state. In the 1890s, Congress began to follow rules adopted by then Speaker of the House Thomas Reed, perhaps the most feared and powerful person ever to hold that post. Congress was deadlocked on tariff policy because coalitions continually unraveled due to free riding and coalition raiding. The minority party used tactics repeatedly to derail legislation favored by the majority. By controlling the agenda more effectively in the House, Reed achieved his goal of raising tariffs. This is a classic example of how institutional changes within the House can bring about policy consequences that have important effects on the economy. **Reed's Rules**, which are still in place, specify procedural guidelines for how the majority–party leadership should determine who sits on which committees, how the order of business should be decided, and how the majority party should limit the powers of the minority party. To a large extent, Congress today operates under the broad guidelines of these rules.

Below the House Speaker in the majority party are the **majority leader** and **whip**, who help the Speaker organize the chamber for business, raise money for elections, and encourage party members to vote for party-sponsored bills. The minority party also elects its leaders, the minority leader and the minority whip. (The term *whip* is derived from the British word for the person who keeps the dogs in line during foxhunts.)

Reed's Rules Procedural guidelines used by the majority-party leadership for determining who sits on which committees, how the order of business should be decided, and how the majority party should limit the powers of the minority party.

majority leader The head of the party holding a majority of seats and, in the Senate, the leader of the Senate. In the House, the majority leader is second to the Speaker of the House.

whip A member of the House or Senate who is elected by his or her party to help party leaders coordinate party members' actions, including enforcing party discipline.

Coordination among party leadership is an important institutional element that shapes legislative behavior and outcomes and helps solve inherent collective dilemmas in Congress. The current Republican party leaders in the House of Representatives are Speaker John Boehner (second from right), Majority Leader Kevin McCarthy (right), and Majority Whip Steve Scalise (far left).

In the Senate, the majority party chooses the Senate majority leader and also a party whip, while the minority party elects the minority leader and minority whip. Additional leadership posts include the chairs of the four party caucuses (one for each party in each chamber) and the four fund-raising committees (again, one for each party in each chamber). Together with the top leaders, these legislators gather often to plan legislative and electoral strategy. The leaders of the majority party determine the content and order of business. For example, they choose which proposed bills will be considered and when, and which bills will be ignored. Both the majority and the minority leaders appoint committee members and select who will be allowed to speak from the floor and in what order.

Proponents of the partisan model of Congress emphasize that party leaders stand at the center of congressional politics. In this view, the winners in the legislature are those currently represented by the majority party. Minority-party members routinely lose in their efforts to pass legislation or gain pork for their district. Majority-party leaders in Congress, when united as a group, rarely allow competing bills to reach the floor for a vote. And party leaders often use their prerogative to punish recalcitrant party members by denying them sought-after committee assignments, and reward loyal party members with plum committee assignments. The leaders devote considerable energy to crafting a theme for the upcoming election and assisting, both financially and administratively, loyal party members who are in danger of losing their seats.

Although it is hard to deny that party leaders are extremely important, their power is limited by the persistent individualism of their members. As a result, political parties in Congress are relatively weak in contrast to their parliamentary counterparts in other countries. This means there is less party unity in voting. It is not uncommon in Congress for as many as 20 percent of a party's members to vote against their party's stated position and the majority of their colleagues. As discussed earlier (and in the following), this type of voting defection is rare in other countries because party leaders effectively choose who can serve in parliament by controlling who gets on the ballot at election time.

Committees

While the leadership orchestrates business, much of the detailed legislative work in Congress occurs in committees. Committees have jurisdictions, which means they have discretion over certain policy areas. For instance, foreign aid bills are sent to the Senate Foreign Relations Committee in that chamber, and most likely to the Appropriations Committee in the House. Farm-related bills go to the agriculture committees, and those for science funding are sent either to the Science Committee in the House or to the Commerce, Science, and Transportation Committee in the Senate.

Types of Committees There are several types of congressional committees. The most well known are the **standing committees**, which remain in existence permanently unless they are formally abolished. Among these are the important House Ways and Means Committee and Senate Finance Committee, which deal with taxes and spending. Committees with more specialized jurisdictions, such as agriculture, science, veterans' affairs, small business, or foreign relations, tend to attract members whose constituents care deeply about or are directly affected by policy in these areas. Agriculture committees, therefore, are primarily composed of members who represent states with large farming sectors, while committees that deal with federal government operations are heavily populated by legislators from Maryland, Virginia, and West Virginia, which are home to the majority of the federal government's offices.[24]

Special (or **select**) **committees** are formed for a specific purpose and are dissolved in principle after accomplishing their tasks. An example is the Joint

standing committee A group of legislators given permanent jurisdiction over a particular issue area or type of policy.

special (or select) committee A committee appointed to consider a special issue or serve a special function that disbands once it has completed its duties.

[24] The boundaries among committees' responsibilities shift over time. Frequently, committees jockey for control of a particular type of policy. The Speaker of the House or the Senate majority leader arbitrates disagreements in the respective chambers. Control over the outcome of these disagreements is one of the sources of a chamber leader's power. See David C. King, *Turf Wars: How Congressional Committees Claim Jurisdiction* (Chicago: University of Chicago Press, 1997).

Select Committee on Deficit Reduction (or its nickname, the Supercommittee), which was created in 2011 to avoid partisan gridlock on budget matters that could have led to the United States defaulting on its loans. The Supercommittee was also an example of a joint committee. **Joint committees** include members from both the House and the Senate—there is a Joint Committee on Taxation, for instance. In recent years, the House and Senate Select Intelligence Committees have acted in tandem, submitting joint reports and regularly meeting together. In practice, many select committees end up being as permanent as standing committees. Three Senate select committees—on Indian affairs, intelligence, and aging—have existed for decades.

joint committee A committee made up of members of both the House and Senate.

Conference committees consist of members of both chambers and are sometimes formed when each chamber passes a different version of the same bill. These committees, which are formed specific to a given bill and at the point in the process when the two chambers agree that reconciliation of the two bills is necessary, play a crucial role in congressional lawmaking. Most bills that pass do not require the formation and use of a conference committee, and often the two chambers work out their differences without conference committees. But conference committees become necessary for many important and controversial bills. Their job is to craft a compromise bill that both chambers will eventually approve.

conference committee A meeting of legislators from the House and Senate to reconcile two bills passed on the same topic.

The House Rules Committee, the traditional vehicle used by the majority party leadership to control House business, deserves special note. It determines which bills get considered for votes, under which amendment rules, and in which order. (We will discuss this committee in more detail later.) In general, since the late nineteenth century, the Rules Committee has been dominated by majority-party members with close ties to the party leadership, and has served as a means for the leadership to stop and start legislative action. The Rules Committee can prevent a bill from being voted on by the chamber. By tradition, the majority party holds 9 of the 13 seats on the Rules Committee, and the Speaker tightly controls which majority-party members sit on the committee.

Committee Membership Each committee has a chair who oversees its work. Chairs of the major committees are powerful people in the American political system. In many instances, they can by themselves determine the fate of legislation. They can defeat a bill by slowing it down in the committee, ignoring it, or encouraging colleagues to amend it to death by watering it down to such an extent that it no longer accomplishes its original purpose. Chairs can also insert items into bills with dramatic consequences. In one instance of major historical importance, Howard Smith of Virginia, chair of the House Rules Committee in the early 1960s, single-handedly inserted into the bill that eventually became the Civil Rights Act of 1964 a provision that gender was to be a protected category similar to race. This meant that people could be sued for discriminating against people because of their sex. He made the provision a requirement of his

The role of committees in allowing members to examine specialized information in specific policy areas is central to the expertise model of Congress. Above, Senator Orrin Hatch discusses data related to the oil industry during a Senate Finance Committee hearing in 2011.

support for the bill. Many historians believe that Smith, who generally opposed new federal civil rights laws for blacks, actually made the addition to kill the bill. He mistakenly thought that his colleagues would reject the new provision and thus the bill.

Furthermore, most standing committees have subcommittees to address specific topics. Composed of members of the full committee, subcommittees can be quite important, with subcommittee chairs wielding considerable power over legislation in their jurisdiction.

Determining committee assignments is a highly political process. As previously noted, members on all committees are assigned by their party leaders, and the majority of seats on each committee are held by majority-party members. In support of the partisan model of Congress, research has shown that party leaders reward loyal party members by granting them their choice of committee assignments. They likewise punish those who have been disloyal by giving them undesirable committee assignments, using the committee assignment process as one tool to keep members in line.

Consequences of the Committee System The committee system is well suited to accomplishing two somewhat contradictory goals: creating better public policy and assisting members in their re-election efforts. First, as proponents of the informational model of Congress point out, the committee system provides expertise to improve lawmaking and is the key, distinctive institutional feature of Congress. Crafting effective public policy that will make constituents content and want to re-elect incumbents is difficult. The average member of Congress may not know much about agricultural price supports, or the finer points of nuclear power, or defense strategy in the Middle East. But by creating a committee system and enabling members to specialize, both the entire legislative body and the entire country benefit. This basic function of committees—to provide better knowledge—is the centerpiece of the informational model.

Second, the committee system is well suited to members' individualism. The system fragments political power and redirects the limelight, enabling members to play a role in crafting legislation and earn credit from constituents. Each member, through his or her role on key committees of concern to constituents, can credibly claim to be powerful and important. Furthermore, as proponents of the distributional model of Congress point out, committees give special opportunities to their members to insert into legislation language granting government projects specifically to one district or state.[25]

[25] Kenneth A. Shepsle, *The Giant Jigsaw Puzzle: Democratic Committee Assignments in the Modern House* (Chicago: University of Chicago Press, 1978).

The internal makeup of the U.S. Congress varies from that of parliaments in other countries mostly because of the power of its committees. Congressional committees act as gatekeepers for nearly all legislation proposed for the national government. Although there are committees in most nations' parliaments, they play a less important role. This is because drafting, amending, and debating legislation usually occurs within the cabinet of the head of government before the legislation is sent to the parliament for approval. The main personnel in the executive departments and the leaders of the government, therefore, have already vetted legislation introduced to the parliaments. Bills are presented to the parliament as *faits accomplis*, to be voted "up" or "down" (almost always up) with little need for committee work. Political party leaders in other countries are far and away the most powerful actors in the legislature, serving as arbiters of which legislative members may speak, propose amendments to legislation, or run for re-election. In short, the existence of powerful committees is a feature that makes the U.S. Congress less hierarchical than its foreign counterparts. Table 5.1 shows the major committees in Congress, plus a few smaller ones.

Other Internal Features

Besides parties and committees, there are other elements that make up the institutional machinery inside Congress. Nonparty caucuses, congressional staffers, and bureaus that carry out research services and other activities play important roles.

Caucuses In addition to the party caucuses in each chamber (made up of the members of that party), nonparty **caucuses** represent a third way for members to group themselves and conduct business. Unlike committees, caucuses are not given formal legislative power, nor do they command much in the way of resources or disciplinary mechanisms to hold their members in line. Rather, they are a means by which groups of members can push agendas that are not pursued within the parties or the committees. Several important caucuses align by racial identity, such as the Congressional Black Caucus, or by ideology, such as the Congressional Progressive Caucus. And some caucuses have only one member![26]

caucus In a legislature, a group of legislators that unites to promote an agenda not pursued within the parties or the legislative committees.

Staff Congressional staff play a large role in Congress. Hired by representatives and senators who have many competing demands on their time, staffers are indispensable. They operate members' offices; communicate with constituents, the press, and other staffers on the members' behalf; organize the members' schedules; and even advise members and help them write legislation. Senior staffers, who make a career of working on Capitol Hill, tend to work directly

[26] The term *caucus* can be confusing. A party caucus is a meeting of party members. Nonparty caucuses are groups of legislators who pursue common policy goals that are more specific than the broad ideological goals pursued by parties.

TABLE 5.1

Selected Congressional Committees, 2014

Committee Name	Description	Number of Members
House Committee on Financial Services	Addresses issues pertaining to the economy, banking system, housing, insurance, and securities and exchanges	61
House Committee on Appropriations	Appropriates all funds that the U.S. Treasury will spend	51
House Committee on Ways and Means	Serves as the chief tax-writing committee in the House	39
House Committee on Homeland Security	Crafts legislations and holds hearings for matters of domestic security.	31
House Committee on Rules	Determines the rules under which the House will receive a piece of legislation	13
Senate Committee on Armed Forces	Responsible for the common defense and all branches of the U.S. military	26
Senate Committee on Banking, House, and Urban Affairs	Charged with the policy areas that include banking, insurance, financial markets, mass transit, housing, and urban development	22
Senate Committee on the Judiciary	Considers presidential nominations for federal judgeships, and oversees the Department of Justice	18
Senate Committee on Foreign Relations	Considers all diplomatic presidential nominations, and responsible for treaties and legislation related to foreign relations	18
Senate Committee on Indian Affairs	Oversees the issues pertaining to American Indian education, health care, economic development, land management, and claims against the United States.	14
Senate Commission on Security and Cooperation in Europe	Monitors and aims to advance European security	9

for a committee and can be very influential in shaping how the committee operates and makes decisions. Staff sizes have grown substantially since the 1950s, although that growth has recently tailed off. There are currently around 11,000 staffers who work for members of Congress.

Separate from staff who work directly on legislative business, members of Congress also hire staff to manage their re-election campaigns. Funding and staffing for legislative work and for campaign work must be kept separate by law, but the growth in numbers of both kinds of staff help explain the

The Congressional Hispanic Caucus focuses on issues that affect minority groups, especially the Hispanic community. Above, the members of the caucus appear with Vice President Joe Biden in 2013.

substantial incumbency advantage. The legislative staff can help work on pork-barrel aspects of legislation and constituency service, while campaign staff can help with the direct work of running the re-election campaign, such as raising money and appealing to constituents for their vote.

Research Services Congress has created its own internal bureaucracy to help its members conduct research and carry out other duties. These congressional bureaus have become increasingly important as counterweights to the bureaus that formally reside in the executive branch. The congressional bureaus, such as the Congressional Budget Office (CBO), were created because members of Congress, especially in the wake of the Nixon administration's Watergate scandal in the 1970s, had become suspicious of the data presented by executive branch agencies. The CBO, for example, was established as a balance to the executive Office of Management and Budget (OMB), which was regarded as too closely tied to the president's own political goals. The Congressional Research Service provides reports on policy topics upon request for members of Congress. One example of such reports is an analysis that shows how well Veterans Administration hospitals are meeting the needs of soldiers returning from war who have experienced trauma leading to mental illness. This report is designed to help the House and Senate Veterans Affairs Committees write legislation to improve matters in these hospitals. Those who regard the informational model of Congress as the most convincing focus on how institutions have grown within the chambers to help members navigate the complexities of modern policies. The expertise provided by staffers and research agencies is part of what makes it possible for members to make knowledgeable decisions.

The Process of Lawmaking

We have learned about the incentives that motivate members of Congress and the institutions inside of Congress. We now turn to the process of lawmaking. In this section, we will see how the institutions inside of Congress work to assist members in overcoming their collective dilemmas and principal-agent problems to pass legislation.

Proposals

Passing a law in Congress begins with at least one member of either the House or the Senate submitting a bill to his or her respective chamber. Only legislators themselves can formally submit a bill; no one else, not even the president, can do so. Some bills are proposed that everyone knows were written by the Office of the President, executive branch agencies, or interest groups, but they must always be submitted by surrogates in Congress. Bills can have multiple sponsors; sponsoring a popular bill can earn kudos from constituents, and sometimes there are dozens and even hundreds of sponsors of a bill.

The volume of proposed bills is huge—around 9,000 per year in recent sessions. Once submitted in either the House or Senate, bills are given a number in each chamber and assigned to a committee and then usually to a subcommittee. With 9,000 bills per year proposed, party leaders have to solve a massive coordination problem. The only way to focus members' attention and effort is to ignore most of the proposed bills so that the members of their party can coordinate action on a select few. Otherwise, members will divide their efforts among too many bills competing for attention. Given the work needed to pass legislation, this would risk none of the bills being passed. In fact, thousands of bills are proposed every year by members knowing that they will not be acted upon, but the members have their own reasons for submitting bills, typically to brag to specific constituents that they did so.

Referrals

Which committee receives a given bill is usually determined by its topic, and the assignment is routinely doled out by the nonpartisan parliamentarian. But for important or controversial bills, the Speaker of the House and Senate majority-party leaders can use the process of referral strategically. For instance, if the Speaker does not like a bill about agricultural trade and has a choice between sending it to the Agriculture Committee or the International Relations Committee, he or she can send it to the one where it is more likely to be ignored or killed. Through these kinds of decisions, the Speaker in effect solves the coordination problem through agenda control, but in a way that suits his or her preferences.

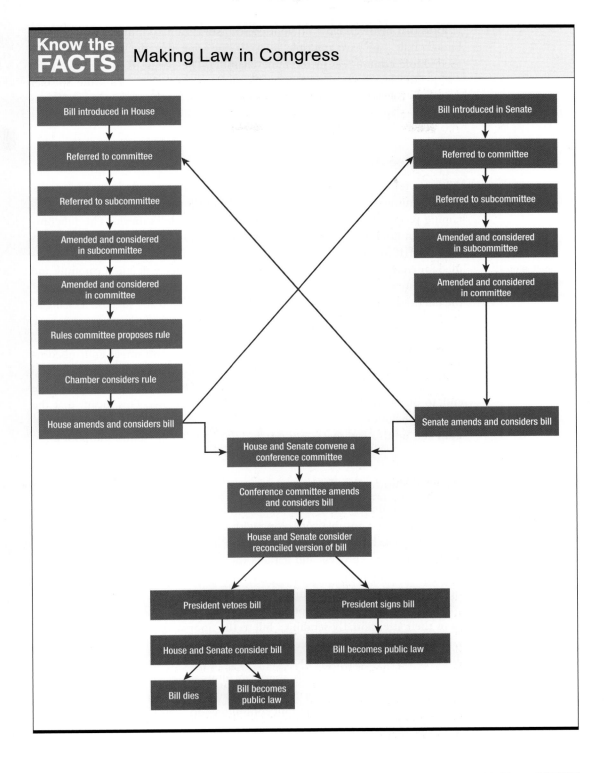

Bills that involve many different policy issues, such as omnibus (multi-issue) budget bills, can have multiple referrals, meaning that the same bill can go to multiple committees in the same chamber. The House Republicans in the 1990s and early 2000s tried to take advantage of rules that permit the Speaker to split a bill into sections and give sections to specific committees. This is known as a **split referral**.

split referral A rule (in place since 1975) that permits the Speaker to split a bill into sections and give sections to specific committees.

Committee Action

All but a few bills are simply ignored by committee and subcommittee chairs. Subcommittees tend to do the bulk of the work for bills taken seriously, entertaining proposed amendments and deliberating the bill's merits. The subcommittee can hold hearings where experts are called in to testify about the merits of the bill. If the subcommittee decides to move forward, then the bill is scheduled for **markup**, which means that the subcommittee will edit it carefully and incorporate any approved amendments. The subcommittee can then "report" the bill (meaning to pass it along with their approval and any suggested changes) to the full committee, which can in turn conduct its own hearings and mark up the bill as well.

markup A committee or subcommittee process where committee members edit and amend bills.

Much of the real politics of Congress occurs in committees and subcommittees, especially in the House. Members must often bargain, compromise, and trade votes with fellow committee members to fashion bills that seem, in the end, to be "lowest-common-denominator" types of laws. This means that the bill only includes provisions that have widespread support; often those provisions add up to a law that is not much different from the status quo policy.

Moving Bills to the Floor

If the full committee wishes to move forward, it sends the bill to the floor of the chamber for a possible vote, along with a written report that explains why it should be passed (this is why we say a bill is "reported"). If a bill passes through the subcommittee process and gathers the support of enough full committee members to be reported to the floor with a positive report, its chances of passage by the full chamber are high.

This process is where proponents of the informational model of Congress focus their attention. By sending a bill to the floor with a recommendation for passage, a committee is in effect saying, "We think this bill will make good law, and you should listen to us because we are specialists on the topic." If that is the main thing committees do—serve as filters to let good laws through and stop bad laws—then the informational model would seem to have considerable merit. In contrast, if the main thing committees do is take legislation and load it up with pork or with other kinds of special favors to specific constituents, then of course the distributional model seems more appropriate for describing Congress.

In the House, as mentioned earlier, the Rules Committee plays a critical role at the point when other committees approve a bill and send it out for consideration by the entire chamber floor. The Rules Committee formally decides the bills to be considered for votes on the floor, what rules will be applied—such as the types of amendments that are permitted as the proposed legislation comes out of committee markup—and how much time will be allotted for debate. Through this committee, House party leaders have greater authority than their Senate counterparts over what happens on the floor of the chamber. Scholars argue that having something like a Rules Committee is vital to the proper functioning of a large chamber like the House. Without an agenda-setter, the House would be far more vulnerable to the problems of unstable coalitions and other collective dilemmas, such as a lack of coordination among different committees working on the same bill.

The House Rules Committee's options for amendments allowable on the floor, for example, include:

- **Open rule**, which means any amendment can be proposed.
- **Closed rule**, which means no amendments can be proposed.
- **Restricted** (or **modified**) **rule**, which specifies that only certain kinds of amendments are allowed. This typically is a "germaneness rule," which means that only amendments pertaining to the original purpose of the bill can be proposed.

open rule A provision that allows any amendment to be proposed once a bill comes to the chamber floor.

closed rule A provision that allows no amendments to be proposed once a bill comes to the chamber floor.

restricted (or modified) rule A provision that allows only certain kinds of amendments to be proposed once a bill comes to the floor, typically only amendments that pertain to the original purpose of the bill.

The majority-party leadership in the House, through the Rules Committee, can choose an amendment rule to thwart its opponents on a bill. Those opponents could be within the majority party or among the minority-party members. Consider several scenarios. First, assuming the leadership likes a bill and wants to see it passed in something similar to its present form, it may worry about the bill being amended to death on the floor so that its main effects are gutted. In this case, the Rules Committee would adopt either a closed or a restricted rule. Second, assuming the leadership does not like a bill in its present form, but wants to pass something along the same lines, then it would adopt a restricted or open rule and let allies on the floor offer amendments to change the bill accordingly. Third, assuming the leadership does not like a bill and wants to see it killed but feels public pressure to allow a floor vote, it may permit the bill to go to the floor under an open rule and let an unrestricted amendment process gut and perhaps even kill the bill. Scholars in favor of the partisan model of Congress often use the centrality of the Rules Committee in the legislative process as evidence to support their claims. Majority-party leadership can use the committee's powers over debate and amendment to get what it wants. The Rules Committee can itself kill a bill, even if that bill has been reported out of another committee.[27]

The Senate's process of moving a bill from committee to the floor is different from that of the House and gives less control to the majority party in that chamber. The Senate has a long tradition of giving more power to individual senators, even those from the minority party, to raise objections, propose amendments, and even halt legislation. Thus, the Senate has a reputation for being the slower, more cautious chamber, with more potential roadblocks put up by senators objecting to a bill.

There is no rules committee in the Senate, and in theory there are no limits on debate or on amendments from the floor. In the House, most of the real action is in the committees, whereas in the Senate, it is at least as common for real action to occur on the floor of the chamber as in committees. Less work happens in committees in the Senate than in the House because of the long-standing tradition of debate and amendment of bills on the floor of the Senate. Why should a committee bother to devote a lot of time to markups if their work will be undone on the floor? Let us explore these aspects and others about the Senate in more detail.

Senate Distinctiveness

unanimous consent agreement Rules under which the Senate debates, offers amendments, and votes on a given bill. All members of the chamber must agree to them, so any senator can object and halt progress on a bill.

Although unlimited debate and open-amendment rules are in theory the way of the Senate, in practice the Senate uses **unanimous consent agreements** for relatively uncontroversial bills. These agreements describe rules for a given bill regarding debate and amendments on the floor. They are unanimous in that all senators must agree to them, and any senator can object and halt progress on a bill. Like the House Rules Committee, these agreements are an institutional means by which the members in the chamber can restrain individual action and solve collective dilemmas. In the absence of a unanimous consent agreement, for instance, the Senate could keep voting repeatedly for newly amended bills, producing voting cycles, because each senator could in theory keep proposing new amendments under the open rules.

filibuster Instances in which senators, once recognized to speak on the floor, talk for an extended period ("hold the floor") in an attempt to block the rest of the Senate from voting on a bill.

Individual senators even have certain powers to halt the progress of a bill they do not like. As mentioned, they can refuse to approve a unanimous consent agreement specifying a rule for debate and amendment. Or they can **filibuster**, which means that once recognized to speak on the floor, a senator can talk for hours, days, or even weeks to prevent any other action from happening

[27] There are rare instances when a majority of the House has used a *discharge petition* to force a regular standing committee or the Rules Committee to report out a bill that would otherwise die in committee. When that happens, members can petition to require a floor debate or a floor vote. If the petition gets a majority of votes, then the Speaker must comply. In a famous example, the Bipartisan Campaign Finance Act (known as the McCain-Feingold Act, after its authors), which eventually passed in 2002, was discharged several times over a four-year period, forcing debate and votes on the floor against the wishes of party leaders, including the Speaker. The discharge petition is rare enough that we can still ascribe very strong agenda-setting powers to the Rules Committee.

on the bill. The filibustering senator hopes that the bill's proponents will get tired or frustrated and drop the proposed legislation. The current record is held by the late Strom Thurmond of South Carolina, who spoke for more than 24 hours straight to prevent his colleagues from voting on a civil rights bill in 1957. In March 2013, Kentucky Senator Rand Paul filibustered the appointment of John Brennan, the candidate whom President Obama nominated to become the director of the CIA, for nearly 13 hours. Although this filibuster did not prevent the appointment, it did ignite considerable support from many conservative Americans. The current rules of the Senate allow for a filibuster to occur simply by invoking it for a specific bill without the requirement that someone actually speak on the floor. This rule allows Senate business to continue on other bills while a given bill is being filibustered. Fellow senators can stop a filibuster by voting to invoke **cloture**, which is a rule to limit debate on a bill to a specific number of hours. For many years, it took two-thirds of the Senate to invoke cloture, but that was changed in 1975. It now takes 60 votes to approve cloture. In practice, this rule means that (with rare exceptions) any bill that is not supported by at least 60 senators will not be approved and will therefore not become law. In 2013 the Democratic majority in the Senate changed the cloture rules so that only 51 votes would be required to invoke cloture when confirming judicial and executive branch appointees (with the exception of Supreme Court justice nominees).

cloture A rule that limits debate on a bill to a specific number of hours. Senate rules require 60 senators to support such a motion to end debate (including filibusters) and proceed to a vote.

The procedures of the Senate tend to keep legislation flowing in spite of the powers of senators to stymie legislation. More than members of the House, senators have developed norms for cooperation and for collegiality in their everyday interactions with each other. Most of the time senators, even from the opposing party, do not object to rules of debate and voting on the floor proposed by the majority-party leadership. They typically give their approval to a unanimous consent agreement by not objecting, unless they feel very strongly about the bill. In other words, the norm among senators is not to abuse their individual prerogatives on issues that are not all that important to them. The norms in the Senate are one way that senators can overcome the various collective dilemmas arising from their temptations to halt any collective actions that they do not like.

There is some evidence that in recent decades, as the major political parties in Congress have polarized ideologically, that the norms just described have frayed somewhat. The use of holds, filibusters, and arcane parliamentary maneuvers to achieve legislative goals has increased, according to scholars. We will discuss these trends in more detail shortly.

Floor Action

Floor debate can be a dramatic event in either chamber, and some of the most memorable moments in congressional history have occurred when members gave rousing speeches about historic pieces of legislation. Particularly eloquent members, such as Senator Henry Clay of Kentucky in the nineteenth century,

Overcoming the Filibuster to Pass a Major Bill

Following the 2008 elections, the Democratic Party controlled the House, Senate, and presidency. They held a 60-seat majority in the Senate, which meant that they had just enough votes to invoke cloture and override any filibuster attempts. With such dominance of the national government, it was expected that their signature campaign proposal—health care reform—would pass.

However, when Democratic senator Edward Kennedy of Massachusetts died in 2009, Republican Scott Brown won a special election to fill the seat. The Democrats now had 59 seats, and the Republicans, who despised the proposed health care reform policies, could in principle filibuster in the Senate and defeat the legislation. The Democrats were one vote short of being able to invoke cloture to stop a filibuster.

Interests

President Obama came into office claiming a mandate to reform the health care system and provide insurance coverage for all Americans. Many voters, interest groups, and party activists who supported Obama and his fellow Democrats urged them to make good on their promises and pass a comprehensive health care reform. Arrayed against them were not only the Republicans in Congress but also numerous interest groups and many voters who intensely disliked the policies being proposed. They resented that the reforms would likely mean higher taxes or premiums for health insurance and larger government bureaucracies. The loud voices against the health care reform were heard clearly by the Republicans, and party members in Congress promised to do what they could to thwart reform efforts.

Institutions

A little-known institutional detail in the U.S. Congress enables leaders in the Senate to bypass the filibuster on rare occasions. A process called budget reconciliation is a tool by which Congress can "reconcile" disparities between the federal budget and entitlement spending or taxes. The Center on Budget and Policy Priorities explains it as a "deficit-reduction tool to force committees to produce spending cuts or tax increases called for in the budget resolution."[1] This procedure allows for a 20-hour limit on debate over legislation involving budget reconciliation. This limit removes the opportunity for senators of the opposition to filibuster a piece of legislation. In addition, for a bill to pass under bud-

The intensity of the debate over health care reform pushed Democrats to use arcane Senate rules to pass the legislation.

get reconciliation, it requires only a simple majority of 51 votes, which the Democratic leaders reasoned would allow health care reform to pass even if a small number of their fellow Democratic senators voted against it.

Outcomes

For Democrats, using the rare budget reconciliation procedure was too tempting to pass up. This maneuver enabled the Democrats to pass one of the most controversial bills in American history—the Patient Protection and Affordable Care Act.

Think About It

Is having the filibuster a good institutional feature? Is allowing for the occasional budget reconciliation procedure a good institutional feature? With a bill of such enormous importance, should either one of these parliamentary maneuvers be allowed?

[1] Center on Budget and Policy Priorities, "Policy Basics: Introduction to the Federal Budget Process," January 3, 2011, www.cbpp.org/cms /?fa=view&id=155 (accessed 11/6/12).

could compel their colleagues to compromise over deeply divisive issues like slavery and tariffs by the sheer force of their rhetoric. But often floor debates are dull, especially in the House, with members taking turns to enhance their reputations back home in front of the television cameras. Members sometimes hold the floor when the chamber is virtually empty—when everyone else is either in committee meetings or otherwise engaged—and talk to a camera so that constituents back home can catch a glimpse of the legislator in action.

After all the debating and amending is completed, the leadership schedules a vote, which on important pieces of legislation occurs by roll call. With a roll-call vote, each member's name is called and he or she responds "yea," "nay," or "abstain." ("Abstain" usually indicates that the member doesn't want to take a position on an issue for political reasons.) The roll call is taken electronically in the House and verbally in the Senate. These final roll-call votes are reported publicly and are important in building a member's reputation with constituents and interest groups. Many interest groups tally the roll-call votes on key bills and use them to craft members' "scores" to determine which members are friends and foes of the group.

Conference Committees

Although both chambers start the entire process with the same text for a bill, the bills that emerge from each chamber may be significantly different from the original bill and from each other. Often the two chambers work it out through informal negotiations or by one chamber just adopting the other chamber's version of the bill. Or sometimes it is clear that one chamber will not compromise, and the bill may just die. But other times, the bill goes to formal negotiating process in a House–Senate conference committee to be "reconciled"—that is, for the differences to be ironed out. If the conference committee cannot reconcile the two versions of the bill into one common bill, then the proposed legislation dies. The death of legislation after going to a conference committee is uncommon, because both chambers have devoted so much energy to the bill already and have built considerable steam behind its passage. More typically, the conference committee agrees on a single text, perhaps after much compromise and haggling among committee members. Very few bills are defeated at this point, as the conference committee members tend to be careful to approve compromises that their own chamber will support. However it happens, through a conference committee or through less formal bargaining processes, the identical bill passed by both chambers is called the "enrolled bill." The enrolled bill must be voted on by both chambers.

Presidential Signature

At this point, the bill's long journey is almost over. It now goes to the president's desk, whereupon the president has several options. He or she can sign the bill and it becomes law. The president can veto the bill and send it back to Congress, where it can still become law if two-thirds of the members of both chambers override the veto. If the president does not sign the bill within 10 days, it automatically becomes law if Congress is still in session. If Congress adjourns before the 10 days have passed, and the president has not signed the bill, the bill is effectively vetoed in what is called a **pocket veto**. Since the outgoing Congress has no opportunity to override a pocket veto, the legislation must wait until the next session, when the new Congress can pass a similar bill and force the president to make an explicit choice between signing and vetoing it. Congress in recent decades has become more careful in the timing of legislation, paying attention to the 10-day deadline prior to adjournment. Thus, the use of the pocket veto has become extremely rare.

pocket veto A veto that occurs automatically if a president does not sign a bill for 10 days after passage in Congress and Congress has adjourned during that 10-day period.

Making Law in a Separation-of-Powers System

In considering how Congress makes law, it is important to note that Congress does not act independently of the other two branches. Its actions do not have much meaning or effect without them. In fact, the executive branch also has legislative powers. No piece of legislation can take effect until the president signs a bill into law (or Congress overrides a veto). A president can thwart congressional action in multiple ways, including the veto. Furthermore, Congress has no capacity to carry out its laws. The executive branch, through executive agencies under the direction of the president, enforces, executes, and promulgates policies described in the laws passed by Congress.[28] As for the judiciary, Congress has no authorized powers or capacity to adjudicate disputes that arise over the interpretations of laws or in the enforcement of laws. Rather, it must rely on the courts that make up the judicial branch to perform this critical task. A noteworthy exception is a presidential impeachment trial, which occurs in the Senate and is presided over by the chief justice of the Supreme Court.

The most contentious and consequential interactions among branches in the national government occur between Congress and the president. The separation of powers often requires that Congress repeatedly bargain with the president over policies. The two branches represent different constituencies and see their roles in the American political system as distinct. We will discuss interbranch politics in greater detail in Chapter 6.

[28] D. Roderick Kiewiet and Mathew D. McCubbins, *The Logic of Delegation: Congressional Parties and the Appropriations Process* (Chicago: University of Chicago Press, 1991); David Epstein and Sharyn O'Halloran, *Delegating Powers: A Transaction Cost Politics Approach to Policy Making under Separate Powers* (New York: Cambridge University Press, 1999).

In Comparison: Legislative Institutions

At various points in this chapter, we have highlighted differences between the U.S. Congress and other legislatures around the world. We have discussed why members of Congress see the success of their careers as being closely linked to their individual reputations for being good agents for the voters in their specific constituencies. In most other democracies, legislators succeed or fail based on how loyal they are to party leaders. Furthermore, inside of Congress much of the action in crafting policy occurs within committees. The details of legislating happen in negotiations among committee leaders, party leaders, and sometimes people in the White House, including the president. In most other democracies, legislation is crafted by the executive and then simply voted on by the parliament.

Compare, for instance, how the French legislature works. French lawmakers get elected to the lower house, the National Assembly, mostly by virtue of working as loyal party members and being nominated by local party committees to run for office in a given district. France has single-member districts but uses a majority runoff system. Party leaders can prevent a legislator from running in a district if that legislator is disloyal to the party. Little of what occurs inside the French parliament resembles the operations of the American Congress. The National Assembly receives proposals for legislation from the French prime minister and the executive cabinet (the heads of the various national bureaucratic ministries). Prime ministers in countries like France are chosen from among parliamentary members by the parliament itself, so the prime minister's government has the support of a majority in the parliament. The Assembly, after receiving the proposed legislation, has a short time to offer suggested revisions and comment on the draft. The members of the Assembly, in public sessions, question members of the prime minister's cabinet about policy matters, but these sessions are largely for show. Then the Assembly votes on the proposed legislation and nearly always approves it. Unlike in Congress, where the work of legislating happens inside the chambers, in France the work of legislating happens inside the prime minister's government. The legislature more or less rubber-stamps what is proposed by the executive officers.

The French system is similar to that of most other democracies. Even in countries with presidential, separation-of-powers systems, such as Brazil or Argentina, parliaments rarely have the kinds of active legislation-writing duties that fall upon the U.S. Congress.

It is also worth noting how state legislatures compare to Congress. The states have intentionally modeled their state-level legislatures on the national Congress. With the sole exception of Nebraska, all states have bicameral legislatures.[29] The procedures for lawmaking, the organization of the chambers, and

---

[29] Nebraska has only one chamber as a result of a 1937 ballot initiative, which abolished the state senate. This initiative succeeded when enough voters became convinced that it would save taxpayers' money.

the electoral rules used to elect state representatives and senators are all similar to those used for the U.S. Congress. Even in architectural style, state capitol buildings tend to resemble the home of Congress in Washington, with large domes and Greek Revival architecture. There is one important exception to these similarities. In the U.S. Senate, as mandated by the Constitution, each state has two senators, regardless of population size. As we discussed earlier in this chapter, with the *Baker* and *Wesberry* rulings, the Supreme Court declared that the *one-person/one-vote* principle must apply to state legislative houses and the U.S. House (but not to the U.S. Senate). This means that state senates have to be organized so that each electoral district within the state is roughly the same size by population. So, state houses and state senates have similar representational schemes (and therefore similar political pressures), though the senates generally have fewer members.

Taking Account of Congress

 We started with a puzzle at the beginning of this chapter: How does Congress overcome its collective dilemmas to work together? As we have seen, the answer is that members of Congress have together developed a set of internal institutions designed to overcome the body's collective dilemmas *and* enable members to sustain individual reputations that lead to re-election. Consider several specific institutional features. Having strong committees allows for party leaders to divide the legislative work. Then maintaining agenda control through the Rules Committee in the House and the office of the majority leader in the Senate helps coordinate and control floor action. These features help solve collective dilemmas. But also having large numbers of staff enables the members of Congress to serve constituents directly and investigate opportunities to insert pork into bills. The institutionalization of staff working on committees and in members' offices sustains a system where high re-election rates are the norm.

Although scholars largely agree that the institutions of Congress enable it to accomplish as much as it does collectively—that is, the institutions allow the members to overcome their collective dilemmas as individually elected representatives and senators, but also continue to get re-elected—they disagree about the fundamental nature of those institutions, their operation, and their consequences. Hence the three different models of congressional institutions discussed previously in this chapter.

Under the distributional model, the institutions of Congress are created to help members deliver pork and other special considerations to their districts, and the winners are those people in geographic areas with effective representatives and senators. The losers are everyone else, and perhaps the taxpayers who foot the bill. This model makes sense to the degree that we see logrolling across groups of legislators on bills providing geographically specific benefits, and that we see less attention paid to legislation with broad benefits across the entire country.

The informational model, in contrast, presumes that members of Congress want to pass legislation after becoming better informed because that is the best means to ensure re-election. Members structure lawmaking rules primarily to yield good information on the consequences of public policy, and they want to satisfy most voters. Some might consider the informational model a somewhat upbeat version of Congress, though such a conclusion depends on how information from committees is used by the rest of the members. If their fellow members learn from committees what will make effective public policy—meaning effective and helpful for a large proportion of people in the country—then the informational model presents Congress in a relatively positive light. If the information from committees is mostly used to improve the targeting of policies toward narrow interests, then the model is not much different in effect from the distributive model but just differs in the mechanisms through which narrow interests are served. For the distributional model, committee membership confers advantages by virtue of being present at the markup stage. For the informational model, all members in the Congress benefit from other committees by learning how best to serve their specific constituencies.

The partisan model proposes an ideological, team-oriented approach to understanding Congress. Party members, when necessary, hold together to overcome their own collective dilemmas, and then act in unison to enable Congress as a whole to get things done. The model is particularly apt if we emphasize the passage of the most bitterly contested bills, which pit the two parties against each other. In these cases, party leadership typically takes a firm, united position, demanding party discipline and staking the party's fortunes on the legislation's success. Winners under this model are the voters living in states and districts with representation by politicians from the majority party.

All three models assume that members of Congress are driven by their desire to win re-election, and their actions reflect that goal. Admittedly, these are simplistic versions of how Congress works. Those who subscribe to the partisan model do not believe that the distributional or informational models are irrelevant—that members of Congress are never motivated to understand or predict the consequences of proposed policies, or by the desire to bring pork to their districts. Likewise, the informational model does not posit that political parties are irrelevant in congressional politics. Rather, scholars who espouse these models claim that the assumptions and conclusions associated with them capture the essence of congressional politics better than other models. Strip away the details and the favored model (one of the three) gets to the heart of the matter.

It may be the case that one model best describes Congress for a given era, while another model is more apt for another era. Some scholars argue that

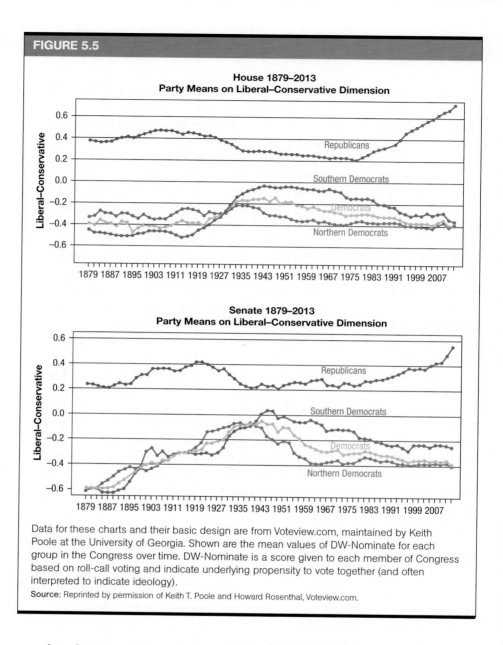

FIGURE 5.5

House 1879–2013
Party Means on Liberal–Conservative Dimension

Republicans

Southern Democrats

Democrats

Northern Democrats

Senate 1879–2013
Party Means on Liberal–Conservative Dimension

Republicans

Southern Democrats

Democrats

Northern Democrats

Data for these charts and their basic design are from Voteview.com, maintained by Keith Poole at the University of Georgia. Shown are the mean values of DW-Nominate for each group in the Congress over time. DW-Nominate is a score given to each member of Congress based on roll-call voting and indicate underlying propensity to vote together (and often interpreted to indicate ideology).

Source: Reprinted by permission of Keith T. Poole and Howard Rosenthal, Voteview.com.

the relevance of the partisan model has fluctuated, and that in our own era it matches the data best. Indeed, the partisan model has gained adherents among political scientists in recent years because of the partisan polarization that has occurred (see Figure 5.5; this is discussed in more detail in Chapter 12). Among members of Congress, since the 1980s Democrats have become more uniformly liberal and Republicans have become more uniformly conservative. There are very few ideological moderates in either chamber, and this has meant less bipartisan cooperation on legislation, more floor and committee votes straight down party lines, and greater use of obstructive tactics by minority parties, especially in the Senate. Political scientists disagree on the causes and consequences of this polarization, but there is little disputing that it has occurred.

The three models focus attention on the inner workings of Congress. There is a fourth, more directly critical view of Congress. These critics focus more attention on the process of election, particularly campaign finance, and less on the workings of internal congressional institutions. They charge that because of the election process, the workings of Congress as a whole are geared toward maintaining a system of governmental benefits for those who are already privileged. They point to the basic fact that wealthy donors provide the vast majority of all the money contributed to congressional candidates. With little public funding for campaigns, American political parties and their candidates must curry the favor of and attract donations from wealthy voters to win elections.[30] The reasonable assumption is that these donors expect favorable legislation in return. Although research linking campaign contributions to legislative favors has largely been inconclusive, these critics argue that the bias toward the wealthy is subtle and really comes in the form of agenda control. The conclusion typically drawn is that policies that would benefit the poor at the expense of the rich do not even make it onto the congressional agenda. The dominance of lobbying and campaign contributions by wealthy corporations means that Congress stands at the center of a political system that maintains privilege for the wealthy in society.

In this chapter, we have analyzed both the workings inside Congress, including three models proposed by political scientists, and the election process that shapes the nature of Congress as a representational institution. The ideas in this chapter—the three models and the criticisms of the election process just described—point to distinct consequences of congressional institutions and give different answers to our opening questions. Given the facts you have learned in this chapter, which ideas are most useful in answering our opening questions, describing Congress, and predicting how it will evolve in the future?

FURTHER READING

★ = Included in *Readings in American Politics*, 3e

Cox, Gary, and Mathew McCubbins, *Legislative Leviathan* (New York: Cambridge University Press, 1992). An account of the House that places great emphasis on how majority-party leaders control committee assignments and

---

[30] Kevin Phillips, *Arrogant Capital* (Boston: Little, Brown, 1994); Thomas Ferguson, *Golden Rule* (Chicago: University of Chicago Press, 1995).

other perks for their party members, and in this way influence the voting decisions of congressional representatives.

★ ———, *Setting the Agenda: Responsible Party Government in the U.S. House of Representatives* (New York: Cambridge University Press, 2005). An account that focuses attention on how leaders of the majority party in the House closely control the agenda, and especially avoid having bills reach the floor that divide the majority-party coalition.

Fenno, Richard, *Congressmen in Committees* (Boston: Little, Brown, 1973). A landmark study of how members of Congress use their prerogatives on committees to serve the specific needs of their constituents.

★ ———, *Home Style: House Members in Their Districts* (Boston: Little, Brown, 1978). A rich account of how members of Congress view their districts, and the kinds of representational styles they use to connect with constituents.

Krehbiel, Keith, *Information and Legislative Organization* (Ann Arbor, MI: University of Michigan Press, 1992). An account that focuses attention on how all decisions made by Congress, including the organization of the chambers, must be approved by the majority—thus, the main purpose of any organizational feature of Congress is to enable the majority to make more informed decisions.

Lublin, David, *The Paradox of Representation: Racial Gerrymandering and Minority Interests in Congress* (Princeton, NJ: Princeton University Press, 1997). Uses comprehensive data to explore whether racial minorities win or lose representation when redistricting works to create districts in which minority groups, such as African Americans, have a majority.

Mayhew, David R., *Congress: The Electoral Connection*, 2nd ed. (New Haven, CT: Yale University Press, 2004). A classic essay that explores the consequences of the basic assumption that members of Congress are primarily motivated by the desire to get re-elected.

Swain, Carol, *Black Faces, Black Interests* (Cambridge, MA: Harvard University Press, 1993). A close exploration of the effects of redistricting efforts designed to increase representation of racial minorities; it argues that in some cases the unintended consequences actually hurt the interests of minority constituents.

Swers, Michele, *The Difference Women Make* (Chicago: University of Chicago Press, 2002). Offers compelling evidence that women in Congress do vote differently than their male counterparts.

KEY TERMS

bicameral legislature (p. 139)

caucus (p. 165)

closed rule (p. 171)

cloture (p. 173)

conference committee (p. 163)

constituency service (p. 150)

delegates (p. 148)

distributional model (p. 155)

filibuster (p. 172)

gerrymandering (p. 146)

incumbency advantage (p. 150)

informational model (p. 155)

joint committee (p. 163)

logrolling (p. 155)

majority leader (p. 160)

markup (p. 170)

open rule (p. 171)

partisan model (p. 156)

party discipline (p. 159)

plurality rule (p. 142)

pocket veto (p. 176)

pork barrel (p. 153)

proportional representation (p. 143)

Reed's Rules (p. 160)

restricted (or modified) rule (p. 171)

single-member district (p. 142)

Speaker of the House (p. 159)

special (or select) committee (p. 162)

split referral (p. 170)

standing committee (p. 162)

trustees (p. 148)

unanimous consent agreement (p. 172)

whip (p. 160)

After seeing that Congress would not pass the DREAM Act that would have stopped the deportation of undocumented immigrants who had come to the United States as children, President Obama issued new guidelines to the Department of Homeland Security restricting deportations. Like most presidents have done, Obama was using certain powers and authorities that allow presidents to shift policy without congressional approval.

6

THE PRESIDENCY

Today, the American presidency is a far more powerful office than the Founders ever envisioned. How have presidents increased their power at the expense of the legislative and judicial branches of government? And why have Congress and the American people allowed this shift in power?

One goal of the first Obama administration was for Congress to pass what was called the DREAM act, which stood for Development, Relief, and Education of Alien Minors. The purpose of the proposed bill was to stop deporting undocumented immigrants who had come to the United States as children with their families and had lived in the country continuously. In 2010, however, the Senate did not pass the bill, to the frustration of the president and his supporters.

A few years later, in the heat of a presidential campaign, President Obama decided to bypass Congress. He made public his administration's change to how federal immigration policy would be implemented. "Effective immediately," Obama announced, "the Department of Homeland Security is taking steps to lift the shadow of deportation" from certain young, undocumented immigrants. More specifically, he set out criteria for people who should not face deportation. They should be age 30 or under who came to the United States under the age 16 and have resided continuously in the country. They must have no federal convictions or significant misdemeanors to their names. Furthermore, they must currently be enrolled in school, graduated high school, earned a general education development certificate, or be an honorably discharged veteran. The president was using his authority to alter the way federal agencies enforced laws against illegal immigration. In this case, it marked a significant change in the types of people the Department of Homeland Security pursued for deportation.

This example would imply that if the president did not like what Congress has done (or not done), the president simply can change how a law is implemented without congressional approval. What is to stop the issuing of such changes whenever Congress stymies what the president wants?

The fact is, the tools available to the president do not give the president complete authority to change how laws are executed. There are constraints on presidential action as we will learn in this chapter. Yet, with immigration and deportation, Obama was clearly using his authority over executive agencies to bypass Congress, achieve his goals, and expand the power of the presidency. He was by no means the first president to do so. Many of his predecessors, including George W. Bush, expanded the authority of the office. Obama, however, while running for president in 2008, criticized his predecessor's actions for overstepping the bounds of legitimate presidential authority. He promised to act differently, consult Congress, and stay well within the limits of the laws as written. Yet Obama has maintained many of Bush's positions on presidential authority. Both Bush and Obama, like other presidents before them, have left or will leave important stamps on the office of the presidency and on the American political system.

According to the Constitution, the presidency is at best equal in power to Congress, and evidence strongly suggests that the Founders generally wanted Congress to be the key decision-making branch. The Founders gave the presidency considerable powers, but they also intended for Congress and the courts to check those powers.

Today, the American presidency is a far more powerful office than the Founders ever envisioned. Presidents, however, have not been the sole advocates of expanding presidential authority. Although the immigration example shows how the president can try to go around Congress, in many cases, Congress and the courts have enabled the presidency to grow stronger.

Why would the other branches of government go along with strengthening the presidency as an institution? If the American people historically have been wary of centralized government power, why do they often support strong presidential powers?

Sources of Presidential Power

Presidential power derives from two main sources. The first source is the Constitution, and includes both enumerated (explicitly described) and implied powers. And the second source is the reputation built from a long history of being the one leader called upon and able to solve collective dilemmas among the states and across the various parts of the national government. Let us explore these sources.

Constitutional Bases of Presidential Power

The Constitutional Convention of 1787 featured intense debate about the organization of the executive branch. Delegates argued over whether to have a single person serve as president or whether an advisory council would be more appropriate. They debated over how the executive was to be chosen—selected by Congress or elected by the people—and over the length of term of office.

Arguments in favor of having a single person as president—made during the Convention and afterward in the *Federalist Papers* by James Madison, Alexander Hamilton, and John Jay—were similar to those used to support a strong national government. Noting the problems that occurred under the Articles of Confederation, promoters of a strong presidency emphasized that states were not meeting their obligations to work toward the collective good of the Union, such as paying their debts from the Revolutionary War. What the country needed, they argued, was a strong executive who would respond decisively to crises, both domestic and foreign, and enforce the laws uniformly and fairly. Thus, the most important aspect of the presidency—one person chosen to lead the executive branch—came about in response to the collective dilemmas that plagued the young United States. A single person given executive and police powers would be able to coerce conflicting groups to cooperate for the good of the whole country.[1]

Although they reached early agreement about having a single person serve as president, the framers of the Constitution debated for another three months over the best method of selection and the length of presidential tenure. Ultimately, the constitutional delegates compromised on the following characteristics.

- *The presidency would not be too democratic.* The president would not be chosen through direct election by the people in which each citizen has one vote. Rather, the president would be chosen for a four-year term by an appointed body known as the electoral college, which in principle represents the people. We say that the president is elected indirectly because there is a layer, the electoral college, between the voters and the choice of president. The electoral college is formally a set of people

[1] See especially the *Federalist Papers,* Nos. 67–77, which focus on the presidency and the executive branch.

chosen in their respective states to vote for the president, and the person winning a majority of electoral college votes becomes president. While it is not specified in the Constitution how electors are chosen by the state, in practice the states hold popular elections to choose a slate of electors pledged to support a particular presidential candidate. Thus, even though the Founders intended the electoral college to be somewhat insulated from popular whim and choose a wise, discerning president regardless of who the people want, in reality today, except in rare circumstances (such as in the very close election of 2000), the winner of the overall popular vote nationwide ends up being the winner of the electoral college vote.

- *The presidency would not be too beholden to the large states.* Recall from Chapter 2 that the Connecticut Compromise created a bicameral Congress, blending equal representation of all the states in the Senate with representation weighted by population in the House of Representatives. The compromise worked because it enabled the large states to be predominant in the House and the small states to have at least equal power in the Senate. The results of the Connecticut Compromise are reflected in the electoral college as well. Representation in the college mirrors the voting weights given to the states in Congress. Each state has as many electoral votes to select the president as it has senators and representatives. Kansas, for example, currently has six electoral votes because it has four representatives in the House and two senators in the Senate. California has 55 electoral votes. Note how this system gives additional weight to the larger states but reserves substantial voting power to the smaller states because every state is guaranteed at least three electoral votes. Even Wyoming has three electoral votes, which is substantially more voting weight in the electoral college than the state would have if the number of electoral votes were determined strictly by population size.

- *The presidency would be checked by the other branches.* The president would not be able to act alone. The president would need the approval of the House and Senate to raise money and declare war, and of the Senate to make appointments and treaties. Furthermore, the president could be impeached and recalled from office by Congress.

- *The presidency would check the other branches.* The Founders wanted the president to be involved in the affairs of the other branches of government. For instance, the office has important legislative powers. The president must sign legislation for it to become law, can force Congress to meet in formal session, and can veto legislation (though Congress can override the veto by a vote of two-thirds of both chambers). The president is also authorized to appoint all federal judges and ambassadors (with Senate approval), and can issue pardons and reprieves for prisoners.

- *The presidency would play the primary role in the conduct of foreign policy and of the military.* The president would be authorized to make treaties with the "advice and consent" of the Senate (meaning that two-thirds of the senators approve), to receive ambassadors from other countries, and most important, to serve as commander in chief of the armed forces.

Despite the consensus on the general characteristics of the presidency, the Constitution left many of the president's powers and responsibilities vague. The Founders envisioned a somewhat regal president, a man of unquestioned prestige who could rise above ordinary, day-to-day politics. George Washington, leader of the Continental army during the Revolution, set this tone immediately and was twice elected unanimously by the electoral college as the first president. Throughout his administration, from 1789 to 1797, Washington exercised his authority through subordinates, retained respect from people on all sides of the day's various debates, and excelled at the ceremonial duties of the office. The Founders anticipated that the president would concentrate on foreign affairs and internal security, leaving most domestic policy matters to the Congress.

The Constitution lists two major roles for the president: executor (enforcer) of the laws, and commander in chief of the armed forces. It was not clear, even to the Founders, how the president would act in these roles. The Constitution says only that "the executive Power shall be vested in a President of the United States of America," that "he shall take Care that the Laws be faithfully executed," and that "the President shall be Commander in Chief of the Army and Navy of the United States, and of the Militia of the several States, when called into the actual Service of the United States." It says little about the specific powers the president can exercise, except for those of appointment, pardon, and the making of treaties.

This constitutional vagueness regarding presidential power—especially the "take Care" clause quoted earlier—has generally worked in the presidency's favor, providing openings for presidents to increase their powers and institutional capacities when they believed circumstances warranted such moves. As we have already seen in the opening story, presidents have taken advantage of this vagueness to assert their authority and at times act decisively without congressional approval.[2] Challenges to presidential power based on constitutional principles have often ended up in the courts. The Supreme Court has generally held that the scope of these powers depends on historical circumstances. The Court has stated that it prefers the president to act "concurrently" with the Congress, but that in some instances the president can act alone. This ambivalence can make Court rulings on presidential powers hard to predict. By and large, the Court has granted wider latitude to the president as military

[2] Stephen Skowronek, *The Politics Presidents Make* (Cambridge, MA: Belknap Press, 1997).

Know the FACTS — Constitutional Powers of the Presidency

ENUMERATED POWERS (EXPRESSED POWERS)
The presidential powers explicitly stated in the Constitution.

- **Power to execute the law:** The Constitution bestows on the president executive power and authority over government. (Article II, Section 1, and Article II, Section 3)

- **Power of military authority:** The Constitution defers authority over the nation's military to the president. (Article II, Section 2)

- **Power to pardon:** The Constitution gives the president power to pardon or grant reprieves. (Article II, Section 2)

- **Power of diplomacy:** The president is given considerable authority in dealing with the nation's foreign relations. The Constitution enables the president to meet with foreign ambassadors and to make treaties. (Article II, Section 3, and Article II, Section 2)

- **Power to veto legislation:** The Constitution gives the president some legislative authority through veto power. After Congress passes a bill, the president can veto it in an attempt to keep it from becoming law. However, Congress can overturn the veto when there is supermajority congressional support for the bill. (Article I, Section 7)

- **Power of appointment:** The president is given the power to nominate and appoint, with the Senate's advice and consent, various political officers, including members of the Supreme Court. (Article II, Section 2)

IMPLIED POWERS (INHERENT POWERS)
Powers not explicitly stated in the Constitution, but rather inferred from it. (These continue to be debated.)

- **Power to wage war:** The Constitution gives Congress the power to declare war. However, presidents have often engaged in military action without such congressional declaration. The president derives authority to take such unilateral military action and effectively "wage war" from the power implied by the title "Commander in Chief of the Army and Navy." Some argue that such action is an abuse of presidential power.

- **Power over domestic security:** Does the president have unilateral authority to dispatch federal troops to address domestic threats? Congress is given explicit constitutional authority to call forth the militia in response to insurrection and invasion. However, the president has called forth the National Guard in response to national emergencies such as Hurricane Katrina in 2005.

- **Power to issue executive agreements:** To avoid the need to obtain Senate approval for treaties, presidents have adopted the use of executive agreements. These agreements, though not addressed in the Constitution, have the effect of a treaty without requiring Senate approval.

- **Executive privilege:** Past presidents have maintained that, given the sensitive nature of information acquired by the executive, the office holds inherent privacy privileges. Presidents from George Washington to Barack Obama have evoked such executive privilege to keep documents and other information confidential despite congressional protests.

commander in chief than as executor of the laws. When President Truman issued an executive order seizing steel mills during the Korean War to prevent a general strike by steelworkers, his action was declared unconstitutional by the Supreme Court on the grounds that he had overstepped his role as executor of the recently passed Taft-Hartley Act. The Court rejected the president's argument that he had acted as commander in chief to prevent disruption of the war effort. However, when Presidents Jimmy Carter and Ronald Reagan concluded an executive agreement with Iran concerning legal claims against the Iranian revolutionary government—a prerequisite for securing the release of American hostages in Tehran—the Court agreed that the president, as commander in chief, had such powers to resolve a foreign policy crisis.

Solving Collective Dilemmas and Principal–Agent Problems since the Founding

The Founders wanted a presidency that was relatively strong by the standards of the time, but the office has grown considerably stronger. The modern presidency emerged through a series of institutional changes that ratcheted presidential power higher in response to specific historical crises. Each crisis required cooperation and coordination among groups—states, members of Congress, bureaucracies, and members of political parties—that faced collective dilemmas. The president was and continues to be the primary solver of collective dilemmas not only in moments of deepest crisis, but also in the achievement of political goals set by him and by his political allies.

Contrast the president with Congress. Because only one person occupies the presidency, the institution does not face the same kind of internal collective dilemmas as Congress. In Chapter 5, we discussed how Congress faces potentially severe collective dilemmas among its 535 members. We learned that Congress must sustain internal institutions that are designed to resolve these dilemmas.

The president encounters different kinds of problems arising from the fact that the executive branch is more hierarchical than the legislative branch.[3] As a single person overseeing a vast administration, the president faces more direct managerial challenges, including recurrent principal-agent problems. First, the president needs information from trusted agents. As the chief executive of the federal government, the president needs to make quick decisions on issues of foreign policy, national security, and the economy, and must have access to information from diverse, trusted sources. It is crucial that the president (the principal) has close advisers (agents) who are loyal and share the president's policy goals. To get useful information, presidents have surrounded themselves with a massive cadre of handpicked advisers working within the White House. We will discuss some of these White House staff members later in this chapter.

Second, the president (as principal) must try to coordinate the bureaucracy (as agents). There are natural coordination problems within the executive branch. To act effectively, the president must get the disparate parts of the executive branch "on the same page" by cultivating loyalty to certain policies among White House staff, among top executive-branch officials, and

---

[3] For a comprehensive account of presidential authority, see Richard Neustadt, *Presidential Power and the Modern Presidents* (New York: Free Press, 1990).

When George Washington was sworn in as president in 1789, most of the Founders wanted a fairly strong executive to help solve collective dilemmas. The Federalists believed that having a single president (rather than a multi-person executive council, for example) was important for a strong central government.

throughout the federal bureaucracy. Later in this chapter, we will discuss how the presidency over time has increasingly used the White House staff, and at times the vice president, to coordinate the federal bureaucracy.

Third, the president is needed to solve broad collective dilemmas, not just those occurring within his group of advisers. The creation—and evolution—of the presidency stemmed from the need to solve collective dilemmas among the states, within Congress, and among various groups within society. The justification among the Founders for having a single person as president was that it was an important component for developing a strong central government. Recall that they (the Federalists, at least) wanted a strong central government to overcome collective dilemmas among the states. Over time, the president's ability to solve broad collective dilemmas has been an underlying cause of the growth in presidential power.

The solving of collective dilemmas and principal-agent problems occurred right away following the Founding. As the first president, Washington set a variety of important precedents. First, he instituted the cabinet system and met regularly with his closest advisers, some of whom were secretaries of such departments as Treasury and State. The creation of the cabinet was Washington's attempt to coordinate the actions of the several executive departments. Second, he firmly maintained that the president had inherent powers that were implied, but not explicitly stated, in the Constitution. These inherent powers included the authorization to conduct a broad array of diplomatic relations with foreign countries, the negotiation of treaties before asking the Senate for approval, and the "federalization" of state militias to keep domestic peace. For example, Washington used state militias in 1794 to end the Whiskey Rebellion, a series of attacks by Pennsylvania farmers on officials charged with collecting federal excise taxes. True to the wishes of the Founders (and in contrast to the problems under the Articles of Confederation—see Chapter 2), Washington acted forcefully, coordinating the disparate state militias to quell internal unrest.

Shaping the Modern Presidency

The American presidency as an institution has changed substantially over time because individual presidents responded to circumstances and built support for stronger institutional powers. The actions of several key presidents continued the trajectory Washington initiated, stretching and expanding the prerogatives of the office, making the presidency more partisan, more populist, and more powerful than the Founders intended.

Nineteenth-Century Changes

Three nineteenth-century presidents were especially influential in changing the institution. Andrew Jackson and Martin Van Buren made the presidency more populist and partisan than was intended by the Founders, then Abraham Lincoln made the presidency more powerful mostly through strong military action.

The President as the Voice of the People Jackson served two terms as president, from 1829 to 1837, and profoundly changed the office. First, more than any previous president, he continually justified his actions as following the people's will. He considered himself the people's legitimate representative in opposition to the economically and politically well connected, and especially against Congress, which he berated as a bastion of special interests. Throughout his administration, he maintained that the presidency was equal to Congress and not subordinate to it. Jackson believed that only the president, as a single person representing the people, could overcome the delay and deadlock caused by disagreements among rival groups within Congress and among the states. In our contemporary terminology, he viewed himself as a solver of collective dilemmas.[4]

The Spoils System and Partisan Goals Jackson also created the **spoils system**, which lasted in full for 50 years and, in some respects, survives to this day. Under the spoils system, loyal partisans who support the president during campaigns for office gain government jobs after the elections. Jackson campaigned for the presidency by harshly criticizing the federal bureaucracy and promising to replace federal employees on a regular basis. The spoils system gave Jackson and subsequent nineteenth-century presidents many opportunities to fill government jobs with party supporters.

spoils system The practice of rewarding loyal partisans with government positions after they demonstrate their support during an election.

Van Buren, Jackson's second-term vice president, won the presidency in 1836 and used the spoils system to create mass parties. Following Jackson's lead, presidential candidates like Van Buren offered federal jobs to supporters if elected. The spoils system helped presidents carry out their policies within the bureaucracy, but it also helped them solidify the loyalties of new voters toward the party in office. From this point forward, presidents routinely provided government jobs to people who supported them *and* their party.

Van Buren's genius was to exploit and build on the rapid expansion of voting rights that occurred in this era. Candidates for president and the presidents themselves needed to mobilize large numbers of voters to win mass elections and accomplish what they wanted to in office. Van Buren saw that the way to mobilize large numbers of voters was to link local, state, and national elections around a common partisan effort. State-level political parties would help themselves win state offices by helping the party's presidential candidate win the national office. Van Buren's goal was to mobilize a national organization in

[4] For more on Jackson's populism, see Robert Remini, *The Life of Andrew Jackson* (New York: Harper and Row, 1998).

support of a single presidential candidate. It was to have a presence at all levels of government and would continue beyond the Van Buren presidency.

Voting in mass elections presents a collective-action problem. Citizens always face the temptation to stay at home and avoid the costs of voting, such as the need in Van Buren's time to travel long distances to polling stations. It is tempting to free ride off the voting of one's fellow citizens. Parties and candidates must overcome these temptations and give citizens compelling reasons to act collectively by voting. In the 1830s and subsequently, they did so by organizing rousing parades, rallies, and pamphlets, by exaggerating the danger of voting for the opposing party, and by going door to door in their canvassing.

Furthermore, political parties in Van Buren's era had to convince state party leaders to support their presidential candidate because the state party leaders picked the delegates to the national convention. State party leaders across the country faced coordination problems in deciding which potential candidates to support. If they failed to agree on a candidate within their party, the opposition party would likely win. Thus, not only did presidential candidates and their supporters need to convince voters to turn out, but also they needed to coordinate their actions among state leaders.

Van Buren's efforts built a partisan presidency based on the mass support and mobilization of many new voters. Turnout for his election in 1836 was even higher than that of 1832, at the peak of Jackson's popularity. Van Buren approached the presidential contest as a partisan effort to gain mass support, and he succeeded in bringing many new participants into the political process.

The President as Military Leader Lincoln's actions during the Civil War set key precedents for how executive power over the militia can solve the deepest of collective dilemmas. Lincoln faced the most serious crisis in American history when the southern states seceded from the Union in 1860–61 and declared themselves a separate country, the Confederate States of America. In order to defeat the southern rebels and reunite the country, he needed to invade the South and protect the North. He was concerned not only about the Confederate army invading the North and capturing Washington, D.C., but also about southern infiltration and sabotage. He had to deal with northern states that were reluctant to send troops, money, and matériel for the war. There was strong resistance to the draft in the North, including violent draft riots. In other words, the northern states' leaders and populations faced deep collective-action problems. They all wanted to defeat the South or end the war or both, yet it was costly to contribute to the effort and there were incentives to free ride.

Lincoln responded forcefully to overcome these problems. With the help of allies in Congress, he created what were at the time massive government bureaucracies to supply the army with troops, materials, food, and transportation and communication networks. When state governments in the North resisted his calls for more draftees to fight the war, he forced their hand by threatening arrests and armed intervention. And he went beyond the provisions of the Constitution in temporarily suspending the writ of *habeas corpus,* allowing federal troops and local officials to arrest people suspected of treason and hold them indefinitely without charge. In essence, he enforced the cooperation of people he needed to contribute to costly collective efforts.

Lincoln often faced a recalcitrant Congress, stubborn state leaders, and many critics within his own party and the army. He pushed on with the war effort, even when some of his own advisers urged him to settle with the South and end the conflict. Institutionally, he pushed the boundaries of presidential power during the Civil War by exploiting ambiguities in the Constitution (which we will discuss in the next section). He expanded the role of commander in chief far beyond what previous presidents had done, and made policy decisions about the war within his administration and sometimes without full congressional approval.

Through Lincoln's efforts, and with the help of political allies who agreed with his political goals (though not necessarily with his institutional methods), the size of the national government and especially the powers of the president grew substantially during the Civil War era. In the years since Lincoln's presidency, Congress and the courts have given presidents more leeway to conduct foreign policy and make war than was likely intended by the Founders. Although many of the bureaucracies Lincoln created to help prosecute the war were abolished after its conclusion, as we saw in Chapter 3, the size of the national government—in terms of both spending and personnel—remained larger after the war than before it.

As this example shows, crises call for quick responses that often require coordination among, and even coercion of, diverse interests and political groups. After the crisis passes, there is often disagreement over whether to return to a weaker presidency or to maintain the new institutionalized powers of the executive office. Thus, we see a persistent dynamic in American political history: an emergency leads first to a stronger presidency and then to ongoing debates and political conflicts over continuing or rescinding presidential power. As illustrated by the cases of Lincoln in the Civil War and Obama with the DREAM Act, the presidency has grown stronger largely as a consequence of individual presidents with enough political support from the other branches to solve collective dilemmas.

Through the Twentieth Century and into the Twenty-First

We have seen from Lincoln's actions during the Civil War how presidents can increase their power in times of crisis. In the twentieth century, the presidency became powerful to a degree beyond the reckoning of the Founders and nineteenth-century Americans. In many ways, this parallels the increasing power of the national government relative to the states, and especially the increasing power of the United States in world affairs. It was not inevitable, however, that the presidency would become as important as it has within the American political system.

Building on the Partisan Presidency As a result of Jackson's and Van Buren's strategies in the nineteenth century, all successful presidential candidates since have had to gain leadership within one of the two major parties and help the party turn out the vote at the national, state, and local levels. As head of the party, the president is expected to solve the collective dilemmas that arise from within the party.

The president today is the leader of the party in two arenas, elections and policy making.[5] Because the president is the public face of the party, his or her popularity shapes the party's fortunes in congressional and state elections. These election contests are deeply affected by people's attitudes toward the president. When the president is relatively popular, candidates for other offices running under the same party label typically benefit by "riding on the president's coattails." This means that candidates receive a boost in their own election fortunes simply by belonging to the same party as a popular president. On the flip side, members of the president's party can face difficulties when the president is relatively unpopular.

Some presidents have followed Van Buren's example and been important builders of political parties as organizations, helping candidates at all levels to mobilize voters, raise money, and create a more permanent party presence in the states and localities. Among recent presidents, Ronald Reagan was noteworthy for traveling around the country to help congressional and state candidates in their efforts to win elections. He spoke at numerous fund-raising events for congressional candidates. Not all presidents relish this role, and some have been criticized for largely ignoring it. Richard Nixon was criticized by members of the Republican Party for not doing enough to help the party as a whole improve its capacity to win elections throughout the country. Barack Obama was criticized for not helping Democrats enough in the midterm congressional elections of 2010.

The president leads his or her party in policy making. For example, in 2009 and 2010, President Obama led the Democrats' efforts to pass a new health care policy. Here, Obama and Democratic members of Congress make a statement to the press about health care reform.

---

[5] Sidney Milkis, *The President and the Parties* (New York: Oxford University Press, 1993); Scott James, *Presidents, Parties, and the State* (New York: Cambridge University Press, 2000).

During presidential campaigns and in the several months after someone takes office in the White House, the president's initiatives shape the policy agenda not only of the party but also of the national government as a whole. Obama campaigned in 2012, as he had in 2008, on a platform of stimulating the economy and improving health care and education. His ideas dominated public debate after both elections and led to major shifts in government policy, including massive federal stimulus spending in 2009, an overhaul of health care in 2010, new immigration policies in 2013, and an education program that has affected every public school in the country. Obama's policy proposals and their aftermath will shape the Democratic Party's reputation for years.

The president relies on his own party members in Congress to support White House initiatives. Although they cannot expect unanimous support from all party members, presidents can count on much more support from members of their own party than from the opposition. Opposition-party members in Congress can be expected to oppose the president on a regular basis, to criticize presidential policies and competence, and to try to thwart White House efforts.

Partly because presidents serve as leaders and standard-bearers for their political parties, they are deeply affected by the partisan makeup of Congress. Presidents can accomplish more of their goals when bargaining with the legislative branches if they have partisan allies at the table. Presidential success in bargaining depends substantially on whether the country has **divided** or **unified government**. The U.S. government is said to be divided when the presidency and at least one chamber of Congress are controlled by different political parties. Under divided government, presidents find it more difficult to get their legislative priorities passed. We will consider this issue later in this chapter in our discussion of the president's veto power.

divided government A government in which the president is from a different party than the majority in Congress.

unified government A government in which the president is from the same party as the majority in Congress.

Developing the Populist Presidency Although Jackson promoted the idea of the president as the voice of the people, most nineteenth-century presidents remained aloof, rarely making public appearances. It was considered undignified, for example, to campaign openly for re-election by giving speeches to the general public. Presidents seldom left Washington, D.C., even during campaign seasons.

In the twentieth century, the presidency became much more populist. Woodrow Wilson, who served two terms from 1913 to 1921, went beyond any previous president in his effort to reach the average man and woman "in the street." In part, this was because automobiles and improved roads gave him technological advantages over his predecessors. Moreover, Wilson's philosophy of democratic governance emphasized the value of direct contact between the president as leader and the people the president serves. He also gave many speeches in Washington trying to woo the press and interest groups in his favor over political opponents.

After Wilson, presidents increasingly reached out to the American people and sought their support as a way of increasing their own power. Presidents

FIGURE 6.1

Presidential Public Activities in the United States (Yearly Average)*

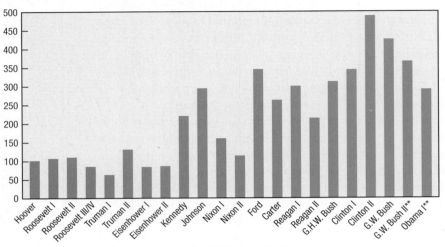

*The yearly average number of public activities by presidents, including major speeches, news conferences, minor speeches, and U.S. appearances, including those in Washington D.C. Excluded are specifically political activities.

**Through 2007 only. Data for Obama I are approximated from available data as of fall 2014.

Source: Lyn Ragsdale, *Vital Statistics on the Presidency,* 3rd ed. (Washington, DC: CQ Press, 2009), p. 207.

going public Action taken by a president to communicate directly with the people, usually through a press conference, radio broadcast, or televised speech, in order to influence public opinion and put pressure on Congress.

today use televised speeches and press conferences to communicate directly with citizens (Figure 6.1). Modern scholars call this **going public**. President Ronald Reagan, who was elected in 1980, raised this art to a new level. A former movie star, he had a warm smile and telegenic looks that endeared him to people and mobilized supporters. Reagan's ability to use his personal popularity to win over the general public, who would then pressure their members of Congress to follow his lead, is legendary. During one of his televised addresses to the country in 1981 about his proposed budget, which was stalled in Congress, he could not have been more explicit: "I urge you again to contact your senators and congressmen. Tell them of your support for this bipartisan proposal. Tell them you believe this is an unequaled opportunity to help return America to prosperity and make government again the servant of the people."[6] Reagan continually battered congressional opponents by encouraging constituents to inundate them with letters. Even after he had been in office for five

[6] Samuel Kernell, *Going Public: New Strategies of Presidential Leadership,* 3rd ed. (Washington, DC: CQ Press, 1997), p. 150.

years, one Democratic member of Congress admitted that "we're still a bit afraid of him."[7]

Besides talking to people directly, presidents—beginning with John F. Kennedy in the early 1960s—have increasingly conducted private polls to measure public opinion about their standing and their prospects for success with legislative initiatives. From new archival research, we now know that Kennedy conducted 15 private polls in less than three years in office, compared with Reagan's 204 in eight years.[8] Presidents use polls on a regular basis to hone their communications with the general public and to gauge their popular approval. Bill Clinton reportedly preferred to pursue policy goals that had the support of 60 percent of the public according to polls.

President Barack Obama, meanwhile, has enthusiastically embraced social media to interact with the public and promote his legislative priorities. Obama communicates directly with nearly tens of millions of followers on Facebook and on Twitter. As part of his presidential campaign for re-election, his team developed its own social network, MyBarackObama.com. This strategy allowed the president direct contact to his supporters, while also giving him access to information about his supporters to be used in the reelection campaign.

The president's connection to the people can be an important source of power. For example, Ronald Reagan successfully used direct appeals to the American people to put pressure on Congress to approve his policies.

Presidents nowadays are often highly responsive to—and constrained by—public opinion.[9] They hire full-time public relations specialists to maximize their appeal nationwide. To win the office, presidents campaign in a personal way, traveling around the country to make speeches in as many localities as they can, and crafting emotional appeals to enhance their reputations for being strong leaders and likable personalities. Once in office, they frequently leave Washington, D.C., to appear in person to announce new policy initiatives, pressure local members of Congress to vote their way, and raise money for congressional and presidential campaigns. They need to press the flesh constantly, be sure to give their speeches before the local television news deadlines, and present themselves in such appealing settings as school classrooms, factory floors, and fields of wheat and corn.

[7] Kernell, *Going Public,* p. 140.

[8] Lawrence R. Jacobs, "Communicating from the White House: Presidential Narrowcasting and the National Interest," in *The Executive Branch,* ed. Joel D. Aberbach and Mark A. Peterson (New York: Oxford University Press, 2005), pp. 174–218.

[9] We will discuss the relationship between politicians and public opinion in Chapter 9.

Enhancing Presidential Power through Military and Economic Means

Three men in the office in the early twentieth century are noteworthy for changing the nature of presidential power: Theodore Roosevelt, Woodrow Wilson, and Franklin Delano Roosevelt (FDR). Republican Theodore Roosevelt served as president from 1901 to 1909. He created a personality cult around the office that had never before existed. An extraordinarily popular president, he was known as much for his larger-than-life personality as for his policies. "Teddy" Roosevelt projected an energetic, athletic, can-do spirit with the help of an increasingly aggressive press corps who covered his daily actions and utterances in detail. Like Andrew Jackson, he governed with the attitude that he alone represented the people.

Roosevelt made effective use of his "bully pulpit"—his privileged place as speaker on behalf of the American people—to pressure those who opposed his agenda. He was careful to cultivate the notion that the presidency was separate from Congress and that the president would not wait for Congress to act if he felt the action was in the people's best interest. Roosevelt demonstrated repeatedly that a president's personal charisma and popularity with the masses could be a powerful political tool. He had no qualms about stirring up popular support for his policies to pressure political opponents, even those within his Republican Party. The personality of the president, particularly his public approval and his performance in office, grew in importance following Roosevelt's tenure.

Like his successors, Roosevelt responded to collective dilemmas among various economic and political groups. The industrialization of the country had created an urban working class that was increasingly militant and demanded a share in the nation's wealth. It also gave rise to enormous industrial corporations (the "trusts") that Roosevelt considered dangerous to the country's economic and social well-being. Many people wanted to rein in these trusts, and a collective effort by various economic interests could have accomplished it. Such action, however, would have been costly because of the trusts' power and ability to punish opponents. Others wanted to counteract the increasing power of a small number of trade unions. Roosevelt responded to pressure from these constituencies by forming regulatory agencies and using litigation as a forceful tool.

For example, rather than wait for a foot-dragging Congress to legislate against the trusts—the huge monopoly corporations that he wanted to break up into smaller companies—Roosevelt decided to sue them directly from the president's office. He initiated 44 lawsuits against companies in his first year in office, an unprecedented strong-arm tactic for any branch of the national government to undertake, let alone the presidency.

Institutionally, Roosevelt took major steps toward creating a national government bureaucracy to regulate the activities of American businesses. His executive branch increasingly regulated the railroads, oil companies, and some forestry industries. This policy expanded the role of the national government in the economy and gave the presidency a substantial boost in power. Although Teddy Roosevelt is credited with setting the regulatory wheels in motion, full-scale regulation of broad sectors of the economy did not come to fruition until after his cousin, Franklin Delano Roosevelt, became president in 1933.

We have already learned how Wilson advanced the populism of the office. With regard to world affairs, Wilson changed the presidency in important ways during and after World War I. He sought to establish the American president as a major voice in international politics, on an equal footing with the leaders of the great powers in Europe. He believed that one of his major roles following World War I was to help the European countries resolve their internal collective dilemmas. Wilson emphasized an internationalist foreign policy and established regular contact with his counterparts abroad. His foreign policy had broad implications for the future of the presidency. Most presidents who followed Wilson, including those who served through the Cold War and into the 1990s, regarded maintaining the peace in Europe, Asia, and Latin America as a prime mission.

No president other than Washington has had a greater impact on the nature of the office than Franklin Delano Roosevelt (known as FDR, to distinguish him from Teddy). Starting in 1932, he won four elections—more than any president before or since—and served three full terms. (He died in 1945, about three months into his fourth term.) The two signature achievements of Roosevelt's presidency, the New Deal and the leadership of the Allies in World War II, led to massive increases in the size, reach, and importance of the national government.

After the Wall Street crash of 1929, the national government under President Herbert Hoover and the Republican Congress seemed unable or unwilling to respond effectively to the economic crisis. Political leaders and various economic interests disagreed over what the national government should do. The Democrats swept into power in the 1932 elections on a wave of optimism, but they too faced uncertainty and internal dissension. FDR devoted his efforts to solving collective dilemmas within his own party and across many diverse and competing interests. Within the first 100 days of taking office in 1933, he laid the groundwork for his New Deal, a set of policies intended to boost the American economy in the face of the Great Depression, to stabilize it once it was back on its feet, and to further regulate the activities of corporations. A by-product of the policies was to redistribute income in favor of retirees, widows, the disabled, and orphans.

The New Deal, discussed in detail in Chapters 3 and 15, was a major overhaul in the way the national government operated within the American political system. It gave the executive branch greater authority than ever before. Under FDR, many new national bureaucracies were created to regulate the economy, with the result that the White House directed economic policies to an unprecedented degree. New Deal policies, including Social Security and unemployment

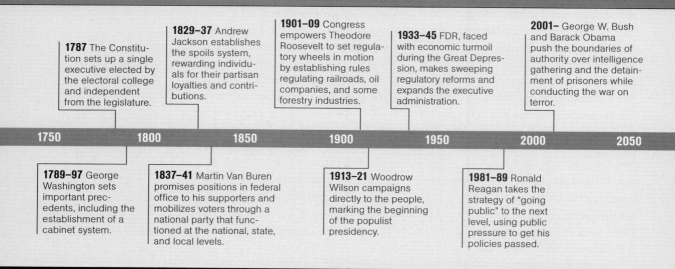

1787 The Constitution sets up a single executive elected by the electoral college and independent from the legislature.

1829–37 Andrew Jackson establishes the spoils system, rewarding individuals for their partisan loyalties and contributions.

1901–09 Congress empowers Theodore Roosevelt to set regulatory wheels in motion by establishing rules regulating railroads, oil companies, and some forestry industries.

1933–45 FDR, faced with economic turmoil during the Great Depression, makes sweeping regulatory reforms and expands the executive administration.

2001– George W. Bush and Barack Obama push the boundaries of authority over intelligence gathering and the detainment of prisoners while conducting the war on terror.

1750   1800   1850   1900   1950   2000   2050

1789–97 George Washington sets important precedents, including the establishment of a cabinet system.

1837–41 Martin Van Buren promises positions in federal office to his supporters and mobilizes voters through a national party that functioned at the national, state, and local levels.

1913–21 Woodrow Wilson campaigns directly to the people, marking the beginning of the populist presidency.

1981–89 Ronald Reagan takes the strategy of "going public" to the next level, using public pressure to get his policies passed.

insurance, increased both the taxes the national government collected from people and the benefits people received from the national government.

In the wake of FDR's New Deal, the political fate of all presidents—including re-election prospects, overall popularity, and ability to get legislation passed in the Congress—has increasingly been tied to the state of the national economy. Because the presidency now wielded so much power, the American people could legitimately blame presidents when the economy was in trouble and reward them when times were good.

As during Lincoln's presidency, the Roosevelt administration's war effort also greatly expanded the size of the national government. The massive mobilization of more than 5 million U.S. soldiers and sailors during World War II (1941–45) necessitated a huge government bureaucracy to oversee their recruiting, training, supply, and transport. Unlike in the past, however, the military did not shrink after the war to a tiny peacetime force, but remained large and strong. FDR's successors, Presidents Harry S. Truman and Dwight D. Eisenhower, carried on many of his policies.

After World War I, the United States had gradually withdrawn from European politics. By the end of World War II, however, the country had by and large abandoned its isolationist foreign policy and become deeply involved in international affairs on every continent. The national government spawned a huge military bureaucracy devoted to gathering intelligence, protecting Europe (and ultimately Korea) from communist aggression, and participating in new international organizations such as the United Nations (UN) and the North Atlantic Treaty Organization (NATO). The victory in World War II under FDR

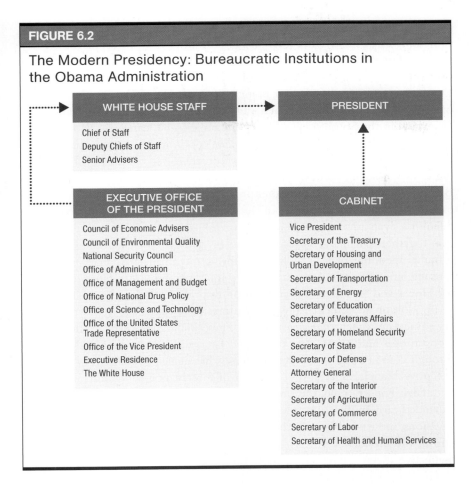

FIGURE 6.2

The Modern Presidency: Bureaucratic Institutions in the Obama Administration

WHITE HOUSE STAFF

Chief of Staff
Deputy Chiefs of Staff
Senior Advisers

PRESIDENT

EXECUTIVE OFFICE OF THE PRESIDENT

Council of Economic Advisers
Council of Environmental Quality
National Security Council
Office of Administration
Office of Management and Budget
Office of National Drug Policy
Office of Science and Technology
Office of the United States Trade Representative
Office of the Vice President
Executive Residence
The White House

CABINET

Vice President
Secretary of the Treasury
Secretary of Housing and Urban Development
Secretary of Transportation
Secretary of Energy
Secretary of Education
Secretary of Veterans Affairs
Secretary of Homeland Security
Secretary of State
Secretary of Defense
Attorney General
Secretary of the Interior
Secretary of Agriculture
Secretary of Commerce
Secretary of Labor
Secretary of Health and Human Services

ushered in a new era of American leadership on the world stage, which in turn raised the American president to new heights of power and influence.

The growth of the federal government spilled over into the president's own office. FDR created a massive bureaucracy within the executive branch devoted to helping him make economic and foreign policy decisions, in addition to implementing policies decided upon by the legislative branch. Figure 6.2 shows the current bureaucracy built around the office of the president. It is important to recognize that none of these bureaucratic institutions, other than the cabinet departments, existed before FDR took office.

Today's Powerful Presidency

The president has a variety of tools to wield authority, many of these tools oriented toward solving collective dilemmas and principal-agent problems. We can divide the tools into informal and formal (or enumerated) powers.

The president's position as head of a major political party and his ability to command public attention and communicate directly with citizens are key sources of presidential power. We call these *informal powers*, and they have grown over time with the actions of successive presidents. They enable the president to influence the actions of other branches of government, of state leaders, and of group leaders in society. When FDR needed the support of Democratic governors in the South for his New Deal policies, he leaned on them heavily, appealing to them as fellow Democrats and pointing out how popular some New Deal programs were among people in the South. He was actively trying to avoid having them defect from partisan cooperation on the New Deal. Barack Obama, like FDR and other presidents, has used his informal powers to pressure Congress to adopt his policies. He too needed to overcome collective dilemmas, even among members of his own Democratic Party, to keep a coalition together. Obama achieved much of his early agenda, including the large stimulus spending plan, health care reform, and financial regulation reform, through a mixture of coaxing and public appeals to prod reluctant members of the House and Senate to vote in favor of his preferred bills.

In addition to informal powers, the president also exercises formal powers, sometimes called *enumerated powers*. These include powers specified by the Constitution and others that developed later and became codified into law through court rulings or statutes. Congress has delegated many powers to the executive branch, especially in the area of foreign policy, but also in domestic affairs. For example, the president's powers as commander in chief were expanded early in the country's history with congressional approval. On several occasions, most notably with the 1973 War Powers Act, Congress has tried to rein in the president's power to wage war, but these curbs have been largely ineffective. (See Chapter 17 for more on the War Powers Act.)

administrative law The body of law created by executive agencies with the purpose of refining general law passed in legislation.

Furthermore, Congress and the courts have permitted the creation of **administrative law**, whereby Congress passes legislation to achieve broad policy goals, and the administrative agencies in the executive branch have the authority to fill in the legislative details. As we will see in Chapter 7, the administrative decisions of the federal bureaucracies overseen by the president can have the force of law.

Finally, in the early years of the Republic, Congress met for less than half the year. (Today Congress is in session almost continuously.) Many major decisions by early presidents, including Thomas Jefferson's Louisiana Purchase, which more than doubled the geographic size of the country, were made while Congress was out of session. The fact that Congress was not always available to consult gave presidents more leeway to act. Over time, presidents seized these opportunities not only to make policy but also to increase the power of their office.

Let us now consider several of the president's formal powers in more detail. Some (the veto and the power to make appointments) are mentioned in the Constitution, while others (executive orders and agreements, signing statements, and access to administrative resources) were asserted by presidents and later sanctioned by Congress and the courts.

The Veto

As we saw in Chapter 5, if Congress passes a bill, the president can either sign it into law or veto it. Congress can override a veto with a two-thirds vote in both chambers. If Congress overrides the president's veto, the bill becomes law without presidential signature. Presidents can also exercise a **pocket veto** by failing to sign legislation at the end of a congressional session. If Congress is not in session, then bills unsigned by the president 10 days after being passed by Congress are considered vetoed. Congress must pass the law again in the next session to keep the bill alive. In recent decades, the pocket veto has been very rare because Congress has learned to anticipate the president's possible action and has paid attention to the timing of legislation to avoid the 10-day cutoff. This does not mean the pocket veto is now unimportant. Rather, the possibility of its usage shapes the nature of congressional action and spurs them to speed things along when the end of a session approaches.

pocket veto A veto that occurs automatically if a president does not sign a bill for 10 days after passage in Congress and Congress has adjourned during that 10-day period.

The earliest presidents used the veto to nullify bills passed by Congress that they felt were unconstitutional. Andrew Jackson was the first president to justify the veto as a strategic tool to bring about policies more to his liking. He vetoed bills simply because he disagreed with them. In other words, Jackson considered the veto as a legislative procedure rather than merely to protect the Constitution. This rankled members of Congress at the time, but Jackson set a precedent that has been followed ever since.

Figure 6.3 shows how some presidents have regularly used the veto to bargain with Congress, while others have used it sparingly. What explains the differences? To answer this question, let us step back a bit and use the logic described earlier for the pocket veto. Contemporary scholars have studied how the mere *threat* of the veto can convince Congress to modify a piece of legislation. So presidents may not actually need to use the veto to achieve their goals. Presidents make so-called **veto threats** by publicly stating that if Congress passes a bill that is not to their liking, they will veto it. Scholars have shown that Congress tends to modify bills after presidents issue veto threats. This is a case of an institutional device, the veto, granting the president considerable power over legislation; the president doesn't actually need to use it, but only to have it available for use if necessary. Thus, the fact that a given president seldom exercises the veto power does not mean that he considers it an unimportant tool.

veto threat A public statement issued by the president declaring that if Congress passes a particular bill that the president dislikes it will ultimately be vetoed.

Partisan control of Congress also helps to explain differences in the use of the veto. In our discussion of divided government and unified government, we saw how partisan control of Congress can affect the success of the president's legislative initiatives. As we might expect, research has shown that presidents veto important legislation much more often under divided government than under unified government.[10]

Bargaining between the president and Congress becomes easier to manage when the president and Congress belong to the same party. The president can typically expect cooperation from members of his own party in Congress.

[10] Charles Cameron, *Veto Bargaining* (New York: Cambridge University Press, 2000).

FIGURE 6.3

Presidential Vetoes

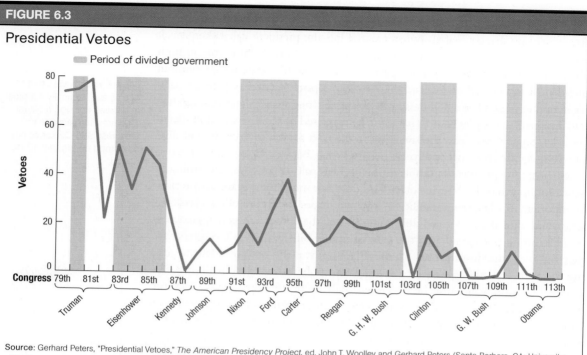

Source: Gerhard Peters, "Presidential Vetoes," *The American Presidency Project*, ed. John T. Woolley and Gerhard Peters (Santa Barbara, CA: University of California, 1999–2013), www.presidency.ucsb.edu/data/vetoes.php (accessed 5/31/13).

Under unified government, Congress does not usually send the president a bill that is destined to be vetoed, because any differences between the two branches have already been smoothed over within the party. Under divided government, the two major parties spar more frequently over legislation, and the presidential veto or veto threat can be a powerful weapon in this partisan conflict.

Congress can play the veto game as well, though. Under divided government, Congress sometimes sends the president a bill that is quite popular but that its members know the president will veto for ideological or political reasons. In this way, congressional leaders hope to embarrass the president and make the public unhappy with his leadership. An example of this tactic occurred in 1992 when the Democratic Congress sent Republican President George H. W. Bush several bills intended to boost the economy during a recession. Bush vetoed them, fulfilling promises he had made to important constituencies in the Republican Party. His popularity fell as a result, and those vetoes contributed to his defeat by Bill Clinton in the 1992 election. Not surprisingly, Congress resorts to this tactic more often just prior to presidential elections than in other years.[11]

[11] Tim Groseclose and Nolan McCarty, "The Politics of Blame: Bargaining before an Audience," *American Journal of Political Science* 45, no. 1 (2001): 100–119.

Appointments

The Constitution grants the president the power to make appointments to executive departments and other bureaus, and to the federal courts. Beginning with George Washington, presidents have shaped their governments by appointing people who agree with them on policy matters. With the growth of the federal government, this prerogative has become even more significant. Today, presidents make thousands of appointments to populate a much larger and more powerful national bureaucracy that affects the well-being of every community in the country

Most presidential appointments that require the Senate's "advice and consent" are routinely approved. High-profile positions, including cabinet secretaries and especially Supreme Court justices, can be controversial, and occasionally the Senate will reject a presidential appointment. But by and large, appointment of personnel at the top of the executive agencies and in the courts occurs as the president sees fit. Certain kinds of positions, especially ambassadorships to foreign countries, are often handed out as rewards to people who helped the president get elected. For example, President George W. Bush appointed David H. Wilkins, a major contributor to his 2004 campaign, as ambassador to Canada. Similarly, President Barack Obama appointed Dan Rooney, owner of the Pittsburgh Steelers football team and an early supporter of Obama's candidacy in Pennsylvania, to be ambassador to Ireland. These appointments followed a long, bipartisan tradition of handing out federal jobs to thank people and curry favor with donors and the party faithful. Although the spoils system is a shadow of what it was in the nineteenth century, vestiges of it survive in these presidential appointments.

In making most appointments, the president looks for candidates who not only have the necessary skills and prestige but also share his broader philosophical views. The president wants to use the appointments as ways to populate the leadership of the bureaucracy and the courts with people who think like the president does on overall policy and legal issues; this goes a long way toward coordinating the executive and judicial branches on common political goals aligned with the president's goals. For instance, the first two Supreme Court justices that Obama appointed, Sonia Sotomayor in 2009 and Elena Kagan in 2010, were liberals who could be expected to support a range of legal interpretations sympathetic to Democrats and their policy agenda in such areas as abortion rights, gun control laws, and restrictions on campaign spending by corporations.

When appointing a federal judge, the president is choosing someone who may stay in that position for life. (Federal judges serve until they resign, die, or are removed from office as a result of an impeachment trial in Congress.) Thus, appointments to the judicial branch provide the president with an opportunity to leave a lasting legacy. In contrast, appointees who lead the bureaucracy and military usually serve much shorter terms. Not only are the heads of the federal bureaucracies typically replaced by new presidents when they come into office, but top officials routinely leave before serving an entire presidential term. Some appointees want to return to their previous careers; others are replaced because the president is displeased with their performance. For example, President Obama repeatedly replaced generals who were leading the war in Afghanistan.

Executive Orders, Executive Agreements, and Signing Statements

executive order An official means by which the president can instruct federal agencies on how to execute the laws passed by Congress.

Modern presidents also have several legal maneuvers at their disposal to bypass Congress. An **executive order** is a regulation or a rule made by the president that has the force of law. In the early years of the Republic, such orders typically dictated the manner in which the federal bureaucracy would implement laws passed by Congress. In more recent years, presidents have used executive orders to make major policy changes and even exercise war powers. Examples include Harry S. Truman's order that desegregated the armed forces, Lyndon Johnson's order that the U.S. government adopt affirmative action, and Bill Clinton's order that led to the use of military force in Kosovo. (Technically, President Obama's action on immigration discussed in the opening story was not formally an executive order but simply a directive for an agency to follow and did not involve formal changes in any laws or regulations.)

All recent presidents have issued executive orders to avoid waiting for legislation that might not be forthcoming from a Congress controlled by the opposition party.[12] Sometimes resistance by members of the president's own party prompts the president to resort to an executive order. Truman desegregated the armed forces in 1948 after bills introduced in Congress to do the same were repeatedly stymied by southern Democrats. Truman issued his executive order in response to a bill proposed by a group of so-called Dixiecrats, which would have given soldiers a choice of whether to serve in biracial units. Truman's order did not offer soldiers a choice. Another reason for the use of executive orders over the past century is that the United States has been engaged in many wars since the 1930s. Executive orders are issued frequently during wartime because presidents do not feel they have the time to wait for congressional action.

The courts generally have upheld the right of presidents to issue executive orders, within limits. In two notable cases, however, federal judges have ruled that the president overstepped the bounds of executive authority and defied laws passed by Congress: Truman's seizure of the steel mills in 1952 (discussed earlier), and Clinton's 1996 order preventing government agencies from contracting with organizations that had strikebreakers on their payrolls. In the latter case, the court held that Clinton's executive order violated established law on labor relations.

Congressional legislation can overturn an executive order, although such a law must generally survive a presidential veto. Thus, if a president is confident

[12] William Howell, *Power without Persuasion* (Princeton, NJ: Princeton University Press, 2003).

of having the support of at least one-third of the members of one chamber of Congress for a given action, an executive order is an effective way to make policy without requiring that a law be passed by Congress. George W. Bush made ample use of this maneuver, for example, when he limited funding for stem-cell research through an executive order. Barack Obama used executive orders to reverse this and several other Bush policies (see the Interests, Institutions, and Outcomes box).

Presidents can also issue **executive agreements**, which are those made between the United States and foreign countries and that are concluded solely with presidential approval. Because such agreements are not treaties they do not need Senate approval. In terms of how they are enforced and their legal status, there is not much difference between a treaty and an executive agreement, except that treaties are more prominent and are considered weightier and more enduring. Since the end of World War II, the United States has been party to more than 10,000 executive agreements involving trade, troop deployments in foreign countries, and cultural exchanges. The federal courts have repeatedly held that such agreements are constitutional.

Finally, presidents can issue **signing statements**. These are public declarations about how the president intends to interpret a law, and they can be controversial both legally and politically. Like their predecessors, George W. Bush and Barack Obama both used signing statements to communicate how laws should be interpreted by federal agencies and the courts. Most experts agree that such statements are within presidential prerogative. In his signing statements, President Bush also indicated which parts of laws he considered unconstitutional and would not enforce. Critics charged that this tactic gave him, in effect, a line-item veto, which is not allowed under current constitutional law. It is unclear whether the courts will allow this latter use of signing statements to continue, but President Bush often issued them in connection with foreign policy matters, where presidents historically have had great discretion. President Obama has used signing statements mostly to clarify where he thinks the line is between executive authority and legislative authority. As Figure 6.4 shows, modern presidents have been increasingly likely to issue signing statements to address constitutional questions.

executive agreement An agreement between the United States and one or more foreign countries. Because it is not a formal treaty, it does not need Senate approval.

signing statement A public statement written by the president and attached to a particular bill to outline the president's interpretation of the legislation.

Administrative and Financial Resources

The power of the presidency has increased over time partly as a result of presidents reacting to crises, including wars, depressions, and civil unrest. One important way presidents "react" to crises is to create new bureaucratic agencies designed to help them implement policy and make decisions. These agencies help coordinate government action across various parts of the government.

The growth of the federal bureaucracy has been particularly dramatic in recent years. When George Washington was president, his cabinet consisted of five people and the national government's budget was a mere $4 million. (Even

Abortion Funding and the Use of Executive Orders

The United States government provides substantial financing to social service agencies and organizations working in foreign countries, especially in poor, developing areas. One major controversy for decades has been whether government funding can go to organizations promoting family planning, including abortions. Since the 1980s, U.S. law has prohibited any federal money going to pay for abortions, and it is a matter of interpretation whether that ban includes giving to organizations that support access to abortion services.

Interests

Opponents of abortion rights favor a strict enforcement of U.S. law, which means banning U.S. federal funds from going to any organization working overseas that promotes, in any overt way, abortion rights. Supporters of abortion rights find this kind of ban counterproductive because it restricts funding to many organizations that provide health care to women and children overseas.

Institutions

One way that the rules around abortion funding can be set is through the use of executive orders handed down by the president. These orders have the force of law, and, historically, presidents have used them to direct the bureaucracy on how to implement the policy. More recently, presidents have issued orders that shift the direction of the policy. Thus, the availability of executive orders are tools for presidents to avoid having to rely on congressional support. Also, executive orders are very difficult for Congress to overturn. Congress can reverse an executive order by passing a bill, but the president can veto that bill, and it would take two-thirds of both chambers of Congress to overturn that veto.

Outcomes

The use of executive orders has caused abortion funding to come and go. Since President Ronald Reagan used executive orders in 1984 to establish what was called the Mexico City Policy—the policy that the U.S. Agency for International Development could not allocate funds to organizations that advocate or perform

Like others before him, President Obama has used executive orders to alter policy without congressional approval.

abortions in foreign nations—the back and forth has coincided with the party of the president; Republican presidents have enforced it while Democratic presidents have not.

On January 22, 2001, just two days after he took office, President George W. Bush issued a memorandum restoring the Mexico City Policy (after President Clinton had revoked it), and the United Nations Population Fund lost $34 million in U.S. aid as a result.[1] Then on January 23, 2009, on his third day in office, President Barack Obama revoked Bush's policy, and in effect allowed the U.S. government to provide funds to family planning organizations overseas that can include abortion services as part of their mission. The organizations that lost funding after Bush's executive order were once again eligible to receive funding.

Think About It:
Will the Mexico City Policy continue to be implemented and repealed every so often? What would have to happen to settle the policy one way or another? Should presidents have such powers through executive orders?

[1] Todd S. Purdum, "U.S. Blocks Money for Family Clinics Promoted by U.N.," *New York Times*, July 23, 2012.

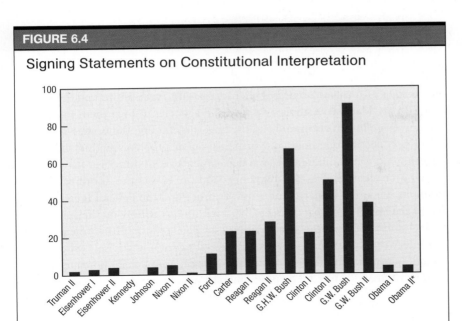

FIGURE 6.4

Signing Statements on Constitutional Interpretation

Presidential Administration

*Includes up to November 2014.

Sources: Lyn Ragsdale, *Vital Statistics on the Presidency*, 3rd ed. (Washington, DC: CQ Press, 2009), pp. 460–62; John T. Woolley, "Presidential Signing Statements," *The American Presidency Project*, ed. John T. Woolley and Gerhard Peters (Santa Barbara, CA: University of California, 1999–2013). Data on Obama II collected by author.

in the late eighteenth century, this was a small figure compared to the size of the American economy.) Today, Barack Obama presides over a vast federal bureaucracy with more than 2 million civilian employees and a budget of $3.8 trillion.

Because presidents have usually acted together with Congress in solving a crisis, the required congressional approval for these new agencies has sometimes been easy to obtain. For example, FDR established the Executive Office of the President (EOP; discussed later) by executive order; Congress did not object and even approved money for the staff. A more recent example is George W. Bush's creation of the Department of Homeland Security, a cabinet department established in 2003 in response to the September 11 terrorist attacks and ongoing terrorist threats. A bill to create Homeland Security was first proposed publicly and then shepherded through Congress by Bush, resulting in the reorganization of existing agencies and the devotion of new resources to protecting the United States from attack and from natural disasters. President Obama created various new agencies to oversee implementation of his three main policy initiatives—reform of health care, financial regulation, and national education standards. For instance, he established the Consumer Financial Protection Agency inside the Federal Reserve Bank to implement aspects of the new financial regulations passed by Congress with his support. While presidents often receive congressional approval, it is also true that the president's powers to issue orders in some areas can be controversial and deeply contested.

Beyond the federal departments and agencies that execute national policies, such as Homeland Security, Defense, Treasury, Agriculture, and the Federal Reserve, presidents have their own staff and agencies to help them make decisions, manage information, and run the government. Presidents need a vast staff to solve collective dilemmas and principal-agent problems within the federal government. When different federal departments are at odds over national policy, who or what resolves the differences and forces them to coordinate? As an example, when the Department of the Treasury and the Federal Reserve Bank both have units to combat financial fraud within banks, how do they coordinate their actions, and also coordinate with the Department of Justice, to enforce the law effectively? President Obama has several economic advisers whose work includes coordinating the actions of these three large federal bureaucracies on matters of financial fraud. The president also has advisers who do central clearance, which means that the White House monitors administrative proposals from federal departments to ensure that they comply with the president's policy goals. This is a form of solving principal-agent problems, with the president as principal and the bureaucracies as agents (see Chapter 7).

The president relies on staff to guide the bureaucracy and constantly seeks advice from them and other people. Three resources especially assist presidents in decision making and in solving collective dilemmas: the White House staff, the EOP, and the vice president.

White House Staff The president relies mostly on White House staff to organize schedules and plot political, legislative, and international strategies. These advisers do not need Senate approval and serve at the pleasure of the president (that is, the president can hire and fire them at will). They are the closest layer of government employees to the president. The White House chief of staff, for instance, controls access to the president and manages presidential duties. This person also is head of the EOP (discussed later). The national security adviser maintains constant contact with the president to help manage foreign relations and the military aspects of the job. Recent presidents have also had political strategists, communications directors, spokespersons, and economic advisers (and their respective staffs) as part of the White House bureaucracy. Additionally, some members of the cabinet are part of the president's intimate circle of advisers. They are the front-line people for the president's desire to solve collective dilemmas and enable effective government action around his goals.

Obama's White House staff, as shown in Figure 6.2, consisted of senior advisers and his chief of staff's office. All told, Obama has around 500 people working for him as part of the White House staff. Besides security personnel, cooks, and personal assistants, most of them work for people who advise the president directly on policy matters.

Executive Office of the President Formally, the White House staff is part of the EOP. We can think of it as the nerve center of the presidency, whereas the remainder of the EOP provides expertise and continuity to the executive branch. The core parts of the EOP, such as the Office of Management and Budget (OMB) and the Office of the United States Trade Representative, stay in place from president to president. Because these offices were legislated into existence by Congress, the people appointed to head them require Senate approval. These are the exceptions, however. Much of the EOP is formed around the agenda of the current president, and the leaders of its various units serve at his pleasure. Obama, for instance, has an Office of Energy and Climate Change Policy, but his predecessor did not.

The EOP is a crucial intermediate layer between the president's core staff (in the White House) and the rest of the federal bureaucracy in the cabinet departments (discussed in detail in Chapter 7). Although all three layers report to the president, their independence from the president's political goals increases as one moves from the White House staff to the EOP and then to the executive departments. The EOP carries out functions of both the White House staff and the executive departments. Like the White House staff, much of the EOP advises the president and helps with the president's policy agenda. But like the executive departments, the EOP also implements policy and provides Congress with credible information.

A good example of this intermediate role is the OMB, which provides information about federal revenues and spending, and assists the entire national government with budget information.[13] The OMB is the primary source of information about the national government's finances. At the same time, it is a crucial source of advice for the president and helps craft the budget proposal sent to Congress every year. The head of the OMB works for the president and helps with the president's policy agenda. The OMB, by being part of the EOP, can be both a source of reliable information and expertise for the entire government and an asset when the president plots and implements strategies for carrying out budget goals.

The Vice President The vice presidency in the modern era is a major resource for the president. But the office hasn't always been this way—or, at least, it hasn't always been seen this way. The Constitution allows for the vice president to take office should the president die or be incapacitated. In the original document ratified in 1788, the vice president was the person who came in second place in the contest for the presidency. This presented problems because the president and vice president had just run against each other. For example, Thomas Jefferson became vice president when John Adams was elected president in 1796. Because they were bitter rivals, Jefferson could hardly be expected to help Adams with his policy programs. Nor would he have been likely to enact similar policies if he had been called upon as vice president to assume the powers of the presidency.

---

[13] The Congressional Budget Office (CBO) is the legislative counterpart to the OMB, and it provides budget information. Often, the OMB and the CBO disagree about financial projections, but they both provide the same data about past government spending.

The Twelfth Amendment (1804) changed the procedure for choosing the vice president. Under the amendment, the vice president runs for election for that office concurrently with the president. In practice, this means that, since the early nineteenth century, presidential and vice-presidential candidates have run together as a pair and been elected as a team. It was common in past eras for vice presidents to be chosen only to placate a disaffected wing of the president's party. According to the Twelfth Amendment, vice presidents must come from a different state than the president. It has made political sense for presidential candidates to choose vice-presidential running mates not only from different states but from different regions of the country in order to "balance" or broaden the appeal of the ticket.

Many vice presidents in the past had few qualifications for the office apart from their political appeal. In fact, over the years, the vice presidency has been the butt of jokes. One vice president even said the office wasn't worth a warm bucket of urine.[14] To comics and critics alike, vice presidents often seem to be idly waiting in the wings and acting as the president's lapdog. Dan Quayle, George H. W. Bush's vice president, was treated harshly by critics; comics and reporters skewered him for his tendency to misspeak and for his callow appearance. When Vice President Gerald Ford became president after Richard Nixon resigned, becoming the first nonelected president in American history (as Ford had been appointed vice president by Nixon following the resignation of Nixon's prior vice president, Spiro Agnew), he was criticized for being unprepared for the office.[15]

Vice President Joseph Biden's foreign policy experience was seen as an important resource for President Obama. In 2013, Biden met with Russian Foreign Minister Sergey Lavrov during bilateral talks at a conference on security policy.

[14] There are conflicting accounts as to whether John Garner told Lyndon Johnson that the vice presidency wasn't worth a bucket of "piss" or "spit." Most historians believe that he said "piss" and that the press made it more palatable by changing it to "spit."

[15] Ford had been appointed by Nixon after Spiro Agnew resigned as vice president.

However, contrary to the old jokes about the office, vice presidents today are powerful people within the administration of the president. Dick Cheney, the vice president for George W. Bush, played a particularly strong role, setting a new standard for being one of the president's closest advisers. Joe Biden, Obama's vice president, had a hand in changing the history of gay rights when his comment during a public interview supporting gay marriage forced Obama to take a position on the controversial issue during the heat of the 2012 presidential campaign. Obama, shortly after Biden's interview, expressed his support for gay marriage, a watershed moment for the gay rights movement. In general, vice presidents today have four crucial roles. First, the vice president must be ready to take over the presidency should the president die or become incapacitated. Thus, he or she needs to be fully informed about all matters that the president deals with in case the vice president is called upon to assume control of the government. Second, the vice president is a key adviser to the president. Since the presidency of Harry S. Truman (1945–53), the vice president has sat on the National Security Council and has regularly counseled the president on foreign and domestic policy. Third, the vice president casts tie-breaking votes in the Senate, a power that has occasionally been historically important. For instance, Al Gore cast a tie-breaking vote in 1993 on a key budget bill.

Fourth, the vice president typically helps the president coordinate federal bureaucratic agencies to achieve presidential goals. Presidents entering office face a massive coordination problem in getting federal agencies focused on their policy agendas. Although vice presidents have been given different specific responsibilities depending on who is president, they have in recent eras been active in promulgating the president's agenda and helping to solve coordination problems. Joe Biden has helped Barack Obama considerably in foreign diplomacy. On the domestic side, Al Gore assisted Bill Clinton in reforming the bureaucracies to make them more efficient.

The vice presidency has become increasingly powerful since the end of World War II. In parallel to the trends in the size of the president's own staff and bureaucracy, vice presidents have developed their own institutional capacity. Vice presidents since Gerald Ford have had their own staffs paid for by the national government. Partly as a result of the Twenty-second Amendment (1951), which limited presidents to two terms, ambitious vice presidents may hope to run for president themselves, ascending naturally as the party's standard-bearer in the election after their predecessor leaves office.

In Comparison: Executive Forms

The institutional form chosen by the Founders for the presidency was not the only one possible. They raised the possibility of a three-person executive, and some people advocated having a single person serve as president for life.

Moreover, the nature of the American presidency, as it has evolved, reflects the particular historical trajectory since the Founding. Recall our discussion of path dependence in Chapter 1, the notion that past decisions about institutions leave legacies for the present that make it difficult to change direction. The American presidency has features distinctive from executives in other countries both because of what the Founders decided and because of specific decisions by individual presidents as discussed throughout this chapter.

The Founders ultimately chose a system that stood in stark contrast to that of Britain, which had both a king or queen who inherited the crown and a prime minister chosen by Parliament. The broad outlines of that system remain in place today in Great Britain, except that the contemporary monarch has no real political power. Great Britain remains a **parliamentary democracy**, which means that the legislature (in this case, the House of Commons) chooses the executive. As in much of Western Europe, as well as in Canada, Australia, Japan, and India, the prime minister and his or her government hold executive power by virtue of their leadership of the majority party in the national parliament. The most important decision the parliaments make in these countries is to elect the executive government. As discussed in Chapter 5, parliaments largely go along with the policies proposed by the executive once the executive is chosen.

Many other parliamentary democracies, like Italy, Ireland, and Israel, have presidents in addition to prime ministers. These presidencies are ceremonial

parliamentary democracy
A form of democracy in which the executive is elected by the legislature and government is responsible to the legislature.

In the United States, the president serves as head of government as well as head of state. As head of state, the American president has a good deal of responsibility for foreign affairs and interacts with the leaders of other countries. Here, President Obama attends a dinner hosted by Indian Prime Minister Monmohan Singh.

posts held by appointees who wield little actual power. They are not the real executives of the government, although they are considered heads of state. Similarly, the British monarch is the (ceremonial) head of state, while the prime minister is head of government and de facto executive. When the president of the United States visits Britain, meetings about real foreign policy issues are held with the prime minister.

By contrast, the American president serves as *both* head of state and head of government. He or she is chosen by the electoral college, which in principle represents the people, and the president governs as the executive independently of Congress. The fact that the president's authority comes not from Congress but from the people is what makes the United States a **presidential system** of government with separation of powers.

France offers an example of a **mixed presidential system**, in which an elected president governs alongside a prime minister chosen by the National Assembly (the French parliament). By tradition, the French president is head of state and deals mostly with foreign affairs, while the French prime minister is head of government and deals mostly with domestic affairs.

The powers of the executive branch vary among presidential systems around the world. In Chile, for example, the president can legislate by decree on many important matters. This means that the Chilean president can make law independently of the legislature. It is up to the legislature to overturn the law, and it often takes more than a majority of legislators to revoke a presidential decree. Note how this reverses the practice used in the United States, where the legislature makes laws and the president has the veto power.

Presidents in certain countries have sole power to propose legislation. In a common variation, presidents can exercise a partial veto, known as a **line-item veto**, to strike down specific parts of legislation passed by the legislature. This is a tremendous advantage for presidents because they do not have to accept a law in its entirety, but can pick and choose what they believe is acceptable and veto accordingly. An executive can virtually mold legislation to his or her liking. (The U.S. Congress approved the presidential line-item veto in 1996, when Bill Clinton was president, but the Supreme Court quickly ruled that it was unconstitutional.) In these countries, institutional rules concerning presidential powers of decree, of proposal, and of partial veto give the chief executive substantially more legislative powers than those granted to the American president.

Other nations' presidents have considerably *less* power than the American executive. In Poland and Portugal, for example, presidents have very limited veto powers and can apply them only to select types of legislation. Some countries' legislatures have the power to dismiss executive cabinet members against the president's wishes. The French president—who, as mentioned earlier, governs in tandem with a prime minister—has only limited powers concerning domestic legislation.

presidential system A form of democracy in which the executive is elected independently and the government is not responsible to the legislature.

mixed presidential system A form of democracy in which the executive is elected independently and shares responsibility for the government with the legislature.

line-item veto A partial veto that allows the executive to strike specific passages from a given bill.

Scholars of comparative government tend to believe that, on balance, American presidents—in comparison with their peers in other countries—have mid-level power relative to the legislature within their own political system.[16]

It is also interesting to compare the powers of the U.S. president to those of the American governors, who are the executives of the 50 state governments. Every state has a governor who is directly elected by voters rather than being chosen by the state legislature. Thus, every state shares with the American national government a separation of powers system, though, unlike the national government, no state has the equivalent of an electoral college. Many formal powers of the governors are modeled after presidential powers, such as the power to veto legislation and the power of appointment. However, governors' powers vary from state to state. All but six governors have some form of line-item veto. More than half of the governors have sole power to propose state budgets. Governors without such powers are at a disadvantage compared with their counterparts. The governor of Vermont, for example, is considered institutionally weak in comparison with most of the others because the office does not have the line-item veto and the legislature has full power to change the governor's proposed budget. When governors have these powers, they can gain an upper hand against the state legislature and direct their state's policies to a larger degree than governors without such powers.

Is the Presidency Too Powerful?

In light of the massive powers discussed in this chapter, it is sometimes said that the United States has an "imperial presidency." In some respects, the phrase makes a good deal of sense. The American presidency revolves around an individual who holds vast powers to influence the course of the U.S. government. Moreover, given the dominant role that the United States plays in world affairs, the president's power *within* the American political system gives him enormous influence *outside* of the United States.

By certain criteria, the power of American presidents is unmatched. No executive anywhere in the world controls anything like the vast administrative and military machinery that the American president uses to influence domestic and world affairs. Since the early twentieth century, the American presidency has evolved into a vast bureaucracy that gives sitting presidents unparalleled access to information, resources, and personnel. They are free to use these resources during times that they themselves define as crises. Although the American president does not have all of the constitutional powers within

[16] Mathew Shugart and John Carey, *Presidents and Assemblies: Constitutional Design and Electoral Dynamics* (Cambridge, UK: Cambridge University Press, 1992).

the political system that are granted to some other countries' chief executives, no reasonable comparison can be made to the sheer power of the American president to affect American and world politics.

The term *imperial* is misleading, however, if it is meant to imply that the president is detached from the American people and not subject to public pressure. The term is also inappropriate if it is meant to imply that the president is unconstrained by the institutional design of the American government—namely, its separation of powers. Two simple but key factors prove these implications false. First, Congress can override presidential vetoes and withhold money for the president's policies. Second, as in any true democracy characterized by the rule of law, the president must obey the law and the Constitution.

Investigations and Impeachment

Courts have occasionally declared actions of the president unconstitutional. More important in recent times, Congress has shown the capacity and will to investigate the president's actions and even exercise its power of impeachment. It has become increasingly common for **special prosecutors** to investigate misdeeds among presidents and White House aides. These investigations—especially since the Nixon administration—have not only led to high-profile hearings, trials, and occasional prison sentences but have also been a significant means for the two major political parties to attack each other and seek advantage in elections. The opposing party often tries to embarrass the president by exposing scandal, dishonesty, and betrayal in the administration.

special prosecutor Independent, private-sector counsel hired by Congress to investigate government officials.

Reserved for the most serious offenses, **impeachment** is the process by which the House of Representatives formally charges a federal government official with, in the language of the Constitution, "Treason, Bribery, or other high Crimes and Misdemeanors." If a president is impeached by the House, the case then goes to the Senate, which votes on whether to recall the president from office. Although the impeachment procedure is rarely used, it represents a powerful check on the president's authority by the legislative branch.

impeachment Process by which the House of Representatives formally charges a federal government official with "Treason, Bribery, or other high Crimes and Misdemeanors."

No president has been forcibly recalled from office by a Senate vote, but three came close: Andrew Johnson (1868), Richard Nixon (1974), and Bill Clinton (1999). Johnson was impeached on a variety of charges, including conspiracy, but was acquitted by the Senate by just one vote. Nixon was not formally impeached but resigned before the full House vote, which was certain to impeach him. Clinton was impeached by the House on two counts of perjury (lying under oath before a grand jury) about his affair with a White House staffer. He was acquitted by the Senate and served out his full term.

It is interesting to place the Nixon and Clinton impeachment crises in the context of how public opinion and the modern political climate shaped decision making. Nixon's public approval ratings, as measured by opinion polls, had sunk to historic lows, with only about one-quarter of those polled approving of his

FIGURE 6.5

Presidential Approval Rating, 1946–2014

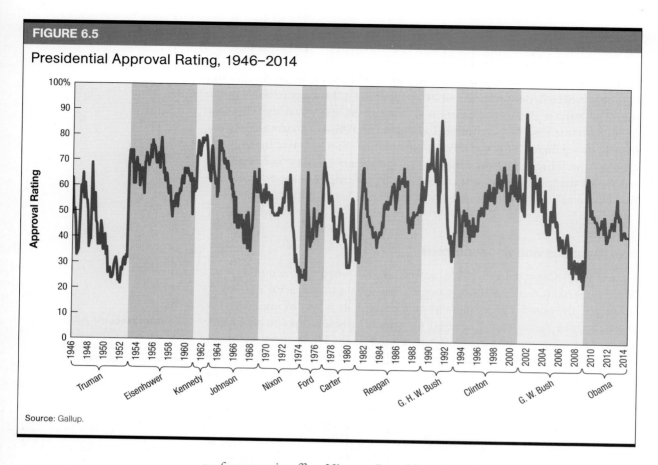

Source: Gallup.

performance in office. His own Republican Party in Congress had made it clear that most would vote to recall him from office. Clinton's approval ratings, in contrast, remained at a high 60 percent throughout his ordeal (Figure 6.5). Not only did he carry on his normal duties as president, he steadfastly refused to respond directly to his Republican opponents about the charges against him. Most of his fellow Democrats in Congress supported him and voted against both impeachment in the House and removal from office in the Senate. Clinton reportedly said after surviving the vote in the Senate, "Thank God for public opinion."[17]

Electoral Pressures

Beyond the formal means of constraining the president—the veto override and other congressional checks, investigations, and impeachment—consider that the president needs to be elected and re-elected by a people who are historically

[17] Bob Woodward, *Shadow: Five Presidents and the Legacy of Watergate* (New York: Simon & Schuster, 1999), p. 513.

suspicious of centralized power, and presidential power in particular. The comparison between the Nixon and Clinton impeachment cases highlights the more general point that modern presidents carry out their duties under the watchful eyes of Congress and are highly responsive to shifting public opinion regarding their performance. Presidents, more than any other members of the U.S. government, are either encouraged or restrained by mass public opinion.[18] They are lightning rods for public anger, taking the blame when the economy turns bad or foreign policy initiatives do not work well. Yet they are heralded when they are seen to perform well, as illustrated by the initial popular support for George W. Bush's response to the September 11 attacks in 2001.

The American people seem to tolerate and even prefer a powerful and decisive president, as long as there are electoral and institutional checks on that power. In the terminology used by political scientists, the people (as principals) have an extremely powerful agent in the president, but one they ultimately want to be able to control at the ballot box.

The president as the elected representative of the entire country has a mandate different from any other, including that of Congress. Congress is composed of 535 people elected to represent specific subconstituencies, and these subconstituencies end up being quite different from one another. How Congress manages to make law given the different interests brought to its chambers by representatives and senators was the subject of Chapter 5. The president pursues policy goals and takes action on behalf of everyone, and this means ultimately that the president is the only person charged with being the agent of every single person regardless of where those people live in the country. What this means in practice is difficult to nail down. As we will study in more detail in Chapter 13, whether elections end up choosing a president who represents the "average" person or voter, or who represents a specific partisan subset of the population, depends on how we think elections work. Prominent models of national elections—though not the only ones used by political scientists—depict the president as the winner of a contest for the allegiance of the average voter, where average is typically interpreted to mean ideologically moderate. And if true, then the president does or should focus on pleasing the average, moderate person with policy actions; in theory, this person best represents what the entire country deserves from government. As we'll see in Chapter 13, though, competing theories regarding elections mean this may not necessarily be the case.

Institutionalizing Presidential Power

Let us now return to our puzzle from the beginning of this chapter. As we have seen, the power of the modern presidency is largely the result of presidents creating new institutions within the executive branch to solve collective

[18] Brandice Canes-Wrone, *Who Leads Whom? Presidents, Policy, and the Public* (Chicago: University of Chicago Press, 2006).

dilemmas. Presidents often expanded their authority in response to crises like the September 11 attacks or the recession of 2008–9 with the approval of Congress and the American people. Such crises demand collective action, yet it is difficult for rival political parties, competitors within the business community, and interest groups to coalesce behind a solution. At key moments in American history, the president's allies in Congress, the states, and society have demonstrated a belief that the presidency is the institution best equipped to solve collective dilemmas bedeviling a nation. Past presidents, like Obama, have relied on this belief to take unilateral actions in a range of policy areas, such as regulating immigration.

Even when the country is not in crisis, the power of the president to direct executive agencies in how to implement a law remains. Once the crisis is over, why has the power of the presidency not fallen back to its precrisis level? The answer has to do with the nature of the political institutions set up to assist presidents and maintain their power. By definition, institutions of government are designed to persist and address various political situations as they arise over time. Institutions are "sticky," they do not come and go easily. Vestiges of institutions can remain in place long after the situation that compelled their creation has passed. As we will see in Chapter 7, many government institutions that persist—for instance, those created by presidents with the approval of Congress and public opinion—take the form of federal bureaucracies that the president can use to implement policy priorities.

FURTHER READING

★ = Included in *Readings in American Politics*, 3e

Cameron, Charles, *Veto Bargaining* (New York: Cambridge University Press, 2000). A sophisticated look at presidents as legislators, and how they use the veto to influence legislation more to their liking than what the Congress would do otherwise.

★ Canes-Wrone, Brandice, *Who Leads Whom? Presidents, Policy, and the Public* (Chicago: University of Chicago Press, 2006). A historical examination of twentieth-century presidents who sometimes followed public opinion and sometimes tried to lead public opinion.

★ Howell, William, *Power without Persuasion* (Princeton, NJ: Princeton University Press, 2003). A detailed look at the tools presidents use unilaterally to make policy, bypassing or forcing the hand of Congress.

James, Scott, *Presidents, Parties, and the State* (New York: Cambridge University Press, 2000). A thoughtful history of how presidents have used the bureaucracy of the national government to serve the goals of their political parties.

★ Kernell, Samuel, *Going Public: New Strategies of Presidential Leadership*, 4th ed. (Washington, DC: CQ Press, 2007). A book rich with data showing how presidents increasingly over the twentieth century spoke directly to the people in order to enhance their bargaining position with Congress.

Madison, James, Alexander Hamilton, and John Jay. *Federalists Papers*, Nos. 67–77. Clear statements of support for a presidency both checked by the other branches but also with enough autonomy to be decisive in times of crisis.

★ Neustadt, Richard, *Presidential Power and the Modern Presidents* (New York: Free Press, 1990). A classic explanation of how presidents wield power, arguing that executives are successful only to the degree that their personal charisma persuades people that helping the president achieve his or her goals is in their interests.

Skowronek, Stephen, *The Politics Presidents Make* (Cambridge, MA: Belknap Press, 1997). A historical account of how different presidents molded different kinds of political coalitions to accomplish their policy goals.

KEY TERMS

administrative law (p. 204)

divided government (p. 197)

executive agreement (p. 209)

executive order (p. 208)

going public (p. 198)

impeachment (p. 219)

line-item veto (p. 217)

mixed presidential system (p. 217)

parliamentary democracy (p. 216)

pocket veto (p. 205)

presidential system (p. 217)

signing statement (p. 209)

special prosecutor (p. 219)

spoils system (p. 193)

unified government (p. 197)

veto threat (p. 205)

The controversy around the Department of Health and Human Services's rule that would require health insurance p[...] including those offered by Roman Catholic hospitals, universities, and charities—to offer free birth control to female em[...] ees illustrates the tensions bureaucrats face. While then–Secretary of HHS Kathleen Sebelius (left) had been appoint[...] President Obama, she and her department also had to be responsive to Congress and the public.

7

THE BUREAUCRACY

The agencies of the federal bureaucracy are responsible for carrying out the policies passed by Congress and the president. However, bureaucrats are not elected and it is not always clear to whom they answer. Who ultimately are their bosses and how can they avoid defying them?

D uring President Obama's first term in office, the U.S. Department of Health and Human Services (HHS) asked teams of prominent medical advisers to provide recommendations for improving women's health. The department then used these recommendations to create guidelines for all health care insurance plans adopted by employers. The HHS guidelines stated that all health care plans by employers should "cover women's preventive services such as well-woman visits, breastfeeding support, domestic violence screening, and contraception without charging a copayment, coinsurance, or a deductible."[1]

These regulatory guidelines met both praise—chiefly from those concerned with women's reproductive rights and preventative health care—and protest. One protesting voice came from the U.S. Conference of Catholic Bishops, who contended that the contraception mandate would force employers who oppose contraception on religious or moral grounds to "subsidize what they believe to be immoral."[2] Kathleen Sebelius, the Secretary of HHS at the time, responded that the guidelines had "carved out" an exemption for religious organizations like churches that primarily employ people who subscribe to that faith. Yet for employers like Catholic hospitals and universities whose employees might be from any faith (including no religious

---

[1] U.S. Department of Health and Human Services, "Affordable Care Act Ensures Women Receive Preventative Services at No Additional Cost," August 1, 2011, www.hhs.gov/news/press/2011pres/08/20110801b.html (accessed 3/1/13).

[2] Timothy Dolan, "HHS Contraception Mandate 'Un-American'," USA Today, January 25, 2012, www.usatoday.com (accessed 3/1/13).

faith), the guidelines eventually would need to be followed. Furthermore, there was no exemption for employers (nonreligious) who merely oppose contraception on moral grounds.

The exemptions did little to mollify the opposition. President Obama and Secretary Sebelius reconsidered the policy slightly and changed the regulations in 2012. The new regulations shifted the responsibility of providing free contraception from the employer to the insurance companies. "Religious organizations won't have to pay for these services," the president said in describing the new HHS changes, "and no religious institution will have to provide these services directly,"[3] accommodating the concerns of religiously aligned hospitals, universities, and charities.

This shift in policy from HHS did not satisfy all opponents, but it did win over some Catholic women's groups, who split with the bishops and expressed satisfaction with the new regulations. Yet the way HHS handled the matter, at first declaring a mandate for employers on providing contraception, and then backtracking slightly to try to appease an important constituency, invited criticisms from members of Congress, both conservative Republicans and liberal Democrats. The HHS was caught between taking the recommendations of scientists and doctors from the medical community and responding to political pressures from important groups in society during a presidential election year. In the years thereafter, the contraception mandate was still mired in legal challenges from religious organizations and employers who opposed contraception for moral reasons.

The HHS, as with all executive bureaucracies, is tasked with implementing legislation. But it can also establish the law, crafting new guidelines that impose certain standards and requirements on citizens to achieve policy goals. Thus, sometimes bureaucrats are also policy makers in that they refine and tailor vague legislation. However, bureaucrats are not elected and it is not always clear to whom they answer, especially when Congress and the president are at odds. The House of Representatives, with a Republican majority, had reasons to be strongly opposed to the contraception mandate, and indeed, the Republican leadership complained loudly. If executive branch bureaucrats have bosses both in Congress and the president, and those bosses disagree, how can they avoid defying their bosses?

[3] Barack Obama, White House address on the revision to the Department of Health and Human Services contraception mandate, "Video: President Obama on New Contraception Rules," Kaiser Health News, February 10, 2012, www.kaiserhealthnews.org (accessed 3/1/13).

What Is the Federal Bureaucracy?

In Chapter 6, we focused on the president, who sits atop the executive branch and is chosen through the process of election. A small portion of the people in the executive branch are appointed by the president. Most people working in the executive branch, however, are not elected and belong to the civil service and military bureaucracies, and are neither appointed by the president nor by any other elected official. Millions of people in these bureaucracies implement the policies that elected officials in Congress and the White House, and occasionally judges, decide upon. They are the ones who, at the federal level, fight wars; protect borders; regulate markets; dispense Social Security payments; coin money and control the money supply; make loans to students, farmers, and small businesses; finance science and applied research; operate national parks; investigate and prosecute federal criminal activity; run prisons; and set interest rates for banks. At lower levels of government, in the states and localities, bureaucrats teach, enforce the law, clean streets, distribute driver's licenses, inspect restaurants, and distribute school lunches. Civilian and military bureaucrats have always been the workhorses of the government.

In a democracy, a government *bureaucrat* refers to anyone working for the government who is not elected.[4] The **government bureaucracy** refers to the agencies and offices devoted to carrying out tasks for the government in a manner consistent with the law. Federal bureaucrats work in **government agencies**, which are the fundamental units within the national government that carry out duties prescribed by Congress or the president. Most bureaucrats in the national government work in the executive branch, although Congress and the courts also have their own small bureaucracies. All bureaucrats working for the government are agents in some way. Thus, Congress and the president are the principals, and the bureaucrats are the agents.[5] As we will see, having two principals presents challenges for federal bureaucracies.

Agencies in the executive branch exist in one of three settings: within a department, as an independent agency, or as a government corporation. Some agencies are part of a **cabinet department**, such as the Department of Agriculture or the Department of Justice. Thus, the Food and Nutrition Service is an agency within the Department of Agriculture. Bureaucrats in the Food and Nutrition Service operate the Supplemental Nutrition Assistance Program (SNAP), which provides food for the poor and various school meals programs, among other things. The cabinet departments encompass hundreds of agencies.

government bureaucracy The agencies and offices devoted to carrying out the tasks of government consistent with the law.

government agency An individual unit of the government responsible for carrying out tasks delegated to it by Congress or the president in accordance with the law.

cabinet departments Departments within the executive branch that encompass many of the agencies that implement federal policy. Secretaries appointed by the president and confirmed by the Senate are given the responsibility of leading these departments and providing advice to the president.

---

[4] For classic accounts of bureaucracy, see the following three texts: Max Weber, *From Max Weber: Essays in Sociology,* trans. H. H. Gerth and C. Wright Mills (London: Routledge & Kegan Paul, 1948); Woodrow Wilson, "The Study of Administration," *Political Science Quarterly* 2 (1887); and James Q. Wilson, *The Politics of Regulation* (New York: Basic Books, 1980).

[5] D. Roderick Kiewiet and Mathew McCubbins, *The Logic of Delegation* (Berkeley: University of California Press, 1991).

Three Types of Government Bureaucracy

Less Independent

More Independent

Cabinet Departments

The cabinet departments are government agencies that report directly to the president. The constitution establishes that the cabinet departments advise the president on subjects relating to the duties of their respective offices. The employment of cabinet officials as well as their job responsibilities rely heavily on the discretion of the president.

Examples:
Department of State, Department of the Treasury, Department of Defense, Department of Agriculture, Department of Justice, Department of the Interior

Independent Agencies

Independent agencies are established by congressional statutes to exist outside the cabinet departments. They are often headed by executive boards or commissions appointed by the president and confirmed by the Senate. The president's authority to remove board members or commissioners is generally subject to greater restriction than members of the cabinet. This restriction, among others, allows independent agencies more autonomy.

Examples:
National Aeronautics and Space Administration, Environmental Protection Agency, National Science Foundation, Federal Exchange Commission, Federal Trade Commission

Government Corporations

Federally owned corporations carry out businesslike tasks with the highest degree of agency independence. Generally, these corporations are motivated to generate revenue while achieving public service goals.

Examples:
U.S. Postal Service, Amtrak, Tennessee Valley Authority, Federal Deposit Insurance Corporation, Corporation for National and Community Service

At the head of cabinet departments are secretaries appointed by the president, such as the secretary of agriculture and the attorney general (the "secretary" of justice). The heads of all the departments are part of the president's cabinet and can be close advisers to the president. (You may want to review the outline of cabinet departments in Figure 6.2 in Chapter 6.)

Other agencies are considered to be independent, meaning that they are not part of one of the cabinet departments. **Independent agencies** are granted more autonomy from the president and Congress than those within departments, and are typically headed by boards or commissions appointed by the president and approved by the Senate. The Environmental Protection Agency (EPA) is an example of an independent agency. These agencies usually regulate the conduct of business corporations in some way. The president and Congress still are ultimately the principals over independent agencies, and they are part of the executive branch. But by virtue of how the laws setting up these agencies were written, the president has more limited removal powers of the people who lead them.

Government corporations are a third type of agency. They are given even more discretion than independent agencies and are charged by Congress with carrying out a task. Sometimes these tasks are regulatory, but often they are businesslike activities that the government wants done by a federal agency. Examples include the U.S. Postal Service and Amtrak, the passenger-railway company. Although technically part of the government, these organizations conduct their affairs and run their businesses with relative independence. They may occasionally receive subsidies from the government, but the expectation is that they will generate enough revenue at least to break even. Their operations are heavily regulated in most cases. For example, the U.S. Postal Service could make more profits if it were allowed to abandon its least profitable rural routes. However, it is required to serve every address in the United States, and its rates are set by a government-appointed commission. Private companies by law are not allowed to compete with the Postal Service to deliver ordinary mail. In many aspects of its work, however, the service operates like a private company. Its overnight mail service faces competition from companies like UPS, DHL, and FedEx, and it is allowed to charge market rates and compete against private companies for certain services. As with independent agencies, the president appoints the boards and commissions of the government corporations, and the appointments must be approved by the Senate.

independent agency An agency that exists outside the cabinet departments and is run with a larger degree of independence from presidential influence.

government corporation A federally owned corporation that generates revenue by providing a public service, operating much like a private business and with a higher degree of autonomy than a cabinet department or an independent agency.

Why Do We Need a Federal Bureaucracy?

Bureaucracies are necessary because someone or some set of people actually has to do the work of government and not just make decisions. For instance, some bureaucratic agencies exist to redistribute resources. The Social Security Administration, an independent agency, is charged with using money collected through taxes to pay for retirement and disability benefits for millions of people.[6] It keeps records on everyone's payroll contributions and their age, and sends people money according to formulas set by Congress.

It turns out bureaucracies make policy decisions as well, as will be discussed shortly. In both implementing policies and in making certain decisions, bureaucracies are crucial parts of governments solving collective dilemmas.

Solvers of Collective Dilemmas

Recall from Chapter 1 that funding and creating public goods involve collective dilemmas. When it comes to public goods—benefits that anyone can enjoy, like national security or national parks—people are tempted to free ride and let others pay for or create them. Some public goods require coordinated action to produce. When government solves collective dilemmas, including those related to public goods, bureaucracies actually implement the solutions. Thus, the main task of many bureaucratic agencies is the implementation of decisions (by Congress and the president) to create public goods. Consider the following public goods and some of the government agencies or departments involved in providing them. These are just a few of the many departments, agencies, and corporations that create public goods.

- *Scientific knowledge.* The National Aeronautics and Space Administration is an independent agency that explores space to gather more knowledge of the physical world and the universe.
- *Security.* The Department of Defense prepares for and fights wars to keep the country and its interests abroad secure.
- *National parks.* The Department of the Interior manages parks to preserve natural resources and enable citizens to enjoy nature.
- *Public health.* The Centers for Disease Control and Prevention (part of the Department of Health and Human Services) conduct research to avoid epidemic outbreaks.
- *Funding for public goods.* The Internal Revenue Service is the part of the Treasury Department that collects taxes, a necessary task that makes everything the government does possible.

Other bureaucratic agencies regulate private and commercial activities to make society function smoothly. They too are creating public goods, but to do so they typically solve coordination problems. The Federal Aviation Administration (part of the Department of Transportation), for example, hires air traffic controllers to manage the flow of airplanes into and out of airports. Without a public authority to help them coordinate, the airline companies, which compete

[6] See Martha Derthick, *Policymaking for Social Security* (Washington, DC: Brookings Institution, 1997), for a classic account.

against each other for business, for slots at airports, and for flying times, might bump into each other—both literally and figuratively—in their quest for profits. Air traffic controllers are government bureaucrats who solve coordination problems every day.

Coordination problems also need solving among the federal bureaucratic agencies. As the chief executive of the national government, the president sets the direction for the executive branch and, in modern times, has a large White House bureaucracy to help make decisions.[7] Presidents and their staff must coordinate the actions of numerous agencies. At times, this can be more than daunting. Take, for example, the government's response to a series of enormous storms hitting various parts of the country. Tornadoes in Alabama in 2011, and Hurricane Sandy along the East Coast in fall 2012, led to massive devastation of property, natural habitats, and people's lives. Numerous national government agencies and tens of thousands of national government employees became involved in responding to these storms. The White House relied to a large extent on the Federal Emergency Management Agency (FEMA) to organize the deployment of first responders, to coordinate with state and local governments, and to bring aid to the thousands of people living in the affected areas. The White House also made sure the EPA played a role in sending scientists and inspectors to assess the damage to coastlines and fragile ecosystems. Meanwhile, the U.S. Coast Guard responded

Scientific knowledge, including knowledge of the universe, is one public good that the government supplies through a bureaucratic agency, NASA. The information gathered through the Space Launch System and other NASA efforts benefits the country as a whole.

to the dangers people faced at sea during the hurricanes. Without a major effort to coordinate their actions, these bureaucracies would have unclear lines of responsibility, duplicate efforts needlessly, and work at cross-purposes.

Sometimes regulatory agencies help solve prisoner's dilemmas.[8] This kind of collective dilemma is common among companies advertising against each other. Suppose two drug companies that make aspirin tablets compete intensely for customers. Because they make basically the same product, the companies must compete on the basis of price and product quality. It is always tempting for each company to exaggerate the claims of its product's

---

[7] Andrew Rudalevige, *Managing the President's Program* (Princeton, NJ: Princeton University Press, 2002); Joel Aberbach, "The U.S. Federal Executive in an Era of Change," *Governance* 16 (2003): 373–99; Terry Moe, "The Politicized Presidency," in *The New Direction in American Politics*, ed. John E. Chubb and Paul Peterson (Washington, DC: Brookings Institution, 1985), pp. 235–71.

[8] For a general discussion of bureaucracy solving collective dilemmas, see Mathew McCubbins, Roger Noll, and Barry Weingast, "Structure and Process, Politics and Policy," *Virginia Law Review* 75 (1989): 431–82.

superiority over the competition, or to claim that the other company's product is inferior or even dangerous. The Federal Trade Commission (FTC) is an independent agency charged with protecting consumers against unfair or deceptive practices, and this includes requiring that companies not lie in their advertising (Figure 7.1).

In policing the claims made by the two drug companies in their advertising, the FTC tries to move the companies away from the "defect-defect" equilibrium where they both lie to consumers. The FTC does this by suing (or threatening to sue) companies on behalf of the American people, claiming that the companies cannot back up the statements made in their advertisements. In the end, the two companies (not to mention consumers) are better off if they don't tear each other down with misinformation in advertising campaigns. Both companies can retain their reputation for safe products, and consumers can have confidence that they are not receiving false information. A regulatory agency is necessary to enforce and monitor this "cooperate-cooperate" outcome.

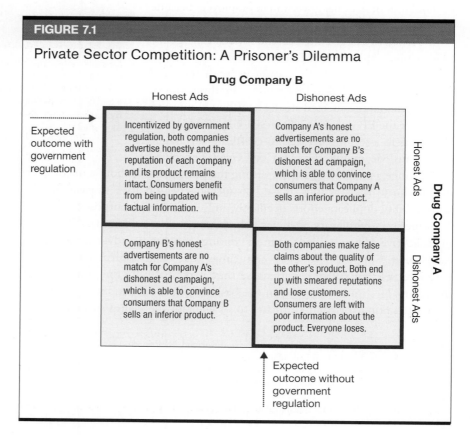

FIGURE 7.1

Private Sector Competition: A Prisoner's Dilemma

Drug Company B

	Honest Ads	Dishonest Ads
Honest Ads (Drug Company A)	Incentivized by government regulation, both companies advertise honestly and the reputation of each company and its product remains intact. Consumers benefit from being updated with factual information.	Company A's honest advertisements are no match for Company B's dishonest ad campaign, which is able to convince consumers that Company A sells an inferior product.
Dishonest Ads (Drug Company A)	Company B's honest advertisements are no match for Company A's dishonest ad campaign, which is able to convince consumers that Company B sells an inferior product.	Both companies make false claims about the quality of the other's product. Both end up with smeared reputations and lose customers. Consumers are left with poor information about the product. Everyone loses.

Expected outcome with government regulation → (points to Honest/Honest cell)

Expected outcome without government regulation → (points to Dishonest/Dishonest cell)

Bureaucrats as Policy Makers

Bureaucrats, like anyone else, have political goals and preferences, and moreover they are called upon to act as policy makers in certain ways. The shorthand version of policy making by the national government—Congress legislates and the president executes by relying on the executive-branch bureaucracy to enforce and implement the law—is overly simplistic. In reality, the executive branch conducts considerable lawmaking activity.

We described **administrative law** in the previous chapter on the presidency. In fact, the vast majority of administrative law is made within the executive-branch bureaucracy, not within the White House. The making of administrative law is referred to as **rule making** by governmental agencies. Laws passed by Congress are often vague, requiring the government to establish a program or to regulate an aspect of commercial, private, or governmental behavior. If a law is vague, the bureaucracy must determine the specific details of the law as it is to be applied in practice.

Most of the rules and regulations for conducting commercial activities in the United States are actually drafted by administrative agencies doing rule making. Congress's immense workload makes it impossible for its members and their staff to write sufficiently detailed legislation. In addition, Congress does not have the technical or scientific expertise that the executive-branch agencies have. Such expertise is necessary to write specific rules for, say, applying pesticides appropriately to avoid harming rare species, protecting workers in coal mines, or setting up the application process for students to request college loans. Interestingly, evidence shows that laws tend to be more vague under unified government than under divided government. This is probably because, under unified government, both branches are controlled by the same political party and Congress trusts the executive branch to implement the laws more faithfully than they would under divided government.[9]

The Administrative Procedures Act (APA) of 1946 established guidelines for agency rule making that are still followed. Specifically, the APA mandated, among other things, that agencies

- make records about all processes used to decide on regulations and rules fully transparent and accessible to the public;
- publish regulations in a timely manner and allow regulated persons time to comply;
- publish proposed regulations and allow public hearings prior to enforcement, during which the agency can make amendments in response to public comment;

administrative law The body of law created by executive agencies with the purpose of refining general law passed in legislation.

rule making The process by which governmental agencies provide details on how laws passed by elected officials will be implemented.

[9] John D. Huber and Charles R. Shipan, *Deliberate Discretion: The Institutional Foundations of Bureaucratic Autonomy* (New York: Cambridge University Press, 2002).

- use trial-like procedures in many cases to adjudicate disputes, including protection for witnesses and defendants, and attorney-client privileges;
- report to Congress regularly on the results of regulations.

Because of the APA guidelines, agencies first propose a new set of rules, then allow for citizens and interest groups to comment on the proposed rules, and then possibly amend the rules in response to comments. If public interest is high for a proposed rule, it is not uncommon for members of Congress to weigh in and require hearings. As an example, in 2012 the EPA and the U.S. Department of Transportation proposed rules requiring that by 2025 all automobiles sold in the United States have 54.5 miles-per-gallon fuel efficiency. This set of rules was decided upon after long comments periods, during which the agencies and the department heard from hundreds of consumer groups, oil companies, auto companies, driver associations, and environmental groups, not to mention members of Congress. Note that the specific fuel standards were set by decisions of bureaucratic agencies and not by legislation passed by Congress, and those fuel standard requirements for automobile companies have the force of law. The bureaucrats were given the mandate by previous laws to set standards to achieve goals set by Congress and the president—to reduce American dependence on fossil fuels, cut costs for consumers who drive automobiles, and improve the environment. It is a multistep process beginning with legislation that grants the bureaucrats the discretion to fill in the details with rule making later.

Besides rule making, bureaucrats act as policy makers in a more general, less formal way. Scholars sometimes refer to the people who most directly implement policies as "street-level" bureaucrats.[10] They staff the offices that interact with citizens and representatives from interest groups and companies; they conduct the inspections or experiments; they write the memos justifying decisions; and they organize small groups of bureaucrats to do the work of government. In each of these day-to-day actions, bureaucrats make important policy decisions. As an example, consider an inspector of meatpacking factories for the Department of Agriculture. He or she decides whether a slaughterhouse is clean enough for slaughtering cows and storing meat to satisfy federal regulations. Or consider a federal prosecutor deciding whether to charge someone with financial fraud. Is there enough evidence of fraud to proceed with charges? These are judgment calls made by individuals on the basis of their knowledge of the laws and their observations. Through their everyday practices, they set standards and create routines of behavior by the government.

---

[10] Michael Lipsky, *Street-Level Bureaucracy* (New York: Russell Sage, 1980).

Development of the Executive Bureaucracy

In the early years of the American republic, national government policies were administered by a few agencies led by groups of people appointed by the Continental Congress. As early as the 1780s, following the ideas of Alexander Hamilton and based on the British model of governmental administration, the government began to create "departments" headed by a single, appointed person called a secretary.

In 1789, there were three executive agencies—the State Department, the Treasury Department, and the War Department (later called Defense)—and the Office of the Attorney General (later a full-fledged department called Justice). The number of agencies and their scope grew slowly. Throughout the nineteenth century, the small size and focused work of the national agencies reflected the limited scope of the national government. Most national bureaucrats in the nineteenth century were post-office workers, soldiers, or customs officials. As the bureaucracy grew more quickly in the late nineteenth and early twentieth centuries, numerous reforms were proposed to make it more effective and efficient.

Growth in Size

In previous chapters, we studied the increasing nationalization of the American political system and the growing power of the presidency. Largely due to these trends, the bureaucracy has grown. By tracking the changes and large spikes in the size of the bureaucracy, one can trace the major eras of reform, the wars, and the establishment of new programs (Figure 7.2).

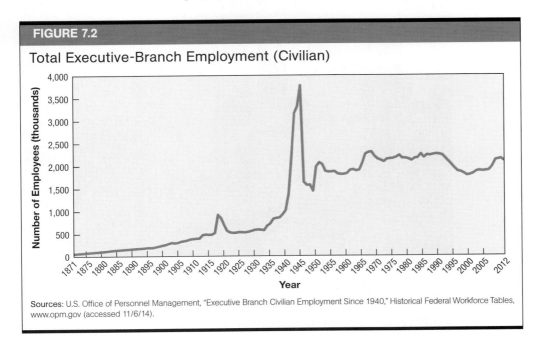

FIGURE 7.2

Total Executive-Branch Employment (Civilian)

Sources: U.S. Office of Personnel Management, "Executive Branch Civilian Employment Since 1940," Historical Federal Workforce Tables, www.opm.gov (accessed 11/6/14).

The first major increase began in the late nineteenth century and continued through the Progressive Era in the early 1900s. The bureaucracy grew as the national government increasingly regulated the national economy and built a larger military. For regulation purposes, the government created a new type of bureaucracy: the independent agency (or commission). The first such agency, the Interstate Commerce Commission, was formed in 1887 to regulate railroads and later trucking and other surface carriers of goods and people. The Federal Trade Commission (1913) and the Federal Reserve Administration (1914) were created to regulate, respectively, financial transactions and the money supply for banks.

Independent agencies were ostensibly designed to have greater autonomy from political officials than executive departments had. People working for the independent agencies could be dismissed only "for cause." This means that employees, even those appointed by the president, could not be fired by the president or their superiors at the top of the agency except for specific reasons having to do with performance or for corruption. With the more traditional executive departments that are part of the president's cabinet, workers in leadership positions who are appointed by the president serve at his or her discretion—that is, the president can fire them for any reason unless the law specifically says otherwise.

The New Deal programs of the 1930s vastly expanded the federal bureaucracy. One of the largest new programs administered by government agencies was the Social Security program. When the program went into effect in 1936, bureaucrats (like the workers in this Social Security office) had to set up and administer accounts for millions of Americans.

The national bureaucracy spiked in size during the 1930s and 1940s, following New Deal legislation and the massive mobilization for World War II. Many New Deal agencies, including executive departments and independent commissions, were created to regulate even more sectors of the economy. Examples include the Transportation Safety Administration and the Social Security Administration. The Department of Defense was created in 1947 through the merger of the Departments of the Army and the Navy and the addition of the Air Force. Its establishment reflected the need to coordinate the global presence of the American military after World War II.

Another notable growth period of the civilian bureaucracy occurred in the 1960s and 1970s with Lyndon Johnson's Great Society programs and related new initiatives under Presidents Richard Nixon and Jimmy Carter. During that era, Congress passed laws creating agencies such as the Department of Housing and Urban Development, the EPA, and the Department of Education, which was spun off from the Department of Health, Education, and Welfare that had been created in 1953.

Since the 1960s the overall the size of the federal bureaucracy in terms of regular employees has plateaued, with occasional small dips or increases. The minor growth in the civilian bureaucracy in the early 2000s resulted largely from the establishment of the new Department of Homeland Security (DHS). The department was created by splitting off some agencies from other parts of the executive-branch bureaucracy, bringing under its umbrella agencies that formerly stood alone and establishing new bureaucratic offices. The new Transportation Safety Administration is part of DHS, as is FEMA, once under the Department of Housing and Urban Development, which was a cabinet-level department prior to being absorbed into DHS.

Figure 7.2 shows the link between major wars and the growth of the military bureaucracy. Large spikes occurred during the two world wars and the Korean, Vietnam, and two Iraq wars. During the Cold War (1946–90), the military stayed relatively large to manage American obligations around the world associated with the containment of communism. When the Cold War ended, the size of the military shrank briefly, only to grow again during the Gulf War (1991–92) and the war in Iraq that started in 2003.

The Spoils System

The nature of presidential appointments has also changed over time. Recall our discussion of Andrew Jackson's presidency in Chapter 6. Because Jackson believed that national bureaucrats should not hold government jobs for long periods, he instituted a rotation system, which had the effect of opening up positions for presidential appointments every four years or so. This conveniently aligned with presidential elections and, in effect, ushered in the *patronage* or *spoils system*: to the victorious party (which won the presidency and did well in congressional elections) went the spoils (jobs). Thus, starting in the 1830s with Jackson's presidency, the national bureaucracy became a favorite vehicle for elected presidents to reward their supporters with government jobs.[11]

This patronage-appointment system had a major impact on the federal bureaucracy, but its excesses soon became obvious as constant turnover and underqualified appointees interfered with the effective implementation of government policies. In the late nineteenth century, Congress passed laws establishing a professional civil service. However, vestiges of the spoils system still exist at the top of the bureaucracy. Presidents continue to fill several thousand leadership positions in the bureaucracy with men and women who either worked directly on or helped fund their campaigns, or who are known to be sympathetic to the ideological and political goals of the president.

One problem with filling bureaucratic positions with political appointees is that campaign supporters and other ideological allies in those positions are not always knowledgeable or professionally trained to do their jobs. President George W. Bush appointed Michael D. Brown, a man with little experience in disaster relief, to be in charge of FEMA. When Hurricane Katrina devastated the Gulf Coast in 2005, the press and members of Congress accused Brown of incompetence in coordinating the federal response. In another example, Bush, wanting to reward a major fund-raiser for his campaign, appointed a man who did not speak French as ambassador to France. Nearly all presidents have made similarly embarrassing appointments, though in the heyday of the spoils system this kind of cronyism was more widespread and reached further down the bureaucratic ranks.

As the national government in the late nineteenth century increased its role in the economy and in building an infrastructure for commerce across regions, many government jobs required a measure of expertise. It became important, for example, for inspectors of meatpacking plants to know something about the science of pathogens and public health. In the 1880s, reformers known as *mugwumps* called for abolishing the spoils system and instituting a more merit-based bureaucracy. Mugwumps were mostly Republicans known for their willingness to support the Democrats when necessary to achieve reforms.[12] Reformers' appeals played well with segments of the population who were shut out from government jobs—pretty much anyone, that is, who was not active in the president's campaign or from a group considered crucial to the president's election efforts. Led by the mugwumps, reformers pressured the national government to take action in the 1880s to do away with the worst excesses of the spoils system. The core idea was to make the bureaucracy more professional and insulated from politicians who want to fill the jobs with their cronies.

[11] Robert Remini, *The Life of Andrew Jackson* (New York: Harper and Row, 1998).

[12] *Mugwump* means "great man" in the Algonquin language. It eventually became a political slur, meaning someone who is indecisive or lacks ideological conviction.

Civil Service Reform

With the Pendleton Act of 1883, the national government began to institute a civil service system. The act made it illegal to require people to pay dues to political parties in order to get national government jobs, and it instituted layers of the national bureaucracy that are "protected," meaning they are not subject to political appointment and are classified or ranked by the skill and education levels required. Other countries, including Britain, France, and Germany, were instituting similar reforms at the same time.

All of these civil services are characterized by a system of evaluation and promotion from within the bureaucracies; tests and training take place to ensure that competent people fill the jobs. It is expected that employees in the bureaucracy can keep their job when a new president or new government is elected, but that the bureaucrats must work on behalf of whoever is in office. Salaries are allocated according to rank, and professional codes of conduct prohibit graft and political favoritism. Today, the vast majority of civilian bureaucrats in the U.S. government are civil servants—that is, their jobs are protected from patronage and they cannot be fired by an incoming president for political reasons. Presidential appointees occupy only the top layers of a typical department.

Civil service reform sought to establish rational, routine procedures for conducting work, communicating among employees, hiring employees, setting salaries, and managing promotions and demotions (or layoffs). One goal was to minimize uncertainty in budgeting and to create a smoothly functioning bureaucracy in which people knew their jobs well and could coordinate their actions for the benefit of the organization. The increasingly technical nature of government work by the late nineteenth century provided further motivation to improve efficiency and performance within the government bureaucracy. Ideally, in jobs that required skill and specific knowledge, experienced bureaucrats who had learned how to do their jobs well would be able to retain those jobs and continue cultivating their expertise. Many people came to realize that it was wasteful for the government to remove a highly skilled worker, or someone who was successfully learning those skills, just to repay a political favor. The rapid turnover of qualified personnel in bureaucracies every time a new president took office represented a lost opportunity to build expertise in the bureaucracy.

Civil service reforms also served to break the grip that certain political party bosses had on specific segments of the national bureaucracy. It was well known in the nineteenth century that party bosses in New York had final say over who could fill the potentially lucrative national bureaucratic positions in the New York customhouses. These officials oversaw imports coming into the United States and collected customs and duties. Plum jobs in these houses afforded many opportunities to accept bribes from importers. The civil service reforms did not do away with all forms of bribery and patronage politics, but they did diminish their incidence and contributed to a much more professionalized, effective government bureaucracy, especially in those realms requiring expertise or some measure of political neutrality.

Beginning in the late 1890s, the Progressive Movement carried on this philosophy of scientific management as it applied to government bureaucracies. The Progressives, like their mugwump predecessors, believed fundamentally in the idea that government could and should be operated in an apolitical and nonpartisan manner based on scientific principles. In the first two decades of the twentieth century, especially with the elections of presidents Theodore Roosevelt and Woodrow Wilson, the national government continued shifting toward a civil service form of bureaucracy and setting up independent agencies. In fact, early in his career as a professor, Wilson had written famous works extolling the virtues of scientific management.

Modern Reforms of the Bureaucracy

In spite of these reforms, and in part because the government bureaucracy at all levels grew throughout the twentieth century even with the implementation of the civil service model, the federal bureaucracy is widely seen today as bloated and inefficient. Many people complain that the bureaucracy grows but never shrinks (in fact, as noted later, its size has remained remarkably stable since the 1950s), and that large bureaucracies waste taxpayers' money and are inherently inefficient. It is often tempting for politicians running for office to tap into the public's wariness of large government agencies. The Republican Party has traditionally been the party of "small government," but throughout the twentieth century presidents of both major parties, as well as a number of third-party candidates, ran for office promising to clean up government "red tape" and provide the same or more government service for less tax money.

Ronald Reagan was openly hostile to government bureaucracy during his first campaign for president in 1980. He complained of runaway government budgets, bloated bureaucracy, regulations that hampered legitimate business activity, and corruption in the distribution of welfare benefits. He promised to reduce government regulation of businesses, cut taxes and government spending, and reorganize agencies to eliminate redundancy, waste, and fraud. Reagan's campaign struck a responsive chord among people upset by media reports of $600 toilet seats purchased by the Department of Defense for government airplanes, or welfare cheats who drove fancy cars while taking advantage of generous government programs. Although some of these stories were exaggerated or apocryphal, many Americans agreed with Reagan that they paid too much in taxes for what they received in public goods and services.

As part of his effort to shrink the federal bureaucracy, Reagan was determined to weaken public employee unions. In 1981, he dramatically fired more than 11,000 federal air traffic controllers who had gone on strike over pay and working conditions. (National government employees were first permitted to

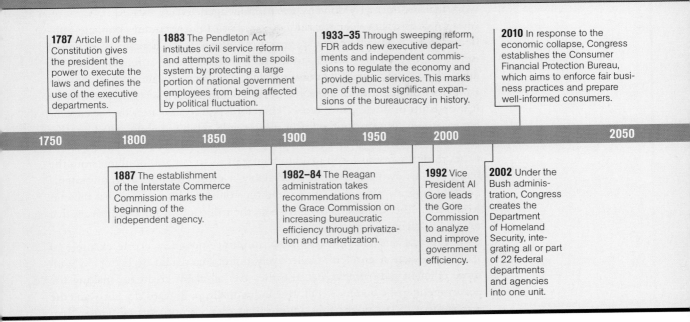

HISTORICAL PATH Development and Reform of the Federal Bureaucracy

1787 Article II of the Constitution gives the president the power to execute the laws and defines the use of the executive departments.

1883 The Pendleton Act institutes civil service reform and attempts to limit the spoils system by protecting a large portion of national government employees from being affected by political fluctuation.

1933–35 Through sweeping reform, FDR adds new executive departments and independent commissions to regulate the economy and provide public services. This marks one of the most significant expansions of the bureaucracy in history.

2010 In response to the economic collapse, Congress establishes the Consumer Financial Protection Bureau, which aims to enforce fair business practices and prepare well-informed consumers.

1750   1800   1850   1900   1950   2000   2050

1887 The establishment of the Interstate Commerce Commission marks the beginning of the independent agency.

1982–84 The Reagan administration takes recommendations from the Grace Commission on increasing bureaucratic efficiency through privatization and marketization.

1992 Vice President Al Gore leads the Gore Commission to analyze and improve government efficiency.

2002 Under the Bush administration, Congress creates the Department of Homeland Security, integrating all or part of 22 federal departments and agencies into one unit.

unionize in 1962, but unlike workers in the private sector, they were prohibited from striking.) In the wake of the strike, the Reagan administration decertified the controllers' union, fined senior union officials, and banned strikers from holding government jobs in the future.

In some cases, complaints about bureaucratic inefficiency and bungling are clearly justified. Individual government agencies often need reform, and the consolidation and coordination of the sprawling federal bureaucracy is an ongoing concern. For example, the September 11 terrorist attacks in 2001 highlighted the lack of communication among law enforcement and intelligence agencies spread across several departments, such as Defense, State, and Justice. Most analysts consider the collapse of financial markets in 2008–09 to have resulted in part because of failed coordination among, and weak enforcement of regulations by, agencies in various government departments.

Sometimes, members of Congress and the president move beyond campaign promises and actually work to reform the bureaucracy by improving laws and regulations or by cutting costs. Agencies are periodically consolidated and jobs eliminated. In fact, since the beginning of the twentieth century, there have been 11 major presidential commissions devoted to reforming the executive branch. These commissions made recommendations, many of which were implemented by Congress and the president, to abolish certain agencies, consolidate others, and privatize much of the work of government.[13] Privatization means that the government contracts with private companies to conduct work that was formerly done by government agencies.

It is not easy, however, for the government to cut jobs and eliminate public programs.[14] Members of Congress from districts that contain government offices targeted for cuts will try to scuttle legislation aimed at reducing bureaucracy, since it may hurt their constituents and thus their chances of re-election. People who benefit from a specific government program will blame Congress if it ends up on the cutting block. Therefore, politicians often find it expedient to support bureaucratic reforms in principle, while avoiding actual, specific reforms that affect a given constituency. In 2010, Secretary of Defense Robert Gates took the unusual step of announcing plans to cut $600 million from the budget of his own department. Predictably, it caused an uproar among members of Congress and politicians around the country who worried that the cuts would force the military to close bases in their districts or hurt companies that relied on defense contracts.

The politicians' reaction to Gates's announcement is a classic example of a collective-action problem. Collectively, politicians would be better off with more efficient government, because they can all claim credit for making the government work better overall. But individually, politicians do not want the government to cut public jobs among their own constituents. So rather than cooperating, they "defect" and vote against reforms that might be unpopular with their constituents, even if the reforms would help the government and the country as a whole.

Nonetheless, many bureaucratic reforms have resulted in reducing the size of the bureaucracy, or at least slowing its growth. As Figure 7.2 shows, starting in the 1950s the overall size of the civilian bureaucracy leveled off at around 2 million workers. It has remained remarkably constant since then, even though the population it serves and the money the government spends have grown significantly.

How can the federal government spend so much more and serve so many more people with fewer workers in the bureaucracy? The gain in efficiency is partly due to technological advances. Computers, for example, have enabled fewer employees to do the work of collecting and distributing government benefits. Before the advent of computers, running the Social Security program entailed keeping paper records for each of the millions of employed, retired, or disabled people in the United States. However, the reduction in the size of the

[13] Paul Light, *The Tides of Reform* (New Haven, CT: Yale University Press, 1997). More recent data can be found in Daniel Carpenter, "The Evolution of National Bureaucracy in the United States," in *The Institutions of American Democracy: The Executive Branch*, ed. Joel Aberbach and Mark Peterson (New York: Oxford University Press, 2005), pp. 41–71.

[14] Hugh Heclo, *A Government of Strangers* (Washington, DC: Brookings Institution, 1977); Paul Light, *The Tides of Reform* (New Haven, CT: Yale University Press, 1997); Glenn Beamer, *Creative Politics* (Ann Arbor: University of Michigan Press, 1999).

bureaucracy is mostly the result of various programs of reform, especially since the 1980s, which limited the growth of the executive branch. These reform efforts have led to a decline in the number of employees and the elimination of numerous agencies. More than half of the federal agencies created between 1947 and 1998—57 percent—have been abolished because of mergers of agencies, creation of new replacement agencies, or simply elimination altogether of the tasks.[15]

Privatization and Marketization

There has been a big push since the 1980s for the national government to privatize and marketize.[16] **Privatization** refers to having private-sector companies or individuals implement government programs. **Marketization** refers to having government agencies adopt principles of private enterprise when making decisions and implementing policies.

Privatization takes numerous forms. One example is when the government hires a company or an organization on a **contract** basis to carry out a task, such as building roads, making military jets, or providing security in Iraq or Afghanistan for American diplomats and military leaders. Such contracts account for a significant portion of the federal government's budget—the 2014 figure was about $408 billion, or approximately 11 percent of the total budget—and have long been accepted practice.

Other types of privatization also account for a large proportion of government spending. The government can give **grants** to people and organizations to perform a task in the public interest, such as conducting research, experimenting with new policy initiatives, attending school, and making art. In 2014, government grants totaled roughly $589 billion. Sometimes, the government partners with private financial institutions to fund public projects. In recent years, this has included partnering with companies to build factories and housing that are jointly used by government agencies and by others. (An example is housing for military personnel and their families that is open to nonmilitary families as well.) The government can rely on volunteers and private donations to conduct work that is sanctioned by the government but directed by a private agency. For instance, the Red Cross is authorized by the government to provide relief to victims of disasters, but it is not formally a public entity. The government can also sell land and other assets to private companies or individuals, a form of privatization that increases government revenue.

Since the 1980s, privatization reform has been a huge factor in flattening the growth of the government bureaucracy. Reagan appointed a prominent

privatization The contracting of private companies by the government to conduct work that was formerly done by government agencies.

marketization Government bureaucratic reform that emphasizes market-based principles of management that are common to the private sector.

government contract An agreement whereby the government hires a company or an organization to carry out certain tasks on its behalf.

government grants Money that the government provides to individuals or organizations to perform tasks in the public's interest.

---

[15] See Daniel P. Carpenter, "The Evolution of National Bureaucracy in the United States," in *The Executive Branch*, ed. Joel D. Aberbach and Mark Peterson (New York: Oxford University Press, 2005), pp. 52–53.

[16] Donald Kettl, *The Transformation of Governance* (Baltimore: Johns Hopkins Press, 2000).

businessman, J. Peter Grace, to lead a commission devoted to reducing the size and cost of the executive branch. The Grace Commission (1982–84) made many recommendations for reform that focused on the idea that the government should emulate the private sector more closely. This recommendation not only entailed privatizing many government tasks but also meant that government bureaucracies should adopt market-based principles of management widely used by private corporations (marketization).

One highly controversial example of marketization sometimes used at the state or local level is government-funded vouchers that parents can "spend" to send their children to private schools. The premise behind vouchers is that failing public schools will improve in order to compete for students and funding. Another example is the use of "pollution rights" that can be traded on the open market. Under these so-called cap-and-trade policies, companies (typically power plants) are allotted permits to pollute the environment with a certain quantity of emissions (up to a limit, or "cap"). They can buy other companies' emissions permits if they need to exceed the cap, or sell their own permits if they succeed in reducing emissions. In theory, the price of emissions permits should adjust so that supply meets demand, while the overall level of emissions (which is set by the government) gradually declines. Like school vouchers, pollution rights and emissions permits are controversial, but both the United States and the European Union have market-based emissions trading programs in place.

The Grace Commission's recommendations, and the underlying concepts of marketization and privatization, have influenced bureaucratic reform efforts by both Republican and Democratic administrations. Promoting privatization is a way for politicians to have their cake and eat it too. They can claim to keep the size of government in check while still maintaining the services that make constituents happy. Critics of privatization charge that private companies are more interested in profits than in the public good. Furthermore, private companies are much less accountable to elected officials than are government bureaucrats. During the Iraq War, for example, numerous private companies provided security for American government officials working in Iraq or actually carried out government-mandated rebuilding efforts in Iraq. There were instances of fraud and recurring complaints about a lack of oversight of these contractors. Without the direct control of the White House or a cabinet secretary, it can be difficult to monitor and coordinate these companies' actions.

In the Iraq and Afghanistan wars, the U.S. military hired private companies to do the work previously handled by government employees. For example, in Iraq, private contractors provided security services and even engaged in some combat operations, raising questions about accountability.

Principals and Agents in the Executive Bureaucracy

The principal–agent problem introduced in Chapter 1 sheds light on the politics of the bureaucracy. To reiterate briefly, principal–agent problems occur because principals cannot always observe what agents are doing. As a result, agents can shirk their duties and even steal from the principals. Let us now consider two major factors that contribute to this problem in the context of the federal bureaucracy: the tendency of government agencies to "drift" from their defined missions, and the often conflicting motivations of bureaucrats and elected officials.[17]

Drift

In the American political system, we often think of elected officials—members of Congress and the president—as the principals and the executive-branch bureaucrats as the agents. Problems arise when bureaucrats gradually change their behavior and stray from what the elected representatives want, working instead toward what the bureaucrats want. This is sometimes referred to as **bureaucratic drift**, in that agents "drift" from the mandates given to them by principals.

Of course, there is another side to this story too. A newly elected Congress or president may change policy preferences after an election and push the bureaucracy to alter its priorities. This situation, when the principals change but the agents stay the same, is known as **coalitional drift**. The agents are expected to adjust to the new political principals, but how quickly? And how completely? See Figure 7.3 for a comparison of bureaucratic and coalitional drift.

To illustrate how the principal–agent problem can apply to bureaucratic politics, let us consider a hypothetical example. Suppose Congress passes a law mandating that the EPA ensure that factories do not dump mercury into rivers. The EPA, as the agent, is supposed to do what Congress, as the principal, has asked it to do. Congress gives the EPA money to carry out these tasks. It instructs the EPA to notify companies of the rule changes, inspect factories regularly, monitor water quality in the rivers, and investigate possible illegal dumping of mercury.

The EPA could drift away from these duties for several reasons. First, the agency may be busy and its leaders may feel that they do not have the resources to do all that Congress and the president ask. If they respond by making choices and prioritizing the agency's many tasks, they may delay implementation of the mercury regulation and focus on other tasks that they consider more urgent.

bureaucratic drift When government agencies depart from executing policy consistent with the ideological preferences of Congress or the president so as to execute policy consistent with their own ideological preferences.

coalitional drift When an ideological shift in elected branches creates disparity between the way an agency executes policy and the way new members of Congress or a new president believes the agency ought to execute policy.

[17] William Niskanen, *Bureaucracy and Representative Government* (Chicago: Aldine, 1971); David Epstein and Sharyn O'Halloran, *Delegating Powers* (New York: Cambridge University Press, 1999).

FIGURE 7.3

Bureaucratic Drift and Coalitional Drift

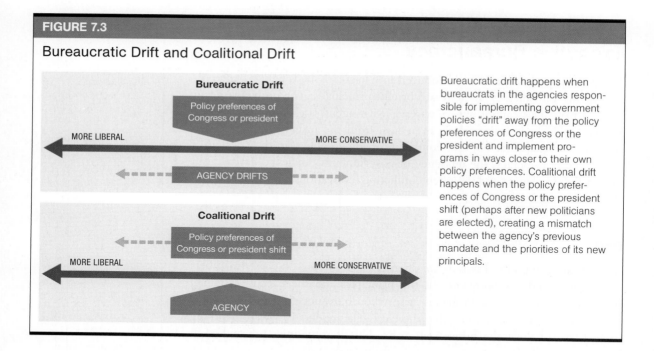

Bureaucratic drift happens when bureaucrats in the agencies responsible for implementing government policies "drift" away from the policy preferences of Congress or the president and implement programs in ways closer to their own policy preferences. Coalitional drift happens when the policy preferences of Congress or the president shift (perhaps after new politicians are elected), creating a mismatch between the agency's previous mandate and the priorities of its new principals.

Congress, however, may want immediate compliance with the mercury law and so view the agency as shirking its duty by delaying.

Second, the EPA has multiple principals who cannot always be satisfied simultaneously. This is a constant problem for executive-branch agencies. The EPA's leaders are appointed by the president but mandated to carry out laws passed by Congress (and usually signed by *a* president, who may no longer be in office). If the mercury law was passed during a previous administration and the new president disagrees with it, the new president or the EPA leaders he or she appointed may instruct the EPA to drag its feet, go easy on offending companies, or simply ignore the law altogether. Although Congress typically sets out the details of the laws to be implemented and controls the budgets, the president nominates the leaders of the agencies and can fire top-level agency employees. These cross-pressures from the different branches of government could lead the EPA to drift away from its congressional mandate.

A third reason for drift could arise from corporations, which may provide compelling arguments for why dumping mercury in rivers is not as bad as disposing of it in waste containers that then get buried. The industry might be able to produce research indicating that the leaching of mercury into the soil from containers poses a greater environmental danger than releasing the chemical into rivers. Perhaps the EPA is convinced by this evidence. Its leaders then face a classic choice for a government bureaucracy: obey Congress's mandate strictly, even if it means doing something they think might be wrong, or rely on their own best judgment.

All three of these examples are forms of drifting away from the congressional mandate. In the third case, critics may accuse the EPA of being "captured" by interest groups—the corporations that supplied the research findings on the matter it was supposed to be regulating. So-called **bureaucratic capture** refers to regulatory agencies being more beholden to the interest groups they regulate than to the principals for whom they work.[18] (We will return to this issue in Chapter 11.)

A fourth, and more general, way for the EPA to shirk its duty as defined by Congress is to spend money it gets from Congress irresponsibly. In an ideal world, government bureaucracies would spend only as much as they need in order to accomplish their mandates, and then return the rest to the public treasury. In doing so, the bureaucracies would be acting as responsible agents for the elected representatives. In the real world, many critics claim, government bureaucracies typically spend all of their money by the end of the fiscal year, regardless of whether the spending is efficient and rational. Then they complain to elected representatives that they do not have enough funding and ask for an increase for the following year. Elected officials cannot keep track of all the spending decisions of government bureaucracies to make sure they are always spending money responsibly.

Fifth, the EPA could simply be corrupt. Its personnel could take bribes from companies and allow illegal pollution of the rivers to go on. This kind of bureaucratic misconduct is rare, but hardly unheard of. In a major scandal in 2006, corporate lobbyist Jack Abramoff was sentenced to prison for corruption of public officials and other crimes related to the defrauding of American Indian tribes. Abramoff's conviction also shed light onto numerous cases of conspiracy by bureaucratic officials, many of whom were later convicted of illegally accepting various gifts under the table.

You might ask, Why does Congress let agencies get away with such less-than-dutiful actions? The truth is that Congress passes so many rules and regulations that it cannot monitor everything that all the agencies do. To return to our hypothetical mercury regulation, Congress may not discover the EPA's shirking unless its members hear complaints about river pollution from environmental groups, or call on the agency to account for its implementation of the regulation. In fact, as we will see later in the section on congressional oversight, Congress has set up internal institutional rules precisely for the purpose of dealing with the fundamental principal–agent problem associated with bureaucratic agencies. Members of Congress want to be informed when agencies "drift" away and shirk the tasks assigned to them.[19]

bureaucratic capture When regulatory agencies are beholden to the organizations or interests they are supposed to regulate.

[18] For a more general argument about capture and drift, see William Niskanen, *Bureaucracy and Representative Government* (Chicago: Aldine, 1971).

[19] Kathleen Bawn, "Political Control versus Expertise: Congressional Choices about Administrative Procedures," *American Political Science Review* 89 (1995): 62–73; Mathew McCubbins, Roger Noll, and Barry Weingast, "Administrative Procedures as Instruments of Political Control," *Journal of Law, Economics, and Organization* 3 (1987): 243–77; David Epstein and Sharyn O'Halloran, *Delegating Powers* (New York: Cambridge University Press, 1999).

The EPA example also shows how easily coalitional drift can occur in such situations. Consider a case involving the most recent change in presidential administrations. Under George W. Bush, the EPA was given low priority for funding and other resources. When asked to regulate companies, the Bush White House pressured the EPA to be lenient and to give companies extra time to comply with regulations. Often, the EPA was instructed to put industry representatives on panels that made administrative laws on environmental issues. When Barack Obama took over as president, the EPA suddenly became a priority for the White House. The EPA was expected to be a more forceful advocate for communities and environmental groups against industry. The Obama White House undid many of the Bush policies concerning the EPA. In this instance, most employees of the EPA welcomed the change in administration because it seemed as though the Obama administration appreciated their main mission more than the Bush administration did. Nevertheless, the EPA employees had to adjust quickly to their new political principals.

New presidential administrations sometimes seek to avoid the most jarring effects of coalitional drift, especially if the heads of agencies or departments are well liked by both political parties. Obama kept in place Bush's last secretary of defense, Robert Gates, because he had the respect of both major parties in Congress and was already moving the wars in Iraq and Afghanistan in the direction favored by Obama. Obama also nominated Bush's choice for chair of the Federal Reserve Bank, Ben Bernanke, for a second term.

The Motivations of Bureaucrats

As mentioned, bureaucrats, like others in government, have policy goals. And as employees, they generally want the same things other workers want from their jobs: clear instructions about what they are supposed to do, autonomy to carry out their tasks in the way they think best, and resources to accomplish their goals. Federal bureaucrats seldom get all three items on their wish list in the right proportions: *clarity in instructions* from Congress and the president, who often disagree and sometimes are from opposing parties; *autonomy* from too much intrusion by the people who pay their budgets and hire their bosses; and enough *resources* (money and staffing) allocated by people who find it easier to get re-elected the more they complain about spending within the bureaucracy.

But bureaucrats are not helpless; they can take actions to gain some autonomy and resources to do their jobs well. The political scientist Daniel Carpenter studied how upper-level civil servants in the early twentieth century cultivated allies across the national government, creating coalitions in favor of granting certain agencies more autonomy from political interference.[20] Until then, for

---

[20] Daniel P. Carpenter, *The Forging of Bureaucratic Autonomy: Reputations, Networks, and Policy Innovation in Executive Agencies, 1862–1928* (Princeton, NJ: Princeton University Press, 2001).

example, the Department of Agriculture was dominated by political patronage appointments. Independent-minded bureaucrats like Seaman Knapp pushed for the department to make decisions based on the science of seeds, crops, and soils. In 1902–3, Knapp was instrumental in convincing members of both parties in Congress that the department deserved money and autonomy to help farmers increase their yields of crops and experiment with new techniques. Largely through the efforts of bureaucrats like Knapp, many parts of the Department of Agriculture gained stature as nonpartisan agencies that provided technical assistance to farmers regardless of their political affiliations, and the department was able to expand with increased funding from Congress and new positions for scientists.

It is clear from Carpenter's research that bureaucrats can act like politicians— not in the sense of having to win elections, but in terms of building coalitions to bring about policy change. Bureaucrats, like all other citizens, have personal opinions and attitudes about policies and social goals. Sometimes they have to refrain from stating their political preferences in the workplace (and in some jobs, they cannot publicly advocate for or against certain controversial policies). Nevertheless, many bureaucrats can—and do—work harder at the tasks they believe they should be doing, and less hard at the tasks they believe they should *not* be doing.

Bureaucrats can also use their position to press for policy change that they see as desirable.[21] One advantage bureaucrats tend to have over members of Congress and the president is expert knowledge of a policy area and information about which policies work and do not work. They can use this information in their reports, in their publicity materials for the news media and for constituents, and in their communications with Congress. Furthermore, because bureaucrats are the government officials who are most directly in contact with the public, they can sometimes encourage people to communicate with Congress. Technically, members of the bureaucracy are not allowed to lobby members of Congress on behalf of their agencies, but they can, in a variety of ways, mobilize constituents to pressure Congress. The National Science Foundation (NSF), an independent agency constantly targeted for budget cuts, is masterful at letting university-based scientists and researchers know who in Congress is currently threatening the agency's independence or its budget (or both). The implication is clear: although the NSF cannot lobby, it can inform, and bureaucrats in the NSF hope that those they inform will act to pressure Congress.

[21] Joel Aberbach, "The U.S. Federal Executive in an Era of Change," *Governance* 16 (2003): 373–99; Terry Moe, "The Politicized Presidency," in *The New Direction in American Politics*, ed. John E. Chubb and Paul Peterson (Washington, DC: Brookings Institution, 1985), pp. 235–71.

Shaping and Influencing the Bureaucracy

We began this chapter indicating how the executive branch bureaucracy has two main principals, Congress and the president. Their direct influence over the bureaucracy occurs through the processes of appointments, budgeting, and oversight.

Appointments

Both the president and the Congress (through the Senate) are involved in appointing the leadership of the bureaucracy; in general, the president proposes and the Senate approves. Although most of the people who work in executive-branch agencies are civil service employees, the top positions are almost always filled by appointees. It is a matter of law which of these appointments must be approved by the Senate; generally, the higher up the person will be in a department or an agency, the more likely it is that he or she must be approved by the Senate.

The appointment of cabinet secretaries, and perhaps of officials one or two layers further down in the hierarchy of an agency, can be politically controversial, especially under divided government. When the Senate was controlled by Democrats during President George W. Bush's tenure in office, the Senate stalled on many of Bush's appointment requests or turned them down. A similar pattern occurred during the Clinton presidency when the Republicans controlled the Senate. Under President Obama, Republican senators, though not in a majority, frequently filibustered to prevent selected appointments of the president.

Moreover, after the appointments are made, there can be tension between the professionals already working in the bureaucracy and the new political appointees.[22] Civil service workers are obligated to do what their superiors ask, regardless of whether they agree. Career bureaucrats in the EPA, who tend to have environmentalist backgrounds and sympathies, were known to resent top-level appointees of Presidents Reagan, George H. W. Bush, and George W. Bush. They viewed the political appointees as favoring business interests more than protection of the environment. Likewise, there is a long history of tension between professional military personnel in the Pentagon and their civilian bosses, both the president and top-level presidential appointees.

Budgeting

While the Senate's role in appointments is substantial, budgeting serves as Congress's major control over the executive-branch bureaucracy. The president is involved as well in proposing an annual budget to Congress. Further, through

---

[22] Joel Aberbach, "The U.S. Federal Executive in an Era of Change," *Governance* 16 (2003): 373–99.

the information provided by the Office of Management and Budget (OMB) and through the president's public statements, the president profoundly shapes the budgets of the various bureaucratic agencies. Nevertheless, Congress in the end controls the "purse strings" of government. The annual budgeting process includes deciding on the specific budgets of all the executive-branch agencies.

There is an important distinction between Congress *authorizing* that something be done by the national government and Congress *appropriating* money to enable the national bureaucracy to implement the law. Even if something is authorized under law, until the money is appropriated by Congress to pay for it, the law will remain a dead letter. Thus, Congress can pass a bill to authorize the building of a new type of aircraft carrier, but until a separate bill is passed that appropriates money for the new fleet of aircraft carriers, nothing can flow to the Department of Defense for that purpose. (Sometimes a single bill can both authorize and appropriate.)

Recall our earlier discussion about how bureaucracies are often accused of spending their full appropriations and then asking for increases the next year, regardless of whether it is the most efficient use of the government's resources. This approach to budgeting is actually acknowledged and indeed expected by elected representatives, who often lack the information they need to make the most efficient spending decisions. In effect, as the principals (primarily Congress) asking the agents (bureaucracies) to spend money to solve problems, the principals cannot micromanage all the spending decisions involving many billions of dollars. To deal with the difficulty of tracking the income and expenditures of government bureaucracies, elected officials have created a system of "incremental budgeting." In this system, most government agencies in any given year can expect to receive approximately the same budget as the year before, with only a small, incremental increase. Thus, in the absence of a substantial change in the government's priorities, agency budgets tend to grow only modestly from year to year. Congress can eliminate any project simply by deleting the relevant line item in the agency's budget. Sometimes Congress may cut—or threaten to cut—an agency's entire budget. The national budget, however, provides departments and agencies with considerable discretion over their expenditures. This means that, short of a law requiring an agency to stop spending money on a particular action, the agency's leaders can often shift money from other parts of the agency to continue funding the project.

Oversight

Oversight refers to the monitoring of bureaucracies, and it is essentially how principals learn information on the agents. Both Congress and the president oversee the workings of the bureaucracy, though Congress plays the more direct and public role through hearings and investigations. Even one executive-branch bureaucracy can oversee or investigate another. Sometimes the Justice

Department will investigate other agencies (or even its own subagencies or personnel) if criminal wrongdoing is alleged, and the General Accounting Office (GAO) oversees the accounting, human resources, and budgeting practices of most of the federal bureaucracies.

In delegating authority to the bureaucracy, lawmakers have set up institutional rules for how bureaucracies should conduct their rule-making and adjudicating roles.[23] We already discussed the APA and the procedures required under that 1946 law. Two other laws are also critical to bureaucratic oversight. The Freedom of Information Act, passed in 1966, requires that government agencies, upon request, disclose information (other than information vital to national security) on their activities if the information has not already been released through public reporting. The Sunshine Act, passed in 1976, requires that, with certain exceptions, all meetings of government agencies must be open to public observation.

fire-alarm oversight Congressional oversight that relies on interest groups and citizens to inform representatives of unwarranted action.

police-patrol oversight Congressional oversight that consists of actively monitoring agencies through routine inspection.

Scholars of bureaucracy have argued that the APA, the Freedom of Information Act, and the Sunshine Act constitute a system of congressional **fire-alarm oversight** of the bureaucracy. In other words, members of Congress hear from constituents when the bureaucracy does not do its job well or conform to congressional mandates. This contrasts with **police-patrol oversight,** in which members of Congress keep constant tabs on bureaucracies, routinely inspecting what they do. By mandating public comment periods before regulations are finally decided, and mandating public hearings in many cases, these laws allow aggrieved constituents to do the job of overseeing the bureaucracy and setting off alarms in Congress if bureaucrats drift too far from their principals' wishes.[24]

The Courts' Influence

Court decisions play a major role in shaping overall bureaucratic responsibilities and influencing their decisions. Lawsuits can lead to court interpretations of laws mandating that bureaucracies play a smaller or larger role in determining public policy. One key decision in 2007, for instance, substantially altered the prerogatives of the EPA. During the George W. Bush administration in 2003, the EPA took the position that it did not have the authority to regulate pollutants for the purpose of controlling greenhouse gases and affecting climate change. A dozen states, including California, plus numerous cities sued, and in a 5–4 decision (labeled *Massachusetts v. EPA*), the Supreme Court sided with the states and local governments. The Court held that the Clean Air Act, originally passed in 1970 and amended since, required that the EPA regulate such pollutants.

[23] For a recent perspective on this topic, see Sean Gailmard and John W. Patty, *Learning while Governing: Information, Accountability, and Executive Branch Institutions* (Chicago: University of Chicago Press, 2013).

[24] Mathew D. McCubbins and Thomas Schwartz, "Congressional Oversight Overlooked: Police Patrols versus Fire Alarms," *American Journal of Political Science* 28 (1984): 165–79.

Defense Budgets and Beef Jerky

The U.S. Department of Defense has an annual budget of $530 billion, and its expressed mission is to "provide the military forces necessary to deter war" and "protect the security" of the country. A portion of its activities, however, involves doing things not directly related to providing military force. Why?

Interests

Politicians in Washington D.C. from both political parties want to claim credit for curbing the size of the bureaucracy as well as supporting exciting research. Democrats especially have new government projects they want to see funded, and are generally in favor of government supporting research and innovation. Republicans, meanwhile, are hesitant to reduce the amount of money to the Department of Defense (DoD). Already the party with a reputation for being strict on controlling the size of the government budget, Republicans, like their Democratic opponents, also want a reputation as supporters of a strong military and military troops. Finally, leaders of the DoD want to receive generous budgets and be given reasonable discretion on how to spend the funds.

Institutions

The DoD has two things going for it institutionally that insulate it from budget cutters. First is bureaucratic autonomy. As with any large government bureaucracy, there is a fundamental principal–agent problem between the elected branches and the DoD. Congress and the president—the principals—have limited information regarding every facet of such an enormous department and budget, and the DoD—the agent—has flexibility and discretion to set the boundaries on what it considers as part of its mission to defend the interests of the country. If the leaders want to spend some of the DoD's money on research, they have enough autonomy to shift resources in that direction. The second feature that insulates the DoD from budget cutters is the nature of its mission. Members of both parties can support funding defense, even if "defense" is defined broadly. Not many politicians from either party want to argue against military spending, and the DoD budget is a place that Congress can locate programs that they otherwise find difficult to fund.

It is difficult for members of Congress to vote against military spending even when it is deemed unnecessary, as it was for an alternative engine for the F-35 fighter, above.

Outcomes

Because of how it is insulated from budget cutting politicians, the DoD uses its funds for projects that seem tangential to the mission of the department or that seem to overlap with the responsibilities of other bureaucracies in the government. (In fact, Senator Tom Coburn, a Republican from Oklahoma, suggested that the department could cut $68 billion in nonmilitary spending from its budget.) It spends money on education, energy, and the Centers for Disease Control and Prevention, among others. For example, it funded research on slang on Twitter and developed a new form of beef jerky. It has become one of the few units in the U.S. government with relatively healthy budget and the flexibility to pursue innovative research and new social programs.

Think About It

Will the Department of Defense continue to be able to fund governmental activities that are not strictly defense related? Should Congress rein in the department? What are the downsides, if any, to having overlapping programs in different departments of the federal government?

An earlier Court decision set an important precedent for lawmaking in general. The 1984 Supreme Court decision in *Chevron v. the Natural Resources Defense Council* established a legal standard for upholding an agency's authority to write law in a specific area. If a person files a lawsuit challenging a bureaucratic agency's authority to write a rule following a congressional statute, the courts are first supposed to examine whether the congressional statute explicitly authorized the agency to write rules of implementation. If so, then the agency has considerable discretion. If, however, as is commonly the case, the legislation is not clear on this point, then the courts are to determine if the agency's interpretation of the statute is "reasonable" or "permissible." In the *Chevron* case, an environmental group had brought suit against the EPA in a lower federal court, arguing that the EPA's reinterpretation of part of the Clean Air Act of 1977 went beyond the agency's authority to interpret the law. The lower court ruled against the EPA, and Chevron, as an affected party, appealed the decision to the Supreme Court. The Supreme Court sided with Chevron and ruled that the EPA had reasonably interpreted the Clean Air Act. Environmental groups liked neither the EPA's interpretation of the act nor the Court's decision, but the legal ruling set an important precedent about the authority of federal agencies.

Interest Groups

Although much interest-group activity is focused on Congress, these groups lobby bureaucratic agencies as well. Groups try to influence those writing administrative laws and complain when their interests are threatened. Often, they enlist help from other parts of the government. Suppose a group of trucking companies is dismayed by the regulatory actions of the Department of Transportation. They may try to convince members of the specialized congressional transportation committees, who make most of the budgetary decisions affecting the department, that their complaints deserve attention. Another way to complain is to request a visit with someone in the White House; that person, assuming he or she agrees with the trucking companies, can put pressure on the Department of Transportation to alter its behavior. Or the trucking companies can take their grievances directly to the bureaucrats themselves and request hearings.

When scholars and other commentators speak of the "iron triangle," they are referring to the special relationships that develop among three types of actors: the interest groups representing the private sector that is being regulated by the government, the congressional committees and subcommittees that write laws regulating that sector, and the bureaucratic agency that implements the laws[25] (Figure 7.4). The concern is that these special relationships may lead to biased regulatory decisions. Specifically, the business interests being regulated by the

---

[25] Hugh Heclo, *A Government of Strangers* (Washington, DC: Brookings Institution, 1977).

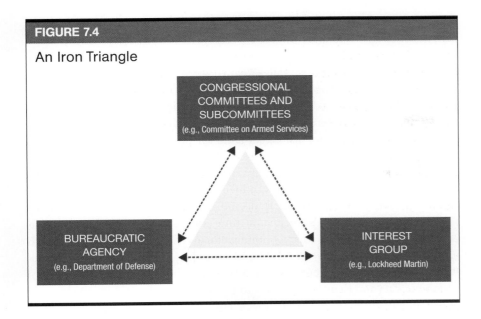

FIGURE 7.4

An Iron Triangle

CONGRESSIONAL COMMITTEES AND SUBCOMMITTEES
(e.g., Committee on Armed Services)

BUREAUCRATIC AGENCY
(e.g., Department of Defense)

INTEREST GROUP
(e.g., Lockheed Martin)

government might have more "insider" status in the bureaucratic agency than the consumers whom the regulations are supposed to protect.

Iron triangles occur when a certain "coziness" develops among the three kinds of actors. People often switch jobs, moving from one corner of the triangle to another. It is common for someone who has worked in a government agency or as a staff member for a congressional committee to go to work as a lobbyist for a regulated business or industry. Lobbying organizations seek out such people because they know not only the laws and regulations but also the right people in the government to help advance their clients' interests. For instance, the lobbying firms representing defense contractors are filled with former members of the military and other government officials who have intimate knowledge of the process by which the Pentagon awards bids. Some observers believe that as consumer, environmental, and other public interest groups have gained power in the American political system since the 1970s, these classic triangular relationships have become less "ironclad," reducing the worst excesses of favoritism and "insiderism."

In Comparison: Bureaucratic Traditions

In all modern democracies, the bureaucracy is accountable to the elected branches of government, at least in principle. But the actual relationships between executive departments and parliaments, and the political power of the bureaucracy, vary across countries.

In parliamentary democracies, executive agencies are accountable only to the parliament, unlike in an American-style separation-of-powers system where they have dual loyalties to the legislature and the president. In countries like Britain, when the government falls—that is, when the parliament votes to dismiss the current government—the ministers of all the executive departments are immediately fired and new people must be chosen by the parliament to replace them. In the American system, by contrast, if the majority party changes in Congress following a popular election but the president remains in office, the heads of the executive departments stay in place at the pleasure of the president.

Japan, a parliamentary democracy, is well known for having a national bureaucracy that carries enormous influence at the national level. In particular, the Ministry of International Trade and Industry (MITI) controls so many aspects of economic regulation that at times in recent Japanese history it has exercised an effective veto over economic reforms of the government. Although it is true that in principle the MITI and other Japanese bureaucratic agencies serve under the government, the bureaucrats use their intimate knowledge of economic data and their connections to private industry to wield considerable power.

In many countries, bureaucratic institutions are the legacies of previous monarchical governments. France, for instance, with a long tradition of a strong centralized government since the 1500s, has always had a prestigious, well-educated bureaucracy that is widely seen as an elite segment of society. The United States has largely adopted the British civil service model, in which a modern, professional bureaucracy offers established career paths for people who mostly remain in nonelected government service. The French and Japanese models of bureaucracy have tended to lead to closer cooperation between the government and private-sector corporations than in the United States. Since World War II, the French and Japanese governments have been much more actively involved in investment decisions regarding industrial development than in either the United States or Britain.

National bureaucracies in many developing countries are less well equipped to do government work than bureaucracies in the developed world. For example, tax compliance is much lower in parts of the developing world because the collection agencies (analogous to the U.S. Internal Revenue Service) are not equipped to gather all of the taxes that people are required to pay. Furthermore, bureaucratic agencies in much of the developing world are filled with patronage appointments. Similar to the earlier eras in the United States when the bureaucracy was filled by the spoils system, so it now goes in places like Nigeria, Bolivia, and the Philippines. When new governments come into power or new presidents are elected in such countries, wholesale changes often occur in the personnel of many government bureaucracies, and entire communities may feel a direct economic impact, depending on how their preferred party fared at the polls.

Two Views of Bureaucracy

Through legislative acts and court decisions, the American federal bureaucracy has been empowered in many instances to conduct work that touches on the three major realms of government activity. Agencies can write statutes or administrative law (legislate), hold hearings and decide cases (adjudicate as quasi-courts), and implement policies (as executive bodies). The last activity, implementation of policy, is the primary reason for the existence of the bureaucracy. Legislative and judicial powers have been specially delegated to bureaucracies by lawmakers on the grounds that the agencies have access to expertise that Congress and perhaps the courts do not have. Moreover, giving agencies rule-making and adjudication powers relieves the burden on the other branches. Let the bureaucracies deal with the details, the thinking goes, while Congress, the president, and the federal courts deal with broad areas of policy.

Because they do the "grunt" work of government, bureaucrats at all levels often feel underappreciated. The words *bureaucrat* and *bureaucracy* can have negative connotations, especially in the United States, and especially in reference to government agencies. Many people have a jaundiced view of bureaucrats as inefficient, impersonal, indifferent government workers who cannot be fired because of civil service laws, regardless of the service they provide to their fellow citizens. Government bureaucrats, especially those at higher levels in an agency, may also feel conflicted over certain responsibilities of their jobs. As the story of the HHS contraception mandate used at the beginning of this chapter highlights, there are two potentially competing visions of what public bureaucracies should do in a modern democracy. We will call them the "progressive" vision and the "democratic" vision.

The Progressive Vision of a Fair, Competent, and Impartial Bureaucracy

In the vision promoted by the mugwumps, and later during the Progressive Era in the early twentieth century, bureaucrats and government agencies should be fair, impartial, and competent. They should help resolve differences and even solve collective dilemmas among politicians and among groups in society in a reasonable and socially productive manner. A prosecutor, for example, should be able to investigate crimes without interference from politicians. A regulator of the oil companies should be free from political pressure by politicians from oil-rich states. The central bank president likewise should decide interest rates independent of any political pressure. Further down the ladder of the bureaucratic hierarchy, the person charged with checking your luggage at the airport should not care about your political party affiliation. It should not matter to the person inspecting industrial plants for pollution controls if the corporation's chief executive officer made campaign contributions to the president.

A bureaucracy independent of political meddling has advantages. By avoiding favoritism and bias, a specific agency can build a reputation across the political spectrum for expertise, integrity, and sound advice. Its staff can make decisions they feel are in the best interests of the country without regard to a particular party's political ideology. And the agency can be trusted to resolve collective dilemmas among social and political groups.

The Democratic Vision of a Bureaucracy Responsive to the Wishes of Politicians Elected by the People

This vision holds that because bureaucrats and government agencies are part of democratically elected governments, they should be responsive to what elected officials tell them to do. If the American people elect a new president from a party different from that of the previous president, they want the government to move in a different direction and the federal bureaucracy to follow suit. One does not need the spoils system of the nineteenth century to have a bureaucracy responsive to election returns. It is enough to replace the top-level secretaries and have them give their underlings directions on how to implement policy consistent with the president's wishes.

Responsiveness may be desirable, but recall the problem of multiple principals that opened this chapter: What does responsiveness mean when principals are in conflict with each other, as was the secretary of HHS, Kathleen Sebelius, in the opening of this chapter? Like all employees of the bureaucracy, she worked for the president. However, Congress believes that people like Sebelius are tasked with carrying out laws that it wrote, amended, and passed. The fact that at times the executive-branch bureaucracy has two principals—the president and Congress—complicates matters considerably for some employees of the U.S. government.

Sometimes political institutions have to change to allow bureaucrats to do their jobs better. During the Watergate scandal under President Richard Nixon in the early 1970s, a special prosecutor hired by Congress to investigate the White House was fired by the president because he did something the president did not like. This action, among others, eventually led to the president's resignation. For our purposes, the lesson is that there are situations that show a flaw in institutional design. It became clear in the Watergate case that the president should not have the power to dismiss a federal prosecutor whom the president has appointed and who happens to be investigating the president's own actions. Four years after President Nixon resigned, a new law was passed that created the independent council's office. A special prosecutor in the independent council's office who is investigating high officials in the government can be dismissed only by the attorney general or a panel of three judges, not the president. This is a good example of a political institution being changed to fix a problem. In this instance, the institutional design of the bureaucracy, which can be depicted as a set of principal–agent relationships between the bureaucracy and the elected branches, was changed to eliminate a flaw.

Nonetheless, the political conflicts within and between the executive and legislative branches continue to affect the bureaucracy. In 2013, a scandal erupted when it was alleged that the Internal Revenue Service (IRS) had targeted conservative political groups in a biased way. The IRS is required to remain politically neutral in all its actions, and the allegations were that rogue agents had violated protocols and audited some groups because of their political leanings. Republicans charged that the actions of the IRS were deliberate by the Obama administration to weaken conservative groups during an election year. The scandal led to a major showdown between the Democrats and Republicans in Congress and between the White House and Congress. The fundamental issue was whether the IRS had been appropriately independent from political pressures.

What is the right balance between the progressive and democratic visions of the bureaucracy? The answer boils down to a trade-off between loyalty and competence. In a democracy, bureaucrats should have a measure of loyalty to the goals of elected officials, and voters should be able to predict what the bureaucracy will do given the preferences of the people the voters elected. At the same time, bureaucrats should be competent, which sometimes means that they act in unexpected but valuable ways. After all, the bureaucrats are experts and often know how to respond to complex situations better than the elected officials.

Ideally, bureaucrats should try to achieve a balance by executing policies in a fair manner consistent with the law and responding to the goals of the elected officials who hire them.[26] However, it can seem at times as if it is impossible to do both well, and thus, many bureaucrats work in a somewhat paradoxical position. How well they balance these sometimes competing pressures is critically important to the effective operation of the American political system. This has been a key purpose of such institutions and procedures as the Administrative Procedures Act, the Freedom of Information Act, and the Sunshine Act—to provide the right incentives so that bureaucrats can be effective while balancing these pressures. The government passed laws setting up institutional procedures to solve the difficult principal–agent problems inherent in the U.S. democratic political system.

[26] Discussion of the trade-off can be found in the following texts: Kathleen Bawn, "Political Control versus Expertise: Congressional Choices about Administrative Procedures," *American Political Science Review* 89 (1995): 62–73; Terry Moe, "Politics of Bureaucratic Structure," in *Can the Government Govern?,* ed. John Chubb and Paul Peterson (Washington, DC: Brookings Institution, 1989), pp. 267–330; and David Epstein and Sharyn O'Halloran, *Delegating Powers* (New York: Cambridge University Press, 1999).

FURTHER READING

★ = Included in *Readings in American Politics*, 3e

★ Carpenter, Daniel, *The Forging of Bureaucratic Autonomy* (Princeton, NJ: Princeton University Press, 2001). An in-depth historical account of secretaries at the top of the federal departments pursuing political clout during the Progressive Era so that they could be free from political meddling.

Epstein, David, and Sharyn O'Halloran, *Delegating Powers* (New York: Cambridge University Press, 1999). Highlights the trade-offs in designating institutions for preventing bureaucratic drift in democratic government.

★ Gailmard, Sean, and John W. Patty, *Learning While Governing: Expertise and Accountability in the Executive Branch* (Chicago: University of Chicago Press, 2013). An examination of how bureaucratic expertise develops on the job and the challenge of ensuring bureaucrats remain loyal to the preferred policies of the president and Congress.

Gordon, Sanford C., "Politicizing Agency Spending Authority: Lessons from a Bush-Era Scandal," *American Political Science Review* 105, no. 4 (November 2011): 717–34. A case study from President George W. Bush's presidency that explores how an administration can apply electoral pressure to federal bureaucracies.

Heclo, Hugh, *A Government of Strangers* (Washington, DC: Brookings Institution, 1977). Describes the politics of bureaucratic agencies, with special attention on iron triangle relationships among congressional subcommittees, bureaucratic agencies, and interest groups.

Huber, John, and Charles Shipan, *Deliberate Discretion* (New York: Cambridge University Press, 2002). A comparative study of different democratic systems and the degree to which legislatures seek to write laws constraining government bureaucracies.

Lipsky, Michael, *Street-Level Bureaucracy* (New York: Russell Sage, 1980). A detailed account of how the everyday actions of bureaucrats affect people's lives and set precedents for future government actions.

McCubbins, Mathew D., Roger Noll, and Barry Weingast, "Structure and Process, Politics and Policy," *Virginia Law Review* 75 (1989): 431–82. A classic article describing how codified administrative procedures solve principal–agent problems between Congress and bureaucracies.

★ McCubbins, Mathew D., and Thomas Schwartz, "Congressional Oversight Overlooked: Police Patrols versus Fire Alarms," *American Journal of Political Science* 28 (1984): 165–79. Describes the contrast between police-patrol and fire-alarm methods of monitoring bureaucratic agencies.

Niskanen, William, *Bureaucracy and Representative Government* (Chicago: Aldine, 1971). A political economy of the inefficiencies inherent in government bureaucracy.

★ Wilson, James Q., *Bureaucracy: What Government Agencies Do and Why They Do It* (New York: Basic Books, 1989). A detailed examination of the goals of government bureaucracies and how those goals can be confusing given the different principals telling them what to do.

————, *The Politics of Regulation* (New York: Basic Books, 1980). A classic account of the relationships between industries being regulated and the agencies designed to regulate them.

KEY TERMS

administrative law (p. 233)

bureaucratic capture (p. 247)

bureaucratic drift (p. 245)

cabinet department (p. 227)

coalitional drift (p. 245)

fire-alarm oversight (p. 252)

government agency (p. 227)

government bureaucracy (p. 227)

government contract (p. 243)

government corporation (p. 229)

government grants (p. 243)

independent agency (p. 229)

marketization (p. 243)

police-patrol oversight (p. 252)

privatization (p. 243)

rule making (p. 233)

The Supreme Court is the governmental institution that is most commonly seen as being independent and above politics. Yet as evidenced by the intense debate and demonstrations—both in government and the public—surrounding its 2012 ruling on the Affordable Care Act, the Court is not detached from political pressures.

8

THE JUDICIARY

The courts—especially the Supreme Court—are sometimes seen as being "above" politics, yet court decisions have enormous political consequences, and courts are often subject to strong political pressures. How has the Supreme Court maintained its place as the respected independent arbiter of the Constitution despite these political pressures?

A signature piece of Barack Obama's first term as president was passage by Congress of the Affordable Care Act in 2010, which greatly expanded the role of the national government in ensuring that all people in the country have access to health insurance. The new law was controversial in part because it was possibly unconstitutional. It placed requirements on individuals and states that might violate liberty guarantees and federalism enshrined in the Constitution. Opponents especially targeted the law's mandate that all individuals obtain medical insurance and states expand their Medicaid coverage or lose federal funding.

In summer of 2012, the fate of the law rested in the hands of the nine members of the U.S. Supreme Court. Supporters and critics of the law were nervous about the Supreme Court's impending decision because it was difficult to predict and so much was at stake. Any decision could either kill the law completely (bad for the supporters of the law) or give it legal sanction (bad for the critics of the law). When the Supreme Court finally ruled on June 28th, in *National Federation of Independent Business v. Sebelius* (2012), its decision shocked people on both sides.

In a 5–4 decision, the Court upheld nearly all aspects of the law, declaring only one part of it unconstitutional: the mandate that states expand their Medicaid coverage, which the majority found too coercive. Otherwise, the other parts of the law were allowed to stand as constitutional. However, Chief Justice John Roberts, who wrote the majority opinion, offered an unexpected legal twist in his justification. His opinion stated that while the law potentially violated the commerce clause because it punished inactivity rather than regulated activity, it was nonetheless consistent with the power of Congress to tax. Thus, nearly all of the law could stand as constitutional.

At issue was the part of the law that would fine people in some circumstances if they did not buy health insurance. Roberts dedicated considerable space in his opinion to explaining why the commerce clause does not grant authority to Congress to require people to make such a purchase. The opinion did acknowledge the Supreme Court's recognition that the interpretation of the commerce clause has expanded from regulating commerce among the states, as explicitly mentioned in the clause, to include activities that "have a substantial effect on interstate commerce."[1] He argued, however, that the commerce clause does not give Congress the authority to regulate a citizen's choice to not purchase an item or a service—that is, the commerce clause does not justify Congress's compelling citizens "to *become* active in commerce."[2] Roberts thus set a precedent in determining one area of personal behavior—nonactivity—that the commerce clause cannot regulate.

Yet Roberts went on to describe the potential penalty as a "tax." And since Article I, Section 8, of the Constitution grants Congress the power "to lay and collect Taxes," Roberts concluded that this controversial feature of the legislation passed constitutional muster. With this conclusion, Roberts shifted the focus of legal attention away from the commerce clause and onto taxing power. In doing so, he and his fellow justices in the majority upheld the law. Some interpreted Roberts to be shying away from having the Court interject itself into social policy by overturning such a major piece of legislation, and that he used what legal means he had at his disposal in doing so.

Conservative commentators and leading members of the Republican Party were outraged by the decision and by Roberts's opinion. "Justice Roberts's opinion provides a constitutional road map for architects of the next great expansion of the welfare state," fumed a former member of the George W. Bush administration.[3] But of course the Court's decision stood and the law went into effect. Roberts's majority opinion not only affected the future of the Affordable Care Act. The legal rationale it conveyed will undoubtedly shape future decisions over the commerce clause, the powers of taxation, and federalism.

The Supreme Court is the least democratic of the branches of the national government. Justices are appointed for life rather than being elected, and once appointed, their decisions are not formally accountable either to voters or other branches of government. As the final arbiter on constitutional matters, the Court has an aura of independence, of being "above" politics. Yet the story of the Court's decision on the Affordable Care Act highlights the fact that the Court is a major participant in American politics and policy making. Because its decisions have enormous political consequences, the executive and legislative branches try to influence the Court directly, through criticism, appointments, and, in rare cases, even threats to change the way the Court acts. How has the Court maintained its aura of independence and its place as the respected arbiter of the Constitution despite these political pressures?

[1] *National Federation of Independent Business v. Sebelius*, 567 U.S. 17 (2012).
[2] *National Federation of Independent Business v. Sebelius*, 567 U.S. 20 (2012).
[3] John Yoo, "Chief Justice Roberts and His Apologists," *Wall Street Journal*, June 29, 2012.

Courts and Collective Dilemmas

In any stable society, courts provide a means of settling disputes peacefully, enforcing contracts, interpreting the law, and holding persons accountable for their actions. As we discussed in Chapter 1, unfettered, ungoverned society is plagued by collective dilemmas. In an effectively governed society, courts are critical for solving certain kinds of collective dilemmas and allowing for productive interactions among people.

Prisoner's Dilemmas

Consider, for instance, the problem of enforcing contracts, which can be depicted as a prisoner's dilemma between any two or more people or groups in society. Suppose John agrees to sell his house to Julie for $200,000. They draw up a contract stating that Julie will pay John the money on July 1 and that John will vacate the house and Julie will have access to it on July 2. In the absence of a court of law, John might be tempted to "defect" from the agreement by taking Julie's money and then denying her access to the house. A court, however, enables Julie to sue John if he does not honor his obligations under the contract. If we depict the relationship between John and Julie as a type of prisoner's dilemma, then when courts enforce contracts, they are making sure the two sides cooperate even though they might be tempted to defect.

Coordination Problems

Courts also solve coordination problems. Interpreting laws or constitutional provisions can be depicted as a coordination problem among different regulatory agencies and among groups trying to comply with the law. Consider the McCain-Feingold campaign finance law that Congress passed in 2002, banning television advertisements for or against specific candidates or political parties by certain groups within 60 days of a general election. Broadly speaking, there were two different interpretations of the law. One side believed that it was narrowly tailored to ban only those advertisements by corporations and labor unions that mention a candidate or party and the election itself ("Vote for Troy Gamble on November 2"). The other believed that the law was broadly intended to ban all advertisements that could hurt or hinder a candidate or party ("We urge you to support candidates who are pro-labor"), even banning issue advertisements by corporations and labor unions within 60 days of the general election. After a series of lawsuits against the Federal Election Committee (FEC), the Supreme Court in *McConnell v. FEC* (2003) and *Citizens United v. FEC* (2010), sided with the first interpretation. In fact, it went even further, ruling that the broader interpretation, if enforced by the FEC, would violate the freedom of speech protected by the First Amendment. In *Citizens United*, the Court declared that those parts of the law that specifically banned advertisements sponsored by corporations and unions were unconstitutional.

The key insight here is that the courts coordinate people's interpretations of the law and the actions they take as a result.[4] If people are not coordinated on a common interpretation of the law, then the result is less effective enforcement: the law is applied differently in different parts of the country or by different government agencies. Everyone is better off with a common interpretation.

Independence and Legitimacy

For the rule of law to work for the benefit of society, people must have faith that the courts will be unbiased and rule fairly based on the law. Courts are central to modern societies because they play the role of impartial enforcers of contractual relationships among people, groups, and companies, as well as between people and the government. It would not undermine the legitimacy of a legislature to craft a policy favoring one particular group simply because that group voted heavily for the majority party in the legislature. But it would

The independence of the judiciary from the other branches of government is especially important when government is a party to a case, as in the cases concerning the treatment of "enemy combatants" and American citizens charged with conspiring with the enemy. The independence of the judicial branch is established by the Constitution.

definitely be considered inappropriate for a court to decide in favor of one side or the other in a case because of that side's political support for particular judges. Economic historians claim that the establishment of courts with legitimacy in the eyes of society—that is, with a reputation for unbiased decision making—to settle disputes over contractual issues was essential to economic growth and the creation of capitalistic economies.[5]

In most modern democracies, the judiciary is independent of the elected branches and serves to check the authority of the government. By "independent," we mean that the courts are free to decide cases on their merits with limited or no pressure from the legislative or executive branches. As John Adams wrote in the Massachusetts Constitution (1780), which was a model for the U.S. Constitution, the democratic ideal was "a government of laws and not of men."

The importance of an independent judiciary is most evident when the government is a party in a court case. This is true both in criminal trials—which always involve a government prosecutor who charges a person with a crime—or when people, organizations, businesses, and other levels of

[4] Keith Whittington, *Constitutional Interpretation* (Lawrence: University of Kansas Press, 1999).

[5] We discuss the legitimacy of the courts in Chapter 4 as well.

government sue or are sued by the national government. If the courts are truly independent, there should be no bias in the government's favor. That is the promise of an independent judiciary, yet it is violated routinely in many countries to the detriment of both democratic processes and the quality of life.

Constitutional Basis

Despite the central importance of courts in democratic societies, the U.S. Constitution says remarkably little about the role of the judicial branch. Article III states that judicial power shall be "vested" in the federal courts, which are headed by the Supreme Court. The Constitution lists the kinds of cases that fall under the jurisdiction of the national courts, including cases where one of the states is a party. The Constitution also requires that the courts be independent from the elected branches. Article III states that Supreme Court justices and lower-court judges are appointed and can hold their offices during good behavior—that is, for life if they are not impeached—and that their salaries cannot be reduced while they are in office. In other words, federal judges cannot be fired or have their pay cut just because Congress or the president becomes unhappy with a court's decisions.

At the same time, the Constitution binds the judicial branch to the other branches, consistent with the notion of checks and balances. Article II gives the president power to appoint Supreme Court judges and implies the same for the judges of any lesser courts established by Congress. The Senate is empowered to give "advice and consent" on such presidential appointments. The courts, as Congress likes to remind judges from time to time, rely on the legislative branch to fund the salaries of judges and prosecutors and maintain offices, courts, and jails.

Establishing Judicial Power

Regarding the judiciary's power to check the other branches, all the Constitution says is that the chief justice of the Supreme Court presides over impeachment trials in the Senate. The judiciary gained its most important powers over time as a result of court decisions that interpret the Constitution and statutory laws. Foremost among those powers is *judicial review*, the power to determine if a law or an act of government conforms to the Constitution. A related power is enshrined in the concept of the *supremacy* of federal courts over state courts. Let us examine these powers in turn, and then see how, beyond its powers to interpret the law, the Supreme Court acts as the court of last resort in settling disputes.

Judicial Review

Soon after the Founding, Congress passed the Judiciary Act of 1789, which laid the groundwork for the federal court system. It established circuit courts and other courts of appeal, and district courts throughout the states. One key aspect of the Act was the provision for federal officials to apply to the Supreme Court for a writ of *mandamus* (a court order) if they believe they have been wronged. With a writ of *mandamus*, federal official A can ask the Court to order person B in the federal government or in a lower government to comply with the terms of official duties, for example, to appoint someone to a new position that the law requires. This provision in the Act played a prominent role in the establishment of judicial review.

judicial review The authority of the judiciary to decide whether a law or any other government action is constitutional.

As we discussed in Chapter 2, the power of **judicial review** was first applied by the Supreme Court in the *Marbury v. Madison* decision in 1803.[6] The origins of this famous case go back to the bitter political battles waged during the administration of the second president, John Adams. Adams was a Federalist, as was his secretary of state, John Marshall. After Adams was defeated in his bid for re-election in 1800, but before his successor took office, he appointed Marshall chief justice of the Supreme Court. Marshall continued to serve in both capacities, only stepping down as secretary of state when Adams left office. Adams also decided to appoint 42 new justices of the peace for Washington, D.C., filling those positions with people sympathetic to the Federalist cause.

On March 3, 1801, the night before Adams turned the presidency over to Thomas Jefferson, the letters of commission granting the appointments for the justices of the peace were placed on a desk in the Department of State. They were supposed to be delivered to the appointees, but were overlooked in the Federalists' haste to vacate the premises. Jefferson, the leader of the Democratic-Republicans, who had defeated Adams for the presidency in a bitter election, took office the next morning, March 4, and discovered the commissions on the desk. He decided not to deliver the letters, thus in his view voiding the appointments.

One of the Federalist appointees, William Marbury, brought suit against James Madison, Jefferson's secretary of state. Under the Judiciary Act, he asked the Supreme Court for a writ of *mandamus* to force Madison either to make the appointment or to compensate him for being wronged. The Act, which gave the Court original jurisdiction in such cases, enjoyed broad support, but that support did not extend to the idea that the Supreme Court could override the states or was the final arbiter on legal matters. Marbury put the Court in a vulnerable position, because if it was seen to overreach in deciding his case, it risked a backlash by the other branches of national government and by the states.

[6] For a classic account, see Alexander Bickel, *The Least Dangerous Branch* (Indianapolis: Bobbs-Merrill, 1962).

In historical terms, the Court's decision in *Marbury v. Madison* was extremely ambitious, but at the time it seemed somewhat convoluted. Chief Justice Marshall's majority opinion brimmed with irony and seeming contradiction. As a Federalist, Marshall blasted the Democratic-Republicans for violating the legal rights of the appointees, while simultaneously ruling that the Supreme Court did not have the authority to settle the matter. The Judiciary Act's provision that the Supreme Court had original jurisdiction was invalid, Marshall reasoned, because the Constitution limited the Court to being an appellate court in such cases. Yet he also took the occasion to declare expansively that "it is emphatically the province and duty of the judicial department to say what the law is." In short, although Marshall and his fellow justices ruled that the Court was not empowered to adjudicate the controversy over the Adams appointments, it *was* empowered to declare laws passed by Congress and signed by the president unconstitutional. The decision narrowly diminished the Court's jurisdiction under the Judiciary Act, but greatly enhanced its powers to determine the constitutionality of all laws.

Although the idea of judicial review—especially the notion that the Supreme Court could declare acts of Congress unconstitutional—was highly controversial, it was hardly new. It had been mentioned in *Federalist 78* and was implicit in other writings of Alexander Hamilton and James Madison. Over the course of the nineteenth century, judicial review gradually became widely accepted as a legal concept. The Supreme Court's reasoning in the infamous *Dred Scott v. Sanford* (1857) decision, for example, relied directly on Marshall's logic in *Marbury v. Madison*. The Court declared that Scott, as a slave, was not entitled to the constitutional protections reserved for U.S. citizens. This decision depended on the assumption that the Supreme Court had the authority to invalidate the Missouri Compromise, a law passed by Congress in 1824. In ruling that the law was unconstitutional, the Court sealed Scott's legal fate and allowed him to be returned to Missouri as a slave.

The Court's use of judicial review fundamentally changed the nature of American government and federalism. In revising its interpretation of the commerce clause over time, the Court opened the door to expansive national power. Through many decisions, the Court prevented the national government from regulating corporations until the late 1930s. In 1935, for instance, the Supreme Court began to strike down key parts of President Franklin Delano Roosevelt's New Deal programs as unconstitutional. In decision after decision, the Court ruled that legislation aspects of the New Deal overreached the constitutional powers of the national government to regulate commercial activity. According to the Court's interpretations of the commerce clause (Article I, Section 8) and the Fourteenth Amendment, the national government could regulate only some aspects of commerce between states, and commerce within states was mostly out of its reach.

The Court's decisions angered FDR, and he proposed the idea of expanding the size of the court to 15 justices, entailing his appointment of six new justices

Despite their independence, as FDR's court-packing plan—and the response to that plan—indicated, the courts are still linked to the other branches of government and to the political goals of elected officials and other groups. In this cartoon, FDR and Congress are telling the judicial branch to "fall in" step with their goals.

to reach that number. He wanted to try to change the Court's composition so that it would be more sympathetic to his policies.

The immediate political response to this court-packing plan, however, was decidedly negative. Even FDR's supporters in Congress felt that he had gone too far. The plan gathered little support in Congress and was not even approved by the Senate Judiciary Committee. Nevertheless, simply by proposing the plan, FDR seemingly had a major effect on the Court. Several months later, the same nine justices decided in favor of a minimum-wage law in the state of Washington, reversing a previous ruling that had declared such laws unconstitutional. A key swing justice, Owen Roberts, changed his position on minimum-wage laws generally and began to vote consistently with the liberals on regulatory questions. The Court, with what was now a 5–4 liberal majority, began to approve New Deal programs and eventually opened the way for Congress to regulate virtually any commercial activity in the country. Many people at the time considered Roberts's change of heart a response to FDR's intimidation of the Court. It was called "the switch in time that saved nine."

Why the Court's power of judicial review has been accepted by the other branches of government is an interesting question, which we will try to answer toward the end of this chapter. Now we will consider another question concerning the power of the courts: How did the Supreme Court establish the supremacy of federal courts over state courts?

Supremacy of Federal Courts and Federal Law

Article VI of the Constitution says that all laws of the United States, and the Constitution itself, shall be "the supreme Law of the Land." After the Founding, however, it was not certain who would have the authority to interpret federal law and the Constitution. *Marbury v. Madison* presented the Marshall Court's view, generally supported by the Federalists, that the Supreme Court would interpret the Constitution as it applied to federal law and the actions of federal officials. But what about the Court's role in reviewing and potentially striking down state laws? Could state courts be the final arbiters about the degree to which state laws conformed to the federal Constitution? Through a set of key decisions after *Marbury*, the Court asserted strong powers of **federal court supremacy** over state law and state courts.

federal court supremacy The arrangement based on the supremacy clause in the Constitution that gives federal courts the authority to overturn state court decisions and to decide on the constitutionality of state laws and actions.

In *Fletcher v. Peck* (1810), the Court for the first time declared a state law unconstitutional. In *McCulloch v. Maryland* (1813) and *Gibbons v. Ogden* (1824), the Marshall Court set precedents for defining the appropriate powers of Congress to regulate commerce, thus confirming the role of the federal courts in drawing the boundaries for relations between the states and the national government. *McCulloch v. Maryland* involved a state law that was intended to impede the operation of the Second Bank of the United States. The Court ruled that Congress, through the necessary and proper clause, has the authority to set commercial policies that do not violate the Constitution, even policies that might intrude on state sovereignty, so long as they serve a rational purpose. Another decision, *Martin v. Hunter's Lessee* (1816), is particularly interesting for the language used by the Court. The Virginia supreme court had ruled that the Judiciary Act of 1789 was unconstitutional because it implied that the federal courts could overrule state courts. In the *Martin* decision, the U.S. Supreme Court first asserted its supremacy over state courts. In view of the potential problem of various state courts offering "jarring and discordant judgments" on the meaning of federal laws, the Court deemed it necessary for a single authority to review the laws so that interpretations would be harmonized. In other words, the Court recognized the dangers posed by coordination problems among different interpreters of law and declared the need for an authoritative court to coordinate on a single interpretation.

Federal courts are sometimes called upon to decide whether, in a given circumstance, it is appropriate to overturn state courts' decisions. Generally, federal courts would rather defer to the state courts if the matter is internal to the states and does not obviously violate national law. But assertions of supremacy occur and are noteworthy. In *American Tradition Partnership v. Bullock* (2012), the Supreme Court ruled that a Montana law banning corporate and union campaign contributions violated the interpretation of federal law given in *Citizens United v. FEC* (2010) (discussed earlier). In doing so, the high court was reversing a decision of the Montana supreme court. It probably did not amuse the U.S. Supreme Court when the Montana court, in upholding the Montana law and prior to the case reaching the national court, wrote that the logic of the *Citizens United* decision was "utter nonsense" and that the U.S. Supreme Court had a "crabbed view of corruption." When it invoked the supremacy clause and precedent, the higher court had the last word.

The Court of Last Resort

The Supreme Court's role as final arbiter of the laws, both state and federal, has put it at the center of numerous political controversies. The *Dred Scott* decision discussed earlier exacerbated regional tensions and contributed to the onset of the Civil War. In 1895, the Court ruled that a personal income tax passed into law by Congress was unconstitutional; that decision was eventually overridden by the Sixteenth Amendment to the Constitution in 1913.

Know the FACTS

Sources of Judicial Power

CONSTITUTIONAL POWER

Article III, Section 1

- Judicial power is vested in a Supreme Court as well as other inferior courts ordained and established by Congress.

- Judges of these courts will "hold their offices during good behavior." In other words, Supreme Court justices and other federal judges are appointed for as long as they are willing serve in good behavior.

Article III, Section 2

- This section defines what types of cases federal courts are allowed to hear. It outlines when the courts have original jurisdiction and when the courts have appellate jurisdiction.

JUDICIAL REVIEW

Marbury v. Madison (1803)
This case marked the first time that the Supreme Court struck down a federal law as unconstitutional, setting the precedent for judicial review.

Dred Scott v. Sanford (1857)
In deciding the case of Dred Scott, a slave who sued for his freedom, the Court ruled that Congress did not have constitutional authority to ban slavery in newly acquired territories (as Congress had attempted to do in the Missouri Compromise). This was the second time the Supreme

Court struck down a federal law for violating the Constitution.

FEDERAL SUPREMACY

Fletcher v. Peck (1810)
The Supreme Court ruled that a Georgia state law violated the contract clause of the Constitution. This was the first time the Supreme Court ruled a state law unconstitutional.

McCulloch v. Maryland (1813)
The Supreme Court ruled that the Constitution allows Congress the authority to establish a bank in Maryland and protects the bank from being taxed by the state. The ruling not only strengthened the power of Congress and federal law under the Constitution, it also established the authority of federal courts to adjudicate disputes between state and federal governments.

Gibbons v. Ogden (1824)
The Court struck down a New York monopoly over steamboat ferry services and ruled that other steamboat ferry companies licensed by Congress could not be prevented from competing with companies licensed by New York. The congressional licenses were valid under the commerce clause of the Constitution. This is another prominent example of federal courts acting as the authoritative arbiter of disputes between state and federal governments.

Throughout the twentieth century, besides the interpretation of the commerce clause, the Court was embroiled in controversies over race and voting rights, segregation in schools, and the rights of criminal defendants. In recent years, the Court has decided on the constitutionality of abortion regulations, laws regulating homosexual conduct, campaign finance laws, affirmative action, antidiscrimination laws, and the rights of enemy combatants during wartime.

Beyond declaring specific laws unconstitutional, the Supreme Court has stepped in as the court of last resort to settle political disputes between the states and the national government, between different branches of government, and between major political parties or candidates. Few cases have been more controversial than the *Bush v. Gore* decision of 2000. That year's presidential election hinged on which candidate, Republican George W. Bush or Democrat Al Gore, had won more votes in Florida and would thus be awarded that state's electoral votes. The popular vote in Florida was almost evenly divided between the two candidates, and disputes arose in several counties over the validity of the ballots. The official count certified by Florida's attorney general came out in Bush's favor (by fewer than 1,000 votes), but the Democrats argued that many votes cast for Gore had not been counted accurately because of confusing ballots and voting machines in some counties. The Florida supreme court ordered a recount of ballots in certain counties. However, the Bush campaign appealed to the U.S. Supreme Court, which reversed the Florida court's ruling by a vote of 5–4, effectively awarding the presidency to Bush.

In deciding the case, the more conservative members of the Supreme Court sided with Bush and the more liberal members with Gore. Many critics accused the Court of basing its decision more on politics than on legal reasoning. The majority opinion, written by Chief Justice William Rehnquist for the conservative bloc, stated that one main reason to overturn the Florida supreme court ruling was that it violated equal protection of the laws to recount the votes in only some but not all counties.[7] Ironically, arguments made on the basis of equal protection of the laws, at least in voting rights cases, are typically made by more liberal groups in society. It has long been a liberal cause to ensure that the votes of all citizens are counted equally in elections. The liberal justices of the Court, in a heated dissent, argued that the majority's argument was flawed. They believed the case was about federalism and urged the Court to let Florida decide for itself how it ran its elections. Again, the irony was that arguments about federalism—states' rights to run their own affairs—are typically made by conservatives. Thus, the legal foundations of both the majority and the dissenting opinions seemed to many to be simply partisan interest cloaked in convenient legal jargon. However, both sides in the case accepted the Court's decision and Bush took office a few weeks later.

Bush v. Gore was an unusual case. But it highlights the fact that, as the highest court in the federal judiciary, the Supreme Court is often asked to adjudicate disputes that other branches or levels of government do not have the legitimacy or the political will to resolve. Because it is the court of last resort in such cases, there can be no further legal appeals. People who are unsatisfied with a Court ruling, however, have several options to effect future change. If it is a matter of interpretation of a statutory law, they can try to convince Congress to pass a different law. If it is a matter of constitutional interpretation, those who disagree with a ruling may have to wait for the composition of the Court to change as justices retire or die, and hope that the new justices will have a different point

---

[7] In fact, seven of the nine justices agreed that equal protection of voters had been violated by Florida's procedures, but two of the seven did not think it sufficiently serious to reverse the Florida court's ruling.

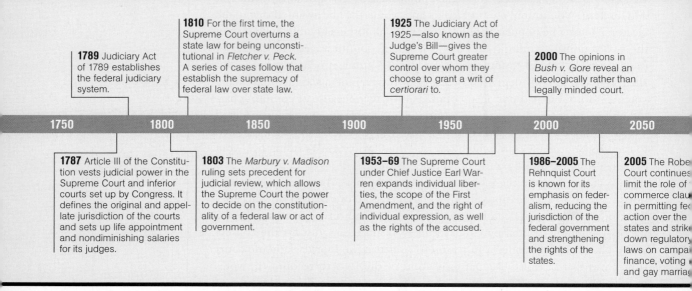

1789 Judiciary Act of 1789 establishes the federal judiciary system.

1810 For the first time, the Supreme Court overturns a state law for being unconstitutional in *Fletcher v. Peck.* A series of cases follow that establish the supremacy of federal law over state law.

1925 The Judiciary Act of 1925—also known as the Judge's Bill—gives the Supreme Court greater control over whom they choose to grant a writ of *certiorari* to.

2000 The opinions in *Bush v. Gore* reveal an ideologically rather than legally minded court.

1750   1800   1850   1900   1950   2000   2050

1787 Article III of the Constitution vests judicial power in the Supreme Court and inferior courts set up by Congress. It defines the original and appellate jurisdiction of the courts and sets up life appointment and nondiminishing salaries for its judges.

1803 The *Marbury v. Madison* ruling sets precedent for judicial review, which allows the Supreme Court the power to decide on the constitutionality of a federal law or act of government.

1953–69 The Supreme Court under Chief Justice Earl Warren expands individual liberties, the scope of the First Amendment, and the right of individual expression, as well as the rights of the accused.

1986–2005 The Rehnquist Court is known for its emphasis on federalism, reducing the jurisdiction of the federal government and strengthening the rights of the states.

2005 The Rober Court continues limit the role of commerce clau in permitting fec action over the states and strike down regulatory laws on campai finance, voting and gay marria

of view and be willing to overturn the precedent. Alternatively, opponents of a ruling can work to pass a constitutional amendment that overrides the Court's decision—something that is rarely achieved.

Organization of the American Judiciary

To understand how the courts carry out their roles in American society, we need to understand the basic characteristics of the American legal system, including the types of cases that come before the courts, standing and jurisdiction, the differences between federal and state courts, and common law and legal precedent.

Types of Cases

criminal case A case in which the government prosecutes a person for a crime against society.

civil case A case in which at least one person sues another person for violating the civil code of conduct.

U.S. courts deal with two kinds of cases, criminal and civil. **Criminal cases** involve the government prosecuting a person for a crime against society. **Civil cases** involve one person suing another person for violating the civil code of conduct. It is important to note that under the law a *person* can be an individual, an organization, a business firm, or a government.

Both criminal and civil cases typically involve two parties: the plaintiff, who brings the charges, and the defendant, who is charged with violating the law. In a criminal case, the plaintiff is always the national or state government. The standard of proof in a criminal case at any level, except for military tribunals, is that a judge or jury must find a defendant innocent unless the evidence shows that she or he is guilty beyond a reasonable doubt. In a civil case, judges or juries merely decide which party's side is better supported by the evidence.

Standing and Class Actions

Standing refers to the official status of being a party to a case in court. Judges determine who has standing to sue or be sued. In lawsuits, huge groups can be granted standing in the same case, as when judges grant **class-action** status to all individuals harmed by the actions of a corporation. Class-action lawsuits arose from a section of the federal rules first promulgated in 1938. The intention was to streamline the hearing of cases in which multiple plaintiffs could press the same claim against a defendant. It is more efficient for multiple cases of harm to be dealt with in a single case. In some extreme situations, hundreds of thousands of people can be considered part of a class-action lawsuit, as when all those taking a particular drug found to be harmful might be entitled to compensation from the drug manufacturing company.

Many class actions are initiated by an entrepreneurial lawyer or law firm that specializes in finding promising lawsuits to bring against corporations. These lawyers make their money by suing companies on behalf of groups of people who have allegedly been wronged. By granting class-action status, a judge is declaring that these lawyers or law firms represent a class of people, even though those people may not be aware of the lawsuit or have never consented to it and might prefer different representation. In recent decades, some states have tried to restrict the ability of plaintiffs' lawyers to bring class-action lawsuits without notifying or identifying each person in the class individually. Similar bills have been introduced in Congress as well. Critics charge that such laws merely protect corporations and give them license to do harm.

standing The official status of a litigant who is entitled to have his or her case decided by the court.

class action A lawsuit in which the plaintiff or defendant is a collective group of individuals.

Federal Courts

The U.S. Supreme Court is the only court specifically mentioned in the Constitution, although Congress was granted the power to establish lower federal courts. The Judiciary Act of 1789 did just that by creating district courts at the lowest level and circuit courts of appeal above them. Subsequent amendments to the Act have expanded on that basic structure. There are currently 94 federal district courts around the country that are organized into 13 circuits, with each circuit hosting a court of appeal, meaning there are 13 circuit appeals courts. Appeals made following a district court verdict go to the circuit containing that district (Figure 8.1). Cases that reach the U.S. Supreme Court can originate in either state or federal courts. Either the Supreme Court or a federal circuit court of appeals can overrule findings of a state supreme court.

FIGURE 8.1

Federal Appeals Court Circuits

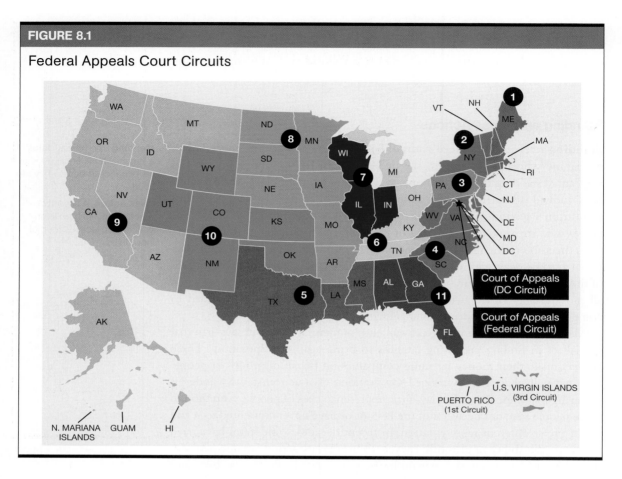

There are also two special courts with national jurisdiction. The U.S. Court of Federal Claims deals with most civil cases in which the national government is a party (usually the defendant). These cases are often disputes over business contracts between private firms and the government. The U.S. Court of International Trade deals with cases involving matters of trade and customs, often with foreign persons as a party.

State Courts and the Electoral Connection

Each state has its own hierarchy of courts, with a court of last resort (usually called the state supreme court) above the others. At the bottom level are state trial courts, where 99 percent of all cases originate. State appellate courts stand between the trial courts and the state supreme court.

The most distinctive feature of state courts in the United States—which sets them apart from the federal courts and most courts around the world—is that a sizable proportion of their judges and prosecutors are elected by voters,

TABLE 8.1

Judicial Selection for State Appellate Courts

Partisan Election	Nonpartisan Election	Legislative Appointment	Gubernatorial Appointment	Merit Plan*	
Alabama	Arkansas	South Carolina	California	Alaska	New York
Illinois	Georgia	Virginia	Maine	Arizona	Oklahoma
Louisiana	Idaho		New Hampshire	Colorado	Rhode Island
New Mexico	Kentucky		New Jersey	Connecticut	South Dakota
Ohio	Michigan			Delaware	Tennessee
Pennsylvania	Minnesota			Florida	Utah
Texas	Mississippi			Hawaii	Vermont
West Virginia	Montana			Indiana	Wyoming
	Nevada			Iowa	
	North Carolina			Kansas	
	North Dakota			Maryland	
	Oregon			Massachusetts	
	Washington			Missouri	
	Wisconsin			Nebraska	

*Merit plans typically involve appointment by the governor from a list of candidates submitted by an independent or quasi-independent judiciary council or commission.

Source: Harold Stanley and Richard Niemi, *Vital Statistics on American Politics, 2009–10* (Washington, DC: CQ Press, 2010), Table 7-1.

rather than appointed by elected officials. In 37 of the 50 states, at least some state judges are chosen by popular election; the remaining states appoint their judges (see Table 8.1, which shows data for state appeals courts). In many states, supreme court justices are elected. State prosecutors, especially district attorneys (the top prosecutors for particular regions in the state), are elected by voters in many states.

In some respects, the election of judges and prosecutors helps democratize the U.S. judicial system. Judges or prosecutors found to be corrupt or too far out of line with voters' preferences can be voted out of office. In general, voters appear to be satisfied with their state-level judges. Re-election for judges in many states is often routine unless a judge has been charged with corruption. Many judicial elections are uncontested, meaning that only the incumbent is on the ballot. District attorney jobs, however, are often hotly contested, and prosecutors get voted out of office more often than judges. In most states, judicial elections are nonpartisan, meaning that judges or prosecutors do not indicate on the ballot their political party affiliation.

However, this electoral connection has a more worrisome side as well. State-level judges and prosecutors must campaign for office, raise campaign funds, and woo interest groups and newspaper editorial boards for endorsements. In many judicial elections, candidates compete by bragging that they have put more people on death row than their opponents. Although such campaigning gives voters some information about the judges' attitude toward the death penalty, it also raises concerns about whether electoral pressures interfere with their incentives to act impartially. We may also ask whether voters have the information they need to make informed decisions about the performance of judges and prosecutors. Available evidence indicates that many voters ignore judicial elections on ballots more often than other races, and that they often vote for the incumbent simply because they have heard his or her name.

Jurisdiction at the Federal and State Levels

As we saw earlier, federal law overrides state law, and the federal courts have jurisdiction to review both state law and legal findings in state courts (Figure 8.2). State courts deal with trials involving state law, while federal courts deal with trials involving federal law. Nearly all felonies, such as murder, rape, robbery, burglary, and car theft, are prosecuted at the state level. In recent decades, however, Congress has legislated on some matters, such as drug offenses, that have

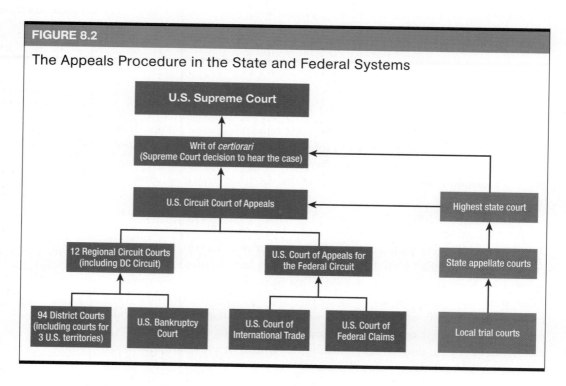

FIGURE 8.2

The Appeals Procedure in the State and Federal Systems

traditionally been the province of the states. The federal courts, for example, have increasingly heard cases involving felonies related to drug offenses because the alleged crimes often involve criminal organizations that operate across several states. In addition, federal statutes usually provide more severe punishments for drug crimes than state statutes, so state prosecutors often allow federal prosecutors to take over the cases.

When courts have *original jurisdiction*, it means that cases start there. When courts have only *appellate jurisdiction*, it means that cases are brought there on appeal by either the plaintiff or the defendant after being decided in a lower-level court. No new evidence or witnesses are brought to an appellate (or appeals) court. The appeals court makes decisions based on the soundness of the procedures used to decide the case at the lower level. Some courts, like the U.S. Supreme Court and state supreme courts, have both original and appellate jurisdiction, depending on the nature of the case and the parties involved. In practice, however, federal and state supreme courts, which can rule on issues of fundamental federal or state constitutional law, almost always hear cases on appeal.

Common Law and Legal Precedent

The United States operates largely under a common law system, as opposed to the civil law system prevalent in Europe and other parts of the world. In a **common law** system, the judiciary at both the federal and state levels has the authority, when deciding cases, to declare how the law is to be interpreted. This contrasts with a **civil law** system in which the law is described in a body of authoritative documents and judges apply the reasoning set forth in those documents to make decisions. Hence, to learn what the law means today in a civil law system, one merely refers to the relevant sections of that country's legal code.[8]

In a common law system, higher-level courts set legal precedents. When a court decides what a law means, then that court and all those below it are supposed to use that meaning to guide decision making in future cases. To learn what the law means today, one refers back to court decisions at the highest-level court that decided on a relevant case and uses that court's reasoning as the basis. The Latin term ***stare decisis***, which means "to stand by the things that have been settled," describes this basic principle.

In effect, the body of laws governing the United States is built not only on the statutes passed by legislatures and on constitutions but also on court precedents. Courts at federal and state levels can set precedents on the interpretation of statutes (laws and regulations), and in doing so create a body of **statutory law** that becomes part of the legal code along with the actual statutes. Lawyers

common law A system of jurisprudence in which the judiciary has the authority to determine how the law is to be interpreted. Under this system, legal precedent established by judges informs future decisions.

civil law A system of jurisprudence in which authoritative documents determine how the law is to be interpreted. Under this system, legal codes and statutes (and not judges) inform future decisions.

stare decisis The legal principle that requires judges to respect the decisions of past court cases.

statutory law The laws passed by legislatures, or administrative agencies empowered by legislatures, and the court decisions interpreting those laws.

---

[8] It is worth noting that Louisiana still uses aspects of civil law because of its legacy of French rule until the early eighteenth century.

and judges then use both the text of the statutes and decisions of the highest court ruling on the matter when making their own decisions. Or, similarly, courts can set precedents on constitutional interpretation; when they do so, they are adding to a body of **constitutional law** whereupon the opinions of the highest courts to rule on a given matter are part of the legal code.

constitutional law The collection of fundamental rules for making statutory laws and regulations, their enforcement, and the court decisions interpreting those rules.

In the relatively rare cases when a legal precedent is overturned by the same level of court that set the original precedent, it is considered a serious decision by any court. Even the U.S. Supreme Court has reversed its own decisions. For example, the Constitution guarantees the right to counsel—that is, to have a lawyer represent you in court. In *Betts v. Brady* (1942), the Court ruled that states are not required to provide lawyers for defendants who are too poor to pay for legal services, and that only the federal government is required to do so in cases at the federal level. Yet 20 years later, in *Gideon v. Wainright* (1962), the Court ruled that the Constitution guarantees the right of counsel for defendants in felony cases at all levels of courts, including the state level. In another example, the Court's *Bowers v. Hardwick* (1986) ruling upheld a Georgia law banning sodomy, but in *Lawrence v. Texas* (2003) the Court struck down a Texas law banning sodomy between consenting adults of the same sex.

Although the *Gideon* and *Lawrence* decisions are noteworthy in that they overturned precedents that were controversial and had garnered a lot of attention, they are often interpreted as examples of how the Court can be sensitive to the tides of public opinion. In both circumstances, the Court changed national legal standards following a period in which gradual changes had been made in state laws around the country. For instance, in 1986, 25 states had laws against some form of sodomy, while by 2003 only 13 states had such laws. There is little doubt that in the years between the *Bowers* and *Lawrence* rulings, American society became more tolerant of homosexuals and their private sexual conduct. Scholars of the Supreme Court disagree as to whether shifts in public opinion actually cause the Court to change direction. In this case, the evidence is compelling. Writing for the Court's majority in *Lawrence*, Justice Anthony Kennedy admitted that increasing tolerance toward homosexuals was a factor in his decision to vote to reverse *Bowers*. It is likely that changes of public opinion influenced the Court (and Kennedy who wrote key opinions) when it made decisions in favor of gay marriage in 2013.

Path of a Supreme Court Case

As we saw earlier, the Supreme Court is the court of last resort in the United States, deciding questions for which there are conflicting opinions among lower courts, or questions that cannot be resolved by the lower courts, the states, or other branches of government. The Court profoundly shapes the legal and political system of the United States, yet few Americans know much about how the justices reach their decisions. Let us take a look at this process, referring to the path of a typical Supreme Court case outlined in Figure 8.3.

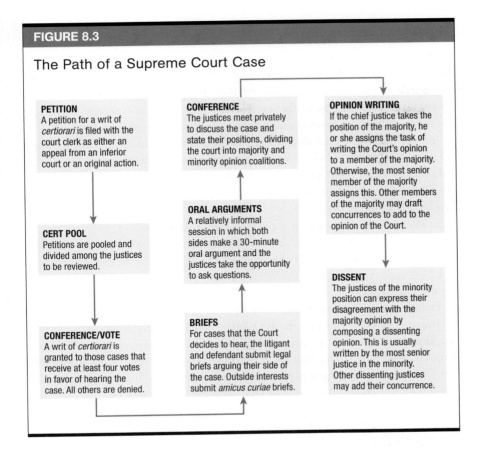

FIGURE 8.3

The Path of a Supreme Court Case

PETITION
A petition for a writ of *certiorari* is filed with the court clerk as either an appeal from an inferior court or an original action.

CERT POOL
Petitions are pooled and divided among the justices to be reviewed.

CONFERENCE/VOTE
A writ of *certiorari* is granted to those cases that receive at least four votes in favor of hearing the case. All others are denied.

CONFERENCE
The justices meet privately to discuss the case and state their positions, dividing the court into majority and minority opinion coalitions.

ORAL ARGUMENTS
A relatively informal session in which both sides make a 30-minute oral argument and the justices take the opportunity to ask questions.

BRIEFS
For cases that the Court decides to hear, the litigant and defendant submit legal briefs arguing their side of the case. Outside interests submit *amicus curiae* briefs.

OPINION WRITING
If the chief justice takes the position of the majority, he or she assigns the task of writing the Court's opinion to a member of the majority. Otherwise, the most senior member of the majority assigns this. Other members of the majority may draft concurrences to add to the opinion of the Court.

DISSENT
The justices of the minority position can express their disagreement with the majority opinion by composing a dissenting opinion. This is usually written by the most senior justice in the minority. Other dissenting justices may add their concurrence.

Choosing Cases

The Supreme Court hears cases for which it has jurisdiction, including all cases involving federal law, cases between states, and cases that deal with a clear federal constitutional issue. (Note that this excludes the vast majority of court cases in the United States.) Since the early twentieth century (by act of Congress), the justices themselves have decided which cases they hear. Under the so-called rule of four, the approval of four of the nine justices is required to grant a **writ of *certiorari***, which means the Court will hear the case. (*Certiorari*, which means "to be informed of" in Latin, is the legal term for the Supreme Court's review of a lower court's decision.) Over the past few decades, the Court has typically accepted fewer than 80 cases per year out of the approximately 8,000 petitions it receives for a writ of *certiorari*.

The Supreme Court can decide not to hear a case because any decision would be considered **moot**, meaning that further legal proceedings would have no effect on at least one of the parties in the case. This can happen when a plaintiff dies, or a new law passed by Congress changes the legal standards, or

writ of *certiorari* An order by the Supreme Court directing an inferior court to deliver the records of a case to be reviewed, which effectively means the justices of the Court have decided to hear the case.

moot The status of a case in which further legal proceedings would have no impact on one or both parties.

the matter in question is no longer relevant. A student suing over college admission standards, for example, may have been admitted in the meantime and thus the case can be declared moot. If a class action is involved, the Court may hear a case even when it is moot for the original plaintiff. In a lawsuit against tobacco manufacturers, for example, even if the original plaintiff has died and thus no longer represents the class of former smokers, the case may continue because of the many millions of former smokers who continue to have standing.

If the Supreme Court decides not to hear a case, the lower court's ruling automatically stands. This does not necessarily mean, however, that the Court upholds the lower court's reasoning or legal opinion. Rather, it could mean that the Court does not want to deal with the constitutional questions raised by the case at that point in time.

Many cases the Court takes are ones raising issues on which different federal courts or state supreme courts have made conflicting opinions. As an example, the Court agreed to take up the issue of the legal status of gay marriage in 2012 because courts around the country, both federal and state, were deciding on the legal merits in contradictory fashion. Its subsequent rulings in 2013 in favor of gay marriage were controversial within the Court (both major decisions were 5–4) and outside the Court. When courts below them conflict, the Supreme Court can in principle use the decisions of specific lower courts as cues about how to decide the case. For instance, conservative justices on the Supreme Court might pay more attention to the rulings of conservative-leaning circuit court opinions, and vice versa for liberal justices.

Legal Briefs

Once a case is granted a writ of *certiorari*, the two sides in the case submit written briefs (legal documents) arguing their positions. For appellate cases, the side challenging the lower court's ruling submits a brief first, and then the side urging the court to uphold the lower court's ruling responds.

Anyone who does not have a direct stake in the outcome of the particular case—including interest groups, government departments, members of Congress, and private citizens—can submit **amicus curiae** ("friend of the court") briefs. These are letters supporting one side or the other in the case. Some *amicus* briefs are requested by the Court. For instance, the justices might ask a historian or an economist to write a brief on an academic matter that would help them reach a decision.

In politically charged cases, it is common for many interest groups and private citizens to submit *amicus* briefs. In the famous *Brown v. Board of Education* (1954) decision that outlawed racial segregation in public education, according to later statements by several of the justices, *amicus* briefs documenting the harmful effects of segregation on African American children played a major role in the Court's decision.

amicus curiae Briefs (letters to the court) in which those who are not parties in a case provide their opinions on how the case should be decided.

Oral Arguments

After the written briefs are submitted, a clerk for the Supreme Court schedules a time for oral arguments. Each side has approximately half an hour to present its case, followed by questions from the justices. If the U.S. government is a party in the case, the solicitor general formally represents the government as its lawyer and will speak. Sometimes those submitting *amicus curiae* briefs are permitted to speak. These sessions are open to the public and are remarkably informal. Justices often interrupt to ask questions, make observations, or challenge attorneys' arguments. During these exchanges, justices may reveal how they are thinking on a case. During the 2012 oral arguments on the constitutionality of the individual health insurance mandate (requiring people to buy insurance under certain circumstances) in the Affordable Care Act, Justice Antonin Scalia inferred that the Act was a power-grab by the federal government, asking the solicitor general where the federal government would be limited if not with respect to mandating health insurance. Scalia questioned, "What is left? If the government can do this, what else can it not do?" Eventually, he suggested that if the government can make people buy health insurance, it would, by the same logic, be able to make people buy broccoli. In asking such questions, Scalia inferred that he thought the individual

During the oral argument phase of a Supreme Court case, some justices, such as Justice Scalia, tend to ask many questions or address comments to the arguing attorneys, while others, such as Justice Thomas, rarely speak. Above, attorney Paul Clement speaks before the Court during *National Federation of Independent Business v. Sebelius.*

mandate was overstepping certain constitutional boundaries, indicating his position against the Act.[9]

Although justices' predispositions may be revealed during oral arguments, scholars have shown that what transpires during arguments can influence how a case is decided. Traces of the discussions between the advocates and the justices during oral arguments often emerge in the Court's majority opinions.[10] Evidence suggests that the Court is somewhat more likely to find for the side whose lawyer presents a higher-quality case during oral arguments.[11]

The Conference

After taking time—often many months—to consider the written and oral arguments, the justices meet in private conference to discuss the case and take a preliminary vote. Political scientists have outlined three principal models of judicial decision making. The **legal model** portrays Supreme Court decisions as determined by the facts of the case at hand in conjunction with the plain meaning of the relevant statutes and constitutional provisions, the intent of the framers of the Constitution, and legal precedent.[12] It is this model that most justices espouse publicly in explaining their decision-making process. Chief Justice John Roberts, for example, commented during his confirmation hearings in 2005 that a judge's job is like that of a baseball umpire who calls balls and strikes—that is, to decide neutrally based on how one sees the facts.

Most political scientists, however, argue that justices are not simply neutral "umpires" but political actors.[13] Supreme Court conferences often resemble "mini-legislatures," with bargaining among the justices over decisions, strategic maneuvers to control the Court's agenda, and complex processes of coalition building. According to the **attitudinal model** of judicial decision making, the individual justices' ideological biases and policy preferences shape how they interpret the facts of a given case and the decision they reach.[14]

This model is useful in grouping the justices into the ideological camps that tend to vote together. Figure 8.4 arrays the members of the Court in 2013 along

legal model A theoretical model where judicial decisions are primarily determined by the case, the plain meaning of the text from the Constitution and statutes, the intent of the framers, and/or legal precedent.

attitudinal model A theoretical model where judicial decisions are primarily determined by the policy goals and ideological agendas of judges.

[9] Some justices rarely or never speak. Justice Clarence Thomas did not speak once in oral arguments between 2006 and 2013.

[10] Timothy R. Johnson, *Oral Arguments and Decision Making on the U.S. Supreme Court* (Albany: State University of New York Press, 2004).

[11] Timothy R. Johnson, Paul J. Wahlbeck, and James F. Spriggs II, "The Influence of Oral Arguments on the U.S. Supreme Court," *American Political Science Review* 100, no. 1 (February 2006): 99–113.

[12] See, for example, Ronald Dworkin, *Taking Rights Seriously* (Cambridge, MA: Harvard University Press, 1988).

[13] Howard Gillman, *The Constitution Besieged* (Durham, NC: Duke University Press, 1993); Larry Kramer, *The People Themselves* (New York: Oxford University Press, 2004).

[14] Jeffrey A. Segal and Harold J. Spaeth, *The Supreme Court and the Attitudinal Model Revisited* (Cambridge, UK: Cambridge University Press, 2002).

an ideological spectrum. Justices Antonin Scalia, Samuel Alito, and Clarence Thomas anchor the conservative or right wing, while Sonia Sotomayer and Ruth Bader Ginsburg anchor the liberal or left wing. Anthony Kennedy is considered the pivotal justice, at least for cases involving issues of traditional morality and economic regulation.

Studies have shown a close correlation between the Court's voting patterns and the issues that divide the two major political parties. In abortion cases, for example, the conservative justices usually reflect the positions of the Republican Party, while the liberals reflect those of the Democratic Party. This is perhaps no surprise given that justices are appointed by presidents who are partisan politicians. The most conservative members of the Court were appointed by Ronald Reagan, George H. W. Bush, and George W. Bush, the three most recent Republican presidents. Most of the liberal members of the Court were appointed by presidents Jimmy Carter, Bill Clinton, and Barack Obama, all Democratic presidents. But note that some justices appointed by Republican presidents ended up in the liberal wing of the Court, and some swing justices were appointed by Democrats. On closely argued cases, these swing justices play the decisive role in the final outcome.

For some political scientists, the explanation of justices' decisions as a reflection of their underlying political preferences is incomplete. Proponents of the **strategic (or rational choice) model** of judicial decision making emphasize the strategic nature of judicial behavior.[15] Justices, they argue, have personal policy goals that they wish to achieve. For a given justice to accomplish particular ends, he or she must consider the preferences and likely actions of fellow justices, but also the institutional context in which the Court operates. For example, under the rule of four—the requirement that at least four members of the Court must agree to hear a case—a justice who wishes a case to be considered needs the agreement of three fellow justices and therefore must tailor arguments to win over at least that many colleagues. The Court's place in the separation-of-powers system also constrains its decision making; Congress, for example, can pass legislation that overrides a ruling of the Supreme Court. Justices keep Congress's potential legislative powers in mind as they write and decide on opinions. All of these constraints influence the way justices decide cases. (See Figure 8.5.)

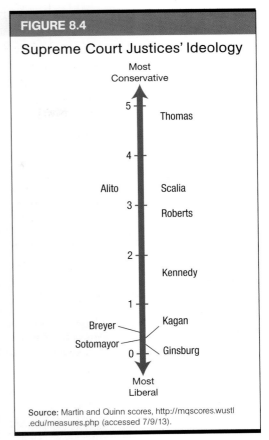

FIGURE 8.4

Supreme Court Justices' Ideology

Source: Martin and Quinn scores, http://mqscores.wustl.edu/measures.php (accessed 7/9/13).

strategic (or rational choice) model A theoretical model where judicial decisions are primarily determined by the policy goals of judges and the various constraints that stand in the way of achieving those goals.

[15] Lee Epstein and Jack Knight, *The Choices Justices Make* (Washington, DC: CQ Press, 1998); Forrest Maltzman, James Spriggs, and Paul Wahlbeck, *Crafting Law on the Supreme Court: The Collegial Game* (New York: Cambridge University Press, 2000).

FIGURE 8.5

Judicial Decision Making

MORE AUTONOMY

ATTITUDINAL MODEL

This model of judicial decision making posits that a judge's behavior can be predicted largely by his or her policy attitudes. It perceives judges of the court as motivated by policy goals and unconstrained by the law. Thus, they decide cases according to ideological preference rather than by the meaning or intention of legal texts or by precedent.

STRATEGIC MODEL

The strategic model acknowledges that judges seek to achieve policy goals. But it also acknowledges that they are subject to certain constraints in doing so. Since they cannot act simply according to preference, they must act strategically to achieve their goals given the constraints.

LEGAL MODEL

The legal model assumes that judges submit to the law when making decisions. If a judge has any personal preference for an outcome in a case, it is assumed that he or she leaves these preferences aside and defers to the facts of the case, the plain meaning of the Constitution or statute, the intention of its framers, or legal precedent when making his or her decision.

LESS AUTONOMY

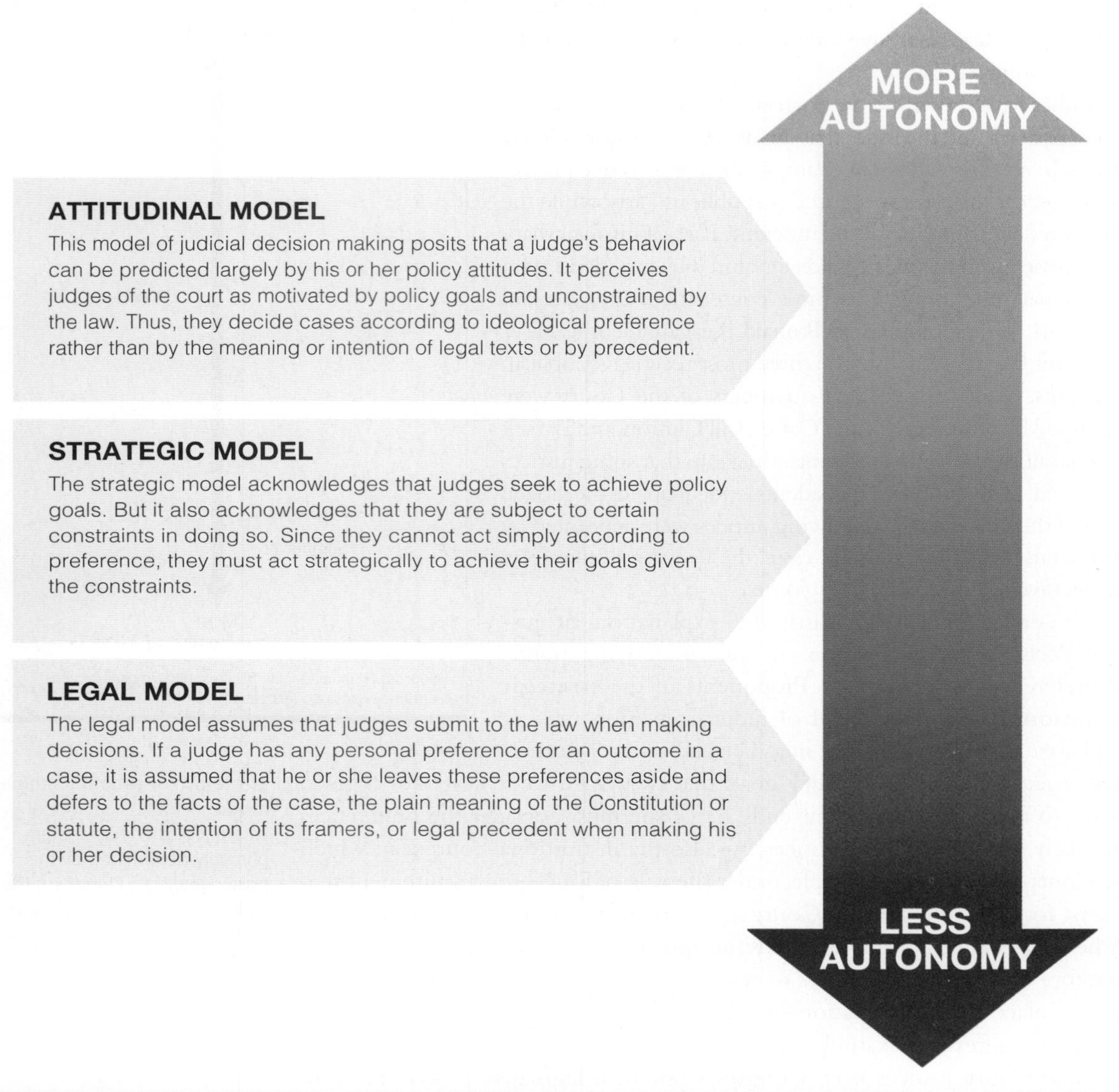

The dynamics of the strategic model can be seen in an interpretation of the *National Federation of Independent Businesses v. Sebelius* (2012) decision described in our opening story. Chief Justice Roberts, by most accounts, would have preferred the Court to limit the scope of the commerce clause through its decisions, including this one. But he did not want the Court to overturn a major piece of social legislation passed by Congress and signed by the president. He thus chose to write the majority opinion so that he could argue that the law could not be based on Congress's power to regulate commerce. Roberts was worried, in this version of the story, that if someone else wrote the opinion or he joined the minority, another justice might convince a majority to sign on to an opinion leading to either one of two outcomes Roberts did not want—to overturn the law based on the commerce clause, or to expand the commerce clause to include regulating inactivity. Roberts pursued the best strategy he could by making sure he wrote the majority opinion. By writing the opinion himself, he could signal both that the interpretation of the commerce clause should not be expanded and maybe even should be scaled back to a more limited form, and also that the Court should not meddle in policy making to a degree called for in overturning this important law.

Opinion Writing

During conference, one of the justices representing the majority is assigned to write the opinion justifying the ruling. As the preceding example illustrates, this choice can have significant consequences. If the chief justice is in the majority, he or she assigns a justice from the majority side to write the opinion. The chief justice can assign it to himself or herself, a key agenda-setting power. If the chief justice is not in the majority, then the senior justice on the majority side assigns the task to a justice representing the majority.

Any justice from the majority may also write a **concurring opinion** to explain why he or she is in the majority but for different reasons than stated in the majority opinion. Likewise, any justice from the minority can write a **dissenting opinion** to give reasons for disagreeing with the majority. Concurrences and dissents often indicate how justices might try to craft a coalition in future cases on the same topic, or signal to Congress how it might write new legislation to overturn the Court's decision. In the early twentieth century, for example, Justice Oliver Wendell Holmes wrote several historic dissents that laid the groundwork for expanding freedom of speech in later Court majority decisions.

Even after the opinions are drafted, justices can change their minds before the Court's decision is announced. In one prominent example, certain justices (reportedly David Souter and Sandra Day O'Connor) belatedly convinced Anthony Kennedy to join them in upholding the logic of *Roe v. Wade,* the Court's landmark decision guaranteeing a woman's right to an abortion, in *Planned Parenthood v. Casey* (1992). Kennedy's shift gave those in favor of upholding abortion rights a majority in the case.

Once the justices have made their final decisions and written their opinions, the chief justice announces the case, and the author of the majority opinion reads it aloud in public session. Dissenting and concurring opinions may also be read aloud. Four-to-four decisions, which can happen if a justice is absent or

concurring opinion An opinion issued by a member of the majority of the Supreme Court that agrees with the decision of the majority but offers alternative legal reasoning.

dissenting opinion An opinion issued by a member of the Supreme Court in opposition to the majority, offering legal reasoning for the decision to oppose.

recuses himself or herself because of conflict of interest, uphold the lower-court ruling. The Court's opinions are then recorded in law indexes and the majority opinion becomes the law of the land.

In Comparison: The Judiciary

We have already compared the American common law system (also used in Great Britain and most of its former colonies) with the civil law system in other countries. Now let us consider two other distinctive features of the American judiciary—the selection of judges and the concept of judicial review—from an international perspective.

Selecting Judges

The American courts, along with those in other countries in Europe, Japan, and Australia, are widely considered models of independence and professionalism. Compared with many other countries, especially in the developing world, there is less bribery and corruption in the ranks of courts in these democracies and less overt partisanship in judicial decision making. At the same time, there are differences even among advanced industrial democracies. The American judiciary is tied to the electoral process more closely than in other countries. Judges and prosecutors are either elected, as in some states, or appointed by elected officials.

In many other countries, judges and prosecutors are appointed by special panels of fellow judges or lawyers—the equivalent of bar associations—which keeps politicians and voters out of the process of choosing judges. In France, judges are technically civil servants appointed by the president on the recommendation of a council of legal experts. A lawyer in France who wishes to become a judge must enter a special course of study at the National School for Magistrates. Similarly, lawyers in Germany who want to become judges must first gain experience as civil servants, working as prosecutors or in some other legal capacity within the government. Only then can they become eligible to be appointed as federal judges by either the upper or lower house of parliament.

From the outside, Great Britain's system looks similar to the American system in that the elected head of government, the prime minister, appoints judges. But in practice, the prime minister chooses from among candidates recommended by a nonpartisan commission in charge of judicial appointments. Most new democracies adopt a European-style judicial system based on the French, British, or German models, rather than an American-style model with elections and a highly politicized appointment process.[16]

[16] For more on European legal traditions, see Alex Stone Sweet, *Governing with Judges* (New York: Oxford University Press, 2000).

Judicial Review

Compared with courts in some other countries, U.S. courts have relatively strong powers of judicial review. For example, in the British model, which is common around the world, judges do not have the power to review the constitutionality of acts of Parliament. British high courts can, however, review cases to clarify the meaning of laws passed by Parliament, and occasionally Parliament grants them authority to investigate alleged wrongdoing by members of the government. In both France and Germany, however, the high courts have powers of judicial review similar to that in the United States, with Germany's Constitutional Court empowered much like the U.S. Supreme Court. In France, cases involving judicial review of government acts or laws arise from members of parliament petitioning the high court for an opinion on a pending piece of legislation, rather than from lower courts ruling on laws already passed.

In all of the countries of the European Union, the European Court of Justice is empowered to declare laws and actions of governments of the member states in violation of European law and European constitutional tradition. Thus, although Britain does not have judicial review in its own judicial system, its laws are subject to judicial review with reference to European law. The United States does not formally recognize any international court as authorized to overrule the U.S. Supreme Court. However, as a party to various international treaties, the United States tends to abide by the rulings of several international courts. Under the North American Free Trade Agreement with Canada and Mexico, for example, international tribunals settle disputes among the three countries or among companies operating within them. When these tribunals make decisions, U.S. domestic courts are supposed to enforce them.

The issue of whether the United States is required to abide by the rulings of international courts continues to be controversial, as illustrated by several recent cases involving potential litigation over the behavior of American soldiers during the Iraq War. Recent presidential administrations have firmly maintained that the United States can voluntarily comply with the rulings of international courts, but is not legally obligated to do so.

How Political Are the Courts?

American courts toe a difficult line in interpreting the law and maintaining their independence. If they stray too far from the path laid down by politics and public opinion, the courts can experience intense criticism and pressure to change or reverse course. They may lose legitimacy among some if they persistently make unpopular decisions. The courts grapple with problems balancing in three areas in particular: minority rights versus majority rule, judicial restraint versus judicial activism, and popular sovereignty versus the rule of law. In all three of these areas, the federal courts are making decisions reacting to and also influencing the actions of Congress and the president, and of the states.

Minority Rights versus Majority Rule

In some eras in American history, groups who felt excluded from the electoral process have used the courts as a means to change policy without having to rely on Congress and the president.[17] For instance, black organizations in the first half of the twentieth century brought lawsuits in federal court to fight Jim Crow laws and violations of voting rights by the states. This strategy served two purposes. It was a way around having to win the support of the U.S. Senate, where civil rights laws had been blocked by southern senators for decades, and it enabled these organizations to avoid bringing the suits in biased state courts in the South. Through rulings like *Brown v. Board of Education,* the judiciary was extremely helpful to African Americans seeking to overturn discriminatory laws. That the courts gave such access to an oppressed minority is a credit to the federal judiciary of that era.

This example shows how an unelected branch of government can not only protect the rights and liberties of minorities from oppressive majorities but also define which rights and liberties need to be protected, the conditions under which they should be protected, and how to trade off rights and liberties against each other. Another set of unpopular minorities, criminal defendants, has an especially difficult time winning protection from legislatures and executives. As a result, federal courts in the mid-twentieth century were instrumental in protecting the constitutional rights of defendants to a fair trial and to freedom from cruel and unusual punishment. In these cases, the courts acted to offset the tendencies of the other branches of government to be responsive to majorities who wanted to be harsh toward criminal defendants.

The courts have not consistently taken the lead in protecting minorities, of course. In fact, a substantial body of scholarship indicates that most changes in the direction of the Supreme Court have occurred *after* shifts in public opinion and majority sentiment. For example, the Court began to approve New Deal legislation only after it became popular and was supported by the other two branches of government. And the Court moved to protect the rights of African Americans *after* majority sentiment across the entire country turned against segregationist attitudes among southern whites.[18]

Some critics caution that groups in democracies who are simply disappointed because they lose in the legislative arena should not be encouraged

[17] Ronald Dworkin, *Taking Rights Seriously* (Cambridge, MA: Harvard University Press, 1978).
[18] Gerald Rosenberg, *The Hollow Hope: Can Courts Bring about Social Change?* (Chicago: University of Chicago Press, 1991).

to pursue their policy goals through the courts. In one example raised by the political scientist Robert Dahl, business groups in the late nineteenth and early twentieth centuries used the courts to keep anti–child labor regulations from becoming law, even though majorities in most states, as reflected in the overwhelming votes of state legislatures, wished to ban child labor. These critics argue that the courts should not be an alternative legislative system by which minorities, including privileged sectors of the business or investor communities, try to bypass the legitimate policy-making system.[19]

Restraint versus Activism

Judges, especially those in the federal circuit courts and in the state and national supreme courts, realize that their actions can have profound political consequences. Yet, in general, American judges do not consider themselves part of the ordinary political process. They insist that they merely interpret the law and do not, or at least should not, make public policy. Judges likewise tend to be uncomfortable stepping into the electoral arena, as the Supreme Court was asked to do in *Bush v. Gore*.

Court observers often categorize judges according to their philosophical approaches to the law. Some judges are referred to as **strict constructionists**, meaning that they believe that the proper role for judges is to interpret the law strictly in accordance with what the people who wrote the law meant at the time it was written. This includes both the Constitution itself and laws passed by Congress. Such judges are said to exercise "judicial restraint" and not to enter into the policy-making process. Rather, they merely interpret what policy makers (or the Founders) wrote down.

strict constructivism The legal philosophy that judges should use the intentions of those writing the law or the Constitution as guides for how to interpret the law.

Other judges are considered to show more **judicial activism**, meaning that they examine how the law as written should be applied to contemporary affairs. The tag of judicial activist refers to judges who go beyond the words of the law and consider how it should be interpreted and applied in light of historical changes. The implication often is that activist judges intrude in the process of policy making, which is properly the function of the legislative and executive branches. Judges have even been accused of inventing constitutional concepts to justify their rulings.

judicial activism Judicial rulings that go beyond interpreting the law in order to promote a judge's personal or political agenda.

The judiciary may be the least politicized of the three branches of government, but it is still deeply political. Traditionally, the divide between strict constructionists and judicial activists mirrored political ideology, with more liberal judges being comfortable making policy, while more conservative judges viewed such activity with discomfort and even disdain. Lately, however, judges on the Roberts Supreme Court have been accused of becoming increasingly activist in overturning the actions of legislatures in pursuit of conservative policies. Whether a judge

[19] Robert A. Dahl, "Decision-Making in a Democracy: The Supreme Court as a National Policy-Maker," *Journal of Public Law* 6 (1957): 279–95.

is being activist or is simply applying the language of the law is a judgment that in itself follows from the ideology of the person making the judgment. These ideological disputes are especially bitter in battles over abortion, the rights of criminal defendants, gun control, homosexual rights, affirmative action, and race.

The Politics of Judicial Appointments

The most potent and long-lasting influence of the political branches on the federal courts is in the appointment of judges. In recent decades, presidential appointments to the federal judiciary have been politically contentious. The more openly ideological the judges, the more controversy they generate during Senate confirmation hearings and in the mass media. This is especially true of Supreme Court nominations, but confirmation rates for nominees to the lower federal courts have also fallen in recent years, as senators from the opposing party block nominations. Nominees to the appeals courts now wait an average of six months to be confirmed, and vacancies on federal district courts typically persist for months before a nominee is even named.[20]

Some scholars claim that the judicial appointment process has always been highly political, as judges, the presidents who nominate them, and the senators who confirm or reject them are themselves political actors.[21] Others contend that the process has become intensely politicized only in recent years. They point to events such as the failed confirmation of Robert Bork to the Supreme Court in 1987 and the increasing emphasis placed on judicial nominations by interest groups as causing a breakdown in the norms of deference and restraint that previously governed the process.[22] Other scholars point to the existence of institutional hurdles such as the Senate's "blue slip" (by which the senators from the state in which a judgeship is located can veto a nomination), the majority party's control of the Senate Judiciary Committee, and the filibuster on the Senate floor. These procedural tools, when wielded in an environment marked by polarized parties that recognize the importance of judges in interpreting federal law, can cause the appointment process to grind to a halt.[23]

All federal judges can hold their office for as long as they are on good behavior (not impeached), which means that a given president's impact on the courts will last far beyond his or her term in office. In the New Deal era,

---

[20] Statistics from Sarah A. Binder and Forrest Maltzman, *Advice and Dissent: The Struggle to Shape the Federal Judiciary* (Washington, DC: Brookings Press, 2009).

[21] Lee Epstein and Jeffrey Segal, *Advice and Consent: The Politics of Judicial Appointments* (New York: Oxford University Press, 2005).

[22] See, for example, Wendy L. Martinek, Mark Kemper, and Steven R. Van Winkle, "To Advise and Consent: The Senate and Lower Federal Court Nominations," *Journal of Politics* 64, no. 2 (2002): 337–61; and Lauren Cohen Bell, *Warring Factions: Interest Groups, Money, and the New Politics of Senate Confirmation* (Columbus: Ohio State University Press, 2002).

[23] Binder and Maltzman, *Advice and Dissent*.

both supporters and opponents of FDR's policies clearly recognized the political dimension of the Supreme Court and the long-range importance of judicial appointments. This remained the case when Barack Obama made his two appointments to the Supreme Court in his first term.

This discussion of appointments and of the role of the other branches, especially the president and Senate in the appointment process, brings us back to the questions posed at the beginning of this chapter. In principle, the Supreme Court should have the independence to make unbiased decisions based on its interpretation of the law. In order for it to do so, however, the president and Congress must refrain from pressuring the Court and need to respect its decisions even if they disagree with them. Though it is tempting to pressure the Court or threaten its independence in some way—such as when FDR threatened to pack the Court with additional justices judged friendly to his policies—by leaving the Court alone the other branches receive the best long-term joint outcome. The situation thus represents a collective dilemma among people who might be tempted to interfere in the Court's business and pressure the Court beyond what is considered acceptable. If they interfere too much, it becomes a form of defection from a cooperative outcome. All are better off preserving the independence of the Court.

FDR's plan to change the composition of the Court during the New Deal Era was a defection in this interpretation. He saw the Court as an obstacle and was tempted, as players are in prisoner's dilemmas, to defect instead of cooperate, threatening to change the composition of the Court in an admittedly legal but politically unacceptable way. Many members of Congress, even from FDR's party, felt that he was violating long-standing norms and traditions that bound the legislative and executive branches to respect the Court's independence. Viewing this as a collective dilemma helps us to understand the anger of Congress, and why people believed FDR was "defecting" from a cooperative outcome. As a blatant attempt to influence the decisions of the Court, his plan offended their sense of how separation of powers ought to work. It would set a bad precedent by allowing the president to control the Court by "packing" it with judges favorable to his policies whenever he disagreed with Court decisions.

The reaction of New Deal supporters in Congress, especially the Senate, and among the general public is telling.

Judicial nominations, especially to the Supreme Court, are often controversial. President Obama's first appointee, Sonia Sotomayor, underwent an especially contentious confirmation hearing by Senate Republicans before ultimately being confirmed.

A majority agreed with FDR's policy goals, and Congress might easily have approved his court-packing plan. Why, then, did they balk? More generally, why are the more political branches—Congress and president—reluctant to exert direct pressure on the Supreme Court, and why is the Court accorded such respect?

The opponents of the Affordable Care Act did not defect as did FDR, though they theoretically could have. The House of Representatives, which was controlled by Republicans, could have threatened to freeze judicial salaries or even instigate investigations into judicial conduct. But Republican party leaders did not, and given the respect the Court enjoys it would clearly have hurt the party's reputation for fair play. Republican leaders complained but begrudgingly went along with the decision and vowed to try through elections and the legislative process to overturn the Act itself.

The reactions to Robert's decision and to FDR's court-packing plan illustrate both the legitimacy of the Court in the eyes of the public and members of the other branches and the difficulties courts face in acting independently. Although the courts are largely independent, they are simultaneously part of the national government under the separation-of-powers system and intertwined with the other branches through checks and balances. This dichotomy—between the ideal of independent courts and the reality of their being tied up with the elected branches—provokes temptation among groups within government to interfere in the courts' business. Fortunately, it is the rare exception that the other branches of government actually do step over the line as FDR did. More often, the outcome is what happened in 2012. Critics of the Court's decision raged, but they opted to try to influence the Court through well-accepted means: trying to capture the presidency and the Senate so that they could affect future appointments to the bench.

To what extent do the courts make decisions on the basis of public or political pressure or judges' personal ideologies, instead of relying on the texts of laws, regulations, and the Constitution?[24] The answer depends on who sits on the court and who appointed them, the partisan divides within and among the other branches of government, and on the specific policy issue involved in the court case. We are currently in an era where Republican presidents seek to appoint conservative justices to the Supreme Court who will generally (though not always, as we saw with Roberts) uphold conservative policies and Democratic presidents seek to appoint liberal justices who will generally (but not always) uphold liberal policies. The Courts are respected and independent in terms of resisting pressure on specific cases, but at a time of deep partisan polarization such as ours, the nature of the judicial appointment process ensures that the courts will be firmly enmeshed in the divisive politics of society at large.

---

[24] For a discussion of these ideas set in historical perspective, see Bruce Ackerman, *We the People* (Cambridge, MA: Harvard University Press, 1991).

The Politics and Strategies of Judicial Confirmations

The Supreme Court today is divided ideologically between conservative and liberal justices because the presidency has gone back and forth between Republicans and Democrats over the past three decades. Republican presidents appointed the conservative justices and Democratic presidents appointed the liberal ones. Many cases on the Supreme Court today, especially the politically sensitive ones, are decided 5–4 or 6–3, with the Court reflecting the partisanship of the appointing presidents.

Interests

Presidents and the people who support them politically want justices appointed to the Supreme Court who are competent and respected, but also who will decide cases consistent with the overall political and legal philosophies of their political party. The people whom the president appoints can serve as a president's legacy. Those who oppose the judicial philosophy of a nominated justice try to influence the relevant decision makers and thwart the candidate. When President Obama nominated Elena Kagan, antiabortion rights groups protested and pressured senators to vote her down because she was known to support *Roe v. Wade* (1973), a decision in favor of abortion rights. Nominees in recent times have had to answer questions during hearings about abortion, affirmative action, campaign finance regulations, press freedom, and executive privilege. Because these issues are political hot buttons, Supreme Court nominations become highly publicized forums for interest groups to press their views.

Institutions

Though Supreme Court justices are not elected, the selection and confirmation processes are not devoid of politics. In fact, the institutions involved in the nomination procedures mean that politics has much to do with *who* is nominated, as well as *how* this person is confirmed.

The president must be strategic because of the fundamental institutional design of the confirmation process. The president proposes a nominee, but the Senate plays a large role in having the nominee confirmed. The people chosen generally share the broad

In recent years, Supreme Court nominations have become highly contentious.

legal philosophies of the presidential administration, but presidents also anticipate what kinds of nominees the Senate will likely approve. Rarely nominated are people that senators will consider too extreme ideologically or in legal philosophy.

Outcomes

Because presidents value both judicial competance and ability to get confirmed, a president's nominee is very likely to be approved by the Senate. Historically, only 16 percent of all people nominated have been rejected or have withdrawn. Even when the presidency and Senate are controlled by different parties, nominees are still routinely confirmed, despite senators peppering nominees with difficult questions. Since 1971, out of the 17 people nominated, 15 were confirmed by the Senate, one was rejected (Robert Bork, who some senators found too conservative), and one withdrew (Harriet Myers, who some claimed was inexperienced). These cases serve as the exceptions to the general pattern and are the most recent examples of when presidents made the rare strategic blunders.

Think About It

If the judicial nomination process is so political, why do most nominees get confirmed?

FURTHER READING

★ = Included in *Readings in American Politics*, 3e

Ackerman, Bruce, *We the People* (Cambridge, MA: Harvard University Press, 1991). A detailed examination of how constitutional interpretation has gone through phases in American history in response to changes in historical circumstances.

Binder, Sarah A., and Forrest Maltzman, *Advice and Dissent: The Struggle to Shape the Federal Judiciary* (Washington, DC: Brookings Press, 2009). A study indicating the many constraints that elected officials face when they try to shape the judiciary through the appointment process.

Clark, Tom, *The Limits of Judical Independence* (New York: Cambridge University Press, 2011). Analyzes in detail how Congress tries to constrain the federal courts and how the federal courts react to Congress.

Epstein, Lee, and Jack Knight, *The Choices Justices Make* (Washington, DC: CQ Press, 1998). Treats justices of the Supreme Court as savvy, rational actors who act strategically to improve the odds of bringing about the kinds of decisions they want.

Epstein, Lee, and Jeffrey Segal, *Advice and Consent: The Politics of Judicial Appointments* (New York: Oxford University Press, 2005). A systematic analysis of the relationship of the branches on judicial appointments, putting weight on political ideology as a motivation.

Johnson, Timothy, *Oral Arguments and Decision Making on the U.S. Supreme Court* (Albany: State University of New York Press, 2004). An innovative study of how oral arguments affect judicial decision making on the Supreme Court.

Kramer, Larry, *The People Themselves* (New York: Oxford University Press, 2004). A clear account of how courts respond to changes in public opinion and election results.

★ *Lawrence v. Texas* (2003). The ruling that overturned *Bowers v. Hardwick* (1986) and declared the sodomy law in Texas (and subsequently other states) unconstitutional.

★ *Marbury v. Madison* (1803). The ruling that established the Supreme Court's power of judicial review.

★ *National Federation of Independent Business v. Sebelius* (2012). The ruling that upheld major provisions of the Patient Protection and Affordable Care Act, including the individual mandate, but deemed its expansion of Medicaid unconstitutional.

★ Rosenberg, Gerald, *The Hollow Hope: Can Courts Bring about Social Change?* (Chicago: University of Chicago Press, 1991). A classic account that questions the notion that courts lead social change, arguing instead that courts have lagged behind the elected branches in responding to changing social conditions and enacting liberal policies.

Segal, Jeffrey A., and Harold J. Spaeth, *The Supreme Court and the Attitudinal Model Revisited* (Cambridge, UK: Cambridge University Press, 2002). A systematic analysis of decision making on the Supreme Court, treating the court like a mini-legislature where the justices act as though they "vote" on policies.

Whittington, Keith, *Constitutional Interpretation* (Lawrence: University of Kansas Press, 1999). A deep and convincing analysis of the changing interpretation of the Constitution throughout American history.

KEY TERMS

amicus curiae (p. 282)

attitudinal model (p. 284)

civil case (p. 274)

civil law (p. 279)

class action (p. 275)

common law (p. 279)

concurring opinion (p. 287)

constitutional law (p. 280)

criminal case (p. 274)

dissenting opinion (p. 287)

federal court supremacy (p. 270)

judicial activism (p. 291)

judicial review (p. 268)

legal model (p. 284)

moot (p. 281)

standing (p. 275)

stare decisis (p. 279)

statutory law (p. 279)

strategic (or rational choice) model (p. 285)

strict constructivism (p. 291)

writ of *certiorari* (p. 281)

Public opinion on same-sex marriage has shifted in recent years from majority sentiment against it to majority support for it. In 2012, President Obama announced his own change in position to one of support for same-sex marriage. It is likely this change was influenced by, and in turn influenced, the evolution in public attitudes.

9

PUBLIC OPINION

Democratic government emphasizes "the will of the people," and at times politicians seem very concerned with following public opinion. Yet at other times, the government goes against what a majority of people want. What is the link between public opinion and politicians' behavior and expressed views?

Until recently, reputable and independent surveys showed that a strong majority of Americans opposed same-sex marriage. In 1996, Bill Clinton, with overwhelming support from Congress, signed the Defense of Marriage Act (DOMA), which legally defined marriage as being between one man and one woman. That year, the Gallup polling company asked the following question: "Do you think that marriages between homosexual couples should or should not be recognized by the law as valid, with the same rights as traditional marriages?" Their results showed that only 27 percent of respondents thought that same-sex marriages should be legal, with 68 percent of the opinion that same-sex marriage should be illegal.

As a candidate for the Senate in 2004, Barack Obama declared his view that marriage should be defined as being between one man and one woman, going so far as to state that marriage is not a civil right, though he did come out in favor of civil unions and various rights that come with marriage. Public support for the idea of same-sex marriage had increased since DOMA passed, but the same Gallup question in 2004 showed that the public still opposed same-sex marriage by a margin of 55 to 42 percent. Around the same time, several states amended their constitutions to codify the traditional definition of marriage and Congress considered an amendment to the U. S. Constitution to do the same.

Over the next few years, the percentage of people reporting opposition to same-sex marriage dropped slightly again. Leading up to the 2008 presidential election, Barack Obama reiterated his support for defining marriage as between one man and one woman. As public opinion continued to shift, though, so too did the resilience of President Obama's position on the issue. In 2010, President Obama said that his feelings on the issue were "evolving" and that he was struggling with his position on same-sex marriage.

In 2011, for the first time since the question began being asked, polling data showed that the public supported same-sex marriage, with support continuing to trend upward and opposition trending downward (see Figure 9.1). Around this time, the president became more publicly supportive of issues affecting the gay community, endorsing New York's decision to recognize same-sex marriage and saying that he supported the repeal of DOMA and would instruct his administration not to defend it in federal courts. Then, in May 2012, Vice President Joe Biden announced his support for same-sex marriage on television, with the president following suit shortly after. President Obama's announcement made headlines around the world.

Though it may appear that Obama made a sudden and radical shift, his public positions had been shifting for several years on the issue in correspondence with changing public opinion. When there was a clear majority opposing same-sex marriage, so too did Senator Obama. As the public's position became less clear, so too did the president's. Finally, as the public became more supportive of same-sex marriage, the president announced his qualified support, until he eventually sided with what was a newly recorded majority position in favor. (Though Obama endorsed same-sex marriage in 2012, he continued to argue that it was an issue that should be left to the states, not handled by the federal government). After the president's announcement, some interest group leaders associated with the president also announced their support, and survey respondents indicated that the president's support affected their views. Meanwhile, the Congress remained opposed and refused to take up changes to DOMA. The Supreme Court in 2013 finally struck down the law as unconstitutional.

At times, politicians seem quite concerned with following public opinion. Yet at other times, people in the government go against what a majority of people want, and in their statements try to sway the public. What is the link between public opinion and politicians' behavior and expressed views? Under what circumstances do politicians respond to the expressed opinions of the public? And when is the public influenced by elite rhetoric and decisions?

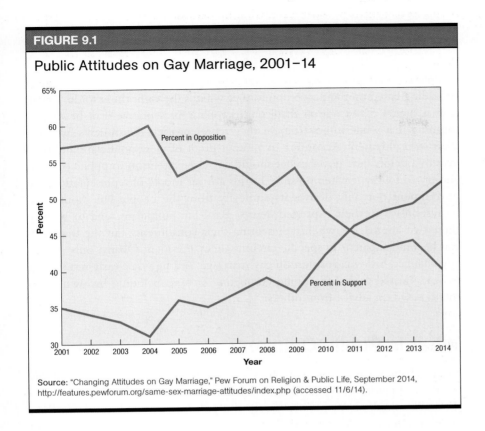

FIGURE 9.1

Public Attitudes on Gay Marriage, 2001–14

Source: "Changing Attitudes on Gay Marriage," Pew Forum on Religion & Public Life, September 2014, http://features.pewforum.org/same-sex-marriage-attitudes/index.php (accessed 11/6/14).

Public Opinion in a Democratic System

In the preceding chapters, we have focused on the institutions of government, the rules and procedures that structure government action. We now switch to analyzing the external factors in society that both shape and are shaped by government action. This chapter is on the most general of these external factors, public opinion. As we saw with changing attitudes about same-sex marriage, public opinion is a crucial "input" in determining government action, but it is also affected by the actions of politicians and other leaders in society. The nature of public opinion, its nuances, how it is communicated and how it changes over time, have been the subject of intense study by social scientists. In later chapters, we will discuss specific means of transmitting public opinion and putting pressure on government, such as voting in elections and lobbying on behalf of various interest groups.

A core philosophical underpinning of the American political system—indeed, of any political system based on the concept of popular sovereignty—is that the government's authority is derived from the people. In the modern era of scientifically valid surveys, summaries of public opinion serve almost as proxies for "the people." Policy makers and mass media communicators often use such measures of public opinion as indicators of what "the people" desire.

Politicians are sometimes criticized for being slaves to public opinion instead of leading based on their own opinions of what is the right thing to do. Recall from Chapter 5 the notion that congressional representatives can be *trustees*, meaning that while in government they represent their constituents by using their own judgment. According to another point of view, politicians and officials in a democratic government should pay close attention to public opinion and try to follow it when possible. In this *delegate* model of representation, the government not only derives its authority from the people but should also be responsive to their expressed desires. Real-life politicians tend to balance these two approaches when representing their constituents, but the trade-offs can become apparent in specific circumstances. President Obama only gradually changed his own position on gay marriage, and he was clearly responding to complicated trade-offs among competing factors, including his own judgments based on advice from others.

What Is Public Opinion?

public opinion The collection of attitudes and preferences of the mass public.

In this chapter, we analyze both how researchers study public opinion (How are surveys conducted?) and what has been learned from that study (What does the public think about political issues and politicians?). Although researchers attempt to measure it by means of surveys and other methods, **public opinion** remains a fundamentally amorphous concept. It is typically defined as the collection of attitudes and preferences of the mass public.

We can further define an attitude in this context as coming in one of two forms. An opinion is an evaluation of a subject such as a politician or a policy. A predisposition is a deeper value or belief about politics that tends to be stable over time (such as an ideology or partisanship). Both opinions and predispositions fall under the broader concept of attitudes. Furthermore, preferences refer to how people rank-order outcomes or experiences. An example of a preference is "I prefer paying fewer taxes and therefore having fewer parks to paying more taxes and having more, high quality parks." These various concepts are certainly related to one another, but noting their differences can help us understand public-opinion formation and expression, as we will learn shortly.

There has been a great deal of high-quality research on public opinion, and many polls about politics are conducted on a daily basis. Quantitative analyses of results from surveys and polls are the most common method of measuring and analyzing public opinion. As we will see, we tend to measure public opinion in terms of what opinion polls or surveys report in response to questions asked of random samples of people. Most of our attention will be on the use of surveys, though we will summarize other methods later in this chapter.

The Challenge of Having Many Principals

The relationship between the public and the government can be viewed as a special kind of principal-agent problem. We might think of an elected politician as an agent with multiple principals. The president, for example, works for all the people. They "hire" the president through their ballots and can fire him or her at the next election. It is true that only approximately 65 million people may vote for the winning presidential candidate in a typical election (given recent turnout rates), but after taking office, the president represents more than 300 million principals. How does he or she know what these 300 million principals want? How does the president incorporate public-opinion information into decision making? Members of Congress face a similar challenge: How can a senator from California, with close to 40 million principals, be a good agent? Can a representative in the House, typically having 650,000 constituents in his or her district, be responsive to all of them?

This challenge is all the more daunting because public opinion can be difficult to discern and follow with consistency. Consider a recent example using real public-opinion data. The following three questions were asked of different national samples by different polling organizations in the same week of May 2013. Each question appears to measure public opinion about a controversy over the Justice Department subpoenaing the phone records of reporters from the Associated Press.

> *Do you approve or disapprove of the Justice Department's decision to subpoena AP phone records as part of investigation into disclosure of classified information?* (Pew)[1]
>
> 36 percent of respondents said they approved.
>
> *As you may know, the Associated Press reported classified information about U. S. antiterrorism efforts, and federal prosecutors have obtained AP's phone records through a court order to find the source of this information. Do you think this action by federal prosecutors is or is not justified?* (*Washington Post*/ABC News)[2]
>
> 52 percent of respondents thought this action was "justified."
>
> *As you may know, after the AP ran news stories that included classified information about U. S. antiterrorism efforts, the Justice Department secretly collected phone records of reporters and editors who work there. Do you think the actions of the Justice Department were acceptable or unacceptable?* (CNN/ORC)[3]
>
> 43 percent of respondents thought this action was "acceptable."

Given these disparate survey results, how can one accurately gauge public attitudes about the Justice Department activities? Is it reasonable to conclude that a majority of Americans support the phone record subpoenas? It is difficult to say. People's support for or opposition to a government action often depends on how a question is posed. In this case, it matters whether the survey

---

[1] Pew Research Center, May 2013.

[2] *Washington Post*/ABC News, May 2013.

[3] CNN/ORC, May 2013.

mentions "U. S. antiterrorism efforts" and how the survey describes what the Justice Department did. Among other aspects of survey design, question wording matters a lot in determining results. These three survey questions could be interpreted as indicating majority support for *or* opposition to the Justice Department's actions. Such mixed signals make it hard for politicians to decipher public attitudes.

Moreover, the public can be fickle. Public opinion fluctuates even over relatively short periods. Consider the pattern of President Obama's approval ratings—the proportion of people who responded that they "approved" of the way he was running the country (Figure 9.2). Obama's ratings have fluctuated throughout the course of his presidency, often in response to events over which he had little control. Even if the public seems to approve of the job a politician is doing, or to support a particular policy, that approval can change relatively quickly. (We will have more to say about presidential approval ratings below.)

Finally, many people are simply uninformed about government and politics, as we will discuss later in this chapter. For instance, pollsters in the 1960s discovered that a significant percentage of people gave what were essentially random answers to questions about their own preferences with regard to public

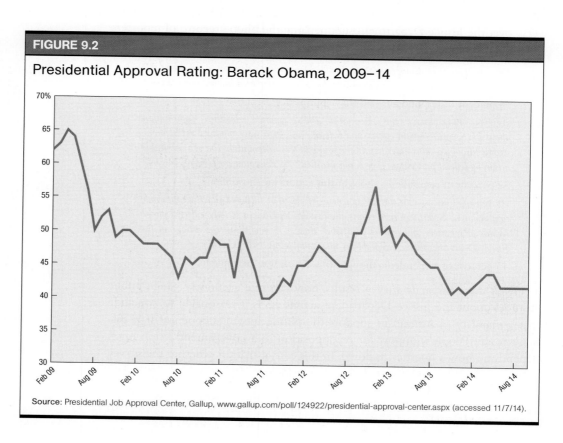

FIGURE 9.2

Presidential Approval Rating: Barack Obama, 2009–14

Source: Presidential Job Approval Center, Gallup, www.gallup.com/poll/124922/presidential-approval-center.aspx (accessed 11/7/14).

policies.[4] Contemporary surveys find low levels of factual knowledge among people about the basic workings of the government.

These challenges point to the fact that public opinion can be complex. People are diverse in their opinions and attitudes (and political knowledge). When we summarize what millions of people think and then refer to a small set of numbers as reflecting public opinion, we can overlook the fundamental difficulties public officials have in responding to that opinion in a coherent way. Acknowledging these challenges may provide a clue as to why Barack Obama claimed such a cautious position on same-sex marriage. Perhaps he understood that public opinion on that issue was too complicated to be measured by a simple set of numbers derived from questions in several public-opinion surveys.

Measuring Public Opinion

The study of public opinion is one of the most developed areas of research in the social sciences. Because of sophisticated methods of survey research and creative experimental techniques, we now know more than ever before about what people think and feel, and about the collective attitudes of the general public.

As agents (or representatives) of their constituents, policy makers find it difficult to follow the wishes of *all* their principals. For example, Americans were deeply split on how to balance spending cuts and tax increases during the "fiscal cliff" crisis of late 2012 and early 2013.

[4] Philip Converse, "The Nature of Belief Systems in Mass Publics," in *Ideology and Discontent*, ed. D. E. Apter (New York: Free Press, 1964), pp. 206–61.

Early Attempts at Measurement

Before the advent of scientific opinion polling, politicians and journalists looked to the size of crowds at rallies, the number of people buying and reading pamphlets, and the incidences of mob action as indicators of public opinion. National magazines regularly published the results of informal "straw polls." *Literary Digest*, for example, would mail out millions of sample ballots to its readers months or weeks before a presidential election, and then record responses from those completed and returned. From 1920 through 1932, these straw polls predicted election results quite accurately, including the margins of victory. When the *Digest* failed to predict Franklin Delano Roosevelt's landslide victory over Alf Landon in 1936, however, these methods were called into question.

Straw polls, which were used as early as the nineteenth century, can get it right sometimes, but they are not scientifically valid in the sense that they are not consciously designed to represent accurately the views of the electorate. Since the late 1940s, public opinion, including people's voting intentions in upcoming elections, has routinely been measured through polling of random samples of people and convincing them to respond to questionnaires. Polls in recent years have been remarkably accurate in predicting the election results in presidential races. Final poll results in the few days before the elections are typically within one percentage point of the actual percentage of votes the winner and loser (or losers) receive on Election Day.

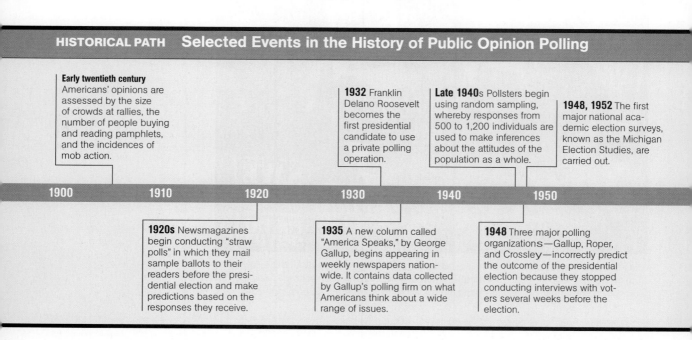

HISTORICAL PATH **Selected Events in the History of Public Opinion Polling**

Early twentieth century Americans' opinions are assessed by the size of crowds at rallies, the number of people buying and reading pamphlets, and the incidences of mob action.

1932 Franklin Delano Roosevelt becomes the first presidential candidate to use a private polling operation.

Late 1940s Pollsters begin using random sampling, whereby responses from 500 to 1,200 individuals are used to make inferences about the attitudes of the population as a whole.

1948, 1952 The first major national academic election surveys, known as the Michigan Election Studies, are carried out.

| 1900 | 1910 | 1920 | 1930 | 1940 | 1950 |

1920s Newsmagazines begin conducting "straw polls" in which they mail sample ballots to their readers before the presidential election and make predictions based on the responses they receive.

1935 A new column called "America Speaks," by George Gallup, begins appearing in weekly newspapers nationwide. It contains data collected by Gallup's polling firm on what Americans think about a wide range of issues.

1948 Three major polling organizations—Gallup, Roper, and Crossley—incorrectly predict the outcome of the presidential election because they stopped conducting interviews with voters several weeks before the election.

Random Sampling

What accounts for the accuracy in predicting election results today? More generally, why can we have any confidence in results from surveys? National polls for the presidential election typically have between 500 and 1,200 respondents. This is an infinitesimal proportion of the voting population of approximately 130 million. It turns out that, with care, social scientists can get an accurate picture of what an entire group will do by sampling a small fraction of randomly selected respondents from that group. The key lies in the tremendous value that comes from statistical analysis of random samples of data.

In the language of statistics, a **population** is the group you want to learn about. Suppose you want to know what proportion of the voters will choose the Democratic candidate for president. Your population is the set of voters in the presidential contest on Election Day. You are trying to predict in advance the behavior of that population. A **sample** is a subset of the population chosen to provide information for analysis. A reputable pollster will choose a sample of people expected to vote in the election using methods of **random selection**, meaning that in principle each person in the population has an equal chance of being chosen to be part of the sample.

As the random sample gets larger, it increasingly approximates the entire population, but it does not need to be anywhere near the size of the true population for the sample data to offer a good approximation. In fact, if people

population In statistical research, the entire group about which you want to learn, such as all adults living in the United States.

sample In statistical research, a subset of the population chosen to provide information for the research about the population.

random selection Choosing a sample such that each member of a population has an equal chance of being selected into the sample.

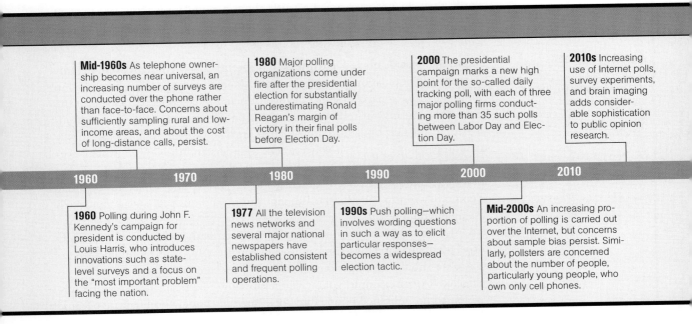

Mid-1960s As telephone ownership becomes near universal, an increasing number of surveys are conducted over the phone rather than face-to-face. Concerns about sufficiently sampling rural and low-income areas, and about the cost of long-distance calls, persist.

1980 Major polling organizations come under fire after the presidential election for substantially underestimating Ronald Reagan's margin of victory in their final polls before Election Day.

2000 The presidential campaign marks a new high point for the so-called daily tracking poll, with each of three major polling firms conducting more than 35 such polls between Labor Day and Election Day.

2010s Increasing use of Internet polls, survey experiments, and brain imaging adds considerable sophistication to public opinion research.

| 1960 | 1970 | 1980 | 1990 | 2000 | 2010 |

1960 Polling during John F. Kennedy's campaign for president is conducted by Louis Harris, who introduces innovations such as state-level surveys and a focus on the "most important problem" facing the nation.

1977 All the television news networks and several major national newspapers have established consistent and frequent polling operations.

1990s Push polling—which involves wording questions in such a way as to elicit particular responses—becomes a widespread election tactic.

Mid-2000s An increasing proportion of polling is carried out over the Internet, but concerns about sample bias persist. Similarly, pollsters are concerned about the number of people, particularly young people, who own only cell phones.

are chosen randomly from the population and surveyed on their preference of presidential candidate, and if they answer the survey honestly and stick to their indicated choice when they actually vote, then a poll of approximately 1,200 respondents will predict the eventual popular-vote winner in a typical presidential election nearly every time.

Well-done surveys that evaluate politicians, consumer products, and other matters of public opinion share similar features, such as selecting a truly random sample. If the sample is random and the responses are honest, then statistical summaries of the sample population will closely resemble characteristics of the entire population.

Information gleaned from samples is not perfectly accurate, of course. Pollsters refer to the **margin of error** as the range of outcomes in the population that we can expect to see given the data generated by the sample. As an example, in a typical presidential election poll surveying 1,200 voters, the margin of error is around 1.5 percent. This means that if a candidate, according to the sample of voters in a survey, will receive 47 percent of the vote on Election Day, we can confidently predict that the real election will lead to that candidate receiving between 45.5 and 48.5 percent of the vote (the range you get when you subtract 1.5 from 47 or add 1.5 to 47).

margin of error In statistical research, the range of outcomes we expect for a population, given the data revealed by a sample drawn from that population.

Possible Biases

Any attempt to measure public opinion will be inexact because measurements based on samples are unavoidably biased to a greater or lesser degree. In other words, they do not measure the truth about a population with 100 percent accuracy. Reputable researchers try to minimize bias, which is often unintentional and a natural outcome of the research process.

biased sample A sample that, because it does not accurately represent the overall population, is likely to lead to erroneous conclusions about the population.

Biased Samples A **biased sample** is one potential problem with polls. In sampling for any population you want to understand, the ideal is for each person in the population to have an equal chance of being selected to participate in the survey. This means not relying on biased sampling schemes where some kinds of people in the population are much more likely to respond to the survey than others. For example, if you wanted to understand the opinions of all college students, you would not simply go to the library on a Saturday evening to interview randomly selected students studying there. The library on Saturday evening draws a specific kind of student (more studious, less social?), and such a sample would be biased.

Unfortunately, many opinion polls reported in the media, and especially those used in marketing campaigns, rely on heavily biased sampling strategies. One should be suspicious of polls in which respondents are allowed to self-select by, for example, voluntarily responding to an e-mail. Telephone surveys based on published phone directories are increasingly problematic because a growing number of people screen their calls or use cell phones rather than land lines. Prior to the 1970s, researchers encountered a different problem: a significant proportion of American households did not have phone service, either because it was too expensive or because the technology was not available in their area.

Response rates to phone surveys—the number of people who actually give interviews as compared to the number selected and solicited through a random process—have been declining for many years and now stand at about 30 percent. Low response rates can make it expensive to complete a survey because of the large number of people who need to be contacted in order to get a representative sample. Low response rates can also introduce substantial bias if those who respond to the survey are in some way different from those who do not respond. Consider a survey about same-sex marriage, for instance. If younger and older voters hold different opinions on the issue, the fact that younger voters tend not to respond to surveys will introduce bias in the results. Reputable survey companies work hard to minimize such bias. Phone surveys are still used for many purposes, but at some point response rates may become so low that other means will become the norm.

Internet polls are increasingly common. If they are not carefully designed, however, they can introduce even more serious biases than phone surveys. There is some evidence that improved Internet technology is providing opportunities to collect good samples. In the mid-2000s, for example, companies such as Knowledge Networks and Polimetrix gave thousands of people an Internet connection for free on the condition that they occasionally answered survey questions. Such techniques can eliminate a built-in bias arising from the fact that people with lower incomes are less likely to have Internet access. This means that Internet surveys run the risk of oversampling people who have the money to buy online access. Some research suggests that surveys that correct for this risk can provide samples that are as reliable as those produced by other, more traditional survey methods, but these research results are controversial.[5]

Question Wording The way questions are worded can introduce other kinds of biased responses in opinion polling. We have already seen how differences in wording affected the poll results about the Justice Department's subpoenas in 2013. Now consider these two differently worded questions about the death penalty:

> *If you could choose between the following two approaches, which do you think is the better penalty for murder—the death penalty or life imprisonment, with absolutely no possibility of parole?* (Gallup, 2005)
>
> 53 percent said "death penalty," while 44 percent said "life imprisonment."

[5] See, for example, Linchiat Chang and Jon A. Krosnick, "National Surveys via RDD Telephone Interviewing versus the Internet: Comparing Sample Representativeness and Response Quality," *Public Opinion Quarterly* 73, no. 4 (Winter 2009): 641–78.

Are you in favor of the death penalty for a person convicted of murder? (Gallup, 2005)[6]
77 percent said "yes."

There is no objective way to determine which preceding question is more "biased." But clearly if people wanted to demonstrate strong support for the death penalty, they would use the second question in their survey. In other words, survey information can be deliberately manipulated so that it yields results that are consistent with specific political goals. By wording a question in a particular way, interest group leaders can publicize results that are favorable to their policy interests. Even researchers who are trying to conduct an accurate, unbiased survey can inadvertently introduce bias depending on how they word their questions.

The most egregious form of biased wording is "push polling," which is not really polling at all, but rather a form of marketing and campaigning. In push polling, people are given information that reflects poorly or well on a particular candidate, and then asked if they would vote for that candidate on the basis of that information. These survey "results" are highly misleading because they are based on responses influenced by selective information. During the 2000 Republican presidential primaries, for example, campaign consultants in favor of George W. Bush's election (possibly without the knowledge or involvement of his official campaign) conducted a poll in which potential primary voters were asked whether they would be likely to vote for or against John McCain after learning that his "campaign finance proposals would give labor unions and the media a bigger influence on the outcome of elections."[7] Clearly, the consultants' goal was not to find out how many people were going to vote for McCain, but to spread negative information about Bush's opponent while posing as pollsters, and eventually to publish poll results that showed McCain's drooping prospects. It is hard to know how widespread push polling is, but it definitely occurs and is troublesome for the polling industry because it heightens peoples' suspicions of pollsters.

Reputable, independent polling organizations, such as Gallup, Pew, and Roper, tend to use defensible methods and have long track records of relatively accurate polling results. By accurate, we mean that the results from polls show up consistently if the polling is repeated or changes in results can be explained. Academic polls such as the General Social Survey and the American National Election Survey are especially careful and have earned a reputation for providing high-quality data on public opinion about politics and public affairs.

---

[6] Both questions are from the Gallup Poll, May 2005.

[7] Matthew J. Streb and Susan H. Pinkus, "When Push Comes to Shove: Push Polling and the Manipulation of Public Opinion," in *Polls and Politics: The Dilemmas of Democracy*, ed. Michael A. Genovese and Matthew J. Streb (Albany: State University of New York Press, 2006), pp. 95–117.

Public Opinion Surveys

In order to evaluate public-opinion results reported in surveys, it is important to understand how surveys are conducted.

- Modern survey research usually relies on *samples from the overall population* of only 500 to 1,200 adults.

- *Numerous groups conduct political surveys*, including media outlets (such as television networks and newspapers), private polling firms, academic researchers, and interest groups. The Gallup Poll, for example, regularly publishes results on the president's approval rating.

- A political survey may ask questions about *policy attitudes* ("Do you support an expansion of offshore drilling?"), *evaluations of political figures* ("Do you approve of the job the president is doing?"), and *future political behavior* ("Which candidate do you intend to vote for in the November elections?").

- *A range of techniques may be used to obtain a sample* for a survey, from random-digit dialing (in which telephone numbers to call are generated at random) to self-selection on the part of the respondents. There is no consensus on the best way to select a sample, but it is clear that the results may be affected by the procedure used.

- *Survey questions may be developed in a number of ways*, including in a manner designed to elicit certain responses. In addition, questions about a given topic may be worded differently by different survey organizations.

- The *response rate*—the number of people from the selected sample who choose to cooperate with the survey—is also an important factor to consider when evaluating a survey. Although consensus exists on how to measure a survey's response rate, experts disagree on how much response rates affect the quality of results.

Alternative Methods to Surveys

It is worth noting that surveys are not the only methods for understanding public opinion. Although we cannot discuss these other methods in detail, six deserve mention. First, researchers can conduct intensive interviews with people and analyze their answers to discover underlying predispositions and mental processes. Second, researchers can run focus groups, in which people gathered in a room discuss answers to questions posed by a moderator. This can help us learn how people express their views in groups, as opposed to in isolation with a survey interviewer or on a questionnaire. The third method offers similar advantages: listening to conversations among groups in everyday environments and discovering how people spontaneously express their political

Political Polling in the Cell Phone Era

By the 1990s, the science of opinion surveys became good enough that most reputable survey companies were able to predict the winner of the presidential election in advance of the actual election itself. Unfortunately, producing quality survey data and forecasting election outcomes have become more difficult, because potential respondents often do not answer their phones and may not even have ordinary phones. Response rates to quality surveys have dropped. Furthermore, for the past three presidential elections, it has become more challenging to predict who will turn out in elections.

Interests

Subscribers to election polling information, including candidates and political parties, campaign consultants, interest groups, and journalists value the ability to predict election results or react to trends in voters' intentions during campaigns. Companies or organizations conducting opinion surveys on voter intentions want to earn money from clients and a reputation for accuracy and providing valuable information. Yet, accurate election polling is expensive and difficult for elections below the presidential, national level.

Institutions

A new trend among institutions conducting surveys and doing election forecasting is the rise of meta-analysis. Meta-analysis enables people to forecast election outcomes by using multiple survey results from a variety of sources. It differs from the work of individual firms like Gallup in that it analyzes the *aggregation* of polls. While the mathematical machinery is complex, the basic idea behind meta-analysis is simple. Consulting a variety of results from different polls and combining them allows one to minimize a variety of potential sources of bias. With meta-analysis, people can take into consideration not only poll results but also well-known patterns, such as voters' responses to new information about economic indicators and the tendency for voters in certain states to change their voting intentions in tandem.[1] Moreover, people can use a given survey's degree of accuracy and make the necessary statistical adjustments to correct for biases.[2] Putting more weight on certain poll results and less weight on others, in effect, minimizes the opportunity for overall error.

Outcomes

One of the most famous people using meta-analysis in the study of elections is Nate Silver, a statistician who

Statistician Nate Silver used meta-analysis techniques to correctly predict the outcomes of the 2012 elections.

has written for the *New York Times*. Prior to the 2012 presidential election, he predicted with perfect accuracy which candidate would win each state. No other well-known analyst or survey firm was as accurate as Silver. In fact, several famous survey firms, including Gallup, had their least accurate predictions in decades. (This was attributed in Gallup's case to inaccurate accounting for voter turnout.) Silver used meta-analysis and aggregated the results from dozens of polls conducted across the country, including those conducted within various states. Anyone who wants to do meta-analysis needs brains, but not necessarily a lot of money. The method does not bear the same costs as traditional random sampling because it uses available data conducted by other entities. Someone needs to conduct the surveys, so everyone cannot do meta-analysis. But meta-analysis is poised to change the way institutions that produce and consume survey information analyze and predict election outcomes.

Think About It

Are there any downsides to using the meta-analysis method for polling? If more and more people are using meta-analysis, what will be the effects on traditional polling firms?

[1] Nate Silver, "Election Forecast: Obama Begins with Tenuous Advantage," FiveThirtyEight, *New York Times*, June 7, 2012, http://fivethirtyeight.blogs.nytimes.com/2012/06/07/election-forecast-obama-begins-with-tenuous-advantage/ (accessed 11/12/12).

[2] Nate Silver, "Election Forecast: Obama Begins with Tenuous Advantage."

opinions during their ordinary routines. Fourth, researchers can run experiments to gain more knowledge of what affects the way people answer surveys or experience a particular emotion at one moment in time versus another, given a stimulus. Fifth, there has been increasing use of brain imaging (MRIs) to study mental processes as people hear or see political information. Sixth, researchers have examined the genetic makeup of people to learn if aspects of their political attitudes come from personality traits inherited from parents. Knowledge from all of these methods can complement the knowledge gained from surveys.

On these fifth and sixth sets of methods, brain imaging and genetic analysis, research has led to noteworthy findings that are spurring deeper study and analysis. Researchers are discovering, for instance, patterns linking specific genes to predispositions toward supporting liberal or conservative ideologies. Genetic attributes do not appear to determine political attitudes, but they do interact with and can be reinforced by social and environmental factors like family influences and traumatic events to tilt people in an ideological direction.[8]

Where Do Political Attitudes Come From?

Scholars of public opinion evaluate data of various kinds with the primary goals of describing people's attitudes and understanding what causes people to have certain attitudes. What are Americans' views toward government and politics? And where do these attitudes come from? In this section, we will summarize some of the fruits of this research, beginning with several fundamental factors that shape people's political attitudes: their backgrounds, underlying interests, group attachments, emotions, and the influence of political elites.

One of the strongest influences on individuals' political views is their parents' political views. Most people—including Texas Republican Representative Ron Paul (R–TX) and his son, Senator Rand Paul (R–KY)—follow in their parents' footsteps when it comes to party identification.

Socialization

Beyond the provocative idea that people might actually have genetically determined traits linked to their political attitudes (discussed earlier), research has shown that the information to which people are exposed in their formative years—usually during the late teens or early twenties—matters tremendously in determining political attitudes, especially predispositions. Studies have found

[8] Peter K. Hatemi and Rose McDermott, "The Political Psychology of Biology, Genetics, and Behavior," *Political Psychology* 33, no. 3 (June 2012): 307–12. Brad Verhulst, Peter K. Hatemi, and Lindon J. Eaves, "Disentangling the Importance of Psychological Predispositions and Social Constructions in the Organization of American Political Ideology," *Political Psychology* 33, no. 3 (June 2012): 375–93.

that parents play a primary role. Chances are high, for example, that if both parents are Democrats, their children will be Democrats as they reach adulthood—not because we can identify a "Democrat" gene, but because of the process of socialization. Likewise for Republicans, or for those who describe themselves as liberals or conservatives. And we know from research that partisanship tends to persist over the course of one's lifetime. Thus, the children of Democrats will typically grow up to be lifelong Democrats.[9] It is certainly the case that most people stay in place on both partisanship and ideology. (We will discuss partisanship and ideology in depth later in the chapter.)

The strong effect of parents' political views and the persistence of individuals' partisanship and ideology are the predominant patterns, but there are exceptions. Some people do change over time. Friends, coworkers, acquaintances, and others can influence one's partisanship and ideology. When asked in surveys with whom they discuss politics, people tend to identify one or two friends or coworkers who are particularly knowledgeable about politics. These knowledgeable people (often called "cue-givers," as we will see later) have been shown to influence the way their peers think about politics and their underlying attitudes toward public issues.[10]

There is evidence also that students who attend college at a liberal campus will tend to become more liberal during their college years, and vice versa for students who attend a conservative college.[11] Major world events, such as wars, recessions, and social movements, can change people's partisanship and ideology, as can such personal events such as becoming a small business owner or a member of the military, which tend to move people in a more conservative direction.[12] These are all factors in the process of socialization, in which the information and views to which people are exposed influence their attitudes and opinions.

Mass media can also be a source of individuals' attitudes. People tend to pay attention to media—newspapers, television stations, websites, blogs—that frame information in ways comfortable to them.[13] Thus, Fox News, widely considered a conservative media outlet, attracts many more conservative viewers than liberal viewers. But it's not clear which way the relationship works. Is Fox News causing people to be more conservative? Or are people who already hold conservative views choosing Fox News because they feel comfortable with the way

[9] Richard G. Niemi and M. Kent Jennings, "Issues and Inheritance in the Formation of Party Identification," *American Journal of Political Science* 35, no. 4 (1991): 970–88.

[10] Robert Huckfeldt and John Sprague, *Citizens, Politics, and Social Communication: Information and Influence in an Election Campaign* (New York: Cambridge University Press, 1995).

[11] Theodore Newcomb et al., *Persistence and Change: Bennington College and Its Students after Twenty-Five Years* (New York: John Wiley & Sons, 1967).

[12] Richard G. Niemi and M. Kent Jennings, "Issues and Inheritance in the Formation of Party Identification."

[13] Norman H. Nie, Darwin W. Miller III, Saar Golde, Daniel M. Butler, and Kenneth Winneg, "The World Wide Web and the U. S. Political News Market," *American Journal of Political Science* 54, no. 2 (2010): 428–39.

it frames the news? The preponderance of evidence suggests that people tend to select media with which they already agree in general.

Interests and Rationality

One seemingly straightforward explanation for someone's expressed attitude in a survey or an interview is that it is "in his or her interest," which might be a way of saying that they have a preference for something and that is that: "My preferences and attitudes follow from what my interests are." To what extent do self-interest and fixed preference determine political attitudes? Are people rational in making decisions based on their interests and preferences and the information that is available to them?

Material Interests The notion of interest is hard to define precisely. It may seem easy to explain why poor people would prefer that the government increase spending on social welfare programs even if taxes need to be raised, and why the rich would prefer that the government cut taxes even at the cost of shrinking social welfare programs. Answers to many survey questions about economic and social issues depend on one's income level. In surveys about health care reform in 2010, data showed that people in families with below-average incomes were significantly more likely to prefer mandatory, government-funded health insurance than people in families with above-average incomes.[14] Public-opinion data from surveys in all advanced industrial countries show that the higher the income or wealth of respondents, the more likely they are to say they prefer to cut taxes and reduce the size of government.

We might say that these preferences make sense because people prefer to be better-off materially and thus prefer particular public policies that would accomplish this. In other words, they are protecting their interests and express their preferences accordingly. By similar reasoning, younger people tend to be more opposed to war than older people because younger people tend to do the fighting. Women prefer more public funding for child care than men. Labor union members favor laws that make it easier for workers to unionize, while business owners do not. African Americans prefer tougher enforcement of racial discrimination laws.

If preferences and attitudes come purely from material interest, it almost inevitably follows that different groups of people will have conflicting preferences and attitudes. If you are taxed heavily to pay for a program that benefits others but not you, then you have an economic interest in changing either the program or the way it is funded.

Most public-opinion researchers, however, broaden the definition of interests to acknowledge that many people have complicated policy preferences and

---

[14] Data analyzed from the Kaiser Family Foundation Tracking Poll (September 11–18, 2009), available from the Roper Center, http://webapps.ropercenter.uconn.edu (accessed 5/11/11).

attitudes that may conflict with their economic interests or their apparent self-interest. In other words, they might include nonmaterial benefits as part of their interests. This broader definition of interests might include altruism, among other things. The noted economist Albert Hirschman wrote that interests were "the totality of human aspiration, [but denoting] an element of reflection and calculation with respect to the manner in which these aspirations [are] to be pursued." Put another way, interests are what people prefer after careful consideration, not merely what they seek at the spur of the moment.[15]

Many researchers would go even further, for purposes of analysis, and argue that someone's interests are whatever he or she says they prefer in surveys or in other settings. Although the general patterns in survey data seem to indicate a relationship between material self-interest and opinions, there are many exceptions. Some rich people prefer even higher taxes than they currently pay, and some poor people prefer to reduce or even eliminate social welfare programs. Some African Americans and women wish to eliminate affirmative action programs, and some teachers prefer that less money be spent on public schools. One might conclude that these people are stating policy opinions and preferences that run contrary to their interests. Others might argue that these respondents are not typical, but that they are entitled to define and express their own interests.

Rationality An idea related to interests is the assumption that people are rational. There is an ongoing debate in the social sciences about whether people's political behavior is fundamentally rational. Traditional models of political institutions often begin with the assumption that people are rational in the sense that they

- pay attention only to relevant information when making choices;
- make their decisions based on what is in their best interests;
- do not systematically make mistakes, but can correct past mistakes and improve decision making.

Researchers who use a "rational choice" framework to study public opinion and politics restrict their attention to interests and information. Given an individual's interests and given the information the individual has at his or her disposal, there is a rational choice to be made when faced with a decision. Deciding on the basis of **rationality** means making the best choice among available options given one's interests and information.

To test whether someone is being rational, we would need to have a complete understanding of their interests and all the information they have before them when making a decision. As a practical matter, since it is often difficult to define someone's interests, it generally makes sense for researchers to assume that people have a certain set of interests—that they prefer to make

rationality The habit of choosing the best choice among available options given one's interests and information.

[15] Albert Hirschman, *The Passions and the Interests* (Princeton, NJ: Princeton University Press, 1977), p. 32.

more money and work fewer hours, for example, or that members of Congress prefer to be re-elected—and protect those interests by acting rationally. Given these assumptions, researchers can predict people's behavior.

However, there is considerable evidence that people violate the principle of rationality. As we will learn later, evidence from surveys shows that many people pay attention to irrelevant information when making their choice among options. Scholars disagree about how often and why people deviate from acting rationally, but much public-opinion research is based on the assumption that people are *not* always rational in the way defined earlier.

Group Attachments

Researchers have discovered that many people express opinions and attitudes in surveys that are inconsistent with their own personal, material interests, but in accord with the collective interests of the groups with whom they affiliate. Quite a few wealthy African Americans, for example, support more liberal social welfare policies than their wealthy white counterparts.[16]

In these cases, group interest, not mere self-interest, guides individuals' political attitudes and opinions. Often, group interests and self-interests are not in conflict, but when they are, surveys show that people tend to respond more in line with their group interests.

This finding can be explained in at least two ways. First, the public has a tendency to see the political world as made up of groups competing, forming coalitions, and winning or losing under each set of policies created by the government. That is, competition for resources at the political level tends to be among groups, not among individuals, and people orient themselves in the political world by connecting cognitively with groups.[17] Moreover, group leaders convince people, rightly or wrongly, that their individual interests are closely tied to group interests, and therefore it is usually best to support group goals. Second, group leaders' endorsements of particular policies (or stances against those policies) give shorthand cues to people to form opinions on topics they do not necessarily understand or pay much attention to. We examine the role of group endorsements as information cues in more detail later in this chapter.

Emotions

Political scientists and psychologists study in great detail how people make political decisions. In addition to the influences discussed earlier, researchers have discovered deeper mental processes that affect things like vote choices and

[16] Michael Dawson, *Behind the Mule: Race and Class in African-American Politics* (Princeton, NJ: Princeton University Press, 1995).

[17] Donald Kinder and Cindy Kam, *Us Against Them: Ethnocentric Foundations of American Opinion* (Chicago: University of Chicago Press, 2010).

Were civil rights supporters motivated by self-interest and the desire for more opportunities as individuals? By group attachments? Or other factors? While researchers have identified numerous influences on individual opinions, it can be difficult to say which influences are decisive in a given instance.

survey responses. What causes some people to choose Republicans over Democrats? Why do some people vote, while others do not? What causes some people to answer "very liberal" when asked about their political ideology?

There have been interesting research results, for instance, about the role of emotion (or "affect"). Some researchers who study political psychology have challenged the assumptions behind the concept of rationality. They have found that people do not always make political decisions based on objective consideration of the options and the information available. In particular, they emphasize that enthusiasm, fear, and other emotions can explain a great deal about attitudes and behavior that rationality cannot. The theory of affective intelligence, for instance, distinguishes between people's dispositions to act in normal situations and how those dispositions can be interrupted when emotion—such as the feeling of being threatened—comes into play.[18]

Researchers have also discovered patterns in how campaign advertisements trigger emotional responses and affect people's choices. Evidence shows, for instance, that positive advertisements laced with emotional images and music tend to make supporters and detractors more enthusiastic about their own positions. In other words, positive ads with emotional appeals polarize viewers. Negative ads have the opposite effect, with disturbing images and tense music that tend to make people less certain of their convictions.[19] This area of research is still somewhat new, but the larger point is that, in addition to the other factors that shape political attitudes and decisions, emotion plays a role.

Influence of Elites

People's attitudes about politics can be affected by the way issues are presented to them by politicians, mass media personalities, pollsters, and interest group leaders. Research into priming and framing is especially instructive. Let us first consider **priming**, which is the psychological process of shaping people's perceptions of a particular issue, figure, or policy. Say voters are being asked to decide whether to build a new county jail. Voters could be primed to think about this decision in a certain way based on how it is portrayed by those in

priming The psychological process of shaping people's perceptions of a particular issue, figure, or policy.

[18] George Marcus, Michael MacKuen, and W. Russell Neuman, *Affective Intelligence and Political Judgment* (Chicago: University of Chicago Press, 2000).

[19] Ted Brader, *Campaigning for Hearts and Minds: How Emotional Appeals in Political Ads Work* (Chicago: University of Chicago Press, 2006).

government or in the media. Overt priming might take the form of negative coverage of the proposal to build the jail, influencing voters to view it negatively (and vice versa for positive coverage). More subtle priming might take the form of a photo of prisoners accompanying a news story about the proposal, cueing a negative connotation in voters' minds and thus *priming* them to consider the issue in a negative light. Conversely, a photo showing contented prison workers from another county might prime voters to consciously or subconsciously associate the building of the jail more positively.

Framing, meanwhile, has to do with establishing the context for an issue in such a way as to emphasize certain aspects over others. In our county jail example, the public could be cued by politicians, pundits, other public figures, and television ads to consider the proposal in terms of its effects on their taxes on the one hand, or as a way to increase the number of jobs available to potential guards, cooks, and social workers on the other. Which consideration ultimately dominates their thinking about the issue may shape their subsequent formation of an opinion on it.

Priming and framing are related, and both can also play a role in measurements of public opinion. For example, in a survey, respondents could be primed to make a positive association with the jail proposal by framing the question in terms of the employment possibilities it offers rather than the higher taxes it threatens:

> To alleviate the county's unemployment problems, some have suggested trying to convince the state to build the new jail here. Do you support or oppose building a new jail in our county?

Framing can also affect how people assess various risks and rewards in politics and other arenas. In a famous survey experiment, the psychologists Daniel Kahneman and Amos Tversky asked a group of undergraduates the following questions, which were separated in the survey by filler questions:

> A. Would you accept a gamble that offers a 10% chance to win $95 and a 90% chance to lose $5?
>
> B. Would you pay $5 to participate in a lottery that offers a 10% chance to win $100 and a 90% chance to win nothing?

Objectively, these two questions describe the same options, but question A frames the $5 as a loss, while question B frames it as a cost incurred in playing a potentially lucrative lottery. In responding to the questions, more than half the subjects chose differently for the two questions, and among those, more than three-quarters answered "no" to A and "yes" to B. Kahneman and Tversky interpreted their results as highlighting two things: the key effect that framing choices has on influencing people's behavior, and the way in which people are biased against choices framed as losses rather than as potential gains.[20]

framing Establishing the context for an issue in such a way as to emphasize certain aspects over others.

[20] Daniel Kahneman and Amos Tversky, *Choices, Values, and Frames* (New York: Russell Sage, 2000).

Whether framing matters, in surveys or in any setting where people are expressing opinions or acting on them, depends very much on the subject matter.[21] In the context of surveys, the more we know about the effects of framing, the more researchers can design surveys to avoid some biases in responses that hinder knowledge about what people really think and feel.

There are several larger lessons we can draw from our discussion of priming and framing. The first is the various biases that are introduced into polls by the possibilities of framing. It is important to be careful both in gathering data on public opinion and in interpreting it. For consumers of public-opinion information, knowing the political interests of the people involved, especially those who are funding the research, is of key importance because, through manipulation of framing, researchers sometimes can get the results they want out of surveys.

Second, in the larger context beyond surveys, framing and attempted priming is done all the time by candidates, political parties, interest groups, advertisers, and public relations specialists. They seek to frame the controversy at hand in a manner favorable to them. Our earlier example of whether to build a new jail makes this point. On the issue of abortion rights, opponents frame it as an issue about the life of the fetus, hoping to tilt people's opinions one way, while supporters frame it as an issue about women's autonomy and life chances, hoping to tilt people's opinions the other way. These so-called wars of frames are intensely political and competitive with much at stake. Researchers have studied these situations in great detail; it is often difficult to predict in advance which framing will work for a given policy controversy.

Predispositions

Research on political attitudes shows that most Americans agree about certain topics. By and large, Americans appear to feel that their system of government is generally good, and they are comfortable with concepts like freedom of speech, religion, and the press. Because so few Americans depart from the norm when answering questions such as those given in Table 9.1, polling firms seldom ask these questions any more.

What some scholars have called the "American Creed" is a set of widely shared values. According to some, this creed has been instrumental in allowing the United States to stay united and relatively free of group-on-group violence since the Civil War. There has not been much support for violent revolution in American society, even when it was quite popular in other countries in the early twentieth century. Nearly all people in the United States agree that on

---

[21] See, for example, James N. Druckman, "Political Preference Formation: Competition, Deliberation, and the (Ir)relevance of Framing Effects," *American Political Science Review* 98, no. 4 (2004): 671–86.

TABLE 9.1

Public Opinion and Democracy

In this survey, respondents were asked whether they thought a democratic political system was a very good, fairly good, fairly bad, or very bad way of governing.

	Very/Fairly Good	Fairly/Very Bad
Australia	89%	11%
Brazil	90	10
Bulgaria	87	13
Canada	92	8
Chile	93	8
China	94	6
Colombia	87	13
Egypt	98	2
Ethiopia	98	2
Finland	90	10
France	90	10
Germany	95	5
Ghana	96	4
Great Britain	91	9
Guatemala	87	13
India	92	8
Iraq	88	12
Italy	95	5
Japan	89	12
Jordan	96	4
Netherlands	92	8
Poland	84	16
Russian Federation	79	21
Slovenia	87	13
South Africa	90	10
South Korea	77	23
Spain	96	4
Switzerland	96	4
Taiwan	93	7
Thailand	93	7
Turkey	93	7
Ukraine	81	19
United States	86	14

Source: World Values Survey, 2005–2008, www.worldvaluessurvey.org (accessed 4/5/11).

balance the political system works pretty well and is worth preserving. They especially believe in the First Amendment rights to freedom of expression and freedom of religion. These rights are ingrained in people at all levels of American society.

Of course, Americans differ in their opinions over what policies governments should adopt. In particular instances, even regarding First Amendment rights, there can be vigorous disagreement. In this section, we will discuss the other side of attitudes—predispositions. Ideology and partisanship are two fundamental predispositions that are usually long term and shape people's opinions toward specific politicians and government policies. By definition, ideology and partisanship divide people into different categories based on their overall perspectives on government and society.

Ideology

ideology A coherent, organized set of ideas and principles that functions as a core on which individuals draw when forming their attitudes about public affairs.

An **ideology** can be defined as a coherent, organized set of ideas founded on basic principles. Ideologies start with a core. When someone in the United States today professes to have a *conservative* ideology, for example, he or she is usually expressing a core preference for tradition—for preserving what currently works well or has worked well in the past. The value of tradition trumps the possibilities that might arise from changing to novel or untried policies. From that core, this individual might conclude that, on specific public issues, it is best to let markets work unhindered by regulation and keep government small, while allowing government to use the force of law to preserve moral standards in society. Note that conservatives can desire change, but usually they prefer to change back to a situation from a previous era.

Alternatively, when someone in the United States today professes to have a *liberal* ideology, he or she is usually expressing a fundamental optimism about change in a new direction and an enthusiasm for the possible benefits of redistribution of resources. From that core, this person might conclude that, on specific public issues, government should be an active agent to improve society, especially economically, and that people should be free to experiment with lifestyles and private behavior without the government interfering in an attempt to protect traditional moral values.

Liberalism and conservatism anchor the predominant ideological differences that animate American politics. The political differences between liberals and conservatives in the modern United States are loosely related to concepts of "left" and "right" that originated in pre-Revolutionary France. In the eighteenth century, members of the French Assembly who were more favorable to the king, the military, and the Church sat to the king's right, while the various representatives of the guilds and artisans, who tended to be critical of the king, sat to his left. The seating arrangements in the French Assembly continue along these lines today, but the meanings of left and right have evolved over time.

FIGURE 9.3

Placement of Political Parties on the Ideological Spectrum

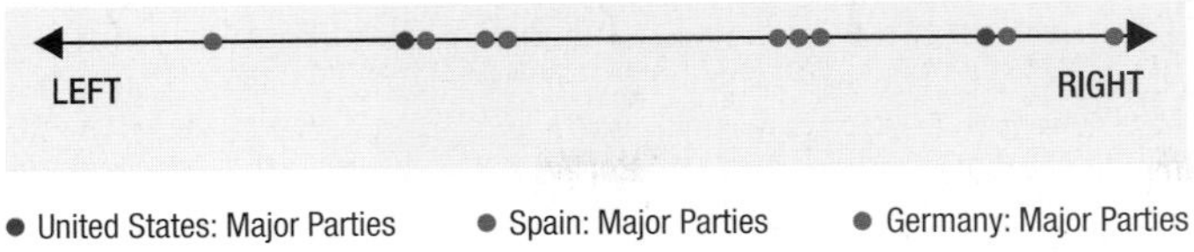

- United States: Major Parties
- Spain: Major Parties
- Germany: Major Parties

Source: Kenneth Benoit and Michael Laver, *Party Policy in Modern Democracies* (New York: Routledge, 2006).

Since the mid-nineteenth century in Western political thought, the predominant set of political ideologies has ranged from communism on the far left (most closely identified with Marxism) to fascism on the far right. These extreme ideologies were discredited in the twentieth century by the actions of the fascist regimes in Germany and Italy, and of the communist regime in the Soviet Union. But communism as a state-sponsored ideology still persists in the world, most prominently in places like Cuba and North Korea.

As Figure 9.3 shows, ideological differences among the political parties in some other countries can be wider than in the United States. In Spain, for instance, some political parties in parliament and their supporters still espouse principles of communism. In Italy (not shown) and Germany, something close to far-right fascism continues to have an appreciable following. In the United States, very few people—and none among serious candidates for national office—profess to support either communism or fascism. The most extreme politicians in the United States today who stand any chance of being elected to national office tend to be (on the left) democratic socialists like Bernie Sanders, a senator from Vermont who espouses a European-style social welfare system, and (on the right) Rand Paul, a populist, libertarian rightist who represents Kentucky in the Senate and supports policies such as auditing the Federal Reserve and withdrawing from the United Nations.

Although ideologies are abstract, they relate to opinions about concrete issues that confront the American government today. Survey research offers a way to conceptualize ideology in a systematic way and trace the connection between abstract principles and specific policy goals. Political scientist Philip Converse provided the concept of ideological "constraint," which means that preferences on one policy correlate with preferences on another policy issue.[22] One's opinion on the death penalty, for instance, might be constrained by one's predisposition toward the rights of the accused or by one's ideology.

[22] Converse, "The Nature of Belief Systems in Mass Publics."

Party Identification

party identification
(or partisanship) Loyalty or
psychological attachment
to a political party.

Loyalty or psychological attachment to a political party is called **party identi-fication** (or **partisanship**). The following is one of the best-known questions in public-opinion research because it has been asked regularly and tracked for many decades:

Generally speaking, do you consider yourself a Democrat, a Republican, an inde-pendent, or what?

Public-opinion researchers use the answer to this question to reveal the respondent's party identification. Figure 9.4 shows how responses to this question have changed since the 1950s. This figure does not tell us whether individuals are stable in their party identification, or whether they change much over time. Some people are changing, but how many? That number is difficult to pin down at any given time. The overall number of Republicans, for example, could be increasing or decreasing over time, while the majority of existing Republicans may be holding steady. Yet more in-depth analysis of party identification from survey research shows that individuals tend to be quite stable. Some do change over time, but most retain their party loyalties over the course of their adulthood.

Research in the 1950s at the University of Michigan showed that the best predictor of how someone would vote in a congressional or presidential election was their party identification, as given in an answer to the question earlier. It even trumped one's evaluation of a candidate's issue positions. The so-called Michigan model of voting, discussed in more detail in Chapter 13, posits that party identification is a psychological orientation to the political world that colors how people evaluate policies and candidates.[23]

What is clear from Figure 9.4 is that the percentage of survey respon-dents who identify with one or the other party has fluctuated over time. This corresponds partially to the success or failures of presidents and to current events. Examine the trajectory in Figure 9.4. The proportion of Republicans relative to the proportion of Democrats drops after the Nixon Watergate scan-dals (mid-1970s) and during the second Iraq War (2006), but it rises during the Reagan administration (1980s) as Reagan succeeded in carrying out key parts of the Republican agenda.

Other Predispositions

People have deeply held predispositions besides ideology and partisanship that affect their opinions. Research has shown, for instance, that some people have rac-ist predispositions that are often not expressed openly (to pollsters, for example) but that still affect opinions on policies and politicians and behaviors such as

---

[23] Angus Campbell, Philip Converse, Warren Miller, and Donald Stokes, *The American Voter* (New York: John Wiley & Sons, 1960).

FIGURE 9.4

Party Identification, 1952–2012

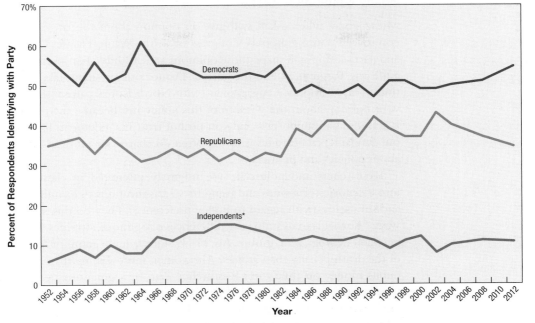

*Independents who "lean" toward one party are included with that party.
Source: American National Election Survey.

voting decisions.[24] More broadly, a person might have predispositions that stem from their being a member of a particular ethnic or racial group. Many people's religious beliefs stay fixed over long periods, if not their lifetimes, and those beliefs shape opinions on issues—especially social issues having to do with marriage, reproduction, women's rights, homosexuality, and the death penalty. As we discuss later, religion plays a distinctive role in American public opinion and political life compared to that of many other advanced industrial democracies.

Opinions on Policies and Politicians

When analyzing attitudes, in addition to predispositions such as ideology, religion, and party identification, we can also consider opinions toward current events and the policies of the government. These opinions are more amenable to

[24] Donald Kinder and Cindy Kam, *Us Against Them: Ethnocentric Foundations of American Opinion.*

change and may be shaped by a number of factors. The lack of durability of these opinions contrasts with the persistence of the predispositions discussed earlier.

Policy Opinions

Most people when asked will give an opinion about the latest major policy controversy rattling around Congress or in the White House. Their ideology and partisanship will shape those opinions and attitudes. For instance, if you are a lifelong Republican and the current Democratic president takes a firm position in favor of policy engagement with North Korea, partisanship may affect your opinion about the wisdom of this policy just because the president, who is a Democrat, supports it and you do not trust his judgment. In other words, our fundamental attitudes can, and often do, shape our more specific attitudes about policies and politicians.

Researchers and politicians are intensely interested in classifying people into categories or groups and using these classifications to examine differences and similarities with regard to policy preferences. They do this in two general ways. The first is to examine the differences of opinions, attitudes, and behaviors between demographic groups. Are blacks, for example, more or less supportive of the death penalty than whites? Are women more willing than men to spend public money on child care? Researchers start by segmenting people based on their relatively immutable or objective characteristics, and then compare their survey responses (see, for example, Table 9.2).

Another way is to classify people according to their opinions and attitudes (both fundamental and specific), and then examine the different behaviors of the various groups (Table 9.3). If people say they value environmental cleanup more than economic growth, for example, are they more willing to vote for tax increases to pay for the cleanup than the people who place a greater value on economic growth? Are liberals less willing to spend government money on crime control than conservatives?

TABLE 9.2

Differences in Attitudes between Demographic Groups

"Do you favor or oppose the death penalty for murder?"

	Whites	Blacks
Favor	69.7%	47.6%
Oppose	30.3%	52.4%

Source: 2012 General Social Survey, National Opinion Research Center, data available at http://sda .berkeley.edu (accessed 5/22/13).

TABLE 9.3

Differences in Attitudes Leading to Differences in Behavior

"What if there was a measure on your local ballot to increase local parcel taxes to provide more funds for the local public schools? Would you vote yes or no?"

	Democrats	Republicans	Independents
Yes	69%	33%	54%
No	29%	65%	43%

Source: Public Policy Institute of California, 2013 Statewide Survey, www.ppic.org (accessed 5/22/13).

Evaluations of Politicians and Government Institutions

Politicians and the people who work for them are often interested in learning how the public evaluates their performance. In the American political system, with re-election campaigns constantly looming for members of Congress and first-term presidents, political leaders want to know if people are angry, frustrated, disappointed, or generally happy with how things are going. More specifically, they want to know how many people are evaluating them negatively and how many are satisfied enough to keep them in office.

One of the great predictors of how presidents will fare—in their re-election efforts, in their relationship with Congress, and in their efforts to convince citizens to support them in their policy goals—is the presidential approval rating. Here is the question Gallup asks a random sample of voting-age Americans at least once a month:

Do you approve or disapprove of the job [X] is doing as president?

As we saw in Chapter 6, approval ratings shift, sometimes dramatically, during each president's term in office. (Figure 6.5 in Chapter 6 tracks the approval ratings for American presidents from the 1950s to the present.) Some scholars of voting behavior put great stock in predicting voting patterns by relying on people's evaluations of the performance of politicians, especially the president. As we will discuss in Chapter 13, voting behavior by people in elections can be partially predicted by learning how people evaluate an incumbent politician's past performance in office.

A related question, but one that earns less attention, asks about Congress:

Do you approve or disapprove of the way Congress is handling its job? (CBS News, 2010)

As we discussed in Chapter 5, people often give negative evaluations of Congress as a whole, while giving a more positive evaluation of their individual representatives or senators. When the preceding question was asked in May 2010, only 15 percent of respondents said they approved of Congress's performance. However, when asked the following question, 47 percent said they approved:

> *How about the representative in Congress from your district? Do you approve or disapprove of the way your representative is handling his or her job?* (CBS News, 2010)[25]

Most incumbents in the House are re-elected easily, despite generally low evaluations of Congress as a whole, while senators face more competition but are usually re-elected as well. Voters appear to separate their opinions about the entire legislative body from their evaluations of their own representatives.[26]

Apathy and Lack of Knowledge

In general, people readily give answers to survey questions, but can we trust their answers to reflect an informed opinion? What if people do not pay attention to politics and their answers simply follow from being polite to the interviewer? Research on the topic of political knowledge can lead to pessimistic conclusions.

We know from surveys, for example, that two-thirds of American adults cannot name the chief justice of the Supreme Court, and one-third cannot name the vice president. Even when shown a list of names, 40 percent of adults are unable to identify the Speaker of the House, while more than one-fourth mention a branch other than the Supreme Court as having the final authority to declare laws unconstitutional, and nearly one-third are unable to name which political party controls the House of Representatives. Only a small percentage can name the leaders of Russia, Germany, China, Canada, Mexico, or France, and a vast majority cannot say with confidence whether Mexico holds elections for its president. (It does.)

The lack of knowledge revealed in these surveys is nothing new. Studies over the last 60 years have shown that a large percentage of Americans have little factual understanding of their government, the governments of other countries, and world affairs.[27] Research in the 1950s and early 1960s revealed not only factual ignorance, but also a lack of basic understanding of the philosophical underpinnings of our government. These studies uncovered that the majorities of those polled could not correctly indicate whether the Democratic or Republican

[25] CBS News Poll, May 2010.

[26] John R. Hibbing and Elizabeth Theiss-Morse, *Congress as Public Enemy: Public Attitudes toward American Political Institutions* (New York: Cambridge University Press, 1995).

[27] Michael Delli Carpini and Scott Keeter, *What Americans Know about Politics and Why It Matters* (New Haven, CT: Yale University Press, 1997).

Party was more conservative on economic issues. Many respondents could not even describe coherently what kinds of policies liberal or conservative politicians tend to pursue. As mentioned earlier, pollsters found that a significant percentage of people gave what were essentially random answers to questions about their own preferences on public policies.

If you happen to follow the news closely and are knowledgeable about politics, it is easy to be smug when you learn of such data. Yet the individual who does not follow the news closely and who would likely get many of the factual answers wrong in a political research poll could reasonably argue, "I am busy with other important things in my life. I know what I need to know to make good choices." Although some people may feel disappointed with their fellow citizens or even superior to them based on their lack of political awareness, others—including some public-opinion researchers—contend that these citizens have enough knowledge to navigate their lives effectively, even if they cannot identify the current chief justice of the Supreme Court. Researchers are generally in agreement on the levels of ignorance about factual information, yet question whether such a prevalent lack of knowledge of public affairs is an important problem.

Who is this man? In recent surveys, a majority of Americans are consistently unable to name John Roberts as the chief justice of the Supreme Court. Can citizens hold meaningful opinions about politics if they lack basic knowledge about government?

On the one hand, some analysts contend that we should be deeply worried that the American people may not be equipped intellectually to make good decisions in the voting booth and choose appropriately given their interests. Perhaps Americans are not up to the task of democracy, of guiding elected officials wisely through the ballot box, through their expressions of opinions in polls, and through lobbying efforts. The Founders expressed such concerns when they designed a set of governmental institutions that were originally quite removed from popular control. In the early years of the Republic, for example, the House of Representatives was the only element of the national government that was comprised of members directly elected by the people. Alexander Hamilton spoke for many political leaders of his generation when he reportedly referred to the people—those who would be the basis of popular sovereignty—as a "beast," a dangerous and unpredictable force that needed to be controlled rather than allowed to control leaders.

Along the same lines, commentators in the early to mid-twentieth century worried that the populace's ignorance would make it easy for manipulative leaders to whip up support for oppressive policies, authoritarian leadership, and even fascism. They saw educating the public as necessary to preserve democracy. Some were deeply concerned that ignorance of public affairs—more pronounced among the uneducated, but also among the poor—only disadvantaged further those at the bottom rungs of society. Knowledge, it is said, is power, and in the American political system, knowledge means knowing when your interests are threatened and how to act to protect them.

A different perspective focuses less on what people do not know and more on whether they have the information they need to choose wisely. We might call this the "need to know" position. It is based on whether people can get the information they need to function properly in our society, and on how much information is widely available. Although many cannot name the chief justice or perhaps not even their senator, maybe they can pick the correct party to vote for in the upcoming election, even if they cannot name the candidate. Since such decisions are often confined to a small number of options—should I vote for the Republican or the Democrat?—it might not be all that difficult for people to have just enough information to choose correctly, given their interests. There is also some evidence that people know more than has been concluded from analysis of surveys.[28]

It is puzzling that the level of public ignorance has remained roughly constant since quality surveys about politics began in earnest in the 1950s, while the education level of Americans has steadily increased over this same period. It is even more surprising given that consumption of media containing political news, especially television, has also increased during this period. Political news, while often crowded out by news of celebrities and sports, is widely available. Certainly it is not for lack of available information that people do not know much about politics.

Rational Ignorance?

One explanation for the low levels of knowledge among the general public focuses on a fundamental collective-action problem. People can engage in what Anthony Downs called "rational ignorance" about politics by free riding off people who happen to like politics or need to know about politics for their jobs.[29]

To understand this concept, consider the following nonpolitical situation. You and seven of your friends are planning to take a flight to a warm destination over the holiday break. Only one of you needs to contact a travel agent and make the reservations for everyone in the group, and presumably that person will keep all the information about the travel arrangements. Your group faces a collective-action problem. Who will take the time to book the reservations and keep all the materials and information together?

It turns out that one of your friends, Rita, volunteers and books everyone on the same flight, which leaves on a Friday. Rita informs you of the time of

---

[28] See, for example, Jeffery J. Mondak and Mary R. Anderson, "The Knowledge Gap: A Reexamination of Gender-Based Differences in Political Knowledge," *Journal of Politics* 66, no. 2 (2004): 492–512; and James L. Gibson and Gregory A. Caldeira, "Knowing the Supreme Court? A Reconsideration of Public Ignorance of the High Court," *Journal of Politics* 71, no. 2 (2009): 429–41.

[29] Anthony Downs, *An Economic Theory of Democracy* (New York: Harper & Row, 1957).

the flight, but you forget to write it down. Is this a big problem? Not really, as long as you can find out from Rita or the others in your party in enough time to make your flight. People ask you, "When is your flight Friday?" You reply, "I don't know. Rita knows. I'll check with her before Friday."

If you are confident that Rita is someone you trust to provide the correct information in time for you to catch your flight, you can free ride off her efforts. In fact, your ignorance about the time of the flight saves you the effort of tracking it until you actually need it.

This way of thinking has led some researchers to a more benign conclusion about the levels of ignorance among the general public. As long as people can learn the necessary information to make wise choices from people they trust and who share their interests—called "cue-givers" because they give small, informative cues to people to help them make decisions—then general ignorance of politics is not a major problem. What matters is the quality of the specific knowledge people need to have and whether they can access that information in a timely manner.[30]

This view is contested by those who put more emphasis on the possibility that those people who know a lot about politics—the cue-givers—do not have the same interests as those who are less knowledgeable and receive the cues. Cue-givers typically include interest groups, politicians, media personalities, commentators, and even knowledgeable friends and relatives. Their cues, some argue, can manipulate situations and get people to make decisions that are not in their best interests.[31]

Apathy and Non-Attitudes

Some scholars are less concerned about the public's lack of knowledge than about its apathy. People simply may not care about politics, or they may display what scholars call **non-attitudes**. That is, people may answer survey questions about an issue even though they have never really thought about it. This could be the result of apathy or of a complete indifference to specific issues that might be of great import to others. We can think of a non-attitude as applying to an issue about which a person either has no opinion or does not let an opinion enter into his or her calculations about voting or taking some other political action. One can easily imagine, for instance, that a typical college student has a non-attitude about policies having to do with specific tax formulas for retirement accounts. But this may not prevent the student from answering survey questions or voting in a referendum on the matter. It is highly likely that more college students have non-attitudes about this kind of policy issue than do people over the age of 65.

non-attitude A lack of opinion on an issue, or an opinion so weakly held that it does not enter into a person's calculations about voting or taking some other political action, even though the person may express an opinion to a pollster.

[30] See, for example, Benjamin Page and Robert Shapiro, *The Rational Public* (Chicago: University of Chicago Press, 1992).

[31] See, for example, Larry Bartels, "Uninformed Votes: Information Effects in Presidential Elections," *American Journal of Political Science* 40, no. 1 (1996): 194–230.

Some scholars have considered using the proportion of people who answer "don't know," "refuse to answer," or "no opinion" to a particular question as an indication of the size of the population with non-attitudes on a specific issue. For example, when asked about the nation's campaign finance laws—a policy issue that rarely bears directly on the quality of life of individual citizens—24 percent of respondents in a Gallup Poll reported having "no opinion."[32] The conclusion these scholars draw is that this issue is of little or no importance to a quarter of the American people.

However, researchers have learned to be careful about interpreting survey responses in this way. Evidence shows that the proportion of people who answer certain kinds of survey questions depends on the race, ethnicity, or sex of the interviewer. People may have strong opinions about some issues on the public agenda, and those opinions matter a lot in evaluating candidates and parties, but the survey respondents may not answer some questions because the issue is sensitive. For instance, people may not answer questions about policies regarding race or gender, not because they have non-attitudes, but because of embarrassment or reticence. When samples of Americans were asked about government efforts to integrate schools racially through busing and redistricting, whites being interviewed by blacks are more likely to answer "don't know" than whites being interviewed by whites.[33] It is important, therefore, to be careful in interpreting nonresponses as non-attitudes. It depends on the topic being addressed.

In Comparison: Public Opinion

To gain perspective on how Americans think about politics and their political system, we can examine the similarities and differences between the United States and other countries. We start with a puzzle. American society is in many respects more diverse than that of any other country. By just about any measure of diversity, the U. S. population is at or near the top of every international ranking. You might conclude that this diversity of wealth, ethnicity, and religion would be reflected in public opinion, and that the population of the United States would hold highly diverse opinions about public policies and controversies, as well as a wide range of ideologies and perspectives.

To a degree, however, comparisons of surveys from around the world contradict this expectation. As we have already discussed, Americans as a group hold a near consensus of views about democracy and forms of government, whereas this is not always the case in other countries. (See Figure 9.4 once again.) We

[32] Gallup Poll, January 2008.

[33] Adam Berinsky, "The Two Faces of Public Opinion," *American Journal of Political Science* 43, no. 4 (1999): 1209–30.

also learned earlier that Americans' ideologies, at least with regard to the candidates and policies they support, are not as widely spread on the spectrum from far left to far right as in other countries that have similar levels of economic development and democracy. So, in two important respects, Americans may have less diverse opinions about broad matters of politics than residents of other countries.

This disparity could be explained by the fact that the United States was founded on basic principles that transcend ethnicity, religion, and class, whereas other countries were organized along ethnic or religious lines. The problem with this explanation is that even in countries like France that share with the United States basic principles of government, public opinion displays wider variation in key ideological dimensions.

The causes of the kind of consensus one observes in the United States relative to other countries is a matter of controversy in the political science literature. Some scholars find that the lack of diversity in some measures of public opinion in the United States stems from the rather bland political news coverage relative to that found in other countries.[34] Others believe that there is plenty of diversity in public opinion in the United States, just not along the left–right continuum.[35] Still others think that the lack of American support for socialist and far-left policies is the main difference between the United States and other countries.[36]

Recall our earlier discussion of redistributive policies and the relationship between social class and support for more active government policies for the poor. Such a relationship is even more pronounced in most other countries. Among the lower classes in Europe, and especially in the developing world, there is intense and consistent support for active government redistribution of income. In the United States, compared with nations with similar economic wealth in Europe, there is less support among the lower classes and more support among the upper classes for generous social welfare spending. In short, social class does not adequately explain support for leftist or rightist government policies.

Another point of comparison between the United States and other countries involves religion. In one important respect, the United States is markedly different from countries of similar wealth and economic development. Americans are decidedly more religious than Europeans, Canadians, Australians, and the developed countries of Asia (such as Japan). A vast majority of Americans (more than 85 percent) indicate in surveys that they believe in God, pray, and attend religious services often. In countries like Sweden, these numbers are

[34] For a summary of this argument, see Diana Mutz, *Impersonal Influence: How Perceptions of Mass Collectives Affect Political Attitudes* (New York: Cambridge University Press, 1998).

[35] See, for example, Robert Axelrod, "The Structure of Public Opinion on Policy Issues," *Public Opinion Quarterly* 31, no. 1 (1967): 51–60.

[36] Kay Lehman Schlozman and Sidney Verba, *Injury to Insult: Unemployment, Class, and Political Response* (Cambridge, MA: Harvard University Press, 1979).

much lower, well below 50 percent. The American pattern on religion surprises many scholars, given that in most other societies religious practice and belief have tended to decline as wealth has grown. In matters of religion, the United States more closely resembles the developing world than the industrialized nations.[37] And the religiosity of Americans appears to shape their opinions on issues such as whether public schools should allow prayer at official functions (most Americans say yes), and whether evolution should be taught in schools (a greater proportion of Americans say no, compared with publics in other countries). Certainly religious behavior correlates with political attitudes and voting behavior. Evidence is consistent that Americans who regularly attend religious services are on average more conservative politically than Americans who do not. This correlation shows up in Europe as well, but many more Americans attend religious services regularly compared with Europeans.

Public Opinion and Policy Making

The information we have covered in this chapter helps us return to the question we posed at the beginning about the conditions under which politicians are responsive to public opinion and when they can affect public opinion. One would hope, given the ideals of the American political system, that public opinion constrains the government, preventing it from enacting grossly unpopular policies on a regular basis. Politicians should *want* to please a majority of the public in order to win election and re-election, though they should not do so in ways that violate the fundamental rights of minorities.

Does Government Policy Follow Public Opinion or Vice Versa?

Public opinion is surely shaped by events, much as politicians' behavior is shaped by those same events. As an example, public support for off-shore drilling of oil dropped dramatically after a major oil spill in the Gulf of Mexico in 2010. And evidence shows that people are more likely to support same-sex marriage if they know gay and lesbians personally, and thus the more people come into contact with openly gay and lesbian people the more public support for same-sex marriage ought to increase. Both public opinion and President Obama's actions regarding same-sex marriage have changed over time. But was Obama reacting to public opinion, getting to know more gays and lesbians, public pressure from interest groups and voters, or something else? In many instances, politicians' reactions can be difficult to predict and understand. In this case, however, it is easy to conclude that when public opinion, events, and the interests within one's own political party all point in the same direction ("Support same-sex marriage"), politicians will likely move in that direction. For

[37] World Values Survey, 2005–2008 wave.

years, Obama was not predictable on the issue because he was trying to be responsive to conflicting pressures from vocal supporters within his electoral coalition and within his own party and from the public. But he was more predictable as majorities started to support change. Polls showing a new majority reinforced the views of key constituencies within his party, and arguably his own predispositions, to support marriage equality.

The question posed at the opening of this chapter presumes that politicians can know with some degree of certainty what public opinion is on a given issue. But, as we have learned, public-opinion data can either be unreliable or reflect a fickle public. As we have seen in exploring how surveys work, there can be biases (often unintentional) in representations of public opinion. It would be wrong to conclude that public-opinion information from surveys and polls is always politically biased or useless. Despite the challenges of interpreting polls, enough good public-opinion data evidently exists to motivate politicians to pay attention and even commission their own private polls. But when information about public opinion sends conflicting signals, it grants leaders a certain freedom to make policy decisions based on other grounds. Although the principals (the public) can be difficult to read at times, the agents (people in government) are quite good at treading a middle ground between being responsive and being steadfast over spans of time.

One reason it is difficult to study the connection between public opinion and government action is that survey questions tend to ask about the broad direction of policy, rather than about specific, technical details that are the stuff of much of public policy making. If surveys reveal, for example, that a majority of people want more money to be spent on primary education, how should that money be spent? Should it be for new schools, more teachers, more rigorous curriculum development, or different programs?

Systematically measuring the actions of government poses another problem. If the government only slightly increases funding for primary school education to keep up with inflation, is that conforming to public opinion? Or is it actually just "standing pat" on policy when the public really seems to want a substantial increase? These kinds of measurement decisions for researchers who study public opinion and policy making are crucial to drawing conclusions that link public opinion to policy making.

Nevertheless, researchers have made some progress in measuring the extent to which government policy follows public opinion or leads it. In certain areas, government policy decidedly does not conform to majority opinion. Take the issue of prayer in public schools (see Chapter 4). The federal courts have interpreted the

To what extent are governmental policies shaped by public opinion? Elected officials must always be mindful of how the policies they support will be perceived by constituents. However, they may focus on pleasing some constituents more than others.

Constitution as forbidding formal prayers, and in some cases even silent prayers, in public schools. Yet public-opinion data quite clearly shows that this policy contradicts majority views. When asked in surveys, between 55 and 75 percent of Americans (depending on question wording) support allowing prayer in public schools.

Yet this kind of issue is the exception that seems to prove the rule. On most politically debated policy issues, the government in fact does what the majority wants, at least according to systematic research on the subject. The political scientists Benjamin Page and Robert Shapiro studied public-opinion data and policies across many issue areas and found that approximately two-thirds of the time the national government was responsive to public opinion.[38] When public opinion moved in one direction, government policy typically changed to accommodate that shift. Why the government responds to majority opinion on some issues and not on others remains a key question. This too is difficult to answer, but we will gain some insights in later chapters, especially Chapter 12, which focuses on interest groups.

In other research, scholars have studied broad patterns of opinion change that suggest the public has "moods" that make it more or less favorable to government activism in the economy. They have been able to trace the relationship between these moods and actual government policies, and the results are striking. Through careful analysis, they have shown that government policy changes in a liberal or conservative direction on economic policy *after* a public-opinion mood change in the same direction. This is further evidence of the overall responsiveness of the national government to public opinion.[39]

As for whether the public is influenced by actions and statements of elites, there are compelling examples from numerous studies to indicate a responsive public. The public is not always movable (maybe not even often movable), but as research into priming and framing (discussed previously) shows, the potential is there. When people receive competing frames, however, and conflicting information or psychological cues, in general they retreat to their predispositions to guide them in what opinions to express and act upon. As an example, if a staunchly conservative person hears information from credible sources that raising taxes will lead to better schools in her area, she may be inclined to increase her support for higher local tax rates. But if she then hears information from competing credible sources that the money will be wasted on inefficient school bureaucracies, she will likely be inclined to follow her conservative predisposition and express opinions or vote against raising local taxes for schools. In a competition for people's allegiance involving different frames or competing

[38] Page and Shapiro, *The Rational Public.*

[39] James A. Stimson, Michael B. Mackuen, and Robert S. Erikson, "Dynamic Representation," *American Political Science Review* 89, no. 3 (1995): 545–65.

information or cues, predispositions are hard to overcome. Liberals will not be able to sway this voter if conservatives get her ear as well.[40]

In sum, research shows that public opinion frequently, but not always, shapes government policy in the United States, and public opinion has the potential to be shaped by elite rhetoric. To determine when and under what conditions this is true, we need to know more about the actual mechanisms that link public opinion to government policy and the actions of government and media elites. The means through which public opinion is packaged and communicated to politicians are not politically neutral. Interest groups, mass media, and partisan groups can shape the collection and communication of opinions in biased ways that have real consequences for how people in government perceive what the public wants. In later chapters, we will study these other mechanisms—elections, political parties, interest groups, and the mass media—in detail. These institutions provide focused, usable information for those who are most active in the political system as they attempt to respond to the people.

Furthermore, there is no *one* public opinion. Instead, there are multiple publics with different opinions, and politicians struggle all the time with how to be responsive to constituents who organize and present their opinions in packages. In other words, politicians, as the agents, want to make the principals happy, but understanding exactly which principals to focus on is a constant challenge.

To return to our opening story, Obama's actions throughout the history of changing public opinion on same-sex marriage should not be ascribed merely to attention to majority sentiment as expressed in public-opinion surveys. Rather, they were reactions to the advice and political support he received from specific groups within his network of supporters and the Democratic Party. Meanwhile, the initial answer to our question is that politicians' behavior does follow public opinion, but mostly in response to broad movements across many issues over relatively long spans of time, or sometimes in response to clear, reasonable, and measurably sharp movements. And the potential is there for public opinion to change with elite priming and framing, though the mass public is constantly barraged by competing frames and new information and cues, and in general their predispositions hold their attitudes mostly in place.

A helpful way to conceptualize the role of public opinion within the American political system is to consider the attitudes of the public as forming a landscape upon which the main actors in the system operate. The landscape determines what the government, and those who wish to influence the government, can do. Features of the landscape make some tasks easier to accomplish and others more difficult. The landscape's basic contours are difficult if

---

[40] James Druckman, "Political Preference Formation: Competition, Deliberation, and the (Ir)relevance of Framing Effects," *American Political Science Review* 98 (2004): 671–86.

not impossible to change and shape. Some parts of the landscape are firm and immutable, while others are soft and can be changed with effort.

There are some policies that will simply not be possible for the government to pursue because public opinion is constraining. If the government takes actions that are too much at odds with public opinion, it will ultimately fail unless public opinion changes to conform. The attempted prohibition of liquor production and transport in the early twentieth century offers an excellent example. Prohibition was a failure as a policy because enough people in the general public were adamantly opposed to it and were willing to break the laws associated with it. As a result, enforcement was impossible. The prohibition policy did not fit into the public-opinion landscape.

FURTHER READING

★ = Included in *Readings in American Politics*, 3e

Bishop, Bill, *The Big Sort: Why the Clustering of Like-Minded America Is Tearing Us Apart* (Boston: Houghton Mills, 2008). An investigation of the political landscape of American neighbors, in particular, the increasing trend in politically homogenous communities and how this contributes to polarization.

Converse, Philip, "The Nature of Belief Systems in Mass Publics," in *Ideology and Discontent*, ed. D. E. Apter (New York: Free Press, 1964), pp. 206–61. A classic article with survey results indicating that many Americans have little knowledge or understanding of the political system and of electoral choices.

Gelman, Andrew, Boris Shor, Joseph Bafumi, and David Park, *Rich State, Poor State, Red State, Blue State: What's the Matter with Connecticut?* (Princeton, NJ: Princeton University Press, 2008). An examination of party identification, socioeconomic status, and the myths associated with their relationship.

Kahneman, Daniel, and Amos Tversky, *Choices, Values, and Frames* (New York: Russell Sage, 2000). A deep analysis of how the framing of decisions affects people's choices.

★ Kinder, Donald, and Cindy Kam, *Us Against Them: Ethnocentric Foundations of American Opinion* (Chicago: University of Chicago Press, 2010). Many people conceive of the political world as comprising ethnic and racial groups that compete with one another, and their political attitudes are shaped by their degree of tolerance toward other groups.

★ Lupia, Arthur, and Mathew McCubbins, *The Democratic Dilemma: Can Citizens Learn What They Need to Know?* (New York: Cambridge University Press, 1998). This book counters the belief that Americans are ignorant about politics, arguing instead that Americans tend to get the information they need when they need it.

Page, Benjamin, and Robert Shapiro, *The Rational Public* (Chicago: University of Chicago Press, 1992). This book makes a compelling argument that, on the whole, the mass public tends to respond in reasonable ways to new information about politics.

Stimson, James A., Michael B. Mackuen, and Robert S. Erikson, "Dynamic Representation," *American Political Science Review* 89, no. 3 (September 1995): 543–65. An article presenting research results indicating that the broad direction of policy by the U. S. government responds to shifts in public opinion.

★ Zaller, John R., *The Nature and Origins of Mass Opinion* (New York: Cambridge University Press, 1992). A theory of how political attitudes are shaped by the combination of predispositions and new information, lending insight into who changes their attitudes and when.

KEY TERMS

biased sample (p. 308)

framing (p. 319)

ideology (p. 322)

margin of error (p. 308)

non-attitude (p. 331)

party identification (or partisanship) (p. 324)

population (p. 307)

priming (p. 318)

public opinion (p. 302)

random selection (p. 307)

rationality (p. 316)

sample (p. 307)

Despite recent increases in voting by 18- to 24-year-olds, younger Americans are still significantly less likely to vote than older Americans. Efforts to register and mobilize voters, as on this college campus, can increase turnout, but political scientists also look at other factors that may influence the decision to participate in politics.

10

POLITICAL PARTICIPATION

Citizens in a democracy influence the government through political participation, especially voting. However, some groups of citizens—for example, young adults, the poor, and racial and ethnic minorities—are less likely to vote than others, meaning that they have less of a say in government. Why do those groups with the greatest interest in changing the status quo have relatively low turnout rates?

Voter turnout in the 2012 election dipped slightly from 2008, but it was still high relative to average turnout in the previous few decades. The high point in turnout came in 2008, and especially among young people. In the 2008 presidential election, voter turnout among 18- to 24-year-olds reached the highest level since 1972. As shown in Figure 10.1, 44 percent of eligible voters in this age group went to the polls, nearly 15 percentage points higher than in 2000. Yet turnout among the young consistently lags behind that of the elderly. In 2012, nearly 70 percent of those 65 years and older turned out to vote, roughly consistent with previous elections. In a typical presidential election, 55 to 65 percent of all eligible voters ages 18 to 24 do not vote. These numbers stand in stark contrast to other age groups, especially the elderly.

The patterns in Figure 10.1 beg for explanation. Citizens in a democracy wield power through political participation, especially voting. However, some groups of citizens are less likely to vote than others, meaning that they have less of a say in government. Besides age, we know that income, race and ethnicity, and education correlate with voter turnout, as we discuss later in this chapter. Wealthier, more educated people vote in higher proportions than poorer and less educated people. Northerners vote in higher proportions than southerners. Whites and African Americans vote in higher proportions than Latinos. And Jews turn out more than Catholics and Protestants.

Many people who would seem to have the most to gain from changing the status quo—the poor, youth, racial and ethnic minorities—turn out to vote in lower numbers than other citizens. Consider what citizens should expect to gain from the actions of

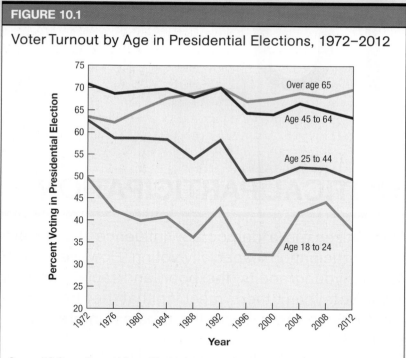

FIGURE 10.1

Voter Turnout by Age in Presidential Elections, 1972–2012

Source: U.S. Census Bureau, Voting and Registration, Historical Time Series Tables, Table A-9, www.census.gov (accessed 5/22/13).

the government from the moment they vote. The typical 20-year-old in the United States, for example, will live for another 60 years and experience many years of potential government benefits, while the typical 70-year-old will live only another decade or so. The poor often rely on government assistance to support themselves, yet they vote in lower numbers than the wealthy, who can rely on their own ample resources.

There also is change over time in turnout rates for different groups. Why did young people begin turning out in higher numbers in presidential elections in the 2000s? It cannot be solely due to the enthusiasm for Barack Obama, because the recent increase in voter turnout among the young began in 2004, but then dipped again in 2012. And was there something similar happening in 1992 when a spike in turnout among young voters also occurred? Other groups also vary in terms of how they participate in politics, over time and as compared with one another. Why, generally, do those groups with the greatest interest in changing the status quo have lower turnout rates? What explains this and other patterns of participation?

Participation and Democratic Politics

In Chapter 9, we studied the attitudes and preferences of individuals toward government and politics. We now move to studying the participation of people trying to influence government. Our focus in this chapter is on general patterns of **political participation**, including the decision of whether or not to vote. We will study elections in more detail in Chapter 13.

As we have noted in previous chapters, democracy is based on the principle of **popular sovereignty**—the rule of the people. Citizens in a representative democracy rule by choosing their leaders through popular elections. The legitimacy of such governments depends on the participation of enough citizens at the polls. Voting in general elections serves as the central act of citizenship in modern democracies like the United States. When immigrants become U.S. citizens, the right to vote is heralded as a key element of their new status.

Political participation, however, is not just a matter of voting. It is also understood to include many other actions intended to influence the government, such as:

- writing or contacting political representatives;
- attending rallies and protests;
- attending meetings of political organizations;
- writing to newspapers, magazines, or blogs about politics;
- wearing campaign buttons, posting political placards, or displaying political bumper stickers;
- giving money to campaigns and political organizations;
- talking to other people about politics.

The conventional forms of political participation listed here play important roles in determining the way democratic political systems function, because they communicate aspects of public opinion to the government or help people form their own opinions and hone their communication skills to pressure government. Most scholars of democratic politics believe that citizen participation is the lifeblood of a vibrant, democratic society. Diverse opinions are communicated through elections, peaceful mass action, deliberation in small or large groups, and direct contact with government representatives.

Some philosophers and political activists have expressed the view that participation makes more public-spirited individuals and thus better citizens. The early democratic theorists Jean-Jacques Rousseau and John Stuart Mill believed that people who participate in politics, even if they are in the minority, more readily accept collective decisions. Moreover, those who participate have a heightened awareness of belonging to a community. Modern researchers have found evidence that people who participate in politics experience joy in self-expression aimed at improving society. They learn about themselves and about

political participation Activities citizens undertake to influence government behavior.

popular sovereignty The principle that the authority to make decisions on behalf of society belongs to the people.

government. They become more engaged with how government affects them and learn how to take advantage of what it has to offer. They acquire valuable skills in navigating government bureaucracy, pressing for change, and organizing others to do so. In short, they experience the full scope of citizenship, to the benefit of both themselves and society.[1]

To establish a successful participatory democracy, simply holding elections is not enough; people must be able to participate and organize freely, without fear. Governments in some countries vigorously repress dissent and citizens' participation, even though they may hold elections. In "democracies" like Iran, Pakistan, and Zimbabwe, citizens are typically intimidated by the government. Although they are allowed to vote, they are afraid to petition political leaders, organize political parties as rivals to the government, or openly express their frustration or anger with government. It is questionable whether such societies have a truly democratic political system. The popular legitimacy of any government depends on tolerance of dissent and criticism, and on freedom of the people to participate in choosing their leaders.

Is More Participation Better for Society?

There are alternative points of view about participation, and these have to do not with the ability of people to participate legally and without fear, but with the question of whether people can choose not to participate for defensible reasons, and whether society is actually better off when many versus few people participate in politics. Some take low levels of political participation to mean that people are generally satisfied and do not speak out or vote because they like things as they are. In other words, the absence of overt dissent signifies the absence of grievances. Others question whether people who are uninformed should choose not to participate and leave decisions to those who choose to become informed. After all, why should we have uninformed people making bad decisions that make society collectively worse off? Why not encourage political participation only for those who are informed on public issues?

Several well-known facts about participation muddy the debates over whether societies should strive for robust participation in politics or merely permit participation but not especially encourage it. In the first place, there is overwhelming evidence that the wealthiest, most materially contented people are the most likely to participate in politics. By one interpretation, those with the least to complain about participate the most, and conversely, those with the most to complain about participate the least. This could be because poorer citizens tend to be less informed about politics than the average citizen. Perhaps many poor people choose to leave decisions over governance to others. In the

---

[1] See, for example, Carole Pateman, *Participation and Democratic Theory* (New York: Cambridge University Press, 1970); and Robert Putnam, *Making Democracy Work* (Princeton, NJ: Princeton University Press, 1993).

second place, low levels of political participation are concentrated in the segments of the population who arguably face individual barriers to participation or who are rarely, if ever, encouraged by organizations and groups to participate. This is a far cry from failing to participate because one is content, or because one chooses to not to because of a lack of information. These facts about patterns of participation are not controversial; what are controversial are interpretations of the causes of those facts and the drawing of conclusions about whether more political participation by more people is desirable.

Conventional and Unconventional Participation

Throughout this chapter, we will focus on conventional (and what are generally considered legitimate) participatory acts during ordinary times. This does not include such acts of violence as rioting, vigilantism, terrorism, or insurgency. Although such actions can communicate opinions and preferences to the government, and may be rationalized as necessary in extreme situations, they are not typically considered legitimate and do not ordinarily contribute to the functioning of a democratic system. Rather, they are unconventional and can generally be considered illegitimate because they detract from the functioning of a political system and a stable society. Yet it must also be noted that these acts often have a major impact.

Sit-ins and some kinds of strikes and protests are unconventional, but they represent a gray area between legitimate and illegitimate acts of civil disobedience. The nature of a political regime can lend an air of legitimacy to such acts. Consider the sometimes-illegal protests of blacks in the South during the civil rights movement in the 1950s and 1960s, or the uprising of gays and lesbians against police raids of gay bars in the 1970s and 1980s. Today, these acts are widely judged to have been legitimate, given the oppression these groups were struggling to overcome. Determining what constitutes a legitimate act of political participation can be controversial and often depends on context and timing. Long after the fact, for example, we can judge as legitimate the 1960 sit-ins by students at lunch counters in Greensboro, North Carolina, to protest "whites-only" seating at restaurants and other Jim Crow barriers, even though those actions violated local laws, the rules of the local businesses, and local customs. We look back and judge these laws and rules of businesses to be unjust and immoral.

Clearly, the morality of existing laws and practices, and the legitimacy of such unconventional forms of political participation, ranging from one-day work stoppages that might be against the law to the nineteenth-century slave rebellions, are in the eye of the beholder. People who break local laws to block traffic (as environmentalists and anti-war protesters have done) or protest in front of abortion clinics believe they ought to be judged similarly as the sit-in leaders during the civil rights movement. Today, Americans venerate the revolutionaries who fought against the British in the American Revolution, but note that they waged war against the established regime, and the British clearly believed the colonists' actions to be illegitimate. Regardless, our focus in this chapter is on conventional modes of participation that are generally considered legitimate in a functioning democracy.

Collective Dilemmas in Participation

Political participation presents a set of collective dilemmas. Voting, for example, is a collective-action problem. Suppose an election for president is coming up. It is costly to vote (in terms of time and trouble), and your vote will almost never matter to the outcome. Therefore, the best outcome, in strictly self-interested terms, is for a potential voter to let others vote and free ride off their efforts.

paradox of voting The notion that people still vote despite the fact that the individual costs of voting often outweigh the individual benefits.

In what is sometimes called the **paradox of voting**, some scholars ask, "Why does anyone ever bother to vote in mass elections?"[2] On presidential Election Day, if you drive or take the bus, or walk anywhere you need to cross the street, the probability of a grave accident, though very small, is still much higher than the probability of swaying a national election with your single vote.

Recall that a presidential election consists of 51 separate elections (the 50 states plus Washington, D.C.). What does it mean to say that your vote could ultimately sway the national election? It means that in your state the vote would have been a tie if you had not voted. That is, of course, extremely unlikely. But compound that small likelihood by the chance that your state is the pivotal state in the national election, that by your one vote you swing the vote in your state, and that your state then swings the entire election. It is easy to see that the probability of such an outcome is very close to zero. The probability of your action being pivotal might be higher for local elections than for national elections, but it is still extremely small most of the time.

Given these odds, it may be reasonable to wonder why you should bother to vote when your vote will have a negligible effect on the outcome of the election. But if everyone thought that way no one would vote, and that would be bad for the country. Most people think it is good for a lot of people to vote because it shows their support for the democratic system. Nevertheless, individuals have an incentive to stay home and let others incur the costs.

The information in Box 10.1 makes this point more generally. In principle, this kind of calculation can apply to any act of political participation. The real monetary costs of donating to a political campaign, for example, or to an interest group, need to be weighed against other uses of that money. Why give to

[2] See, for example, Anthony Downs, *An Economic Theory of Democracy* (New York: Harper, 1957).

The Paradox of Voting

An individual's "utility" from voting in a general election can be understood as:

$$p B - C$$

p is the probability that an individual's act of voting will influence the outcome of the election.

B is an individual's share of the benefit derived from the election outcome occurring to his or her liking.

C is the costs of voting, including risks of harm, loss of wages, and time taken away from other activities.

Is the value of *p B − C* greater than or less than zero? If it is greater than zero, the individual will vote; if it is less than zero, the individual will not vote. The paradox is that, because *p* is typically so small, the costs (*C*) will almost always be larger than *pB*, and the value will be less than zero—yet large numbers of people still vote.

Source: William Riker and Peter Ordeshook, "A Theory of the Calculus of Voting," *American Political Science Review* 62, no. 1 (1968): 25–42.

a political group if your donation will not make much of a difference? Why not let others do it? You could use your money for other things. Why write a letter to members of Congress to express your views on an issue that matters to you? Others will write such letters and yours probably won't matter much, unless you are a figure of importance like the president of a huge corporation, a celebrity, or a leader of a state or local government. If your letter will not matter much, why not spend your time in other ways?

For people who give money or spend time writing letters or attending rallies and protests, the cost of participation could potentially be much higher than that of voting. Why do people attend rallies and protests in authoritarian states, where police may be armed with batons, tear gas, or even live ammunition? The presence of one more or one less protestor is unlikely to affect the outcome. Yet people frequently risk their lives to participate in collective protests against government actions or regimes. When protestors have taken to the streets in Iran to rail against the governing regime, they have literally risked death. Many Syrians were killed by government-backed forces when their allegiance to the rebellion against the government became known. Syria's and Iran's governments have executed numerous people in recent years who have participated in or organized protest rallies or rallies in support of rebellion.

These examples focus our attention on the choices people make when faced with the collective-action problem inherent in political participation. How large are the potential costs relative to the gain attained through an individual's participation?

Social scientists propose the collective-action problem as a way to think about the act of voting and other forms of mass action, not as a suggestion that people ought to free ride. Most people who teach civics and who study political participation strongly encourage individuals to participate in the electoral process (and other conventional kinds of participation). They believe people should resist individual temptation and focus on the collective good engendered by widespread participation. And, of course, tens of millions of people in the United States, and hundreds of millions of people in other democracies around the world, participate in politics and overcome ordinary kinds of collective dilemmas such as those that occur in national elections.

Collective-action problems are not the only kinds of dilemmas facing citizens when they consider political participation. They also face persistent coordination problems. Suppose you have decided to write a letter to members of Congress regarding an issue about which you care strongly. It would be most effective if others who share your goals sent letters saying similar things, or sent those letters to the same members of Congress on the same committees. Ideally, people who share views should coordinate their efforts and communicate a focused message. They should also target those communications to the members of Congress who are poised to do something about the issue in their favor. How do people who share the same political goals coordinate if they don't know each other or live in different parts of the country?

As we will see in Chapter 11, interest groups often solve coordination problems as a way to help mobilize people to participate in politics. To take a specific example, the American Farm Bureau Federation, the nation's largest agricultural lobbying group, sent a newsletter to its members in 2012 regarding proposed Environmental Protection Agency rules, urging them to "share your story and concerns, use the #stoptheflood hashtag on Twitter and the campaign's Stop the Flood of Regulation Facebook page." Their intention was to get their members to pressure their representatives in Congress. We see these kinds of communications—solutions to coordination problems, really—all the time in interest-group flyers, newsletters, websites, and advertisements. In the absence of this kind of coordination, like-minded people would be less effective in pressuring Congress because their messages would vary and would not target the same, pivotal legislators.

Analyzing participation through the lens of collective dilemmas focuses our attention on the costs and benefits of voting and of participation more generally. It also sheds light on the importance of mobilization, the active attempt by organizations and leaders to encourage people to participate. Mobilization can be seen as the effort both to reduce the costs of participating and to increase the perceived benefits. Let us analyze these costs and benefits in more detail, and discuss how mobilization might affect change.

Tallying the Costs and Benefits of Participating

There are many individual and social reasons why people vote and participate in politics. They feel a sense of duty. They are pressured to vote and participate by friends, family members, or coworkers. They do not want to be embarrassed to admit they did not vote. They want to indicate that they support their group. One way to explain why people still vote and participate even when the possible costs appear to outweigh the likely benefits is that people do not always think strictly in terms of their own individual, instrumental benefits. Among the collective benefits of participation is the possibility that your action, in concert with the similar actions of others, could have an impact on government policies. If many members of a group vote and participate in disproportionately high numbers, this may sway government policies in that group's direction. In school board elections at the local level, for example, it is well known that teachers and school administrators turn out in high numbers relative to other groups in the community. Similarly, business owners and executives, highly paid professionals, scientists, community leaders, and other groups have good reason to feel that their participation in politics—especially in the forms of contacting elected officials, organizing campaign contributions, and writing blogs, op-eds, and letters to the editor—has a discernible impact on governmental decisions affecting their well-being.

These may all be valid benefits to consider, but the paradox presented in Box 10.1 exposes a central fact about the cost side of voting (and all forms of political participation): as the costs of participation rise, fewer people will participate because the costs will increasingly outweigh the likely benefits of a favorable outcome, as weighted by the probability that one's actions will affect the outcome of the election or the outcome of any political process.

More important for our discussion, which focuses just on voting for the moment, the costs of voting do not have to be high to discourage some people from doing it. Even minor personal and bureaucratic barriers can dampen participation, especially among those for whom the costs loom large in their lives and the benefits seem remote.

There are costs associated with voting. For example, voters may have to wait in long lines in order to cast their votes and give up time that could be spent on other activities.

Registering to Vote

U.S. citizens must register to vote, whereas most other nations permit their citizens to vote based simply on whether they are listed as residents and citizens of a town, city, or community. Under the

voter registration A process by which citizens enroll themselves with the government to gain permission to vote in an election.

requirements of **voter registration**, Americans who wish to vote must fill out forms and provide personal information to their state government. Citizens used to have to make a special trip to a local office to register. In 1994, however, President Bill Clinton signed the Motor Voter Bill, requiring that when you apply for a driver's license in your home state, you must be offered the chance to register to vote. And some states now have same-day registration (SDR), which allows people to register at the polls immediately before voting.

The impacts of the Motor Voter Bill and SDR on voter registration and participation have been studied by political scientists, and their conclusions are mixed. Some scholars have provided evidence that Motor Voter registration has increased participation among those who voted only occasionally. However, the bill appears to have done little to increase voting among those who never vote. In other words, even if people who habitually do not vote register when they get their driver's license, they still typically do not go to the polls on Election Day.[3] As for SDR, among states adopting this reform (13 states had done so as of fall 2014), voter turnout is about 10 percentage points higher than the average of the other states. But it is a matter of debate whether SDR caused this increase or whether the reform occurred in states with already high turnout rates.[4]

Gathering Information

political knowledge A general understanding of how the political system works, and who runs the government.

As we discussed in Chapter 9, the level of **political knowledge** varies widely within the population, and most people are not well informed. Some people like to follow politics, but most rely on friends or coworkers, or on simple "cues" from news stories or advertisements, to get the information they need to make political choices. Many people pay virtually no attention to politics.

People who habitually do not vote tend to pay little attention to politics. The same is true for people who almost never participate in any way in politics. This pattern raises some interesting questions. Is lack of information the cause or the effect of the failure to participate? Do people who find it too costly to become informed also find it too costly to vote? Do they simply believe that as uninformed people they should not vote? Or do people who do not vote tend to ignore politics because they know they will not participate in the process? These are difficult questions to answer with available data.

This much we do know: becoming informed about politics takes time and effort. Thus, the costs of becoming informed are higher for certain types of people than others. Wealthier and more-educated people know more about politics for a variety of reasons, including their schooling, their jobs and com-

[3] For a general discussion of how electoral reforms retain voters from election to election without expanding the population of those who participate, see Adam J. Berinsky, "The Perverse Consequences of Electoral Reform in the United States," *American Politics Research* 33, no. 4 (2005): 471–91.

[4] See www.projectvote.org/same-day-reg.html (accessed 11/6/14).

munity organizations, and the fact that they are routinely mobilized.[5] They also systematically follow political news in mass media more than other citizens. Alternatively, for the poor and less educated, becoming knowledgeable about politics often has to happen on their own and they are not routinely mobilized. The individual costs for becoming informed on average are relatively higher, and they are exacerbated by the tendency of the less-educated to choose entertainment over news in mass media. The discrepancies in the extent to which the wealthy and poor are mobilized perpetuate their different levels of participation. When people are mobilized to participate (to vote, attend meetings, and go to rallies) by organizations and personal contacts, they learn about politics, which further spurs them to continue participating in the future. So, if people consider being informed a prerequisite for participation, then the costs of gathering information will dampen participation among those who experience or perceive higher costs in becoming informed, specifically poorer and less-educated citizens.

Voting

Casting a ballot is never completely without cost, but the burdens vary depending on the rules and procedures. In the United States, for instance, national Election Day always falls on a Tuesday in November. This day became traditional when the United States was an agrarian society because it was after the harvest season, was not on a Sunday (a holy day for the largely Christian country), and gave people relying on foot or horseback one full day after Sunday to travel to the polls. Voting at all levels and in other months (in primaries, for example) also tends to occur during the week and not on weekends, as in many other countries. For some people, missing work to vote is not a problem, but others might lose wages if they are paid hourly, or they might work in remote locations that make it difficult for them to get back to their polling place to vote.

States, moreover, can impose various rules at the polls that make it harder or easier to vote on Election Day. Some aspects of voting have become easier. We already discussed same-day registration (SDR). Casting absentee ballots has become widespread in recent elections as more people travel for work, and the military has pressed Congress to make it easier to allow troops overseas to vote. New voting machines, especially since the controversy surrounding the 2000 presidential election in Florida (see Chapter 8), have reportedly been easier to use than older machines.

Following the 2000 presidential election, Congress acted to help the states administer elections more effectively. The **Help America Vote Act of 2002** was intended to spur states to adopt electronic voting machines and to make it easier to vote in general. States could apply for federal funding to modernize much of their

Help America Vote Act of 2002 A federal law meant to reduce barriers to participation in elections.

[5] See, for example, W. Russell Neuman, *The Paradox of Mass Politics: Knowledge and Opinion in the American Electorate* (Cambridge, MA: Harvard University Press, 1986).

Democracy is based on the principle of popular sovereignty, meaning the people rule. In practice, the people generally do not make government decisions directly but instead elect leaders by voting in elections. Several factors may limit who participates through voting.

- **Formal barriers can limit voting.**

  - In most cases, an individual must be registered to vote.

  - For much of American history, women, nonwhites, and poor people without property were prevented from participating in elections.

  - Today, there are still some limits on who can vote. For example, many states bar convicted felons from voting. Americans under the age of 18 cannot vote.

  - Only citizens may vote, so immigrants who have not achieved citizen status cannot participate in elections.

- **There are costs associated with voting.**

  - Individuals may lack information about where and how to vote.

  - Individuals may lack information about which policies or candidates will best serve their interests.

  - Polls are typically open for only a few hours after regular work hours which makes voting costly for those who cannot take time off to vote.

- **Electoral reforms and voter mobilization efforts are often aimed at removing barriers and minimizing the costs associated with voting.**

  - Civic organizations play a critical role in mobilizing citizens to participate in politics.

  - Older people are more likely to belong to these groups, and they participate in elections and politics at relatively high rates.

  - Young people are less likely to belong to a civic organization and are relatively less likely to vote or participate in politics.

equipment at the polls, including purchasing or renting more accurate machines. This legislation has had at least one perverse effect. States have reduced the number of voting precincts by almost 40 percent because of the costs of updating voting equipment. Fewer precincts means fewer machines to buy and lower costs for the states, even with federal funding assistance. It also means that, as compared with the early 2000s, there are fewer places for people to vote on Election Day, longer lines, and less convenient polling locations. In the 2012 national election, many voters, especially in large cities, complained about long voting lines.

A number of states now permit and even encourage **voting by mail**, including Oregon, Washington, and Colorado. As with other reforms discussed above, the evidence on whether voting by mail leads to higher turnout is mixed. Early research suggested that voting by mail has increased turnout and encouraged people to become regular voters. It seemed that voting by mail lowered the costs of voting for enough people to make a difference. More recent research has questioned these findings and indicated that voting by mail has little to no effect on federal election turnout, but it can boost participation in local elections that typically have low turnout.[6] Note that voting by mail can potentially increase turnout only among those who have already registered to vote; it can have no direct effect on people who have not registered, because ballots are mailed only to registered voters.[7]

The Help America Vote Act also permitted states to adopt antifraud measures that might not have been allowed under previous law. States increasingly require citizens to show proof of citizenship and identity in the form of a photo ID, passport, or birth certificate. The trend toward stronger antifraud measures tends to create an obstacle for those who do not drive or are elderly and may have difficulty finding their birth certificate. We discuss some of these measures again later.

vote by mail A program in many states that allows voters to mail in their ballots rather than appearing in person at a polling place.

Participation beyond Voting

The costs and benefits of participating in politics in other ways than voting vary from person to person and from one type of participation to another. Depending on one's life circumstances, spending money or time tallies up differently. People with plenty of money of course find it easier to donate money to political campaigns, organizations, and causes. So the difficulty of donating $100 to a candidate is lower for the rich than for the poor. As a percentage of income, spending that $100 is more "costly" for people the less money they have.

We discussed earlier in the context of political knowledge how costs and benefits fall differently on people. Similar patterns occur regarding time and skills. The following types of people, for instance, find it less difficult (and more beneficial) than the average person to contact elected officials directly through e-mail, letters, personal visits, and petitions:

- highly educated people;
- people who write and fill out forms as a regular part of their job—that is, people in generally higher paying jobs, as opposed to those who mostly work with their hands;

[6] Kevin Arceneaux, Thad Kousser, and Megan Mullin, "Get Out the Vote-by-Mail? A Randomized Field Experiment Testing the Effect of Mobilization in Traditional and Vote-by-Mail Precincts." *Political Research Quarterly* 65 (2012): 882–94; Thad Kousser and Megan Mullin, "Does Voting by Mail Increase Participation? Using Matching to Analyze a Natural Experiment," *Political Analysis* 15 (2007): 428–45.

[7] Adam J. Berinsky, Nancy Burns, and Michael W. Traugott, "Who Votes by Mail? A Dynamic Model of the Individual-Level Consequences of Voting-by-Mail Systems," *Public Opinion Quarterly* 65, no. 2 (2001): 178–97.

Voter ID Laws: Fighting Fraud or Reducing Turnout?

State governments in the United States have recently passed dozens of laws requiring voter identification at election polling stations. At the same time, many states have passed laws making it easier to vote. These laws are controversial and deeply divide Democrats and Republicans.

Interests

In general, Republicans and conservatives express concern about fraud and want to restrict voting access to those who can prove identity with an ID like a driver's license. Democrats and liberals maintain that restrictive measures like voter identification laws place an undue burden on racial minorities, elderly citizens, students, and low-income voters, many of whom tend to vote for Democratic candidates. During the 2012 presidential election, Rep. Mike Turzai, a Republican from Pennsylvania, described voter identification laws as the tool that would "allow Governor Romney to win Pennsylvania."[1] This remark caused quite a stir, for it laid bare the alleged partisan motivation behind such legislation.

Institutions

Voter identification laws vary from state to state. Some require proof of citizenship, while others expect photo identification. State legislatures controlled by Republicans have increasingly tightened voter identification requirements. The state of Texas, dominated by Republicans in the legislature and governor's office, banned university-issued student identification, but allowed licenses to carry a concealed handgun as acceptable proof of identity at the polls.

Meanwhile, some states are moving in the other direction, with more of them, especially those controlled by Democrats, permitting early voting (i.e., before Election Day), registration over the Internet, and Election Day Registration.

Outcomes

What people in both political parties seem to agree on is that such laws as those requiring voter identification have considerable political consequences: determining who can vote can determine which candidates

Many states, including Pennsylvania, have pushed for laws requiring people to present photo identification before voting. Critics say this will greatly reduce voter turnout.

win. Evidence from research, however, is mixed, and it will take a few years to assess the effects of these relatively new laws. On the question of whether voter identification laws reduce turnout, some studies have suggested that it reduces turnout by around 2 percent, but those results have been contested.[2] State legislatures will continue to be battlegrounds over legislation on voter requirements and policies, which some argue combat fraud while others argue reduce turnout. Aside from situations where courts step in to decide legal questions about the constitutionality of the laws, partisan control of state legislatures will determine who wins those battles.

Think About It

Given their goals and preferences, are there places or situations in which Republicans or conservatives would want to encourage turnout? Are there places or stiuations in which Democrats or liberals would want to discourage turnout?

[1] "Turzai: Voter ID Will Allow Romney to Win Pa.," Youtube, Pa. House Democratic Caucus, June 25, 2012, www.youtube.com/watch?v=EuOT1bRYdK8 (accessed 11/11/12).

[2] Robert S. Erikson and Lorraine C. Minnite, "Modeling Problems in the Voter Identification—Voter Turnout Debate," *Election Law Journal* 8, no. 2 (2009). See also www.brennancenter.org/analysis/research-and -publications-voter-id (accessed 7/16/13).

- people who tend to join organizations or who are in leadership positions within organizations;
- people who have experience communicating with public officials.

On this last factor in particular (experience), note how the elderly might incur less "cost" in communicating with public officials compared with younger people simply because they have lived longer and have had more opportunities. Those who are more educated and wealthier may be more likely to attend the meetings of political organizations in part because they are more likely to make beneficial business contacts through such participatory actions. Who, for instance, would reap more benefits from regularly attending meetings of a local chapter of an environmental group—someone who owns her own business selling advertising for small businesses in the area, or someone who works in a factory piecing together components for television sets? The former will see political participation in such an organization not only as a good thing to do but also as a potential benefit for her business. She could get to know people who might become clients and buy her advertising services. Small business owners, professionals, and entrepreneurs especially benefit from participating in local meetings because they can make personal contacts and market their services and products.

These examples help us to see how analyzing costs and benefits can help explain patterns in participation. We see a general pattern of costs and benefits falling favorably on those who are already advantaged in society. In other words, the individual costs are smaller and individual benefits potentially bigger for wealthier, more-educated people. Exceptions to the general pattern, however, can be seen in the acts of protesting or rallying. Largely because a major portion of protests and rallies in the United States are organized by labor unions in the form of strikes or walkouts, the costs of participating are somewhat equalized across different income groups in society. Labor unions substantially reduce the costs for unionized workers to learn about politics and to know how to participate to effect change. Working-class people, especially those in unionized jobs, have many opportunities to join in these kinds of collective efforts. Note, however, that these costs are not lowered for the poorest members of society: the unemployed and those in the lowest-wage, nonunionized jobs.

Some people believe that the rise of the Internet since the late 1990s has created a new kind of political participation, where people blog and get their information from websites, and can organize political action easily by using e-mail and social-networking sites. The potential has been evident in the protests in the Middle East following the Arab Spring of 2011, for example. The availability of these means of communication allows organizers to communicate even though their governments might crack down on other forms of news dissemination. The Internet, they argue, has altered costs and benefits. This argument relies on the idea that the participation of people on the Internet is fundamentally different from, or has different effects than, more traditional, nonelectronic forms of participation. It has lowered the costs so much that inequalities in participation should go away. Anyone can communicate rapidly with others and receive information about participation options.

Other arguments leading to the opposite conclusion fall along two lines. First, there is the fact that the Internet is also available to the government and other powerful institutions to monitor and possibly suppress dissent. Second, there is the possibility that Internet usage can solidify inequalities in participation. Online participation is similar to older modes of participation—communicating with others, learning news about politics, writing political rhetoric for others to react to and comment on (this was done as early as the Founding era), mobilizing people—but it can happen more rapidly and with greater impact on the Internet because of the large numbers of people who can be reached in a few moments. Evidence from studies in the 2000s points to an overall inequality in Internet usage for politics. Higher-income people and younger people use the Internet more often than others. By the late 2000s, however, the gap between income groups using the Internet to discuss or learn news about the election was very small, not only in the United States but in many other countries as well.[8] Research continues to be conducted on the impact of Internet usage and availability. As of now, there is not much systematic evidence in the United States that the Internet has increased active participation in politics generally, though certainly in some instances electronic communication has eased the organizing of mass action.

How people live, what kinds of jobs they have, and what resources they have affect whether they accept the costs of voting and other forms of participation as so minor that they participate anyway, or as so significant that they are discouraged from participating. But people who either are not allowed to participate or are discouraged from participating can overcome their collective dilemmas and push for change. Let us now consider struggles for equality of opportunity in political participation.

The Struggles for Voting Rights

the franchise (or suffrage)
The right to vote.

Voting is the most fundamental participatory act in any democracy. The right to vote, also known as **the franchise** (or **suffrage**), was denied to many types of people from the very beginning of the United States. Gradually, however, the country extended the franchise to the point where today virtually all American adults are eligible to vote.

[8] Aaron Smith, "The Internet's Role in Campaign 2008," *Pew Internet and American Life Project*, February 2009, www.pewinternet.org (accessed 4/29/13).

Restricting the Right to Vote

Democracies all over the world set boundaries on who can and cannot vote. Most advanced democracies allow citizens to vote by age 18 and have few restrictions beyond that. In the American political system, the states formally control the franchise, but they must conform to federal law and the Constitution. States typically restrict voting to citizens who have resided in the state for a certain number of months, with a common threshold being three months. States vary when it comes to extending voting rights to former prisoners with felony records and to those with mental illness. Voting restrictions based on mental capacities, criminal record, and residency have been deemed constitutional by courts, and the diversity of laws across states is widely acknowledged and accepted as complying with current constitutional law. Many laws affecting turnout were instituted during the Progressive Era in response to abuses by the political parties and candidate organizations that committed fraud or intimidated citizens. There is a long history of questionable election practices in the United States, especially in the nineteenth century.

There are subtle restrictions to voting that are considered questionable by the courts and affected groups. Certain laws and their implementation can indirectly disenfranchise specific population groups, or at least raise their costs of voting. Some restrictions are devised by local political parties, candidate organizations, or government officials with the obvious intent of limiting the franchise. Southern states in the twentieth century, for example, required that people registering to vote pay a poll tax or pass a literacy test. At the local level, these measures were implemented unevenly, with registrars requiring them more often of blacks than of whites. Even if they were implemented evenly, their effects fell disproportionately on blacks because of their poverty and lower educational status relative to whites in the South at the time.

Most of these kinds of restrictions were ultimately abolished by legislatures and the courts. The key legal change was the **Voting Rights Act of 1965**, which devised a wide-ranging set of federal protections of voting rights for minorities, especially in the South. Until 2013, parts of the South were designated as areas of special scrutiny by the U. S. Justice Department because of their history of disenfranchising specific groups. The Justice Department was empowered to monitor and enforce equal voting rights for racial minorities in these areas. The Supreme Court in 2013 struck down continued application of the Voting Rights Act to these specific areas, but the Court invited Congress to use contemporary information to identify the targeted areas.

Voting Rights Act of 1965
A federal law that made it a priority of the national government to enforce provisions of the Fourteenth and Fifteenth Amendments, leading to major improvements in voting rights for blacks, other minorities, and the poor.

Some barriers are less obvious than poll taxes or literacy tests and may not be deliberate, yet they still result in unequal access to voting. In many states, for example, precincts in poorer neighborhoods have fewer voting machines and less up-to-date technologies for voting. This could be intentional or it could be a result of more benign policy choices, such as concluding that the need for more and better voting technology is less in these neighborhoods where voter turnout tends to be lower. Whatever the motivation, the result is often that lines for voting are longer in poorer neighborhoods than in wealthier ones, which may discourage some citizens from going to the polls.

In voting rights cases, the courts attempt to determine whether a given action by a local or state government should be struck down on constitutional grounds. If a state or local government designs and implements a system for voting that restricts the right to vote for minority groups that have been historically disenfranchised or underrepresented in government, then federal courts usually rule against the state or local government.

In recent years, there has been intense controversy over the implementation of voter ID requirements at the polls. The laws, passed in some form by most states, require that voters present a government-issued photo identification in order to prove identity and eligibility. The battles over these laws are occurring in state legislatures and state and federal courts, and they engender heated public debate. People disagree over whether this is a legitimate reform to combat voter fraud or an attempt to suppress turnout among population groups less likely to have ID or intimidated to show ID. The federal courts have generally allowed the laws to exist at the state level, but permit the U.S. Justice Department to monitor how they are implemented.

Challenges to Reforms Intended to Increase Turnout

Some groups have been denied voting rights because others hold deep prejudices against them or find it politically advantageous to restrict the franchise. The Founders generally believed that only white male property owners, who (in their view) could be trusted to take the common good into account, should be eligible to vote. Racism and xenophobia led people to support restrictions on voting by blacks, Catholics, Mormons, Jews, and immigrants. Many people, including some women, argued that women should not be eligible to vote because they were inherently less intelligent than men. These prejudices have been, and continue to be, widespread in some parts of the world. They have often bolstered the case for restrictions on voting.

Overcoming such restrictions is complicated by the self-interest of incumbent politicians. Extending the franchise can be difficult because it typically requires the support of politicians who attained office when the restrictions were in place. When officials elected under one set of rules are asked to consider changing those rules to admit a new set of voters into the electoral process, they naturally tend to resist. The incumbent politician is likely to think, "Why rock the boat? Why not preserve the status quo? After all, the existing electorate elected me, so why should I take the risk and allow a new set of people to vote?"

When it comes to reforming voting rules, prejudices and self-interest often go hand in hand. For example, even after the Fifteenth Amendment stated in 1870 that voting rights could not be denied on the basis of race, white politicians in the South continued to resist removing the barriers that disenfranchised African Americans until the 1960s. Politicians elected in the South during this period used arguments about the inferiority of blacks as a justification for withholding their voting rights. The politicians' self-interest in maintaining the status quo and their belief in racial inferiority conspired to keep blacks from voting. Proponents of women's right to vote encountered similarly stiff resistance. They had to convince male lawmakers that it was right and just, as well as politically wise, to extend the franchise to women. It took more than seven decades for women to win the right to vote. The struggle began in earnest in the 1850s, when the argument for women's suffrage was linked to the abolition of slavery, and concluded with the passage of the Nineteenth Amendment in 1920.

Today it is common for the two major parties to disagree over proposed reforms that might affect the costs of voting. Republican candidates tend to attract voters on the higher end of the scale for income and education, while Democrats tend to attract voters at the lower end. Not surprisingly, Democrat-sponsored reforms aimed at making it easier to vote or to register to vote are frequently opposed by Republicans. Making it easier to register or to vote tends to boost turnout among those who are less inclined to turn out—that is, those lower down the income and education scale. This would likely increase support for Democrats, or so goes the thinking of many Republicans. Republicans often claim that making it too easy to vote invites fraud and have even proposed making it somewhat harder to vote, or at least harder to satisfy the requirements to be eligible to vote. Thus, the conflict over voter ID laws. Not surprisingly, when introduced, these bills have typically been supported by Republicans and opposed by Democrats. Eric Holder, Obama's previous attorney general, compared such laws to the poll taxes of previous eras. The courts have generally upheld such laws, though some state supreme courts have recently overturned a few voter ID laws and the Obama administration challenged laws in Texas, South Carolina, North Carolina, Ohio, and Wisconsin under the Voting Rights Act and the Fourteenth Amendment. Federal courts have issued conflicting opinions on specific instances, but as mentioned, states are permitted to have these laws if implemented in a way consistent with certain guidelines.

Removing Barriers to Voting

By the 1840s, nearly all the states had removed the requirement that only property owners could vote and had extended the franchise to all (white) free men. This was mostly because budding political parties—the Jacksonian Democrats and the Whigs—were in fierce competition and hungry to appeal to a new set of voters. Religious barriers took longer to dismantle. Even though Article VI of the U.S. Constitution states that "no religious Test shall ever be required as a Qualification to any Office or public Trust under the United States," Catholics were not allowed to vote or hold office in many states in the late eighteenth

century, and Jews earned the right to vote in Maryland only in 1828. Yet by the 1860s, the United States had the most expansive franchise in the world, meaning that larger percentages of the male population were allowed to vote than anywhere else.

After the Civil War, all African Americans were formally enfranchised by the Fifteenth Amendment (1870), which states: "The right of citizens of the United States to vote shall not be denied or abridged by the United States or by any State on account of race, color, or previous condition of servitude." Nevertheless, for more than 90 years many southern states continued systematically to deny blacks their voting rights through intimidation and various legal and illegal barriers. In 1940, the state of Louisiana reported that 886 "colored" people had registered to vote, out of a population of 473,000 blacks in the state, Numbers in Mississippi, South Carolina, and Alabama were similar. Many whites were also effectively disenfranchised by some of these restrictions—voter turnout rates in the South were around 10 percent in some years—but blacks were denied more comprehensively based strictly on the color of their skin.[9]

Women were denied the right to vote in many states until the passage of the Nineteenth Amendment. From the mid-nineteenth century until the passage of the amendment in 1920, women's suffrage groups argued for this right.

Throughout the twentieth century, the franchise expanded through mass mobilization, court decisions, constitutional amendment, and the actions of the national government. As noted above, women were granted the right to vote in all federal and state elections upon passage of the Nineteenth Amendment (1920). The Voting Rights Act of 1965 made it a priority of the national government to enforce provisions of the Fourteenth and Fifteenth Amendments. Amendments to the act in 1970, 1975, and 1982 largely removed the barriers to voting that had disproportionately disenfranchised blacks in the South. While the Supreme Court in 2013 struck down specific parts of the Voting Rights Act, arguing that aspects of it were no longer relevant, in general, Court's interpretations of the act and the Fourteenth Amendment (specifically the equal protection clause) have led to major improvements in voting rights for blacks, other minorities, and the poor. Today, voting rates among blacks across the country largely match those of other racial groups.

Group Struggles

Throughout American history, disenfranchised citizens have fought hard through the legal system, collective action, and political pressure on lawmakers to change the rules and allow new groups of people to vote. The legal foundation for opening the franchise could not have been established without group struggle. In the late 1960s, for example, college students in California

[9] V. O. Key, *Southern Politics in State and Nation* (New York: Knopf, 1949), p. 519.

launched a campaign called "Let Us Vote," or "LUV," to lower the minimum legal voting age from 21 to 18. The movement appealed to citizens of all ages and earned the support of such mainstream organizations as the League of Women Voters and the American Legion. Responding to public opinion and student pressure, Congress passed a law that mandated voting rights for 18- to 20-year-olds in all federal elections beginning in 1970. The Supreme Court, however, delivered a setback to this legislation, ruling that states had the right to set their own voting-age restrictions as long as they conformed to the Fourteenth Amendment, which mandated voting rights at age 21 for all elections, including state and local contests. This led to a bizarre situation in which some states were not coordinating effectively with the national government. Many young people on Election Day in 1970 had to be given separate ballots because they were permitted to vote only for the federal offices.

Congress quickly solved this coordination problem by passing a constitutional amendment in March 1971, which took just two months and seven days for 38 states to ratify (the shortest ratification time on record). The Twenty-sixth Amendment mandated that people 18 years of age and older had the right to vote in federal, state, and local elections, thus coordinating voting ages among all the states and the federal government.

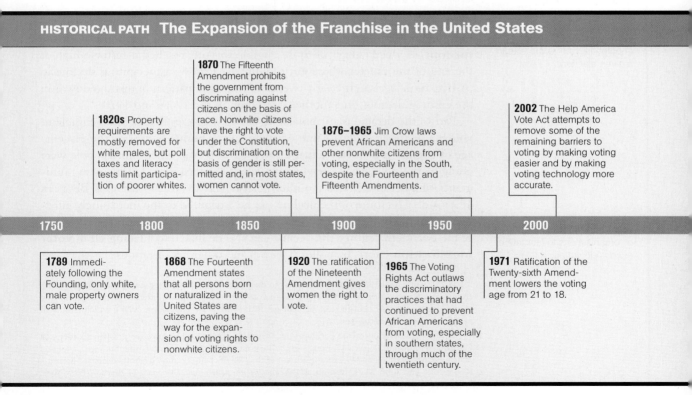

HISTORICAL PATH **The Expansion of the Franchise in the United States**

1820s Property requirements are mostly removed for white males, but poll taxes and literacy tests limit participation of poorer whites.

1870 The Fifteenth Amendment prohibits the government from discriminating against citizens on the basis of race. Nonwhite citizens have the right to vote under the Constitution, but discrimination on the basis of gender is still permitted and, in most states, women cannot vote.

1876–1965 Jim Crow laws prevent African Americans and other nonwhite citizens from voting, especially in the South, despite the Fourteenth and Fifteenth Amendments.

2002 The Help America Vote Act attempts to remove some of the remaining barriers to voting by making voting easier and by making voting technology more accurate.

1750 — 1800 — 1850 — 1900 — 1950 — 2000

1789 Immediately following the Founding, only white, male property owners can vote.

1868 The Fourteenth Amendment states that all persons born or naturalized in the United States are citizens, paving the way for the expansion of voting rights to nonwhite citizens.

1920 The ratification of the Nineteenth Amendment gives women the right to vote.

1965 The Voting Rights Act outlaws the discriminatory practices that had continued to prevent African Americans from voting, especially in southern states, through much of the twentieth century.

1971 Ratification of the Twenty-sixth Amendment lowers the voting age from 21 to 18.

The students' activism paid dividends for future generations; they overcame their collective dilemmas to produce a public good (a protected right to vote for millions). Moreover, they acted at an opportune time. Politicians in both major parties realized that it looked good to be on record as supporting the lower voting age. They also calculated that giving 18- to 20-year-olds the right to vote would help them win future elections. It is important to note the two stages of participation at work here. People first had to participate in politics—mass action, protests, organizing, pressuring policy makers—in order to earn the second, more regular form of political participation—the opportunity to vote.

Patterns of Participation in the United States

Much like the study of public opinion, the study of political participation is quite advanced in the social sciences. Surveys reveal broad patterns of participation: what types of people tend to participate, how often they participate, and how participation compares over time and across countries. Much of this research focuses on voting habits, but we will also look at other forms of participation.

Trends in Voter Turnout

voter turnout The proportion of potential voters who vote in a given election.

In the nineteenth century, American political parties and other organized movements expended massive efforts to turn out voters on Election Day. **Voter turnout**, as a percentage of those eligible to vote, reached a historic high at the end of the nineteenth century. Figure 10.2 shows a precipitous decline in participation levels in the early twentieth century, a pattern of ups and downs in the ensuing decades, and another steep drop in the 1960s and 1970s.[10]

Part of the decline is attributable to the new groups that became eligible to vote but did not participate immediately in large numbers, causing the percentage of eligible voters who actually voted to drop even when more people were going to the polls. These newly enfranchised groups included women, immigrants who became citizens, southern blacks, and 18- to 20-year-olds. Between 1890 and 1920, some of the decline can be attributed to the increasingly effective denial of voting rights to African Americans in the South. In the latter half of the twentieth century, the decline can also be linked to a falling off in **voter mobilization** efforts by political parties and other organizations.[11]

voter mobilization Efforts by organizations to facilitate or encourage voting.

[10] This discussion, including Figure 10.2, refers to the percentage of the voting-*eligible* population (VEP), counting only those citizens who are eligible to vote as the base. Slightly different percentages may be obtained if turnout is calculated as a percentage of the voting-*age* population (VAP), which counts all people of voting age as the base.

[11] For one consideration of the participation of newly enfranchised groups, see J. Kevin Corder and Christina Wolbrecht, "Political Context and the Turnout of New Women Voters after Suffrage," *Journal of Politics*, 68, no. 1 (2006): 34–49. For a treatment of the role of changing mobilization efforts, see Steven J. Rosenstone and John Mark Hansen, *Mobilization, Participation, and Democracy in America* (New York: Longman, 1993).

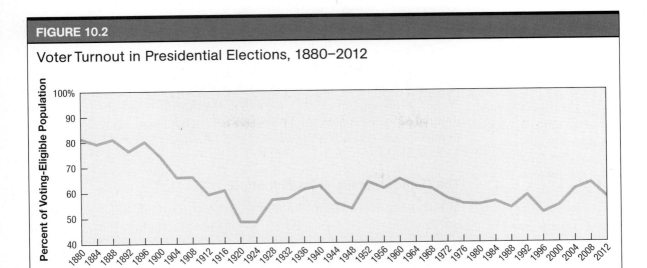

FIGURE 10.2

Voter Turnout in Presidential Elections, 1880–2012

Percent of Voting-Eligible Population

Year

Sources: For years before 1920, data are from Walter Dean Burnham, *Voting in American Elections* (Bethesda, MD: Academica Press, 2010); for years after 1920, data are from the Center for the Study of the American Electorate, American University, www.american.edu/spa/cdem/csae.cfm (accessed 5/22/13).

Recent years, however, have seen an overall upturn in turnout in presidential elections. The major political parties have begun to conduct large-scale efforts, especially in key states like Ohio and Florida, to mobilize people who do not ordinarily vote. It is estimated that 600,000 more people voted in Ohio in the 2004 presidential election than in 2000, largely as a result of the intense mobilization efforts of both parties (but primarily the Republicans). Moreover, there was an 11 percent increase between 2000 and 2004 in nationwide voter turnout in presidential elections, and another 2.5 percent increase between 2004 and 2008. There was a slight dip in national turnout in 2012. Turnout in Ohio, meanwhile, was slightly lower in 2012 compared to 2008 (about a 2 percent decrease) but still high by historical standards.

Elections for the presidency and Congress have been extremely competitive since 2000. Margins of victory were small in the 2000 election in many races, which may help explain the upturn in voter participation in 2004. Although the 2008 and 2012 presidential elections were not as close as in 2000 and 2004, many state-level and local races across the country were very tight.

Research conducted on congressional elections shows that more competitive races tend to lead to increased turnout. If the races are expected to be close, then at least three related patterns emerge:

- Voters might believe their votes actually matter.
- Political organizations might expend greater effort to turn out voters because of heightened competition.

- The sense of drama causes the media to cover the race more closely, making it easier for people to get information and become excited about the race.

Two economists studying this phenomenon have analyzed data on different types of American elections and concluded that a 1 percent change in the predicted closeness of an election (toward a tied outcome) stimulated efforts by campaign organizations to mobilize more voters, leading to an average increase in turnout of 0.34 percent.[12]

The Demographics of Participation

In analyzing who participates and why, it is important to focus not only on the costs and benefits of participation generally but also on how different people respond to these costs and benefits. As noted earlier, the costs of political participation fall hardest on those who face other disadvantages in society, such as the poor, the unemployed, the least educated, and those whose English-language skills are weak. Wealthier, more-educated people tend to enjoy the lowest costs and the most benefits from participating.

Socioeconomic Status and Participation Differences in the costs and benefits of voting go far back in American history. Consider this description of the act of voting just after the Founding in 1788:

> Voting . . . may require a lengthy ride from the farm to the county seat and back. Many . . . will be deprived of suffrage "by the necessity of traveling nearly fifty miles, passing over many mountains and cross many watercourses (frequently so high at the time of holding elections as to make it dangerous to pass the same)." Having reached the polling place, you may find it open or you may not: the length of the election (one to four days in Virginia) and the hours when the polls are open fluctuate according to the sheriff's humor and inclinations.[13]

Who would travel this far and be away from home for so long? Those who could afford to take time away from their work, those with healthy horses to transport them, or those with money to pay others to transport them. Among the landholding class eligible to vote, those near the top of the heap faced the fewest barriers. It is not so difficult to get to the polls today, but the costs of voting still fall differently across groups in the population.

To help understand who is advantaged and disadvantaged in society, social scientists employ the concept of **socioeconomic status (SES)**—the relative degree of status persons enjoy in society by virtue of their wealth, income, education, and profession. The distribution of SES in the United States looks

socioeconomic status (SES) A measure of the way that individuals are regarded within a society by virtue of their wealth, income, education, and profession.

[12] Ron Shachar and Barry Nalebuff, "Follow the Leader: Theory and Evidence on Political Participation," *American Economic Review* 89, no. 3 (1999): 525–47.

[13] Neil Spitzer, "The First Election," *The Atlantic* (November 1988): 18–19.

similar to that in other advanced industrial societies in Europe and Asia. Most people are middle class or below, with a smaller proportion earning high incomes and having advanced educational degrees. Studies dating back to the 1950s clearly show that the higher a person's SES, the more likely he or she is to be engaged in politics, to vote, and to join political organizations. In the language of social science, higher SES among people correlates positively with higher probabilities of voting and other kinds of political participation. This finding of class bias among those who turn out to vote, contact elected officials, donate money to campaigns and political parties, openly communicate their political views, and talk politics is robust and has changed little in the United States over the last 60 years.[14]

Studies of voting patterns in the United States have shown that educational status matters more than economic status in predicting voter turnout.[15] In other words, the key factor driving voter turnout is education; more-educated people turn out to vote more often than less-educated people, when controlling for other factors such as wealth, income, race, region, and age.

Other Factors Looking beyond SES and voting, we discover other factors that correlate with participation. Figure 10.3 shows patterns across different kinds of political participation (self-reported by survey respondents). We see, for example, that voting among Hispanics is lower than other racial or ethnic groups. This disparity is not surprising, given the language barriers that many immigrants in the Hispanic community face and their on average lower SES. The data on participation for African Americans is revealing, however. Studies have shown that African Americans tend to be mobilized quite effectively by civil rights organizations and churches, and thus, blacks actually have

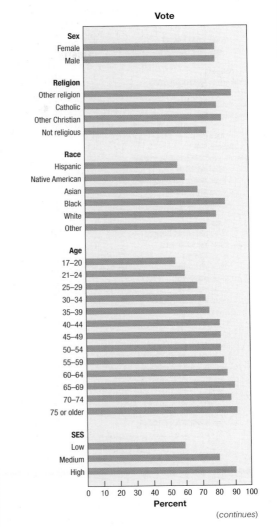

FIGURE 10.3

Participation, by Social Group, 2012

Source: American National Election Studies. These percentages reflect results from surveys which give self-reported participation.

[14] See, for example, Sidney Verba and Norman H. Nie, *Participation in America* (New York: Harper & Row, 1972) or, more recently, Joe Soss and Lawrence R. Jacobs, "The Place of Inequality: Non-Participation in the American Polity," *Political Science Quarterly* 124, no. 1 (2009): 95–125.

[15] Raymond E. Wolfinger and Steven J. Rosenstone, *Who Votes?* (New Haven, CT: Yale University Press, 1980).

FIGURE 10.3 (cont.)

Participation, by Social Group, 2012

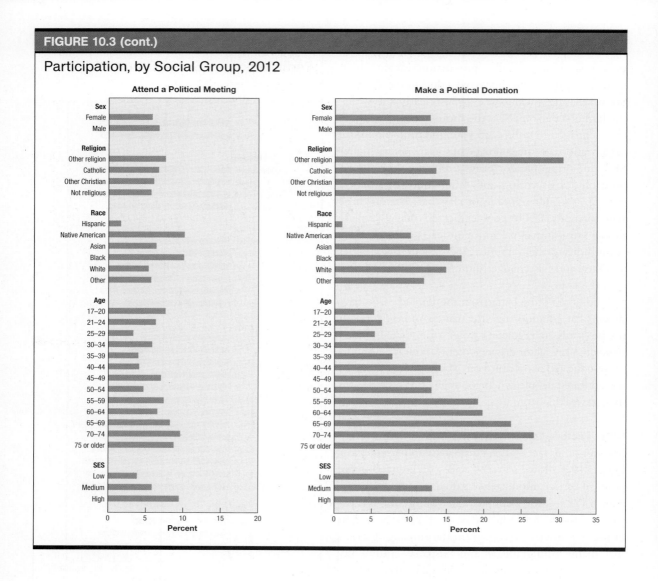

turned out in about the same or even higher proportions as their white counterparts in recent national elections.

Lower voter turnout in southern states remains a persistent pattern (not shown). This is mostly due to the greater numbers of poor and rural residents in the region. Nationwide, participation outside the biggest cities continues to be higher among suburbanites than among rural citizens. Mainline Protestants and Jews (reflected in Other Christian and Other Religious categories) turn out in slightly higher numbers than Catholics, who turn out in higher numbers than evangelical Protestants (data not broken out). Evangelical Protestants are closing the gap, though, because of the intense mobilization of this group by the Republican Party in recent decades.

In the past, more men voted than women. In recent years, however, women have turned out in proportions roughly equivalent to men, if not higher in some elections, though any difference is very slight. The reasons for this change are unclear, but available evidence indicates that in some groups, especially among African Americans, women are mobilized effectively through church and other organizational affiliations.[16]

None of the differences across groups mentioned here compare to the differences between those whose education is above average and below average. If we control for education and, to some extent, wealth, then almost all of the other differences become insignificant. In other words, the different turnout rates between religious groups or regions to the country, for example, merely reflect differences across those groups in average levels of education and wealth.

The effect of SES on participation in activities other than voting is even clearer (Figure 10.4). Higher SES leads to substantially higher participation in such activities as financial contributions to campaigns and contacting public officials. More educated people join political organizations and attend meetings more often than those with less education. And people with higher SES participate in campaign activities more frequently than those with lower SES. As previously mentioned, the exception is that lower SES groups tend to protest and rally more often than those higher up on the SES scale.

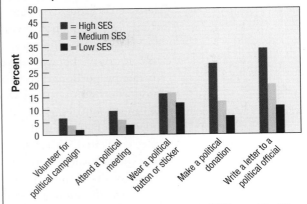

FIGURE 10.4

Socioeconomic Status (SES) and Political Participation

Note: For information on the measurement of SES, see http://tinyurl.com/pv8g29t.
Source: American National Election Studies.

In Comparison: Political Participation

In virtually every country for which political participation has been surveyed and studied systematically, there is a correlation between status—measured by levels of education and income (or the equivalent of SES in other countries)—and rates of political participation. That is, the wealthier and more educated a person is, the more likely he or she will be to participate in politics, including

---

[16] Sidney Verba and Norman H. Nie, *Participation in America* (New York: Harper & Row, 1972); Steven J. Rosenstone and John Mark Hansen, *Mobilization, Participation, and Democracy in America* (New York: Longman, 1993).

voting, attending meetings, working on an electoral campaign, and directly contacting a public official. This pattern shows up repeatedly in data from democratic countries around the world. Some exceptions exist in India and parts of Latin America, where data show either no differences in turnout across SES groups, or slightly higher rates of voting participation among the rural poor than among wealthier people in the cities.

Yet there are differences in the overall levels of participation from country to country. We know from years of research that Americans consistently vote in smaller proportions than citizens in other countries. We also know that a higher proportion of Americans work in campaigns and belong to organizations than in other countries. How can we explain this seeming paradox? Let us first consider voter participation. Figure 10.5 shows that Americans rank low in turnout rates compared with citizens of other countries. This may seem strange given that voting turnout correlates with wealth and education, and the United States is one of the wealthiest and best-educated countries in the world. Even more puzzling, education and wealth levels have been increasing in the United States faster than in other countries, yet participation rates here have fallen overall, despite recent increases.

There is more to this story, however. First, social scientists disagree about how to measure turnout, and there are disparities in how turnout is measured across countries. Most scholars who study turnout across countries believe that the typical way voting participation is measured in the United States understates real turnout, though controversy persists among scholars over which is indeed the best way to compare turnout across countries. The conclusion is that the gap between the United States and other countries is likely not as large as the most widely used measures indicate.

Second, even acknowledging the controversy that exists over measurement methods and accepting the commonly cited differences across countries, as it happens, voter turnout rates declined in all long-standing, major democracies in the latter half of the twentieth century. Unfortunately, social scientists have no adequate explanation for this overall decline. Some claim that it is a result of the decline of labor unions around the world. Unions are a major source of voter mobilization among working-class voters; if they decline in numbers and importance, so does the mobilization of those who are below average in income and education.[17]

Others claim that political parties around the world have changed, as we will discuss in Chapter 12. Parties have relied more on electronic media, especially television, to communicate with voters, instead of sending campaign workers door to door to whip up enthusiasm not only for party candidates but for

[17] Mark Gray and Miki Caul, "Declining Voter Turnout in Advanced Industrial Democracies, 1950 to 1997: The Effects of Declining Group Mobilization," *Comparative Political Studies* 33, no. 9 (2000): 1091–122.

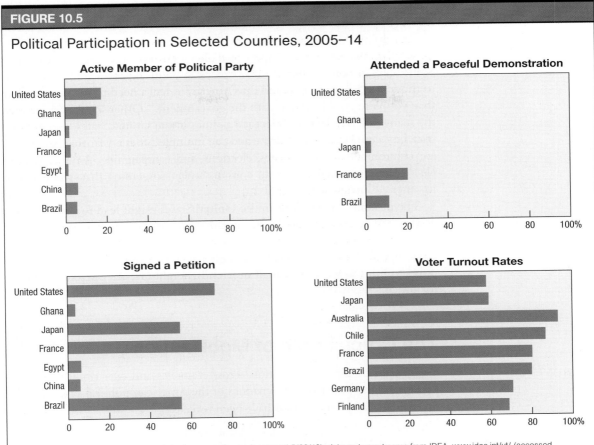

FIGURE 10.5

Political Participation in Selected Countries, 2005–14

Active Member of Political Party

United States
Ghana
Japan
France
Egypt
China
Brazil

0   20   40   60   80   100%

Attended a Peaceful Demonstration

United States
Ghana
Japan
France
Brazil

0   20   40   60   80   100%

Signed a Petition

United States
Ghana
Japan
France
Egypt
China
Brazil

0   20   40   60   80   100%

Voter Turnout Rates

United States
Japan
Australia
Chile
France
Brazil
Germany
Finland

0   20   40   60   80   100%

Source: World Values Survey, 2005 Codebook, wvsevsdb.com (accessed 5/22/13); data on turnout come from IDEA, www.idea.int/vt/ (accessed 11/6/14), except for the U.S. data, which come from the United States Elections Project, http://elections.gmu.edu/voter_turnout.htm (accessed 5/22/13); turnout data shown are the most recently available from presidential elections under presidential systems and parliamentary elections under parliamentary systems, and show votes as percentage of voting eligible population (VEP).

the act of voting itself. Among the evidence supporting this claim is that the increase in turnout in the last two U.S. presidential elections has followed the increasing use of old-fashioned, direct-contact mobilization efforts by parties and political organizations. Recent studies using experimental methods confirm that in-person contacts increase voter turnout more than impersonal appeals on radio or television.

Now let us consider other kinds of participation. As Figure 10.5 shows, people in other countries are more likely than Americans to be active in a political party or attend a demonstration. However, a higher proportion of Americans participate in election campaigns than their counterparts in other countries by giving money to candidates, attending political meetings, wearing campaign buttons, displaying bumper stickers and yard signs, and writing letters to their political representatives.

Why do Americans participate at higher rates in ways other than voting? Some scholars point to the fact that American political parties are weak relative to those in other countries, and thus Americans feel a need to use means other than voting to communicate with the government.[18] Other scholars emphasize the many different levels of electoral politics in the United States—school district, city, county, state, country—and the multiple times a year that Americans are confronted with candidates, elections, and campaigning. Americans even elect county coroners and drain commissioners, something that is unheard of in other countries (see Chapter 13).

The ubiquity of elections in the United States might lead to voter fatigue. This, in turn, might explain the paradox mentioned earlier: the fact that Americans tend to turn out in relatively small numbers for national elections, but participate at relatively high levels in other activities that offer opportunities to work on behalf of friends, neighbors, or coworkers running for office.[19]

The Crucial Role of Mobilization

Comparing political participation across countries and over time helps us to understand the patterns and dynamics of the American political system. Based on such analysis, four patterns have been revealed:

- Wealthier and more highly educated people participate more in politics than others in the population. This is a widespread pattern in democracies around the world.

- Voter turnout—the percentage of those voting among those eligible to vote—declined overall in the United States from the late nineteenth century to 2000, but it has increased somewhat in recent presidential elections.

- Americans turn out to vote in lower percentages than people in most other democratic countries (even accounting for differences in measurement).

- Americans participate in campaigns and join organizations in higher percentages than people in most other democracies.

[18] See, for example, Elisabeth S. Clemens, "Organizational Repertoires and Institutional Change: Women's Groups and the Transformation of American Politics, 1890–1920," *Civic Engagement in American Democracy*, ed. Theda Skocpol and Morris Fiorina (Washington, DC: Brookings Institution Press, 1999), pp. 81–110.

[19] See, for example, Richard W. Boyd, "The Effects of Primaries and Statewide Races on Voter Turnout," *Journal of Politics* 51, no. 3 (1989): 730–39.

What explains these patterns? First, it is widely accepted that wealthier and more highly educated people face lower costs when voting and participating in politics in other ways. They find the bureaucracy of voting easier to navigate, including filling out forms, not to mention the fact that salaried workers don't have to sacrifice wages when they leave their workplace to vote on a workday. And people in this segment of society are generally more attuned to politics and current events than those making less money and with less education.

A second, related consideration is that organizations intent on mobilizing voters and participants in other kinds of activities find it easier to contact and convince people to participate if these people have above-average wealth and education. In other words, richer and better-educated people are generally more receptive to organizations' appeals to participate. It is more efficient—more successful mobilization of people for lower costs—to mobilize people higher up the status scale, which is why these types of people are mobilized more frequently.[20]

Third, the kinds of organizations that specialize in mobilizing working-class and poorer people, such as unions and leftist, community-based organizations, have been declining in reach and importance in most developed democracies over the past 35 years.[21] Some argue that a consequence of this decline was a commensurate decline in participation in the United States and in other countries. The revival of such groups over the past decade—especially leftist organizations and church organizations devoted to mobilizing voting and campaign contributions—goes a long way toward explaining the upturn in voting rates.

Finally, not only was the decline of unions steeper in the United States than in other countries in the latter half of the twentieth century, but even going back 100 years, these kinds of American organizations have played a less powerful role in politics than their counterparts in other long-standing democracies.[22]

What about the high percentages of Americans belonging to organizations? Research shows that group members, especially those who attend meetings, are more likely to vote and participate in politics in other ways than those who do not belong to an organization.[23] Churches, for example, play a much greater role in educating people about politics and mobilizing them to participate in the United States compared with other democracies, and Americans tend to be more religious than citizens of other countries.

[20] Steven J. Rosenstone and John Mark Hansen, *Mobilization, Participation, and Democracy in America* (New York: Longman, 1993).

[21] See, for example, Michael Goldfield, *The Decline of Organized Labor in the United States* (Chicago: University of Chicago Press, 1987); and Benjamin Radcliff and Patricia Davis, "Labor Organization and Electoral Participation in Industrial Democracies," *American Journal of Political Science* 44 (2000): 132–41.

[22] Gary Marks, *Unions in Politics: Britain, Germany, and the United States in the Nineteenth and Early Twentieth Centuries* (Princeton, NJ: Princeton University Press, 1989).

[23] Sidney Verba, Kay Lehman Schlozman, and Henry E. Brady, *Voice and Equality: Civic Voluntarism in American Politics* (Cambridge, MA: Harvard University Press, 1995).

Participation in organizations is highly correlated with income, wealth, and education, and there has been a decline in organizational affiliation among Americans, along with a decline in voter participation. Church attendance is the exception. If Americans did not attend church in higher numbers than those in other countries, the data suggest that the differences in voter participation between the United States and other countries would be even greater.

All this is to say that the patterns over time in political participation in the United States, and the differences between the United States and other countries, stem in large part from differences in the nature of nongovernment institutions that mobilize people to participate in politics. Inequalities arise partly from the fact that poorer, less-educated people are less likely to participate in politics. But inequalities also stem from the different rates of mobilization by organizations such as political parties, interest groups, churches, and other associations. Moreover, these organizations continue to vary across countries in their commitments to mobilizing the working class and unemployed. As we have seen throughout this book, there are consequences when institutions constrain, encourage, and generally shape behavior within political systems. Most observers believe it matters a great deal that older, wealthier, more-educated people vote and participate in politics at much higher rates than others. It is hard to imagine that the government is not more responsive to those whose

Concert tours are one way organizations like Rock the Vote, a nonpartisan voter mobilization group, connect and engage with young voters.

voices they hear and whose votes they seek than to those who fail to participate in the electoral process.

To return to our puzzle at the beginning of this chapter concerning why a lower percentage of the young, poor, and racial and ethnic minorities turn out to vote than other age groups, we need to examine both the costs and the benefits of voting. On balance, young, poor, and racial and ethnic minorities are less likely to be mobilized by organizations and institutions. For one thing, these people are less likely to be employed. Employment not only connects people with others who share similar interests and discuss politics, it also directly connects government policies to financial well-being. Furthermore, these people are less likely to belong to associations that might mobilize them to vote and participate in politics.

Let us focus on age differences. As people age, they generally become more involved in their community, local schools, churches, and clubs, and in work-related organizations such as unions and trade associations. In contrast, the elderly not only have more time to gather information about politics, but also generally have more money to devote to organizations, institutions, and politics. Perhaps most important, they are mobilized. They have the largest lobbying organization in the country, AARP (formerly the American Association of Retired People), along with many other similar organizations. The organizations and institutions that mobilize people to participate are more apt to target retired people who have the resources and the time to help the organizations and institutions thrive.

Being mobilized reduces information costs because the mobilizing group is typically telling you how to vote or what to do in a participatory act ("Write to this senator on this Senate committee"). Being mobilized improves your knowledge of the benefits of your side winning the election, while also increasing your own sense of efficacy and feelings of fulfilling your duty.[24] So although it is true that young people will on average have more years to reap the benefits of government policies, those benefits seem vague and spread out over many years. More important and more generally, the costs of participation seem higher for the young, poor, and minorities than for other groups, and there are fewer organizations around to lower those costs for them. In recent years, however, the increasing turnout among some of these groups seems to have encouraged organizations to make a greater effort to reach them, so perhaps the pattern will change.

[24] Sidney Verba, Kay Lehman Schlozman, and Henry E. Brady, *Voice and Equality: Civic Voluntarism in American Politics*; Steven J. Rosenstone and John Mark Hansen, *Mobilization, Participation, and Democracy in America*.

FURTHER READING

★ = Included in *Readings in American Politics*, 3e

Burns, Nancy, Kay Lehman Schlozman, and Sidney Verba, *The Private Roots of Public Action: Gender, Equality, and Political Participation* (Cambridge, MA: Harvard Univerity Press, 2001). An extensive study of how women and men differ in their political participation.

Chong, Dennis, *Collective Action and the Civil Rights Movement* (Chicago: University of Chicago Press, 1992). Applies the concepts of collective action problems and other collective dilemmas to study which people participated in the civil rights movement of the 1950s and 1960s.

Green, Donald P., and Alan S. Gerber, *Get out the Vote: How to Increase Voter Turnout* (Washington, DC: Brookings Institution Press, 2008). An assessment of various techniques for mobilizing voters and running effective campaigns.

Pateman, Carole, *Participation and Democratic Theory* (New York: Cambridge University Press, 1970). A classic argument that political participation improves citizenship and self-worth.

★ Putnam, Robert, *Bowling Alone: The Collapse and Revival of American Community* (New York: Simon & Schuster, 2000). Shows extensive data indicating that American participation in voluntary organizations and in political participation more generally declined over the second half of the twentieth century. This had negative consequences for American civil life.

★ Rosenstone, Steven, and John Mark Hansen, *Mobilization, Participation, and Democracy in America* (New York: Longman, 1993). Presents convincing evidence that the decline in political participation in the second half of the twentieth century was because of declining mobilization by political organizations that in the past mobilized the poor and working class.

Verba, Sidney, Kay Lehman Schlozman, and Henry Brady, *Voice and Equality: Civic Voluntarism in American Politics* (Cambridge, MA: Harvard Univerity Press, 1995). A complete analysis of who participates in American politics.

★ Wong et al., *Asian American Political Participation: Emerging Constituents and Their Political Identities* (New York: Russell Sage Foundation, 2011). An examination of Asian American political participation in the United States as captured in the 2008 National Asian American Survey.

KEY TERMS

An anti-National Rifle Association protestor from the group Code Pink interrupts NRA Executive Director Wayne LaPierre during an NRA press conference. Following a mass shooting at Sandy Hook elementary school in Connecticut, the NRA and

11

INTEREST GROUPS AND SOCIAL MOVEMENTS

How can well-organized, narrow interests influence government in ways that go against the preferences of a majority of Americans? Why are some interests more successful than others in achieving their political goals?

Gun control has been controversial for many decades in American politics, pitting those who claim a constitutional right (from the Second Amendment) to own guns for self-protection against those who want to see stricter regulations. We learned about the legal debates over the Second Amendment in Chapter 4. The political controversy over gun control heated up substantially in late 2012 after a man in Sandy Hook, Connecticut, shot and killed six adults and 20 small children in an attack on an elementary school. This followed a wave of deadly mass shootings since 2009 in movie theaters, on military bases, in government offices, and in factories.

These attacks, especially at Sandy Hook, prompted calls at the beginning of the second term of the Obama administration for stricter regulations for private ownership of guns. President Obama himself pledged in his second inaugural address to do whatever he could to tighten regulations on gun ownership. Politicians from both major political parties vowed to expand background checks on gun buyers, improve notices between mental health professionals and law enforcement offices when people make statements about their potential use of guns to kill, and limit the size of bullet magazines for semi-automatic weapons. Victims' families personally visited members of Congress and pleaded with them to enact stricter gun control regulations.

Surveys over the course of 2012 and 2013 revealed an ambivalent and divided public opinion on gun control. A sizable majority indicated that they favored stricter background checks and a few other relatively minor regulations. But when asked in national polls whether, for instance, the government should control gun ownership or should protect the constitutional right to own guns, the mass public showed a roughly 50-50 split in responses.

The National Rifle Association (NRA), which represents gun owners, has always taken a stance opposing stricter regulations on gun ownership. When faced with the increasing attention to the issue after the Sandy Hook shootings, the NRA stood firm. In fact, during the previous year they had launched a drive to turn back any efforts at gun control and even to repeal existing regulations. Then even after the Sandy Hook shootings later that year, Wayne LaPierre, the executive vice president of the NRA, said in a defiant news conference, "The only way to stop a bad guy with a gun is with a good guy with a gun," and promoted the idea of armed law enforcement officers at elementary and secondary schools in response to the shooting and other similar ones.

With 3.5 million members, the NRA is widely considered one of the most powerful interest groups in the country. The group has a fearsome reputation, not only for publicly attacking politicians who support gun control, but most crucially, for mobilizing its members to contribute money and use their votes to turn those politicians out of office. Historically, the NRA has been a major campaign contributor in election races across the country, usually trying to get anti–gun control Republicans to defeat pro–gun control Democrats.

In 2013, the NRA's aim, in the face of increasing pressure on Congress from gun control advocates—including the president—to tighten regulations, was to thwart momentum toward new laws limiting freedoms to own and use guns. The NRA lobbied intensely in the halls of Congress to water down and eventually defeat gun control bills. The implicit message in that lobbying was the following: supporting gun control measures may cost you your job as a member of Congress, because we can turn out contributors and voters for your opponents within your party and in the other party. The NRA's lobbying work, on top of its mobilization work in the electorate, was successful in ensuring that no major gun control policy reform was enacted in 2013, even after the horrendous violence in Sandy Hook had spurred action in Congress. Each of several attempts to pass a major gun control bill introduced in spring 2013 was met with defeat in the Senate because of filibustering.

This story highlights two essential truths about interest groups and lobbying in American politics. First, direct, person-to-person lobbying is not always enough to convince members of Congress to support the NRA's position. The ultimate tactic available to groups trying to influence legislators is to criticize them and mobilize against them at election time. Second, well-organized, highly motivated groups can influence government in ways that go beyond the effects of public opinion as measured by surveys. Why are some groups more successful at these tactics and influencing government than other groups? For example, why didn't groups fighting *for* gun control have at least as much clout as the NRA?

What Are Interest Groups and What Do They Do?

This chapter focuses on *group politics*—the activities of interest groups and social movements. Unlike the relatively undifferentiated and unorganized general public that we considered in Chapter 9, these groupings of people are more organized in pressing their claims on the government. We start with analyzing interest groups. Social movements are discussed later in this chapter.

An **interest group** can be defined as any group other than a political party that is organized to influence the government. By implication, such groups are represented by formal organizations. Interest group politics occur primarily as interactions between organized groups (often represented by lobbyists working for those organizations) and people in government. It is important to note the distinction between interest groups and political parties. Parties, as we will learn in Chapter 12, are oriented toward gaining positions of power within the government. Interest groups, in contrast, do not seek positions in government, but rather try to influence those who are in government.

interest group Any group other than a political party that is organized to influence the government.

For many interest groups, seeking to influence the government is not their primary purpose, even though they engage in that activity. Labor unions, corporations, trade associations, nonprofit organizations, and foundations can all act as interest groups, even though their day-to-day work focuses on something else. The United Auto Workers is an interest group that tries to influence the government at times, but its main mission is to represent workers in their relations with their employers. Microsoft Corporation acts as an interest group, but it exists primarily to make and sell products and earn profits for its shareholders. Some interest groups do exist primarily to advocate policy goals to government officials—the NRA is an example—but they are only a small portion of active interest groups.

Lobbying refers to attempts to influence public officials by speaking to them directly or by pressuring them through their constituents. Much lobbying in the United States is directed at Congress and the White House. In fact, the term *lobbying* originated from the notion that people trying to influence the legislative process speak to legislators outside of the chamber, in the lobby. As we will see, lobbying today involves much more than just talking to lawmakers in person. Also, groups lobbying the government can attempt to use the courts to promote their cause, through lawsuits or court briefings. Likewise, lobbying can be directed at bureaucratic agencies, such as when a business trade group tries to influence the interpretation or setting of a rule or regulation by an executive branch agency when that rule would affect business firms.

lobbying An attempt to influence public officials by speaking to them directly or by pressuring them through their constituents.

Thousands of interest groups and lobbyists are active today in Washington, D.C., and many thousands more are found in state capitals. Interest groups can either have their own staff lobbyists or hire lobbyists who work for professional lobbying firms, much like hiring a lawyer or an accountant. Thousands of groups have their headquarters in Washington, D.C., to be near government decision makers.

Most interest groups in the United States represent business corporations, business trade associations, and professional organizations. Large corporations such as Microsoft typically have their own lobbying units, but so do trade associations such as the American Petroleum Association, which represents numerous companies in the oil industry in pursuing their collective interests. Similarly, professional organizations such as the American Medical Association, representing medical doctors, can be quite powerful in lobbying on medical issues.

A smaller but still important portion of the interest group world is populated by labor unions and by what are called *public interest groups*. Public interest groups are defined as organizations that "seek a collective good, the achievement of which will not selectively or materially benefit the membership or activists of the organization."[1] The Child Welfare League of America—devoted to furthering the cause of foster children and other vulnerable children—is a classic example of a public interest group.

Figure 11.1 shows a distribution of interest group types according to a recent study. Simply counting groups can lead to the impression that business interests are much more heavily represented in the interest group community than other kinds of groups. Although this is undoubtedly true, it is not so easy to determine the degree of imbalance between business interests and other types of interests, or whether this imbalance gives businesses an unfair advantage in the policy-making process. Many of the largest organizations are not business associations. For example, AARP (formerly the American Association of Retired Persons), which considers itself a public interest group in its lobbying role, has more than 37 million members and is by far the largest voluntary interest group with dues-paying members in the country, dwarfing any specific business association. Likewise, the AFL-CIO claims to speak on behalf of all of organized labor and in some instances all workers (including nonunionized workers), not just its own members.

Nonetheless, a sizable majority of paid lobbyists and the bulk of campaign contributions from interest groups are oriented toward the promotion of business interests. When those interests are united for or against a specific policy, it is hard for the major political parties or for Congress to ignore them. Such unity in the business community is extremely rare, however. Most of the time, industry lobbyists compete, as various business interest groups find themselves on opposite sides of policy issues.

As an example, a bill proposed in Congress to lengthen the life of patents for medicines would likely be supported by many large pharmaceutical companies but opposed by health insurance companies, many doctors' and hospital

---

[1] Jeffrey M. Berry, *Lobbying for the People: The Political Behavior of Public Interest Groups* (Princeton, NJ: Princeton University Press, 1977).

FIGURE 11.1

Interest Groups in 2014 (by Type)

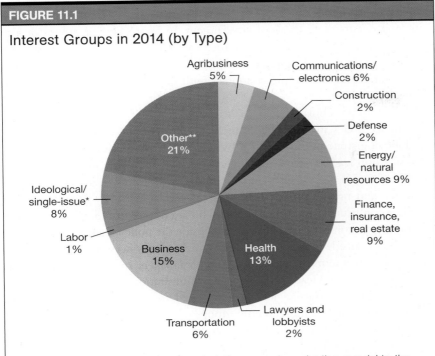

Agribusiness 5%

Communications/electronics 6%

Construction 2%

Defense 2%

Energy/natural resources 9%

Finance, insurance, real estate 9%

Health 13%

Lawyers and lobbyists 2%

Transportation 6%

Business 15%

Labor 1%

Ideological/single-issue* 8%

Other** 21%

*Includes groups that focus primarily on single issues, such as abortion, gun rights, the environment, and foreign policy.

**Includes groups that represent government employees (excluding unions), nonprofits, religious groups, and members of the armed forces.

Source: "Interest Groups: Industries by Sector," The Center for Responsive Politics, 2014, www.opensecrets.org (accessed 11/6/14).

groups, and certainly the companies that make generic (non-brand name) drugs. Consider the interests involved. The pharmaceutical companies that develop drugs want longer patents so that they can avoid competition from other companies for the drugs they have developed. They want higher prices and argue that they should be able to reap the profits from products they developed after spending money on research. In contrast, companies that make generic drugs want the patents to run out quickly so that they can copy the drug formulas, sell the same drugs as the original developer, and compete on price. By the same token, doctors, hospital groups, and insurance companies favor shorter patents so that generic drug companies can make drugs more affordable to their patients and clients.

As this example shows, there is typically no unified "business interest" with respect to a policy issue that is being debated and voted on in Congress and discussed within presidential administrations. Instead, different industry groups usually compete for the attention of lawmakers.

Inside and Outside Lobbying

Lobbying occurs at all levels of government. In fact, lobbying groups devote substantial resources to state-level efforts as well as to the federal level.[2] All lobbyists use a range of strategies and tools to influence policy makers. Some of these strategies involve direct contact with politicians, while others involve mobilizing constituents.

Interest group scholars refer to a "toolkit" that group leaders can draw from to influence policy makers. The kit includes two types of tools: inside and outside lobbying strategies. **Inside lobbying** refers to activities by lobbyists and interest group leaders who make direct contact with policy makers by speaking with them in person, testifying at committee hearings, or giving money to them at a fund-raiser. **Outside lobbying** refers to activities by group leaders to mobilize constituents and other people who are not part of the policy-making community to contact or pressure people inside the policy-making community. Examples of outside lobbying include organizing letter-writing or e-mail campaigns for constituents to apply pressure on lawmakers, running advertisements on a policy issue, and leading protests or demonstrations.[3]

Both inside and outside lobbying are used to try to influence Congress and the White House, and certainly groups often use inside lobbying in their interactions with bureaucratic agencies. As we learned in Chapter 7, these agencies have to pay attention to groups in society for multiple reasons. Groups unhappy with the decisions and actions of an agency can complain to Congress, and this can get agency leaders in hot water with the people who fund the agency. (Recall from Chapter 7 the fire alarm model of monitoring the bureaucracy.) Alternatively, groups representing firms and organizations regulated by agencies can have productive and cooperative relationships with those agencies simply by staying in touch and keeping the lines of communication open with regulators, an important purpose of inside lobbying. Finally, groups often want to have their leaders and members comment on potential regulatory or rules changes proposed by agencies. As we know from Chapter 7, agencies are required to post potential rules and regulation changes and invite commentary from the public. Most such commentary occurring in hearings devoted to receiving this feedback comes from interest group leaders and spokespeople. Thus, participating in hearings at agencies is a major inside lobbying task of many interest groups.

When targeting bureaucratic agencies, outside lobbying is less effective and used less often by groups, because the leverage from outside lobbying comes from convincing elected officials that their constituents might care enough about the issue to alter their voting decisions in the next election. Bureaucrats

inside lobbying Activities by lobbyists and interest group leaders that involve direct contact with policy makers.

outside lobbying Activities by interest group leaders that seek to mobilize constituents and others outside the policy-making community to contact or pressure policy makers.

[2] Virginia Gray and David Lowery, *The Population Ecology of Interest Representation: Lobbying Communities in the American States* (Ann Arbor: University of Michigan Press, 1996).

[3] Ken Kollman, *Outside Lobbying* (Princeton, NJ: Princeton University Press, 1997).

do not face re-election. Any outside lobbying directed at bureaucratic agencies would also usually have Congress or the White House as intended targets.

Another strategy that interest groups can use to influence policy does not fit easily into our typology of inside and outside lobbying: using the courts to promote an agenda. Interest groups use the courts in a number of ways to pursue their goals. They advocate for or against the confirmation of nominees for federal judgeships based on how they believe those nominees would rule on questions important to them.[4] They file *amicus curiae,* or "friend of the court," briefs in Supreme Court cases (see Chapter 8). These types of briefs allow individuals or organizations that are not party to a case, but who care about its outcome, to provide the Court with information that can aid its decision making. Research suggests that these types of filings by interest groups do have an effect on the Court's opinions[5]; in particular, evidence indicates that a litigant's status can be improved by the presence of an *amicus* brief filed by an interest group ally.[6] Interest groups may even go as far as filing their own lawsuits.[7] Scholars have found that this approach has been particularly popular with conservative groups and has been used with less frequency on behalf of disadvantaged populations.[8]

Campaign Financing

One straightforward way to try to influence a politician is to give money in support of his or her election or re-election. Under American law, and under the law of other democracies, outright bribery is illegal. Suppose a politician who receives a contribution from an interest group soon thereafter makes policy decisions unduly favorable to that group, and suppose someone (an accuser in court) can establish a direct cause-and-effect link between the contribution and the policy decisions. This is by definition a bribe.

Altogether, interest groups in the United States give billions of dollars a year to federal candidates, and they do not give that money for charitable reasons. They intend to spend their money in a way that will further the cause of their group interest.

[4] Lauren Cohen Bell, *Warring Factions: Interest Groups, Money, and the New Politics of Senate Confirmation* (Columbus: Ohio State University Press, 2002); Nancy Scherer, Brandon L. Bartels, and Amy Steigerwalt, "Sounding the Fire Alarm: The Role of Interest Groups in the Lower Federal Court Confirmation Process," *Journal of Politics* 70 (2008): 1026–39.

[5] Paul M. Collins Jr., *Friends of the Supreme Court: Interest Groups and Judicial Decision Making* (New York: Oxford University Press, 2008).

[6] Ryan C. Black and Christina L. Boyd, "U.S. Supreme Court Agenda Setting and the Role of Litigant Status," *Journal of Law, Economics, and Organization* (2010), first published online February 19, 2010.

[7] Frank R. Baumgartner and Beth L. Leech, *Basic Interests: The Importance of Groups in Politics and in Political Science* (Princeton, NJ: Princeton University Press, 1998), chap. 8.

[8] Karen O'Connor and Lee Epstein, "The Rise of Conservative Interest Group Litigation," *Journal of Politics* 45 (1983): 479–89; Dara Z. Strolovitch, *Affirmative Advocacy: Race, Class, and Gender in Interest Group Politics* (Chicago: University of Chicago Press, 2007).

In fund-raising situations, party leaders or candidates often come close to suggesting that large contributions to a campaign can result in favorable treatment by the government. "Please ask Panhandle Eastern Chairman Dennis Hendrix to donate $10,000 to join the Democratic Party's Business Council," read one internal memo to a National Democratic Party fund-raiser. "President Clinton ... was instrumental in getting deep water drilling rights in the Gulf of Mexico through Congress."[9] The implication is clear: we, the Democrats, helped your company; now it's your turn to help us. (Republican politicians are no less averse to such quid pro quos, of course.) Scholars sometimes refer to this as the "holdup" potential by members of Congress, meaning that since they can influence the fortunes of any company or organization, they can virtually force an interest group to make campaign contributions, much as a robber can force a victim to hand over his or her money (Figure 11.2). Although such behavior may be unseemly at times, it is not illegal.

The American campaign finance system is unusual. In most industrialized democracies, the government distributes money to political parties to enable candidates to run for public office. In most developing countries that are democracies, money is funneled more or less secretly to candidates and political parties; the public knows little about where the money comes from and how much is raised. In the United States, by contrast, campaign money for candidates

[9] Juliet Eilperin, "Old Memos Detail Link of Money to Influence," *Washington Post*, May 17, 2003.

FIGURE 11.2

Interest Groups and Campaign Contributions

In a simple model of why interest groups contribute to campaigns, an interest group contributes funds for the politician's election/re-election campaign and . . .

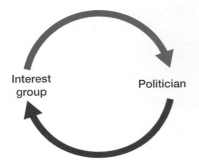

Interest group   Politician

. . . the politician is more likely to work on behalf of the group's goals.

Often, an interest group finds itself in a "holdup," knowing that if it does not contribute to the politician's campaign . . .

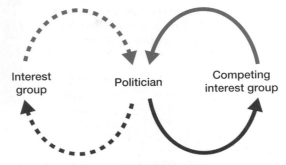

Interest group   Politician   Competing interest group

. . . the politician loses an incentive to work for the group's goals. The politician may even begin to work toward goals of competing groups.

and parties mostly comes from wealthy individuals and interest groups. Since the 1970s, however, these contributions have been heavily regulated, so we know a lot about where the money comes from and how much is given.

In private, Washington lobbyists often complain about having to attend so many fund-raisers. Many believe that their contributions will have little effect on an upcoming election or in changing policy. After all, if it takes hundreds of thousands, if not millions, of dollars to win a House or Senate seat, a lobbyist's $5,000 contribution will not make much difference.

Why, then, do lobbyists make any campaign contributions? This is not a straightforward question to answer, even if we approach it from the perspective of collective dilemmas. Consider, first, a collective-action problem among interest group leaders and lobbyists who might in general be supportive of a particular candidate. Since any single lobbyist's contribution is small relative to the amount the candidate needs to campaign seriously for office, why don't lobbyists save their money and free ride off the efforts of others who are willing to contribute?

One answer is that campaign contributions, unlike many other types of collective action, *are* noticed by candidates, parties, and politicians. Candidates (and those who win and become public officials) pay attention to who gives and who does not. So it is not the case that a group's contribution will both be ineffective

The Tea Party's Tax Status

Some organizations in American society are tax exempt, which means they do not have to pay certain taxes. Also, people can donate to certain organizations and deduct the cost of the donations from their taxable income, reducing their tax burden. The United States tax code distinguishes among nonprofit organizations based on their purposes and activities. What are the political implications of these distinctions?

Interests

Leaders of organizations that rely on private donations have an interest in obtaining tax-exempt status for three reasons. First, it lowers the costs of doing their work by avoiding various taxes. Second, it gives incentives for people to donate to their organizations if those people can deduct the cost of the donation from their income taxes. Third, being tax exempt typically means less regulation and scrutiny from the Federal Election Commission (FEC) if the organization is politically active. One recent example is the tax status of local Tea Party organizations. The Tea Party is a loose coalition of conservative groups opposed to expansive government and high taxes. Supporters and leaders of Tea Party groups want to enjoy the benefits of tax-exempt status if possible.

Institutions

Tax codes should be considered part of the institutional fabric of the political system. The government uses the tax code to affect the incentives of people and organizations and influence their behavior. If an organization's primary purpose is to engage in endorsing and/or funding political campaign activities, then it is not tax exempt. In contrast, the Internal Revenue Service provides a tax-exempt status to entities called "social welfare organizations," which are "civic leagues or organizations not organized for profit but operated exclusively for the promotion of social welfare."[1]

Outcomes

Many organized groups create multiple units for different purposes, and in doing so gain tax exemption for some of their activities. A group of local citizens who support the Tea Party might create a local political action committee (PAC) to raise money and provide campaign contributions to conservative candidates. This PAC will be taxed according to standard IRS rules

Tea Party activists rallying against the Internal Revenue Service and their alleged targeting of conservative groups for greater scrutiny.

and regulated by the FEC. The group might create another organization with the purpose of educating citizens and working to spread the word about the virtues of the Tea Party ideals. This latter organization could earn tax-exempt status by claiming that promoting social welfare, and not engaging in political activities, is their primary purpose.

There was a controversy in summer 2013 over allegations that the Obama administration had ordered the IRS to investigate and enforce potential tax law violations among local Tea Party organizations. Critics charged that the administration, during the 2012 election year, specifically targeted conservative organizations because of their ideas and sought to intimidate them. Some Republicans in Congress called for investigations into the administration's (and the IRS's) actions.

The tax code details and the ambiguity of definitions of what is "political" put the IRS at the center of politically sensitive decisions over the financial well-being of organizations that try to influence the public, the government, or both.

Think About It

Isn't there something intrinsically political about promoting social welfare? How can government effectively regulate these activities?

[1] U.S. Internal Revenue Service, "Types of Organization Exempt under 501(c)(4)," March 25, 2013, www.irs.gov/Charities-&-Non-Profits/Other-Non-Profits/Types-of-Organizations-Exempt-under-Section-501(c)(4) (accessed 6/5/13).

in determining the outcome and go unnoticed. On the contrary, as we noted in the previous section, the recipients often try to give the contributing group more access and perhaps more attention when considering policy decisions.

Two useful ways to understand campaign contributions are to consider these situations first as prisoner's dilemmas and second as opportunities to make investments. Let us start with considering prisoner's dilemma situations (Figure 11.3). Suppose there are two interest groups on opposite sides of an issue. If a member of Congress running for re-election receives money from only one group, then that member is more likely to invite that interest group in to talk about the issue, to testify at hearings, and to use the assistance of the group in crafting legislation. But if both groups contribute, the member of Congress will gladly accept both contributions and be more evenhanded in the granting of access and in relying on both groups for advice. Thus, contribution-contribution is akin to a defect-defect outcome in a classic prisoner's dilemma situation. Each group is worse off if it doesn't contribute when the other group does.

If we consider contributions as investments, then an interest group is paying to support a politician who might win and also supports the group's goals. Especially important is investing in a politician early in his or her career because that investment may pay off for a long time if the politician makes a career out of being in government. As with any uncertain investment, there is risk of little or no return. Campaign contributions (as investments) may not pay off where *paying off* means

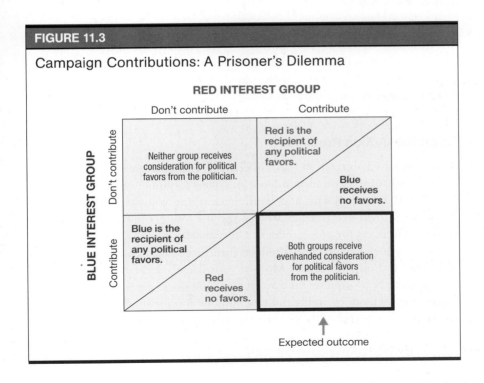

FIGURE 11.3

Campaign Contributions: A Prisoner's Dilemma

RED INTEREST GROUP

Don't contribute / Contribute

BLUE INTEREST GROUP

Don't contribute:
- Neither group receives consideration for political favors from the politician.
- Red is the recipient of any political favors. Blue receives no favors.

Contribute:
- Blue is the recipient of any political favors. Red receives no favors.
- Both groups receive evenhanded consideration for political favors from the politician.

↑ Expected outcome

that the politician regularly grants the group's leaders access to discuss key issues or looks favorably on the group's proposals for changes in policy or for preventing changes in policy. Interest groups that can afford to give generously know the risks on return, and mindful that there is only the potential of reward, they invest in many different politicians, hoping that some portion will pay off, so to speak.

Finally, and related, following the Supreme Court's decision in *Citizens United v. FEC* (2010), wealthy interest groups and wealthy people, including corporations, are permitted under the law to give unlimited contributions to groups that advocate on behalf of political ideas, ideologies, issues, and in support of candidates and parties. These relatively unregulated groups (often called super PACs) cannot give directly to candidates and parties, but they can advertise, mobilize, inform, and organize groups of citizens to promote political causes—that is, they can engage in forms of outside lobbying. The *Citizens United* decision has opened up the campaign contribution landscape to allow huge contributions to political groups from many wealthy people and interests, including famous billionaires and the world's largest corporations. (We will discuss campaign finance regulations in more detail in Chapter 13.)

Collective Dilemmas and Interest Group Politics

Interest group politics are fraught with collective dilemmas (as are social movements, which we discuss later in this chapter). In fact, the study of collective dilemmas in political science originated among scholars of interest groups who sought to explain why some groups gained organizational strength while others failed to spawn an organizational base.[10]

Collective-Action Problems

As we saw in Chapters 1 and 10, collective-action problems plague groups of people who share a common interest in trying to influence the government. To illustrate such problems and solutions, imagine you work in Greeneville, Tennessee, a town that is dependent on the zinc mining industry and on government contracts for zinc products. Greeneville is the home of Jarden Zinc Company, which manufactures products made from zinc for automobiles, coins, plumbing, and other products. Most of your friends and family work for the zinc industry. Now suppose the government announces plans to stop using zinc for some of its products in the military. Suppose too that there is a bill pending in Congress to get rid of the penny coin, which includes zinc.

---

[10] Mancur Olson, *The Logic of Collective Action* (Cambridge, MA: Harvard University Press, 1971).

Leaders in Greeneville, and of Jarden Zinc, ask the citizens of the town to contribute to the common cause of preserving the economic health of the community. They form a group called Americans for Common Cents and try to enlist the support of people from the town and around the country to "save the penny" from elimination and showcase the value of zinc more generally. They ask for financial contributions from people like you to create an organization with headquarters in Washington, D.C.; to pay a lobbyist; and to run advertisements in specialized journals and magazines extolling the virtues of the penny and of zinc as the basis of industrial products.

Do you contribute financially to the cause? Do you agree to write to your member of Congress explaining how angry you are about the proposed bill, as requested by the leaders of Americans for Common Cents? You see the common good it will do for your community if the group succeeds. Moreover, you personally will benefit if the group helps defeat the bill in Congress and convinces the government to continue the use of zinc in its military vehicles. But as one of the thousands of residents of Greeneville, your financial contribution will make little, if any, difference in the outcome. If the group succeeds in defeating the bill, but you do not contribute financially or give of your time, you will get the benefits from saving the government contracts for Jarden Zinc (and for your town) anyway. Why not free ride off the efforts of others?

This scenario is based on the true story of the Jarden Zinc Company, including its location in Tennessee, the 1989–90 bill to eliminate the penny (which was eventually defeated), and the name of the interest group formed and largely funded by Jarden.[11]

Overcoming Collective-Action Problems

Groups facing common problems or seeking common goals constantly face collective-action problems. The process of forming an interest group requires solving such problems and convincing people to contribute to a common cause in spite of the incentives to free ride. In this case, the residents of Greeneville shared an interest in protecting their jobs and local industry, but until they mobilized to form an organized group, that interest was merely **latent**. We say an interest is latent when the potential to form an active group and affect politics based on common interests exists, but that potential remains unrealized until the people take collective action.

latent interest A concern shared by a group of people on which they have not yet chosen to act collectively.

Interest groups tend to be successful in organizing and in being active (as opposed to being latent) under two conditions.[12] First, groups are more likely to succeed in organizing on behalf of shared political interests if they exist

---

[11] David Owen, "Penny Dreadful: They're Horrid and Useless. Why Do Pennies Persist?" *New Yorker* (March 31, 2008): 60.

[12] Olson, *The Logic of Collective Action*.

primarily for reasons other than to influence politics. They may be corporations or business associations formed to share expertise among employees within an industry. They may also be labor unions formed to bargain collectively with companies on behalf of workers. The political activities conducted by such interest groups are **by-products** of organizing for other purposes. These groups were not formed by the voluntary contributions of members to further a political cause. Thus, they do not have to solve collective-action problems in order to come together on behalf of shared political interests because they are already organized for some other purpose.

by-product A political activity conducted by groups whose principal organizational purpose is the pursuit of some nonpolitical goal.

The second condition related to success has to do with the problem of free riding: organizations that exist primarily for the purpose of political advocacy and that rely on the voluntary contributions of members are more likely to organize successfully if they have figured out a systematic method for overcoming people's incentives to free ride off others. Voluntary membership groups can overcome this kind of collective-action problem through selective incentives, special donors, or entrepreneurs. Let us consider these strategies one at a time.

Recall that a public good is something that everyone can enjoy without necessarily having to pay for it, and for which one person's enjoyment of it does not inhibit the enjoyment of it by others (see Chapter 1). A **selective incentive**, in contrast, is a *private* good offered by group leadership to an individual on the condition that the individual contributes to group goals. This means that an individual enjoys that good in such a way that others cannot enjoy it at the same time. For example, interest groups can offer benefits such as T-shirts, discounts on insurance, or journal subscriptions to entice potential members to participate in a collective effort. In other words, by creating selective incentives, groups offer private goods to get people to contribute toward the creation of a public good.

selective incentive A benefit that a group can offer to potential members in exchange for participation as a way to encourage that involvement.

Selective incentives do not have to be material goods, such as financial discounts, vacation packages, or calendars. They can also be social goods, such as the private benefits you might get from attending meetings of the interest group. Perhaps you will make new friends at a meeting of an interest group on your campus, or you might make business contacts at a local meeting of an interest group.

special donor A potential participant in a group for whom the cost of participating is very low and/or the benefits of participating are very high.

Large or noticeable contributions from **special donors** can also make a difference in overcoming collective-action problems. Groups can lean on potential participants who experience the lowest costs and/or derive the highest benefits from participation. In some instances, there are potential beneficiaries who might be willing to pay *all* of the costs of the collective effort because the payoff is large enough for them. As an example, the executives of the Jarden Zinc Company might have been willing to pay the entire cost of lobbying Congress over the bill to eliminate the penny. The company's well-being depended on defeating the bill to such an extent that the free-riding temptation no longer existed. It made sense for the executives to contribute to the cause, both because they alone could fund the lobbying effort (they could afford it) and because their contribution made a huge difference in the success of the collective effort (they knew their money would matter).[13]

Groups may also rely on **entrepreneurs**, people who are so committed or so skilled in pursuit of a political goal that they do not need selective incentives. These political entrepreneurs are willing to join a common cause and take on the risks of failure and the high costs of starting something new. Because these people see the benefits as so compelling that just about any cost is worth paying, and are skilled enough to seize the right opportunities when they arise, they are not (as) tempted to free ride. Although risk-taking political entrepreneurs are rare, they have made a huge difference in the world. Martin Luther King, Jr., who took enormous risks to create and sustain several organizations within the civil rights movement, is a canonical example of a political entrepreneur. He was likewise skilled at choosing protest strategies for maximum media impact. Ralph Nader, who started several consumer rights organizations in the 1960s, took fewer personal risks, but was skilled at publicity and pressuring the right corporations and policy makers at the right time.[14]

entrepreneur A leading group participant who is so committed to the group's goals, and/or so skilled in the pursuit of those goals, that he or she does not need selective incentives.

Coordination Problems

The collective-action problem poses the main dilemma for latent groups with common interests in pressuring the government. However, groups also face coordination problems. Political action is most effective when groups can pressure the government in coordinated fashion, but different people or different groups might have different views of the best ways to coordinate.

Coordination means several things in interest group politics. First, it means finding a common message that can be delivered to government representatives from a variety of sources. Suppose two interest groups oppose a bill. One group says it opposes the bill because it is too expensive and prefers to support another, less costly bill. The other group says it opposes the bill, not because of the price tag, but because it will spread those costs unequally across population groups. The people in government who hear these two different messages might become confused and ask, "Should we scrap the bill, or amend it? If the latter, how should it be changed?" Although the two groups agree on the ultimate policy goal, they advocate different strategies for amending the bill or introducing a new bill. It would be better for both

[13] Terry M. Moe, *The Organization of Interests: Incentives and the Internal Dynamics of Political Interest Groups* (Chicago: University of Chicago Press, 1980), esp. chap. 3; Theda Skocpol, "Voice and Inequality: The Transformation of American Civic Democracy," *Perspectives on Politics* 2 (2004): 3–20.

[14] Jack L. Walker, *Mobilizing Interest Groups in America: Patrons, Professions, and Social Movements* (Ann Arbor: University of Michigan Press, 1991); Kenneth T. Andrews et al., "Leadership, Membership, and Voice: Civic Associations That Work," *American Journal of Sociology* 115, no. 4 (2010): 1191–242.

Groups on the same side of any given issue may have trouble coordinating on a strategy to influence policy makers. For example, when the anti-abortion group Always Life put up billboards in African American communities highlighting the demographics of abortion, the strategy was controversial even among other anti-abortion groups.

groups, therefore, to coordinate on a common message to achieve their shared goal of killing the bill.

Second, coordination means organizing action to focus lobbying on the same key people in the government. If one group fighting a specific government regulation focuses its lobbying on the executive-branch agency in charge of interpreting and implementing the statutes, while another focuses on the congressional committee charged with writing the statutes, the two groups might lack the coordination necessary to be effective. It would be better, therefore, for the groups to decide jointly on lobbying targets. Is the problem with the interpretation or implementation of the statute? (If so, then target the agency.) Is the problem with the statute itself? (If so, then target Congress.) Then they can join forces and apply pressure to the specific parts of the government that can further their cause.

Third, coordination means organizing strategies so as not to overlap too much or miss opportunities. For instance, two interest groups trying to influence Congress might divide tasks. One group might focus on lobbying members of Congress, meeting with them in Washington and providing written reports on the value of proposed legislation. The other group might devote more attention to rallying support for or opposition to a bill among the constituents of key legislators, using advertisements, e-mail and Web campaigns, and direct mail. Group leaders do well to coordinate their strategies with others.

Coordination problems are acute across interest groups. This is why organizations in Washington spend a lot of time working to form coalitions—groups of groups, if you will. Interest group leaders sometimes want to go it alone and lobby as they see fit, but often enough they join forces with other interest group leaders to create broader coalitions. This demonstrates to policy makers the breadth of concern across different kinds of groups representing different interests in society. Leaders of groups face recurrent coordination problems that need to be solved in order to make their activities effective.

Although these examples of collective dilemmas—both collective-action problems and coordination problems—are drawn mostly from interest groups, the same logic applies to group politics in general. Leaders of social movements face the same types of dilemmas and need to find ways to solve them (as discussed later).

Determining Interest Group Influence

Washington, D.C., churns with group politics. Thousands of lobbyists swarm the Capitol daily while Congress is in session and make appointments to speak to executive-branch bureaucrats. They press their cases, provide information, and become friendly with politicians and their staff. They attend frequent fund-raisers, make donations to re-election campaigns, and in general show their support for politicians. The Mall, the large, grassy strip between the Capitol and the Lincoln Memorial, hosts protest groups on many weekends of the year. Demonstrators wave placards, march in unison, sing songs, and shout catchy slogans. Interest groups and the people mobilized by them create much of the buzz of Washington.

It is difficult to imagine that so much money and time would be invested in the formation of organized groups, and in lobbying activities and campaign contributions, if people did not think that lobbying mattered, or if people who contributed to causes or candidates did not believe that they would get a return on their investment. Do such groups really influence the decisions of policy makers? If so, which groups have influence over policy, and how much? These are difficult questions to answer, in part because it is hard to isolate the effects of lobbying from all the other influences on policy makers' decisions.

Consider, for example, the possible influences on a senator's decision to vote yes or no on a controversial bill. The senator could draw upon any of the following in making his or her decision: personal beliefs on the issue, constituents' opinions, pressure from party leaders, pressure from other senators, or lobbyists' activities. To claim that lobbying matters, one would need to identify specific situations in which the senator reversed his or her inclination to vote yes or no on the bill as a result of lobbying by interest groups. Unfortunately, there are not many instances in which we can know for sure that pressure from lobbyists was the deciding factor.

The fact that members of Congress are typically lobbied from various sides of an issue reveals a second, related problem. When the senator decides to vote one way or another, his or her actions almost certainly will be consistent with the wishes of *some* lobbying group. The question is, how do we know that the senator made his or her decision as a direct result of the lobbying group's actions?

Moreover, lobbyists tend to lobby legislators or agency bureaucrats who agree with them.[15] If an interest group wants a bill to pass, its lobbyists tend to focus on those legislators who are generally sympathetic to the group's goals. By making sure that it has the votes of these legislators, the group lays a solid foundation for its broader campaign. Given this tendency, it is hard to make the case that, absent the interest group's lobbying, the legislator would have chosen to do the opposite of what he or she actually did after being lobbied by the group.

---

[15] Marie Hojnacki and David Kimball, "Organized Interests and the Decision of Whom to Lobby in Congress," *American Political Science Review* 92 (1998): 775–90.

It is likewise difficult to draw definitive conclusions about the impact of campaign contributions. Suppose you wanted to know whether a $5,000 contribution from an interest group influenced a candidate once he or she was in office. It is almost impossible to determine whether the contribution itself changed the actions of the member once in office; whether contributions from other groups mattered more or less than the $5,000 from this particular group; or whether the member of Congress would have acted this particular way regardless of the contribution. Scholars who have attempted to understand the relationship have generally found limited effects of campaign contributions on legislators' voting behavior.[16]

Despite the difficulties in linking groups' actions to legislative behavior, scholars have used creative research strategies to discern the effects of lobbying and of campaign finance. The political scientist Robert Dahl in his book, *Who Governs?*, concluded that American government at its various levels was pluralist.[17] By this he meant that no one group dominated decision making; rather, within different policy areas certain groups were influential, but these groups did not all contain the same people. Dahl examined in close detail the decisions of the city government of New Haven, Connecticut. He then connected those decisions to the various groups that were actively pressuring the mayor and city council. He found that each group sometimes was influential and sometimes not. His work refuted the widely held view that a small number of prominent people within towns and cities dominate the politics of those places. Dahl's study of New Haven was important because he appeared to capture how power was dispersed across groups in American politics, not only in New Haven but at all levels of government. It was also influential for its style of research: learning through interviews and observation what various groups want to achieve and then observing which groups win out in any particular political conflict.

Building on Dahl's research, other pluralist scholars described American politics as an arena in which many groups were active, but none was dominant. Critics of the pluralist viewpoint, however, contended that Dahl and others missed the underlying bias in favor of the interests of the wealthy. As one scholar put it, "The flaw in the pluralist heaven is that the heavenly chorus sings with an upper-class accent."[18] Another set of scholars pointed out that Dahl and his fellow pluralists limited their studies to policy issues that were actually being proposed and debated. But what about those issues that never came up for consideration? Dahl's critics argue that dominant—that is, wealthy—

[16] Stephen G. Bronars and John R. Lott, "Do Campaign Donations Alter How a Politician Votes? Or, Do Donors Support Candidates Who Value the Same Things That They Do?" *Journal of Law and Economics* 40 (October 1997): 317–50; Gregory Wawro, "A Panel Probit Analysis of Campaign Contributions and Roll-Call Votes," *American Journal of Political Science* 45, no. 3 (2001): 563–79.

[17] Robert Dahl, *Who Governs?* (New Haven, CT: Yale University Press, 1961).

[18] E. E. Schattschneider, *The Semisovereign People* (1960; repr., Hinsdale, IL: Dryden Press, 1975), pp. 34–35.

interest groups keep controversial policies that might redistribute wealth and income off the legislative agenda.

The concept of pluralism is not as widely accepted among scholars of interest groups as it once was. Who has power in any given political situation has been difficult if not impossible to determine by rigorous scientific methods. Moreover, many scholars believe that power depends on institutional context—be it the U.S. House of Representatives, a city council, or an agency of the federal bureaucracy—and on the issue at stake. Scholars today tend to focus on the potential influence of lobbying or campaign contributions in specific contexts, rather than making general claims about the power of one group in society over others across a wide range of issues.

Research in the past few decades has sharpened our knowledge of lobbying and the role of interest groups in campaign finance. We know, for instance, that interest groups are vital sources of information for policy makers as they try to predict the consequences of policy changes on industries, companies, communities, and groups in the population. Interest groups often act as proxy "staff" for a member of Congress. They can help write, amend, and lobby other members on behalf of a particular bill that the member wants passed. They can also help maneuver a bill through complex legislative processes. The groups and the member of Congress want the same thing, and the groups help the member achieve his or her goals. Of course, groups can give biased information, but policy makers repeatedly attest to the importance of dealing with lobbyists on a basis of mutual trust.[19] If a lobbyist misleads a policy maker even once, he or she loses credibility and jeopardizes future opportunities to enlist support.

Research has also shown that when policy makers are subjected to "cross pressure" from various interest groups on opposite sides of an issue, those policy makers tend to decide consistently with public opinion in their district or with their political party leaders.[20]

In an attempt to influence policy, people like Michael Correia (above), director of government relations for the National Cannabis Industry Association, regularly meet with legislators and their staff. It is unclear how much effect direct lobbying has on the outcome of legislation, though there is evidence that lobbyists can help legislators achieve policy goals by sharing information or helping to move a bill through the legislative process.

[19] Richard Hall and Alan Deardorff, "Lobbying as Legislative Subsidy," *American Political Science Review* 100 (2006): 69–84.

[20] John Kingdon, *Congressmen's Voting Decisions* (Ann Arbor: University of Michigan Press, 1989); Gene M. Grossman and Elhanan Helpman, *Special Interest Politics* (Cambridge, MA: MIT Press, 2001).

Finally, there is some limited evidence that members of Congress tend to grant more direct access to two types of groups: ones that represent constituents, as opposed to ideological groups representing broad national goals[21]; and ones that contribute to their campaigns.[22] Similarly, White House officials tend to grant more direct access to groups that contribute to the president's campaign. In other words, if two groups seek a meeting with a policy maker and only one of them contributed money to that policy maker's campaign *and* represents constituents, that group is more likely to get the meeting.

Social Movements

social movement A loose coalition of groups and organizations with common goals that are oriented toward using mass action to influence the government.

Social movements are more difficult to define than interest groups, mostly because they do not have clear boundaries. We can define a social movement as a loose coalition of groups and organizations with common goals that are oriented toward mass action and popular participation and share the intention of influencing the government. Interest groups can be part of a social movement, and new interest groups may be spawned by the activities of a broader social movement. But interest groups are formal organizations, while social movements are coalitions of many groups and individuals, some well organized and others less so.

Social movements are like the constellations of stars that make up a galaxy. Together, the clusters of various groups form a movement, but within the movement we can see all sorts of nuances and potential divisions. A major challenge for social movement leaders is to coordinate the actions of disparate and sometimes competing organizations, all of which might agree on large philosophical goals and work toward common policy goals (see Figure 11.4).

The quintessential example of a social movement is the civil rights movement, which began in the early 1950s and lasted as a major popular force until the late 1960s. The movement produced such monumental policy successes as the Civil Rights Act of 1964 and the Voting Rights Act of 1965, which shaped American politics and society as few other pieces of legislation have. Although the movement's most famous leader was Martin Luther King, Jr., it was composed of many groups and encompassed many mass actions and leaders. Throughout the 1950s and 1960s, people and groups in the movement targeted racial segregation, unequal treatment of African Americans, and

[21] John R. Wright, "PAC Contributions, Lobbying, and Representation," *Journal of Politics* 51 (1989): 713–29; Michelle L. Chin, "Constituents versus Fat Cats: Testing Assumptions about Congressional Access Decisions," *American Politics Research* 33 (November 2005): 751–86; Paul D. Jorgensen, "Campaigning on Fruit, Nuts, and Wine," *Political Research Quarterly* 63, no. 1 (2010): 16–22.

[22] John R. Wright, "Contributions, Lobbying, and Committee Voting in the U.S. House of Representatives," *American Political Science Review* 84, no. 2 (1990): 417–38; Micky Tripathi, Stephen Ansolabehere, and James M. Snyder Jr., "Are PAC Contributions and Lobbying Linked? New Evidence from the 1995 Lobby Disclosure Act," *Business and Politics* 4, no. 2 (2002): 131–55.

FIGURE 11.4

Social Movements and Interest Groups

Individuals share a common interest in an issue, such as civil rights.

INDIVIDUALS across the United States who were concerned about civil rights

They locate other individuals with similar interests and begin to organize into **groups**.

STUDENT GROUPS **RELIGIOUS GROUPS** **LIBERAL GROUPS**

These groups coordinate their actions to gain greater leverage for change and, in doing so, form a **movement**.

CIVIL RIGHTS MOVEMENT

Often, one or more **interest groups** related to the social movement become established as mainstream Washington organizations.

NAACP
National Association for the Advancement of Colored People

RAINBOW COALITION

MALDEF
Mexican-American Legal Defense and Education Fund

NOW
National Organization for Women

HUMAN RIGHTS CAMPAIGN

disparities in wealth and access to social advancement. Local leaders throughout the country (especially in the South) organized protests, sit-ins, boycotts, and educational forums to press the case that African Americans deserved the same rights to citizenship and the same privileges enjoyed by whites.

Although its goals are very different and its scale smaller, the Tea Party movement launched in 2009 initially shared many of these characteristics. A few charismatic leaders, such as Glenn Beck and Sarah Palin, helped to coordinate the action of numerous local groups to pressure for policy changes, including balanced budgets, lower taxes, and traditional interpretations of the Bill of Rights. More than the civil rights movement, however, the Tea Party movement devoted special attention to electoral politics—specifically, helping movement-backed candidates win Republican primaries and defeat Democratic candidates in elections. The Tea Party movement ultimately morphed into a faction within the Republican Party. By 2014, though it had elements remaining of a social movement—loosely organized groups around the country mobilized to achieve change and occasionally coordinating their actions—the strategic focus of its various groups became almost solely electoral victory in Republican primaries for its favored Congressional candidates and pressure on existing members of Congress to stay firm on cutting the federal deficit and reducing the size of government.

The Occupy movement in 2011 and 2012 also had classic elements of a social movement. It began as Occupy Wall Street in September 2011 when a group of protesters set up tents and lived in lower Manhattan in New York City to show their distaste for lax financial regulations and, in their view, the resulting inequalities between rich and poor. Their mantra became that the government ought to take action to help support "the 99%" as opposed to the wealthy "1%." Similar protests involving small tent cities sprang up around the country, in Washington D.C., nearly all major cities with large financial sectors (Chicago and San Francisco, for instance), and even college towns (including New Haven, Berkeley, Ann Arbor, and Madison). The tent cities and occasionally boisterous protests continued for many months, though participation waned somewhat in winter, and were rebuilt again in smaller form in spring and summer of 2012. After that, Occupy lost momentum, and by 2013, it had become mostly dormant. Still, the possibility of its revival remained, or at least the revival of another similar social movement focused on issues of inequality.

Prominent social movements, such as the suffrage movement for women's right to vote, the civil rights movement, the consumer rights movement, or the Christian conservative movement, have played major roles in American history. Movements come in different forms and have different modes of action. The civil rights movement had identifiable leaders and constituent organizations, was covered extensively by the mass media, used protest and nonviolent resistance as its main mode of operation, and—at least until the mid-1960s, a full 10 years after it began—had several clear policy goals that drove members' participation, including the repeal of Jim Crow laws and full civil and political rights for African Americans.

The consumer rights movement also had several identifiable leaders, such as Ralph Nader, but it relied less on protest and disruption than on publications, demonstrations of product dangers for mass-media consumption, and more traditional forms of lobbying. The Prohibition movement in the nineteenth and early twentieth centuries had a few identifiable leaders, such as Carrie Nation in the 1880s, but was oriented mostly toward convincing candidates for public office at all levels of government—from local city boards to Congress—to support a nationwide ban on the sale of alcoholic beverages. Again, there were some protests and social disruption on the part of movement activists, but generally they worked through the electoral process and other accepted means to effect change.

Despite their diversity of form, social movements share certain features that set them apart from interest groups. One common feature is that social movements typically arise out of groups of people who feel excluded, or have deliberately excluded themselves, from the mainstream political process. In fact, many scholars define a social movement as a form of resistance by disadvantaged segments of society.[23]

Just as protest is a staple of many, though not all, social movements, not all social movements are leftist in orientation, though most are. Recall from Chapter 9 that a leftist is someone who generally opposes inequalities of class, wealth, and status in society, and who advocates redistributing wealth to the poor and increasing the representation of the marginalized and disadvantaged. The leftist tendency of social movements stems from the fact that groups that are part of social movements tend to use strategies and tactics outside the mainstream, which are regarded as the only tools available to those who feel excluded from the centers of power. In comparison with leftist groups, centrist or rightist organizations tend to have more support among those at the top of the social hierarchy and thus can work within the existing system of representation.

Exceptional rightist social movements—for example, Christian conservatives, Tea Partiers, or Prohibitionists—arise and sustain themselves for the same reason as leftist groups. The people behind the Christian conservative and Tea Party movements have felt excluded from decision making and often use protest to achieve their objectives. Protest from the right is commonly associated with the issues of abortion, health care reform, immigration, and government spending. Many Christian conservatives have also felt excluded by the mass media and some state-level political parties when it comes to decision making in local schools.

Two yardsticks are often used to measure the "success" of a social movement. First, a movement can succeed in mobilization by encouraging people to participate, by raising the profile of a cause, and by placing a specific set of policy

---

[23] This is sometimes referred to as a *political process approach* to social movements. See, for example, Doug McAdam, *Political Process and the Development of Black Insurgency, 1930–1970* (Chicago: University of Chicago Press, 1982); and Doug McAdam, Sidney Tarrow, and Charles Tilly, *Dynamics of Contention* (New York: Cambridge University Press, 2001).

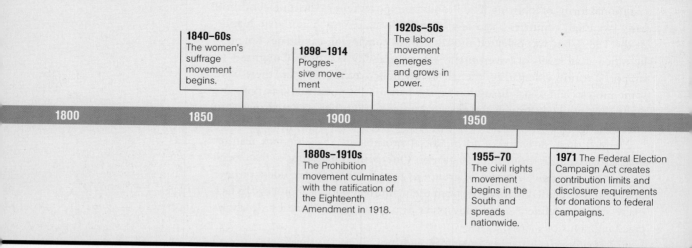

1840–60s
The women's suffrage movement begins.

1898–1914
Progressive movement

1920s–50s
The labor movement emerges and grows in power.

1800   1850   1900   1950

1880s–1910s
The Prohibition movement culminates with the ratification of the Eighteenth Amendment in 1918.

1955–70
The civil rights movement begins in the South and spreads nationwide.

1971 The Federal Election Campaign Act creates contribution limits and disclosure requirements for donations to federal campaigns.

changes on the agenda. Alternatively, a movement can succeed by changing government policy and achieving most of its desired reforms. The first kind of success does not automatically lead to the second kind. Not every social movement, even ones that are large and mobilize many people, succeeds in achieving the goals of the groups under its umbrella. Nevertheless, social movements have profoundly shaped the political agenda and changed the nature of government and public policy. For example, in the absence of social movements that brought popular pressure to bear on the government, women would probably not have the right to vote, there would be few environmental laws, and labor unions would have a much more difficult time operating, if they were allowed to exist at all.

Deeper Analysis of Social Movements

Scholars ask some of the same questions about social movements that they ask about interest groups: Are social movements influential? If so, when and how? And why do some social movements get off the ground and take lasting shape, while others do not?

We have defined a social movement as a loose coalition of groups and organizations with common goals, oriented toward mass action and popular participation. One question that continually intrigues scholars of mass behavior is, what explains why some social movements succeed in mobilizing people to participate, while other movements fail? "Failed" social movements are usually hard to study because we do not hear about them, and they are not in our history books because they never got off the ground. In recent times, leaders of antiwar groups

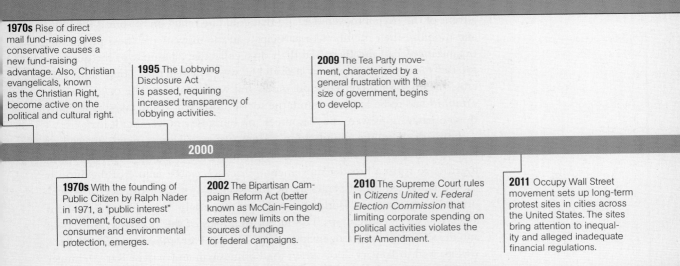

1970s Rise of direct mail fund-raising gives conservative causes a new fund-raising advantage. Also, Christian evangelicals, known as the Christian Right, become active on the political and cultural right.

1995 The Lobbying Disclosure Act is passed, requiring increased transparency of lobbying activities.

2009 The Tea Party movement, characterized by a general frustration with the size of government, begins to develop.

2000

1970s With the founding of Public Citizen by Ralph Nader in 1971, a "public interest" movement, focused on consumer and environmental protection, emerges.

2002 The Bipartisan Campaign Reform Act (better known as McCain-Feingold) creates new limits on the sources of funding for federal campaigns.

2010 The Supreme Court rules in *Citizens United* v. *Federal Election Commission* that limiting corporate spending on political activities violates the First Amendment.

2011 Occupy Wall Street movement sets up long-term protest sites in cities across the United States. The sites bring attention to inequality and alleged inadequate financial regulations.

tried to mobilize a mass movement to oppose the wars in Iraq and Afghanistan, but by most measures they did not succeed. There were spotty protests, but little in the way of sustained, large-scale mass action against the wars.

Let us consider two approaches to the study of social movements that may help us understand why some succeed and some fail. First, one might focus attention on collective dilemmas—specifically, collective-action problems. Explaining why some groups in society are able to organize for mass action and form successful social movements is analogous to explaining why some latent groups are able to overcome their collective-action problems. Perhaps some groups are just lucky in having talented political entrepreneurs who are willing to pay the up-front costs of early organizing, and who then can use selective incentives to build the organizations. As for why the antiwar movement failed to gain traction, the explanation has less to do with people's opposition to the wars in Iraq and Afghanistan—after all, poll numbers showed that many millions of Americans were deeply opposed—than with the failure of the movement's potential leaders to overcome people's incentives to free ride off others.[24]

A second approach draws on what is sometimes called a *resource mobilization perspective*, a set of ideas borrowed from sociology. This perspective takes some of the lessons from the study of collective dilemmas, but it also incorporates knowledge of the organizations that predate the social movement itself. It is well

[24] See, for example, Dennis Chong, *Collective Action and the Civil Rights Movement* (Chicago: University of Chicago Press, 1991); and Marc Schneiberg, Marissa King, and Thomas Smith, "Social Movements and Organizational Form: Cooperative Alternatives to Corporations in the American Insurance, Dairy, and Grain Industries," *American Sociological Review* 73 (August 2008): 635–67.

known, for instance, that the civil rights movement was built on a network of churches and student organizations that had existed for many decades before the advent of the overall movement, and that could be relied on to spread the word and mobilize their members to participate in the movement. These preexisting organizations had already solved their own collective dilemmas, so the question for the success of the broader movement was whether they could also solve cross-organizational collective dilemmas and work together. The original organizations had to be in place before the social movement could take shape. Thus, these organizations were the "resources" mobilized by movement leaders.[25]

From the resource mobilization perspective, social movements succeed or fail depending on the existence of established, organized groups that can be knit together to form a broader movement. For example, the failure of the antiwar movement is explained primarily by the weakness or nonexistence of peace-oriented organizations. Both of these approaches help us understand different aspects of social movements. The recent examples of the Tea Party movement and the Occupy movement are instructive. The Tea Party movement, for instance, was sparked in January 2009 when the businessman and activist Karl Denniger used the Internet to urge readers to send tea bags to their congressional representatives to protest the government's bailout of large banks and auto companies. The symbolism of the tea bag was important. It referred to the Boston Tea Party of 1773, when colonists protested against onerous taxes imposed by the British Crown. Following Denniger's appeal, "tea parties" sprang up around the country. These were demonstrations and protests by conservatives against Democratic president Barack Obama's policies expanding government programs to stabilize and grow the economy during the recession. (In reality, some of these programs had been initiated by the previous Republican president, George W. Bush.) It is estimated that 300,000 people participated in Tea Party demonstrations nationwide on April 15, 2009, the day taxes are due to the national government.

In February 2010, a National Tea Party Convention was held in Nashville, Tennessee. It was organized by Tea Party Nation, one of several groups around the country that claimed to represent the movement, including Tea Party Patriots and the Tea Party Unity Movement. The first meeting in Nashville was disappointing for many supporters because it ended up revealing disagreements among the groups about what the movement stood for and who should be considered part of it. A second convention aimed at fostering a sense of cohesion among the collection of smaller groups took place in October 2010, just ahead of the November elections. That fall, many candidates endorsed by the Tea Party movement were voted into office in what was widely interpreted as a strong protest against the economic policies of the Obama administration.

[25] See, for example, John D. McCarthy and Mayer N. Zald, "Resource Mobilization and Social Movements: A Partial Theory," *American Journal of Sociology* 82 (1977): 1212–41; and D. Michael Lindsay, "Evangelicals in the Power Elite: Elite Cohesion Advancing a Movement," *American Sociological Review* 73, no. 1 (2008): 60–82.

It revived again in 2012. Unlike most social movements, the Tea Party increasingly was able to enlist the support of extremely wealthy contributors and wealthy organizations. With these resources, the movement remained a potent force in Republican primaries around the country, helping defeat moderate Republicans, such as Richard Lugar, long-standing senator from Indiana, and supporting more conservative Republican candidates. In the presidential race, Tea Party supporters were lukewarm at best toward Mitt Romney until late in the campaign, but rallied around him against Barack Obama.

Occupy, as mentioned, started with protest occupations near Wall Street and then spread outward to other cities. The initial organizers of the movement drew upon the ideas of bloggers and writers complaining about inequality and the damage that distorted financial regulations have on the poor. Certainly around the country there are many local organizations devoted to fighting for the rights of the poor and verbally attacking the coziness of financial industries and government regulators. Some of these organizations joined together to assist in the Occupy protests and mobilized their own supporters to participate in the larger movement. By 2013 it seemed to have run its course as a movement.

Both movements struggled to establish local organizations ("resources") and then to solve broader collective-action and coordination problems across those local groups. Their efforts at grassroots mobilization met with mixed success. It remains to be seen whether the Tea Party will succeed in overcoming these collective dilemmas and have a lasting impact on American politics.

In Comparison: Group Politics

The American political system is widely considered to have more active and numerous interest groups than any other democratic country in the world. Scholars have explained this activity as a consequence of the many points of access in the U.S. national government. For instance, in the United States, if you want to change a particular regulatory rule that adversely affects your company, you can try to influence the bureaucrats in the regulatory agency to alter their interpretation and implementation of the rule. You can also try to influence the White House, and maybe even the president (if the company or industry is large and important enough and represents a huge constituency), to lean on the regulatory agency. Or you can try to influence the majority-party leadership in Congress to make changing the rule a legislative priority. Another route is to try to influence the chairs or members of the relevant committees or subcommittees in Congress to attach an amendment to a future bill changing the rule. You may also try to take your case to court and influence the legal interpretation of the rule.

In other words, given the separation of powers in American government, you can seek access to all three branches of government, any one of which might be able to improve the lot of your company. In parliamentary democracies there are fewer points of access to influence the government. The governing cabinet tightly controls the flow of legislation in countries such as Britain, Germany, and Canada. Committees in these legislatures have little power. If you operate a company in Britain and you want to change a rule that affects your company, you have to make your case to a small number of people in the cabinet, most likely the minister in charge of the bureaucratic ministry that directly regulates the industry or environment in which your business operates.

Furthermore, in many countries, laws severely restrict the kinds of lobbying that can occur. Many countries have what is called a corporatist style of interest representation. Under corporatism, the government grants recognition to a particular group to represent a set of people in society, and then the government grants access to that group alone. In Germany, for example, the government invites representatives from employer organizations and from labor unions to meet with government ministers to hash out legislation affecting workers. The government confers on specific interest groups the right to represent workers in society, and those interest groups are invited to such meetings.

This stands in contrast to American-style group politics, in which any group can form and press its cause on government officials. Under **pluralism**, as we saw earlier, groups compete with each other for influence, even within a particular policy realm and industry. There is no process that results in members of Congress granting access only to specific interest groups. In other words, the United States has a more laissez-faire system of interest representation.

pluralism A view of the American political system that emphasizes the fact that a large number of diverse interest groups are involved in the political process, and that any given group may be influential on some occasions and not on others.

Organized Forms of Public Pressure

In Chapter 9, we explored how public opinion is studied and how it forms the basis of political competition. We compared public opinion to a landscape on which politics occurs. Public opinion sets the stage for what is possible in politics—for what kinds of constraints people in the government face when they try to make, implement, or interpret public policies.

How is public opinion actually communicated? We learned about polling as one method elected officials use to learn about public opinion. But it is more common for elected officials and upper-level bureaucrats in the government to hear from the representatives of groups in the population than from the people themselves.

If you ask a politician to specify how he or she learned about public opinion on a controversial policy issue, more often than not the politician will refer to interest group leaders who bring their concerns forward. "I heard from the local business community that this would be a bad bill for my state," is a typical response. Many different groups are trying to pressure the government, and the saying "The squeaky wheel gets the grease" is especially relevant to the American political system, with its multiple levels and layers of authority.

A group becomes "squeaky" when it acts collectively, hiring lobbyists or organizing protests or letter-writing campaigns, and puts pressure on government officials.

Interest groups and social movements can be thought of as organized clumps of public opinion. They help form the public opinion landscape. What politicians learn from interest groups is not always a fair rendering of public opinion. Often the opposite is true, in that the groups politicians hear from are those that have organized themselves most effectively to capture the attention of politicians. These interest groups, no matter how widespread, are not typically representative of the entire public. Thus, although interest groups seek to encapsulate public preferences in order to target government officials more effectively, their representations are hardly synonymous with public opinion. Many people in the population, including many directly affected by public policies in question, are not represented by any group active on a given issue. Interest groups and social movements represent the public in biased, unrepresentative ways, but in ways that are nevertheless important and deeply consequential.

Let us return to the example of the NRA discussed at the beginning of this chapter. Members of the NRA are not wealthier than the general population, and they generally are not business leaders, but they are well organized. It would seem that the NRA, through its campaign actions, has gained a reputation for being able to influence election outcomes, even though its position on the issue of gun control is not always popular. Evidence shows that gun control groups have not been as focused as the NRA on local-level organizing, and this mostly explains their weakness relative to the NRA.[26] It is because the NRA has focused on grassroots organizing that it could mobilize voters based on that one issue (gun control), convince them steadfastly to oppose pro–gun control politicians, and raise and spend money to defeat these politicians *and* influence voters. Any group with that kind of organizational muscle, and with as many members and as much money as the NRA has, will be influential in American politics. Only a few groups wield such clout. The NRA is successful because it repeatedly solves collective dilemmas among gun owners, targeting its efforts in a coordinated fashion and working to defeat its political foes in election contests across the

Interest groups and social movements can be thought of as organized expressions of public opinion. As public opinion shifted more strongly in favor of civil rights in the 1950s and 1960s, the civil rights movement provided a dramatic expression of these preferences—and ultimately influenced public policy.

[26] Kristin Goss, *Disarmed: The Missing Movement for Gun Control in America* (Princeton, NJ: Princeton University Press, 2006).

country. A well-organized and coordinated minority of voters can achieve a reputation for voting as a bloc and swinging elections.

The NRA example is unusual in that any single interest group is rarely able to flex its muscles so effectively at election time, mostly because it is hard to do and can be politically risky. What if your targeted incumbents win? You might then lose access to them in the future. But when such a group displays its power and actually appears to swing an election, this can have an enormous impact. One example from long ago is well known even today: In 1994, the speaker of the House, Thomas Foley of Washington State, lost his seat in Congress when he crossed the NRA on an assault weapons ban. These examples stick in the minds of politicians and become the stuff of lore in Washington, D.C. "Be careful of the interest groups you cross," politicians tell each other. "If the interest groups have enough clout with voters, they can cause you to lose your job."

Underlying whatever influence interest groups have over incumbents is the perception that they represent an important set of constituents whom incumbents want to keep happy. That constituency can represent a large number of voters or a significant bloc of campaign contributors. Either way, politicians pay attention to interest groups because they know that these groups can affect the outcome of an election.

It is important to keep this "ultimate weapon" in mind when assessing the impact of lobbying and campaign contributions, and social movement politics, on policy making by legislatures and executives. An interest group can try to work through the courts if the other branches are not receptive. But if there is no electoral connection whereby a politician sees the link between what a group wants him or her to do and what will happen in the next election, then the interest group will have little influence on legislatures and executives.

FURTHER READING

★ = Included in *Readings in American Politics,* 3e

Ainsworth, Scott, *Analyzing Interest Groups: Group Influence on People and Policies* (New York: Norton, 2002). A comprehensive overview of theories of interest groups and lobbying.

Baumgartner, Frank R., and Beth L. Leech, *Basic Interests: The Importance of Groups in Politics and in Political Science* (Princeton, NJ: Princeton University Press, 1998). A broad overview of research findings on interest groups and campaign finance.

Dahl, Robert, *Who Governs?* (New Haven, CT: Yale University Press, 1961). A clear statement of pluralism, coming out of a study of political power in the city government of New Haven, Connecticut.

★ Gilens, Martin, *Affluence and Influence: Economic Inequality and Political Power in America* (Princeton, NJ: Princeton University Press, 2012). An analysis of political inequality and its impact on American democracy.

Goss, Kristin, *Disarmed: The Missing Movement for Gun Control in America* (Princeton, NJ: Princeton University Press, 2006). A detailed study comparing the success of pro- and anti-gun control organizations in mobilization and advocacy.

★ Kollman, Ken, *Outside Lobbying: Public Opinion and Interest Group Strategies* (Princeton, NJ: Princeton University Press, 1997). An analysis of interest group strategies, with special focus on decisions to use grassroots mobilization as opposed to insider lobbying.

Moe, Terry M., *The Organization of Interests: Incentives and the Internal Dynamics of Interest Groups* (Chicago: University of Chicago Press, 1980). A collective-action based analysis of the way interest group leaders persuade people to participate in group activities and lobbying.

★ Olson, Mancur, Jr., *The Logic of Collective Action: Public Goods and the Theory of Groups* (Cambridge, MA: Harvard University Press, 1971). A classic book describing the collective-action problem and applying it to the study of political organizations.

Schattschneider, E. E., *The Semisovereign People* (1960; repr., Hinsdale, IL: Dryden Press, 1975). An account of popular mobilization that emphasizes the importance of who controls the participants in a political conflict; a critique of pluralism.

Strolovitch, Dara Z., *Affirmative Advocacy: Race, Class, and Gender in Interest Group Politics* (Chicago: University of Chicago Press, 2007). A creative study about organizations that advocate for the poor and marginalized, and about how well they represent the interests of the people they claim to represent.

KEY TERMS

by-product (p. 390)

entrepreneur (p. 391)

inside lobbying (p. 382)

interest group (p. 379)

latent interest (p. 389)

lobbying (p. 379)

outside lobbying (p. 382)

pluralism (p. 404)

selective incentive (p. 390)

social movement (p. 396)

special donor (p. 390)

Americans frequently claim to dislike partisanship, but parties play an important role in politics and government. For example, parties help organize Congress. After the Republicans won a majority in the Senate in 2014, Senate Majority Leader Mitch McConnell (left) and House Speaker John Boehner (right) will work together to set the Republican agenda in Congress.

12

POLITICAL PARTIES

 Why are political parties and partisanship so widely criticized—but also so indispensable in a democratic system?

During the 2012 presidential campaign, Mitt Romney bragged that even though he was the Republican nominee he had often crossed party lines and cooperated with Democrats when he was governor of Massachusetts. He promised to end partisan rancor in Washington, D.C. Barack Obama, first as a Democratic candidate in 2008 and then as president, has repeatedly extolled the virtues of bringing together members of both major political parties to solve the country's problems. After taking office, and then in the 2012 re-election campaign, he criticized the polarizing effects of partisan attacks in Congress.[1]

Romney and Obama are not alone. A favorite theme of recent candidates for president and Congress has been that they can rise above the bitter partisan atmosphere in Washington, D.C. The news media also play on concerns that party politics distracts government from important goals. Reporters and commentators often contend that the parties are merely interested in winning elections and not necessarily in doing what is good for the country. "Party Gridlock in Washington Feeds Fear of a Debt Crisis" and "Partisan Clashes Jeopardize Small Business, Energy Bills," declare two typical recent headlines.[2] Critics charge that leaders of the two major parties want to embarrass each other more than they want to work together to pass bipartisan legislation.

A large majority of Americans identify themselves in surveys as either Republicans or Democrats, but even among partisan loyalists, the two parties are usually seen as necessary evils. In fact, according to surveys, most Americans think that parties in general are bad for democratic politics—that they are corrupt, lead to gridlock in government, and make people inflexible in dealing with new problems as they arise. In one national survey in 2010, for example, 48 percent of respondents said they were

---

[1] Alec MacGillis and Paul Kane, "As Obama Talks of Bipartisanship, Definitions Vary," *Washington Post*, February 2, 2009.

[2] Jackie Calmes, *New York Times*, February 16, 2010; and Naftali Bendavid and Stephen Power, *Wall Street Journal*, July 30, 2010.

angry at both parties, a much larger percentage than expressed anger at only one or neither party.[3]

The tendency to deride political parties is not new. James Madison in *Federalist 10* describes the inevitability of factions (similar to what we know as political parties) competing for influence in a republic. He and the other Founders were motivated to design political institutions precisely to control and soften the negative effects of factional conflict. In one of his final public speeches as the country's first president, George Washington warned that parties were threatening the health of the young republic, and that if politicians continued to divide into parties they would damage the country's viability. In the late nineteenth and early twentieth centuries, election reforms were driven by a widespread perception that corruption in government was due in large part to corruption among state and local party leaders. We continue to see this distrust today: when presidential candidates claim to be able to break through partisan conflict, they are tapping into a long-standing tradition in American history of frustration with partisan rigidity.

A majority of Americans seem to believe that partisan disagreement in Washington is bad for American democracy and that parties do more harm than good in our political system. Political scientists who study parties, however, usually make the opposite argument. They tend to agree with E. E. Schattschneider, who claims that "modern democracy is unthinkable save in terms of political parties."[4] Americans typically vote along partisan lines, and as we saw in Chapter 9, their attitudes toward policies and candidates are profoundly shaped by their partisanship. Politicians in Washington unite with fellow partisans to work toward common goals and thwart opponents. Indeed, as we will learn in this chapter, parties solve a variety of collective dilemmas in the American political system, as well as in other systems. They grease the wheels of democracy. Why are parties and partisanship so widely criticized—but also so indispensable in a democratic system?

---

[3] CNN/Opinion Research Corporation Poll, January 22–24, 2010.

[4] E. E. Schattschneider, *Party Government* (New York: Farrar and Rinehart, 1942).

What Are Parties?

A **political party** can be defined as a group of candidates and elected officials organized under a common label for the purpose of attaining positions of public authority.[5] Parties are not formally part of the American government—the Constitution nowhere mentions them—yet they are key intermediate institutions in the American political system. They are intermediate in the sense that they mediate between the mass public and the government to help make democracy work.

Parties are ubiquitous in the national politics of representative democracies and, in the view of most scholars, essential to the functioning of elections and governing. Parties seem to "sprout and grow" under the right conditions, taking forms that are both influenced and shaped by that environment. In fact, data show that wherever mass elections are conducted freely and fairly, and wherever a legislature has meaningful policy power, political parties arise and play a central role. This is just as true in the newest democracies in the least developed parts of the world as it is in cities and most localities across the United States.[6]

The preceding definition seems simple enough, but it obscures a fundamental fact: parties are complex organizations, especially in the American political system. One reason many Americans view parties negatively is that they often do not understand what parties do. Parties organize politics in the American political system, but they are not singular, tightly unified organizations. Each of the major parties consists of multiple organizations that are linked by labels and by loose ideological affinity. Their complexity makes it more difficult to appreciate the purpose parties serve in the American political system.

Scholars have sought to help people understand parties by dividing their functions and operations into three categories:

- *Parties in government:* Parties organize governmental action, especially in legislatures and parliaments. They influence how people in public office cooperate with one another to form teams and achieve policy goals.

- *Parties as organizations:* Parties organize efforts of candidates, politicians, and voters to win elections. They choose candidates to be on election ballots, help these candidates raise money, run campaigns, and turn out voters.

- *Parties in the electorate:* Parties orient voters' thinking by providing intellectual categories. Identifying with a party helps people link the party's values with their own beliefs and interests, engendering loyalty in the voting booth. Party labels also make it easier for citizens who share common

> **political party** A group of candidates and elected officials organized under a common label for the purpose of attaining positions of public authority.

---

[5] The party can include close supporters who work on behalf of candidates and public officials.

[6] Exceptions in American politics occur when states or localities mandate that elections be "nonpartisan," which means that candidates for office are not identified by party label on election ballots. In this case, laws inhibit some party functions. Many cities have formally nonpartisan elections for their city councils, and the Nebraska state legislature formally has nonpartisan elections at all levels, though it is important to note that within the legislature the members behave as though they belong to parties.

beliefs and interests to coordinate their actions during elections, including voting and donating time and money, toward a unified goal.

These three functions reinforce each other. For example, the Republican Party members in Congress and (when in power) in the presidency work together to enact conservative policies—lower taxes and lower government spending, a robust U.S. military policy, and traditional social mores. This example illustrates the party in government.

Republican members of Congress sit in those seats because Republican Party organizations throughout the country appeal to people who want those things, and the party organizations try to get those people to donate to the party. The organizations distribute donated money among candidates, assist candidates in developing campaign advertisements touting conservative values, and help turn out conservative voters on election days. This is the party as organization, serving candidates and politicians in their desire to win and keep office.

The actions by Republicans in government also help increase the appeal of the party to voters who want conservative policies. These voters, in turn, develop loyalties to the Republican Party. The party reputation among potential voters creates groups of loyal voters, and those groups of loyal voters make up the party in the electorate.

Success in one area contributes to success in the other two. Let us now discuss each of these functions in more detail, referring to Figure 12.1.

Parties in Government

In every mature democracy in the world, including the United States, national governments are run by political parties. That is, the leaders of the government are also leaders of their political parties, and they use the machinery of their parties to organize the activities of the government—to draft and pass legislation, to place top bureaucrats in the executive agencies, and to formulate broad policy goals.

Party leadership and governmental leadership are fused in most countries. In parliamentary democracies such as Britain, Germany, or Japan, the prime minister or other head of government is the leader of his or her party. If the party decides to change leaders, the prime minister steps down and gives way to the new party leader. Moreover, as we will discuss in more detail later, members of the parties in the parliament almost always vote as blocs, with rare defections.

The role of parties in the U.S. government is more complicated because of the separation-of-powers system. Generally, the president is considered the head of his party, while the speaker of the House and the Senate majority leader are among the top leaders in their parties. In light of the possibility of divided government—the situation in which one party controls the presidency while another controls at least one chamber of Congress—we cannot always say that one party or the other controls the national government. Only if one party controls the presidency, the House, and the Senate can we say that it controls

FIGURE 12.1

Three Roles of Parties

Parties operate in the electorate by shaping the way voters understand the political world. They are instruments of political identification, affiliation, and information for voters. Parties also are organizations by which candidates and interested citizens can aggregate to effect policy change. In this light, they serve as infrastructure for candidates to gather resources for elections. Parties organize government action in that collective decisions like passing legislation are made by coalitional work among like-minded lawmakers.

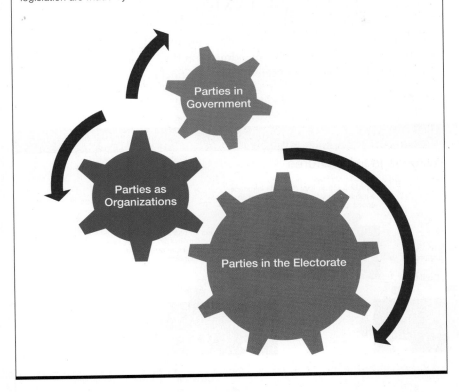

the government. Moreover, party control of a chamber of Congress is by no means straightforward. Unlike legislators in many other countries, members of Congress do not always vote according to their party leaders' recommendations. (We discussed this topic in Chapter 5 and will return to it later in this chapter.)

Why are parties so central to governing, especially in legislatures? To answer this question, it is helpful to consider a process of making policy decisions in the absence of parties. The following story highlights the role that parties play in controlling agendas and keeping policy-making coalitions together, and, more generally, in solving collective dilemmas inside legislatures.

Unstable Coalitions in Legislatures In Chapter 1, we discussed the concept of an unstable coalition, which is one kind of collective dilemma. We revisited the concept in Chapter 5 with an example from a hypothetical legislature. Let us now reconsider the situation in a new hypothetical legislature, which we will call the House of Delegates. (See Figure 12.2.)

Suppose for the sake of argument that there are three roughly equal-sized groups in the House and that they each vote as blocs—that is, each legislator within a group votes as the leader of that group says to vote. One group represents students, another represents veterans, and another represents farmers. As expected, they legislate by majority rule, and here this means that any two of the groups joining together can pass a law. A bill can be proposed by any one leader of a group, and a vote is held—yea or nay—on the bill. Before voting on a bill, though, the leader of any other group can stand up and propose an amendment. Members can propose as many amendments as they wish. Each of the amendments must be approved or rejected before the final bill is voted on.

FIGURE 12.2

Parties and Unstable Coalitions in Legislatures

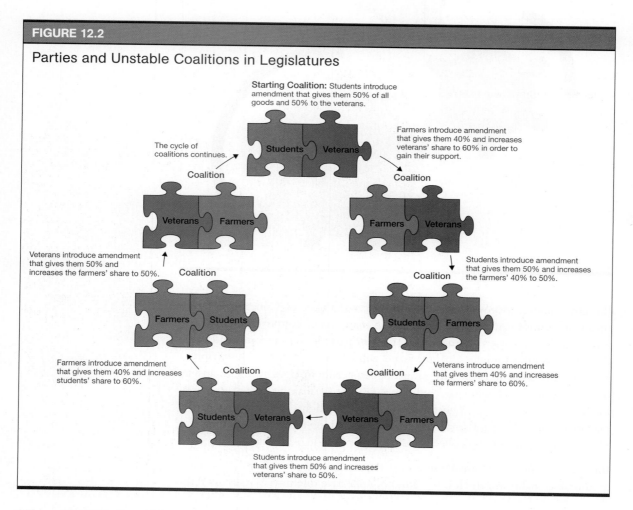

Starting Coalition: Students introduce amendment that gives them 50% of all goods and 50% to the veterans.

Farmers introduce amendment that gives them 40% and increases veterans' share to 60% in order to gain their support.

Students introduce amendment that gives them 50% and increases the farmers' 40% to 50%.

Veterans introduce amendment that gives them 40% and increases the farmers' share to 60%.

Students introduce amendment that gives them 50% and increases veterans' share to 50%.

Farmers introduce amendment that gives them 40% and increases students' share to 60%.

Veterans introduce amendment that gives them 50% and increases the farmers' share to 50%.

The cycle of coalitions continues.

Coalition

In our simple scenario, the members of the House are intent on passing legislation to benefit the people they represent. The ideal bill for, say, the students would tax farmers and veterans and give all the benefits to students. But such a bill would not be supported by the representatives of either the veterans or the farmers. The student group needs to propose legislation that at least one of the other two groups will support. So the student group proposes a bill to tax farmers and spread the benefits between students and veterans in a bid to get the support of the representatives of the veterans. In short, students and veterans get everything they want under this bill, and farmers get nothing but higher taxes.

Now let's say that the leader of the farmers group proposes an amendment that effectively changes the entire bill. Under the amendment, veterans and farmers benefit from the public good and the taxes fall entirely on students. To win the support of the representatives of the veterans, the farmers group offers slightly more of the public good to veterans than the previous students' bill was proposing. In short, veterans and farmers get everything they want, while students get nothing but higher taxes.

Before any of this can be voted on, however, the student group proposes an amendment to the farmers' amendment. As you might guess, the goal of the students is to entice the farmers to join with the students and to tax veterans. Then the representatives of the veterans respond by attaching an amendment to the students' amendment, this time proposing a coalition of veterans and farmers, with students paying for the public good with taxes. In theory, this amendment process can go on forever. Note that eventually, the House will end up repeating the coalitions, sometimes students and farmers, sometimes students and veterans, and so on, as it repeats the process. The coalitions can "cycle" if no one controls the agenda.

In Chapter 1, we noted that coalition cycles can be prevented by putting institutions in place to assign agenda-setting control to specific members of a decision-making body. In our simple example, policies and coalitions can cycle indefinitely and end up anywhere the process stops. Imagine how cycling could occur in a representative body as large as the real U.S. House of Representatives, with 435 members representing many more groups than students, veterans, and farmers! All it would take to upset any existing coalition in favor of a bill is for one person to propose an amendment.

Political parties are the key institutions that prevent coalition cycling in legislatures around the

Party leaders in legislatures, like House minority leader Nancy Pelosi, keep coalitions together by imposing discipline on their members. They may use pressure and enticements to ensure that their members vote in line with the party's overall goals.

world. How do parties do this? Members who form parties essentially promise to support each other's bills most of the time and not to propose distracting or potentially divisive amendments. In our example, perhaps farmers and students create a durable coalition by promising to support each other's proposals most of the time, and not to propose something that will split their votes. In this way, parties create reputations for groups of politicians. Students and farmers could label their group something (the Liberal Party, for example) and try to convince voters that they are the reliable representatives for their districts. They signal to voters, "We will support each other in the legislature and thus pass helpful policies for you." The need for a positive reputation among voters gives them incentives to stay consistent in their support for certain kinds of policies and allied with others who tend to agree with them ideologically.

You might ask, why not form a universal party coalition, with farmers, students, and veterans all together? Well, someone needs to pay for the benefits, and those who pay more than the others will need to be left out of the winning coalition and will be unhappy and form the opposition. The view of those who are left out is that hopefully in the next round of elections they can win enough seats to form a majority. The prospect of new elections avoids a situation where opposition parties believe that they will be in opposition forever (and thus is the main difference between a one-party state and a true democracy).

The preceding scenario illustrates why parties are useful, and perhaps even necessary, in any legislative body. Although our example is greatly simplified, there is strong evidence that in the early sessions of Congress, just after the Founding, politicians formed parties in just this manner. At first there were many shifting coalitions, and members of Congress were unhappy with the uncertainty and the difficulty in getting things done. Then, as parties formed and Congress divided into stable coalitions under the party labels, Federalist and Republican—they did so to establish reputations to run for election against their opponents—Congress was able to pass key policies and avoid coalition cycles.[7] In the earliest Congress, the Federalists formed a majority and passed legislation whose costs were imposed primarily on the constituencies of the Republicans. Later, the Republicans won control of the Congress and turned the tables, passing the costs onto the constituencies of the Federalists.

The same function for parties holds true in modern times. We learned in Chapter 5 that parties are key to the workings of Congress. Recall that the two major parties hold their own caucuses (meetings of all party members in Congress) and elect leaders, such as the speaker of the House (if the party holds the majority in that chamber) and the majority-party leaders, whips, the committee and subcommittee chairs, and the leaders of the campaign committees. Of particular importance in the House is the Rules Committee (discussed in Chapter 5), which the majority-party leadership uses to set the agenda for the entire chamber.

[7] John H. Aldrich, *Why Parties? A Second Look* (Chicago: University of Chicago Press, 2011).

In the contemporary Congress, the Republicans have a challenging divide between mainstream Republicans, who tend to be strong on national defense and moderate to conservative on fiscal affairs, and Tea Party Republicans, who favor much smaller government. Both factions within the Republicans tend to favor conservative policies on social issues. A major task of the leaders of the Republican Party is to hold their coalition together and avoid being divided by counter-proposals from the Democrats. When the parties have such factional divides, the potential threat of "cycling" and unstable voting coalitions becomes more palpable, and the need within the party for strong agenda control of the legislative process becomes paramount.

Because political parties are present wherever there are free and fair elections and representative government, and because they largely succeed at controlling agendas, we rarely see the kinds of coalition cycles described earlier within legislative bodies. Parties actively seek to prevent their members from peeling away from coalitions by imposing as much discipline as possible, although, as we will discuss later, they do not always succeed. Besides agenda control, party leaders may apply pressure on reluctant members in the legislature or offer them enticements to vote for party-favored bills, such as pork-barrel projects for their districts (see Chapter 5) or funding for their re-election campaigns.[8]

Parties are also important for presidents and other executives (such as governors), especially in aligning their goals and actions with those of legislatures. President Obama, besides being identified and running for office as a Democrat, received assistance in enacting his policies from Democratic Party organizations both inside and outside Congress. He struggled and competed against the majority Republicans in the House of Representatives. Likewise, his Republican predecessor, George W. Bush, relied on Republicans in Congress and on Republican organizations throughout the country to help achieve his policy goals, and also competed against (at the time) majority Democrats in the House of Representatives.

Parties as Organizations

Outside of the government, the parties' activities mainly have to do with winning elections. Parties as organizations nominate candidates, help candidates get their messages out to potential voters and supporters, hire campaign workers, raise money, and turn out voters on election days. They do this at multiple levels. The national party organizations focus mostly on presidential elections, while state and local organizations focus on congressional elections and elections for state legislatures and governorships.

---

[8] Gary Cox and Mathew McCubbins, *Legislative Leviathan: Party Government in the House*, 2nd ed. (New York: Cambridge University Press, 1993).

Organizational Features In general, American parties are quite loosely organized. They are not strongly hierarchical. The major American parties are large, sprawling, decentralized organizations, much like the government as a whole. In fact, the organizational chart of the Republican and Democratic parties reflects the structure of the federal system within which they operate (Figure 12.3).

In addition to the national party organizations there are state-level party organizations, and within each state there are county-level, and often city-level, units. Local party offices help local candidates with fund-raising and public relations, answer questions from the press and from potential voters, and sometimes act as campaign offices for specific candidates. Candidates for federal office—either the presidency or Congress—also set up their own campaign organizations. So it is not unusual for a given city to have parallel offices supporting the same candidate—one for the candidate's campaign organization and one for the local party. The degree to which these offices coordinate with each other varies tremendously.

The Republican National Committee and the Democratic National Committee oversee the operation of their parties over the entire country. The two **national committees** plot their party's strategy, decide on rules for nominating elections and conventions, and try to coordinate candidates on common campaign themes. These committees are populated by politicians, activists, and major donors. The heads of the committees are often former politicians who

national committee Officials who oversee the operation of their party nationwide.

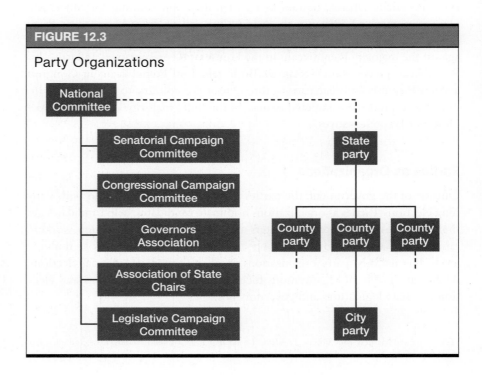

FIGURE 12.3

Party Organizations

National Committee — Senatorial Campaign Committee — Congressional Campaign Committee — Governors Association — Association of State Chairs — Legislative Campaign Committee

State party — County party, County party, County party — City party have standing within the party and untarnished credentials as party loyalists and successful fund-raisers. They can be influential in reshaping the organization of the parties. In the 1980s, for instance, several leaders of the Republican National Committee pushed and prodded state and local party organizations to use direct-mail fund-raising strategies to increase revenues for election campaigns and voter-turnout drives. Similarly, today leaders of both parties work to coordinate Internet fund-raising for their national organizations.

Every four years, the two national committees organize the **national party conventions**, where each party showcases its top politicians (including the candidates for president and vice president) before a nationwide television audience. The national conventions were once the events where the parties actually decided who was going to run for president under their banners. In 1976, for example, it was uncertain going into the Republican national convention whether Gerald Ford or Ronald Reagan would be the party's candidate. (The nomination eventually went to Ford, the incumbent president.) Today, each party's candidates are chosen prior to the convention in a series of state-level primary elections and caucuses. National conventions have become well-scripted celebrations designed to crown the victor within the party. With delegates from all the state-level parties in attendance, conventions tend to resemble pep rallies for sports teams.

Although the national committees set the rules for the national conventions (including who is invited), they have little operational control over lower-level party organizations. They occasionally use punishments or rewards to try to compel lower-level units to comply with national standards or goals. When the national committee is displeased with a state or local organization, for example, it can refuse to seat the organization's delegation at the national convention. In the early 1960s, as the national Democratic Party became more liberal on racial issues, it closed the door to delegations from several southern states in which the local Democratic Party discriminated against black voters and candidates.

Political party organizations at any level—national, state, and local—consist of diverse people with various levels of commitment to the party. Political scientist James Q. Wilson draws a useful contrast between party professionals and party amateurs. **Party professionals** work directly for the party, are loyal to its goal of winning elections, and stay with it over long periods through multiple election cycles. **Party amateurs**, by contrast, are issue activists who are mostly interested in specific policy areas—such as environmentalism, pro-choice or pro-life abortion policies, gun control or gun rights, and health care reform—and work for the party, or for specific politicians within the party, to advance those goals. Amateurs have less direct loyalty to the party than professionals and are often paid by outside interest groups. Wilson's main point is that professionals make the parties run on a day-to-day basis, whereas amateurs push for change within parties when warranted, and sometimes even switch parties.[9]

national party convention The meeting where the party formally nominates its presidential candidate.

party professional A person who works directly for the party, is loyal to its goal of winning elections, and stays with it over long periods through multiple election cycles.

party amateur An issue activist who is mostly interested in specific policy areas and works for the party, or for the specific politicians within the party, to advance these goals.

[9] James Q. Wilson, *Political Organizations* (Princeton, NJ: Princeton University Press, 1995).

Solving Collective Dilemmas among Candidates and Voters Parties as orga-nizations also solve two kinds of collective dilemmas: coordination problems among candidates and voters, and collective-action problems among voters.

One of the major tasks political parties perform is to coordinate candi-dates to run for office. Early in American history, party leaders chose candidates in meetings that were essentially private. These caucuses were often depicted as taking place in **"smoke-filled rooms,"** where party leaders haggled and traded favors to get their chosen candidates on the ballots. Today, most state-level parties hold **primary elections** to choose candidates. As discussed in Chapters 5 and 13, primary elections occur months before Election Day and allow voters to select the candidates who will appear on the ballot under a given party label. In most states, voters can take part in only one of the two parties' primaries. Even when parties hold caucuses today, voters usually need to be registered party members to participate in the process of choosing party leaders. Thus, caucuses are no longer political horse-trading sessions so much as quasi-elections with a selective electorate.

By choosing only one candidate for each office to run under the party label, the party is, in effect, solving the coordination problem for its voters. Once again, let us consider a simplified example. Suppose three people want to win election to Congress from a given district; we'll call them Andy, Bob, and Carla. Andy and Bob are liberal and would like to be listed as Democrats on the ballot, while Carla is the lone conservative and would like to be listed as the Repub-lican nominee. According to polls, 60 percent of the district's voters are liberals who generally vote Democratic and 40 percent are conservatives who generally vote Republican (Figure 12.4).

Early in the campaign, neither Andy nor Bob will step aside to let the other run as the sole liberal Democrat. If only one runs, he can virtually guarantee a vic-tory over Carla, and the majority of liberals in the district will get their preferred

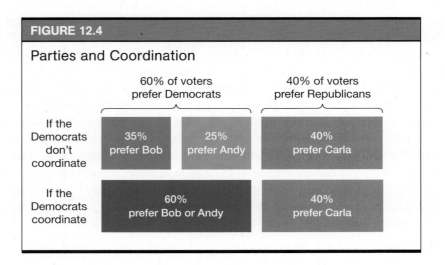

FIGURE 12.4

Parties and Coordination

	60% of voters prefer Democrats		40% of voters prefer Republicans
If the Democrats don't coordinate	35% prefer Bob	25% prefer Andy	40% prefer Carla
If the Democrats coordinate	60% prefer Bob or Andy		40% prefer Carla

ideology represented in Congress. If Andy and Bob both run, however, they may split the liberal vote and throw the election to Carla. The liberals in the district need to find a way to coordinate their efforts on a single candidate. If they fail to coordinate, they may lose the election even though a majority of voters in the district support their ideology. In this case, the local Democratic Party might, with the assistance of the state government, hold a primary election or a caucus to determine which candidate should be listed on the ballot as the Democratic nominee.

There are two important caveats to the notion that parties solve these kinds of coordination problems. First, they need help from the laws regulating elections. The key to parties' ability to solve the coordination problem is that the election laws enforce the rule that the parties "own" their spots on the ballot. Thus, if Andy beats Bob in the party primary, then the Democrats mandate that Bob cannot run for election as a Democrat. The law enforces the rule that the parties control how many people can run under their labels. In principle, Bob could leave the party and run under another party label or as an independent, but unless he is extraordinarily popular, he will likely lose, given party loyalties in the electorate. It is rare in the United States for someone running for national or state office to lose a primary election and then quit the party to run under another party label.[10]

Second, party organizations must do more than just solve coordination problems among candidates and voters; they must also solve such problems between voters, funders, and publicists. As we've seen, parties take strong action to set the agenda for voters, which essentially means choosing the set of candidates available on ballots. But beyond just the leaders of parties, other elite actors, including the major funders, interest group leaders, and activists, play a predominant role in throwing their support behind a small number of viable candidates, signaling to primary voters and party leaders that these are the candidates on which to coordinate.[11]

Also, as we learned in Chapter 10, voters face a collective-action problem in deciding whether to participate in elections. Because voting can be costly and elections almost never turn on a single vote, it may be rational for people to stay home, free ride, and let others vote. The problem for political parties is that they need "their" voters to turn out to defeat the other parties' candidates. The party that best solves the collective-action problem among its loyal voters stands the best chance of winning the election. Thus, party organizations try to make it easier for voters to understand their options and get to the polls. They subsidize transportation to the polls, make phone calls to convince voters

---

[10] It can happen, of course. In 2010, Florida's incumbent governor, Republican Charlie Crist, lost his party's primary for a Senate seat and ran in the general election as an independent against Republican and Democratic opponents. The Republican, Marco Rubio, won the general election.

[11] Marty Cohen, David Karol, Hans Noel, and John Zaller, *The Party Decides: Presidential Nominations Before and After Reform* (Chicago: University of Chicago Press, 2008).

that their votes count, and highlight the benefits that the party's candidates will bring to the district (or the damage their opponents will do if they get elected).[12] Organizations advertise the parties' messages widely. They try to make voters see the high stakes involved in the election contests. Party organizations devote considerable efforts to convincing people to turn out to vote and not to free ride off others.

Parties in the Electorate

party identification A psychological attachment or loyalty to a political party.

When scholars refer to parties in the electorate, they mean the large numbers of people with **party identification**, defined as attachment or loyalty to a political party. At any given moment, the political parties have a level of base support among the population—the proportion of people who consider themselves loyal to the party and nearly always vote for its candidates in elections. The Democratic Party, for example, has millions of people who consider themselves loyal Democrats, and that loyalty can be manifest in a variety of ways, from donating money to working for Democratic candidates, supporting the party itself, or simply voting consistently for Democrats. The same is true for the Republican Party.

In Chapter 9, we saw how party identification in the electorate as a whole fluctuates over time in response to world events and the actions of the government. The population samples used in Figure 9.3 are representative of millions of people. Switching our attention now to the individual voter, scholars conceive of party identification in various ways: as a psychological attachment, an informational shortcut, and a running tally of politicians' performance.

Psychological Attachment Many scholars think of party identification as a stable psychological attachment, the perceptual filter through which people learn about politics and evaluate government and politicians. As we learned in Chapter 9, this has been called the Michigan model, after a group of researchers at the University of Michigan in the 1950s and 1960s who promoted this view.[13] People have allegiances to particular parties, allegiances that color how they perceive the political world and how they make voting decisions. The key aspect of this approach is that party identification introduces a bias. When a Democrat learns of a policy action by President Barack Obama, he or she is more inclined than a Republican to trust the president and believe he is doing the right thing, even if the policy is moderately conservative. Although it is generally true that Democrats are more liberal and Republicans more conservative, party identification in this model is more than a proxy for ideology; it structures how individuals perceive the trustworthiness and incentives

[12] See the discussion of negative campaigning in Chapter 13.

[13] Angus Campbell et al., *The American Voter,* unabridged edition (Chicago: University of Chicago Press, 1980).

of people in government, and how they evaluate policies depending on who supports those policies. For Democrats, for example, Democratic politicians are "on their team," and thus Democrats trust that the Democratic politicians act more in their interest than Republicans do.

Informational Shortcut A slightly different way to think about party identification is as an informational shortcut. As discussed in Chapter 9, many people do not pay much attention to politics. Even those who vote regularly often have difficulty grasping all of the information necessary to make good sense of the political system and how it operates. The American political system is complex, and there are many different kinds of elections across levels of government, with numerous candidates and policies at stake. Party identification in the electorate helps people make sense of this complexity. In recent decades, for example, Democratic candidates have generally supported abortion rights, while Republican candidates have opposed them. People can reasonably categorize candidates and politicians simply on the basis of party labels. By making it easier to navigate the political world, such labels substantially reduce the costs of becoming informed.[14]

Running Tally A third way to think about party identification in the electorate is as a "running tally" of the performance of party leaders. The thinking goes like this: I will be a Republican (or a Democrat) as long as the party leaders perform well and to my liking. If my party disappoints me repeatedly and I think the other party might offer better performance, I will switch my allegiance. In this respect, party identification is like loyalty to a brand or individual based on the consistent quality of their products. Just as with your favorite singer or band, politicians with labels like Democrat or Republican have certain features that we want to rely on. We know, for instance, that our favorite band produces great songs and so we continue to pay attention to what they produce and buy their music. But if they then produce a string of songs we do not like, they might cease to be our favorite band and we may cease to buy their music. A party label is not only an informational shortcut but also a marker of quality that has to be repeatedly earned by politicians.

The fact that party labels are like brands helps to explain why officials in the government have incentives to cooperate with one another. For instance, members of Congress from the same party tend to support each others' bills. Cooperation among politicians within the legislature makes it possible for voters to group them under labels such as Democrats (liberals) and Republicans (conservatives). By the same token, political parties seek to build brand loyalty and expand the number of people who support them. Thus, Republicans and Democrats compete to improve their brand to try to win people's loyalty and perhaps induce enduring party identification.

[14] Arthur Lupia and Mathew D. McCubbins, *The Democratic Dilemma: Can Citizens Learn What They Need to Know?* (New York: Cambridge University Press, 1998).

The latter two ways of considering party identification—as an informational shortcut and as a running tally (brand)—differ from the Michigan model in considering party identification less as a psychological bias than as a rational response to complex information or to the performance of people in government.[15] What is not in dispute among anyone who studies public opinion and voting behavior is that party identification is the best predictor of how people will vote in elections.[16] As we will discuss in Chapter 13, party identification within the electorate, in democracies across the world, is the most important factor in determining people's decisions at the polls. Even if a voter is a loyal Democrat who did not like the job that Barack Obama was doing, chances are quite strong that she voted to re-elect Obama in 2012. Her party identification likely overrode her dissatisfaction with the president.

Some scholars have tried to probe more deeply to understand how and why people develop party identification. Not surprisingly, if you are born into a household of loyal Republicans, you will tend to become a loyal Republican as you attain voting age and retain your party loyalty for the rest of your life. That is the usual pattern, but the exceptions are noteworthy. Over the course of several elections, some people do switch their party identification. In the longer term, whole communities and regions commonly switch loyalties in response to changing circumstances. For example, African Americans by and large switched from being loyal Republicans in the early twentieth century to being loyal Democrats by the mid-twentieth century. Conversely, white southerners became increasingly Republican between the 1960s and 1990s. Studies of new democracies have shown that, in situations in which people are voting in a country's first few elections, party identification appears to develop over multiple elections and not right away. The habit of voting for one party because the voter likes the ideology of its candidates tends to lead to lifelong partisan loyalty that often extends across generations as young people adopt the party identification of their parents.

The History of the American Party System

That parties sprout and grow as democratic processes unfold is illustrated by the early American experience. Also apparent throughout the history of American parties is the role that factional splits, and occasional third and minor parties, play in altering the popular coalitions that form around the two major parties.

The world's first modern political parties, the Federalists and Republicans, were born in the United States in the 1790s. There were earlier entities that

[15] Morris Fiorina, "An Outline for a Model of Party Choice," *American Journal of Political Science* 21 (August 1977): 601–25.

[16] Larry M. Bartels, "Partisanship and Voting Behavior, 1952–1996," *American Journal of Political Science* 44 (January 2000): 35–50.

bore some resemblance to parties: in the 1600s, for instance, British members of Parliament divided themselves into groups that tended to vote together. Similarly, the American colonies had party-like organizations within their assemblies, and some of these party labels appeared on election ballots both before and after the Revolution. But such party-like groups were fundamentally different from political parties as we know them today. All modern parties combine the three functions described earlier: they organize government action, field slates of candidates to compete in mass elections, and appeal to voters based on labels. Such parties originated in the era immediately following ratification of the U.S. Constitution. Political scientists divide the history of American political parties into six periods, or systems, that reflect the dynamics between the major parties.

The First Party System

Even though George Washington warned against the formation of parties, the Federalists and Republicans became locked in tight competition for control of Congress and the presidency in the second half of the 1790s. Both parties needed to mobilize voters throughout the country to win elections. Compared to contemporary parties, they operated on a small scale, even relative to the size of the country. As we learned in Chapters 2 and 10, few men were eligible to vote in the early years of the republic, and Congress was relatively small. Nevertheless, these two loosely organized parties resembled modern political parties in linking their partisan labels to policy programs and then asking voters to choose candidates on the basis of those labels. For instance, the Federalists favored a strong national government and leaned toward England, while the Republicans favored states' rights and leaned toward France. Scholars refer to the Federalist versus Republican era, roughly from 1796 to 1824, as the First Party System in the United States.

The Second Party System

By the 1820s, the Federalist Party had become defunct, having lost its popular support because of its opposition to the War of 1812. During the "Era of Good Feelings" that followed, the Republicans faced little opposition and were increasingly being called the Democratic-Republicans, and eventually, the Democrats. The Second Party System began in 1832 with the rise of the Whig Party, which united remnants of the old Federalist Party with disenchanted Democratic-Republicans. The Democratic-Republicans split over presidential candidates in 1828 and 1832; those who followed the leadership of Andrew Jackson became the Democrats, while most others became Whigs. The modern Democratic Party is the oldest active political party in the world, tracing its origins to the 1832 election (even though it emerged out of the older Republican Party).

This Second Party System of Whigs and Democrats lasted until 1860. The Whigs favored active commercial policies to assist manufacturers and business development in the West and Midwest, while the Democrats favored tariffs and states' rights with respect to issues such as slavery. Most presidents in this era were Democrats, but the Whigs won a few national elections and controlled several sessions of Congress in the 1840s.

A major development in political parties occurred during the Second Party System. The Democrats, through state-level organizations and under the guidance of President Martin Van Buren, developed the capacity to mobilize tens of thousands of voters to win congressional seats and choose presidential electors. The parties became oriented toward solving collective dilemmas among voters and getting voters to the polls. This required tremendous organizing skills and the development of complex state-level party organizations. State party conventions not only served as forums to select candidates for election ballots, but also became large, raucous affairs designed to stir up the party faithful and mobilize voters. The Democrats led the way in organizing, but the Whigs made similar gains. By the late 1840s, the Second Party System included two well-organized parties that were adept at turning out vast numbers of voters, or, as we would say today, "energizing their base." Many new voters entered the electoral process because of the mobilizing actions of these two parties. Patronage by presidents also helped in the process by giving citizens incentives to support one party or the other (see Chapters 6 and 7).

The Third Party System

The discord leading up to the Civil War on the issues of slavery and westward expansion split the two major parties and ultimately destroyed the Whigs as a party. Both Whigs and Democrats had anti- and proslavery factions, and the new Republicans, initially a third party challenging the Whigs and Democrats,

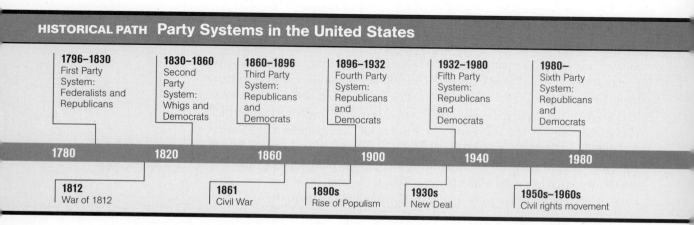

HISTORICAL PATH Party Systems in the United States

1796–1830
First Party System: Federalists and Republicans

1830–1860
Second Party System: Whigs and Democrats

1860–1896
Third Party System: Republicans and Democrats

1896–1932
Fourth Party System: Republicans and Democrats

1932–1980
Fifth Party System: Republicans and Democrats

1980–
Sixth Party System: Republicans and Democrats

1780   1820   1860   1900   1940   1980

1812
War of 1812

1861
Civil War

1890s
Rise of Populism

1930s
New Deal

1950s–1960s
Civil rights movement

emerged from the ashes of the Whig Party in the late 1850s as it split apart. The new Republicans' aim had been to unite antislavery voters from both parties with people who generally favored Whig economic policies, and indeed, most antislavery Democrats became Republicans. In a close race with multiple candidates, Abraham Lincoln won the presidency as a Republican in 1860.

Throughout the Civil War and well into the twentieth century, the Republican Party was identified as mostly northern and to some extent western, and in favor of national policies designed to help manufacturers and mining interests. The Democrats survived the Civil War intact. The South remained staunchly Democratic for another 110 years, largely because of the identification of the Republicans with the Union cause. The Democrats also began to prosper in the latter half of the nineteenth century in large, northern cities. Among working-class and poor (mostly Catholic) immigrants, the Democrats were the partisan counterbalance to the mostly Protestant Republicans. What historians refer to as the Third Party System, which lasted from 1860 to 1896, was evenly balanced (after the Civil War) between Republicans and Democrats, but with a strong sectional flavor. Republicans mostly dominated the Northeast and Midwest, while the Democrats were stronger in the South and in large cities. The two parties were more or less equally strong in the West.[17]

In this era, both parties, but especially the Democrats, developed a system of "machine politics" in northern cities such as Boston, New York, Baltimore, and Chicago. A **political machine** is a local organization that controls the city or county government to such an extent that it can reward whole neighborhoods, wards, and precincts with benefits such as jobs and government programs, in return for supporting the party's candidates. Party machines relied on the use of patronage by local officials to win the loyalty of voters. In the late nineteenth century, political machines were often strong in cities that had large immigrant populations. They devoted considerable effort to obtain citizenship for immigrants so they could vote in elections and support the appropriate party's candidates. The incorporation of new immigrant voters into the electoral process fostered a strong connection between northern, urban Catholics and the Democratic Party.

political machine A local organization that controls the city or county government to such an extent that it can reward whole neighborhoods, wards, and precincts, or other groups with benefits such as jobs and government programs, in return for supporting the party's candidates.

The Fourth Party System

The election of 1896 was a watershed moment that ushered in the Fourth Party System. The election pitted William Jennings Bryan, nominated by both the Democrats and the Populists (a third party), against William McKinley, a pro-business Republican with ties to northern manufacturers and financiers who was intent upon developing the West for the expansion of commerce.

---

[17] William E. Gienapp, *The Origins of the Republican Party, 1852–1856* (New York: Oxford University Press, 1994).

This image shows members of Tammany Hall, a powerful political machine in New York, helping to naturalize immigrants in exchange for votes for the Democratic Party in the 1856 election. As indicated by the man with a club in his hand, this process was not always an innocent one.

At stake in the election was the fate of a brand of government activism promoted by the Populists and some Democrats that would redistribute wealth and power from industrial titans to farmers and the poor. The Populist/Democratic coalition foundered on its own internal splits over racial issues (mostly between southern and northern wings of the Democrats) and over the specific policy proscriptions for redistribution. McKinley won the election by a decisive margin. There was continued sectionalism in this era as well—the South remained strongly Democratic, while the North and Midwest were strongly Republican.

Known mostly for Republican dominance of the national government for the next 34 years, the Fourth Party System saw the rise of the Progressives in 1912, the most potent third party in American history in terms of capturing votes in national elections. The Progressives were mostly former Republicans who mistrusted Democrats—and believed that machine-style politics was hopelessly corrupt—but were in favor of more government regulation than traditional Republicans.

As a political party, the Progressives did not really become prominent until 1912, under the leadership of former President Theodore Roosevelt. But progressive ideals had been a focus of attention in American politics for more than a decade. For most of the nineteenth century, candidates were chosen either informally by local party leaders or by caucuses composed of party leaders and activists. During the first decade of the twentieth century, as part of progressive reforms to reduce corruption in politics, the parties began to use primary

Political Parties

The American Political Parties

- The United States has had two major parties throughout its history, though the identities of those two parties have changed. Currently, the Democratic and Republican parties dominate local, state, and national elections.

  - Other major parties have existed over the course of American history.

    - Most notably, the Federalists, who were infuential in the decades following the Founding, were replaced by the Whigs, who were then replaced by the Republicans.

    - The Democratic Party emerged from the Democratic-Republicans, a party that first arose to compete with the Federalists early in American history.

- Third parties occasionally have influenced politics in the United States.

  - The most important example of such a party is the Progressive Party, which emerged in the late nineteenth century. This party advocated for electoral reforms and for more government intervention in the economy. As with most third-party movements, elements of the Progressives' platform were incorporated into the major parties' platforms.

The American Party System

- Duverger's Law (named after the French political theorist Maurice Duverger) suggests that in a winner-take-all (plurality) electoral system, like that of the United States, where the candidate with the most votes wins a single seat in an election, the number of parties competing to hold office will generally be two.

elections to choose candidates for the general-election ballots. By 1920, most state parties had switched to using primaries for congressional candidates, and the trend in presidential elections during the early twentieth century was an increasing use of primaries. Although the Progressives succeeded in enacting many reforms, they did not last as a political party.

The Fifth Party System

The Fifth Party System, sometimes called the **New Deal Party System**, began in 1932 with the election of Democratic president Franklin Delano Roosevelt (FDR). It was solidified in 1936 with FDR's landslide re-election and the overwhelming victory of the Democrats in Congress. This system lasted until 1980.

New Deal Party System A political alliance between southern Democrats, big-city Democrats, rural voters, and African Americans that endured for several decades after the election of Franklin Roosevelt in 1932.

FDR's New Deal coalition united several large voting blocs for the purpose of winning national elections:

- the southern wing of the Democratic Party
- big-city Democrats from the North and Midwest
- farmers who benefited from New Deal programs and policies
- increasing numbers of African Americans who favored the New Deal and began to see the Democrats as more supportive of their goals

The last two groups—farmers and African Americans—had favored Republicans before the 1930s, so FDR's success in earning their votes for Democrats was a major change. In fact, it ushered in nearly four decades of Democratic dominance of national government.

In the latter half of the twentieth century, as a result of the New Deal policies and the Fifth Party System, Democrats were clearly identified as the more liberal party, emphasizing active government intervention in the economy, civil rights for African Americans and other minorities, and openness to nontraditional social mores. Republicans were identified as the more conservative party, meaning that they preferred less government intervention in the economy, less government spending in general on domestic programs, and more traditional social values. In addition, during the Cold War, Republicans were seen by voters as the more anticommunist of the two parties, advocating an aggressive foreign policy against the Soviet Union.

The Democrats' New Deal coalition was the predominant partisan coalition in American politics in the mid-twentieth century. By the 1980s, however, it began to fray. Largely as a result of the two parties' positions on civil rights, increasing numbers of southern whites switched their support to the Republicans, and by the mid-1990s the once "solidly Democratic" South had become solidly Republican. Meanwhile, Republicans improved their support among Catholics throughout the country. Many Catholics had left big cities to settle in the suburbs, and they supported Republicans because of their stand against abortion rights. The process of Republicans increasingly attracting white southerners and Catholics began under President Richard Nixon, who was first elected in 1968, and came to fruition in the 1980s, when Ronald Reagan won over many former Democrats and helped create the contemporary relationship between the parties.

The Sixth Party System

Most scholars believe that we are now in the Sixth Party System (Table 12.1). It is characterized by many of the same policy positions the two parties took in the New Deal Era, with Democrats generally favoring more activist intervention in the economy and Republicans favoring smaller government. Yet

TABLE 12.1

The Sixth Party System

Democratic votes tend to come from:	Republican votes tend to come from:
Residents of the large cities of the East, Upper Midwest, and West Coast	White suburban residents
African Americans	White rural residents
Jews	Whites in the South
Latinos	Residents of the Mountain West and High Plains
Labor union members	Business owners and executives
Lower income earners	Wealthy retirees
Moderately paid professionals	Well-paid professionals
Gays and lesbians	Religiously observant Christians
Strong environmentalists	Conservatives
Liberals	

the breakdown of voters by region and locale (urban, suburban, and rural) has changed since the Fifth Party System. On average, suburban and rural voters are more Republican than big-city residents. Moreover, the South has switched sides, so to speak, from Democrat to Republican. It is important to emphasize, however, that this partisan imbalance springs from the overwhelmingly Republican leanings of white southerners; African Americans, Hispanics, Jews, and other groups in the South continue to favor the Democrats.

A prominent feature of the Sixth Party System is that the national parties are stronger as organizations than they have ever been. Although they still cannot control lower-level parties to the degree that national parties can in other countries, they have more money and more influence than in any previous era. The strengthening of national party organizations was a key development of the 1980s. Until then, the Democratic and Republican parties functioned primarily as collections of state-level parties that met every four years to choose presidential candidates. Both national parties were relatively weak. They had small budgets, little power over state and local parties, and loose rules for how states chose delegates to the national conventions and candidates for national office.

By the 1980s, led by the Republicans, the two parties developed vast nationwide organizations to raise money for their candidates. The parties began to enforce national rules that reduced the autonomy of the state-level parties. Whereas the state-level parties had been responsible for raising money and mobilizing voters for their own candidates and for the presidential candidates, today's national organizations raise money and dispense it to congressional candidates throughout the country. They often set up their own organizations in the states to assist the party's presidential candidate. These national party organizations now work in parallel with state-level organizations.

As a result, the national parties' power today far exceeds the power they held in the nineteenth and early twentieth centuries. In the 2008 presidential primary season, for example, the national Democratic Party refused for a time to recognize delegates from Michigan and Florida because these states did not strictly follow national party guidelines for when they could hold their primary elections. This was not the first time that something like this had occurred, but instances of the national party imposing its rules on state-level parties have become more frequent in recent decades.[18]

A continuing threat to the contemporary parties is the possibility of internal splits and even third and minor parties appealing to enough voters to thwart election victory. We have already discussed the role the Tea Party has played within the Republican Party. Members of the Tea Party faction have remained mostly loyal to the Republicans in their general elections against Democrats, but within Congress and certainly during the party primaries to choose Republicans candidates, the presence of the Tea Party continues to challenge the Republican leadership as it tries to hold together a unified set of people and principles. Always looming is the possibility that some candidates will run as Tea Party candidates against Republicans and Democrats in races at the local, state, and federal levels; this fills Republican leaders with dread because support for the Tea Party would drain support mostly from Republicans.

Likewise, on the Democratic side, there have been constant complaints from leftists that Presidents Clinton and Obama were not and have not been sufficiently liberal, governed with moderate policies, and compromised too much with Republicans to get policies passed. This sentiment manifested itself concretely when Ralph Nader, a leftist activist who started as a consumer-rights advocate in the 1960s, ran as a third-party candidate for president in the 2000 and 2004 elections (in reaction to the direction the party had taken under Bill Clinton's presidency). There is compelling evidence that Nader's presence in the races sopped voters from Democrats and damaged the candidacies of the party's candidates (Al Gore in 2000 and John Kerry in 2004), taking away just enough popular votes in certain states to cost electoral votes.

Understanding Transitions to New Party Systems

Let's explore more systematically how party coalitions shift and change over time. We know a lot about specific shifts, such as from the Second to the Third Party System in the 1850s, when the slavery issue split both parties and they realigned along sectional lines. But some political scientists and historians have gone further and offered more general explanations that apply across historical periods. In developing theories of partisan realignment, they often focus on transformative elections, such as those of 1896 and 1932. These have been called realigning

[18] John H. Aldrich, *Why Parties? A Second Look.*

The American South experie strong party realignment. For the first half of the twentieth century, the South was solic ocratic. Even segregationist candidates like George Wallace (pictured here campaig Governor of Alabama) were Democrats. In light of the civil rights movement, this bega ange, and by the 1990s, the South was solidly Republican.

(or critical) elections bec ley showcased a transition from one party system to another.[19] In 1932, for e e, many farmers and working-class voters switched to the Democratic Party g the groundwork for the New Deal coalition.

More recent researc altered this picture somewhat, demonstrating that realignments of party c ns usually happen more gradually. For instance, the changes that culminate the New Deal Party System actually began in the 1920s. Likewise, the st shift of southern whites into the Republican Party began as early as the 1 By the 1990s, the emergence of the solidly Republican South was largely lete, but it is misleading to focus exclusively on 1980 as the critical election s important, but so were the elections of 1964, 1968, 1988, and 2000.

One group of sch has proposed a theory of partisan coalition change that pays close attenti the role of activists within the parties in pushing for two kinds of alteratia party strategies. First, activists can convince political leaders within a p to exploit opportunities to win over voters from the other party. Second, ists can mobilize voters to switch party allegiance in line with the appeal oliticians.[20]

[19] V. O. Key, "A Theory o cal Elections," *Journal of Politics* 17 (January 1955): 3–18; Walter Dean Burnham, *Critical Election e Mainsprings of American Politics* (New York: Norton, 1970).

[20] Norman Schofield and Miller, "Elections and Activist Coalitions in the United States," *American Journal of Political Science* y 2007): 518–31.

The abortion issue offers an excellent exa[...]any Democrats in the 1970s and early 1980s—especially Catholics, b[...]working-class evangelical Christians—became disenchanted with the[...]'s position on abortion. The Democrats were pro-choice—that is, in f[...]abortion rights and of upholding the *Roe v. Wade* Supreme Court dec[...]ntiabortion, or pro-life, activists convinced Republican leaders to back[...]tly antiabortion candidates within their party, such as Ronald Reagan,[...]e goal of winning over these Democrats. Meanwhile, these same Repub[...]tivists worked through church organizations and conservative political g[...]o convince voters that the Republican Party was more in tune with the[...]s than the Democratic Party. These activists worked at the elite and mass[...]o gain many new voters for the Republicans. It can be said that pro-[...]activists succeeded in doing the exact opposite for the Democrats—w[...]at the elite and mass levels to convince pro-choice voters to become D[...]ats.

Abortion is only one of many major issues that[...]ffected partisan coalitions. In the late nineteenth century, the issue that[...]d the Democrats and strengthened the Republicans, leading to the Fo[...]arty System, was the controversy over the role of government in regulat[...]economy and redistributing wealth to poorer, more rural parts of the[...]try. In the 1850s and 1860s, as we have seen, it was the issue of slavery[...]tered the makeup of partisan coalitions.

We have told the history of American parties thr[...]he six party systems. By way of summary, let us now consider three long-t[...]ends in the development of parties and the American party system:

- *Increasing democratization:* The parties became[...]e oriented toward including all voters in their decision making ove[...], especially with the advent of primaries to choose candidates to ru[...]er the party labels. By the early twentieth century, the two major [...] were mostly using primary elections instead of party caucuses (smal[...]tings of party loyalists) to choose local candidates and candidates fo[...]gress.

- *More centralized organizations:* The parties becam[...]re nationalized, as distinct from collections of local parties with l[...]n common. Much of this change occurred in the last part of the[...]tieth century and paralleled the increasingly centralized nature of A[...]an federalism (see Chapter 3). These two trends are related, and the[...] strong reasons to believe that the centralization of the political syste[...]used the nationalization of the political parties. This has especially [...]the case since the 1970s, when the major parties became adept at r[...] money for their congressional and presidential candidates.

- *The enduring two-party system:* There has been [...] turbulence and strife in American party history, with some parties [...]g to survive (the Whigs) and others rising (the modern Republica[...]nd some parties being dominant for long periods (as the Republica[...]re between 1896 and 1932). But one thing has stayed constant: the number of serious competitors for control of Congress and of the presidency has always been limited to two.[21] Minor parties have played important roles at times, and have even garnered a significant share of the vote in national elections. Nevertheless, the United States is undeniably the classic case of a two-party system.

Why Two Parties?

Ever since the First Party System pitted the Federalists against the old Republicans in the 1790s, the United States has generally been considered to have a two-party system. Although the names of the major parties have changed, at any given moment in history only two parties have stood a serious chance of capturing the presidency or Congress. Today, and historically since the early twentieth century, more than 95 percent of the votes cast in nearly all elections for national office are for Democrats or Republicans. The occasional exceptions when third parties do reasonably well in runs for president (1912, 1968, 1980, 1992, 2000), or when independents win state-wide or congressional races, are newsworthy because they are unusual (and in the case of presidential third parties, consequential).

No one disputes that the United States has long had a two-party system. Yet throughout American history, minor parties have won a significant share of the popular vote in congressional and presidential elections. This was especially true during the political upheavals of the 1850s and 1890s, when such parties as the Greenbacks, the Union Party, the Populists, and the Progressives all won seats in Congress. Even in the twentieth century, the impact of third-party presidential candidates was significant at times. When Theodore Roosevelt ran as the Progressive candidate in 1912, he won more popular votes and considerably more electoral votes than the Republican incumbent, William Howard Taft, although he lost the election to Democrat Woodrow Wilson. In 1992, independent presidential candidate Ross Perot won 19 percent of the popular vote; in two states, he came in second to Democrat Bill Clinton and ahead of Republican George H. W. Bush (Maine and Utah, respectively).

Beginning in the 1920s, minor parties ceased to win many votes, at least in congressional races. But it is wrong to conclude from this fact that they have not been influential. It is common for minor parties to burst onto the scene, only to have their main issues taken up by the major parties. The income tax, for example, was first proposed by the Populist Party in the early 1890s, promoted by both the Democrats and Progressives, and eventually passed into law in the form of a constitutional amendment. Perot's third-party candidacy brought government deficits to the forefront of presidential politics in the early 1990s, but it was a Democratic

[21] The one possible exception was in 1912, as we will see later.

Though third parties have a very difficult time winning national or even statewide elections, they can influence election outcomes. Third-party candidate Ralph Nader ran for President in 2000 and 2004, and many believe he siphoned off just enough votes from the Democratic candidates to help Republican George W. Bush win both elections.

president, Bill Clinton, who embraced the issue and balanced the federal budget.[22]

The two-party system is unusual outside the United States. Nearly every other country in the world that holds free and fair elections has more than two political parties that compete seriously for national office. It is true that in certain historical periods, two dominant parties in countries such as Great Britain, Uruguay, and Australia have competed for office with no serious opposition from smaller parties. But no other country has had as long a tradition of uninterrupted two-party dominance as the United States.[23] Scholars point to several possible explanations for this example of American exceptionalism, including the electoral system, the changing relationship between the national government and the states, and the actions of the major parties.

The Electoral System

It is well established that countries that hold elections for the national legislature on the basis of single-member districts and plurality voting have fewer political parties than countries that use proportional representation or have more than one representative per district. Put another way, one reason the United States has two major parties as opposed to three, four, or five is the use of single-member legislative districts, in which only one candidate is elected to a given office and whoever gets the most votes wins. This regularity is sometimes referred to as **Duverger's Law**, after the political scientist Maurice Duverger, who wrote in 1954 that "the simple majority, single ballot system favors the two-party system."[24]

In a plurality-rule, single-member-district electoral system, any candidate who fails to win the most votes in a district receives no seat in the legislature or no position in the government. In other words, the losing candidate gets

Duverger's Law A regularity that only two parties tend to compete for control of the government in countries that have single-member, plurality electoral systems.

[22] Note that the Tea Party movement was influential in the 2010 elections, though not as a party but as a movement within a party. This is akin to how the Progressives were a movement within the Republican Party in the early twentieth century. The Progressives only later became their own political party with a brief moment of influence on election outcomes.

[23] Pradeep K. Chhibber and Ken Kollman, *The Formation of National Party Systems: Federalism and Party Competition in Canada, Great Britain, India, and the United States* (Princeton, NJ: Princeton University Press, 2004).

[24] William Riker, "The Two Party System and Duverger's Law," *American Political Science Review* 76 (1982): 753–66; Maurice Duverger, *Political Parties* (London: Methuen, 1954).

nothing in terms of representation, even though he or she may have received only slightly fewer votes than the winner of the election. This is sometimes referred to as the mechanical effect that contributes to Duverger's law.

On a psychological level, Duverger's Law predicts the response among voters to the "winner take all" effect of plurality elections in single-member districts. Suppose there are three people running in a congressional district named Jack, Kerry, and Lisa, and Jack is expected to get small numbers of votes relative to the other two candidates. Now consider all the voters who prefer Jack to the other two candidates; they might vote for Kerry or Lisa to make their votes matter in the election. If a voter's preferred candidate is seen to be unlikely to win, that voter is less likely to support that candidate, thus making the candidate even less likely to win. The candidate's chances of winning the election spiral downward because voters "drop off" in their support as they learn of others dropping off. As a result, only two major candidates are left to contest the election.

This is the heart of Duverger's argument: that voters do not like to waste their votes on candidates or parties that have little or no chance of winning an election, even if the voters prefer those candidates or parties to any other. When countries have proportional representation electoral systems, in contrast, voters can support a minor party and still receive representation. Under proportional representation, in principle, when a party receives 20 percent of the vote it receives 20 percent of the seats. It makes sense, then, that voters feel better about supporting minor parties in proportional representation systems than they do in plurality systems. They get representation despite supporting a party not at the top of the list of vote-getters. The tendency of voters to choose competitive candidates in a plurality system with single-member districts naturally leads to a two-party system, because parties that are expected to come in third (or further behind) in elections cannot convince voters to support them instead of one of the two front-runners.

National–State Political Relations

Some scholars point to the fact that most minor-party activity, especially in congressional elections, died out by the 1930s as evidence that the increasing centralization of American politics at the national level has largely wiped out minor parties. In previous eras, they argue, minor parties tended to derive their strength from specific regions and states. But as power migrated from the states to the national government, voters and potential candidates saw the need to support strong parties across multiple regions, if not the whole country. The American two-party system—comprised of two dominant parties that compete to control Congress and the presidency—has always existed, but a deeper two-party system, with two major parties receiving well over 90 percent of the national vote, has been the reality only since the 1930s. This "deepening" of the two-party system, the argument goes, has been caused by political centralization.[25]

---

[25] Chhibber and Kollman, *The Formation of National Party Systems.*

Ballot Access for Minor Parties

Gary Johnson, the presidential candidate for the Libertarian Party in 2012, sought to have his name and party on ballots in all 50 states plus Washington D.C. It was an arduous process, requiring compliance with different registration rules across many states. Why is this process difficult for minor parties?

Interests

Leaders and candidates from minor political parties, such as the Libertarians, the Greens, and the Constitution parties, and the voters who want to support them wish for fair (and relatively easy) access to ballots in all states. They cannot win more than a few votes if they are not on the ballots. The leaders and candidates from the two major parties, Democrats and Republicans, generally have a shared interest in maintaining dominance and making it difficult for minor parties to get on the ballots in the states. Minor party vote totals are difficult to predict and they siphon votes from the major parties. Meanwhile, state government leaders who manage the electoral process have an interest in making sure that frivolous parties and parties that will garner very few votes will not be on the ballot, because it clutters the ballots, adds work to tally the votes and trivializes an important political process. In their view, only serious parties should have access.

Institutions

The single member, simple plurality electoral system in use in most of the United States makes it difficult for more than two political parties to survive. In addition, the major parties controlling state governments have instituted onerous rules for minor parties to get on state-level ballots, including presidential election ballots. Michigan, for instance, has a "sore loser law," which prohibits a candidate who lost in one party's primary election to run as another party's candidate in the following general election. For example, because Gary Johnson formally ran in the Michigan Republican primary election and lost, this law forbade him from running under the Libertarian Party. As it turns out, Johnson's campaign sent an email to the Michigan Secretary of State stating his intent to withdraw from the primary race.[1] This email, received at 4:03 P.M. on the relevant day, did not meet the 4:00 P.M. withdrawal deadline. As a result, his name appeared on the Michigan ballot as a contender in the Republican primary.

Libertarian Party candidate Gary Johnson running for president in 2012. The rules around American elections make it difficult for third-party candidates to compete with Republicans and Democrats.

The Libertarian Party sued the secretary of state. The court sided, ultimately, with the state of Michigan and against the Libertarian Party.

Outcomes

In the 2012 general election, Johnson's name failed to appear on the presidential election ballot in two states, Michigan and Oklahoma. Johnson's predicament reflects the issue of ballot access, and the difficulty that third-party candidates experience in trying to gain a spot on the ballot due to different kinds of state laws. Most minor party candidates are not nearly as successful as Johnson, who received 1.2 million votes nationwide.

Republicans and Democrats enjoy a duopoly—that is, they receive the majority share of the electorate's votes, usually much more than 90 percent in statewide and national elections. In addition to the plurality rules, legislation like the "sore loser law" at the state level enable the party duopoly to continue.

Think About It

Is the two-party system healthy for American democracy? Should the electoral rules be changed to make it easier for third parties to get on ballots and survive?

[1] *Libertarian Party of Michigan et al. v. Ruth Johnson,* 12-cv-12782, September 7, 2012, www.ca6.uscourts.gov/opinions.pdf/13a0121p–06.pdf (accessed 11/26/12).

Major-Party Actions

A related argument is that the two major parties, in response to calls for cleaning up corruption within the parties during the Progressive Era, succeeded in passing state laws that made it difficult for minor parties to challenge them. Laws that require a high number of signatures on a petition, make it difficult for parties to get on general-election ballots, or hinder minor parties in running their own primaries can solidify major-party dominance. Perhaps that is why minor parties competing for Congress and state offices "died out" starting in the 1910s, such that they were almost completely gone by the 1930s. This argument is appealing, but it has been challenged by scholars who point to the strength of several minor parties—the Progressives in 1912, the Socialists in the 1930s, and the Prohibitionists in the 1910s and 1920s—in many congressional races after restrictions on minor parties were common.

In Comparison: Parties

The durability of the American two-party system is unusual. Moreover, the makeup of the Democratic and Republican parties, and the way they operate, are unusual in comparison with parties in other countries.

Two Parties versus More Parties

Nearly every other democratic country in the world has more than two parties that compete seriously for seats in the national parliament and have a chance to participate in the government. Most advanced industrial democracies have at least four major parties that win seats in the parliament. Furthermore, governments typically consist of multiple parties. That is, in most democracies, no one party controls a majority of seats in the parliament, and thus multiple parties join together to form a majority and elect the government.

There is great variation in party systems across the world. Germany has six parties that compete seriously for parliament and regularly win seats, while Italy has six parties that win seats in parliament, but more than 27 smaller parties that form coalitions with the six major parties. India has an unusually high number of parties in the national parliament (as many as 26 in recent years); this is largely because there are many state-level parties that send representatives to the national parliament. If the pattern in India were replicated in the United States, it would be as though many states had both national parties—the Democrats and Republicans—running candidates for office, but being challenged seriously by a state party with an entirely different label and pursuing state-specific interests. Imagine if Florida elected to Congress members of a party called the Florida First Party, and these members were not directly aligned with either major national party. This is what happens in India, and in a few other countries such as Brazil and Spain.

Party Discipline

Apart from the larger number of parties and the multiparty composition of governments, parties in other countries tend to be more ideologically cohesive, more centralized, and more disciplined than American parties. By discipline, we mean the degree to which party members in the legislature vote together on bills. A party is said have strict **party discipline** if all its members routinely support its positions and vote accordingly. The degree of party discipline varies across countries. Once again, discipline—or the lack of discipline—is an unusual facet of the American political system in comparison with parties in other democracies.

It is relatively common in the United States for members of a given party in the House or Senate to be divided on a given bill, some voting yea and some voting nay. American politicians' party loyalty is often a matter of degree and depends on context.[26] American political parties are less disciplined in this sense than parties in most Western European countries and in other advanced industrial democracies. In most other democracies, especially parliamentary democracies, it is rare for a member of parliament to vote against the wishes of his or her political party. In fact, some scholars have criticized American parties for being undisciplined and fostering an individualistic set of norms within Congress (see Chapter 5).

The difference in discipline between American parties and parties in other countries is directly related to the process by which candidates get on the ballots. In the United States, who appears on the ballot is determined either by many voters (in a primary election) or by many party members (in a party caucus). This means that if a member of Congress votes against his or her party leadership, it may not matter—in the sense that he or she cannot be left off the next election ballot—as long as voters or party members from the district or state choose that person to run again under the party label. The only people a member of Congress absolutely needs to please are his or her constituents.

To be sure, party leaders can make life uncomfortable for mavericks who vote against the party too often. Parties do this by, for example, funding an opponent in the primary or denying the member of Congress committee assignments that help him or her win re-election. But it is a matter of degree. In the American system, a politician who is popular with his or her constituents does not have to pay much attention to party leaders. This explains why American parties are not terribly disciplined in Congress, at least relative to parties in other countries. As we discussed in Chapter 5, members of Congress operate more as individual politicians with their own bases of popular support, than parliamentarians in other countries. That said, there has a been a rise in party discipline in recent decades because of strong party leadership in Congress.

[26] Gary Cox and Mathew McCubbins, *Setting the Agenda: Responsible Party Government in the U.S. House of Representatives* (New York: Cambridge University Press, 2005).

In contrast, in parliamentary democracies such as the United Kingdom, Canada, or Germany, the national party leaders determine who runs under the party label in the various districts around the country. A member of parliament who votes against the party risks being dropped off the ballot under the party label. His or her political career depends directly on the good wishes of the top leaders of the party. This is because the parties are centralized, and they punish or reward their members depending on how often they vote with the rest of the party. In this rather simple way, parties in parliamentary democracies remain highly disciplined and vote as blocs.

Parties in parliamentary systems are highly disciplined for another reason: if a majority party fails to support the government's position in a so-called **confidence vote**, as a result of which the government is forced to resign and call new elections, then members of parliament risk losing the party's endorsement in the next election. Parliamentarians from the majority are strongly motivated to support the government so as not to risk new elections and the possibility of defeat.

confidence vote A vote held in a parliamentary system that, if it fails, brings on an election and possibly a new set of party leaders.

Another way in which American parties have differed from those in other countries, at least until recently, is in their increasing orientation toward high-profile, personalized campaigning by the parties' leaders. In any given national election in the United States, the candidate for the presidency is the focus of attention and the most visible symbol of the party. He or she appears on television to represent the party's views and sets its priorities following the election. Parties in other democracies have traditionally been more team-based. Candidates ran for election to the parliament under the party label and communicated with the public as a group on the basis of a party platform (a manifesto of policies the party will pursue once in office). The image of the party was what the party stood for collectively. This appears to be changing in many parts of the world. When commentators in other countries refer to the "Americanization" of national elections, they are referring in part to the increasing prominence of the top party leaders as the symbols of the parties—and they do not always mean it as a compliment.

Although there are differences across countries in how parties operate within parliaments and how they are organized, they all share certain common features: they solve collective dilemmas in government, in society at election time (as organizations), and among voters (within the electorate).

Key Intermediate Institutions of Democracy

Parties manage democratic processes by running legislatures, organizing campaigns and elections, and helping voters navigate a complicated political system to guide their choices. The word *ingenious* has been applied to political parties by some scholars because they play so many roles and solve so many problems. This description, however, is somewhat misleading because it implies that someone intentionally designed parties in a certain way. In fact, parties seem to emerge simply because politicians find them useful. People active in politics see their necessity in a variety of different situations. It happens that politicians run as independents and win, and it happens that they switch parties, but these actions are rare, both in the American context and in other democracies.

As we have said, political parties are also "intermediate" institutions. That is, although they are not part of the formal institutions of government—to repeat, they are mentioned nowhere in the Constitution—they are key institutions that mediate between the public and the government to help make democracy work. Parties themselves operate within formal institutions, such as the legislature and system of elections, and serve to aggregate and represent broad interests in society.

To return to the question posed at the beginning of this chapter, we have learned why parties are useful, but why do some people react negatively to parties? Surely voters are uncomfortable with conflicts among politicians that seem to be based more on party labels than on policy positions. But media portrayals of partisan bickering in Washington and in state capitals often ignore the broader context—namely, the integral functions that parties perform in a democracy, indeed in any democracy in the world.

Although voters often take their cues from journalists and commentators who complain about politicians being overly partisan, these same voters use party labels to make their decisions more manageable. A lot of information is contained in a single party label on a ballot; if all politicians were completely independent and no party labels were used, voters would be at a loss when trying to figure out who was responsible for what in the government. Conflict is inevitable in any society. In democracies, parties channel that conflict into legislative and electoral divisions instead of violent opposition and separatism.

FURTHER READING

★ = Included in *Readings in American Politics*, 3e

★ Aldrich, John H., *Why Parties? A Second Look* (Chicago: Chicago University Press, 2011). A direct and complete argument that political parties solve collective dilemmas in government and in society.

Bartels, Larry M., "Partisanship and Voting Behavior, 1952–1996," *American Journal of Political Science* 44 (January 2000): 35–50. Presents evidence from the 1990s that the Michigan model of voting held true in American elections.

Burnham, Walter Dean, *Critical Elections and the Mainsprings of American Politics* (New York: Norton, 1970). A readable account of transformative presidential elections (1800, 1828, 1860, 1896, 1932) shaping the party system.

★ Campbell, Angus, Philip E. Converse, Warren E. Miller, and Donald Stokes, *The American Voter*, unabridged edition (Chicago: University of Chicago Press, 1980). A classic book on voting behavior, influencing voting studies all over the world; presents the Michigan model of voting.

Chhibber, Pradeep K., and Ken Kollman, *The Formation of National Party Systems: Federalism and Party Competition in Canada, Great Britain, India, and the United States* (Princeton, NJ: Princeton University Press, 2004). Argues that the degree of political centralization explains why the United States has two parties, while other countries have more than two parties.

★ Cohen et al., *The Party Decides: Presidential Nominations Before and After Reform* (Chicago: University of Chicago Press, 2008). An in-depth study of the presidential nomination process and the powerful way in which parties wield influence.

Cox, Gary W., and Mathew D. McCubbins, *Legislative Leviathan: Party Government in the House*, 2nd ed. (New York: Cambridge University Press, 1993). A careful argument for parties organizing legislative action and serving the interests of party members.

Duverger, Maurice, *Political Parties* (London: Methuen, 1954). Discusses various facets of parties, especially their organization and the nature of party systems across countries.

Schattschneider, E. E., *Party Government* (New York: Farrar and Rinehart, 1942). A classic argument in favor of the responsible party model of democratic government.

Schofield, Norman, and Gary Miller, "Elections and Activist Coalitions in the United States," *American Journal of Political Science* 51 (July 2007): 518–31. Ties the behavior of party activists to the shifting policy positions of the Democrats and Republicans.

Sundquist, James L., *Dynamics of the Party System: Alignment and Realignment of Political Parties in the United States* (Washington, DC: Brookings Institution, 1983). An insightful study of shifting party coalitions in American history.

KEY TERMS

confidence vote (p. 441)

Duverger's Law (p. 436)

national committee (p. 418)

national party convention (p. 419)

New Deal Party System (p. 429)

party amateur (p. 419)

party discipline (p. 440)

party identification (p. 422)

party professional (p. 419)

political machine (p. 427)

political party (p. 411)

primary election (p. 420)

"smoke-filled room" (p. 420)

Barack Obama and challenger Mitt Romney spent a record-breaking $1 billion on advertising, travel, and extensive campaign organizations during the 2012 presidential election. But did all this campaigning change the outcome of the election?

13

ELECTIONS AND CAMPAIGNS

Research shows that most voters have made up their minds how to vote in national elections well before Election Day and are unlikely to be swayed by campaign messages. Do campaigns matter in national elections, and if so, how?

In 2012, challenger Mitt Romney and incumbent president Barack Obama mounted massive fund-raising appeals to win the presidency. Together, their campaigns collected $1 billion in contributions from thousands of individuals and groups. The money was used for large-scale campaign organizations, for travel and staff salaries, and especially for advertising to promote their candidacies. Moreover, groups outside the candidates' campaign organizations spent an estimated $700 million to try to convince voters to support one or the other of the candidates.

Each presidential candidate tried to define the other as the wrong choice for this time in history. Obama's campaign tagged Romney with being out of touch with ordinary Americans and as someone willing to send American jobs overseas so that a few can become rich. Obama charged that Romney's business experience was mostly in the kinds of activities that Americans do not want—financial transactions that shift money around but do not create jobs. The president claimed that his administration needed more time to complete what he promised in 2008 in his first presidential campaign. He took office during a severe recession, and the economy during his first term was slowly but steadily improving. Romney focused on how the economy was sputtering. He tried to turn his business experience to his advantage, claiming that he knew how to create jobs. Above all, Romney attacked Obama's record, saying repeatedly, "If I become president I'll get America working again. The president hasn't. I will." Romney's central campaign strategy was to remind voters of what they did not like about the results of Obama's presidency. Both men traveled the country, campaigning right up to the morning of Election Day.

Presidential campaigns have been called the grand feasts of American democracy. They rouse millions of people to participate in the political process. In the months and weeks preceding elections, potential voters are bombarded with messages, either from the candidates themselves or from people commenting on the election. Ideally, if not always in practice, presidential campaigns constitute ongoing conversations in which the candidates and the American people deliberate over challenging issues about governance and the country's priorities.

But do campaigns matter for the outcome of national elections? This question may seem strange, given the resources devoted to campaigns and the attention they garner. Consider, however, that the two major-party presidential candidates are usually household names by the time they campaign in the general election. The typical voter tends to know the candidates' positions on the issues of most importance to the voter. Unlike in most presidential primary elections, where the candidates are all from the same party, party identification matters a great deal in determining how individuals vote in general elections (see Chapters 9 and 12). Evidence shows that in national elections for the presidency and Congress, as many as 85 percent of voters have made up their mind well before Election Day. Moreover, according to researchers who study public-opinion trends and campaign rhetoric, few voters are swayed by campaigns in the general election at the presidential level. The state of the economy and people's attitudes toward the incumbent administration are much more important than campaign messages. Finally, most states are sewn up by one candidate by early fall, leaving only a few states up for grabs. Why, then, do candidates and parties raise and spend billions of dollars in national campaigns? Why do they continue to seek national media attention up to the day of the election? If campaigns do in fact sway enough undecided voters to influence the outcome of elections, how does this happen?

What Do Elections Accomplish?

Popular elections are the means by which "government by the people" becomes reality. According to the ideals of democracy, the people should have the final say over who governs them, and this is accomplished through voting in elections. In this chapter, we will analyze the conduct and consequences of American electoral institutions and electoral campaigns. We bring together many of the concepts and topics we have already studied in previous chapters, such as political parties, public opinion, interest groups, and participation. This chapter serves partially as the culmination of earlier topics of study, though it offers new concepts and ways to understand elections and campaigns at a deeper level.

Let us first consider the fundamental purposes of elections. If elections are central to democracy, what do they accomplish? Put another way, what consequences should we expect from our elections? Wise, efficient government decisions? Government that is responsive to public opinion? Scholars have different views about the role of elections in the American-style two-party system, and in democracy in general. We will focus on using a principal-agent framework to understand the purposes of elections because voters (as principals) choose representatives and leaders (as agents) to work on their behalf.

Choosing Competent, Noncorrupt Leaders

Some people argue that elections are primarily about preventing corruption or promoting competence in government, or both. That is, because politicians generally want to win election (and re-election) and stay in office, they have incentives to behave in a manner that pleases constituents. Incompetence and corruption surely are present in politics, but if the electoral institutions are operating properly, most dishonest or incompetent politicians should be weeded out by losing elections.

If promoting competence in government and reducing corruption are the main purposes of democratic elections, then we have two additional ways to consider how elections work. Elections can be a good means for selecting the right types of people to be in office (selection), or they can be a good means for giving incentives to people in office to work hard or be honest (accountability). Let us consider these possible functions of elections using the principal-agent framework that we introduced in Chapter 1 and discussed in detail in Chapter 7.

The selection effect assumes that the goal of elections is to choose good leaders. If we consider voters to be the set of principals who hire an agent to represent them, then as we learned, the agent is an elected official—a member of Congress, a governor, or the president. Recall that the principal-agent "problem" is that agents do not always act the way principals want them to behave. Usually, this is because they do not have exactly the same preferences. The politician may not pay attention to issues that the voters care about, may not want to work as hard as the principals expect, or may want to get rich rather than pass good public policy.

The key is the information about candidates that is revealed *before* the election. When campaigns are truly informative for voters about candidates' strengths and weaknesses, and the parties end up nominating strong candidates, then elections enable the voters (as principals) to choose good government officials (as agents). Voters can make good choices, and the electoral system works. We would say that elections select good politicians and do not select bad ones. Politicians come in different types—some are corrupt or incompetent, for example, and some are neither. The selection effect assumes elections are screening devices to filter out the wrong types of politicians.[1]

The accountability effect assumes that the main function of elections is to give leaders the right incentives. In this view, the reason to have regular elections is to ensure that badly behaving or incompetent government officials are thrown out of office—that is, they are defeated in their bids for re-election. The prospect of losing the next election focuses elected officials on staying honest and working hard to represent voters well. Elections hold politicians accountable once they are in office. The selection effect has to do with what happens before and during the election—choosing good government officials on the basis of the information voters have *before* they vote. The accountability effect, by contrast, focuses on what happens *after* the election—encouraging government officials to avoid the temptation to be lazy or corrupt, and helping voters be aware of how incumbents have been behaving.[2]

What is at stake in depicting elections as mechanisms of either selection or accountability? They offer insight into the kinds of reforms that might be called for when elections do not work well. If elections too frequently lead to the choosing of corrupt politicians—politicians who were corrupt even before the election—we might question the parties' nominating procedures and ask why voters did not have enough information to avoid electing these characters. It could be that the election system is not doing a good job of selecting the right types of politicians. In contrast, politicians may tend to become corrupt once they are in office and then secure re-election time and again because of built-in biases in the system. In that case, we would say that the election system does not do a good job of holding politicians accountable. Is the problem the lack of information during campaigns or the lack of information about what government officials do once in office? Neither way of conceptualizing elections is always valid, and you do not need to choose either the selection approach or the accountability approach as accurate or inaccurate.

---

[1] James Fearon, "Electoral Accountability and the Control of Politicians: Selecting Good Types versus Sanctioning Poor Performance," in *Democracy, Accountability, and Representation*, ed. Adam Przeworski, Susan C. Stokes, and Bernard Manin (New York: Cambridge University Press, 1999), pp. 55–97.

[2] Morris P. Fiorina, *Retrospective Voting in American National Elections* (New Haven, CT: Yale University Press, 1981).

Determining Policy Direction and Ideology

Some people argue that elections are not primarily about preventing corruption and promoting competence, but rather that elections are the means by which the people elect representatives to carry out specific policies—in other words, elections communicate policy intent and steer the directions of government ideologically. Representatives in government can move the country in a liberal direction or a conservative direction, or pursue more moderate policies, depending on the voters' wishes.

By way of illustration, consider two approaches to American national elections that link election outcomes and the ideological direction of government. These two approaches focus on the competition between the two national parties for control of the presidency and Congress.

One approach examines the pressures of the two parties to converge on moderate positions. This approach is an extension of a famous argument from theoretical economics called the **median voter theorem.** The theorem holds that if voters are arrayed along a line according to their ideology, and none of the voters controls the agenda, the voter at the exact midpoint of that line will get exactly the policies he or she favors. The median voter's most preferred ideology will prevail. The logic is that any majority coalition of voters supporting a proposal would have to include the median voter, who can "hold out" until exactly what he or she wants is proposed. This approach assumes that politics can be depicted as a competition along a single-dimension line and that no voters abstain.[3]

median voter theorem
A mathematical result showing that the voter with the ideological preference in the middle of the ranking of voters must be satisfied and approve of a majority-rule winning outcome.

A corollary to the median voter theorem holds that if two candidates are competing for votes and can shift their ideological positions to attract new voters, their only equilibrium position is that held by the median voter. This means that if either candidate campaigns based on a position that is not the position of the median voter, then he or she has an incentive to shift toward the median voter and do better in the election. So using this way of thinking, we can predict that candidates in two-party elections will converge on the median voter (again, assuming that no one abstains). And moreover, the median voter is the one principal that the winning candidate (as the agent carrying out policy once in office) has to please.

If all these assumptions hold, we can expect the two candidates to end up being moderate and trying to win over moderate voters, instead of taking ideologically extreme positions. In two-candidate elections, if everyone votes, the voters on the extremes have no choice but to vote for the candidate who is closer to them; hence a candidate can feel comfortable moving as close to the other candidate as possible without crossing over to their ideological side. The other candidate is in the same situation. The two parties are locked in competition to

---

[3] Duncan Black, "On the Rationale of Group Decision-Making," *Journal of Political Economy* 56 (1948): 133–46; Anthony Downs, *An Economic Theory of Democracy* (New York: Harper, 1957).

attract a majority of voters. In order to win, they need to convince the most persuadable voters, the middle-of-the-roaders who may be open to voting for either party depending on how much they like a certain candidate. Thus, the candidates converge on the median voter because to move anywhere else along the line would spell certain defeat.

There is undoubted validity to this line of thinking. In comparison with political parties in other advanced industrial democracies, especially in Europe, the two major American parties are moderate, as we learned in Chapters 9 and 12. There is evidence that presidential candidates seek their nominations by appealing to the party base in primary elections, and then moderate their rhetoric to win over the moderate voters in the general election. Consider this all-too-common scenario: in the primary elections, candidates need to appeal to the median voter *in their parties* to win the nomination; if they win the nomination, they must then appeal to the median voter *in the electorate as a whole*. This means that candidates tend to be more extreme ideologically in primary elections and then moderate their stands during general elections. By the end of the campaign, the candidates will not be very far apart on policy issues; they will both moderate their positions to try to attract independent voters because they know they have their partisans locked up. Following this argument, the policies that gain prominence will not be all that different no matter which party controls the presidency and Congress.[4] Consider that during the 2012 presidential election campaign season, by one interpretation Mitt Romney had to diverge toward extreme Republican primary voters to win the Republican nomination, but then during the general election—facing the Democrat Barack Obama—Romney and his running mate Paul Ryan had to appear more moderate and soften their previously strong conservative positions on issues like immigration, Medicaid, and abortion.

An alternative approach focuses on pressures for candidates or parties to diverge toward the ideological extremes in order to win elections. Candidates and parties need the support of intense partisans, generous donors with strong policy views, and people on the more extreme ends of the ideological spectrum who might not participate if the parties become too moderate. Parties, this line of thinking emphasizes, will respond to their core supporters and will seek to deliver policies favoring distinct industry and population groups (see Figure 13.1). Proponents of this way of thinking of elections note that the two parties

In primary elections, candidates from the same party compete with one another. Here, 2012 presidential candidates Rick Santorum, Mitt Romney, Newt Gingrich, and Ron Paul share the stage at a Republican primary debate. Because primary voters tend to be intense partisans, candidates in primaries often try to appeal to more extreme interests of their parties.

[4] For a classic account of this process, see Benjamin I. Page, *Choices and Echoes in Presidential Elections* (Chicago: University of Chicago Press, 1978).

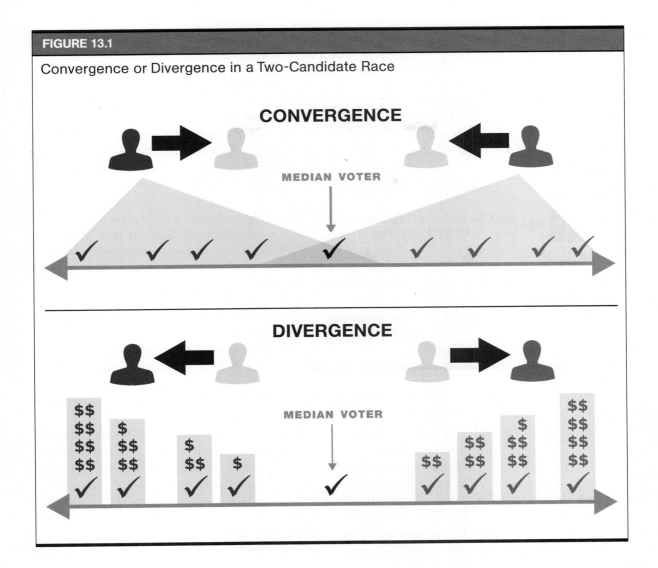

FIGURE 13.1

Convergence or Divergence in a Two-Candidate Race

CONVERGENCE

MEDIAN VOTER

DIVERGENCE

MEDIAN VOTER

often advocate contrasting positions on major policy questions. In the 2012 campaign, for example, Obama and Romney took opposed positions on the Obama health care reforms that had passed in 2012 (Romney promised to repeal the plan if elected), on the desirable size of government, and on weighing women's right to abortion against the possibility of government regulation of abortion. Determining what policies will be pursued after an election depends on which party gets elected; Democrats will adopt different kinds of policies than Republicans.[5]

[5] J. M. Snyder, "Safe Seats, Marginal Seats, and Party Platforms: The Logic of Platform Differentiation," *Economics & Politics* 6, no. 3 (1994): 201–13.

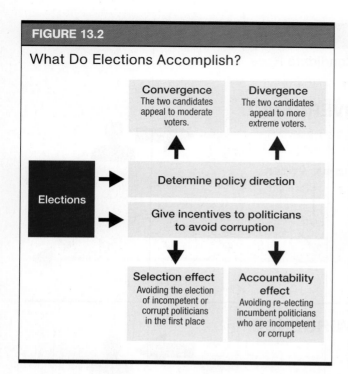

FIGURE 13.2

What Do Elections Accomplish?

Elections

Determine policy direction

→ **Convergence** The two candidates appeal to moderate voters.

→ **Divergence** The two candidates appeal to more extreme voters.

Give incentives to politicians to avoid corruption

↓ **Selection effect** Avoiding the election of incompetent or corrupt politicians in the first place

↓ **Accountability effect** Avoiding re-electing incumbent politicians who are incompetent or corrupt

Which approach to elections and ideological outcomes makes more sense? The different approaches are intended to provide insight into election processes, not to predict outcomes for a specific election. But the reasonable answer to the question is that each approach makes sense in specific contexts. Where candidates end up ideologically in American elections depends to a large extent on how voters at the ideological extremes behave, and on which issues are important to voters and are being considered. If voters at the extremes abstain when candidates get too far from them ideologically, or voters on the extremes are the ones donating money and expecting policies in return for campaign contributions, then the theory that candidates will diverge toward the extremes will prevail. If voters on the extremes vote anyway and are resigned to candidates appealing to moderate voters, and if campaign contributions come from voters across the ideological spectrum, then perhaps the theory that candidates will converge toward the center (that is, the median voter) makes more sense.

It is worth making an intriguing connection from the overall discussion here of the purposes of elections (see Figure 13.2). We have discussed four approaches overall, two having to do with whether elections hinder corruption and promote competence, and two having to do with whether election processes and outcomes guide the government ideologically. Note that if in two-candidate elections the candidates converge on a common ideological position for the reasons discussed earlier, then competence or corruption may be the only feature that distinguishes one from the other. Put simply, if both candidates end up advocating similar issue and ideological positions, then voters have only competence or other nonissue characteristics to use in judging the candidates.

American Electoral Institutions

Elections can lead to desirable goals only if the rules for the conduct of elections are mostly fair and work reasonably well in practice. These rules constitute some of a country's most important political institutions, and they give advantages to some people while disadvantaging others. This does not mean the institutions are necessarily unfair (though they can be at times), but rather that, like all political institutions, their particular features have consequences for who gets what in society, consequences that are not always well understood even by those participating in the electoral processes.

Electoral rules account for the following:

- *How votes are counted and seats are allocated in legislatures.* In the United States, most elections for government office are conducted under plurality rules, which means the person with the most votes wins and there are no runoff elections, and with single-member districts, which means that for a given office only one person is elected from the district.

- *How executives are chosen.* State governors are typically chosen according to plurality rules in statewide elections. The U.S. president is chosen by the electoral college. Electoral college members are elected by plurality rules in most states. This means that the presidential candidate with the most votes in the statewide election wins all the electoral college votes from that state. The candidate with the majority of the college's vote then wins the presidency.

- *Whether, when, and how direct democracy is practiced.* Some elections held in the United States at the state or local level do not elect representatives or executives to office, but rather allow citizens to vote directly on policy issues. Such elections are of two types, referendums and initiatives.

- *How eligible electorates are determined.* The states are charged with maintaining voter registration rolls. Certain federal laws control who is eligible to vote and who must be permitted easy access to voting, but the states still have some leeway to set rules for eligibility. (Most discussion of voter eligibility and turnout occurs in Chapter 10.)

Voting in elections is a hallmark of American democracy, but the institutions of American elections have evolved over time. For example, in the nineteenth century, before the introduction of the "Australian ballot," votes were not private and political parties often printed their own ballots.

These institutional details have important implications for politics and policy. For instance, in some states former felons cannot vote, whereas in other states they can. It has been shown that countries (like the United States) with single-member districts tend to have fewer political parties than other countries, and that the presence of fewer parties tends to lead to more pro-business economic policies compared with countries that have more political parties.[6] These are just a couple of examples of how the nature of the electoral institutions shapes the outcomes that citizens experience in the American political system.

Let us now take a closer look at three aspects of American elections: the role of state-level election laws, plurality rules, and election ballots.

[6] Torsten Persson, Gerard Roland, and Guido Tabellini, "Electoral Rules and Government Spending in Parliamentary Democracies," *Quarterly Journal of Political Science* 2 (2007): 1121–61.

FIGURE 13.3

2012 Electoral Vote Distribution

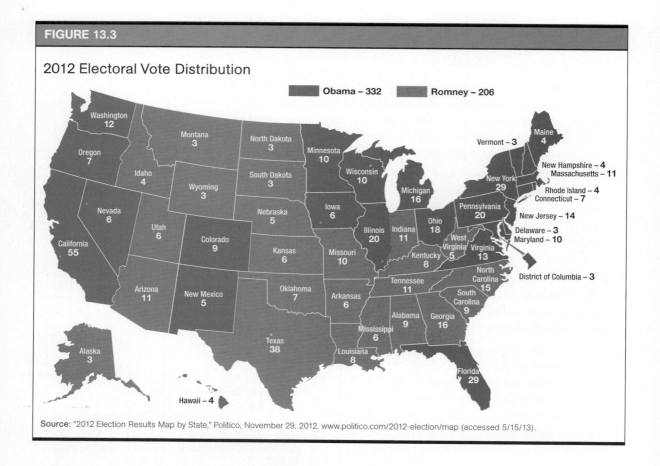

Source: "2012 Election Results Map by State," Politico, November 29, 2012, www.politico.com/2012-election/map (accessed 5/15/13).

State-Level Election Laws

In the United States, as mandated by the Constitution, elections are regulated and operated at the state level. This is true even for elections to national office. In presidential elections, for instance, the Constitution specifies how the electoral college works, how many votes each state has in the college, and what occurs if no candidate receives a majority of the votes (Figure 13.3). The Constitution does not, however, indicate how states should choose their electors for the college. That they are chosen by plurality vote within the states has become customary over time.[7]

By the same token, nothing in the Constitution mandates how states should elect members to the House of Representatives; it says only that they are to be

---

[7] States can alter the methods of choosing electors; in Maine and Nebraska, for instance, electors are chosen in districts, so it is possible that Maine and Nebraska's electoral college votes can be split across multiple candidates (which occurred in Nebraska in 2008). But this is not the typical practice among the states.

chosen "by the people of the several states." Nevertheless, the Constitution does grant Congress broad powers to regulate state-level elections for national office. Article I, Section 4, states: "The Times, Places and Manner of holding Elections for Senators and Representatives, shall be prescribed in each State by the Legislature thereof; but the Congress may at any time by Law make or alter such Regulations."

The states control—under federal supervision in some cases—how electoral districts are drawn for Congress and for state legislatures. Depending on who draws the district boundaries, this can greatly benefit one or the other political party. We have already discussed in Chapter 5 how gerrymandering works and how national courts have, in order to correct for discrimination against disadvantaged minorities, regulated some aspects of how states draw district boundaries. Seats in Congress are reapportioned every 10 years following the national census, and district boundaries for state legislatures and for Congress are often redrawn afterward. Because state governments control the process of drawing district boundaries, the political party in control of a state's government in the few years after a census has the power to draw districts to its advantage. The states also regulate the registration of voters, the counting of ballots, the staffing of polling places, and to varying degrees campaign finance for state office and the operation of primary and general elections.

Beginning in the late nineteenth century, the national government started to mandate certain features of state elections. As a result of congressional statutes, electoral rules have become highly uniform across the 50 states. Congress passed a series of laws requiring the states to hold elections for national office on specific dates, to use single-member districts, and in recent decades to manage voter registration in certain ways. (One example is the Motor Voter Bill, discussed in Chapter 10.) Furthermore, national laws and Supreme Court interpretations of the Constitution have compelled states to change electoral procedures that resulted in systematic discrimination against certain population groups, or violated either the principle of one person/one vote or the First Amendment protections of freedom of speech and association. As we saw in Chapters 4 and 10, much of the federal oversight of state elections resulted from discrimination against African Americans, often in the South.

Nevertheless, the states continue to have wide latitude in running elections. Through the Help America Vote Act of 2002, for example, they can receive money from the national government to improve technology for voting and counting ballots. States that apply for federal funding choose which voting machines to use, how many polling stations to set up, and how to monitor them. In sum, the details of elections are mostly decided upon and entirely implemented by the states.

plurality rule A method for determining an election's winner in which the candidate who receives the most votes wins.

single-member district An electoral district in which a single person is elected to a given office.

Plurality Rule

Most American elections for national office are conducted according to **plurality rule** in **single-member districts**. Typically, each electoral race is

- **Votes and Seats**

  - Nearly all winners of American elections for legislatures and governors are determined in single-member districts and are elected directly by plurality rule with no runoffs.

  - The president and the vice-president are elected indirectly by an electoral college. Each state is allocated a number of electors equal to the total number of its members in the House and Senate. Each elector is given one vote for the president and one vote for the vice-president, and the candidates with an absolute majority of the electoral votes in their respective contests wins the presidency and vice-presidency. (The Twelfth Amendment outlines the procedure invoked when no candidate wins a majority of electoral votes.)

  - Currently, all states choose their electors by a popular vote.

- **How districts are drawn**

  - States divide their seats for the House of Representative into geographic regions called districts. Each district must be of roughly equal population size. However, where the district boundaries are drawn is left primarily to the discretion of state governments.

  - Members of the legislature can use the power to redraw district boundaries in a way that advantages them or their party in future elections. When states draw strangely shaped districts to give a political advantage to one group, it is called gerrymandering.

- **How candidates are chosen**

  - Parties do not want more than one of their members running for a given office at once. Parties hold internal elections to determine their candidates. The elections vary in form.

  - **Primaries** are mass public elections that take place through the ballot process prior to an election for public office.

  - Primaries can either be **open** or **closed**. If only party members are allowed to vote in their party's primary, then the primary election is considered closed. If any registered voters can choose to vote in a party's primary, regardless of membership, then the primary election is considered open.

  - **Caucuses** are formal gatherings of party members who convene to elect their party's candidate for office. Rather than through a public ballot, voting takes place in a private venue (or multiple private venues) where members are asked to vote for the candidate they want to run under the party label.

for a single office from a district or state. The person who receives the most votes wins the election, and there is no runoff to obtain a majority. If more than two candidates run for the office, it is not uncommon for the winner to receive less than 50 percent of the vote. Increasingly, however, states, especially in the South and West, are moving toward a runoff system in which candidates receiving the first or second place finish but not receiving a majority of votes face a runoff election between those top two candidates. The number of states using this system especially for state and local offices has grown but is still small relative to the number using plurality rules.

We have already discussed how elections using single-member districts shape the incentives of members of Congress (Chapter 5) and tend to lead to the two-party system (Chapter 12). Under plurality rule and especially single-member districts, members of Congress work hard to develop reputations for individual competence and willingness to fight for the interests of their single district or state. Moreover, plurality rule combined with single-member districts tends to drive out minor parties because those parties cannot win any representation in Congress unless they win the most votes in district elections.[8] In proportional representation systems with multi-seat districts, by contrast, small parties can gain seats with small proportions of the vote.

As mentioned, other kinds of voting systems are sometimes used, and a few states even depart from plurality rule for national office. In Georgia, for example, a victorious Senate candidate has to receive at least 50 percent of the vote. If no candidate receives 50 percent, a runoff election must be held between the top two vote-getters. Louisiana and Washington State hold an unusual kind of election for national, state, and local offices: candidates from all parties, including multiple candidates from the same party, run together in one primary election. If any candidate receives more than 50 percent of the vote, he or she wins the office. If no one receives more than 50 percent of the vote, there is a runoff between the top two vote-getters, regardless of their party affiliation. So two people from the same party could conceivably face each other in the general election.

Election Ballots

Political parties played a major role in organizing elections until the end of the nineteenth century. Not surprisingly, elections were frequently marred by corruption and bias, as each party tried to skew the results in its favor. For instance, party leaders often handed out distinctively colored party ballots (or had them printed in newspapers) for voters to take into the voting booth. Alternatively, people were simply asked at the voting booth to state their voting intentions orally. Either way, it was difficult in many cases to know if people were being coerced into voting for a particular party. Moreover, because voters' choices were not private, party officials could reward their own voters with bribes or punish voters for the other parties.

As a result of reforms passed during the Progressive Era (in the late nineteenth and early twentieth centuries), state governments stepped in to regulate elections and loosen the grip of the two major parties on the vote-counting process and the allocation of government positions. Supporters of the progressive reforms were primarily motivated by a philosophical preference for transparency in government and fairness in electoral systems, but many progressives also wanted to end the domination of the Republicans and Democrats and open the way for minor parties like the Progressive Party.

[8] Maurice Duverger, *Political Parties* (New York: John Wiley & Sons, 1963); Gary Cox, *Making Votes Count* (Cambridge, UK: Cambridge University Press, 1997).

Australian ballot A type of ballot that lists all candidates running for each office and allows voters to cast their votes secretly and for specific individual candidates.

One key reform was the introduction of the **Australian ballot**, so named because it was first widely used in that country. The Australian ballot, in contrast to a party ballot, is printed by the state government and contains the names of all the candidates or parties participating in the election. Because all ballots look the same, and because voters mark their ballots in the privacy of a voting booth, no one else can know how they voted. This reform greatly reduced the incidence of fraudulent elections. It also enabled voters to "split" their ballots by voting for candidates from different parties, instead of having to choose a single party's slate of candidates for all offices. The Australian ballot is now widely used around the world.

Direct Democracy

Voters who participate in referendums and initiatives are exercising a form of direct democracy that was once common—in ancient Greece, for example—but is relatively rare in the modern world. The initiative and referendum were among the major institutions championed by progressive reformers in the early twentieth century as a way of making the political process more transparent and responsive to the popular will.

referendum An election in which citizens vote directly on whether to overturn a bill or a constitutional amendment that has been passed by the legislature.

Referendums enable voters to accept or reject legislative acts—either laws or constitutional amendments—that have been passed by the state legislature. The legislature controls the agenda in this institutional setup, in the sense that voters react to what has been proposed, rather than proposing legislation themselves. In some states, referendums are held in response to petitions signed by voters who are reacting to what the legislature has done; in other states, the legislature sets the process in motion by, for example, passing a bill that includes a provision mandating a popular referendum on whether it should ultimately become law. **Initiatives** enable voters to decide on questions proposed by a group of citizens. A certain number of signatures on a petition is required to get a question on the ballot. (The number varies from state to state.) Through the initiative process, citizens can place items on the agenda with or without the support of the government in power. State commissions uphold requirements and standards for ballot initiatives, such as ensuring that the question on the ballot is clear and not self-contradictory.

initiative An election held to vote directly on a ballot proposition that was proposed by a group of individuals.

The 50 American states differ on what kinds of direct democracy they allow. Some states hold only referendums, some hold only initiatives, some allow for both, and some do not permit either. The national government does not hold referendums or initiatives.

Direct democracy is controversial. In some quarters, these elections, especially initiatives, are seen to be dominated by special interest groups that pay companies to gather signatures supporting a ballot initiative. Initiatives are often originated by organizations such as environmental or gun control groups or groups seeking to change a state's constitution regarding such matters as

States employ varying methods of direct democracy, including referendum and initiative. Here, teachers, activists, and parents rally support to vote against education reform propositions passed by the Idaho legislature. Voters in Idaho resoundingly rejected these proposals that would have implemented more rigorous evaluations of public school teachers, made it easier to fire teachers, and required more technology in classrooms.

abortion rights or same-sex marriage. Some referendums or initiatives attract a great deal of media attention and cause voters to turn out in high numbers to vote on that one issue. There have been numerous state referendums and initiatives on such controversial issues as medical marijuana, gay marriage, affirmative action, and immigration reform. But many pertain to low-profile issues that few voters care about, or that are arcane or technical. In 2012, voters in Colorado passed an initiative that, among other things, required for state employees that "merit-based appointments be made through a comparative analysis process." Not surprisingly, there was not much media coverage of the initiative relative to a marijuana legalization ballot initiative, though state employees cared about the one on their appointments a great deal.

Some researchers believe that fears of special-interest dominance in direct democracy are largely unfounded. They point to the following common pattern as an example: an initiative is proposed that sounds reasonable, and opinion polls show that voters favor it. Interest groups on both sides of the issue air television advertisements, which give citizens the opportunity to learn about both sides of the argument and make decisions that are on average consistent with their economic interests. Many initiatives fail because the more citizens learn about the consequences of passage, the more skeptical they become. In other words, most voters, using the cues from advertisements on ballot issues, tend to "get it right" in the voting booth. Instead of being persuaded to vote one way or another against their own interests, they learn a good deal from the campaigning on the issue.[9]

American Electoral Campaigns

When voters are choosing representatives or executives in elections, candidates for those positions work hard to win. Winning office through election in the American political system is a process that involves numerous steps. Candidates must obtain a position on the ballot, raise money, decide on a strategy for appealing to voters, get their message out to voters, and let the voters decide. In this section, we will take a closer look at each of these steps.

Getting on the Ballot

For elections to accomplish something meaningful, voters must have meaningful options on the ballots. How do states determine which choices—both for political parties and individual candidates—to present to voters?

In a typical presidential election, numerous political parties other than the Democrats and Republicans are listed on the ballot. (This is also true in elections for Congress or state-level offices.) In 2012 and then again in the 2014 congressional elections, for instance, it was common to see candidates representing the Greens, the Libertarians, or the Independent Party. The names of the parties on the ballot vary from state to state, but the Democratic and Republican parties always appear.

States have generally made it difficult for independent candidates (those who are not affiliated with an organized party) to obtain positions on the general election ballot. Both new parties and independent candidates must satisfy one of two general conditions. Either they need to have secured a certain percentage of the vote (usually 10 or 15 percent) in the previous election for the same office, or they need to submit a petition requesting a space on the ballot signed by a certain number of registered voters. The required number of signatures varies across the states; naturally, the larger it is, the more onerous and expensive is the process of getting on the ballot.

As we discussed in Chapter 12, a key task of political parties is to choose candidates to run under party labels on election ballots. When several people want to run for the same office under the same party label, the party must have some means of choosing among them. Otherwise, the votes of party supporters would be divided among candidates in the general election, which would

---

[9] Elisabeth Gerber, Arthur Lupia, Mathew McCubbins, and Roderick Kiewiet, *Stealing the Initiative* (New York: Prentice Hall, 2000); Arthur Lupia and Mathew D. McCubbins, *The Democratic Dilemma: Can Citizens Learn What They Need to Know?* (New York: Cambridge University Press, 1998).

reduce the party's chances of winning. By choosing who runs under their label in the general election, parties are essentially performing a key act of agenda-control in the American political system. They are determining the slate of candidates that voters can choose among on the general election ballot. Sometimes the parties choose their candidates through meetings (called caucuses, as discussed in Chapter 12) open only to formal party members. But more often parties choose their candidates through primaries.

Recall that primary elections are used in most states to choose candidates for Congress, for state and local offices, and for delegates to the national political conventions that nominate presidential candidates. A primary is a form of mass election and the ballot process is generally open to the public. (In a few states, candidates are selected by party caucuses composed of party members.) Some states hold **open primaries** in which any registered voter can vote, while others hold **closed primaries** in which only those voters registered with a specific political party can vote. By tradition, most states use plurality rules and the candidate who receives the most votes wins.

The differences between primary elections and general elections include the fact that at least two serious candidates within the same party often compete in the primaries. Primaries also generate lower voter turnout than general elections. Research has shown that the average voter in a primary election tends to be more committed to the party cause, more ideologically motivated and extreme, and more affluent and educated than the average voter in a general election,[10] though more recent work suggests that this trend may be changing.[11] Primary elections thus tend to be battles among candidates who claim to be the most authentically committed to the party's goals, but who also must appear to have a good chance of winning the general election against the opposition party's candidate. At this stage in the electoral process, candidates tend to describe themselves less in terms of moderation than in terms of devotion to policy goals that energize activists and garner votes in the primary election.

The nomination of presidential candidates is a long process, beginning in earnest the year before the election. As many as a dozen candidates may compete to become the party's nominee, and in its early stages the competition can seem like a free-for-all. Candidates run in state-level contests, either primary elections or in party caucuses, to earn seats at the national party convention for "their" delegates. The delegates formally select the party's nominee at the convention, but the primary and caucus outcomes prior to the convention make the outcome of the convention a foregone conclusion.

Candidates "test the waters," usually in the Iowa caucuses and the New Hampshire primary, two of the earliest contests. During this preliminary phase

open primary A primary election in which any registered voter can vote, regardless of party affiliation.

closed primary A primary election in which only voters registered with the party can vote.

---

[10] See, for example, Barbara Norrander, "Ideological Representativeness of Presidential Primary Voters," *American Journal of Political Science* 33, no. 3 (1989): 570–87.

[11] See, for example, Alan Abramowitz, "Don't Blame Primary Voters for Polarization," *The Forum* 5, no. 4 (2008).

of the election, the presidential candidates focus on appealing to core party constituencies and often end up criticizing members of their own party. The state contests proceed at a rapid pace. On several key dates, multiple contests are held that often tip the balance toward one of the party's candidates. While Iowa and New Hampshire are important, they are not determinative. Rick Santorum won Iowa in the 2012 Republican nomination process, but ended up losing the nomination. After a lengthy battle throughout the winter, including winning New Hampshire, Mitt Romney surged ahead of his rivals in April 2012 with big wins in five states on the same day, including New York and Pennsylvania. The wins that day essentially locked up the Republican nomination.

Over time, the presidential nomination process has oscillated between granting power to voters and ensuring that key party officeholders have a strong voice in the nomination. In the nineteenth century, nominations often resulted from bargaining among state party chairs and congressional leaders in back rooms at the national conventions; power was clearly in the hands of party leaders. During the twentieth century, the states steadily moved toward adopting primaries and letting the voters choose candidates. This trend culminated in the 1970s when a number of victorious "dark-horse" candidates took party leaders by surprise. In 1972, for example, George McGovern won the Democratic nomination, but lost badly in the general election to Richard Nixon.

The parties reacted by changing the rules in the 1980s and 1990s to offset the power of voters in the primaries. The goal was to give party leaders, who presumably have a better understanding of candidates'"electability" than rank-and-file voters, a larger say in the nomination process. As a result, the modern system of nominating presidential candidates is once again tilted in favor of party power brokers. The Democrats grant heavily weighted votes to so-called PLEO (party leaders and elected officials) delegates to the national convention. The Republicans award states bonus delegates in proportion to how well they delivered Republican votes in previous national elections. Hence, these bonus delegates represent the strongest Republican states with visible, relatively loyal Republican party leaders.

Raising Campaign Money

It costs a lot of money to run a campaign and win office at the national level in the United States. Candidates in Senate races typically raise and spend millions of dollars. House races involve somewhat lower expenditures (the average in the 2014 election cycle was $582,000 for major-party House candidates). Presidential campaigns are vastly more expensive. All told, major-party candidates in the 2012 presidential election, including campaigns for primaries and the general election, raised nearly $1.2 billion.

Election campaigns for Congress and the presidency are largely funded by private contributions. Only presidential candidates are eligible to receive public funding, though the major-party candidates tend not to take the public funds (discussed later). Federal candidates use the money they raise to hire campaign staff, rent offices and equipment, travel, run advertisements, and make and distribute lawn signs, bumper stickers, and T-shirts. Most campaign contributions come from wealthy individuals, interest groups, or groups of wealthy individuals who have a large stake in policies adopted by the national government. Candidates and parties raise money through fund-raising events, direct mail solicitations, and increasingly Internet and e-mail appeals.

Private campaign financing flows through various organizational channels. Individuals can donate directly to a candidate or party. **Political action committees (PACs)** are organizations that raise money for candidates or parties. They can be set up by the employees of a company, members of a union, or any other set of people with common interests. An interest group will often form a PAC (a side organization) with the express purpose of enabling its members to contribute to candidates or parties because the interest group itself is not permitted to give directly. Not surprisingly, the groups that give the most money to candidates in federal elections are those with a huge financial stake in the policy decisions made in Washington, D.C. (Table 13.1).

Since 1974, all such private donations have been regulated by the **Federal Election Commission (FEC)** through a series of laws passed in response to the Watergate scandal. In the first of a series of rulings, the Supreme Court in *Buckley v. Valeo* (1976) established the important precedent that expenditures on behalf of candidates but independent of them could not be regulated because they qualify as First Amendment–protected political speech. The Court did, however, allow the FEC to limit and regulate campaign contributions made directly to candidates and parties. Table 13.2 summarizes the regulations as of 2014. Some regulations limit the amount an individual or organization can give to a political campaign; others prohibit certain kinds of organizations, such as corporations and unions, from contributing directly to candidates or parties.

When the major Supreme Court decision *Citizens United v. FEC* (2010) was announced, striking down many regulations limiting contributions of corporations and unions, the lid was off for campaign contributions. As a result of the ruling, spending "on behalf of" candidates or parties—that is, spending not directly given to candidates or parties or coordinated with them—has no limit even for corporations and unions. Thus, spending by independent groups, especially in television advertising, increased dramatically, to an estimated $1.3 billion for the 2012 federal elections ($700 million in the 2014 midterm elections). This does not count what was spent on state and local campaigns by independent groups.

Individual donations toward candidates and parties are still regulated, but donors can get around many of these legal restrictions by setting up PACs or acting as "bundlers" in order to provide more money to their favored candidate or party. Less formal than PACs, bundlers coordinate the donations of many

political action committee (PAC) A type of organization regulated by the Federal Election Commission that raises money from donors to support the election campaigns of federal political candidates.

Federal Election Commission (FEC) The federal agency that regulates campaign donations to and spending by candidates for Congress and the presidency.

TABLE 13.1

Top Hard Money Contributors to Federal Candidates in the 2014 Election Cycle

	Total Expenditures	Percent to Democrats	Percent to Republicans
ActBlue	$40,511,141	100%	0%
Honeywell International	$4,981,610	42%	58%
National Association of Realtors	$4,665,515	50%	50%
Comcast	$4,532,021	54%	46%
Blue Cross/Blue Shield	$4,311,857	40%	60%
Northrop Grumman	$4,296,324	42%	58%
International Brotherhood of Electrical Workers	$4,090,218	97%	2%
Lockheed Martin	$4,054,674	40%	60%
AT&T	$4,036,101	35%	66%
National Beer Wholesalers Association	$3,972,700	41%	59%
General Electric	$3,953,423	40%	60%
Koch Industries	$3,634,985	1%	99%
Goldman Sachs	$3,407,796	38%	62%
Raytheon Co.	$3,386,648	35%	65%
American Bankers Association	$3,369,323	27%	73%
Berkshire Hathaway	$3,337,908	37%	64%
Operating Engineers Union	$3,251,567	81%	19%
Verizon Communications	$3,189,936	38%	62%
New York Life Insurance	$3,183,881	49%	52%
Deloitte	$3,131,090	39%	61%

Source: The Center for Responsive Politics, "Top Organization Contributors: Hard Money," www.opensecrets.org (accessed 11/6/14).

super PACs A type of organization regulated by the Federal Election Commission that can spend unlimited sums of money to advocate for the election or for the defeat of a candidate, but is prohibited from contributing funds directly to federal campaigns and parties.

individuals and channel them to specific candidates. Through fund-raisers, bundlers combine these individual donations—which are limited by law to $2,600 per candidate—into one lump sum, often tens of thousands of dollars. Jeffrey Katzenberg, chief executive officer of DreamWorks Animation, raised more than $2.3 million as a bundler in the 2012 election. And so-called **super PACs** are those created to spend money independent of the candidates or parties. Following the various court rulings and the resulting hands-off approach of the FEC, there is no limit to how much individuals, corporations, unions, and organizations can

TABLE 13.2

Campaign Contribution Limits for 2013–14

Donors	Recipients				Special Limits
	Candidate Committee	**PAC[1]**	**State, District, and Local Party Committee**	**National Party Committee**	
Individual	$2,600* per election	$5,000 per year	$10,000 per year combined limit	$32,400* per year	
State, District, and Local Party Committee	$5,000 per election combined limit	$5,000 per year combined limit	Unlimited transfers to other party committees		
National Party Committee	$5,000 per election	$5,000 per year	Unlimited transfers to other party committees		$45,400* to Senate candidate per campaign[2]
PAC, Multicandidate[3]	$5,000 per election	$5,000 per year	$5,000 per year combined limit	$15,000 per year	
PAC, Not Multicandidate	$2,600* per election	$5,000 per year	$10,000 per year combined limit	$32,400* per year	

*These limits are increased for inflation in odd-numbered years.

[1] A contribution earmarked for a candidate through a political committee counts against the original contributor's limit for that candidate. In certain circumstances, the contribution also may count against the contributor's limit to the PAC.

[2] This limit is shared by the national committee and the Senate campaign committee.

[3] A multicandidate committee is a political committee with more than 50 contributors that has been registered for at least six months and, with the exception of state party committees, has made contributions to five or more candidates for federal office.

Source: Federal Election Commission, "Contribution Limits for 2013–2014," www.fec.gov (accessed 5/16/13).

donate to and spend through a given super PAC. Ordinary PACs are regulated by the FEC and generally give directly to candidates and parties, while super PACs are subject to very light regulation and spend on behalf of candidates or parties, or in favor of one side on an issue or in favor of an ideological approach.

In the parlance of campaign finance, donations by individuals or PACs to parties or candidates are considered **hard money**, as distinct from **soft money**, which is not given directly to a candidate or party (see Table 13.1 for a list of top hard money contributors in 2014). Soft money is spent on advertising, voter mobilization drives, or other efforts to promote the candidacy of specific people or parties. Much soft money is associated with organizations called **527s** (after the section of the tax code that applies to them) and super PACs, which advocate publicly in favor of a candidate or a position on a ballot initiative. Some of these nonparty organizations have created television ads that are more notable than what the candidates or parties themselves create.

hard money Campaign funds that are given directly to candidates or parties to support a particular candidate, and thus are subject to FEC regulations.

soft money Campaign funds that are given to parties or other organizations to support voter mobilization or voter education activities, and thus typically are not subject to FEC regulations.

527s Organizations that are independent of any party or candidate, and thus are not regulated by the FEC, as they advocate publicly for or against specific candidates, parties, or policies.

In the 2004 presidential election, for example, a coalition of veterans groups and 527s ran commercials attacking Democrat John Kerry for exaggerating his military record. Outside groups in the 2012 election ran advertisements claiming that Mitt Romney was lying about his past actions as a business leader and as a governor, others that Barack Obama was responsible for policies that were actually undertaken by the previous presidential administration of George W. Bush. These commercials were criticized for being misleading, but they were more memorable (and arguably more effective) than other commercials coming from the specific campaign organizations or parties. A recent innovation in political finances comes from the invention of political entities classified as "social welfare" nonprofit groups under the tax code as opposed to 527 groups, which have electoral aims as their primary purpose. By law, these groups are not required to reveal their donors. Their activities, however, have called into question their proper classification (as either political or social welfare), and beginning in 2012, the IRS began to closely scrutinize groups like Crossroads GPS, a conservative social welfare nonprofit group headed by former George W. Bush adviser Karl Rove, that spent millions advocating against President Obama and congressional Democrats.

A few states, including Maine, Vermont, Connecticut, and Arizona, have public funding of election campaigns. Candidates who qualify are given money by their state governments to run their campaigns. Public funding for presidential elections is provided by a special program instituted in the 1970s. The amount of money available is determined by the number of people who check off a special box on their income tax returns indicating that they want to allocate a certain amount (currently three dollars) of their taxes to the presidential candidates. Under this system, candidates who win a certain proportion of the votes during the primaries can tap into the national treasury to pay for their campaigns. In addition, the major-party candidates who end up winning their parties' nominations automatically qualify for a large amount of public funding to run their summer and fall campaigns.

If a state-level candidate accepts public money from his or her state, or if a presidential candidate accepts money from the national government, the candidate must abide by spending limits. Neither Barack Obama nor Mitt Romney accepted public money, and therefore they could spend as much as they wanted. John McCain, likely the last major candidate to do so under the existing system, accepted public money in the 2008 presidential campaign and was able to spend $83 million on the general election. In 2008 Barack Obama chose to forgo public money from the U.S. Treasury. This decision gave him a huge financial advantage in the general election, as he was able to spend nearly three times more than McCain.

Citizens United v. FEC (2010) has clearly changed the campaign-finance landscape. In striking down existing FEC restrictions on corporate and union spending on campaigns, the Court ruled that corporations and unions were "persons" deserving equality under the law and should not be prohibited from exercising their right of free speech in election campaigns, including the right to advertise on behalf of a candidate or party. Some have concluded that the *Citizens United* decision will give a huge advantage in the political system to wealthy corporations and wealthy people. All told, about $6 billion was spent on federal election campaigns in 2012—a record amount by far, even factoring in inflation—and much of that money was given by rich people and rich organizations (though to both major parties). Approximately $3.5 billion was spent on the 2014 federal elections. Yet how much it has or will bias election outcomes systematically has yet to be determined and will be difficult to determine with confidence. Until several campaign cycles have occurred, we will not be able to evaluate the implications of this important ruling by the Court. It is worth noting that many thought the ruling would favor the Republicans, but at least for the presidential election in 2012, pro-Romney and pro-Obama groups spent approximately the same amount. In the 2014 midterm elections, spending by the parties, candidates, and outside groups was roughly equal between the two parties and their supporters.

Campaign Rhetoric and Prisoner's Dilemmas

With money available for campaigning, candidates need to get out their message and motivate their supporters to turn out on Election Day. Candidates have to be strategic in their campaign messages, to consider carefully what the other candidates are communicating, and sometimes to react quickly. They typically use a mixture of messages in their campaigns. For example, they can:

- promote their own qualities and positions on issues (what we might call positive campaigning);
- criticize their opponents for their character and/or their stands on issues (negative campaigning);
- criticize politicians and government in general and claim to be reformers.

Generally, once in the electoral arena, candidates for the major parties consider winning as the ultimate goal. If they believe that negative campaigning will improve their chances of winning, more often than not they will do it. When pressed, many candidates after the election say that they regret having to "go negative." All things being equal, they seem to want to run positive campaigns. However, most candidates would prefer to win by running a negative campaign than to lose by running a positive campaign.

Campaigns between two candidates are like prisoner's dilemmas. In Chapter 1, we discussed the example of two candidates facing off in an election and having to decide whether to spend money and time campaigning. If neither campaigned, the outcome might turn out the same as if they had. But if one campaigns and the other does not, then the campaigning candidate will surely win. One possible reason researchers do not detect many effects of campaigns on election outcomes is that we so rarely observe the situation where only one candidate campaigns. Instead, we observe both

Campaign Finance after *Citizens United*

A fundamental tension in politics concerns the appropriate regulation of campaign spending. The right to engage in political speech—including television commercials, print advertisements, demonstrations and protests—is vigorously protected because the First Amendment guarantees it. The tension is whether something like television advertising on behalf of a candidate, which can cost millions of dollars, should be a right protected under the First Amendment or instead can be restricted because it is an expensive means of communication that gives an unfair advantage to wealthy interests.

Interests

Wealthy people and organizations want to be able to use their resources to try to influence voters and candidates, and they believe they have a right to do so under the Constitution. People and organizations who advocate for the poor and middle class or who feel threatened by the actions of wealthy organizations want more equitable access to the means of communication. They believe the government should be able to restrict some kinds of political speech so that their voices are not drowned out by those who can pay more or that lower cost forms of communication should be made available. Free speech advocates want the government to let all voices be heard in political campaigns.

Institutions

For several decades, the Federal Election Commission (FEC) implemented laws that restricted certain kinds of advertising by corporations and unions prior to an election. In 2010, the Supreme Court struck down these restrictions. The Court ruled in *Citizens United v. Federal Election Committee* that the First Amendment's protection of freedom of speech extends to corporations and unions in the same way that it does for an individual person.[1] In addition, the U.S. Court of Appeals for the District of Columbia decided in that same year in *Speechnow.org v. Federal Election Commission*[2] that organizations and people engaged in independent political speech—that is, money spent on speech and not contributed directly to candidates or parties—could not be subjected to the limits on contributions and spending. Spending limits was an unconstitutional restriction of freedom of speech for such organizations.

After these crucial court decisions, a new kind of campaign finance organization was born, formally called "independent expenditures-only committees" by the

Super PACs are highly controversial. Politicians like Senators Charles Schumer (D–NY), left, and Al Franken (D–MN) sometimes rail against PACs' size and their ability to postpone disclosing names of donors.

FEC. Most people call them super PACs. According to the FEC, these groups can advocate "the election or defeat of clearly identified federal candidates.... [but] expenditures may not be made in concert or cooperation with, or at the request or suggestion of, a candidate, the candidate's campaign or a political party."[3]

Outcomes

By the end of 2014, 1,236 super PACs were registered, spending $340 million to influence the midterm elections. The groups spanned a variety of ideological positions and issues, and a few had very deep pockets. For example, super PAC Freedom Partners Action Fund does not indicate in its public materials that it necessarily supports any one party over another, but it spent $21 million in favor of Republicans or against Democrats in the 2014 midterm elections.

Think About It

Following the 2010 court decisions, there is nothing stopping organizations from spending billions to try to influence voters through advertisements and voter mobilization in federal elections. Is this a problem? If so, how can it be fixed?

[1] "Citizens United v. Federal Election Commission," SCOTUS blog, Bloomberg Law, www.scotusblog.com/case-files/cases/citizens-united-v-federal-election-commission/ (accessed 5/15/13).

[2] 599 F.3d 686 (D.C. Cir. 2010).

[3] 599 F.3d 686 (D.C. Cir. 2010).

candidates campaigning and the outcome being virtually the same as if neither had campaigned. In this situation, the two campaigns "cancel each other out."

Now consider a related situation, this time involving two candidates who are deciding whether to campaign positively or negatively. Suppose, for the sake of argument, that both candidates believe that negative campaigning works better than positive campaigning in persuading voters, but also that negative campaigning harms the overall electoral process.

In Figure 13.4, each of the two candidates has to choose between positive and negative campaigning. All things being equal, both candidates would prefer to campaign positively. Voters would like that too—it would keep the debate surrounding the election enlightened and civil. However, it is all too tempting to campaign negatively. If only one candidate goes negative, he or she wins handily. If they both go negative, the election results (in terms of vote percentages and who wins) are pretty much what they would have been if both stayed positive, but the tone of the election becomes degrading and turns off many voters (and pundits in the media). The equilibrium outcome is negative campaigning by both because they are locked in a prisoner's dilemma–like situation. The temptation to go negative is too great because of the potential payoff.

As in all our prisoner's dilemma depictions, Figure 13.4 leaves out complicating factors. Suppose, for instance, that one of the candidates in the preceding story uses more effective negative campaigning and so the two campaigns do not cancel each other out but instead give one candidate an advantage that would not have occurred without the campaigning. Our depiction here leaves out that factor in order to keep matters simple and to focus on explaining this puzzle: Why would candidates simultaneously campaign negatively and complain about having to do it?

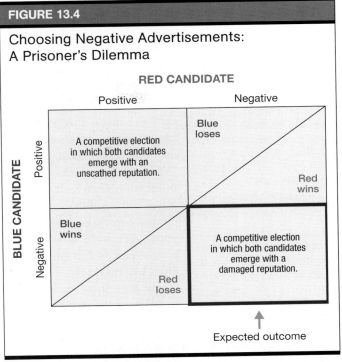

FIGURE 13.4

Choosing Negative Advertisements: A Prisoner's Dilemma

Campaigning with Modern Technologies

A vast majority of elections in the United States, particularly for state and local offices, are conducted on a small scale, with handshakes at fairs, door-to-door leaflet drops, and yard signs and bumper stickers. In nearly all federal elections and statewide elections, by contrast, candidates rely to a considerable extent on electronic media to communicate with voters. These means of electronic communication have profoundly shaped the way campaigns for public office are conducted. (We will discuss the topic of journalism and the general mass media in more detail in Chapter 14.)

We can think of electronic or mass media campaign messages as being relayed to voters in one of two ways: directly, in the form of advertising and speeches, or indirectly, through coverage by journalists, pundits, or bloggers. The former is considered "paid" media, the latter "free" media. Obviously, candidates appreciate free media that portrays them in a positive light. The problem is that they cannot control what others say about them. With paid media, candidates can at least control the messages they are sending to voters.

Before the age of electronic media—that is, before the advent of the telegraph in the mid-nineteenth century—presidential candidates could travel to different places and say different things to different groups of people. A candidate could promise one group of voters a vigorous stand against competition from imported goods, then travel down the road and promise another group of voters a set of policies designed to encourage foreign trade. Since neither group knew what the other had been told, it was unlikely that they would hold the candidate's words against him. Speeches in public squares and essays published in local party newspapers were the primary means of communicating with voters in this era.

Contrast this decentralized mode of campaigning with the situation today, when electronic media transmits a candidate's words around the world in a matter of seconds. This phenomenon began with the telegraph and was extended with the advent of radio, television, the Internet, and now text messaging. Words spoken by or written about politicians can reach all kinds of voters virtually instantaneously. Consequently, candidates are obliged to send out consistent messages, avoid contradictory rhetoric or promises to different groups of voters, and be mindful of the diverse groups that will end up hearing, seeing, or reading a given speech.

This simple observation—that electronic communication has forced candidates to be more careful in what they say—illustrates a broader point: specific kinds of electronic media have changed the nature of campaigns and elections in many fundamental ways. For example, the rapidity with which messages or images can be transmitted has forced candidates to tighten control over the campaign promises they make to voters. It has imposed a certain kind of discipline on candidates and their supporters—a need to stay focused on common themes and messages, and to control the content of all communications.

The advent of television was perhaps the most important turning point in election campaigns. Television offers a highly intimate and immediate method of communication. Beginning in the 1950s and especially the 1960s, when most American families owned televisions, politicians not only had to be eloquent, they also had to look good on the television screen. They needed to communicate in a way that conveyed the force of facial image, voice, and gesture to appeal simultaneously to vast numbers and different kinds of voters. In short, television caused politicians to become mass-marketed products with a consistent brand image across all parts of the country.

Political debates began to be televised in the 1960s. The first televised presidential debates, between Richard Nixon and John F. Kennedy in 1960, were noteworthy for the respective powers of television (visual) and radio (audio). According to polls conducted afterward, more voters watching the debates on television thought Kennedy performed better than Nixon, while more voters listening on the radio thought Nixon performed better than Kennedy. Kennedy, as the more telegenic candidate, represented the wave of the future; ever since then, presidential candidates have had to "win" on television. In the 2008 campaign, Barack Obama, a largely unknown first-term senator from Illinois, became familiar to millions of voters around the country through his performances on television. He was comfortable enough with the medium to buy several 30-minute television advertisements in the last weeks of the campaign, in which he spent much of the time talking directly to the camera. Telegenic candidates like Ronald Reagan, Bill Clinton, and Barack Obama can overcome a lack of experience in the national government or national exposure through powerful performances in this hugely popular format.

Television is also the preferred medium for the short, 15- or 30-second advertisements that are the staple of modern campaigning. Increasingly, television ads are migrating to the Internet through forums like YouTube. These ads range from attacks on opponents to feel-good messages with pleasant images

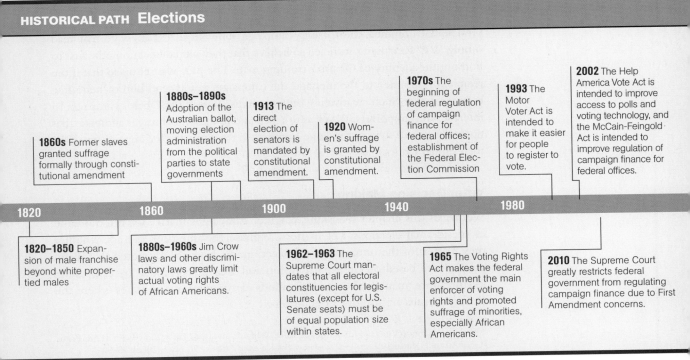

HISTORICAL PATH Elections

1860s Former slaves granted suffrage formally through constitutional amendment

1880s–1890s Adoption of the Australian ballot, moving election administration from the political parties to state governments

1913 The direct election of senators is mandated by constitutional amendment.

1920 Women's suffrage is granted by constitutional amendment.

1970s The beginning of federal regulation of campaign finance for federal offices; establishment of the Federal Election Commission

1993 The Motor Voter Act is intended to make it easier for people to register to vote.

2002 The Help America Vote Act is intended to improve access to polls and voting technology, and the McCain-Feingold Act is intended to improve regulation of campaign finance for federal offices.

1820 — 1860 — 1900 — 1940 — 1980

1820–1850 Expansion of male franchise beyond white propertied males

1880s–1960s Jim Crow laws and other discriminatory laws greatly limit actual voting rights of African Americans.

1962–1963 The Supreme Court mandates that all electoral constituencies for legislatures (except for U.S. Senate seats) must be of equal population size within states.

1965 The Voting Rights Act makes the federal government the main enforcer of voting rights and promoted suffrage of minorities, especially African Americans.

2010 The Supreme Court greatly restricts federal government from regulating campaign finance due to First Amendment concerns.

Today, candidates take advantage of social media to reach new voters and mobilize supporters. Barack Obama's 2012 presidential campaign used Facebook extensively to target key groups of voters and provide them with information that could persuade them to go to the polls. As of fall 2014, Obama's Facebook page had over 43 million "likes."

and upbeat music. The creators of these ads use subtle devices to evoke certain emotions or responses from viewers, in much the same way that television commercials deliberately manipulate our feelings about certain products or services. It has been demonstrated, for example, that when viewers are shown images of racial minorities in campaign advertisements, they tend to use more racist reasoning in making political choices, such as voting or expressing support for certain policies. These same viewers indicate that they are not conscious of the effects of the advertisements on their choices. In other words, much like in product advertising in the business world, political advertising provokes subconscious feelings that affect choices and attitudes.[12]

Beyond the use of television, candidates and parties are increasingly deploying the Internet, social-networking feeds, and cell phones to raise money, communicate their positions on issues to voters and journalists, and mobilize voters. In 2012, both the Romney and the Obama campaigns used these "new media" to connect with potential supporters. The two candidates set up sophisticated websites, promoted themselves on YouTube and Facebook, and stayed in touch with supporters by means of cell phones and text messaging. In 2008, before announcing the vice-presidential nominee, the Obama campaign sent out a text message that read simply, "VP." Recipients were led to believe that they would be among the first to find out the identity of Obama's running mate. The ploy was set up so that if the recipient responded to the message, the campaign would send him or her a free bumper sticker. Such creative use of new media allowed the Obama campaign to interact with supporters, as well as to reach and mobilize a younger audience that normally fails to turn out in large numbers at the polls. Both campaigns in 2012 used similar tactics.

Voter Decision Making

We began this chapter by asking whether campaigns matter for the outcome of presidential elections. Let us now rephrase the question and ask whether they matter for the outcome of *any* election. We have already noted that many people vote based on their partisanship and are not persuaded by campaigns. Furthermore, many make up their minds early on or live in states where the election results are forgone conclusions.

---

[12] Nicholas Valentino, Vincent Hutchings, and Ismail White, "Cues that Matter: How Political Ads Prime Racial Attitudes during Campaigns," *American Political Science Review* 96, no. 1 (2002): 75–90.

Of course, campaigns are not just about persuading people to vote for one candidate or another. They are also about exciting people, mobilizing them to go to the polls, and convincing them to vote for one particular party. In a larger sense, campaigns are part of the process of defining the problems and issues that voters want the government to address.

In some instances, elections come down to a very small number of voters who are genuinely undecided. Swaying a comparative handful of voters in key states could make the difference between winning and losing an election. This happened in the 2000 presidential contest when George W. Bush narrowly won Florida's popular vote by only a few hundred votes (and thus its all-important votes in the electoral college), and again in 2008 when Al Franken won a Senate seat in Minnesota by a paper-thin margin of 312 votes (out of roughly 3 million votes cast). The 2012 presidential election was quite close, with a final popular vote difference of about 3 million, or less than 3 percent. More importantly, key swing states like Ohio and Florida were decided by small margins. This explains why late in the fall of an election year candidates tend to focus their attention on the few geographical areas where undecided voters live. Presidential candidates continue to advertise nationally to make sure voters stay engaged, even in states where they seem to have a secure lead, but they spend most of their time visiting and giving speeches in the so-called swing states.

In previous chapters on public opinion (Chapter 9) and political parties (Chapter 12), we discussed how different groups in the population develop loyalties toward one party or the other. Party identification, we learned, is the best predictor of how most people will vote on Election Day. Other factors matter as well, however, such as evaluations of the incumbents, candidates' positions on issues, and news about corruption and scandal. Voters have been shown to depart often enough from their partisan leanings that the outcome of elections cannot be predicted simply by counting the number of Democrats and Republicans in a given state or congressional district. People might lean toward one party, but in a given election vote for the other party's candidate on the basis of his or her trustworthiness or competence. Moreover, we must not forget that many voters are truly independent and show no consistent preference for one party over another. By one estimate, independent voters comprise roughly 12 percent of the electorate nationwide.

To explain why individuals vote in a certain way, political scientists have developed theories of voter decision making. The following are the four most prominent models of voting that appear in the social science literature.

The Partisan Model This model, also known as the Michigan model, was developed by researchers at the University of Michigan in the 1950s, culminating in publication of the classic book *The American Voter*. The model emphasizes that party identification is a deep psychological attachment to a particular party, and that a voter's partisanship shapes his or her perceptions of facts and issues. For example, Democrats and Republicans will observe certain economic data—say, a troublesome rise in inflation—and assign blame differently to politicians. Democrats are inclined to blame Republicans for causing the inflation, while Republicans are inclined to blame Democrats. The point is that people filter information through their partisanship and come to biased conclusions.[13]

The Retrospective-Voting Model This model emphasizes the many ways in which voters rely on politicians' past performance to make judgments about their competence in office. If the economy is doing poorly, then voters of either party are inclined to blame the incumbent president, or the incumbent president's party, for the problems, and be less inclined to support that party in the next election. Voters look to the past to predict how politicians will fare in the future. The model's logic is rooted in the competence and skill of politicians rather than party identification as a psychological category leading to biased assessments.[14]

The Spatial Model This model considers issues or ideology to be the most important factors in influencing a person's vote. It is called "spatial" because researchers depict voters and politicians as existing in a common space of competition. It is assumed that people vote for the candidate or party closest to them in ideological space. As we discussed in the section on elections as a determinant of policy and ideology direction, competition for office among politicians can be depicted as a movement along an imaginary ideological line in an effort to win over voters. In this model, the key to understanding voting is the assumption that voters know which competitor is closest to them on the line and vote accordingly. In other words, they weigh the candidates' issue positions or ideologies heavily in deciding how to vote.[15]

The Directional Model This model also focuses on ideology, but offers a different interpretation of voting decisions than the spatial model. Voters are interested in knowing in which direction the various parties will shift policy. Voters to the left of the current policy want a party that will be dedicated to moving the policy to the left, while voters to the right of the current policy want a party that will move the policy to the right. The key is not how far away a party or candidate is in a policy space in comparison to the voter's preferred positions (as in the spatial model), but rather on how intensely a party pursues these policies. Thus, leftist voters want candidates or parties to prioritize leftist policies, and vice versa for rightist voters. In spatial terms, leftist voters want parties that are far to the left.[16]

Although political scientists might hold that one or another of these theories is best at explaining voting decisions, it is possible to compromise among several

---

[13] Angus Campbell, Philip E. Converse, Warren E. Miller, and Donald Stokes, *The American Voter* (New York: John Wiley & Sons, 1960).

[14] Fiorina, *Retrospective Voting in American National Elections.*

[15] Anthony Downs, *An Economic Theory of Democracy* (New York: Harper, 1957).

[16] George Rabinowitz and Stuart Elaine Macdonald, "A Directional Theory of Issue Voting," *American Political Science Review* 83 (1989): 93–121.

of them. Evidence remains strong, for example, that party identification is the best predictor of voting, but many scholars have argued that party identification *summarizes* or encompasses these other concepts. That is, voters develop loyalties to parties because those parties appeal to them on the issues, or have in their fold competent incumbent government officials.

Recent research has provided further insight into the conditions under which campaigns can matter in influencing voters. Some scholars have suggested that the presence of a field operation in an area can yield modest effects on a candidate's vote share,[17] while other research has found that both door-to-door canvassing and commercial phone-bank calls can have strong effects on voting choices.[18] In addition, a recent study of presidential campaign advertising suggests that ads can persuade enough voters to swing some elections, even if they do not increase the overall turnout.[19]

In Comparison: Elections

As we have seen in this and previous chapters, American elections have certain well-known features: two-party dominance; candidate-centered elections; freewheeling, open-ended campaigning; fund-raising from private sources; and multiple elections for offices at all levels of government. These features are not found everywhere. Through knowledge of other countries, we can become informed about the consequences of the specific aspects of American institutions, and about what changes might be possible to the American system.

Different Formal Electoral Institutions

The range of electoral rules across countries is too vast to detail here, but we can offer several generalizations. First, several major countries hold single-member plurality elections for the national parliament: the United States, Great Britain, India, and Canada are four examples. This type of electoral system is unusual, however, and is mostly restricted to Britain and its former colonies. Second, it is common for countries to have some form of proportional representation in which the proportion of seats a party holds in parliament is related to the proportion of votes it receives in elections. Third, many countries have complicated voting systems whereby voters can vote for multiple candidates or

---

[17] Seth E. Masket, "Did Obama's Ground Game Matter? The Influence of Local Field Offices during the 2008 Presidential Election," *Public Opinion Quarterly* 73, no. 5 (2009): 1023–39.

[18] Kevin Arceneaux, "I'm Asking for Your Support: The Effects of Personally Delivered Campaign Messages on Voting Decisions and Opinion Formation," *Quarterly Journal of Political Science* 2, no. 1 (2007): 43–65.

[19] Gregory A. Huber and Kevin Arceneaux, "Identifying the Persuasive Effects of Presidential Advertising," *American Journal of Political Science* 51, no. 4 (2007): 957–77.

parties, or can specify a second-favorite choice so that their votes can be transferred to more competitive parties. Fourth, electoral systems around the world tend to encourage the establishment of multiple political parties and to lead to governments in which multiple parties are knit together to form a majority in the parliament. The United States and a few other countries, such as Britain and Canada, are unusual in having single-party majorities controlling the national parliament most of the time.

Party-Centered, Ideological Elections

We discussed in Chapter 12 that national elections in other countries are usually tied more directly to parties and their platforms than to individual politicians. This kind of party-centered election is common in long-standing industrial democracies in Europe, as well as in Australia, Canada, and Japan. In parliamentary contests in the Netherlands, Israel, Italy, or Sweden, voters hardly know the names of the candidates; rather, their vote is based on their favored party. Moreover, voting in other countries tends to involve making selections for a party overall (like voting straight tickets in the United States), while U.S. voters typically choose individual candidates in dozens of elections for various offices. Voters in Oregon, for example, often have more than 100 choices to make on Election Day.

Party-centered campaigning in other countries is more prevalent than in the United States in part because these nations have more competing parties. We described earlier how in the United States there are incentives for candidates of the two major parties to move to the middle to appeal to moderate voters, while taking it for granted that voters who hold more extreme beliefs will vote for them anyway. When there are many parties competing, each party attempts to win as many voters as it can in a relatively narrow range of the ideological space. Party ideology rarely moves much compared to the ideologies of U.S. presidential candidates, which tend to shift toward the moderate center of their party's ideological spectrum. By not shifting positions, the parties in other countries emphasize their ideological credentials.

Limited Campaigning

In many other countries, campaigning for national elections is heavily regulated by the government. For instance, it is common to limit the campaign period to several months before the election. Advertising on television, posting signs, and holding campaign rallies are prohibited before and after the campaign period. Many countries do not allow campaign commercials in the few days prior to an election. All of this might seem appealing to Americans, who experience nearly two years of campaigning for the presidential elections. In South Korea and a few other countries, candidates cannot attack each other verbally. This restriction is interpreted and enforced quite strictly. In political debates, South Korean candidates must stick to descriptions of their policy programs, and they are not permitted to question the character or judgment of the opposition candidates. Such regulations on campaigning are unheard of in the American system, where the legal system places tremendous value on the freedom of political speech.

Public Financing of Campaigns

Although the United States has limited public funding for campaigns, the bulk of money spent on campaigning comes from private sources such as individuals and interest groups. Private campaign financing was common in other countries earlier in the twentieth century. For the past four or five decades, however, it has become the norm in other developed countries for the government to fund campaigns for political parties that stand a realistic chance of winning seats in parliament. Typically, formulas are used to determine how much money a party receives based on its performance in previous elections. The idea behind these policies is that private money can be corrupting. So, by giving every party some government funds, voters will get the information they need to make the appropriate choices and politicians will not feel beholden to special interests that donated to their campaign.

In sum, from a comparative international perspective, American elections and campaigns are unusual. Other countries have different features, often stemming from changes to their election rules in the twentieth century designed to achieve specific purposes. Are there aspects of American elections and campaigns that could be improved? Put another way, what, if anything, can we learn from other countries?

Is There a Need for Reform?

We began this chapter with a question: Do campaigns matter? There are two ways of approaching an answer. First, we can summarize research on how individual voters react to campaign messages. We have learned that campaigns probably do not matter for most voters, but for the small number who might switch from one party to another, they can be decisive. In two-party elections, under the ideas that follow from the median voter theorem discussed earlier in the chapter, the parties can be similar in their ideologies. Furthermore, it might be the perceptions among voters about competence or corruption that distinguish the parties or candidates. Thus, if we accept the convergence theory and the selection effect, elections can hinge on that small number of voters who listen to campaign messages about the individual characteristics of the candidates. So, yes, campaigns can change some voters' minds, though that number is relatively small.

Second, we can think about campaigns in terms of their overall effects on election outcomes, and also on candidates' motivations for campaigning in particular ways. A prisoner's dilemma framework is useful here. If only one of the two major-party candidates conducted a vigorous campaign, then campaigning would likely matter. But since ordinarily both major-party candidates campaign with intensity, the two campaigns may cancel each other out, and it can seem as though campaigning does not matter much. In fact, campaigning matters for each candidate in canceling out the effects of the campaigning of the other. If, however, campaigns reveal information about candidates that tilt voters toward one candidate or the other, then campaigns do not cancel each other out but can shift the outcome.

Now consider a different question: Do the specific electoral institutions in the United States matter? The institutions we have studied throughout this book address a range of collective dilemmas relating to how political parties are organized and mobilize voters; how interest groups and PACs endorse candidates and fund them; how mass media outlets inform voters; how primary elections or party caucuses lead to voter and candidate coordination; and how state-level regulations, intraparty organizations, and campaign finance affect elections.

Some of these institutions or institutional features are more successful than others. The American political parties do quite well in coordinating voters and candidates and in mobilizing fund-raisers. They perhaps do less well in mobilizing voters, but maybe well enough, given the limited number they expect to support them in elections. It is safe to say that the institutions of American electoral democracy do not do terribly well in preventing campaigns in which the two major-party candidates hurl personal and often untrue or misleading accusations at each other. During the 2012 and 2014 congressional election campaigns, candidates in debates and in television commercials accused their opponents of lying, corruption, and in one colorful case, being a "low-life scumbag" and a "gutter dweller." There were many instances in 2014 of name-calling and personal attacks, often based on flimsy or false information.

Beyond considering what discourse is appropriate in election campaigns, we need to ask a more general question: Do American elections work as they should? Do they choose capable, responsive leaders? What reforms, if any, are called for? The following electoral reforms have been proposed in recent decades. Although all have been adopted in other countries, there is little or no chance that any of them will soon be adopted in the United States, given the current political climate. The reforms are listed in order from the least likely to the most possible.

- Limit campaign rhetoric to positive messages. This change would certainly be found to violate the First Amendment's protection of political speech.

- Move toward proportional representation and away from plurality voting. This would require changes in state laws.

- Abolish the electoral college in favor of a pure popular voting system for president. This would require a constitutional amendment, as the Constitution specifies that the president is to be chosen by the electoral college.

- Limit the amount of time for campaigning by prohibiting campaign advertisements and public messages before a certain date prior to the election. This would possibly be found unconstitutional under the First Amendment's protection of political speech, but it could conceivably be achieved by congressional statute.

- Fund all campaigns for federal and state office with public money provided by the government. This could be mandated by congressional statute.

- Make it easier for third and minor parties to get on election ballots. This would require changes in state laws.

- Adopt further limits on the amount of money candidates or parties, and other people, can raise and spend in or on behalf of campaigns. This would require new congressional statutes and state laws, and a different constitutional interpretation by the Supreme Court of whether corporations and unions are persons under the law deserving of protection of freedom of speech under the First Amendment.

- Adopt regulations promoting more transparency and public information about who gives money to candidates and parties, and how that money is spent. This would require new congressional statutes.

Would any of these reforms improve elections in the United States? If so, what would the consequences be? The ideas about elections that we have studied in this chapter, including the conduct of elections in other countries, will enable you to discuss these questions in an informed manner.

FURTHER READING

★ = Included in *Readings in American Politics*, 3e

Brader, Ted, *Campaigning for Hearts and Minds* (Chicago: University of Chicago Press, 2006). A detailed study of the role of emotion in determining how voters respond to campaign advertisements.

★ Campbell, Angus, Philip E. Converse, Warren E. Miller, and Donald Stokes, *The American Voter* (New York: John Wiley & Sons, 1960). A classic book on voting behavior, influencing voting studies all over the world; presents the Michigan model of voting.

★ *Citizens United v. Federal Election Commission* (2010). The ruling that declared that corporations and unions share similar First Amendment rights as individuals, including the right to advertise on behalf of a candidate or party during election campaigns.

Cox, Gary, *Making Votes Count* (Cambridge, UK: Cambridge University Press, 1997). A detailed study of how electoral systems affect the number of parties and candidates in elections around the world.

Downs, Anthony, *An Economic Theory of Democracy* (New York: Harper, 1957). Gives a rational-choice account of democracy, with special focus on electoral processes.

Duverger, Maurice, *Political Parties* (New York: John Wiley & Sons, 1963). A classic book on various facets of parties, especially their organization and the nature of party systems across countries.

Fiorina, Morris P., *Retrospective Voting in American National Elections* (New Haven, CT: Yale University Press, 1981). A study of voting behavior, arguing that many voters choose candidates based on past performance of incumbents.

Gerber, Elisabeth, Arthur Lupia, Mathew McCubbins, and Roderick Kiewiet, *Stealing the Initiative* (New York: Prentice Hall, 2000). Shows in detail the process that occurs when referendums and initiatives are proposed to great fanfare and then lose at the polls.

Huber, Gregory A., and Kevin Arceneaux, "Identifying the Persuasive Effects of Presidential Advertising," *American Journal of Political Science* 51, no. 4 (October 2007): 957–77. A careful analysis of which voters are swayed by campaign advertisements.

Magleby, David, *The Change Election: Money Mobilization, and Persuasion in the 2008 Federal Elections* (Philadelphia: Temple University Press, 2010). Explains well the innovations in campaign strategy employed across a number of federal elections in 2008.

Page, Benjamin I., *Choices and Echoes in Presidential Elections* (Chicago: University of Chicago Press, 1978). An account of how presidential candidates become more moderate over time to try to win general elections.

Rabinowitz, George, and Stuart Elaine Macdonald, "A Directional Theory of Issue Voting," *American Political Science Review* 83 (1989): 93–121. The original article espousing the directional model of voting, where candidates seek to appeal to ideological voters.

Sides, John, and Lynn Vavreck, *The Gamble: Choice and Chance in the 2012 Presidential Election* (Princeton, NJ: Princeton University Press, 2012). The issues, events, and campaign strategies in the 2012 presidential election.

Sulkin, Tracy, *The Legislative Legacy of Congressional Campaigns* (New York: Cambridge University Press, 2011). Examines how reliable congressional members have been in fulfilling campaign promises, finding that congressional promises are good indicators of what policies an elected official will pursue.

Valentino, Nicholas, Vincent Hutchings, and Ismail White, "Cues that Matter: How Political Ads Prime Racial Attitudes during Campaigns," *American Political Science Review* 96, no. 1 (2002): 75–90. Experiments show that voters unconsciously respond to racial appeals in campaign advertisements and sometimes change their voting behavior.

KEY TERMS

527s (p. 465)

Australian ballot (p. 458)

closed primary (p. 461)

Federal Election Commission
(FEC) (p. 463)

hard money (p. 465)

initiative (p. 458)

median voter theorem (p. 449)

open primary (p. 461)

plurality rule (p. 455)

political action committee
(PAC) (p. 463)

referendum (p. 458)

single-member district (p. 455)

soft money (p. 465)

super PACs (p. 464)

The media coverage surrounding Raymond Davis's shooting of two men in Pakistan shows that when reporting the news, the media face intense pressures and difficult choices. These pressures can lead to media bias, which is usually more subtle than simply favoring one party or ideology over another.

14

MASS MEDIA AND THE PRESS

Mass media and the press play an important role in providing the information people need to make political decisions. However, news outlets don't passively report objective facts. Is media bias a problem in American politics?

In January 2011, two Pakistani motorcyclists were shot and killed on a busy street in Lahore, Pakistan. U.S. citizen Raymond Davis shot the two men from his vehicle while stopped at a red light, but conflicting accounts of the incident render a muddled picture of the event. Davis maintained self-defense, but officials in Lahore arrested and detained him.

Following the shooting, protests erupted in Pakistan, marking national outrage over the deaths of these two men. President Obama publically urged Pakistan to recognize Davis as a U.S. diplomat, a recognition that would afford him diplomatic immunity. U.S. officials repeatedly declined to divulge the exact nature of Davis's work in Pakistan, saying only that he was a "member of the administrative and technical staff" at the U.S. Consulate in Lahore.[1]

Some press publications overseas stated what the U.S. government would not confirm or deny. *The Guardian*, a British publication, stated that Davis was "a C.I.A. agent who was on assignment at the time."[2] Back in the United States, however, the press demonstrated considerable discretion in sharing Davis's involvement in the Central Intelligence Agency (CIA). At the request of the Obama administration, the *New York Times* temporarily withheld information about Davis's ties to the CIA.[3]

[1] Jake Tapper and Lee Ferran, "President Barack Obama: Pakistan Should Honor Immunity for 'Our Diplomat'," ABC News, February 15, 2011, www.abcnews.go.com/Blotter/raymond-davis-case-president-barack-obama-urges -pakistan/story?id=12922282 (accessed 3/29/13).

[2] Declan Walsh and Ewen MacAskill, "American Who Sparked Diplomatic Crisis Over Lahore Shooting Was CIA Spy," *The Guardian*, February 20, 2011, www.theguardian.com/world/2011/feb/20/us-raymond-davis-lahore-cia (accessed 3/29/13).

[3] Mark Mazzetti et al., "American Held in Pakistan Worked with CIA," *New York Times*, February 21, 2011, www .nytimes.com/2011/02/22/world/asia/22pakistan.html?pagewanted=all (accessed 3/29/13).

The *New York Times* was not the only American news outlet to show a tenor different from foreign reporting. Consider the difference between the reporting of *The Guardian* and ABC News on this same event. *The Guardian* described Davis as "the subject of widespread speculation since he opened fire with a semi-automatic Glock pistol on the two men who had pulled up in front of his car at a red light on 25 January."[4] ABC News in the United States stated, quite differently, that "Davis, 36, was arrested on Jan. 27 after allegedly shooting and killing two men, who the U.S. State Department said were trying to rob him, on the streets of Lahore, Pakistan."[5]

The distinctions are subtle; the words chosen by each publication elicit different meanings. *The Guardian* discloses that Davis was armed with a semi-automatic weapon, but not much about motive for the shooting. Meanwhile, the ABC News article provides the circumstances of the incident, suggesting that Davis acted in self-defense.

Politicians in the United States often complain about partisan or ideological media bias. Conservatives claim that the political news reporting has a liberal bias. Liberals claim that large media corporations report news in a manner favorable to big business. The events surrounding Raymond Davis in Pakistan reveals that media bias may not always, or primarily, be about partisanship or ideology. Media companies and political reporters face different kinds of pressures to cover the news in particular ways for American consumers, sometimes even directly from the government. What are those pressures and when do they occur? And what explains the consistent complaints over ideological bias when there are potentially other kinds of media bias?

---

[4] Declan Walsh and Ewen MacAskill, "American Who Sparked Diplomatic Crisis Over Lahore Shooting Was CIA Spy."

[5] Jake Tapper and Lee Ferran, "President Barack Obama: Pakistan Should Honor Immunity for 'Our Diplomat'."

Mass Media and the Press in a Democracy

Media generally refers to the methods or technologies people use for communication, such as phones, radio, newspapers, television, or the Internet. *Private media* enables people to communicate information with an understanding that it will not necessarily be shared with others. Information disseminated by **mass media**, in contrast, is intended to be publicly available, or at least targeted at large numbers of people. Early in American history, political information was commonly transmitted by means of letters sent on foot or on horseback across large distances. As media technologies changed, they transformed the nature of politics. For example, the rise of cheap daily newspapers in the late nineteenth century brought to millions of people readable political information quickly for the first time. The increasing prominence of television, starting in the 1950s, dramatically affected the way candidates and political parties campaigned for public office. And the Internet, which became widely used in the late 1990s, created new possibilities for organizing mass action and raising money for campaigns and political causes.

The **press** refers to the people and organizations that provide content—news and commentary—that is disseminated across media.[6] In most of this chapter, we will focus on the role of the press in using mass media to disseminate political news. Although people receive the bulk of their political news and commentary through mass media, they can learn about politics and public affairs through private media as well. The difference between private and mass media can be subtle and the lines blurred. Certain contemporary technologies are used for both. Corresponding privately through e-mail, the Internet, or Twitter is different from sending out massive numbers of e-mails, tweets, or Facebook notices. Blogs may or may not be read by a broad audience, but they are public in the sense that they are typically available to anyone who wants to find them. Blogs, mass e-mails, and tweets would usually be considered mass media, while directed e-mail and Facebook notices would usually be considered private. Another example of private media is someone who posts information about an upcoming political event on a personal site on Facebook, but allows only friends access to that site.[7]

Regardless of the specific media used, a free press is vital to modern democracy. By "free" we mean that news, information, and commentary can be gathered and disseminated without being subject to government controls. If the government can censor the press or control content, it may be able to maintain its authority without being checked by an informed people. Citizens are directly involved in choosing government leaders in a democracy, and they

media The methods or technologies people use for communication, such as phones, radio, newspapers, television, and the Internet.

mass media Media that is intended to be publicly available, or at least targeted at large numbers of people.

press The people and organizations that provide content about public affairs—news and commentary—that is disseminated across media.

---

[6] The press is distinct from paid consultants, who are hired to provide content that is intended to be used by those with political interests.

[7] In our era, private media exchanges can fall into the wrong hands and be made public as content for mass media. Politicians and those in government need to be aware of this possibility.

need information to choose and evaluate their leaders. Effective rule by the people requires a free press leading to an informed citizenry. Let us now explore in more detail what a free press through mass media can do.

Providing Essential Information

At a minimum, mass media ought to do two things in a democracy. First, it should enable politicians to communicate with the people. The mass media can be a means for candidates and parties to make their case for why they should be in government, while giving citizens the information they need to evaluate their options on Election Day. Second, the mass media, usually through the press, should provide information to citizens about their communities, their country, and the wider world so they can form reasonable policy opinions and preferences. How do you find out about what your state government is doing, or about a new war brewing in the Middle East? Through mass media. Even if you learn about political news from friends, they have usually been made aware of the story by the press through mass media.

These two basic functions—providing information about potential leaders and about events in the world—are considered necessary in a democracy. This is why freedom of the press is guaranteed in the First Amendment (and in similar clauses in other democratic countries' constitutions).

Evaluating and Interpreting

The press does more than passively report events and the actions of governments and people. It also actively monitors and investigates the government and interprets developments in government and society.

In serving as a "watchdog," operating independently of opposing political parties, the press can monitor and evaluate government officials and expose wrongdoing or incompetence. In 1972 and 1973, Bob Woodward and Carl Bernstein of the *Washington Post* pursued evidence linking associates of President Richard Nixon to a break-in at the Watergate Hotel and other illegal activity, an investigation that ultimately led to Nixon's resignation. In 2012, when a U.S. ambassador was killed in Benghazi, Libya, reporters from CNN uncovered discrepancies between the statements of government officials and what actually happened. The incident and allegedly misleading statements by State Department officials were major points of contention between congressional Republicans and the Obama administration during Obama's second term. A government report later confirmed CNN's information and corrected the State Department's official stance.[8]

[8] Investigative Reporters and Editors, Inc., "2012 IRE Award Winners," www.ire.org/awards/ire-awards/winners/2012-ire-award-winners/ (accessed 7/31/13).

Verifying Political Statements

Candidates make factual claims about their or their opponents' records. Throughout his re-election campaign, President Obama boasted that within one month of assuming the office of the presidency, his administration "signed into law the biggest middle-class tax cut in history."[1] His opponent, Mitt Romney, claimed that his work in the private sector "created over 100,000 jobs."[2] Are there institutions in place to check their facts?

Interests

Candidates want to win and in the heat of competition will say what is necessary to boost their chances. Most voters want candidates to be truthful in their claims, or at least not be outright liars. Members of the media covering campaigns have several interests that can be in tension. First, they want to maximize the number of readers and viewers of their news and thus want to report compelling claims by politicians. Second, they want to demonstrate concern for truth to consumers and thus want to offer factual corrections. Third, some media personalities stake out ideological positions and publicize their opposition to specific candidates, and thus become persistent critics of one side or the other in election campaigns.

Institutions

There is a new proliferation of "fact checking" in contemporary political news outlets. Fact checkers affirm or deny the validity of statements made by candidates. News shows, newspapers, and websites have devoted space to separating defensible candidate statements from bogus claims. Politifact, for instance, is a project of the *Tampa Bay Times* and won the Pulitzer Prize for National Reporting in 2009 for its coverage and fact checking during the 2008 presidential election. FactCheck.org is a nonpartisan, nonprofit "consumer advocate" for voters sponsored by the Annenberg Public Policy Center of the University of Pennsylvania.

Outcomes

If it emerges as a trusted source, a fact checking project not only helps voters make informed decisions, but also gives candidates incentives to minimize false claims and misleading exaggerations. The scrutiny of fact checkers among political media may compel candidates to be more truthful.

FactCheck.org is just one of several media outlets designed to verify claims made by politicians. It remains to be seen how the existence of such services will change what politicians say.

Fact checkers, of course, may not necessarily maintain that objectivity. They too can cater to biases, and as a result, their findings may amplify ideologically charged coverage. A fact checker could, for instance, neglect to reveal one candidate's misstatements while exposing only those of the other candidate.

The increasing presence of fact checking among political media programs reflects a desire for more objective coverage among an important set of media consumers and voters. Considering the current hyper-partisan political news, there is a (perhaps growing) niche for outlets catering to voters who want more objectivity.

Think About It

Will vigilance by some media companies against false campaign statements improve the tenor of campaigns and make them more informative? Or are fact checkers subject to, and contributors to, the same biases found in other media coverage of politics?

[1] "Remarks by the President at Detroit Labor Day Parade," The White House Office of the Press Secretary, September 5, 2011, www.whitehouse.gov/the-press-office/2011/09/05/remarks-president-detroit-labor-day-event (accessed 10/31/12).

[2] Mitt Romney, interviewed by Mark Halperin, "The Page Romney Interview: Bain Capital Excerpt," *Time Magazine* (December 22, 2011), http://thepage.time.com/2011/12/22/the-page-romney-interview-bain-capital-excerpt/#ixzz1iRAJdBk4 (accessed 10/31/12).

The press through mass media also helps people interpret information. If the only information you received about your local government's budget was a set of numbers, with no context and no interpretation, the numbers would not be very useful. Mass media can help you learn, for example, why this year's budget is larger than last year's. Media stories may help you plan your household finances by indicating the likelihood that your taxes will go up this year based on the local government's budget. The press can also provide a more pointed interpretation by, say, observing that "the city government's budget is full of giveaways to friends of the mayor," which might make you decide to vote against the mayor in the next election.[9]

Helping Solve Collective Dilemmas

As we know, people face various kinds of collective dilemmas in politics. Access to reliable information from mass media plays a major role in solving these dilemmas.

Even if people are willing to participate in political action, they may not know enough about the urgency of a situation, what their fellow citizens are doing, or the trustworthiness and competence of people in government. This kind of information is nearly always conveyed to citizens through the mass media. For individuals contemplating strategies for political behavior (Which candidate should I vote for? Should I attend a certain rally?), it is especially useful to rely on information about politics and public affairs that others receive as well.

The press can help citizens prioritize the various problems that need to be solved. In recent years, press coverage of potential flu epidemics has spurred tens of millions of Americans to get flu shots, and it also has led to pressure on the government to ensure that there are sufficient vaccine supplies available even if private companies cannot provide enough. The local and national press can convey the urgency of the situation ("This year's flu strain is potentially deadly") and provide information about which public officials you and other interested citizens can contact to give your opinions on the need for vaccine supplies.

The press can also coordinate the actions of citizens who want to influence politics but do not know how. Modern forms of media, both broadcast (radio and television) and the Internet, give ordinary people the means to work together for political action. If you are worried about the quality of the schools in your town, for example, you and others who share your concerns will be much less effective in pressuring the local government if you fail to coordinate your efforts and inadvertently split into different groups that meet in more than one location. Better to join forces in common meetings, decide on a common

---

[9] In a related vein, the press can help people orient their own opinions and values to the values of the community. Political theorist Harold Lasswell called this the media's socialization function. People, especially if they are young or new to a community, can use mass media to become more familiar with and accustomed to the culture in a society. See Harold Lasswell, "The Structure and Function of Communication in Society," in *The Process and Effects of Mass Communication*, ed. Wilbur Schramm and Donald F. Roberts (Urbana: University of Illinois Press, 1971), pp. 84–99.

message, and present a united front to the local school board or the local or state government.

Of course, in providing information that might lead to effective collective action, the press can exaggerate and mislead, as we will discuss later. The more trustworthy the media source, the more helpful the information will be in solving a collective dilemma.

Trends in Media and the Press

Media technologies in the United States have evolved over time, and this has had implications for politics. In the nineteenth century, handwritten letters gave way to typed and printed handbills, newsletters, newspapers, and magazines. Later, radio and television became the primary sources of information, and now we have the Internet. Any technological means of communicating political news and commentary can be more or less objective. Historically, technological changes in media have gone hand in hand with changes in the professional norms of the press, especially in news reporting. In brief, we can divide the history of American political mass media into three eras:

- The country began with a highly partisan press that communicated through print media.
- The trend toward more objective reporting by the press coincided with the appearance of large-scale, mass-appeal media outlets based on electronic technologies (such as newspaper wire-service reports, radio, and television) in the twentieth century.
- Today we live in an era when many kinds of media coexist: professionalized, intentionally objective news reporting, mostly promulgated through corporate television, Internet, and hard-copy outlets, exists alongside plenty of ideologically charged, partisan news and commentary distributed through a variety of electronic sources, including cable television and the Internet.

The Eighteenth and Nineteenth Centuries

Americans in the late eighteenth and early nineteenth centuries received much of their political news by word of mouth, or by attending local meetings and rallies. Mass media primarily took the form of an unapologetically partisan press operating through print outlets, such as newspapers and party pamphlets. Many party-sponsored newspapers or pamphlets slanted political coverage to be as critical as possible of the other parties and candidates and as laudatory as possible of the sponsoring party. There was no expectation of objectivity in the press.

Commercial newspapers became increasingly popular during the nineteenth century. To sell as many copies as possible, stories were written to appeal to consumers of various political persuasions. At the same time, the telegraph, which became widely used in the 1840s, made it possible for news to travel over long distances almost instantaneously. The people who produced the news in printed form responded by focusing on straightforward facts about events across the country that local reporters could shape to their own purposes. The founding of the Associated Press in 1848 heralded a new era of centralized gathering and dissemination of relatively unbiased news. This is not to say that partisan bias disappeared entirely, however. Most towns still had competing newspapers that openly supported one political party or another.

By the late nineteenth century, the costs of printing, and of sharing information via telegraph or telephone, had become low enough that newspapers like the *New York Sun* could be sold for a penny—a fraction of the price papers had charged a few years earlier. The era of truly mass media had begun. The "penny press" specialized in reporting bizarre occurrences, society gossip, and sensational news. In a famous example, William Randolph Hearst's *New York Journal* criticized Spain for sinking the U.S. battleship *Maine* in 1898, despite a lack of conclusive evidence. Most historians today consider the explosion in Havana harbor an accident. Nevertheless, the newspaper's tendentious coverage was instrumental in stirring up public opinion in favor of starting the Spanish-American War later that year.

Alongside the sensational press, there arose in the late nineteenth century a new breed of professional journalist working for prestigious, nonpartisan newspapers like the *New York Times* and the *Chicago Daily News*. New codes of journalistic conduct emphasized objective reporting. Professional journalism societies and schools sprang up throughout the country, and journalists increasingly resisted pressure from media owners and editors to publish news with an obvious partisan or ideological slant. By the mid-twentieth century, openly biased reporting was frowned upon at magazines like *Time* and *Newsweek*, and at newspapers like the *New York Times*, *Los Angeles Times*, and *The Christian Science Monitor*.

Network Television Comes to Predominate

Beginning in the 1920s, radio became an important medium for disseminating political news. Some large stations broadcast objective news reporting and commentary, much like the big-city newspapers mentioned earlier. Other stations, many of which had smaller audiences, provided content geared toward specific population groups.

In the late nineteenth century, the "penny press" frequently published sensational, highly biased stories. The *New York Journal*'s misleading coverage of the sinking of a U.S. battleship notoriously whipped up support for the Spanish-American War in 1898.

The different parts of the radio spectrum, and the relatively low cost of radio transmission, encouraged such specialized programming.

After television sets became common in American homes in the 1950s, television quickly replaced newspapers and radio as the main source of political news for most Americans. Because the cost of producing programs for television was considerably higher than for radio, a few large media companies came to dominate television news. By 1960, more than 80 percent of American households owned a television that received the nightly news broadcasts aired by the three major national networks, CBS, ABC, and NBC. The number of competitors was limited both by technology and by government regulation of the television industry; as a result, the content of the network news programs was generally politically moderate, neither strongly conservative nor strongly liberal. At the very least, network news programs generally presented two sides of a controversial issue corresponding to the mainstream ideological positions of the two major political parties. These same limitations encouraged large numbers of citizens who were only slightly interested in politics, but who enjoyed watching network television, to become better informed about public affairs.

The norm of unbiased news coverage—meaning nonpartisan and reasonably objective in reporting the facts—was well established in television news by the 1960s. In the latter third of the twentieth century, the three national networks covered the news in a manner that attracted huge nightly audiences. They presented war footage, political news, personal interest stories, and health information. They also covered the news in a relatively unbiased way—at least, the reports were ostensibly nonpartisan in tone. Government regulation contributed to this state of affairs, a topic discussed in more detail later.

Thus, through big-city newspapers, radio, and the national television networks, national political news in the late twentieth century typically was presented in a manner meant to appeal to people from either party—liberals and conservatives alike—and avoid offending large groups of citizens. There were important exceptions to this model, however. In several large cities, thriving black newspapers competed with the mainstream media for business among African Americans. The *Chicago Defender* and the *New York Amsterdam News* provided alternative points of view on politics, entertainment, and sports. Black radio and (after the advent of cable) television stations similarly targeted the African American community. Other minority groups, especially those with large numbers who spoke a language other than English at home, developed their own media outlets.

Rise of New Media

The contemporary era can be said to have begun with the rapid rise of cable television in the 1980s. Suddenly, dozens and then hundreds of television stations were competing with the three major networks. As a result, programmers were free to appeal to specific groups of people with particular tastes—and, in the realm of news and commentary, particular political attitudes.

Equally important, people with only a slight interest in politics were no longer exposed to political news just because they felt like watching network television. The proliferation of cable stations meant that viewers could opt for biased news, or for entertainment of an entirely different sort—a cooking show, for instance. As we will discuss later, cable television led to the development of "soft news" programs, or "infotainment."

The expansion of the Internet in the 1990s magnified this trend by enabling media companies and individuals supplying political news and commentary to target ever-smaller slivers of demographic groups. The Internet has altered the mass media landscape in two significant ways. First, there are now few limits on reaching specific segments of the population instantaneously through websites, e-mail, cell phones, and social-networking groups. So it is easier than ever to tailor narrow messages to specific people. Second, the costs of sending out information to large numbers of people have dropped, and virtually no marginal costs are incurred in reaching more people directly after the content is produced and disseminated. Each additional e-mail, tweet, or Facebook contact costs nothing to post beyond the time it takes to find the address and add it to a contact list.

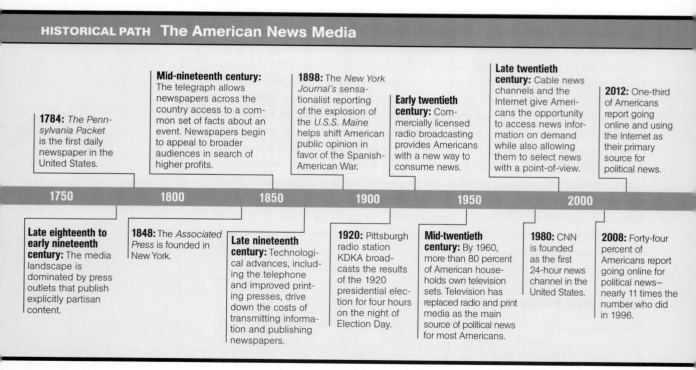

HISTORICAL PATH **The American News Media**

1784: *The Pennsylvania Packet* is the first daily newspaper in the United States.

Mid-nineteenth century: The telegraph allows newspapers across the country access to a common set of facts about an event. Newspapers begin to appeal to broader audiences in search of higher profits.

1898: The *New York Journal's* sensationalist reporting of the explosion of the *U.S.S. Maine* helps shift American public opinion in favor of the Spanish-American War.

Early twentieth century: Commercially licensed radio broadcasting provides Americans with a new way to consume news.

Late twentieth century: Cable news channels and the Internet give Americans the opportunity to access news information on demand while also allowing them to select news with a point-of-view.

2012: One-third of Americans report going online and using the Internet as their primary source for political news.

1750   1800   1850   1900   1950   2000

Late eighteenth to early nineteenth century: The media landscape is dominated by press outlets that publish explicitly partisan content.

1848: The *Associated Press* is founded in New York.

Late nineteenth century: Technological advances, including the telephone and improved printing presses, drive down the costs of transmitting information and publishing newspapers.

1920: Pittsburgh radio station KDKA broadcasts the results of the 1920 presidential election for four hours on the night of Election Day.

Mid-twentieth century: By 1960, more than 80 percent of American households own television sets. Television has replaced radio and print media as the main source of political news for most Americans.

1980: CNN is founded as the first 24-hour news channel in the United States.

2008: Forty-four percent of Americans report going online for political news—nearly 11 times the number who did in 1996.

The Internet now plays an enormous role in the conduct of elections and in political fund-raising. People can get up-to-date information on politics instantaneously through news websites and sites sponsored by interest groups, parties, and private individuals. As more and more information about politics flows through the Internet, television has had to play catch-up and repeat what has already been reported on websites. Television programs, newspapers, and magazines typically have their own websites that continuously update information and post news instantaneously. These websites are now vital means of marketing and staying in contact with readers and viewers. And naturally, candidates post their policy stances and their answers to critics on their Web pages. Barack Obama made history in 2008 by raising hundreds of millions of dollars from Internet appeals, and nearly all candidates today follow his lead. All serious presidential candidates in 2012, from the Republican primaries through the general election, used websites to raise money, post information about their policy positions, answer questions, and coordinate supporters.

With the rise of new media and mobile technology, political news is accessible nearly all the time. In addition, more and more politicians are using text messaging and social media to connect with supporters, and campaigns have developed mobile applications to allow volunteers to make phone calls and share campaign messages easily.

The Internet has dramatically altered how the press is organized and how media companies operate. Scores of major newspapers around the United States either have gone out of business or have severely limited their print versions because more and more people are getting their news from the Internet instead of buying print newspapers. Print magazines struggle to survive as businesses. No longer is it necessary for journalists to join a large news organization to write and spread their content. Blogging has become a standard form of professional journalism, allowing individuals to set up their own Web sites and seek dedicated audiences.

At the same time, there has been somewhat of a return to an era of available partisan sources of the news. This is not because traditional newspapers and magazines have become more politically biased. Rather, it is because of the rise of certain heavily subscribed news outlets, most of which are on the Internet or cable television, which offer openly biased, partisan news and opinion programming. We will have more to say about this trend later in this chapter.

Researchers continue to study how "new media" have transformed the spread of political news. There is little question that the Internet, increasingly accessed through cell phones, has become a central outlet for news. Twenty-eight percent of Americans who are registered voters say they used their cell phones to keep up with political news and with candidates during the 2014 election campaigns. While television is still the most popular source of political information, the Internet is becoming a common means for people, especially younger people, to follow politics. During the 2014 campaign, 22 percent of registered voters under age 49 followed candidates and politics using social media.[10]

[10] Pew Research Center's Internet Project, "Cell Phones, Social Media, and Campaign 2014," November 3, 2014, www.pewinternet.org/2014/11/03/cell-phones-social-media-and campaign-2014/ (accessed 11/7/14).

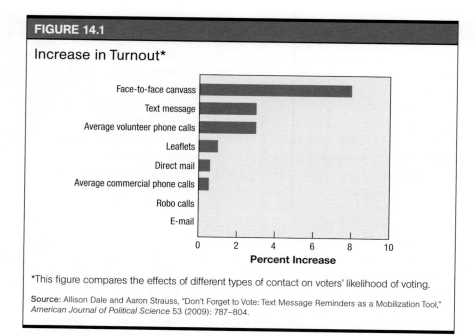

FIGURE 14.1

Increase in Turnout*

Percent Increase

*This figure compares the effects of different types of contact on voters' likelihood of voting.

Source: Allison Dale and Aaron Strauss, "Don't Forget to Vote: Text Message Reminders as a Mobilization Tool," *American Journal of Political Science* 53 (2009): 787–804.

This generational difference appears to carry over to new forms of civic engagement unique to the Internet. In areas where the Internet simply provides a new way to carry out long-established political activity, such as making a donation or contacting an elected official, both old and young citizens use it at similar rates. But in instances where the Internet allows for a new kind of activity—social networking and blogging, for example—young people use it much more than their elders.[11] As Figure 14.1 shows, some forms of new media can be effective in encouraging people to vote.

As we saw with the rise of cable television, the greater volume of accessible information does not mean that people are learning more about politics. Whereas network television, when it dominated political news, tended to expose all sorts of people to daily political happenings, viewers now have a wider range of entertainment options with which political news must compete. Recent surveys suggest that people interested in politics are learning more about it than ever before, but that people with other primary interests know less about politics than in the past.[12] These interests and knowledge levels correlate with people's education and economic status. As discussed in Chapter 10,

---

[11] For more on the role of the Internet in politics, see the Pew Internet and American Life Project, "The Internet and Civic Engagement" and "The Internet's Role in Campaign 2008," www.pewinternet.org (accessed 9/4/13).

[12] Markus Prior, *Post-Broadcast Democracy: How Media Choice Increases Inequality in Political Involvement and Polarizes Elections* (New York: Cambridge University Press, 2007).

the more education and income people have, the more likely they are to seek out political news and entertainment that includes political commentary, while the less education and income people have, the less likely they are to seek out political news and instead watch and listen to entertainment that has little political content. Research also suggests that people who get their political news mostly from cable television and the Internet receive different information than those who get their political news mostly from network television. As an example, network news overwhelmingly focuses on the president and the White House, while cable news covers a broader range of governmental institutions and Washington agenda-setters.[13]

Mass Media Companies and the Profit Motive

Although recent years have been tumultuous for media companies, largely because of the rise of new media, the United States still has a vibrant private media industry. Some media companies that provide political content are struggling to make money through the Internet, but the industry as a whole is thriving in the sense that competing publications, networks, and mass media companies continue to provide content through multiple channels. Most people get their political news and commentary from private media businesses, as opposed to public media companies that are common in other countries. And while there is a huge number of private sources of political news as opposed to public (i.e., government owned) media companies, and each source that survives finds its audience (whether large or small), the overwhelming size of Web and television audiences for news programming produced by a few corporate conglomerates dwarfs the audience sizes for all the other sources combined. Political news produced by, for example, the News Corporation (which owns Fox News and the *Wall Street Journal*), The Disney Company (which owns ABC), The New York Times Company, The Washington Post Company, Gannett, CBS, and General Electric (which owns NBC) collectively reach through their multiple media platforms vastly more people with their political programming than all other sources put together.

There is a publicly owned side of media in the United States as well. The U.S. government supports public television and radio enterprises through the Corporation for Public Broadcasting, which receives funding from both public and private sources. Although the government funds these public enterprises, and at times, politicians pressure public broadcasters, in practice there are few restrictions on the content they provide. In addition, most cities and towns have

---

[13] Matthew Baum and Sam Kernell, "Has Cable Ended the Golden Age of Presidential Television?" *American Political Science Review* 93 (March 1999): 99–114.

Because they seek to hold an audience's interest, the news media tend to focus on stories that involve controversy, conflict, and scandal. In 2012, the press devoted considerable attention to controversial private remarks made by Mitt Romney that 47 percent of Americans are dependent on government and would automatically vote for Obama.

community-based "public-access" television and radio stations that document the affairs of local governments and offer citizens the chance to present their views.

The vast majority of journalists who cover American politics are either employed by private, for-profit companies or work for these same companies as independent freelancers. The underlying profit motive means that these outlets are compelled to present the news in ways that sell newspapers and magazines, get people to watch or listen to a particular news program, or attract people to a particular website. When people joke that "if it bleeds, it leads," they are referring to the tendency of local news programs to put lurid, graphic news—typically violent crime stories—up front to grab and hold viewers' attention. In similar fashion, newspaper headlines and magazine covers often highlight conflict, controversy, and scandal. News stories need a narrative hook, a way to capture an audience that is willing to pay. This makes it worthwhile for journalists to cover stories that are of interest to large numbers of people, preferably those targeted by advertisers—that is, people with money to spend on certain consumer products. The local government's budgeting process that affects people's taxes and education goals may be quite important, but it is not likely to push sports, crime, or scandal off the front page, or bump the top story from the local television newscast.

The drive for profits also determines how media companies allocate resources. These resources can be personnel (journalists and editors), space in publications or time in newscasts, or money spent on travel. Few American newspapers or news websites devote nearly as many resources to international news coverage or national political news as they do to sports, fashion, food, or celebrity gossip. More often than not, the news that gets covered is a function of what will sell rather than what is most critical to a reader's well-being. Consumers of news might well know that the local government's budget process is important, but they might reason, "I don't need to know much about it, and I find it boring to read about."

Journalists often draw a distinction between news and entertainment, but the line is clearly blurred in practice. It is entertaining to read news about celebrities, but it may not be the kind of news that will improve our decisions as citizens. In contrast, it may be entertaining or depressing, depending on one's point of view, to read about scandals involving politicians, but this kind of news may actually help us make better choices in elections.

Infotainment has become an increasingly important way for Americans to get their political news and commentary. Infotainment refers to mass media programming that is intended primarily to entertain, but also provides political news. Shows like *Dateline NBC* or *20/20* mix in political news with news about celebrities and health. Quite a few young people today receive the bulk of their political news from comedy shows such as the *Daily Show* or the *Colbert Report,* in which entertainers comment on the current news in a way that is both funny and informative. These two shows spoof the press and news, but also provide content in the process. Audiences for some of these shows are relatively large and, importantly for advertisers, include disproportionately high numbers from groups such as 20- to 35-year-olds who are hard to reach with more straightforward news programming.[14]

infotainment Mass media programming that is intended primarily to entertain, but also provides political news.

Government Regulation

Because of the First Amendment and the tradition of a free press, governments at various levels in the United States are severely restricted from interfering with the content and dissemination of political information. But this does not mean that government actions do not matter. Government regulation has had an impact on what political information people receive and how it is conveyed by the press. Such regulation of the press and mass media in the United States has focused almost entirely on television and radio broadcasters, as opposed to print media. Newspapers and magazines have been largely protected from government regulation because of First Amendment guarantees. The situation is different for broadcast media because, under U.S. law and the laws of most other countries, the airwaves for television or radio are public property. The rationale for making companies pay for airwave space is that, since the airwaves are publicly owned, the government has the right to sell off and regulate their use. Also, in the absence of government regulation, private companies might trample on each other's airwave space. This is a classic coordination problem. Radio and television stations are all better off with a means of dividing up the airwaves and permitting every station to be heard without interference from other broadcasts. Government regulation is seen as necessary to enforce coordinated use of the airways.

Since the early twentieth century, the federal government has sold to media companies rights of access to specific portions of the airwaves, in return for which the companies have agreed to codes of conduct. For many decades, these codes stipulated that the airwaves be used to promote the common good and provide information useful to all citizens. In practice, this meant that radio

---

[14] Research has shown that "soft news" shows that are intended to entertain draw attention to dramatic stories, especially crises in foreign countries, and away from domestic news about politics that might directly affect Americans. Matthew Baum, "Sex, Lies, and War: How Soft News Brings Foreign Policy to the Inattentive Public," *American Political Science Review* 96 (2002): 91–109.

Government Regulation of Mass Media

- Until 1987, the **Fairness Doctrine**, which stated that holders of broadcast licenses were required to present information on important issues in a way that was honest, equitable, and balanced, was enforced by the Federal Communications Commission (FCC) and influenced American media coverage. The Fairness Doctrine is now defunct.

- Another important provision still somewhat enforced by the FCC is the **Equal Time Rule**, which requires broadcasters to give equal time to competing candidates for political office. For example, if a television station gives one candidate a free minute of airtime, then the station must make the same free airtime available to his or her opponent(s).

- In the broadcasting realm, most current government regulation falls under the purview of the **Telecommunications Act of 1996**, which sought to remove regulatory entry barriers for new firms in the media marketplace.

- A key legal doctrine involves **prior restraint**, which refers to the ability of governmental actors to prevent media outlets from publishing particular material because the government believes that information will jeopardize public safety and/or national security. Federal courts in the United States have ruled that prior restraint may only be exercised in extraordinary circumstances.

and television stations were required to produce news programming and make some time slots available to nonprofit organizations or local governments. In addition, the Federal Communication Commission's Fairness Doctrine, which stood in place until 1987, required that television and radio stations present at least two sides of every controversial public issue. By the same token, if one candidate for office was interviewed on a news program, the other viable candidates for that same office had to be invited for an interview as well.

As a result of trends toward deregulation in business law—and consensus among politicians from both major political parties that the Fairness Doctrine was unworkable, unwise, or both—the federal government has largely ceased regulating content of mass media. The Fairness Doctrine was abandoned after having been left mostly unenforced by the Reagan administration in the 1980s.[15] "Public interest" broadcasting requirements began to be interpreted very broadly. Today there are few restrictions on content for mass media in the United States. Many scholars argue that the rise of cable television and the Internet—media that do not face the same public domain issues as traditional broadcasting—made those restrictions irrelevant anyway.[16]

Likewise, government regulations regarding media ownership, which were on the books and enforced for many years, have largely been abandoned. Strict

[15] See the discussion in Chapter 7 about Reagan's broad attack on the federal bureaucracy in the 1980s, including his complaints about government regulation.

[16] See, for example, Brian Lehrer, "A Million Little Murrows: New Media and New Politics," *Media Law and Policy Review* 17 (September 2008): 1–18.

rules against ownership of multiple broadcast companies by a single group or individual, for example, arose from attempts to avoid concentrating control over the flow of information to the public in a few hands. The rules loosely applied to print media as well. Since the 1980s, however, these regulations have fallen out of favor, and many have been repealed.

As a result, concentrated ownership of major media outlets has become the norm. Large media conglomerates now own newspapers, radio stations, television stations, and cable television stations across multiple states and within the same urban areas. By the 1990s, it had become common for the same company to own the one or two dominant local newspapers in the same town, eliminating any sense of competition between them. Today, many cities have either one or no daily newspaper. Even if one survives, it is likely to be owned by the same company that owns one of the main television stations in town.

The consequences of concentrated media ownership on public discourse and political knowledge are unclear. Some scholars argue that with less competition within local areas, the quality of political information has declined.[17] Evidence of such an effect is hard to come by, however, in part because of the survival of some small-scale media. Certainly, in smaller cities and towns there is little competition among private companies providing local political news. But taking the national-level view, the mass media landscape contains numerous relatively small companies around the country that find their own niche consumer bases, mostly around certain issues people care about. More importantly, national political news and news in large cities is dominated by programming produced by about five or six enormous conglomerates that compete among themselves for huge audience shares. Thus, some argue, competition exists across media companies of various sizes, and, it may be argued, competition at any level causes media companies to provide quality programming. We return to this discussion about the effects of media concentration shortly.

In Comparison: Mass Media

Journalists and media companies in other parts of the world often envy the freedom of their American counterparts to publish what they want. In countries like Iran or China, the government owns nearly all the mass media and closely controls access and content. Even in countries that are considered partial democracies, journalists are arrested and jailed for writing or broadcasting information that offends the government.

Differences across democracies in the conduct of the press and in mass media mostly stem from how media companies are owned and regulated. In

[17] See, for example, Peter Clarke and Eric Fredin, "Newspapers, Television, and Political Reasoning," *Public Opinion Quarterly* 42, no. 2 (1978): 143–60; and Martin Gilens and Craig Hertzman, "Corporate Ownership and News Bias: Newspaper Coverage of the 1996 Telecommunications Act," *Journal of Politics* 62 (2000): 369–86.

In many countries, the media are more heavily regulated than they are in the United States. When news outlets in Iran were prevented by the government from covering protests in Tehran in 2010, people used cell phones to send images and information outside the country.

the United States, a multitude of private media companies, sometimes regulated but not controlled by the government, compete with each other for consumers of news and entertainment. The sheer number and the overwhelming presence of private media companies are unusual features of the American political system.

In many other democracies, public media companies are at the center of political news gathering. One might think that such publicly owned companies would be beholden to the government and rarely criticize its leaders, but this is not the case, particularly in long-standing democracies. The British Broadcasting Corporation (BBC), for example, has earned a reputation as an aggressive news gatherer. In general, the BBC has complete freedom to cover and comment on the news as it wishes. It is seen as acting independently of the government and more than willing to criticize. A similar claim can be made for the public media companies in Canada, France, Australia, and other countries.

In a few countries, private ownership is concentrated in the hands of a small number of individuals, a situation that would probably not be permitted under American antitrust laws. Such concentration can be problematic, especially when the individuals are members of the government. In Italy in the early twenty-first century, for example, Prime Minister Silvio Berlusconi owned four of the five major television companies. Again, the consequences of concentrated media ownership are unclear. Critics are quick to show evidence that the media in countries like Italy offer either bland or biased news coverage, but scholarly research has not established this definitively across various countries or over time.[18]

Many countries have government-enforced restrictions on political content in the media that would not be allowed in the United States because of the First Amendment. Thus, as discussed in Chapter 13, political campaigning—when and where it takes place, and what is said—is heavily regulated in most other democracies. Even political advertisements need to be approved by government regulators in other countries, something that is unheard of in the United States.[19]

[18] See, for example, Kees Brants, "Who's Afraid of Infotainment?" *European Journal of Communication* 13, no. 3 (1998): 315–35.

[19] U.S. television and radio stations have been permitted to refuse to broadcast offensive images or words, even when coming from a political candidate, but this practice has been challenged and sometimes the courts have sided with the candidates. One candidate in 1992 wanted to show bloody fetuses in a campaign ad to highlight his opponent's pro-choice stance. A federal appeals court in *Becker v. FCC* ruled that broadcasters had to allow the ads. See Carol Lomicky and Charles Salestrom, "Anti-Abortion Advertising and Access to the Airwaves: A Public Interest Doctrine Dilemma," *Journal of Broadcasting & Electronic Media* 42, no. 4 (1998): 491–506.

Ironically, in the realm of private media, the U.S. has been somewhat more open to government regulation and monitoring, and to corporate monitoring, of individuals than other countries, especially in comparison with Europe. First, the U.S. government and military branches have aggressively prosecuted individuals accused of leaking classified military and diplomatic information to the entire world community through the Web (through sites such as WikiLeaks). Second, the United States has led the way in allowing government agencies to monitor the e-mails, tweets, cell phone calls and texts, and blogs of people suspected of crimes, especially of abetting terrorism. Third, the U.S. government has been reluctant to pass additional regulations prohibiting companies like Google, Facebook, and Microsoft from collecting personal information on software users so that those companies can market products and advertise more efficiently through their own software portals. On the one hand, this last example is unusual in that, contrary to the norm, here the U.S. privacy protections for individuals are less strict than Europe's protections. On the other hand, it is consistent with a broader difference between the United States and Europe: in Europe, there is more widespread acceptance of corporate regulations.

Are the American Press and Mass Media Biased?

We now return to the subject of our opening story—media bias—in light of our discussion of the history of the press and media. With this context in mind, we can consider the nature of media bias and findings from systematic research.

Discerning Bias

Scholars of media and politics agree that media bias is difficult to discern, let alone define consistently. We might say for our purposes that bias is the notion that someone is being subjective in a way that serves his or her political interest. If a conservative journalist writes a blog that consistently criticizes liberal politicians and praises conservatives, we can confidently say that he or she has an ideological bias. Likewise, if a liberal journalist selectively chooses to report only facts that make liberals look good and conservatives look bad, this reflects a bias. Or, if a news outlet owned by a large corporation always reports in a manner that reflects well on that corporation and avoids reporting negative factual information that is actually in the public's interest to know, then we would say this news outlet is biased.

Bias is not inherently bad. Many publications are widely considered to have an ideological bias and openly admit to it. *National Review* is a conservative magazine, the *Nation* a leftist magazine. The *Rachel Maddow Show* reflects a liberal point of view, the *O'Reilly Factor* a conservative one. Fox News is conservative and pro-Republican, and it has an enormous following in relative terms, while MSNBC has been quite liberal and pro-Democratic in recent years, but with much less market share than Fox News, and only recently outperforming the more ideologically balanced CNN. Many people would argue that, as in a judicial setting where both sides have an opportunity to make their best case, an adversarial system in the press is the best means of uncovering information relevant to the political process. Certainly ideological bias, especially one that is known and acknowledged, is less troublesome than bias by a news outlet against reporting important negative news about its parent corporation.

In fact, most major national news producers, such as the *New York Times* or the *Wall Street Journal*, take pains to avoid the appearance of bias. Even the "liberal" *Times*, which generally supports Democratic candidates over Republicans on their editorial page, would deny having a partisan bent toward the Democrats. The *Times* prides itself on presenting differing points of view in its news stories and routinely publishes unedited comments from a "public editor" charged with investigating bias in the paper's reporting. At the same time, its editorials and other opinion columns clearly lean to the left. The line between news reporting and opinion writing can be blurry at times, but people in the news business, especially at prestigious newspapers and national television networks, try hard to maintain it.

Even when reporters try to avoid bias, they cannot escape the fact that they are making choices about content that are shaped by their own values and experiences. Consider the reporting of facts. What information should be reported when a given event occurs? In theory, any statement, even a purely factual one, is biased because the reporter chooses to report some facts instead of others. Suppose a television reporter noted that "Twelve American soldiers were killed in Afghanistan yesterday." This sentence, if true, would be considered unbiased by most observers. But suppose that 100 Taliban insurgents were killed as well. Someone might say that the news report focused on the American deaths and thus distorted what happened. Now suppose someone stated on television, "Twelve soldiers of the American occupying army were killed by noble Afghan fighters yesterday." Quite biased, you might say. But what about not covering the story at all? Is that biased? Or what if the reporter said, "Twelve American soldiers were killed in Afghanistan yesterday, the largest one-day toll in months." Is that biased? It may be biased because highlighting a one-day surge in deaths may lead people to believe the American military engagement is going badly.

Journalism has professional norms of conduct that require disclosure and honesty to a degree rare in other professions. Journalists known for unbiased reporting are praised and rewarded by their peers. Several prominent television journalists were suspended by their networks in 2010 after it was discovered that they had made campaign contributions to Democratic candidates. The point is that they had violated both a norm in the profession and a corporate policy about the "appropriate," unbiased behavior of journalists who cover politics. Nevertheless, it is hard to refute a charge of bias if someone wants to make one. Such judgments are themselves subjective and depend on one's point of view.

Ideological versus Other Kinds of Bias

We can divide types of bias along several lines. Let us first contrast ideological bias from other kinds. Allegations of media bias by both liberals and conservatives are common in the United States. Both sides have some reason to be concerned. Surveys reveal the press to be, on the whole, more liberal than conservative,[20] suggesting that, consciously or not, individual journalists' decisions about which stories to cover and how to cover them might take on a liberal flavor (Figure 14.2). Yet publishers and owners of media organizations are businesspeople, typically a conservative constituency, and it is conceivable that they exert a subtle influence on how editors, anchors, and reporters convey the news.

Note that the liberal-conservative dimension is not the only area in which the media can potentially exhibit bias. Various scholars have argued, for instance, that the media are biased in favor of capitalism, nationalism, and minimal

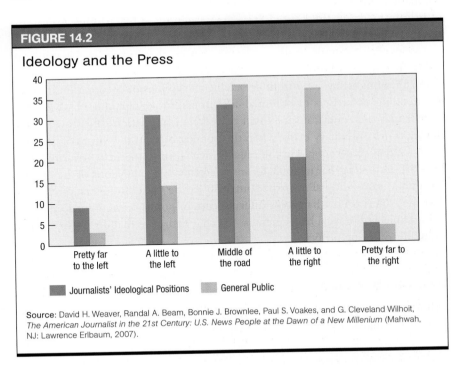

FIGURE 14.2

Ideology and the Press

Journalists' Ideological Positions — General Public

Source: David H. Weaver, Randal A. Beam, Bonnie J. Brownlee, Paul S. Voakes, and G. Cleveland Wilhoit, *The American Journalist in the 21st Century: U.S. News People at the Dawn of a New Millenium* (Mahwah, NJ: Lawrence Erlbaum, 2007).

[20] D. Domke et al., "The Politics of Conservative Elites and the 'Liberal Media' Argument," *Journal of Communication* 49, no. 4 (1999); David Niven, *Tilt: The Search for Media Bias* (Westport, CT: Praeger, 2002).

government. Another vein of research finds that the local media's emphasis on crime has led to an unfavorable, distorted picture of minorities.[21] These quandaries over what is biased and what is not are no easier to sort out than the liberal-conservative divide.

In fact, most scholars of the mass media would focus less on ideological bias of the sort that divides Republicans from Democrat, and the typical Fox News watcher from the typical reader of the *Nation*. This kind of ideological difference gets attention in political circles because politicians can gain some traction among constituents by complaining about news coverage and media bias, but its impact in reality is much less notable. Instead, scholars tend to focus attention on the pressures of private companies to gain more market share and expand their audiences. This biases coverage toward what is sensational and attention-grabbing, and in turn gives incentives for politicians and other government officials to shape their information in certain ways to grab the attention of news reporters hungry for news that sells.

Finally, some critics of American media believe that bias among the press is quite subtle. As we have learned, in terms of content and media ownership, mass media in the United States is less regulated than in other countries. There are thousands of mass media outlets peddling political news, but a few huge companies dominate in terms of market share. Ironically, given the plethora of private media in the United States, many observers believe that Americans actually receive less diversity of viewpoints *on selected topics* than people in other countries. For example, most media companies that create and disseminate political news derive the bulk of their profits from advertising. Private media companies might shy away from criticizing the actions of corporations for fear of offending advertisers or potential consumers.[22] Likewise, there is always the danger that the American press will be reluctant to criticize the government during times of military crisis, when the population is in the throes of patriotic fervor. When some people in the press criticized the American government at the start of the Iraq War in 2003, for instance, there were boycotts of the offending publications and calls for the journalists to be fired. Some critics contend that the American media avoids offering certain points of view for fear not of being subjected to legal harassment, as in other countries that do not have a free press, but of losing profits.

gatekeeping bias The tendency for the media or a particular media outlet not to report stories of a particular nature.

How Can Bias Occur?

Scholars have another way of dividing media bias, into three categories for how it occurs: gatekeeping bias, coverage bias, and statement bias. **Gatekeeping bias**

[21] R. M. Entman and A. Rojecki, *The Black Image in the White Mind: Media and Race in America* (Chicago: University of Chicago Press, 2000).

[22] See, for example, James T. Hamilton, *All the News That's Fit to See: How the Market Transforms Information into News* (Princeton, NJ: Princeton University Press, 2004), especially chap. 3.

is the tendency systematically not to report stories of a particular nature. In the absence of gatekeeping bias, media organizations can still exhibit **coverage bias**, whereby certain kinds or aspects of stories receive less attention in terms of column space or air time. Finally, the media can exhibit **statement bias**, the interjection of opinions into the coverage of an issue.[23]

This classification is far from perfect. To measure gatekeeping bias, for instance, one needs to know how many stories *might* have been reported, which is inevitably a matter of opinion. To measure coverage bias, one needs to decide whether certain aspects of a given story require more attention because of their novelty or complexity. Still, where researchers have undertaken to sort these issues out, a fairly positive picture emerges. Across dozens of studies, newspapers and magazines exhibited no consistent bias in one direction or another. Television networks exhibited slight liberal coverage and statement biases, but on balance it seems that, according to researchers, both liberals and conservatives have ample opportunity to be heard.[24] Now, whether voices on one side or the other are louder and drown out the opposition at times, this can occur, but the available studies do not add up to a conclusion that one side consistently overwhelms the other in politics.

coverage bias The tendency for the media or a particular media outlet to give less attention in terms of column space or air time to certain kinds of stories or aspects of stories.

statement bias The tendency for the media or a particular media outlet to interject opinions into the coverage of an issue.

Media Effects

So far in this chapter, we have focused on the evolution of mass media content, media companies, and government regulation of media. That is, we have studied the *supply* side of media. What about the *demand* side? What is the nature of media consumption? How has consumption of media content changed over time, and what does that mean for politics?

There has been much research on the effects of media on individuals and public opinion. For example, researchers have conducted careful experimental studies of people's responses to campaign advertising. Others have analyzed what people know about politics and how that relates to their choice of media sources. Some of the findings from this research have already been summarized in Chapters 9 and 13.

For our purposes, we can divide questions about media effects into two types: those that ask what media people use and why, and those that ask how specific kinds of media content affect people's attitudes, opinion, and actions. The former type of question examines the decisions people make to read newspapers, watch television, or browse the Internet for information about politics, as well as which newspapers, television programs, or Web sites they select. The latter type examines the consequences of those decisions on how people think and reason.

[23] On this type of bias in presidential election coverage, see D. D'Alessio and M. Allen, "Media Bias in Presidential Elections: A Meta-Analysis," *Journal of Communication* 50, no. 4 (2000): 133–56.

[24] D'Alessio and Allen, "Media Bias in Presidential Elections."

Who Chooses Which Media Content and Why?

Researchers have explored three different hypotheses about why people choose specific media outlets. The *partisan hypothesis* says that people choose media programming on the basis of its partisan or ideological slant. Although this seems plausible on the surface—after all, Fox News clearly attracts more conservative and more Republican viewers (and in fact, many more viewers period) than does MSNBC—studies provide little support for this hypothesis. Subjects in experiments typically appear to choose media content for other reasons.[25]

The *agenda hypothesis* asserts that people choose media programming on the basis of personal interest in the issues and policy areas the outlet tends to emphasize. A news outlet that devotes considerable attention to health care stories, for example, will attract viewers or readers who are especially interested in such stories (such as the elderly). The same appears to be true of such issues as foreign policy, environmentalism, hunting, sports, or local business reports. Experimental and survey evidence strongly supports this agenda hypothesis.[26]

Do people choose to watch the *Rachel Maddow Show* because they want political information with a liberal slant? Do they choose *The O'Reilly Factor* for a conservative slant? Research shows that factors other than partisanship or ideology may be more important.

[25] See, for example, Shanto Iyengar, Kyu S. Hahn, Jon A. Krosnick, and John Walker, "Selective Exposure to Campaign Communication: The Role of Anticipated Agreement and Issue Public Membership," *Journal of Politics* 70 (2008): 186–200.

[26] See, for example, Doris Graber, *Processing the News: How People Tame the Information Tide* (New York: Longman, 1984).

The *engagement hypothesis* contends that some people are generally interested in politics, while others are not. Nearly everyone (or at least some members of each household) is interested in some combination of weather, movies, sports, scandal, and celebrity gossip, but consuming in-depth political news and commentary is almost like a hobby for "political nerds." To show which media outlets people gravitate toward, we can simply find out how interested people are in politics in general and then anticipate that they will access those outlets that offer the corresponding amount of political coverage, from very little (for those uninterested in politics) to very much (for those highly interested in politics).[27]

This last hypothesis turns out to be largely confirmed, and the consequences are important for political equality. Consider the well-known pattern discussed in Chapters 9 and 10: interest in politics is highly correlated with higher levels of education and income. And as a result, because interest in politics leads to people seeking out information about politics, political knowledge is significantly higher among those who are more educated and wealthier. Evidence from surveys and experiments overwhelmingly supports these patterns. Exceptions can occur during heated presidential campaigns or times of economic or foreign policy crisis, when people from all income, wealth, and education groups seek out more political news and commentary.[28]

It is hard to square the minimal evidence for the first hypothesis with the incontrovertible fact that conservatives tend to watch conservative shows on channels like Fox News more than liberals, while liberals prefer to watch liberal shows on such channels as MSNBC, or read the *Nation* or even the *New York Times*. Perhaps different ideological groups pay more attention to different issues, and the various media outlets take advantage of these different focuses. Thus, perhaps Fox News covers wasteful government spending and budget deficits more than MSNBC because Fox viewers, being more conservative, focus their attention on issues related to taxation and spending. This explanation could make sense of the agenda hypothesis and the different viewer bases of various cable channels.

What Is the Effect of Specific Media Content?

In recent decades, researchers have conducted many experiments and surveys to try to understand what difference specific content makes in individual decision making.

[27] Markus Prior, *Post-Broadcast Democracy: How Media Choice Increases Inequality in Political Involvement and Polarizes Elections* (New York: Cambridge University Press, 2007).

[28] On the relationship between education, income, and political knowledge, see Michael X. Delli Carpini and Scott Keeter, *What Americans Know about Politics and Why It Matters* (New Haven, CT: Yale University Press, 1996). On media usage being stratified by income and education, see H. Brandon Haller and Helmut Norpoth, "Reality Bites: News Exposure and Economic Opinion," *Public Opinion Quarterly* 61, no. 4 (1997): 555–75. On media consumption during times of crisis, see Scott L. Althaus, "American News Consumption during Times of National Crisis," *PS: Political Science & Politics* 35, no. 3 (2002): 517–52.

Some scholars have studied whether media content is both informative and persuasive. If media stories are informative, then people learn new facts about the world that they did not know before watching or reading them. Not surprisingly, evidence suggests that people learn most of what they know about current events from the media, as opposed to from direct observation or from neighbors or coworkers.[29] Evidence for the educational value of media overall is more mixed than one might imagine, however. Many studies have shown that people who are generally uninformed about politics retain very little factual information even a short time after observing media content; the information does not stick for long among vast portions of the general public.[30]

Some researchers think that this finding slights people's ability to learn about politics. They may not remember rote facts, but this does not mean that media content did not help them form considered opinions. Think about a movie you saw five years ago. Although you may have forgotten many details of the characters and plot, you probably still remember whether you liked or disliked it. There is evidence that much political information works this way: people discard the details once they have used them to update their *feelings* toward a person or party.[31]

As for persuasion, research has shown that single news stories are rarely enough to prompt someone to change his or her mind about whom to vote for or how to evaluate candidates or government officials. But repeated exposure to negative information about a candidate reduces enthusiasm for voting for that candidate. In other words, mass media content can persuade people to be more or less supportive of something, but usually this occurs only through repetition.[32] But as with other findings, some groups of people are more easily persuaded than others. Interestingly, both the people who are least informed and the people who are the most informed about politics tend to be difficult to persuade. The former (least informed) are difficult to persuade with information from media because they are less engaged and pay less attention. The latter (most informed) are difficult to persuade with information from media because their advanced levels of knowledge mean that additional information is only a small part of all the considerations they use to make decisions. It is the group in the middle—the moderately informed, who occasionally pay attention to politics and know some but not a great deal about politics—that is most amenable to being persuaded by new information provided in news programming via mass media.

[29] Shanto Iyengar and Donald R. Kinder, *News That Matters* (Chicago: University of Chicago Press, 1987).

[30] See, for example, W. Russell Neuman, "Patterns of Recall among Television News Viewers," *Public Opinion Quarterly* 40, no. 1 (1976): 115–23.

[31] Milton Lodge, Kathleen McGraw, and Patrick Stroh, "An Impression-Driven Model of Candidate Evaluation," *American Political Science Review* 83, no. 2 (1989): 399–419; Milton Lodge, Marco Steenbergen, and Shawn Brau, "The Responsive Voter: Campaign Information and the Dynamics of Candidate Evaluation," *American Political Science Review* 89, no. 2 (1995): 309–26.

[32] Benjamin I. Page and Robert Y. Shapiro, *The Rational Public: Fifty Years of Trends in Americans' Policy Preferences* (Chicago: University of Chicago Press, 1992).

Agenda-setting by the mass media has also been a focus of research. People place increased importance on certain social problems and government agenda items based on media coverage. As one scholar observed, "The media may not be successful much of the time in telling people what to think, but [it] is stunningly successful in telling its readers what to think *about*."[33] This is especially true when people are incessantly exposed to a variety of media sources that agree on the need to tackle a given problem. For example, surveys show that most people believe that violent crime is a growing problem, despite the fact that the incidence of such crime has actually fallen in the country as a whole. Why this disconnect between facts and perceptions? Scholars point to data showing the increased coverage of violent crime in the mass media over the 1990s and 2000s, which clearly influenced people en masse to prioritize crime fighting on the government's agenda.[34]

Priming and framing research offers telling insights into media impact. (See Chapter 9.) *Priming* is the psychological process of shaping people's perceptions of a particular issue, figure, or policy. Research shows that mass media reports have a direct bearing on whether people focus on personal character, appearance, performance, competence, or other attributes when evaluating political candidates. The more media content highlights an individual politician's philandering, for instance, the more likely people are to view that politician negatively despite other qualities that might recommend him or her. Moreover, people will be more likely to judge *all* politicians by that criterion.[35]

In much the same way, media reports can influence the weight people attach to certain aspects of a complicated problem or policy issue. The actions by those giving the information, such as reporters and media personalities, is known as *framing*. Research shows that the effects of framing can be very large in shaping people's attitudes. These effects can be attenuated, and in some rare instances eliminated altogether, when people are exposed to multiple media sources that display different ideological or partisan biases.[36] (See Chapter 9 for more discussion of framing.)

What media content people use and how it influences their political behavior is one of the more exciting areas of research in the social sciences. Scholars of media effects are in general agreement that mass media profoundly affect public opinion, at least at the level of framing specific issues in certain ways and shaping attitudes toward certain politicians; they study the details of how, when,

[33] B. Cohen, *The Press and Foreign Policy* (Princeton, NJ: Princeton University Press, 1963), p. 13; emphasis in original.

[34] Maxwell E. McCombs, *Setting the Agenda: The Mass Media and Public Opinion* (Malden, MA: Blackwell Publishing, 2004), chap. 2.

[35] See, for example, James N. Druckman, "Priming the Vote: Campaign Effects in a U.S. Senate Election," *Political Psychology* 25, no. 4 (2004): 577–94; and Nicholas A. Valentino, "Crime News and the Priming of Racial Attitudes during Evaluations of the President," *Public Opinion Quarterly* 63, no. 3 (1999): 293–320.

[36] James N. Druckman, "Political Preference Formation: Competition, Deliberation, and the (Ir)relevance of Framing Effects," *American Political Science Review* 98, no. 4 (2004): 671–86.

and to whom such effects occur. New survey and experimental techniques have given us deeper insight into the causes and consequences of individuals' access to different kinds of political news and commentary.

The Media as Principals and Agents

We began this chapter by posing questions about bias in mass media content and later analyzed the concept of bias in some detail. Some scholars of media politics concede that many Americans are often getting news with a strong partisan bias but question whether this is a problem.[37] Consumers may choose sources that reinforce their own biases. But to call people biased simply means that they have a specific point of view that is shaped by their preferences for political outcomes. Evidence shows that partisan-biased television shows get people engaged in politics and may in fact mobilize them to participate more.[38] As long as people have access to multiple news sources with different biases, then a partisan press may produce a more engaged and active citizenry.[39] It may also be that other kinds of bias, besides the ideological kind, are more consequential.

Let us return to the "why" of our opening puzzle: What explains the nature of American coverage of events in Pakistan in comparison with richer accounts in other countries? What motives drive media companies and reporters? The major answer from our analysis in this chapter is that today companies find it both possible and profitable to tailor their content for specific audiences. But part of the answer also lies in the fact that people appear to find it interesting or useful to read, watch, or listen to political content created by those who share their own political attitudes.

As consumers of political news and commentary, it behooves us to pay close attention to the media sources we use, and especially to their motivations. Reporters have incentives to get an interesting story and are usually in a hurry to get it. They interview and gather information from a variety of sources—the more convenient, the better. Much of their information comes from people in the government, who generally seek to avoid negative coverage. Reporters also get information from candidates and parties challenging incumbents, who naturally want to make the incumbent party and the government look bad. Finally, reporters get information from interest-group leaders, who also have incentives to influence how the news is framed for public consumption.

[37] Shanto Iyengar and Jennifer A. McGrady, *Media Politics: A Citizen's Guide* (New York: Norton, 2006).

[38] See, for example, Stefano DellaVigna and Ethan Kaplan, "The Fox News Effect: Media Bias and Voting," *Quarterly Journal of Economics* 122, no. 3 (2007): 1187–234.

[39] How informed that citizenry becomes because of the press is a different matter, as was addressed in Chapter 9 and earlier in this chapter.

To communicate their content to mass audiences, reporters rely on mass media companies, which have their own complicated set of incentives. In understanding the roles these companies play, it helps to draw on insights from the principal-agent problem we discussed in previous chapters. (See especially Chapters 1 and 7.) American mass media companies, both public and private, play multiple roles and affect the political system in multiple guises. At times they act as principals, and at other times, as agents.

The Press and Mass Media as Principals

Mass media companies *control the means of communication* between people, and between institutions and people. They own the television and radio stations, operate the cables and cable boxes that deliver television programs, license portions of the public airwaves and satellite frequencies, create the technology and towers for cell phone transmissions, and own the billboards and periodicals bearing political advertisements. Mass media companies and their personnel also *produce programming content about politics*, including news programs, opinion and talk shows, written stories and editorials, blogs, and candidate debates. In other words, media companies make products that are disseminated through the forms of transmission mentioned earlier. In this capacity, media companies can act as principals when their own employees produce commentary, news, and forums for debate and discussion.

Like other interest groups, mass media companies try to influence the government to protect and advance their interests by lobbying, making political donations, and appealing to the public. In this respect, they are similar to auto or oil companies, or any other businesses. But unlike any other type of interest group, media companies can use their capacities as owners of means of communication and producers of content to bolster their political influence.

Despite the strong tradition in the journalistic profession of separating business decisions from editorial decisions, there is little question that some media owners use their companies to promote certain lines of argument in politics. For example, Rupert Murdoch, the owner of many newspapers (including the *Wall Street Journal*) and other mass media outlets (including Fox News) in the United States, England, and Australia, is known to be politically conservative and to push his publications to favor conservative points of view. He openly supports Republican candidates in elections and donates to the Republican Party.

The Press and Mass Media as Agents

The government, interest groups, political parties, and candidates all communicate to the mass public through radio, television, the Internet, cell phones, and public billboards and notices. The public communicates with political elites using some of the same means. In other words, media companies allow for communication in several directions. We can say that, in this guise, media companies are the agents, hired by principals (candidates, for example) to carry their messages or to bring them messages.

If mass media producers are merely agents of other principals—such as political parties, candidates, or the government—then the question of bias is really about who gets access to the most effective means of mass communication. We know partisan elites are biased; we expect them to be. In the same way, media producers can shape the news in biased ways by deciding which voices are heard.

In sum, media companies act both as principals *and* as agents, and it is hard to fault them for doing what we, as consumers, encourage them to do when we select content that agrees with our own attitudes. But when critics of the media allege media bias, are they referring mostly to the selective access they give politicians and other political organizations that actually supply the content? Or are they referring to the media companies themselves, producing their own content through their paid journalists and commentators? If the former, then perhaps a return to something like the Fairness Doctrine would improve public discourse. If the latter, new regulations would almost certainly run afoul of interpretations of the First Amendment protections of the press and recent Supreme Court rulings, making it difficult to impose any changes in news content.

FURTHER READING

★ = Included in *Readings in American Politics*, 3e

★ Baum, Matthew, *Soft News Goes to War* (Princeton, NJ: Princeton University Press, 2003). A detailed study of how people learn about international news from soft news, which is media programming that is intended to entertain but contains political information.

Delli Carpini, Michael X., and Scott Keeter, *What Americans Know about Politics and Why It Matters* (New Haven, CT: Yale University Press, 1996). Indicates the deep inequalities in political knowledge, and how this inequality tilts government programs toward the more knowledgeable.

Druckman, James, "Political Preference Formation: Competition, Deliberation, and the (Ir)relevance of Framing Effects," *American Political Science Review* 98 (2004): 671–86. Presents experimental evidence demonstrating that framing effects on people's political attitudes depend on whether they receive one-sided frames or counteracting frames.

Entman, R. M., and A. Rojecki, *The Black Image in the White Mind: Media and Race in America* (Chicago: University of Chicago Press, 2000). Discusses evidence that media coverage of crime and government social welfare programs reinforces racism among certain segments of society.

Hamilton, James T., *All the News That's Fit to Sell: How the Market Transforms Information into News* (Princeton, NJ: Princeton University Press, 2004).

Probes deeply into the incentives of media companies and the press to report political facts.

Iyengar, Shanto, and Donald R. Kinder, *News That Matters* (Chicago: University of Chicago Press, 1987). Describes how the reporting of political information shapes perceptions of social groups, reinforces stereotypes, and shapes political choices.

Iyengar, Shanto, and Jennifer A. McGrady, *Media Politics: A Citizen's Guide,* 2nd ed. (New York: Norton, 2011). A comprehensive resource for the current state of knowledge on media and politics.

Ladd, Jonathan M., *Why Americans Hate the Media and How It Matters* (Princeton, NJ: Princeton University Press, 2012). An argument contending that increased competition within the media and political parties has amplified citizens' distrust of the mainstream media.

Lodge, Milton, Marco Steenbergen, and Shawn Brau, "The Responsive Voter: Campaign Information and the Dynamics of Candidate Evaluation," *American Political Science Review* 89, no. 2 (1995): 309–26. Presents evidence that people retain very little information about candidates from campaign advertising.

Niven, David, *Tilt? The Search for Media Bias* (Westport, CT: Praeger, 2002). Data showing that reporters tend to be slightly more liberal than the general population, and that editors and owners of media companies are slightly more conservative than the general population.

Prior, Markus, *Post-Broadcast Democracy: How Media Choice Increases Inequality in Political Involvement and Polarizes Elections* (New York: Cambridge University Press, 2007). An argument that usage of new media has improved political knowledge among those voters already informed and has reduced political knowledge among those less informed.

Valentino, Nicholas A., "Crime News and the Priming of Racial Attitudes during Evaluations of the President," *Public Opinion Quarterly* 63, no. 3 (Fall 1999): 293–320. Argues that people unconsciously absorb racial cues in news coverage, and these cues shape people's evaluations of politicians.

KEY TERMS

coverage bias (p. 505)

gatekeeping bias (p. 504)

infotainment (p. 497)

mass media (p. 485)

media (p. 485)

press (p. 485)

statement bias (p. 505)

APPENDIX

The Declaration of Independence

In Congress, July 4, 1776

The unanimous Declaration of the thirteen united States of America,

When in the Course of human events, it becomes necessary for one people to dissolve the political bands which have connected them with another, and to assume among the powers of the earth, the separate and equal station to which the Laws of Nature and of Nature's God entitle them, a decent respect to the opinions of mankind requires that they should declare the causes which impel them to the separation.

We hold these truths to be self-evident, that all men are created equal, that they are endowed by their Creator with certain unalienable Rights, that among these are Life, Liberty and the pursuit of Happiness.—That to secure these rights, Governments are instituted among Men, deriving their just powers from the consent of the governed.—That whenever any Form of Government becomes destructive of these ends, it is the Right of the People to alter or to abolish it, and to institute new Government, laying its foundation on such principles and organizing its powers in such form, as to them shall seem most likely to effect their Safety and Happiness. Prudence, indeed, will dictate that Governments long established should not be changed for light and transient causes; and accordingly all experience hath shewn, that mankind are more disposed to suffer, while evils are sufferable, than to right themselves by abolishing the forms to which they are accustomed. But when a long train of abuses and usurpations, pursuing invariably the same Object evinces a design to reduce them under absolute Despotism, it is their right, it is their duty, to throw off such Government, and to provide new Guards for their future security.—Such has been the patient sufferance of these Colonies; and such is now the necessity which constrains them to alter their former Systems of Government. The history of the present King of Great Britain is a history of repeated injuries and usurpations, all having in direct object the establishment of an absolute Tyranny over these States. To prove this, let Facts be submitted to a candid world.

He has refused his Assent to Laws, the most wholesome and necessary for the public good.

He has forbidden his Governors to pass Laws of immediate and pressing importance, unless suspended in their operation till his Assent should be obtained; and when so suspended, he has utterly neglected to attend to them.

He has refused to pass other Laws for the accommodation of large districts of people, unless those people would relinquish the right of Representation in the Legislature, a right inestimable to them and formidable to tyrants only.

He has called together legislative bodies at places unusual, uncomfortable, and distant from the depository of their public Records, for the sole purpose of fatiguing them into compliance with his measures.

He has dissolved Representative Houses repeatedly, for opposing with manly firmness his invasions on the rights of the people.

He has refused for a long time, after such dissolutions, to cause others to be elected; whereby the Legislative powers, incapable of Annihilation, have returned to the People at large for their exercise; the State remaining in the mean time exposed to all the dangers of invasion from without, and convulsions within.

He has endeavoured to prevent the population of these States; for that purpose obstructing the Laws for Naturalization of Foreigners; refusing to pass others to encourage their migrations hither, and raising the conditions of new Appropriations of Lands.

He has obstructed the Administration of Justice, by refusing his Assent to Laws for establishing Judiciary powers.

He has made Judges dependent on his Will alone, for the tenure of their offices, and the amount and payment of their salaries.

He has erected a multitude of New Offices, and sent hither swarms of Officers to harrass our people, and eat out their substance.

He has kept among us, in times of peace, Standing Armies without the Consent of our legislatures.

He has affected to render the Military independent of and superior to the Civil power.

He has combined with others to subject us to a jurisdiction foreign to our constitution, and unacknowledged by our laws; giving his Assent to their Acts of pretended Legislation:

For Quartering large bodies of armed troops among us:

For protecting them, by a mock Trial, from punishment for any Murders which they should commit on the Inhabitants of these States:

For cutting off our Trade with all parts of the world:

For imposing Taxes on us without our Consent:

For depriving us in many cases, of the benefits of Trial by Jury:

For transporting us beyond Seas to be tried for pretended offences:

For abolishing the free System of English Laws in a neighboring Province, establishing therein an Arbitrary government, and enlarging its Boundaries so as to render it at once an example and fit instrument for introducing the same absolute rule into these Colonies:

For taking away our Charters, abolishing our most valuable Laws, and altering fundamentally the Forms of our Governments:

For suspending our own Legislatures, and declaring themselves invested with power to legislate for us in all cases whatsoever.

He has abdicated Government here, by declaring us out of his Protection and waging War against us.

He has plundered our seas, ravaged our Coasts, burnt our towns, and destroyed the lives of our people.

He is at this time transporting large Armies of foreign Mercenaries to compleat the works of death, desolation and tyranny, already begun with circumstances of Cruelty & perfidy scarcely paralleled in the most barbarous ages, and totally unworthy the Head of a civilized nation.

He has constrained our fellow Citizens taken Captive on the high Seas to bear Arms against their Country, to become the executioners of their friends and Brethren, or to fall themselves by their Hands.

He has excited domestic insurrections amongst us, and has endeavoured to bring on the inhabitants of our frontiers, the merciless Indian Savages, whose known rule of warfare, is an undistinguished destruction of all ages, sexes and conditions.

In every stage of these Oppressions We have Petitioned for Redress in the most humble terms: Our repeated Petitions have been answered only by repeated injury. A Prince whose character is thus marked by every act which may define a Tyrant, is unfit to be the ruler of a free people.

Nor have We been wanting in attentions to our Brittish brethren. We have warned them from time to time of attempts by their legislature to extend an unwarrantable jurisdiction over us. We have reminded them of the circum-stances of our emigration and settlement here. We have appealed to their native justice and magnanimity, and we have conjured them by the ties of our common kindred to disavow these usurpations, which, would inevitably interrupt our connections and correspondence. They too have been deaf to the voice of justice and of consanguinity. We must, therefore, acquiesce in the necessity, which denounces our Separation, and hold them, as we hold the rest of mankind, Enemies in War, in Peace Friends.

We, Therefore, the Representatives of the United States of America, in General Congress, Assembled, appealing to the Supreme Judge of the world for the rectitude of our intentions, do, in the Name, and by Authority of the good People of these Colonies, solemnly publish and declare, That these United Colonies are, and of Right ought to be Free and Independent States; that they are Absolved from all Allegiance to the British Crown, and that all political connection between them and the State of Great Britain, is and ought to be totally dissolved; and that as Free and Independent States, they have full Power to levy War, conclude Peace, contract Alliances, establish Commerce, and to do all other Acts and Things which Independent States may of right do. And for the support of this Declaration, with a firm reliance on the protection of divine Providence, we mutually pledge to each other our Lives, our Fortunes and our sacred Honor.

The foregoing Declaration was, by order of Congress, engrossed, and signed by the following members:

John Hancock

NEW HAMPSHIRE
Josiah Bartlett
William Whipple
Matthew Thornton

MASSACHUSETTS BAY
Samuel Adams
John Adams
Robert Treat Paine
Elbridge Gerry

RHODE ISLAND
Stephen Hopkins
William Ellery

CONNECTICUT
Roger Sherman
Samuel Huntington
William Williams
Oliver Wolcott

NEW YORK
William Floyd
Philip Livingston
Francis Lewis
Lewis Morris

NEW JERSEY
Richard Stockton
John Witherspoon
Francis Hopkinson
John Hart
Abraham Clark

PENNSYLVANIA
Robert Morris
Benjamin Rush
Benjamin Franklin
John Morton
George Clymer
James Smith
George Taylor
James Wilson
George Ross

DELAWARE
Caesar Rodney
George Read
Thomas M'Kean

MARYLAND
Samuel Chase
William Paca
Thomas Stone
Charles Carroll, of Carrollton

VIRGINIA
George Wythe
Richard Henry Lee
Thomas Jefferson
Benjamin Harrison
Thomas Nelson, Jr.
Francis Lightfoot Lee
Carter Braxton

NORTH CAROLINA
William Hooper
Joseph Hewes
John Penn

SOUTH CAROLINA	GEORGIA
Edward Rutledge	*Button Gwinnett*
Thomas Heyward, Jr.	*Lyman Hall*
Thomas Lynch, Jr.	*George Walton*
Arthur Middleton	

Resolved, That copies of the Declaration be sent to the several assemblies, conventions, and committees, or councils of safety, and to the several commanding officers of the continental troops; that it be proclaimed in each of the United States, at the head of the army.

The Articles of Confederation

Agreed to by Congress November 15, 1777; ratified and in force March 1, 1781

To all whom these Presents shall come, we the undersigned Delegates of the States affixed to our Names, send greeting. Whereas the Delegates of the United States of America, in Congress assembled, did, on the fifteenth day of November, in the Year of Our Lord One thousand Seven Hundred and Seventy seven, and in the Second Year of the Independence of America, agree to certain articles of Confederation and perpetual Union between the States of Newhampshire, Massachusetts-bay, Rhodeisland and Providence Plantations, Connecticut, New-York, New-Jersey, Pennsylvania, Delaware, Maryland, Virginia, North-Carolina, South-Carolina and Georgia in the words following, viz. "Articles of Confederation and perpetual Union between the states of Newhampshire, Massachusettsbay, Rhodeisland and Providence Plantations, Connecticut, New-York, New-Jersey, Pennsylvania, Delaware, Maryland, Virginia, North-Carolina, South-Carolina and Georgia.

Art. I. The Stile of this confederacy shall be "The United States of America."

Art. II. Each state retains its sovereignty, freedom and independence, and every Power, Jurisdiction and right, which is not by this confederation expressly delegated to the United States, in Congress assembled.

Art. III. The said states hereby severally enter into a firm league of friendship with each other, for their common defence, the security of their Liberties, and their mutual and general welfare, binding themselves to assist each other, against all force offered to, or attacks made upon them, or any of them, on account of religion, sovereignty, trade, or any other pretence whatever.

Art. IV. The better to secure and perpetuate mutual friendship and intercourse among the people of the different states in this union, the free inhabitants of each of these states, paupers, vagabonds and fugitives from Justice excepted, shall be entitled to all privileges and immunities of free citizens in the several states; and the people of each state shall have free ingress and regress to and from any other state, and shall enjoy therein all the privileges of trade and commerce, subject to the same duties, impositions and restrictions as the inhabitants thereof respectively, provided that such restriction shall not extend so far as to prevent the removal of property imported into any state, to any other state, of which the Owner is an inhabitant; provided also that no imposition, duties or restriction shall be laid by any state, on the property of the united states, or either of them.

If any Person guilty of, or charged with treason, felony, or other high misdemeanor in any state, shall flee from Justice, and be found in any of the united states, he shall, upon demand of the Governor or executive power, of the state from which he fled, be delivered up and removed to the state having jurisdiction of his offence.

Full faith and credit shall be given in each of these states to the records, acts and judicial proceedings of the courts and magistrates of every other state.

Art. V. For the more convenient management of the general interests of the united states, delegates shall be annually appointed in such manner as the legislature of each state shall direct, to meet in Congress on the first Monday in November, in every year, with a power reserved to each state, to recall its delegates, or any of them, at any time within the year, and to send others in their stead, for the remainder of the Year.

No state shall be represented in Congress by less than two, nor by more than seven Members; and no person shall be capable of being a delegate for more than three years in any term of six years; nor shall any person, being a delegate, be capable of holding any office under the united states, for which he, or another for his benefit receives any salary, fees or emolument of any kind.

Each state shall maintain its own delegates in a meeting of the states, and while they act as members of the committee of the states.

In determining questions in the united states, in Congress assembled, each state shall have one vote.

Freedom of speech and debate in Congress shall not be impeached or questioned in any Court, or place out of Congress, and the members of congress shall be protected in their persons from arrests and imprisonments, during the time of their going to and from, and attendance on congress, except for treason, felony, or breach of the peace.

Art. VI. No state without the Consent of the united states in congress assembled, shall send any embassy to, or receive any embassy from, or enter into any conference, agreement, or alliance or treaty with any King, prince or state; nor shall any person holding any office or profit or trust under the united states, or any of them, accept of any present, emolument, office or title of any kind whatever from any king, prince or foreign state; nor shall the united states in congress assembled, or any of them, grant any title of nobility.

No two or more states shall enter into any treaty, confederation or alliance whatever between them, without the consent of the united states in congress assembled, specifying accurately the purposes for which the same is to be entered into, and how long it shall continue.

No state shall lay any imposts or duties, which may interfere with any stipulations in treaties, entered into by the united states in congress assembled, with any king, prince or state, in pursuance of any treaties already proposed by congress, to the courts of France and Spain.

No vessels of war shall be kept up in time of peace by any state, except such number only, as shall be deemed necessary by the united states in congress assembled, for the defence of such state, or its trade; nor shall any body of forces be kept up by any state, in time of peace, except such number only, as in the judgment of the united states, in congress assembled, shall be deemed requisite to garrison the forts necessary for the defence of such state; but every state shall always keep up a well regulated and disciplined militia, sufficiently armed and accoutred, and shall provide and constantly have ready for use, in public stores, a due number of field pieces and tents, and a proper quantity of arms, ammunition and camp equipage.

No state shall engage in any war without the consent of the united states in congress assembled, unless such state be actually invaded by enemies, or shall have received certain advice of a resolution being formed by some nation of Indians to invade such state, and the danger is so imminent as not to admit of a delay, till the united states in congress asssembled can be consulted; nor shall any state grant commissions to any ships or vessels of war, nor letters of marque or reprisal, except it be after a declaration of war by the united states in congress assembled, and then only against the kingdom or state and the subjects thereof, against which war has been so declared, and under such regulations as shall be established by the united states in congress assembled, unless such state be infested by pirates; in which case vessels of war may be fitted out for that occasion, and kept so long as the danger shall continue, or until the united states in congress assembled shall determine otherwise.

Art. VII. When land-forces are raised by any state for the common defence, all officers of or under the rank of colonel, shall be appointed by the legislature of each state respectively, by whom such forces shall be raised, or in such manner as such state shall direct, and all vacancies shall be filled up by the state which first made the appointment.

Art. VIII. All charges of war, and all other expences that shall be incurred for the common defence or general welfare, and allowed by the united states in congress assembled, shall be defrayed out of a common treasury, which shall be supplied by the several states in proportion to the value of all land within each state, granted to or surveyed for any Person, as such land and the buildings and improvements thereon shall be estimated according to such mode as the united states in congress assembled, shall from time to time direct and appoint.

The taxes for paying that proportion shall be laid and levied by the authority and direction of the legislatures of the several states within the time agreed upon by the united states in congress assembled.

Art. IX. The united states in congress assembled, shall have the sole and exclusive right and power of determining on peace and war, except in the cases mentioned in the sixth article—of sending and receiving ambassadors—entering into treaties and alliances, provided that no treaty of commerce shall be made whereby the legislative power of the respective states shall be restrained from imposing such imposts and duties on foreigners, as their own people are subjected to, or from prohibiting the exportation of any species of goods or commodities -whatsoever—of establishing rules for deciding in all cases, what captures on land or water shall be legal, and in what manner prizes taken by land or naval forces in the service of the united states shall be divided or appropriated—of granting letters of marque and reprisal in times of peace—appointing courts for the trial of piracies and felonies committed on the high seas and establishing courts for receiving and determining finally appeals in all cases of captures, provided that no member of congress shall be appointed a judge of any of the said courts.

The united states in congress assembled shall also be the last resort on appeal in all disputes and differences now subsisting or that hereafter may arise between two or more states concerning boundary, jurisdiction or any other cause whatever; which authority shall always be exercised in the manner following. Whenever the legislative or executive authority or lawful agent of any state in controversy with another shall present a petition to congress stating the matter in question and praying for a hearing, notice thereof shall be given by order of congress to the legislative or executive authority of the other state in controversy, and a day assigned for the appearance of the parties by their lawful agents, who shall then be directed to appoint by joint consent, commissioners or judges to constitute a court for hearing and determining the matter in question: but if they cannot agree, congress shall name three persons out of each of the united states, and from the list of such persons each party shall alternately strike out one, the petitioners beginning, until the number shall be reduced to thirteen; and from that number not less than seven, nor more than nine names as congress shall direct, shall in the presence of congress be drawn out by lot, and the persons whose names shall be so drawn or any five of them, shall be commissioners or judges, to hear and finally determine the controversy, so always as a major part of the judges who shall hear the cause shall agree in the determination: and if either party shall neglect to attend at the day appointed, without shewing reasons, which congress shall judge sufficient, or being present shall refuse to strike, the congress shall proceed to nominate three persons out of each state, and the secretary of congress shall strike in behalf of such party absent or refusing; and the judgment and sentence of the court to be appointed, in the manner before prescribed, shall be final and conclusive; and if any of the parties shall refuse to submit to the authority of such court, or to appear to defend their claim or cause, the court shall nevertheless proceed to pronounce sentence, or judgment, which shall in like manner be final and decisive, the judgment or sentence and other proceedings being in either case transmitted to congress, and lodged among the acts of congress for the security of the parties concerned: provided that every commissioner, before he sits in judgment, shall take an oath to be administered by one of the judges of the supreme or superior court of the state, where the cause shall be tried, "well and truly to hear and determine the matter in question, according to the best of his judgment, without favour, affection or hope of reward:" provided also, that no state shall be deprived of territory for the benefit of the united states.

All controversies concerning the private right of soil claimed under different grants of two or more states, whose -jurisdictions as they may respect such lands, and the states which passed such grants are adjusted, the said grants or either of them being at the same time claimed to have originated antecedent to such settlement of jurisdiction, shall on the petition of either party to the congress of the united states, be finally determined as near as may be in the same manner as is before prescribed for deciding disputes respecting territorial jurisdiction between different states.

The united states in congress assembled shall also have the sole and exclusive right and power of regulating the alloy and value of coin struck by their own authority, or by that of the respective states—fixing the standard of weights and measures throughout the united states—regulating the trade and managing all affairs with the Indians, not members of any of the states, provided that the legislative right of any state within its own limits be not infringed or violated—establishing and regulating post-offices from one state to another, throughout all the united states, and exacting such postage on the papers passing thro' the same as may be requisite to defray the expences of the said office—appointing all officers of the land forces, in the service of the united states, excepting regimental officers—appointing all the officers of the naval forces, and commissioning all officers whatever in the service of the united states—making rules for the government and regulation of the said land and naval forces, and directing their operations.

The united states in congress assembled shall have authority to appoint a committee, to sit in the recess of congress, to be denominated "A Committee of the States," and to consist of one delegate from each state; and to appoint such other committees and civil officers as may be necessary for managing the general affairs of the united states under their direction—to appoint one of their number to preside, provided that no person be allowed to serve in the office of president more than one year in any term of three years; to ascertain the necessary sums of Money to be raised for the service of the united states, and to appropriate and apply the same for defraying the public expenses—to borrow money, or emit bills on the credit of the united states, transmitting every half year to the respective states an account of the sums of money so borrowed or emitted,—to build and equip a navy—to agree upon the number of land forces, and to make requisitions from each state for its quota, in proportion to the number of white inhabitants in such state; which requisition shall be binding, and thereupon the legislature of each state shall appoint the regimental officers, raise the men and cloath, arm and equip them in a soldier like manner, at the expense of the united states; and the officers and men so cloathed, armed and equipped shall march to the place appointed, and within the time agreed on by the united states in congress assembled: But if the united states in congress assembled shall, on consideration of circumstances judge proper that any state should not raise men, or should raise a smaller number than its quota, and that any other state should raise a greater number of men than the quota thereof, such extra number shall be raised, officered, cloathed, armed and equipped in the same manner as the quota of such state, unless the legislature of such state shall judge that such extra number cannot be safely spared out of the same, in which case they shall raise officer, cloath, arm and equip as many of such extra number as they judge can be safely spared. And the officers and men so cloathed, armed and equipped, shall march to the place appointed, and within the time agreed on by the united states in congress assembled.

The united states in congress assembled shall never engage in a war, nor grant letters of marque and reprisal in time of peace, nor enter into any treaties or alliances, nor coin money, nor regulate the value thereof, nor ascertain the sums and expenses necessary for the defence and welfare of the united states, or any of them, nor emit bills, nor borrow money on the credit of the united states, nor appropriate money, nor agree upon the number of vessels of war, to be built or purchased, or the number of land or sea forces to be raised, nor appoint a commander in chief of the army or navy, unless nine states assent to the same: nor shall a question on any other point, except for adjourning from day to day be determined, unless by the votes of a majority of the united states in congress assembled.

The congress of the united states shall have power to adjourn to any time within the year, and to any place within the united states, so that no period of adjournment be for a longer duration than the space of six Months, and shall publish the Journal of their proceedings monthly, except such parts thereof relating to treaties, alliances or military operations, as in their judgment require secrecy; and the yeas and nays of the delegates of each state on any question shall be entered on the Journal, when it is desired by any delegate; and the delegates of a state, or any of them, at his or their request shall be furnished with a transcript of the said Journal, except such parts as are above excepted, to lay before the legislatures of the several states.

Art. X. The committee of the states, or any nine of them, shall be authorised to execute, in the recess of congress, such of the powers of congress as the united states in congress assembled, by the consent of nine states, shall from time to time think expedient to vest them with; provided that no power be delegated to the said committee, for the exercise of which, by the articles of confederation, the voice of nine states in the congress of the united states assembled is requisite.

Art. XI. Canada acceding to this confederation, and joining in the measures of the united states, shall be admitted into, and entitled to all the advantages of this union: but no other colony shall be admitted into the same, unless such admission be agreed to by nine states.

Art. XII. All bills of credit emitted, monies borrowed and debts contracted by, or under the authority of congress, before the assembling of the united states, in pursuance of the present confederation, shall be deemed and considered as a charge against the united states, for payment and satisfaction whereof the said united states and the public faith are hereby solemnly pledged.

Art. XIII. Every state shall abide by the determinations of the united states in congress assembled, on all questions which by this confederation are submitted to them. And the Articles of this confederation shall be inviolably observed by every state, and the union shall be perpetual; nor shall any alteration at any time hereafter be made in any of them; unless such alteration be agreed to in a congress of the united states, and be afterwards confirmed by the legislatures of every state.

And Whereas it hath pleased the Great Governor of the World to incline the hearts of the legislatures we respectively represent in congress, to approve of, and to authorize us to ratify the said articles of confederation and perpetual union. Know Ye that we the undersigned delegates, by virtue of the power and authority to us given for that purpose, do by these presents, in the name and in behalf of our respective constituents, fully and entirely ratify and confirm each and every of the said articles of confederation and perpetual union, and all and singular the matters and things therein contained: And we do further solemnly plight and engage the faith of our respective constituents, that they shall abide by the determinations of the united states in congress assembled, on all questions, which by the said confederation are submitted to them. And that the articles thereof shall be inviolably observed by the states we respectively represent, and that the union shall be perpetual. In Witness whereof we have hereunto set our hands in Congress. Done at Philadelphia in the state of Pennsylvania the ninth day of July, in the Year of our Lord one Thousand seven Hundred and Seventy-eight, and in the third year of the independence of America.

The Constitution of the United States of America

PREAMBLE

We the People of the United States, in Order to form a more perfect Union, establish Justice, insure domestic Tranquility, provide for the common defence, promote the general Welfare, and secure the Blessings of Liberty to ourselves and our Posterity, do ordain and establish this Constitution for the United States of America.

Article I

SECTION 1

[LEGISLATIVE POWERS]

All legislative Powers herein granted shall be vested in a Congress of the United States, which shall consist of a Senate and House of Representatives.

SECTION 2

[HOUSE OF REPRESENTATIVES, HOW CONSTITUTED, POWER OF IMPEACHMENT]

The House of Representatives shall be composed of Members chosen every second Year by the People of the several States, and the Electors in each State shall have the Qualifications requisite for Electors of the most numerous Branch of the State Legislature.

No Person shall be a Representative who shall not have attained to the Age of twenty five Years, and been seven Years a Citizen of the United States, and who shall not, when elected, be an Inhabitant of that State in which he shall be chosen.

Representatives and *direct Taxes*[1] shall be apportioned among the several States which may be included within this Union, according to their respective Numbers, *which shall be determined by adding to the whole Number of free Persons, including those bound to Service for a Term of Years, and excluding Indians not taxed, three fifths of all other Persons.*[2] The actual Enumeration shall be made within three Years after the first Meeting of the Congress of the United States, and within every subsequent Term of ten Years, in such Manner as they shall by Law direct. The Number of Representatives shall not exceed one for every thirty Thousand, but each State shall have at Least one Representative; *and until such enumeration shall be made, the State of New Hampshire shall be entitled to chuse three, Massachusetts eight, Rhode-Island and Providence Plantations one, Connecticut five, New-York six, New Jersey four,*

[1] Modified by Sixteenth Amendment.
[2] Modified by Fourteenth Amendment.

Pennsylvania eight, Delaware one, Maryland six, Virginia ten, North Carolina five, South Carolina five, and Georgia three.[3]

When vacancies happen in the Representation from any State, the Executive Authority thereof shall issue Writs of Election to fill such Vacancies.

The House of Representatives shall chuse their Speaker and other Officers; and shall have the sole Power of Impeachment.

SECTION 3

[THE SENATE, HOW CONSTITUTED, IMPEACHMENT TRIALS]
The Senate of the United States shall be composed of two Senators from each State, *chosen by the Legislature thereof*[4] for six Years; and each Senator shall have one Vote.

Immediately after they shall be assembled in Consequence of the first Election, they shall be divided as equally as may be into three Classes. The Seats of the Senators of the first Class shall be vacated at the Expiration of the second Year, of the second Class at the Expiration of the fourth Year, and of the third Class at the Expiration of the sixth Year, so that one third may be chosen every second Year; *and if Vacancies happen by Resignation, or otherwise, during the Recess of the Legislature of any State, the Executive thereof may make temporary Appointments until the next Meeting of the Legislature, which shall then fill such Vacancies.*[5]

No Person shall be a Senator who shall not have attained to the Age of thirty Years, and been nine Years a Citizen of the United States, and who shall not, when elected, be an Inhabitant of that State for which he shall be chosen.

The Vice President of the United States shall be President of the Senate, but shall have no Vote, unless they be equally divided.

The Senate shall chuse their other Officers, and also a President pro tempore, in the Absence of the Vice President, or when he shall exercise the Office of President of the United States.

The Senate shall have the sole Power to try all Impeachments. When sitting for that Purpose, they shall be on Oath or Affirmation. When the President of the United States is tried, the Chief Justice shall preside: And no Person shall be convicted without the Concurrence of two thirds of the Members present.

Judgment in Cases of Impeachment shall not extend further than to removal from Office, and disqualification to hold and enjoy any Office of honor, Trust or Profit under the United States: but the Party convicted shall nevertheless be liable and subject to Indictment, Trial, Judgment and Punishment, according to Law.

[3] Temporary provision.
[4] Modified by Seventeenth Amendment.
[5] Modified by Seventeenth Amendment.

SECTION 4

[ELECTION OF SENATORS AND REPRESENTATIVES]

The Times, Places and Manner of holding Elections for Senators and Representatives, shall be prescribed in each State by the Legislature thereof; but the Congress may at any time by Law make or alter such Regulations, except as to the Places of chusing Senators.

The Congress shall assemble at least once in every Year, and such Meeting shall be on the first Monday in December, unless they shall by Law appoint a different Day.[6]

SECTION 5

[QUORUM, JOURNALS MEETINGS, ADJOURNMENTS]

Each House shall be the Judge of the Elections, Returns and Qualifications of its own Members, and a Majority of each shall constitute a Quorum to do Business; but a smaller Number may adjourn from day to day, and may be authorized to compel the Attendance of absent Members, in such Manner, and under such Penalties as each House may provide.

Each House may determine the Rules of its Proceedings, punish its Members for disorderly Behaviour, and, with the Concurrence of two thirds, expel a Member.

Each House shall keep a Journal of its Proceedings, and from time to time publish the same, excepting such Parts as may in their Judgment require Secrecy; and the Yeas and Nays of the Members of either House on any questions shall, at the Desire of one fifth of those Present, be entered on the Journal.

Neither House, during the Session of Congress, shall, without the Consent of the other, adjourn for more than three days, nor to any other Place than that in which the two Houses shall be sitting.

SECTION 6

[COMPENSATION, PRIVILEGES, DISABILITIES]

The Senators and Representatives shall receive a Compensation for their Services, to be ascertained by Law, and paid out of the Treasury of the United States. They shall in all Cases, except Treason, Felony and Breach of the Peace, be privileged from Arrest during their Attendance at the Session of their respective Houses, and in going to and returning from the same; and for any Speech or Debate in either House, they shall not be questioned in any other Place.

No Senator or Representative shall, during the Time for which he was elected, be appointed to any civil Office under the Authority of the United States, which shall have been created, or the Emoluments whereof shall have been encreased during such time; and no Person holding any Office under the United States, shall be a Member of either House during his Continuance in Office.

---

[6] Modified by Twentieth Amendment.

SECTION 7

[PROCEDURE IN PASSING BILLS AND RESOLUTIONS]

All Bills for raising Revenue shall originate in the House of Representatives; but the Senate may propose or concur with Amendments as on other Bills.

Every Bill which shall have passed the House of Representatives and the Senate, shall, before it become a Law, be presented to the President of the United States: If he approve he shall sign it, but if not he shall return it, with his Objections to that House in which it shall have originated, who shall enter the Objections at large on their Journal, and proceed to reconsider it. If after such Reconsideration two thirds of that House shall agree to pass the Bill, it shall be sent, together with the Objections, to the other House, by which it shall likewise be reconsidered, and if approved by two thirds of that House, it shall become a Law. But in all such Cases the Votes of both Houses shall be determined by yeas and Nays, and the Names of the Persons voting for and against the Bill shall be entered on the Journal of each House respectively. If any Bill shall not be returned by the President within ten Days (Sundays excepted) after it shall have been presented to him, the Same shall be a Law, in like Manner as if he had signed it, unless the Congress by their Adjournment prevent its Return, in which Case it shall not be a Law.

Every Order, Resolution, or Vote to which the Concurrence of the Senate and House of Representatives may be necessary (except on a question of Adjournment) shall be presented to the President of the United States; and before the Same shall take Effect, shall be approved by him, or being disapproved by him, shall be repassed by two thirds of the Senate and House of Representatives, according to the Rules and Limitations prescribed in the Case of a Bill.

SECTION 8

[POWERS OF CONGRESS]

The Congress shall have Power

To lay and collect Taxes, Duties, Imposts and Excises, to pay the Debts and provide for the common Defence and general Welfare of the United States; but all Duties, Imposts and Excises shall be uniform throughout the United States;

To borrow Money on the credit of the United States;

To regulate Commerce with foreign Nations, and among the several States, and with the Indian Tribes;

To establish an uniform Rule of Naturalization, and uniform Laws on the subject of Bankruptcies throughout the United States;

To coin Money, regulate the Value thereof, and of foreign Coin, and fix the Standard of Weights and Measures;

To provide for the Punishment of counterfeiting the Securities and current Coin of the United States;

To establish Post Offices and post Roads;

To promote the Progress of Science and useful Arts, by securing for limited Times to Authors and Inventors the exclusive Right to their respective Writings and Discoveries;

To constitute Tribunals inferior to the supreme Court;

To define and punish Piracies and Felonies committed on the high Seas, and Offences against the Law of Nations;

To declare War, grant Letters of Marque and Reprisal, and make Rules concerning Captures on Land and Water;

To raise and support Armies, but no Appropriation of Money to that Use shall be for a longer Term than two Years;

To provide and maintain a Navy;

To make Rules for the Government and Regulation of the land and naval Forces;

To provide for calling forth the Militia to execute the Laws of the Union, suppress Insurrections and repel Invasions;

To provide for organizing, arming, and disciplining, the Militia, and for governing such Part of them as may be employed in the Service of the United States, reserving to the States respectively, the Appointment of the Officers, and the Authority of training the Militia according to the discipline prescribed by Congress;

To exercise exclusive Legislation in all Cases whatsoever, over such District (not exceeding ten Miles square) as may, by Cession of particular States, and the Acceptance of Congress, become the Seat of the Government of the United States, and to exercise like Authority over all Places purchased by the Consent of the Legislature of the State in which the Same shall be, for the Erection of Forts, Magazines, Arsenals, dock-Yards, and other needful Buildings;—And

To make all Laws which shall be necessary and proper for carrying into Execution the foregoing Powers, and all other Powers vested by this Constitution in the Government of the United States, or in any Department or Officer thereof.

SECTION 9

[SOME RESTRICTIONS ON FEDERAL POWER]

The Migration or Importation of such Persons as any of the States now existing shall think proper to admit, shall not be prohibited by the Congress prior to the Year one thousand eight hundred and eight, but a Tax or duty may be imposed on such Importation, not exceeding ten dollars for each Person.[7]

The Privilege of the Writ of Habeas Corpus shall not be suspended, unless when in Cases of Rebellion or Invasion the public Safety may require it.

No Bill of Attainder or ex post facto Law shall be passed.

No Capitation, or other direct, Tax shall be laid, unless in Proportion to the Census or Enumeration herein before directed to be taken.[8]

[7] Temporary provision.

[8] Modified by Sixteenth Amendment.

No Tax or Duty shall be laid on Articles exported from any State.

No Preference shall be given by any Regulation of Commerce or Revenue to the Ports of one State over those of another; nor shall Vessels bound to, or from, one State, be obliged to enter, clear, or pay Duties in another.

No Money shall be drawn from the Treasury, but in Consequence of Appropriations made by Law; and a regular Statement and Account of the Receipts and Expenditures of all public Money shall be published from time to time.

No Title of Nobility shall be granted by the United States: And no Person holding any Office of Profit or Trust under them, shall, without the Consent of the Congress, accept of any present, Emolument, Office, or Title, of any kind whatever, from any King, Prince, or foreign State.

SECTION 10

[RESTRICTIONS UPON POWERS OF STATES]

No State shall enter into any Treaty, Alliance, or Confederation; grant Letters of Marque and Reprisal; coin Money; emit Bills of Credit; make any Thing but gold and silver Coin a Tender in Payment of Debts; pass any Bill of Attainder, ex post facto Law, or Law impairing the Obligation of Contracts, or grant any Title of Nobility.

No State shall, without the Consent of the Congress, lay any Imposts or Duties on Imports or Exports, except what may be absolutely necessary for executing its inspection Laws: and the net Produce of all Duties and Imposts, laid by any State on Imports or Exports, shall be for the Use of the Treasury of the United States; and all such Laws shall be subject to the Revision and Control of the Congress.

No State shall, without the Consent of Congress, lay any Duty of Tonnage, keep Troops, or Ships of War in time of Peace, enter into any Agreement or Compact with another State, or with a foreign Power, or engage in War, unless actually invaded, or in such imminent Danger as will not admit of delay.

Article II

SECTION 1

[EXECUTIVE POWER, ELECTION, QUALIFICATIONS OF THE PRESIDENT]

The executive Power shall be vested in a President of the United States of America. *He shall hold his Office during the Term of four Years, and, together with the Vice President, chosen for the same Term, be elected, as follows*[9]

Each State shall appoint, in such Manner as the Legislature thereof may direct, a Number of Electors, equal to the whole Number of Senators and

---

[9] Number of terms limited to two by Twenty-second Amendment.

Representatives to which the State may be entitled in the Congress: but no Senator or Representative, or Person holding an Office of Trust or Profit under the United States, shall be appointed an Elector.

The electors shall meet in their respective States, and vote by ballot for two Persons, of whom one at least shall not be an Inhabitant of the same State with themselves. And they shall make a List of all the Persons voted for, and of the Number of Votes for each; which List they shall sign and certify, and transmit sealed to the Seat of the Government of the United States, directed to the President of the Senate. The President of the Senate shall, in the Presence of the Senate and House of Representatives, open all the Certificates, and the Votes shall then be counted. The Person having the greatest Number of Votes shall be the President, if such Number be a Majority of the whole Number of Electors appointed; and if there be more than one who have such Majority, and have an equal Number of Votes, then the House of Representatives shall immediately chuse by Ballot one of them for President; and if no Person have a Majority, then from the five highest on the List the said House shall in like Manner chuse the President. But in chusing the President, the Votes shall be taken by States, the Representation from each State having one Vote; A quorum for this Purpose shall consist of a Member or Members from two thirds of the States, and a Majority of all the States shall be necessary to a Choice. In every Case, after the Choice of the President, the person having the greatest Number of Votes of the Electors shall be the Vice President. But if there should remain two or more who have equal Votes, the Senate shall chuse from them by Ballot the Vice President.[10]

The Congress may determine the Time of chusing the Electors, and the Day on which they shall give their Votes; which Day shall be the same throughout the United States.

No Person except a natural born Citizen, or a Citizen of the United States, at the time of the Adoption of this Constitution, shall be eligible to the Office of President; neither shall any Person be eligible to that Office who shall not have attained to the Age of thirty five Years, and been fourteen Years a Resident within the United States.

In Case of the Removal of the President from Office, or his Death, Resignation, or Inability to discharge the Powers and Duties of the said Office, the Same shall devolve on the Vice President, and the Congress may by Law provide for the Case of Removal, Death, Resignation or Inability, both of the President and Vice President, declaring what Officer shall then act as President, and such Officer shall act accordingly, until the Disability be removed, or a President shall be elected.

The President shall, at stated Times, receive for his Services, a Compensation, which shall neither be increased nor diminished during the Period for which he shall have been elected, and he shall not receive within that Period any other Emolument from the United States, or any of them.

---

[10] Modified by Twelfth and Twentieth Amendment.

Before he enter on the Execution of his Office, he shall take the following Oath or Affirmation:—"I do solemnly swear (or affirm) that I will faithfully execute the Office of President of the United States, and will to the best of my Ability, preserve, protect and defend the Constitution of the United States."

SECTION 2

[POWERS OF THE PRESIDENT]

The President shall be Commander in Chief of the Army and Navy of the United States, and of the Militia of the several States, when called into the actual Service of the United States; he may require the Opinion, in writing, of the principal Officer in each of the executive Departments, upon any Subject relating to the Duties of their respective Offices, and he shall have Power to grant Reprieves and Pardons for Offences against the United States, except in Cases of Impeachment.

He shall have Power, by and with the Advice and Consent of the Senate, to make Treaties, provided two thirds of the Senators present concur; and he shall nominate, and by and with the Advice and Consent of the Senate, shall appoint Ambassadors, other public Ministers and Consuls, Judges of the supreme Court, and all other Officers of the United States, whose Appointments are not herein otherwise provided for, and which shall be established by Law: but the Congress may by Law vest the Appointment of such inferior Officers, as they think proper, in the President alone, in the Courts of Law, or in the Heads of Departments.

The President shall have Power to fill up all Vacancies that may happen during the Recess of the Senate, by granting Commissions which shall expire at the End of their next Session.

SECTION 3

[POWERS AND DUTIES OF THE PRESIDENT]

He shall from time to time give to the Congress Information of the State of the Union, and recommend to their Consideration such Measures as he shall judge necessary and expedient; he may, on extraordinary Occasions, convene both Houses, or either of them, and in Case of Disagreement between them, with Respect to the Time of Adjournment, he may adjourn them to such Time as he shall think proper; he shall receive Ambassadors and other public Ministers; he shall take Care that the Laws be faithfully executed, and shall Commission all the Officers of the United States.

SECTION 4

[IMPEACHMENT]

The President, Vice President and all civil Officers of the United States, shall be removed from Office on Impeachment for, and Conviction of, Treason, Bribery, or other high Crimes and Misdemeanors.

Article III

SECTION 1

[JUDICIAL POWER, TENURE OF OFFICE]

The judicial Power of the United States, shall be vested in one supreme Court, and in such inferior Courts as the Congress may from time to time ordain and establish. The Judges, both of the supreme and inferior Courts, shall hold their Offices during good Behaviour, and shall, at stated Times, receive for their Services, a Compensation, which shall not be diminished during their Continuance in Office.

SECTION 2

[JURISDICTION]

The judicial Power shall extend to all Cases, in Law and Equity, arising under this Constitution, the Laws of the United States, and Treaties made, or which shall be made, under their Authority;—to all Cases affecting Ambassadors, other public Ministers and Consuls;—to all Cases of admiralty and maritime Jurisdiction;—to Controversies to which the United States shall be a Party;—to Controversies between two or more States;—*between a State and Citizens of another State;*—between Citizens of different States,—between Citizens of the same State claiming Lands under Grants of different States, *and between a State,* or the Citizens thereof, *and foreign States, Citizens or Subjects.*[11]

In all Cases affecting Ambassadors, other public Ministers and Consuls, and those in which a State shall be Party, the supreme Court shall have original Jurisdiction. In all the other Cases before mentioned, the supreme Court shall have appellate Jurisdiction, both as to Law and Fact, with such Exceptions, and under such Regulations as the Congress shall make.

The Trial of all Crimes, except in Cases of Impeachment, shall be by Jury; and such Trial shall be held in the State where the said Crimes shall have been committed; but when not committed within any State, the Trial shall be at such Place or Places as the Congress may by Law have directed.

SECTION 3

[TREASON, PROOF, AND PUNISHMENT]

Treason against the United States, shall consist only in levying War against them, or in adhering to their Enemies, giving them Aid and Comfort. No Person shall be convicted of Treason unless on the Testimony of two Witnesses to the same overt Act, or on Confession in open Court.

The Congress shall have Power to declare the Punishment of Treason, but no Attainder of Treason shall work Corruption of Blood, or Forfeiture except during the Life of the Person attainted.

---

[11] Modified by Eleventh Amendment.

Article IV

SECTION 1

[FAITH AND CREDIT AMONG STATES]

Full Faith and Credit shall be given in each State to the public Acts, Records, and judicial Proceedings of every other State. And the Congress may by general Laws prescribe the Manner in which such Acts, Records and Proceedings shall be proved, and the Effect thereof.

SECTION 2

[PRIVILEGES AND IMMUNITIES, FUGITIVES]

The Citizens of each State shall be entitled to all Privileges and Immunities of Citizens in the several States.

A Person charged in any State with Treason, Felony or other Crime, who shall flee from Justice, and be found in another State, shall on Demand of the executive Authority of the State from which he fled, be delivered up, to be removed to the State having Jurisdiction of the Crime.

No person held to Service or Labour in one State, under the Laws thereof, escaping into another, shall, in Consequence of any Law or Regulation therein, be discharged from such Service or Labour, but shall be delivered up on Claim of the Party to whom such Service or Labour may be due.[12]

SECTION 3

[ADMISSION OF NEW STATES]

New States may be admitted by the Congress into this Union; but no new State shall be formed or erected within the Jurisdiction of any other State; nor any State be formed by the Junction of two or more States, or Parts of States, without the Consent of the Legislatures of the States concerned as well as of the Congress.

The Congress shall have Power to dispose of and make all needful Rules and Regulations respecting the Territory or other Property belonging to the United States; and nothing in this Constitution shall be so construed as to Prejudice any Claims of the United States, or of any particular State.

SECTION 4

[GUARANTEE OF REPUBLICAN GOVERNMENT]

The United States shall guarantee to every State in this Union a Republican Form of Government, and shall protect each of them against Invasion; and on Application of the Legislature, or of the Executive (when the Legislature cannot be convened), against domestic Violence.

---

[12] Repealed by the Thirteenth Amendment.

Article V

[AMENDMENT OF THE CONSTITUTION]

The Congress, whenever two thirds of both Houses shall deem it necessary, shall propose Amendments to this Constitution, or, on the Application of the Legislatures of two thirds of the several States, shall call a Convention for proposing Amendments, which, in either Case, shall be valid to all Intents and Purposes, as Part of this Constitution, when ratified by the Legislatures of three fourths of the several States, or by Conventions in three fourths thereof, as the one or the other Mode of Ratification may be proposed by the Congress; *Provided that no Amendment which may be made prior to the Year One thousand eight hundred and eight shall in any Manner affect the first and fourth Clauses in the Ninth Section of the first Article;*[13] and that no State, without its Consent, shall be deprived of its equal Suffrage in the Senate.

Article VI

[DEBTS, SUPREMACY, OATH]

All Debts contracted and Engagements entered into, before the Adoption of this Constitution, shall be as valid against the United States under this Constitution, as under the Confederation.

This Constitution, and the Laws of the United States which shall be made in Pursuance thereof; and all Treaties made, or which shall be made, under the Authority of the United States, shall be the supreme Law of the Land; and the Judges in every State shall be bound thereby, any Thing in the Constitution or Laws of any State to the Contrary notwithstanding.

The Senators and Representatives before mentioned, and the Members of the several State Legislatures, and all executive and judicial Officers, both of the United States and of the several States, shall be bound by Oath or Affirmation, to support this Constitution; but no religious Test shall be required as a Qualification to any Office or public Trust under the United States.

Article VII

[RATIFICATION AND ESTABLISHMENT]

The Ratification of the Conventions of nine States, shall be sufficient for the Establishment of this Constitution between the States so ratifying the Same.[14]

---

[13] Temporary provision.

[14] The Constitution was submitted on September 17, 1787, by the Constitutional Convention, was ratified by the conventions of several states at various dates up to May 29, 1790, and became effective on March 4, 1789.

Done in Convention by the Unanimous Consent of the States present the Seventeenth Day of September in the Year of our Lord one thousand seven hundred and Eighty seven and of the Independence of the United States of America the Twelfth. *In Witness* whereof We have hereunto subscribed our Names,

G:⁰ *WASHINGTON—*
Presidt. and deputy from Virginia

NEW HAMPSHIRE
John Langdon
Nicholas Gilman

MASSACHUSETTS
Nathaniel Gorham
Rufus King

CONNECTICUT
Wm. Saml. Johnson
Roger Sherman

NEW YORK
Alexander Hamilton

NEW JERSEY
Wil: Livingston
David Brearley
Wm. Paterson
Jona: Dayton

PENNSYLVANIA
B Franklin
Thomas Mifflin
Robt. Morris
Geo. Clymer
Thos. FitzSimons
Jared Ingersoll
James Wilson
Gouv Morris

DELAWARE
Geo: Read
Gunning Bedford jun
John Dickinson
Richard Bassett
Jaco: Broom

MARYLAND
James McHenry
Dan of St Thos. Jenifer
Danl. Carroll

VIRGINIA
John Blair—
James Madison Jr.

NORTH CAROLINA
Wm. Blount
Richd. Dobbs Spaight
Hu Williamson

SOUTH CAROLINA
J. Rutledge
Charles Cotesworth Pinckney
Charles Pinckney
Pierce Butler

GEORGIA
William Few
Abr Baldwin

Amendments to the Constitution

Proposed by Congress and Ratified by the Legislatures of the Several States, Pursuant to Article V of the Original Constitution.

Amendments I–X, known as the Bill of Rights, were proposed by Congress on September 25, 1789, and ratified on December 15, 1791.

Amendment I

[FREEDOM OF RELIGION, OF SPEECH, AND OF THE PRESS]

Congress shall make no law respecting an establishment of religion, or prohibiting the free exercise thereof; or abridging the freedom of speech, or of the press; or the right of the people peaceably to assemble, and to petition the Government for a redress of grievances.

Amendment II

[RIGHT TO KEEP AND BEAR ARMS]

A well regulated Militia, being necessary to the security of a free State, the right of the people to keep and bear Arms, shall not be infringed.

Amendment III

[QUARTERING OF SOLDIERS]

No Soldier shall, in time of peace be quartered in any house, without the consent of the Owner, nor in time of war, but in a manner to be prescribed by law.

Amendment IV

[SECURITY FROM UNWARRANTABLE SEARCH AND SEIZURE]

The right of the people to be secure in their persons, houses, papers, and effects, against unreasonable searches and seizures, shall not be violated, and no Warrants shall issue, but upon probable cause, supported by Oath or affirmation, and particularly describing the place to be searched, and the persons or things to be seized.

Amendment V

[RIGHTS OF ACCUSED PERSONS IN CRIMINAL PROCEEDINGS]

No person shall be held to answer for a capital, or otherwise infamous crime, unless on a presentment or indictment of a Grand Jury, except in cases arising in the land or naval forces, or in the Militia, when in actual service in time of War or in public danger; nor shall any person be subject for the same offence to be twice put in jeopardy of life or limb; nor shall be compelled in any criminal case to be a witness against himself, nor be deprived of life, liberty, or property, without due process of law; nor shall private property be taken for public use, without just compensation.

Amendment VI

[RIGHT TO SPEEDY TRIAL, WITNESSES, ETC.]
In all criminal prosecutions, the accused shall enjoy the right to a speedy and public trial, by an impartial jury of the State and district wherein the crime shall have been committed, which district shall have been previously ascertained by law, and to be informed of the nature and cause of the accusation; to be confronted with the witnesses against him; to have compulsory process for obtaining witnesses in his favor, and to have the -Assistance of Counsel for his defence.

Amendment VII

[TRIAL BY JURY IN CIVIL CASES]
In suits at common law, where the value in controversy shall exceed twenty dollars, the right of trial by jury shall be preserved, and no fact tried by a jury, shall be otherwise reexamined in any Court of the United States, than according to the rules of the common law.

Amendment VIII

[BAILS, FINES, PUNISHMENTS]
Excessive bail shall not be required, nor excessive fines imposed, nor cruel and unusual punishments inflicted.

Amendment IX

[RESERVATION OF RIGHTS OF PEOPLE]
The enumeration in the Constitution, of certain rights, shall not be construed to deny or disparage others retained by the people.

Amendment X

[POWERS RESERVED TO STATES OR PEOPLE]
The powers not delegated to the United States by the Constitution, nor prohibited by it to the States, are reserved to the States respectively, or to the people.

Amendment XI

[Proposed by Congress on March 4, 1794; declared ratified on January 8, 1798.]

[RESTRICTION OF JUDICIAL POWER]

The Judicial power of the United States shall not be construed to extend to any suit in law or equity, commenced or prosecuted against one of the United States by Citizens of another State, or by Citizens or Subjects of any Foreign State.

Amendment XII

[Proposed by Congress on December 9, 1803; declared ratified on September 25, 1804.]

[ELECTION OF PRESIDENT AND VICE PRESIDENT]

The Electors shall meet in their respective states and vote by ballot for President and Vice-President, one of whom, at least, shall not be an inhabitant of the same state with themselves; they shall name in their ballots the person voted for as President, and in distinct ballots the person voted for as Vice-President, and they shall make distinct lists of all persons voted for as President, and of all persons voted for as Vice-President, and of the number of votes for each, which lists they shall sign and certify, and transmit sealed to the seat of the government of the United States, directed to the President of the Senate;—the President of the Senate shall, in presence of the Senate and House of Representatives, open all the certificates and the votes shall then be counted;—The person having the greatest number of votes for President, shall be the President, if such number be a majority of the whole number of Electors appointed; and if no person have such majority, then from the persons having the highest numbers not exceeding three on the list of those voted for as President, the House of Representatives shall choose immediately, by ballot, the President. But in choosing the President, the votes shall be taken by states, the representation from each state having one vote; a quorum for this purpose shall consist of a member or members from two-thirds of the states, and a majority of all the states shall be necessary to a choice. And if the House of Representatives shall not choose a President whenever the right of choice shall devolve upon them, before the fourth day of March next following, then the Vice-President shall act as President, as in the case of the death or other constitutional disability of the President.—The person having the greatest number of votes as Vice-President, shall be the Vice-President, if such number be a majority of the whole number of Electors appointed, and if no person have a majority, then from the two highest numbers on the list, the Senate shall choose the Vice-President; a quorum for the purpose shall consist of two-thirds of the whole number of Senators, and a majority of the whole number shall be necessary to a choice. But no person constitutionally ineligible to the office of President shall be eligible to that of Vice-President of the United States.

Amendment XIII

[Proposed by Congress on January 31, 1865; declared ratified on December 18, 1865.]

SECTION 1

[ABOLITION OF SLAVERY]
Neither slavery nor involuntary servitude, except as a punishment for crime whereof the party shall have been duly convicted, shall exist within the United States, or any place subject to their jurisdiction.

SECTION 2

[POWER TO ENFORCE THIS ARTICLE]
Congress shall have power to enforce this article by appropriate legislation.

Amendment XIV

[Proposed by Congress on June 13, 1866; declared ratified on July 28, 1868.]

SECTION 1

[CITIZENSHIP RIGHTS NOT TO BE ABRIDGED BY STATES]
All persons born or naturalized in the United States, and subject to the jurisdiction thereof, are citizens of the United States and of the State wherein they reside. No State shall make or enforce any law which shall abridge the privileges or immunities of citizens of the United States; nor shall any State deprive any person of life, liberty, or property, without due process of law; nor deny to any person within its jurisdiction the equal protection of the laws.

SECTION 2

[APPORTIONMENT OF REPRESENTATIVES IN CONGRESS]
Representatives shall be apportioned among the several States according to their respective numbers, counting the whole number of persons in each State, excluding Indians not taxed. But when the right to vote at any election for the choice of electors for President and Vice-President of the United States, Representatives in Congress, the Executive and Judicial officers of a State, or the members of the Legislature thereof, is denied to any of the male inhabitants of such State, being twenty-one years of age, and citizens of the United States, or in any way abridged, except for participation in rebellion, or other crime, the basis of representation therein shall be reduced in the proportion which the number of such male citizens shall bear to the whole number of male citizens twenty-one years of age in such State.

SECTION 3

[PERSONS DISQUALIFIED FROM HOLDING OFFICE]
No person shall be a Senator or Representative in Congress, or elector of President and Vice-President, or hold any office, civil or military, under the

United States, or under any State, who, having previously taken an oath, as a member of Congress, or as an officer of the United States, or as a member of any State legislature, or as an executive or judicial officer of any State, to support the Constitution of the United States, shall have engaged in insurrection or rebellion against the same, or given aid or comfort to the enemies thereof. But Congress may by a vote of two-thirds of each House, remove such disability.

SECTION 4

[WHAT PUBLIC DEBTS ARE VALID]

The validity of the public debt of the United States, authorized by law, including debts incurred for payment of pensions and bounties for services in suppressing insurrection or rebellion, shall not be questioned. But neither the United States nor any State shall assume or pay any debt or obligation incurred in aid of insurrection or rebellion against the United States, or any claim for the loss or emancipation of any slave; but all such debts, obligations and claims shall be held illegal and void.

SECTION 5

[POWER TO ENFORCE THIS ARTICLE]

The Congress shall have power to enforce, by appropriate legislation, the provisions of this article.

Amendment XV

[Proposed by Congress on February 26, 1869; declared ratified on March 30, 1870.]

SECTION 1

[NEGRO SUFFRAGE]

The right of citizens of the United States to vote shall not be denied or abridged by the United States or by any State on account of race, color, or previous condition of servitude.

SECTION 2

[POWER TO ENFORCE THIS ARTICLE]

The Congress shall have power to enforce this article by appropriate legislation.

Amendment XVI

[Proposed by Congress on July 2, 1909; declared ratified on February 25, 1913.]

[AUTHORIZING INCOME TAXES]

The Congress shall have power to lay and collect taxes on incomes, from whatever source derived, without apportionment among the several States, and without regard to any census or enumeration.

Amendment XVII

[Proposed by Congress on May 13, 1912; declared ratified on May 31, 1913.]

[POPULAR ELECTION OF SENATORS]

The Senate of the United States shall be composed of two Senators from each State, elected by the people thereof, for six years; and each Senator shall have one vote. The electors in each State shall have the qualifications requisite for electors of the most numerous branch of the State legislatures.

When vacancies happen in the representation of any State in the Senate, the executive authority of such State shall –issue writs of election to fill such vacancies: Provided, That the legislature of any State may empower the executive thereof to make temporary appointments until the people fill the vacancies by election as the legislature may direct.

This amendment shall not be so construed as to affect the election or term of any Senator chosen before it becomes valid as part of the Constitution.

Amendment XVIII

[Proposed by Congress December 18, 1917; declared ratified on January 29, 1919.]

SECTION 1

[NATIONAL LIQUOR PROHIBITION]

After one year from the ratification of this article the manufacture, sale, or transportation of intoxicating liquors within, the importation thereof into, or the exportation thereof from the United States and all territory subject to the jurisdiction thereof for beverage purposes is hereby prohibited.

SECTION 2

[POWER TO ENFORCE THIS ARTICLE]

The Congress and the several States shall have concurrent power to enforce this article by appropriate legislation.

SECTION 3

[RATIFICATION WITHIN SEVEN YEARS]

This article shall be inoperative unless it shall have been ratified as an amendment to the Constitution by the legislatures of the several States, as provided in the Constitution, within seven years from the date of the submission hereof to the States by the Congress.[1]

---

[1] Repealed by the Twenty-first Amendment.

Amendment XIX

[Proposed by Congress on June 4, 1919; declared ratified on August 26, 1920.]

[WOMAN SUFFRAGE]

The right of citizens of the United States to vote shall not be denied or abridged by the United States or by any State on account of sex.

Congress shall have power to enforce this article by appropriate legislation.

Amendment XX

[Proposed by Congress on March 2, 1932; declared ratified on February 6, 1933.]

SECTION 1

[TERMS OF OFFICE]

The terms of the President and Vice President shall end at noon on the 20th day of January, and the terms of Senators and Representatives at noon on the 3rd day of January, of the years in which such terms would have ended if this article had not been ratified; and the terms of their successors shall then begin.

SECTION 2

[TIME OF CONVENING CONGRESS]

The Congress shall assemble at least once in every year, and such meeting shall begin at noon on the 3d day of January, unless they shall by law appoint a different day.

SECTION 3

[DEATH OF PRESIDENT-ELECT]

If, at the time fixed for the beginning of the term of the President, the President elect shall have died, the Vice President elect shall become President. If a President shall not have been chosen before the time fixed for the beginning of his term, or if the President elect shall have failed to qualify, then the Vice President elect shall act as President until a President shall have qualified; and the Congress may by law provide for the case wherein neither a President elect nor a Vice President elect shall have qualified, declaring who shall then act as President, or the manner in which one who is to act shall be selected, and such person shall act accordingly until a President or Vice President shall have qualified.

SECTION 4

[ELECTION OF THE PRESIDENT]

The Congress may by law provide for the case of the death of any of the persons from whom the House of Representatives may choose a President whenever the right of choice shall have devolved upon them, and for the case of the death of any of the persons from whom the Senate may choose a Vice President whenever the right of choice shall have devolved upon them.

SECTION 5

[AMENDMENT TAKES EFFECT]
Sections 1 and 2 shall take effect on the 15th day of October following the ratification of this article.

SECTION 6

[RATIFICATION WITHIN SEVEN YEARS]
This article shall be inoperative unless it shall have been ratified as an amendment to the Constitution by the legislatures of three-fourths of the several States within seven years from the date of its submission.

Amendment XXI

[Proposed by Congress on February 20, 1933; declared ratified on December 5, 1933.]

SECTION 1

[NATIONAL LIQUOR PROHIBITION REPEALED]
The eighteenth article of amendment to the Constitution of the United States is hereby repealed.

SECTION 2

[TRANSPORTATION OF LIQUOR INTO "DRY" STATES]
The transportation or importation into any State, Territory, or Possession of the United States for delivery or use therein of intoxicating liquors, in violation of the laws thereof, is hereby prohibited.

SECTION 3

[RATIFICATION WITHIN SEVEN YEARS]
This article shall be inoperative unless it shall have been ratified as an amendment to the Constitution by conventions in the several States, as provided in the Constitution, within seven years from the date of the submission hereof to the States by the Congress.

Amendment XXII

[Proposed by Congress on March 21, 1947; declared ratified on February 27, 1951.]

SECTION 1

[TENURE OF PRESIDENT LIMITED]
No person shall be elected to the office of President more than twice, and no person who has held the office of President or acted as President, for more than two years of a term to which some other person was elected President shall be elected to the office of the President more than once. But this Article shall not apply to any person holding the office of President when this Article

was proposed by the Congress, and shall not prevent any person who may be holding the office of President, or acting as President, during the term within which this Article becomes operative from holding the office of President or acting as President during the remainder of such term.

SECTION 2

[RATIFICATION WITHIN SEVEN YEARS]

This article shall be inoperative unless it shall have been ratified as an amendment to the Constitution by the legislatures of three-fourths of the several States within seven years from the date of its submission to the States by the Congress.

Amendment XXIII

[Proposed by Congress on June 16, 1960; declared ratified on March 29, 1961.]

SECTION 1

[ELECTORAL COLLEGE VOTES FOR THE DISTRICT OF COLUMBIA]

The District constituting the seat of Government of the United States shall appoint in such manner as the Congress may direct:

A number of electors of President and Vice President equal to the whole number of Senators and Representatives in Congress to which the District would be entitled if it were a State, but in no event more than the least populous State; they shall be in addition to those appointed by the States, but they shall be considered, for the purposes of the election of President and Vice President, to be electors appointed by a State; and they shall meet in the District and perform such duties as provided by the twelfth article of amendment.

SECTION 2

[POWER TO ENFORCE THIS ARTICLE]

The Congress shall have power to enforce this article by appropriate legislation.

Amendment XXIV

[Proposed by Congress on August 27, 1962; declared ratified on January 23, 1964.]

SECTION 1

[ANTI-POLL TAX]

The right of citizens of the United States to vote in any primary or other election for President or Vice President, for electors for President or Vice President, or for Senator or Representative of Congress, shall not be denied or abridged by the United States or any State by reason of failure to pay any poll tax or other tax.

SECTION 2

[POWER TO ENFORCE THIS ARTICLE]

The Congress shall have power to enforce this article by appropriate legislation.

Amendment XXV

[Proposed by Congress on July 6, 1965; declared ratified on February 10, 1967.]

SECTION 1

[VICE PRESIDENT TO BECOME PRESIDENT]
In case of the removal of the President from office or his death or resignation, the Vice President shall become President.

SECTION 2

[CHOICE OF A NEW VICE PRESIDENT]
Whenever there is a vacancy in the office of the Vice President, the President shall nominate a Vice President who shall take the office upon confirmation by a majority vote of both houses of Congress.

SECTION 3

[PRESIDENT MAY DECLARE OWN DISABILITY]
Whenever the President transmits to the President pro tempore of the Senate and the Speaker of the House of Representatives his written declaration that he is unable to discharge the powers and duties of his office, and until he transmits to them a written declaration to the contrary, such powers and duties shall be discharged by the Vice President as Acting President.

SECTION 4

[ALTERNATE PROCEDURES TO DECLARE AND TO END PRESIDENTIAL DISABILITY]
Whenever the Vice President and a majority of either the principal officers of the executive departments, or of such other body as Congress may by law provide, transmit to the President pro tempore of the Senate and the Speaker of the House of Representatives their written declaration that the President is unable to discharge the powers and duties of his office, the Vice President shall immediately assume the powers and duties of the office as Acting President.

Thereafter, when the President transmits to the President pro tempore of the Senate and the Speaker of the House of Representatives his written declaration that no inability exists, he shall resume the powers and duties of his office unless the Vice President and a majority of either the principal officers of the executive department, or of such other body as Congress may by law provide, transmit within four days to the President pro tempore of the Senate and the Speaker of the House of Representatives their written declaration that the President is unable to discharge the powers and duties of his office. Thereupon Congress shall decide the issue, assembling within forty eight hours for that purpose if not in session. If the Congress, within twenty one days after receipt of the latter written declaration, or, if Congress is not in session, within twenty one days after Congress is required to assemble, determines by two-thirds vote of both Houses that the President is unable to discharge the powers and duties of his office, the Vice President shall continue to discharge the same as Acting President; otherwise, the President shall resume the powers and duties of his office.

Amendment XXVI

[Proposed by Congress on March 23, 1971; declared ratified on July 1, 1971.]

SECTION 1

[EIGHTEEN-YEAR-OLD VOTE]
The right of citizens of the United States, who are eighteen years of age or older, to vote shall not be denied or abridged by the United States or by any State on account of age.

SECTION 2

[POWER TO ENFORCE THIS ARTICLE]
The Congress shall have power to enforce this article by appropriate legislation.

Amendment XXVII

[Proposed by Congress on September 25, 1789; declared ratified on May 8, 1992.]

[CONGRESS CANNOT RAISE ITS OWN PAY]
No law varying the compensation for the services of the Senators and Representatives, shall take effect, until an election of representatives shall have intervened.

The Federalist Papers

No. 10: Madison

Among the numerous advantages promised by a well constructed Union, none deserves to be more accurately developed than its tendency to break and control the violence of faction. The friend of popular governments never finds himself so much alarmed for their character and fate, as when he contemplates their propensity to this dangerous vice. He will not fail therefore to set a due value on any plan which, without violating the principles to which he is attached, provides a proper cure for it. The instability, injustice, and confusion introduced into the public councils have, in truth, been the mortal diseases under which popular governments have everywhere perished, as they continue to be the favorite and fruitful topics from which the adversaries to liberty derive their most specious declamations. The valuable improvements made by the American constitutions on the popular models, both ancient and modern, cannot certainly be too much admired; but it would be an unwarrantable partiality to contend that they have as effectually obviated the danger on this side, as was wished and expected. Complaints are everywhere heard from our most considerate and virtuous citizens, equally the friends of public and private faith and of public and personal liberty, that our governments are too unstable, that the public good is disregarded in the conflicts of rival parties, and that measures are too often decided, not according to the rules of justice and the rights of the minor party, but by the superior force of an interested and overbearing majority. However anxiously we may wish that these complaints had no foundation, the evidence of known facts will not permit us to deny that they are in some degree true. It will be found, indeed, on a candid review of our situation, that some of the distresses under which we labor have been erroneously charged on the operation of our governments; but it will be found, at the same time, that other causes will not alone account for many of our heaviest misfortunes; and, particularly, for that prevailing and increasing distrust of public engagements and alarm for private rights which are echoed from one end of the continent to the other. These must be chiefly, if not wholly, effects of the unsteadiness and injustice with which a factious spirit has tainted our public administration.

By a faction I understand a number of citizens, whether amounting to a majority or minority of the whole, who are united and actuated by some common impulse of passion, or of interest, adverse to the rights of other citizens, or to the permanent and aggregate interests of the community.

There are two methods of curing the mischiefs of faction: the one, by removing its causes; the other, by controlling its effects.

There are again two methods of removing the causes of faction: the one, by destroying the liberty which is essential to its existence; the other, by giving to every citizen the same opinions, the same passions, and the same interests.

It could never be more truly said than of the first remedy, that it is worse than the disease. Liberty is to faction what air is to fire, an aliment without which it instantly expires. But it could not be a less folly to abolish liberty, which is essential to political life, because it nourishes faction, than it would be to wish the annihilation of air, which is essential to animal life, because it imparts to fire its destructive agency.

The second expedient is as impracticable, as the first would be unwise. As long as the reason of man continues fallible, and he is at liberty to exercise it, different opinions will be formed. As long as the connection subsists between his reason and his self-love, his opinions and his passions will have a reciprocal influence on each other; and the former will be objects to which the latter will attach themselves. The diversity in the faculties of men, from which the rights of property originate, is not less an insuperable obstacle to a uniformity of interests. The protection of these faculties is the first object of Government. From the protection of different and unequal faculties of acquiring property, the possession of different degrees and kinds of property immediately results; and from the influence of these on the sentiments and views of the respective proprietors, ensues a division of the society into different interests and parties.

The latent causes of faction are thus sown in the nature of man; and we see them everywhere brought into different degrees of activity, according to the different circumstances of civil society. A zeal for different opinions concerning religion, concerning Government, and many other points, as well of speculation as of practice; an attachment to different leaders ambitiously contending for pre-eminence and power; or to persons of other descriptions whose fortunes have been interesting to the human passions, have in turn divided mankind into parties, inflamed them with mutual animosity, and rendered them much more disposed to vex and oppress each other, than to co-operate for their common good. So strong is this propensity of mankind to fall into mutual animosities, that where no substantial occasion presents itself, the most frivolous and fanciful distinctions have been sufficient to kindle their unfriendly passions, and excite their most violent conflicts. But the most common and durable source of factions has been the various and unequal distribution of property. Those who hold and those who are without property have ever formed distinct interests in society. Those who are creditors, and those who are debtors, fall under a like discrimination. A landed interest, a manufacturing interest, a mercantile interest, a moneyed interest, with many lesser interests, grow up of necessity in civilized nations, and divide them into different classes, actuated by different sentiments and views. The regulation of these various and interfering interests forms the principal task of modern Legislation, and involves the spirit of party and faction in the necessary and ordinary operations of Government.

No man is allowed to be judge in his own cause, because his interest would certainly bias his judgment and, not improbably, corrupt his integrity. With equal, nay with greater reason, a body of men are unfit to be both judges and parties at the same time; yet what are many of the most important acts of legislation but so many judicial determinations, not indeed concerning the rights of single persons, but concerning the rights of large bodies of citizens; and what are the different classes of legislators but advocates and parties to the causes which they determine? Is a law proposed concerning private debts? It is a question to which the creditors are parties on one side and the debtors on the other. Justice ought to hold the balance between them. Yet the parties are, and must be, themselves the judges; and the most numerous party, or in other words, the most powerful faction must be expected to prevail. Shall domestic manufacturers be encouraged, and in what degree, by restrictions on foreign manufacturers? are questions which would be differently decided by the landed and the manufacturing classes, and probably by neither with a sole regard to justice and the public good. The apportionment of taxes on the various descriptions of property is an act which seems to require the most exact impartiality; yet there is, perhaps, no legislative act in which greater opportunity and temptation are given to a predominant party to trample on the rules of justice. Every shilling with which they overburden the inferior number is a shilling saved to their own pockets.

It is in vain to say that enlightened statesmen will be able to adjust these clashing interests and render them all subservient to the public good. Enlightened statesmen will not always be at the helm. Nor, in many cases, can such an adjustment be made at all without taking into view indirect and remote considerations, which will rarely prevail over the immediate interest which one party may find in disregarding the rights of another or the good of the whole.

The inference to which we are brought is that the *causes* of faction cannot be removed and that relief is only to be sought in the means of controlling its *effects*.

If a faction consists of less than a majority, relief is supplied by the republican principle, which enables the majority to defeat its sinister views by regular vote. It may clog the administration, it may convulse the society; but it will be unable to execute and mask its violence under the forms of the Constitution. When a majority is included in a faction, the form of popular government, on the other hand, enables it to sacrifice to its ruling passion or interest both the public good and the rights of other citizens. To secure the public good and private rights against the danger of such a faction, and at the same time to preserve the spirit and the form of popular government, is then the great object to which our enquiries are directed. Let me add that it is the great desideratum by which alone this form of government can be rescued from the opprobrium under which it has so long labored and be recommended to the esteem and adoption of mankind.

By what means is this object attainable? Evidently by one of two only. Either the existence of the same passion or interest in a majority at the same time must be prevented, or the majority, having such co-existent passion or interest, must be rendered, by their number and local situation, unable to concert and carry into effect schemes of oppression. If the impulse and the opportunity be suffered to coincide, we well know that neither moral nor religious motives can be relied on as an adequate control. They are not found to be such on the injustice and violence of individuals, and lose their efficacy in proportion to the number combined together, that is, in proportion as their efficacy becomes needful.

From this view of the subject it may be concluded that a pure Democracy, by which I mean a Society consisting of a small number of citizens, who assemble and administer the Government in person, can admit of no cure for the mischiefs of faction. A common passion or interest will, in almost every case, be felt by a majority of the whole; a communication and concert results from the form of Government itself; and there is nothing to check the inducements to sacrifice the weaker party or an obnoxious individual. Hence it is that such Democracies have ever been spectacles of turbulence and contention; have ever been found incompatible with personal security or the rights of property; and have in general been as short in their lives as they have been violent in their deaths. Theoretic politicians, who have patronized this species of Government, have erroneously supposed that by reducing mankind to a perfect equality in their political rights, they would at the same time be perfectly equalized and assimilated in their possessions, their opinions, and their passions.

A Republic, by which I mean a Government in which the scheme of representation takes place, opens a different prospect and promises the cure for which we are seeking. Let us examine the points in which it varies from pure Democracy, and we shall comprehend both the nature of the cure and the efficacy which it must derive from the Union.

The two great points of difference between a Democracy and a Republic are: first, the delegation of the Government, in the latter, to a small number of citizens elected by the rest; secondly, the greater number of citizens and greater sphere of country over which the latter may be extended.

The effect of the first difference is, on the one hand, to refine and enlarge the public views by passing them through the medium of a chosen body of citizens, whose wisdom may best discern the true interest of their country and whose patriotism and love of justice will be least likely to sacrifice it to temporary or partial considerations. Under such a regulation it may well happen that the public voice, pronounced by the representatives of the people, will be more consonant to the public good than if pronounced by the people themselves, convened for the purpose. On the other hand, the effect may be inverted. Men of factious tempers, of local prejudices, or of sinister designs, may, by intrigue, by corruption, or by other means, first obtain the suffrages, and then betray the interests of the people. The question resulting is, whether small or extensive Republics are most favorable to the election of proper guardians of the public weal; and it is clearly decided in favor of the latter by two obvious considerations.

In the first place it is to be remarked that however small the Republic may be, the Representatives must be raised to a certain number in order to guard against the cabals of a few; and that however large it may be they must be limited to a certain number in order to guard against the confusion of a multitude. Hence, the number of Representatives in the two cases not being in proportion to that of the Constituents, and being proportionally greatest in the small Republic, it follows that if the proportion of fit characters be not less in the large than in the small Republic, the former will present a greater option, and consequently a greater probability of a fit choice.

In the next place, as each Representative will be chosen by a greater number of citizens in the large than in the small Republic, it will be more difficult for unworthy candidates to practise with success the vicious arts by which elections are too often carried; and the suffrages of the people being more free, will be more likely to centre on men who possess the most attractive merit and the most diffusive and established characters.

It must be confessed that in this, as in most other cases, there is a mean, on both sides of which inconveniencies will be found to lie. By enlarging too much the number of electors, you render the representative too little acquainted with all their local circumstances and lesser interests; as by reducing it too much, you render him unduly attached to these, and too little fit to comprehend and pursue great and national objects. The Federal Constitution forms a happy combination in this respect; the great and aggregate interests being referred to the national, the local and particular to the State legislatures.

The other point of difference is the greater number of citizens and extent of territory which may be brought within the compass of Republican than of Democratic Government; and it is this circumstance principally which renders factious combinations less to be dreaded in the former than in the latter. The smaller the society, the fewer probably will be the distinct parties and interests composing it; the fewer the distinct parties and interests, the more frequently will a majority be found of the same party; and the smaller the number of individuals composing a majority, and the smaller the compass within which they are placed, the more easily will they concert and execute their plans of oppression. Extend the sphere and you take in a greater variety of parties and interests; you make it less probable that a majority of the whole will have a common motive to invade the rights of other citizens; or if such a common motive exists, it will be more difficult for all who feel it to discover their own strength and to act in unison with each other. Besides other impediments, it may be remarked, that where there is a consciousness of unjust or dishonorable purposes, communication is always checked by distrust in proportion to the number whose concurrence is necessary.

Hence, it clearly appears that the same advantage which a Republic has over a Democracy in controlling the effects of faction is enjoyed by a large over a small republic—is enjoyed by the Union over the States composing it. Does this advantage consist in the substitution of representatives whose enlightened views and virtuous sentiments render them superior to local prejudices and to schemes of injustice? It will not be denied that the representation of the Union will be most likely to possess these requisite endowments. Does it consist in the greater security afforded by a greater variety of parties, against the event of any one party being able to outnumber and oppress the rest? In an equal degree does the increased variety of parties comprised within the Union increase this security? Does it, in fine, consist in the greater obstacles opposed to the concert and accomplishment of the secret wishes of an unjust and interested majority? Here again the extent of the Union gives it the most palpable advantage.

The influence of factious leaders may kindle a flame within their particular States but will be unable to spread a general conflagration through the other States: a religious sect may degenerate into a political faction in a part of the Confederacy; but the variety of sects dispersed over the entire face of it must secure the national Councils against any danger from that source: a rage for paper money, for an abolition of debts, for an equal division of property, or for any other improper or wicked project, will be less apt to pervade the whole body of the Union than a particular member of it; in the same proportion as such a malady is more likely to taint a particular county or district than an entire State.

In the extent and proper structure of the Union, therefore, we behold a republican remedy for the diseases most incident to Republican Government. And according to the degree of pleasure and pride we feel in being republicans ought to be our zeal in cherishing the spirit and supporting the character of federalist.

PUBLIUS

No. 51: Madison

To what expedient, then, shall we finally resort, for maintaining in practice the necessary partition of power among the several departments as laid down in the constitution? The only answer that can be given is that as all these exterior provisions are found to be inadequate the defect must be supplied, by so contriving the interior structure of the government as that its several constituent parts may, by their mutual relations, be the means of keeping each other in their proper places. Without presuming to undertake a full development of this important idea I will hazard a few general observations which may perhaps place it in a clearer light, and enable us to form a more correct judgment of the principles and structure of the government planned by the convention.

In order to lay a due foundation for that separate and distinct exercise of the different powers of government, which to a certain extent is admitted on all hands to be essential to the preservation of liberty, it is evident that each department should have a will of its own; and consequently should be so constituted that the members of each should have as little agency as possible in the appointment of the members of the others. Were this principle rigorously adhered to, it would require that all the appointments for the supreme executive, legislative, and judiciary magistracies should be drawn from the same fountain of authority, the people, through channels having no communication whatever with one another. Perhaps such a plan of constructing the several departments would be less difficult in practice than it may in contemplation appear. Some difficulties, however, and some additional expense would attend the execution of it. Some deviations, therefore, from the principle must be admitted. In the constitution of the judiciary department in particular, it might be inexpedient to insist rigorously on the principle: first, because peculiar qualifications being essential in the members, the primary consideration ought to be to select that mode of choice which best secures these qualifications; second, because the permanent tenure by which the appointments are held in that department must soon destroy all sense of dependence on the authority conferring them.

It is equally evident that the members of each department should be as little dependent as possible on those of the others for the emoluments annexed to their offices. Were the executive magistrate, or the judges, not independent of the legislature in this particular, their independence in every other would be merely nominal.

But the great security against a gradual concentration of the several powers in the same department consists in giving to those who administer each department the necessary constitutional means and personal motives to resist encroachments of the others. The provision for defence must in this, as in all other cases, be made commensurate to the danger of attack. Ambition must be made to counteract ambition. The interest of the man must be connected with the constitutional rights of the place. It may be a reflection on human nature that such devices should be necessary to control the abuses of government. But what is government itself but the greatest of all reflections on human nature? If men were angels, no government would be necessary. If angels were to govern men, neither external nor internal controls on government would be necessary. In framing a government which is to be administered by men over men, the great difficulty lies in this: You must first enable the government to control the governed; and in the next place oblige it to control itself. A dependence on the people is, no doubt, the primary control on the government; but experience has taught mankind the necessity of auxiliary precautions.

This policy of supplying, by opposite and rival interests, the defect of better motives, might be traced through the whole system of human affairs, private as well as public. We see it particularly displayed in all the subordinate distributions of power, where the constant aim is to divide and arrange the several offices in such a manner as that each may be a check on the other; that the private interest of every individual may be a sentinel over the public rights. These inventions of prudence cannot be less requisite in the distribution of the supreme powers of the State.

But it is not possible to give to each department an equal power of self-defense. In republican government, the legislative authority necessarily predominates. The remedy for this inconveniency is to divide the legislature into different branches; and to render them, by different modes of election and different principles of action, as little connected with each other as the nature of their common functions and their common dependence on the society will admit. It may even be necessary to guard against dangerous encroachments by still further precautions. As the weight of the legislative authority requires that it should be thus divided, the weakness of the executive may require, on the other hand, that it should be fortified. An absolute negative on the legislature appears, at first view, to be the natural defense with which the executive magistrate should be armed. But perhaps it would be neither altogether safe nor alone sufficient. On ordinary occasions it might not be exerted with the requisite firmness, and on extraordinary occasions it might be perfidiously abused. May not this defect of an absolute negative be supplied by some qualified connection between this weaker branch of the stronger department, by which the latter may be led to support the constitutional rights of the former, without being too much detached from the rights of its own department?

If the principles on which these observations are founded be just, as I persuade myself they are, and they be applied as a criterion to the several State constitutions, and to the federal Constitution, it will be found that if the latter does not perfectly correspond with them, the former are infinitely less able to bear such a test.

There are, moreover, two considerations particularly applicable to the federal system of America, which place that system in a very interesting point of view.

First. In a single republic, all the power surrendered by the people is submitted to the administration of a single government; and usurpations are guarded against by a division of the government into distinct and separate departments. In the compound republic of America, the power surrendered by the people is first divided between two distinct governments, and then the portion allotted to each subdivided among distinct and separate departments. Hence a double security arises to the rights of the people. The different governments will control each other, at the same time that each will be controlled by itself.

Second. It is of great importance in a republic not only to guard the society against the oppression of its rulers, but to guard one part of the society against the injustice of the other part. Different interests necessarily exist in different classes of citizens. If a majority be united by a common interest, the rights of the minority will be insecure. There are but two methods of providing against this evil: The one by creating a will in the community independent of the majority—that is, of the society itself; the other, by comprehending in the society so many separate descriptions of citizens as will render an unjust combination of a majority of the whole very improbable, if not impracticable. The first method prevails in all governments possessing an hereditary or self-appointed authority. This, at best, is but a precarious security; because a power independent of the society may as well espouse the unjust views of the major as the rightful interests of the minor party, and may possibly be turned against both parties. The second method will be exemplified in the federal republic of the United States. Whilst all authority in it will be derived from and dependent on the society, the society itself will be broken into so many parts, interests and classes of citizens, that the rights of individuals, or of the minority, will be in little danger from interested combinations of the majority. In a free government the security for civil rights must be the same as that for religious rights. It consists in the one case in the multiplicity of interests, and in the other in the multiplicity of sects. The degree of security in both cases will depend on the number of interests and sects; and this may be presumed to depend on the extent of country and number of people comprehended under the same government. This view of the subject must particularly recommend a proper federal system to all the sincere and considerate friends of republican government: Since it shows that in exact proportion as the territory of the Union may be formed into more circumscribed Confederacies, or States, oppressive combinations of a majority will be facilitated; the best security, under the republican form, for the rights of every class of citizens, will be diminished; and consequently the stability and independence of some member of the government, the only other security, must be proportionally increased. Justice is the end of government. It is the end of civil society. It ever has been and ever will be pursued until it be obtained, or until liberty be lost in the pursuit. In a society under the forms of which the stronger faction can readily unite and oppress the weaker, anarchy may as truly be said to reign as in a state of nature, where the weaker individual is not secured against the violence of the stronger: And as, in the latter state, even the stronger individuals are prompted, by the uncertainty of their condition, to submit to a government which may protect the weak as well as themselves: So, in the former state, will the more powerful factions or parties be gradually induced, by a like motive, to wish for a government which will protect all parties, the weaker as well as the more powerful. It can be little doubted that if the State of Rhode Island was separated from the Confederacy and left to itself, the insecurity of rights under the popular form of government within such narrow limits would be displayed by such reiterated oppressions of factious majorities that some power altogether independent of the people would soon be called for by the voice of the very factions whose misrule had proved the necessity of it. In the extended republic of the United States, and among the great variety of interests, parties, and sects which it embraces, a coalition of a majority of the whole society could seldom take place on any other principles than those of justice and the general good; and there being thus less danger to a minor from the will of the major party, there must be less pretext, also, to provide for the security of the former, by introducing into the government a will not dependent on the latter, or, in other words, a will independent of the society itself. It is no less certain than it is important, notwithstanding the contrary opinions which have been entertained, that the larger the society, provided it lie within a practicable sphere, the more duly capable it will be of self-government. And happily for the *republican cause*, practicable sphere may be carried to a very great extent by a judicious modification and mixture of the *federal principle*.

PUBLIUS

GLOSSARY

527s Organizations that are independent of any party or candidate, and thus are not regulated by the FEC, as they advocate publicly for or against specific candidates, parties, or policies.

administrative law The body of law created by executive agencies with the purpose of refining general law passed in legislation.

affirmative action Efforts to redress previous discrimination against women and minorities through active measures to promote their employment and educational opportunities.

agenda setter An authority that controls what options are decided on by a group.

amicus curiae Briefs (letters to the court) in which those who are not parties in a case provide their opinions on how the case should be decided.

Antifederalists Those who opposed adopting the Constitution as written because they feared that it created an overly strong national government.

Articles of Confederation The constitution drafted by the Second Continental Congress in 1777 and ratified by the states in 1781. It set up a weak central government consisting of a congress with limited legislative power and virtually no authority over the execution of its laws.

attitudinal model A theoretical model where judicial decisions are primarily determined by the policy goals and ideological agendas of judges.

Australian ballot A type of ballot that lists all candidates running for each office and allows voters to cast their votes secretly and for specific individual candidates.

authoritarianism A political system in which there is no expectation that the government represents the people, and the institutions of government do not give the people a direct voice in who will lead.

ballot initiative An election in which citizens vote directly on a proposition raised by a group of fellow citizens.

biased sample A sample that, because it does not accurately represent the overall population, is likely to lead to erroneous conclusions about the population.

bicameral legislature A legislature consisting of two chambers or houses.

Bill of Rights The first 10 amendments to the Constitution, which enumerate a set of liberties not to be violated by the government and a set of rights to be protected by the government.

block grants Sums of money transferred to lower-level governments such that, as long as the general purpose of the grant is met, the lower-level governments are allowed considerable freedom in deciding how the money is spent.

bureaucracy An agency or office devoted to carrying out tasks for the government in a manner consistent with the law.

bureaucrat Any government employee who is not part of the ruling powers.

bureaucratic capture When regulatory agencies are beholden to the organizations or interests they are supposed to regulate.

bureaucratic drift When government agencies depart from executing policy consistent with the ideological preferences of Congress or the president so as to execute policy consistent with their own ideological preferences.

by-product A political activity conducted by groups whose principal organizational purpose is the pursuit of some nonpolitical goal.

cabinet departments Departments within the executive branch that encompass many of the agencies that implement federal policy. Secretaries appointed by the president and confirmed by the Senate are given the responsibility of leading these departments and providing advice to the president.

categorical grants Grants that narrowly define how the funds are to be spent. These grants normally come with conditions that need to be satisfied in order for the money to be used.

caucus In a legislature, a group of legislators that unites to promote an agenda not pursued within the parties or the legislative committees.

checks and balances An arrangement in which no one branch of government can conduct its core business without the approval, tacit or expressed, of the other branches.

civil case A case in which at least one person sues another person for violating the civil code of conduct.

civil law A system of jurisprudence in which authoritative documents determine how the law is to be interpreted. Under this system, legal codes and statutes (and not judges) inform future decisions.

civil liberties Freedoms protected from interference by the government, such as freedom of speech and freedom of religion.

civil rights Rights that (1) enable individuals to engage in activities central to citizenship or legal immigrant status, such as voting or petitioning the government; (2) ensure all individuals receive due process and equal treatment under the law; or (3) guarantee freedom from discriminatory actions by others that seek to deny an individual's full status as an equal member of society.

civil rights movement A social movement of the 1950s and 1960s focused primarily on the situation of African Americans, but also promoting the goals that all people be treated as equals under the law and that discrimination based on race, religion, ethnicity, gender, and place of origin be eliminated.

class action A lawsuit in which the plaintiff or defendant is a collective group of individuals.

closed primary A primary election in which only voters registered with the party can vote.

closed rule A provision that allows no amendments to be proposed once a bill comes to the chamber floor.

cloture A rule that limits debate on a bill to a specific number of hours. Senate rules require 60 senators to support such a motion to end debate (including filibusters) and proceed to a vote.

coalitional drift When an ideological shift in elected branches creates disparity between the way an agency executes policy and the way new members of Congress or a new president believes the agency ought to execute policy.

collective-action problem A situation in which people would be better off if they all cooperated; however, any individual has an incentive not to cooperate as long as others are cooperating.

collective dilemma A situation in which there is conflict between group goals and individual goals or self-interest.

commerce clause An enumerated power listed in Article I, Section 8, of the Constitution that grants Congress the power to "regulate Commerce with foreign Nations, and among the several States, and with the Indian Tribes."

common law A system of jurisprudence in which the judiciary has the authority to determine how the law is to be interpreted. Under this system, legal precedent established by judges informs future decisions.

concurring opinion An opinion issued by a member of the majority of the Supreme Court that agrees with the decision of the majority but offers alternative legal reasoning.

confederation A political system with multiple levels of government, in which lower-level governments retain full sovereignty and cannot be compelled by the national government to act.

conference committee A meeting of legislators from the House and Senate to reconcile two bills passed on the same topic.

confidence vote A vote held in a parliamentary system that, if it fails, brings on an election and possibly a new set of party leaders.

Connecticut Compromise An agreement reached at the Constitutional Convention that there would be a bicameral legislature, with an upper house (the Senate) composed of equal representation from each state and a lower house (the House of Representatives) composed of representation from each state in proportion to its population.

constituency service A legislator directly helping a constituent in dealing with government bureaucracy.

constitutional law The collection of fundamental rules for making statutory laws and regulations, their enforcement, and the court decisions interpreting those rules.

cooperative federalism A political system in which both levels of government—national and state—are active in nearly all areas of policy and share sovereign authority.

coordination problem A situation in which two or more people are all better off if they coordinate on a common course of action, but there is more than one possible course of action to take.

coverage bias The tendency for the media or a particular media outlet to give less attention in terms of column space or air time to certain kinds of stories or aspects of stories.

criminal case A case in which the government prosecutes a person for a crime against society.

delegates Representatives who listen carefully to what their constituents want and make decisions based on feedback from constituents.

democracy Rule by the people; in practice today this means popular election of the government and basic protections of civil rights and liberties.

dictatorship An authoritarian political system in which sovereign power is vested in one individual.

dissenting opinion An opinion issued by a member of the Supreme Court in opposition to the majority, offering legal reasoning for the decision to oppose.

distributional model The view that the internal institutions of the congressional chambers are designed primarily to help members of Congress secure economic benefits for only their constituents, not the general public.

divided government A government in which the president is from a different party than the majority in Congress.

dual federalism A political system in which each level of government—national and state—is sovereign in its own sphere of policy authority.

due process The right to legal protections against arbitrary deprivation of life, liberty, or property.

Duverger's Law A regularity that only two parties tend to compete for control of the government in countries that have single-member, plurality electoral systems.

elastic clause (necessary and proper clause) The provision in Article I, Section 8, of the Constitution that states that Congress can make whatever laws are "necessary and proper" in order to provide the means to carry out its enumerated powers.

electoral college The electors appointed by each state to vote for the president.

entrepreneur A leading group participant who is so committed to the group's goals, and/or so skilled in the pursuit of those goals, that he or she does not need selective incentives.

equal protection The principle that laws passed and enforced by the states must apply fairly to all individuals.

executive agreement An agreement between the United States and one or more foreign countries. Because it is not a formal treaty, it does not need Senate approval.

executive order An official means by which the president can instruct federal agencies on how to execute the laws passed by Congress.

expressed powers (enumerated powers) Those powers specifically described in the Constitution.

federal court supremacy The arrangement based on the supremacy clause in the Constitution that gives federal courts the authority to overturn state court decisions and to decide on the constitutionality of state laws and actions.

Federal Election Commission (FEC) The federal agency that regulates campaign donations to and spending by candidates for Congress and the presidency.

federalism A political system with multiple levels of government, in which each level has independent authority over some important policy areas.

Federalists Those who favored adopting the Constitution as written because they believed that a strong national government was needed to solve the collective dilemmas facing the states.

federal system A political system with multiple levels of government, in which each level has independent authority over some important policy areas.

filibuster Instances in which senators, once recognized to speak on the floor, talk for an extended period ("hold the floor") in an attempt to block the rest of the Senate from voting on a bill.

fire-alarm oversight Congressional oversight that relies on interest groups and citizens to inform representatives of unwarranted action.

framing Establishing the context for an issue in such a way as to emphasize certain aspects over others.

the franchise (or suffrage) The right to vote.

free riding Benefiting from a public good while avoiding the costs of contributing to it.

gatekeeping bias The tendency for the media or a particular media outlet not to report stories of a particular nature.

gerrymandering Drawing strangely shaped district boundaries to gain political advantage.

going public Action taken by a president to communicate directly with the people, usually through a press conference, radio broadcast, or televised speech, in order to influence public opinion and put pressure on Congress.

government agency An individual unit of the government responsible for carrying out tasks delegated to it by Congress or the president in accordance with the law.

government bureaucracy The agencies and offices devoted to carrying out the tasks of government consistent with the law.

government contract An agreement whereby the government hires a company or an organization to carry out certain tasks on its behalf.

government corporation A federally owned corporation that generates revenue by providing a public service, operating much like a private business and with a higher degree of autonomy than a cabinet department or an independent agency.

government grants Money that the government provides to individuals or organizations to perform tasks in the public's interest.

grants-in-aid Money that is distributed to lower-level governments with the purpose of funding special projects.

hard money Campaign funds that are given directly to candidates or parties to support a particular candidate, and thus are subject to FEC regulations.

Help America Vote Act of 2002 A federal law meant to reduce barriers to participation in elections.

home rule The constitutional or legal authority held by local governments that allows them to govern themselves with little or no interference from the state.

ideology A coherent, organized set of ideas and principles that functions as a core on which individuals draw when forming their attitudes about public affairs.

impeachment Process by which the House of Representatives formally charges a federal government official with "Treason, Bribery, or other high Crimes and Misdemeanors."

incorporation The process by which rights and liberties established by the Bill of Rights are applied to state and local governments through the Fourteenth Amendment.

incumbency advantage The advantage current officeholders have in an election, in particular as it relates to the high rates at which congressional legislators win re-election.

independent agency An agency that exists outside the cabinet departments and is run with a larger degree of independence from presidential influence.

informational model The view that the internal institutions of the congressional chambers are designed to help Congress make more informed decisions.

infotainment Mass media programming that is intended primarily to entertain, but also provides political news.

initiative An election held to vote directly on a ballot proposition that was proposed by a group of individuals.

inside lobbying Activities by lobbyists and interest group leaders that involve direct contact with policy makers.

institutions Rules or sets of rules or practices that determine how people make collective decisions.

interest group Any group other than a political party that is organized to influence the government.

intergovernmentalism A system in which multiple levels of government are active in a given policy area.

intergovernmental relations The relationship between the different levels of government. For example, it may pertain to the struggle between the national government and the states for authority over a specific policy domain, or it may pertain to the coordination of action between the levels in an effort to achieve common goals.

intermediate scrutiny An intermediate standard used by the Supreme Court to determine whether a law is compatible with the Constitution. A law subject to this standard is considered constitutional if it advances "an important government objective" and is "substantially related" to the objective.

Jim Crow laws Laws passed after the Civil War to establish a system of segregation of public facilities and private establishments that made African Americans second-class citizens.

joint committee A committee made up of members of both the House and Senate.

judicial activism Judicial rulings that go beyond interpreting the law in order to promote a judge's personal or political agenda.

judicial review The authority of the judiciary to decide whether a law or any other government action is constitutional.

latent interest A concern shared by a group of people on which they have not yet chosen to act collectively.

legal model A theoretical model where judicial decisions are primarily determined by the case, the plain meaning of the text from the Constitution and statutes, the intent of the framers, and/or legal precedent.

line-item veto A partial veto that allows the executive to strike specific passages from a given bill.

lobbying An attempt to influence public officials by speaking to them directly or by pressuring them through their constituents.

logrolling An instance of two or more legislators agreeing to vote in favor of one another's proposed bills or amendments.

majority leader The head of the party holding a majority of seats and, in the Senate, the leader of the Senate. In the House, the majority leader is second to the Speaker of the House.

margin of error In statistical research, the range of outcomes we expect for a population, given the data revealed by a sample drawn from that population.

marketization Government bureaucratic reform that emphasizes market-based principles of management that are common to the private sector.

markup A committee or subcommittee process where committee members edit and amend bills.

mass media Media that is intended to be publicly available, or at least targeted at large numbers of people.

media The methods or technologies people use for communication, such as phones, radio, newspapers, television, and the Internet.

median voter theorem A mathematical result showing that the voter with the ideological preference in the middle of the ranking of voters must be satisfied and approve of a majority-rule winning outcome.

minimum winning coalition The smallest-size coalition necessary to achieve a goal.

mixed presidential system A form of democracy in which the executive is elected independently and shares responsibility for the government with the legislature.

monarchy A political system in which a ruler (usually a king or queen) is chosen by virtue of being the heir of the previous ruler.

moot The status of a case in which further legal proceedings would have no impact on one or both parties.

national committee Officials who oversee the operation of their party nationwide.

national party convention The meeting where the party formally nominates its presidential candidate.

New Deal Party System A political alliance between southern Democrats, big-city Democrats, rural voters, and African Americans that endured for several decades after the election of Franklin Roosevelt in 1932.

New Jersey Plan A plan proposed at the Constitutional Convention by William Paterson of New Jersey to amend, rather than replace, the standing Articles of Confederation. The plan called for a unicameral legislature with equal representation among the states, along with a plural (multiperson) executive appointed by the legislature.

non-attitude A lack of opinion on an issue, or an opinion so weakly held that it does not enter into a person's calculations about voting or taking some other political action, even though the person may express an opinion to a pollster.

oligarchy A political system in which power resides in a small segment of society.

one-party state A political system in which one party controls the government and actively seeks to prevent other parties from contesting for power.

open primary A primary election in which any registered voter can vote, regardless of party affiliation.

open rule A provision that allows any amendment to be proposed once a bill comes to the chamber floor.

outside lobbying Activities by interest group leaders that seek to mobilize constituents and others outside the policy-making community to contact or pressure policy makers.

paradox of voting The notion that people still vote despite the fact that the individual costs of voting often outweigh the individual benefits.

parliamentary democracy A form of democracy in which the executive is elected by the legislature and government is responsible to the legislature.

partisan model The view that majority-party leaders dominate the workings of Congress and ensure that most legislative benefits come to majority-party members.

party amateur An issue activist who is mostly interested in specific policy areas and works for the party, or for the specific politicians within the party, to advance these goals.

party discipline Pressure on party members to vote on bills that have the support of the party leadership. Also, the tendency for members of a legislative party to vote as a bloc.

party identification A psychological attachment or loyalty to a political party.

party professional A person who works directly for the party, is loyal to its goal of winning elections, and stays with it over long periods through multiple election cycles.

path dependence The notion that earlier events or decisions deeply affect current and future policy decisions or outcomes.

pluralism A view of the American political system that emphasizes the fact that a large number of diverse interest groups are involved in the political process, and that any given group may be influential on some occasions and not on others.

plurality rule A method for determining an election's winner in which the candidate who receives the most votes wins.

pocket veto A veto that occurs automatically if a president does not sign a bill for 10 days after passage in Congress and Congress has adjourned during that 10-day period.

police-patrol oversight Congressional oversight that consists of actively monitoring agencies through routine inspection.

political action committee (PAC) A type of organization regulated by the Federal Election Commission that raises money from donors to support the election campaigns of federal political candidates.

political knowledge A general understanding of how the political system works, and who runs the government.

political machine A local organization that controls the city or county government to such an extent that it can reward whole neighborhoods, wards, and precincts, or other groups with benefits such as jobs and government programs, in return for supporting the party's candidates.

political participation Activities citizens undertake to influence government behavior.

political party A group of candidates and elected officials organized under a common label for the purpose of attaining positions of public authority.

political system The way a society organizes and manages its politics across various levels of public authority.

politics The process of making collective decisions, usually by governments, to allocate public resources and to create and enforce rules for the operation of society.

popular sovereignty The principle that the authority to make decisions on behalf of society belongs to the people.

population In statistical research, the entire group about which you want to learn, such as all adults living in the United States.

pork barrel Government spending that benefits a narrow constituency in return for electoral support or some other kind of political support, including campaign donations.

preferences The outcomes or experiences people want or believe they need.

presidential system A form of democracy in which the executive is elected independently and the government is not responsible to the legislature.

press The people and organizations that provide content about public affairs—news and commentary—that is disseminated across media.

primary election An election held before Election Day to allow voters to select which candidates will appear on the ballot under a party label.

priming The psychological process of shaping people's perceptions of a particular issue, figure, or policy.

principal–agent problem (delegation problem) An instance in which one actor, a principal, contracts another actor, an agent, to act on the principal's behalf, but the actors may not share the same preferences, and the principal lacks the means to observe all of the agent's behavior.

prisoner's dilemma An interaction between two strategic actors in which neither actor has an incentive to cooperate even though both would be better off if they both cooperated.

private good A product or benefit provided such that its enjoyment can be limited to specific people, and one individual's consumption of it precludes others from consuming it.

privatization The contracting of private companies by the government to conduct work that was formerly done by government agencies.

proportional representation A method for allocating seats in a legislature in which the number of seats a party receives in a district or nationwide is proportional to the votes it receives in the elections.

public good A benefit provided to a group of people such that each member can enjoy it without necessarily having to pay for it, and one person's enjoyment of it does not inhibit the enjoyment of it by others.

public opinion The collection of attitudes and preferences of the mass public.

public policies Programs and decisions by the government that are enforced by the rule of law.

random selection Choosing a sample such that each member of a population has an equal chance of being selected into the sample.

rational basis test The lowest-level standard used by the Supreme Court to determine whether a law is compatible with the Constitution. A law subject to this standard is assumed to be constitutional as long as its goals are clearly linked to its means.

rationality The habit of choosing the best choice among available options given one's interests and information.

recall election An election during the term of an elected government official in which citizens vote directly on whether to remove the individual from office.

Reed's Rules Procedural guidelines used by the majority-party leadership for determining who sits on which committees, how the order of business should be decided, and how the majority party should limit the powers of the minority party.

referendum An election in which citizens vote directly on whether to overturn a bill or a constitutional amendment that has been passed by the legislature.

republic A political system in which public officials are chosen to represent the people in an assembly that makes important policy decisions.

reserved powers Those powers not granted to the national government by the Constitution, and therefore reserved to the states.

restricted (or modified) rule A provision that allows only certain kinds of amendments to be proposed once a bill comes to the floor, typically only amendments that pertain to the original purpose of the bill.

revenue–sharing A principle whereby the national government and the lower-level governments cooperate in funding a project.

rule of law A system in which all people in a society, including governing officials, are subject to legal codes that are applied without bias by independent courts.

rule making The process by which governmental agencies provide details on how laws passed by elected officials will be implemented.

sample In statistical research, a subset of the population chosen to provide information for the research about the population.

selective incentive A benefit that a group can offer to potential members in exchange for participation as a way to encourage that involvement.

separation of powers An arrangement in which specific governmental powers are divided among distinct branches of government; typically, this means having an executive who is chosen independently of the legislature, and thus executive power and legislative power are separated.

signing statement A public statement written by the president and attached to a particular bill to outline the president's interpretation of the legislation.

single-member district An electoral district in which a single person is elected to a given office.

"smoke–filled room" A situation in which party elites make important decisions away from the scrutiny or influence of party membership.

social movement A loose coalition of groups and organizations with common goals that are oriented toward using mass action to influence the government.

socioeconomic status (SES) A measure of the way that individuals are regarded within a society by virtue of their wealth, income, education, and profession.

soft money Campaign funds that are given to parties or other organizations to support voter mobilization or voter education activities, and thus typically are not subject to FEC regulations.

Speaker of the House The constitutionally designated leader of the House of Representatives. In the modern House, he or she is always the leader of the majority party.

special donor A potential participant in a group for whom the cost of participating is very low and/or the benefits of participating are very high.

special (or select) committee A committee appointed to consider a special issue or serve a special function that disbands once it has completed its duties.

special prosecutor Independent, private-sector counsel hired by Congress to investigate government officials.

split referral A rule (in place since 1975) that permits the Speaker to split a bill into sections and give sections to specific committees.

spoils system The practice of rewarding loyal partisans with government positions after they demonstrate their support during an election.

standing The official status of a litigant who is entitled to have his or her case decided by the court.

standing committee A group of legislators given permanent jurisdiction over a particular issue area or type of policy.

stare decisis The legal principle that requires judges to respect the decisions of past court cases.

statement bias The tendency for the media or a particular media outlet to interject opinions into the coverage of an issue.

statutory law The laws passed by legislatures, or administrative agencies empowered by legislatures, and the court decisions interpreting those laws.

strategic (or rational choice) model A theoretical model where judicial decisions are primarily determined by the policy goals of judges and the various constraints that stand in the way of achieving those goals.

strict constructivism The legal philosophy that judges should use the intentions of those writing the law or the Constitution as guides for how to interpret the law.

strict scrutiny The highest-level standard used by the Supreme Court to determine whether a law is compatible with the Constitution. A law subject to this standard is considered unconstitutional unless it advances a "compelling state interest" and represents the least intrusive means.

super PACs A type of organization regulated by the Federal Election Commission that can spend unlimited sums of money to advocate for the election or for the defeat of a candidate, but is prohibited from contributing funds directly to federal campaigns and parties.

supremacy clause The section of Article VI of the Constitution that states that the Constitution and the subsequent laws of the United States are to be the "supreme law of the land," meaning that they supersede any state and local laws.

trustees Representatives who make decisions using their own judgments about what is best for their constituents.

unanimous consent agreement Rules under which the Senate debates, offers amendments, and votes on a given bill. All members of the chamber must agree to them, so any senator can object and halt progress on a bill.

unified government A government in which the president is from the same party as the majority in Congress.

unitary system A political system in which the national government holds ultimate authority over all areas of policy and over the actions of subunit governments.

unstable coalition An instance in which three or more people must make a collective choice from a set of alternatives, but any voting coalition in favor of an alternative can be divided by consideration of another alternative.

veto threat A public statement issued by the president declaring that if Congress passes a particular bill that the president dislikes it will ultimately be vetoed.

Virginia Plan A plan proposed at the Constitutional Convention by Edmund Randolph of Virginia, which outlined a stronger national government, with an independent executive and a bicameral legislature whose membership in both houses would be apportioned according to state population.

vote by mail A program in many states that allows voters to mail in their ballots rather than appearing in person at a polling place.

voter mobilization Efforts by organizations to facilitate or encourage voting.

voter registration A process by which citizens enroll themselves with the government to gain permission to vote in an election.

voter turnout The proportion of potential voters who vote in a given election.

Voting Rights Act of 1965 A federal law that made it a priority of the national government to enforce provisions of the Fourteenth and Fifteenth Amendments, leading to major improvements in voting rights for blacks, other minorities, and the poor.

whip A member of the House or Senate who is elected by his or her party to help party leaders coordinate party members' actions, including enforcing party discipline.

writ of *certiorari* An order by the Supreme Court directing an inferior court to deliver the records of a case to be reviewed, which effectively means the justices of the Court have decided to hear the case.

PHOTO CREDITS

Chapter 1: Page 2: AP Photo; p. 5: Jeremiah Robinson/Demotix/Corbis; p. 8 (left): Fotog/Tetra Images/Corbis; (right): Shawn Thew/epa/Corbis; p. 13: Camera Press/Tina Paul/Redux. **Chapter 2:** Page 30: Granger Collection; p. 35: Granger Collection; p. 36: Granger Collection; p. 46: Wadsworth Atheneum Museum of Art/Art Resource, NY; p. 56: Philippe Wojazer/Reuters/Corbis; p. 59: Brian C. Frank/Reuters; p. 61: Chuck Nacke/Alamy. **Chapter 3:** Page 66: AP Photo; p. 69:Istockphoto; p. 78: Bettmann/Corbis; p. 80: Corbis; p. 89: AP Photo; p. 96: Reuters/Anthony Bolante/Newscom. **Chapter 4:** Page 100: Bill O'Leary/The Washington Post/Getty Images; p. 108: Pornchai Kittiwongsakul/AFP/Getty Images; p. 110: Tami Chappell/Reuters; p. 114: AP Photo; p. 117: AP Photo; p. 127: Ron Sachs/CNP/Corbis; p. 128: Reuters/Gary Cameron/Newscom. **Chapter 5:** Page 136: AP Photo; p. 142: Eric Gay/Associated Press; p. 161: Melina Mara/The Washington Post/Getty Images; p. 164: AP Photo;p. 167: © Eddie Arrossi; p. 174: Steve Rhodes/Demotix/Corbis. **Chapter 6:** Page 184: David McNew/Reuters/Corbis; p. 192: Granger Collection; p. 196: Ron Sachs/Pool/CNP/Corbis; p. 199: Bettmann/Corbis; p. 210: Joshua Roberts/Bloomberg via Getty Images; p. 214: Tobias Hase/dpa/picture-alliance/Newscom; p. 216: Pete Souza/White House/Handout/Corbis. **Chapter 7:** Page 224: Stephen Crowley/The New York Times/Redux; p. 231: NASA; p. 236: AP Photo; p. 244: AP Photo; p. 253: HO/Reuters/Corbis. **Chapter 8:** Page 262: Suzannah Hoover/Sipa USA/Newscom; p. 266: Reuters/Corbis; p. 270: Granger Collection; p. 283: AP Photo; p. 293: Brendan Smialowski/The New York/Redux; p. 295: Win McNamee/Getty Images. **Chapter 9:** Page 298: Aude Guerrucci/Polaris/Newscom; p. 305: Joe Raedle/Getty Images; p. 312: AP Photo; p. 313: AP Photo; p. 318: Steve Schapiro/Corbis; p. 329: Roger L. Wollenberg/Pool/Corbis; p. 335: Pete Marovich/ZUMA Press/Corbis. **Chapter 10:** Page 340: AP Photo; p. 349: AP Photo; p. 354: AP Photo; p. 360: Photo by Chusseau-Flaviens/George Eastman House/Getty Images; p. 372: AP Photo. **Chapter 11:** Page 376: Evelyn Hockstein/Polaris/Newscom; p. 386: AP Photo; p. 392: Emily Anne Epstein/Corbis; p. 395: Melina Mara/The Washington Post/Getty Images; p. 405: Flip Schulke/Corbis. **Chapter 12:** Page 408: Michael Reynolds/epa/Corbis; p. 415: AP Photo; p. 428: Everett Collection/Agefotostock; p. 433: AP Photo; p. 436: AP Photo; p. 438: Eddie Moore/ZUMA Press/Corbis. **Chapter 13:** Page 444: Bruce Bennett/Getty Images; p. 450: AP Photo; p. 453: Granger Collection; p. 459: AP Photo; p. 468: Bill Clark/CQ Roll Call/Getty Images; p. 472: The White House/Facebook. **Chapter 14:** Page 482: Arif Ali/AFP/Getty Images; p. 487: Courtesy of Factcheck.org; p. 490: Granger Collection; p. 493: Jonny White/Alamy; p. 496: Patrick Farrell/MCT/Newscom; p. 500: Reuters via Your View; p. 506 (left): Virginia Sherwood/MSNBC/NBCU Photo Bank; (right): AP Photo.

INDEX

new initiatives, 237
presidential appointments, 285
categorical grants, 82
caucuses, 165, 456, 461–62
CBO (Congressional Budget Office), 167, 213n
CBS network, 491, 495
cell phones:
electoral campaigns and, 472
political polling and, 312
Center on Budget and Policy Priorities, 174
Centers for Disease Control and Prevention, 230
Central Intelligence Agency (CIA), 483–84
centralization of power, 71, 77
centrists, 399
checks and balances:
definition of, 48
for judicial branch, 48, 188, 267
for legislative branch, 48, 188
for presidential power, 188
Cheney, Joe, 215
Chevron v. the Natural Resources Defense Council, 254
Chicago Daily News, 490
Chicago Defender, 491
Child Welfare League of America, 380
Chile, 217
China, 24, 499
Chong, Dennis, 15
Christian conservative movement, 398–99
The Christian Science Monitor, 490
CIA (Central Intelligence Agency), 483–84
circuit courts of appeal, 275–76
citizenship, rights of, 105
Citizens United v. FEC (2010), 265–66, 271, 384, 388, 401, 463, 466–68
city governments, 90
civil cases, 274–75
civil disobedience, 345
civil law, 279
civil liberties:
around the world, 128–31
Bill of Rights on, 59–60, 104
definition of, 25, 103–4
failures in, 110–14
Fourteenth Amendment and Bill of Rights, 117–20
government responses to discrimination, 120–28

gun restrictions, 101–2
origins of, 104–6
reasons for protecting, 131–33
special role of courts in, 106–10
civil rights:
around the world, 128–31
definition of, 103–4
failures in, 110–14
Fourteenth Amendment and Bill of Rights, 117–20
government responses to discrimination, 120–28
Obama on marriage, 299
origins of, 104–6
popular demands for more, 114–17
reasons for protecting, 131–33
special role of courts in, 106–10
Civil Rights Act (1964), 120, 163, 396
civil rights movement, 115–16, 345–46, 396–98
civil service reform, 239–40
Civil War:
about, 69–70
Dred Scott case and, 271
Lincoln as military leader, 194–95
skeleton analogy and, 33
slavery and, 111–12
class action, 275
Clay, Henry, 173–74
Clean Air Act (1977), 252, 254
Clement, Paul, 283
Clinton, Bill:
1992 election, 206, 435
balancing the budget, 436
Defense of Marriage Act, 299
executive orders, 208, 210
going public, 199
impeachment and, 219–21
interest groups and, 384
line-item veto, 217
performance on television, 471
presidential appointments, 250, 285
on voter registration, 350
war powers, 57
closed primaries, 456, 461
closed rule, 171
cloture, 173–74
CNN, 486, 492, 502
coalitional drift, 245–48
coalition raiding, 19, 157

Coast Guard, U.S., 231
Cold War, 237, 430
collective-action problems:
about, 11–13
Articles of Confederation and, 40, 69
Congress and, 153–54
definition of, 12, 18
elections and, 194, 421–22
examples, 27–28
interest groups and, 385, 388–91
mass elections, 194
Occupy Wall Street, 12–13
in political participation, 346–48
political parties and, 420–22
prisoner's dilemma and, 14
social movements and, 401
collective dilemmas:
Congress and, 178, 191
definition of, 10, 18
federalism as response to, 71–72
government bureaucracies and, 230–32
interest groups and, 388–92
judicial branch and, 265–67
mass media and, 488–89
need for government and, 9–11
in political participation, 346–48
political parties and, 420–22
presidency and, 191–92, 200
press and, 488–89
social movements and, 401
types of, 11–19
unstable coalitions and, 157
colonial charters, 35
commerce clause:
Affordable Care Act and, 264
on centralization of power, 77
definition of, 58, 76
committees:
congressional, 162–66, 170, 175, 245–55
national, 418–19
PAC, 386
common law, 54, 279
communism, 323
Communist Party, 24, 108
concurring opinion, 287
confederation, federation and, 69–72
conference committees, 163, 175
confidence vote, 441

Congress, U.S.:
administrative law, 204
bicameral nature of, 45–46,
139–40, 188
budget process, 250–51
bureaucracy and, 241–42
checks and balances, 48, 188
codes for behavior, 159
collective-action problems, 153–54
collective dilemmas, 178, 191
commerce clause, 58
congressional elections, 141–53
congressional politics, 153–56
congressional staff, 165–67
constituency services, 149–50
constitutional debates and
compromise, 41–44
constitutional prerogatives, 139–41
creating agencies, 237
divided government, 197, 412
election campaigns, 462–63
EOP and, 213
establishment of, 39
evaluations of, 327–28
executive orders and, 208–10
on government spending, 4
on gun control, 378
historical path timeline, 160
individualism in, 142–48, 164
interest groups and, 380–81, 393–96
internal institutions of, 156–67
lawmaking process, 140–41, 164,
168–76
as legislative branch, 7
lobbying and, 384
McCarthy era, 108–9
OMB and, 213
oversight and, 251–52
partisan presidency and, 197
party discipline in, 440
party leaders, 159–62
presidents legally bypassing, 208–9
principal-agent problems, 20–21,
245–48, 303
recent amendment debates, 50
relative powers of, 55–58
research services, 167
roll-call votes, 175
separation-of-powers system, 176
social movements and, 398–99
taking account of, 178–81
term limits proposal, 50
unicameral, 31

vetoes and, 205–6
see also House of Representatives,
U.S.; Senate, U.S.
Congressional Black Caucus, 153, 165
Congressional Budget Office (CBO),
167, 213*n*
congressional committees:
about, 162
chairs of, 163–64
consequences of, 164–65
"iron triangle" and, 254–55
lawmaking process, 170, 175
membership on, 163–64
selected list of, 166
types of, 162–63
congressional districts:
drawing boundaries, 144–47, 456
redistricting, 144–47, 150, 152
representatives for, 148–53
single-member districts, 142–43, 453,
455–57
congressional elections:
about, 141
additional factors, 147–48
constituency services, 149–50
drawing district boundaries,
144–47, 456
incumbency advantage, 150–52
minority representation, 152–53
other electoral factors, 147–48
plurality rule, 142–43
primary elections, 143
representing districts or states,
148–53
single-member districts, 142–43, 453,
455–57
Congressional Hispanic Caucus, 167
congressional politics, 153–56
Congressional Progressive
Caucus, 165
Congressional Research Service, 167
congressional staff, 165–67
Connecticut Compromise, 43, 188
conservatives:
about, 322–23
Christian conservative movement,
398–99
discerning bias in, 501–3
partisan hypothesis for media
content, 506
political parties and, 423, 432
primary elections and, 450
constituency services, 149–50

Constitution, U.S.:
about, 33–34
amending, 50
comparison with national
constitutions, 54–55
consequences of, 60–63
court reliance on, 75–78
federalism and, 75–78
institutional features of, 44–50
on institutions of American
government, 22
on judicial branch, 267, 272
as "living constitution," 55–60
origins of American political system,
34–44
on presidential power, 187–91
ratification debate, 50–54
religion in politics and, 56
skeleton analogy, 33–34
on system of representation, 8–9
on vice presidency, 213
see also Bill of Rights; *specific
amendments*
Constitutional Convention (1787):
about, 35
colonial and state constitutions and,
38–39
constitutional debates, 40–42
on institutions of government, 32
on presidential power, 187
on system of representation, 22
timeline, 52
constitutional law, 280
constitutional monarchies, 25
Constitution Party, 438
constitutions:
of the 1780s, 38–39
accomplishments of, 33–34
national, 54–55
constraint, ideological, 323
Consumer Financial Protection
Agency, 211
consumer rights movement, 399, 432
Continental Congress, 36–40
contracts, government, 243
Converse, Philip, 323
cooperative federalism, 73
coordination problems:
about, 16–17
definition of, 16, 18
interest groups, 391–92
judicial branch and, 265–66
political parties and, 16–17, 421

grants:
  block, 83
  categorical, 82
  definition of, 243
  grants-in-aid, 82
  state revenues from, 83–84
grants-in-aid, 82
Great Britain, *see* United Kingdom
Great Society Era, 81, 237
Greenback Party, 435
Green Party, 438, 460
Griswold v. Connecticut (1965), 59, 106
group attachments and public
  opinion, 317
group politics, *see* interest groups; social
  movements
The Guardian, 483–84
Gulf War, 237
gun control:
  controversy over, 376–78
  public pressure and, 405–6
  right to bear arms and, 53, 101–2,
    376–78, 405–6
Gun-Free School Zones Act (1990), 77

Hamilton, Alexander:
  about, 51
  on constitutional authority, 139, 141
  on governmental administration, 235
  on judicial review, 269
  on people as a "beast," 329
  on presidential powers, 187
Hancock, John, 36, 40
hard money, 465–66
Hatch, Orrin, 164
head of government, 216–17
head of state, 216–17
Health, Education, and Welfare,
  Department of, 237
Health and Human Services, Department
  of, 224–26, 230
health care system, reforming, 174,
  196–97, 262–64
Healthy, Hunger-Free Kids Act
  (2010), 83
Hearst, William Randolph, 490
Heller, Dick, 102–3
Help America Vote Act (2002), 351–53
Hendrix, Dennis, 384
Henry, Patrick, 40
Hirschman, Albert, 316
Hobbes, Thomas, 10–11, 34
Holder, Eric, 359

Homeland Security, Department of:
  deportation of immigrants, 184–85
  establishment of, 211, 237
  terrorist attacks and, 97
home rule, 90
Honest Leadership and Open
  Government Act (2007), 384
Hoover, Herbert, 201
Hoover, J. Edgar, 114
House of Representatives, U.S.:
  average tenure, 158
  bicameralism and, 45, 139–40, 188
  codes for behavior, 159
  direct elections of, 58
  drawing district boundaries,
    144–47, 456
  election campaigns, 462–63
  on government spending, 3
  impeachment process, 219
  institutional features of
    Constitution, 45
  party discipline in, 440
  party leaders, 159–62
  Rules Committee, 156, 163,
    171–72, 416
  Speaker of the House, 159–60
  system of representation in, 22–23, 85,
    87, 140
  trustee-delegate representation, 148–49
  Ways and Means Committee, 158
Housing and Urban Development,
  Department of, 237
HUD (Department of Housing and
  Urban Development), 237
Human Rights Campaign, 397
Hussein, Saddam, 57

ideological bias, 502–4
ideological constraint, 323
ideology:
  definition of, 322–23
  elections and, 449–52, 476
  median voter theorem, 449
  primary elections and, 461
  public opinion and, 326
  socialization and, 314
  of Supreme Court judges, 285, 295
immigration policies:
  deportation of immigrants, 184–86
  drafting new, 197
  DREAM Act and, 184–85
  illegal immigrants and, 66–68
  treatment of immigrants, 112–13

impeachment:
  definition of, 219–20
  judicial power, 176
  legislative power, 48, 176
  presidential power and, 188
implied powers (inherent powers), 190
implied rights, 59
income tax, 50, 435
incorporation, 118–19
incumbency advantage, 150–52, 328
independent agencies, 228–29, 236
Independent Party, 460
India:
  centralization of political control
    and, 93
  civil rights and liberties in, 130
  electoral institutions in, 475
  executive forms, 216
  political participation in, 368
  political parties in, 439
individualism in Congress, 142–48, 164
informal powers, 204
informational model, 155–56, 170–72, 179
infotainment, 497
inherent powers (implied powers), 190
initiatives, 458–59
inside lobbying, 382–83
institutions:
  about, 6–9
  budget reconciliation process, 174
  congressional, 156–67, 177–78
  Constitution on, 44–50
  definition of, 6
  designing, 21–24
  electoral, 452–60
  evaluations of, 327–28
  examples of, 6
  Federalist Papers on, 51
  key intermediate, 441–42
  legalized marijuana, 89
  national government, 24–27, 32
  state government, 86–87
  types of, 24–27
interest groups:
  about, 379–82
  bureaucratic agencies and, 254–55
  campaign financing, 383–88
  collective-action problems, 385,
    388–91
  collective dilemmas and, 388–92
  comparing with other countries,
    403–4
  coordination problems, 391–92

mixed presidential system, 217
modified (restricted) rule, 171
monarchies, 24–25
Montesquieu (philosopher), 39
moot, 281
Motor Voter Bill (1994), 350, 455
mugwumps, 238
Murdoch, Rupert, 511
Myers, Harriet, 295

NAACP (National Association for the Advancement of Colored People), 397
Nader, Ralph, 391, 399, 401, 432, 436
NASA (National Aeronautics and Space Administration), 230–31
Nation, Carrie, 399
National Aeronautics and Space Administration (NASA), 230–31
National Association for the Advancement of Colored People (NAACP), 397
National Cannabis Industry Association, 395
National Cemetery Administration, 137
national committees, 418–19
National Federation of Independent Business v. Sebelius (2012), 81, 83, 263, 283, 286
national government, *see* government, U.S.
nationalism, 42–43, 503
National Organization for Women (NOW), 397
national party conventions, 419
National Review, 501–2
National Rifle Association (NRA), 102, 376, 405–6
National Science Foundation (NSF), 249
National Security Council, 215
Nation magazine, 502
NATO (North Atlantic Treaty Organization), 202
NBC network, 491, 495, 502
necessary and proper clause (elastic clause), 46, 49–50, 76–77
Netherlands, 476
New Deal Era:
    about, 80–81, 201–4
    bureaucracy growth and, 236
    judicial appointments and, 293–94
    judicial review of, 269–70
    Sixth Party System and, 430
New Deal Party System, 429–30, 433
New Jersey Plan, 42–43

News Corporation, 495
Newsweek magazine, 490
New York Amsterdam News, 491
New York Journal, 490, 492
New York Times, 114, 312, 483–84, 490, 502
New York Times Company, 495
New Zealand, 54
Nigeria, 256
Nineteenth Amendment, 104–5, 117, 360
Ninth Amendment, 59, 106
Nixon, Richard M.:
    1960 election, 471
    1972 election, 462
    approval rating of, 220
    bureaucracy growth and, 237
    Fifth Party System, 430
    Great Society Era and, 81
    impeachment and, 219, 221
    partisan presidency and, 196
    resignation of, 214
    Watergate scandal, 167, 258, 486
non-attitudes, 331–32
nonpartisan elections, 411*n*
North American Free Trade Agreement, 289
North Atlantic Treaty Organization (NATO), 202
North Korea, 54, 323
Norway, 130
NOW (National Organization for Women), 397
NRA (National Rifle Association), 102, 376, 405–6
NSF (National Science Foundation), 249

Obama, Barack:
    2008 election, 471
    2012 election, 403, 444–45, 450–51, 466, 472, 487
    administrative and financial resources, 211–12
    ambassador to Libya, 486
    approval ratings, 220, 304
    bureaucratic institutions and, 203, 215
    Davis's shooting in Pakistan, 483–84
    on deportation of immigrants, 184–86, 195, 208
    diplomacy and, 215
    disaster relief, 137
    economic policy, 82
    on education standards, 98
    EPA funding and, 248
    executive orders, 209–10

going public, 199
government expansion programs, 402, 466
on government spending, 3
on gun control, 377
as head of state, 216
health care reform, 174, 196–97, 262–64
HHS role and, 224–26
on legalized marijuana, 89
partisan presidency and, 196–97, 409, 417
presidential appointments, 173, 207–8, 250, 285
on same-sex marriages, 126, 215, 299–300, 302, 305, 337
signing statements, 209
on Tea Party tax status, 386
vice presidents under, 215
war powers, 57
Occupy Wall Street movement, 12–13, 398, 401–2
O'Connor, Sandra Day, 287
Office of Management and Budget (OMB), 167, 213
Office of the Attorney General, 235
Office of the United States Trade Representative, 213
oil spills, 334
oligarchies, 24
OMB (Office of Management and Budget), 167, 213
one-party states, 24
one-person/one-vote principle, 178
open primaries, 456, 461
open rule, 171
opinion polls, *see* measuring public opinion
opinion writing, 287–88
oral arguments, 283–84
organizations, political parties as, 411, 413, 417–22
original jurisdiction of courts, 279
outside lobbying, 382–83
oversight, 85, 251–52

PACs (political action committees), 386, 463–65
Page, Benjamin, 336
Pakistan, 482–84
Palin, Sarah, 398
paradox of voting, 346
pardons, 190

Port Authority of New York and New
    Jersey, 88
Portugal, 54, 217
Powell, Adam Clayton, 15
predispositions in public opinion, 320–25
preferences, 5
presidency:
    administrative and financial resources,
        209–15
    appointments, 190, 207–8, 250
    approval ratings, 220
    bureaucratic institutions and, 203, 215
    campaigning for, 461–62
    checks and balances, 48, 188
    comparison of executive forms, 215–18
    divided government, 197, 412
    election campaigns, 462–67
    electoral college and, 8
    enhancing presidential power,
        200–203
    evaluations of, 327–28
    executive agreements, 209
    as executive branch, 7
    executive orders, 208–11
    historical path timeline, 202
    increasing power of, 185–86
    institutional features of Constitution,
        45, 55
    institutionalizing power of, 221–22
    legal moves bypassing Congress, 208–9
    nineteenth-century changes, 193–95
    oversight and, 251–52
    partisan, 194, 196–97
    political parties and, 417
    populist, 197–99
    presidential signature, 175–76
    principal-agent problem, 20
    questioning power of, 218–22
    relative powers of, 55–58
    shaping of modern, 192–99
    signing statements, 209, 211
    sources of presidential power, 187–92
    term limits, 215
    today's powerful, 203–15
    twentieth century to present, 195–99
    veto power of, 48, 176, 190, 205–6,
        208–10
    see also executive branch of
        government; specific presidents
presidential systems, 61–62, 217
press:
    biases of, 501–5
    definition of, 485

in a democracy, 485–88
eighteenth and nineteenth centuries,
    489–90
evaluating and interpreting
    information, 486–88
freedom of the, 59, 113–14, 485–86
government regulation, 497–99
ideology and, 502–4
profit motive, 495–96, 498–99
solving collective dilemmas, 488–89
trends in, 489–95
primary elections, 142, 149, 420, 456, 461
priming, 318–19, 506
principal-agent problems (delegation
    problems):
    about, 19–21
    Congress and, 154, 245–48, 303
    definition of, 19
    EPA example, 245–48
    mass media, 510–12
    presidency and, 191–92
    public opinion example, 303–5
prior restraint doctrine, 498
prisoner's dilemma:
    about, 13–15
    collective-action problems and, 14
    definition of, 14, 18
    electoral campaigns, 14–15, 387,
        467–69
    judicial branch and, 265
    private sector competition
        example, 232
privacy, right to, 59
private goods, 12, 390
private media, 485
private property, 53
privatization, 242–43
Progressive Era:
    about, 79–80
    executive bureaucracy and, 236
    government regulation and, 457
    political parties and, 439
    voter rights and, 357
Progressive Movement, 240
Progressive Party, 428–29, 435
progressive vision of bureaucracy, 257–58
Prohibition, 399, 439
proportional representation, 143
proposals for bills, 168
public-access television, 495
Public Citizen movement, 401
public education, 130
public goods, 11–12, 230

public interest groups, 380
public opinion:
    apathy and lack of knowledge in,
        328–32
    comparing other countries, 332–34
    definition of, 302
    in democratic system, 301–2
    interest groups and, 405
    measuring, 305–13
    organized forms of public pressure,
        404–6
    on politicians, 325–28
    predispositions, 320–25
    presidency and, 199
    principal-agent problem of, 303–5
    public policies and, 325–28, 334–38
    shaping decision making, 219–20
    social movements and, 405
    sources of political attitudes, 313–20
public policy:
    committee system and, 164
    definition of, 21
    elections determining, 449–52
    interest groups and, 382–83
    public opinion and, 326–27, 334–38
push polling, 310

Qaddafi, Mu'ammar, 24, 57
Quayle, Dan, 214

"race to the bottom," 72, 96
racial discrimination:
    affirmative action and, 123–24
    federalism and, 85–86
    government responses to, 118, 120–24
    Korematsu v. United States, 113
    predisposition toward, 324–25
    racial gerrymandering, 145–46
    school integration and, 78, 122,
        282, 290
    voting rights and, 358–59
Rainbow Coalition, 397
Randolph, Edmund, 41
random sampling, 307–8
random selection, 307
rational basis test, 121
rational choice (strategic) model, 285–86
rational ignorance, 330–31
rationality, 316–17
Reagan, Ronald:
    on abortion, 434
    bureaucracy and, 240–41, 243–44
    on drinking-age standard, 83, 98

SES (socioeconomic status), 364–67
Seventeenth Amendment, 45–46, 59
Seventh Amendment, 106
Shapiro, Robert, 336
Shays, Daniel, 31
Shays's Rebellion, 30–31, 57
signing statements, 209, 211
Silver, Nate, 312
Singh, Monmohan, 216
single-member districts, 142–43, 453, 455–57
Sixteenth Amendment, 50, 271
Sixth Amendment, 106
Sixth Party System, 426, 430–32
Slaughter-House Cases, 118
slavery:
    abolishing, 44, 50, 105
    African Americans and, 111–12
    constitutional debates and compromise over, 42–44
    constitutional protections and, 269
    rights of citizenship, 105
Smith, Howard, 163
"smoke-filled rooms," 420
SNAP (Supplemental Nutrition Assistance Program), 227
social contract theory, 38
socialism, 323
Socialist Party, 439
socialization, 313–15, 488n
social media, 199, 472, 493–94, 501
social movements:
    collective-action problems, 401
    collective dilemmas, 401
    comparing with other countries, 403–4
    definition of, 396
    examples of, 396–99
    historical path timeline, 400–401
    interest groups and, 397
    measuring success of, 399–403
    public opinion and, 405
    resource mobilization perspective, 401–3
social rights, 130
Social Security Administration, 229–30, 237
Social Security program, 80, 236
social welfare organizations, 386
social welfare programs. *see also specific programs*
socioeconomic status (SES), 364–67
soft money, 465–66

"soft news," 497n
"sore loser law," 438
Sotomayer, Sonia, 207, 285, 293
Souter, David, 287
South Korea, 476–77
Spain, 323, 439, 490
Spanish-American War, 490, 492
spatial model, 474
Speaker of the House, 159–60
special (select) committees, 162–63
special districts, 90–91
special donors, 390–91
special prosecutors, 219, 258
speech, freedom of, 52, 59, 129, 131
Speechnow.org v. Federal Election Commission (2010), 468
split referral, 170
spoils system, 193–94, 207, 237–38
Stamp Act (1765), 40
standing, 275
standing committees, 162
stare decisis, 279
state courts, 276–78
State Department, 235, 486
state governments:
    Australian ballots, 458
    campaign financing, 466–67
    constitutions of 1780s, 38–39
    drawing district boundaries, 146–47, 456
    executive forms, 218
    federalism and, 86–88
    Federalist Papers on, 52
    home rule and, 90
    institutional features of Constitution, 45, 49
    institutions of, 86–87
    interest groups and, 382
    legalized marijuana, 89
    legislative institutions in, 177–78
    prerogatives of, 73
    recent trends, 81–82
    relative powers of, 58
    reserved powers for, 49–50
    revenue and expenditures, 88
    selecting judges, 277–78
    separation of powers, 86
    sources of power, 77, 87–88
    state courts, 276–78
    state-level election laws, 453–55
statement bias, 505
states' rights, 85, 95
state supreme courts, 276

statutory law, 33, 279–80
strategic (rational choice) model, 285–86
street-level bureaucrats, 234
strict constructivism, 291–92
strict scrutiny, 121
suffrage (the franchise), 356, 360–61, 398
Sunshine Act (1976), 252, 259
super PACs, 388, 464–65
Supplemental Nutrition Assistance Program (SNAP), 227
supremacy clause, 49, 77, 89, 271
Supreme Court, U.S.:
    on abortion rights, 124–25
    on Affordable Care Act, 262–64
    on bureaucratic responsibilities, 252–54
    on campaign financing, 463
    on centralization of power, 77
    checks and balances, 48, 188
    commerce clause and, 58
    constitutional basis, 266
    court of last resort, 271–74
    on Defense of Marriage Act, 300
    on discrimination, 118, 121–24
    on education, 130
    FDR's court-packing plan, 269–70, 293–94
    federal court supremacy, 270–72
    on gerrymandering, 147
    ideology of, 285, 295
    on immigration policy, 66–68
    institutional features of Constitution, 46–47, 54–55
    interest groups and, 383
    as judicial branch, 7
    on line-item veto, 217
    on lobbying, 384
    on national government rights, 76
    on New Deal programs, 269–70
    path of a case, 280–88
    presidential appointments, 207–8, 293–94
    on presidential power, 189–90
    Progressive Era and, 79
    reliance on Constitution, 75–78
    on reserved powers, 49–50
    on rights and liberties, 59, 102
    on states' rights, 95
    on system of representation, 22–23, 87
    unstable coalitions and, 19
    on voiding appointments, 268–69
    voting patterns of, 285